From Radio to the Big Screen

ALSO BY HAL ERICKSON
AND FROM MCFARLAND

*Military Comedy Films: A Critical Survey
and Filmography of Hollywood Releases Since 1918* (2012)

*The Baseball Filmography,
1915 through 2001*, 2d ed. (2002; pb 2010)

*"From Beautiful Downtown Burbank":
A Critical History of Rowan and Martin's
Laugh-In, 1968–1973* (2000; pb 2009)

Encyclopedia of Television Law Shows, 1948–2008 (2009)

*Sid and Marty Krofft: A Critical Study of Saturday Morning
Children's Television, 1969–1993* (1998; pb 2007)

*Television Cartoon Shows: An Illustrated Encyclopedia,
1949 through 2003*, 2d ed. (2005)

Syndicated Television, 1947–1987 (1989; pb 2001)

*Religious Radio and Television
in the United States, 1921–1991* (1992; pb 2001)

From Radio to the Big Screen

Hollywood Films Featuring Broadcast Personalities and Programs

Hal Erickson

McFarland & Company, Inc., Publishers
Jefferson, North Carolina

LIBRARY OF CONGRESS CATALOGUING-IN-PUBLICATION DATA

Erickson, Hal.
From radio to the big screen : Hollywood films featuring broadcast personalities and programs / Hal Erickson.
    p.   cm.
Includes bibliographical references and index.

ISBN 978-0-7864-7757-9 (softcover : acid free paper) ∞
ISBN 978-1-4766-1558-5 (ebook)

1. Motion pictures—United States. 2. Radio personalities—United States. 3. Radio programs—United States. I. Title.
PN1993.5.U6E75 2014   791.430973—dc23   2014015515

BRITISH LIBRARY CATALOGUING DATA ARE AVAILABLE

© 2014 Hal Erickson. All rights reserved

No part of this book may be reproduced or transmitted in any form or by any means, electronic or mechanical, including photocopying or recording, or by any information storage and retrieval system, without permission in writing from the publisher.

Cover images iStock/Thinkstock

Printed in the United States of America

*McFarland & Company, Inc., Publishers
Box 611, Jefferson, North Carolina 28640
www.mcfarlandpub.com*

**To my dear friend and colleague
Carl Bobke
(1950–2012)**

*"K-ZAM-bo Radio hits the spot,
1200 kilocycles, that's a lot!
From noon 'til three and six 'til nine,
We're the station that's really NEAT!
(Thought it was gonna rhyme, didn't ya, kids?)"*

Table of Contents

Acknowledgments ix

Introduction 1

THE PERSONALITIES,
THE PROGRAMS, THE PICTURES 9

Bibliography 285

Index 289

Acknowledgments

Imagine the excitement of writing a book about two of your favorite subjects, classic Hollywood films and old-time radio. Now imagine the heavy-duty research and sleepless nights involved in writing a book combining these two subjects—not separately or consecutively, but both at the same time.

I have loved classic films since I learned to operate a TV channel dial by myself (remember TV channel dials?), and have been a fan of old-time radio since hearing a rebroadcast of the venerable suspense series *The Shadow* in the fall of 1962. Whereas once upon a time it was considered geekish to harbor an affection for entertainment of the past, in this second decade of the 21st century I personally know scores of similar enthusiasts who aren't the least bit timid or ashamed about proclaiming their devotion to vintage films and radio.

Curiously, not many people share my fondness for films built around popular radio personalities or based upon popular radio programs. After screening my copy of the Fred Allen movie vehicle *It's in the Bag* (1945) for an old-time radio fan club, I was surprised that the picture elicited very few laughs, and was blown off as a waste of time once the screening ended. However, these same radio aficionados have no problem listening to radio adaptions of popular Hollywood films on such anthologies of the 1930s and 1940s as *Lux Radio Theater* and *Screen Director's Playhouse.* The only explanation I can come up with for this paradox is that fans of classic radio (or even modern-day radio) prefer to exercise their imaginations and conjure up images of their favorite stars and programs, and feel a bit resentful when these "word pictures" are literalized on film by others, almost as if some enemy force had invaded their minds and imposed an alien set of images.

Be that as it may, I still enjoy watching radio-inspired motion pictures; the good ones are very good, and even the bad ones have their own peculiar entertainment value. Forsaking further analysis, I hereby declare simply that I wrote this book because the subject matter appeals to me—and is there any *other* reason to write something unless you've been assigned an essay on how you spent your summer vacation?

Since no writer really works in a vacuum even though it sometimes seems that way, I take this opportunity to thank several individuals who have supplied me with valuable information, insight, input and research materials, not to mention lots of moral support and encouragement. In alphabetical order: Cari and David Bobke, Jim Feeley, Wayne and Rita Hawk, Tim Hollis, Cole Johnson, Milton Knight, Miles Kreuger, Bruce Lawton, Steve Massa, Jim Neibaur, Trav S.D., Ivan G. Shreve Jr., Roger Sorenson and Brent Walker. And not in alphabetical order, my wonderful wife Joanne and two terrific sons Brian and Peter.

Unless otherwise noted, the illustrations in this book are from my own collection (eBay got a *lot* of my business this time around). Also, the essay on the films of Kay Kyser is an expanded version of an article I wrote for *Classic Images* in July 1993, and is reprinted with permission.

Both enthusiasm and criticism are subjective things, so I don't expect every reader to share my enthusiasm or agree with my criticism. All I ask is that such radio-generated movies as *The Big Broadcast*, *That's Right—You're Wrong*, *Buck Benny Rides Again*, *Reveille with Beverly*, *My Friend Irma*, *Here Come the Nelsons* and *A Prairie Home Companion* be given an opportunity to stand or fall on their own merits. I therefore entreat you for your consideration and indulgence for the next several hundred pages.

And we'll be back with our book after this pause for author identification...

Hal Erickson

Introduction

There's a lot of truth to the old wisecrack that the "Golden Age" of anything generally occurred just before you were born. This writer came into the world in the decade when the predominance of big-time network radio was drawing to a close; most of my contact with the programs of that era has taken place "after the fact," by way of vintage recordings and the many books on the subject. Most other modern-day enthusiasts of what is generally accepted as the Golden Age of Radio were not only born after that Age came and went, but *long* after.

It's easy to pinpoint the beginning of the Golden Age as November 15, 1926, the day that the National Broadcasting Company (NBC), the first nationwide radio network, signed on the air. The end date, however, depends on one's point of view. Some argue that the Golden Age ended just as the era of network television began in the late 1940s, but this opinion doesn't take into account the number of excellent and innovative radio programs—*Dragnet, Gunsmoke, Crime Classics, CBS Radio Workshop, The Stan Freberg Show*—that came into existence in the years 1949 through 1957. I prefer to go along with encyclopedic radio scholar John Dunning, who has stated that the final day of the Golden Age was September 30, 1962, when the last two surviving CBS dramatic programs, *Yours Truly, Johnny Dollar* and *Suspense,* concluded their runs. While a few stragglers from the 1930s like *The Lutheran Hour* and *Grand Ole Opry* can still be heard to this day, and the weekly public-radio variety show *A Prairie Home Companion* (created in 1974) valiantly carries on the old tradition into the 21st century, for all intents and purposes the Golden Age of Radio was confined to the 36 fabulous years between 1926 and 1962.

So it is that with two exceptions, the films discussed in this book are likewise limited to those 36 years. After a very brief stopover in 1926 with the earliest known radio personality to be groomed for film stardom (Ann Howe, "The Radio Girl"), our story begins with the 1929 Rudy Vallee vehicle *The Vagabond Lover,* the first feature film to fully capitalize on the popularity of radio. Outside of Howard Stern's 1997 biopic *Private Parts* and the 2006 film adaptation of *Prairie Home Companion,* and allowing for titles like *The Legend of the Lone Ranger* (1981) and *The Green Hornet* (2010) which are cited in context with the earlier films based on those properties, our story essentially wraps up with *Pete Kelly's Blues* (1955), the last major Hollywood film to be inspired by a Golden Age radio series.

Note the qualifier "Hollywood." As much as I was tempted to include the many motion pictures derived from British radio programs, I just don't have the time, space and fortitude to include them. (Too bad: I had a ball watching such BBC-generated feature films as *Band Waggon, Hi Gang!, It's That Man Again* and *Dick Barton, Special Agent*). Hopefully this will get me off the hook for not including *Hitchhiker's Guide to the Galaxy* (2005), which though made by an American studio and starring American actors was based on a British radio serial and thus (reluctantly) omitted. There are other qualifiers and omissions to come in these pages, but we'll get to them in due time.

The number of radio-inspired motion pictures produced at any given time has been determined by prevailing show business cycles. The earliest influx of these films occurred during the first few years of the talking picture era, when it was finally feasible to hear as well as see one's radio favorites on the big screen. RKO Radio Pictures, a company with strong corporate ties to the NBC radio network, was the first studio to acknowledge radio's popularity with 1929's *The Vagabond Lover,* 1930's Amos 'n' Andy vehicle *Check and Double Check,* and 1931's *Way Back Home,* a film inspired by radio's *Sunday Evening at Seth Parker's.* While each of these films performed well at the box office, once the public's curiosity was satisfied there was a significant drop-off in ticket sales, discouraging RKO from producing any sequels and temporarily scaring off the other studios from likewise promoting radio personalities as movie stars. The few later exceptions like Ed Wynn's 1933 MGM starrer *The Chief* only served to demonstrate anew that the public is disinclined to pay admission for something they can get at home for free.

By 1932 there was no longer any novelty value in talkies, so the studios sought out other gimmicks to attract customers. One such method was the "all-star" film, exemplified by MGM's *Grand Hotel* and *Dinner at Eight.* For the price of a single ticket, the moviegoer could luxuriate in the spectacle of "more stars than there are in heaven," an experience that would have been cost-prohibitive on the Broadway stage or network radio. Paramount Pictures harnessed the all-star format to showcase several radio personalities whom they'd put under contract with their 1932 musical comedy *The Big Broadcast.* The strategy was masterful: Maybe the public wouldn't "buy" Bing Crosby for the length of an 87-minute feature, but it hardly mattered since the film also featured such broadcast favorites as George Burns & Gracie Allen, Kate Smith, Arthur Tracy, the Mills Brothers, Vincent Lopez, Cab Calloway, the Boswell Sisters and Donald Novis. And let's see them top *that* on any weekly radio program! The success of *The Big Broadcast* yielded other all-star extravaganzas, allowing the public to choose which radio stars they'd like to see on a solo basis in future films. In addition to Crosby and Burns & Allen, this formula advanced the film careers of such "radio people" as Bob Hope, Jack Benny, Martha Raye, Bob Burns and Joe Penner. It might have performed the same magic for singer Russ Columbo, whose appearance in the all-star Darryl F. Zanuck production *Broadway Through a Keyhole* (1933) demonstrated beyond doubt that his mass-audience appeal was equal to if not greater than Bing Crosby's. Tragically, no sooner had Columbo completed his starring vehicle *Wake Up and Dream* (1934) than he was killed in a shooting accident.

Beginning in 1939 we find another major cycle of radio-to-movie properties involving such stars as Kay Kyser, Edgar Bergen & Charlie McCarthy and Fibber McGee & Molly, and programs like *Dr. Christian, Lum & Abner* and *The Great Gildersleeve.* This can be attributed to the looming likelihood that commercial television would soon be the prevailing form of mass entertainment. Perusing the many radio fan magazines of the late 1930s, one finds article after article about the inevitability of TV, their titles always using the word "When" instead of "If" while discussing the still-experimental medium. The successful public demonstration of television at the 1939 New York World's Fair seemed to cinch the deal: Once the production and retail costs could be brought under control, there would a TV receiver in every American home. Rather than react with panic at this probability (as they would ten years later!), the major radio networks—NBC, the Columbia Broadcasting System (CBS) and Mutual—seemed to welcome the challenge of transitioning their operations to television, while the leading radio personalities expressed optimism that they would be just as popular seen as heard. But just to be on the safe side, let's make a few movies to find out if the public will accept radio stars and radio programs visually as well as aurally.

America's entry into World War II put a temporary halt to talk of the oncoming television "boom," as TV technologists moved away from entertainment considerations to focus on military activities. This didn't stop Hollywood from continuing to churn out films based on such programs as *Reveille with Beverly, The*

Whistler and *Take It or Leave It,* but this was mainly due to the double-feature policy followed by most American movie houses. With demand for motion picture entertainment increasing as the public sought escapism during the war years, it was necessary for the studios to make as many films as possible featuring as many different personalities and plotlines as traffic would allow. Network radio was by this time as potent and viable a source of movie material as novels or magazines. The difference between the radio-inspired films of the 1940s and those of the 1930s is that the later films were not treated as "specials" but as just another profitable genre like the western or the murder mystery. Even after the war, when Paramount produced a feature-film version of Lucille Fletcher's classic radio drama *Sorry Wrong Number,* it was not promoted as a novelty in the manner of such earlier radio-related films as *Chandu the Magician* (1932) or *Myrt and Marge* (1933), but primarily as a star vehicle for Barbara Stanwyck.

While big-time radio was bigger than ever in the immediate postwar era, some changes had been wrought in Hollywood. By government decree, the major studios had been forced to divest themselves of the theater chains that had long been the main conduit for their product; for example, Paramount Pictures was no longer linked with the Paramount theater circuit which had been its bread and butter in previous years. They were also compelled to drop the policy of block-booking, in which a studio could force an exhibitor to show all of its films in a given year—even the turkeys—in order to get the "prestige" titles that the exhibitor really wanted. The elimination of these business practices resulted in a drop-off of Hollywood revenue and a corresponding drop in the number of films annually produced by each studio. The individual production firms now had to carefully pick and choose which radio properties they would attempt to translate to film; no longer would there be mass production of "B" pictures inspired by such programs as *The Crime Doctor* and *I Love a Mystery.* Also, now that television technology was freed up for commercial development, Hollywood filmmakers—working in concert with the people making deals on behalf of radio stars and producers—showed a preference for radio properties that might conceivably lead to weekly TV shows. Hence the post–1948 movie adaptations of *A Date with Judy, The Life of Riley, My Friend Irma, Queen for a Day, Ozzie and Harriet* (*Here Come the Nelsons*) and *Pete Kelly's Blues.*

As network radio and its cornucopia of general-entertainment programs were overtaken by the ever-growing marketplace dominance of local stations and highly specialized formats (top–40 record shows, ethnic programming, religious broadcasts, all-news, all-sports and all-talk), Hollywood became uninterested in bringing individual radio programs and personalities to the screen. When time came to offer movie adaptations of such radio-originated efforts as *Dragnet* (the 1954 version), *Our Miss Brooks* and *The Lineup,* the films were patterned after the TV adaptations of these programs. Thus, films of this nature have not been included in this book, though I have made an exception with the 1950 filmization of the long-running radio program *The Goldbergs.* Even though the movie featured the cast from the TV version of the property and was heavily influenced by that version, it came close enough to the radio original both chronologically and stylistically to quality for inclusion.

So now we've arrived at the traditional "What's *not* in this book" tabulation that always seems necessary whenever an author feels compelled to keep the word and page count as low as possible. We've already eliminated a potentially long-winded "history of old-time radio" introduction, bypassing the usual references to the powerful influence of radio on the American public in the 1930s, 1940s, and 1950s, avoiding the nostalgic tally of the great shows, stars and catchphrases, and dispensing with the standard mournful elegy over how much pleasure was lost to future generations when television became the primary form of free popular entertainment. If you've chosen to read this book, you're more than likely familiar with this sort of introduction and don't need to read it again. Moreover, with nearly 200,000 recordings of vintage radio broadcasts presently circulating in archives, in CD form, on various commercial- and public-radio nostalgia shows and streaming on the Internet, there is no reason why the pleasures of Old Time Radio should be lost to anyone. They're there for the asking—and all that is missing is the thrill of listening to these programs live and for the first time.

In focusing on films inspired by radio programs, I have generally limited myself to movies based on properties that originated on radio. You won't find the film appearances of such fictional characters as David Harum, Bulldog Drummond, Ellery Queen, Sam Spade, Philip Marlowe, Mr. and Mrs. North, Nick and Nora Charles, Mike Hammer, the Falcon, Andy Hardy or Dr. Kildare. Even though all these characters had their own radio programs, they were based upon literary or movie properties, and therefore not radio originals. Again, however, I've tweaked the rules by including the *Henry Aldrich* and *Scattergood Baines* B-picture series, the former rooted in a Broadway play and the latter derived from a series of short stories dating back to 1917. They are included because I have determined that neither of the two film properties would have come to pass were it not for the success of the radio adaptations of *Henry Aldrich* (*The Aldrich Family*) and *Scattergood Baines*.

A similar criteria has been followed in the selection of radio personalities in this book. Entertainer Eddie Cantor was undeniably a major radio name, and certainly the same people who listened to him weekly also queued up to see his films. But Cantor was a superstar long before launching his radio program, not only on Broadway but also in films from 1926. His popularity on the airwaves was not ignored by Hollywood publicists, as witness the trade-paper advertisements for the 1933 reissue of his 1930 movie vehicle *Whoopee*: Though the film was originally released some time before Eddie hit it big on radio, the ad copy urged exhibitors to "CASH IN on the vast new audience created by Cantor on the air—the 40,000,000 people who follow his coast-to-coast broadcasts!" But given Cantor's long-standing popularity, it is likely that his films would have done just as well without any sort of radio tie-in. Also, Cantor

A film star long before he entered radio, Eddie Cantor (seen here in 1943) flourished in both mediums.

was careful not to appear in films that exploited his radio fame but instead were accessible even to those who never tuned him in on the Stromberg-Carlson console. When standing before the microphone Eddie played "himself," while in films he played characters different from the image he projected on radio. Perhaps significantly, the only one of Cantor's films for producer Sam Goldwyn to lose money was *Strike Me Pink* (1936), in which Eddie referenced his radio work by featuring his on-the-air stooge Harry "Parkyakarkus" Einstein.

Like Eddie Cantor, Bob Hope managed to separate his radio persona from his screen image by playing characters dissimilar to "himself." An argument can be made that Hope owed his film success in great part to his radio career. Though Bob had been a vaudeville and Broadway headliner and had appeared in a group of two-reel

Trumpeting his Pepsodent-sponsored radio program in the 1948 *Radio Annual,* Bob Hope didn't let us forget that he was also a top Paramount film personality.

Though both Cantor and Hope are referenced throughout this book, their actual entries are titled **The Eddie Cantor Connection** and **The Bob Hope Connection**. This is because I have not analyzed the multifaceted careers of these two entertainers, but instead focused on some of the supporting players who were heard on their respective radio series: comedians like Parkyakarkus, Bert "The Mad Russian" Gordon and Jerry Colonna, whose film careers were wholly a result of—and sometimes totally reliant upon—their radio work. The same applies to many of the other personalities cited in their own entries, among them Jack "Baron Munchausen" Pearl, Joe Penner, Fibber McGee & Molly, Bergen & McCarthy and Kay Kyser. True, some of these worthies had made film appearances before hitting it big on radio, but whatever movie stardom they subsequently enjoyed was a function of their radio fame—notably Penner, whose movie and radio popularity faded at virtually the same time.

In some instances I have delved rather deeply into personalities whose film work predated their radio stardom, notably Ed Wynn and Jack Benny. Their entries deal only summarily with their pre-radio work: The main focus is on the films they starred in that were directly related to their radio popularity—or to be blunt, films which probably wouldn't have been made were it not for their vast following on radio. Thus, when discussing Jack Benny we deal almost exclusively with *Buck Benny Rides Again, Love Thy Neighbor,* etc., leaving such Benny vehicles as *To Be or Not to Be* and *The Meanest Man in the World* to some future author who might wish to publish a "Complete Films of Jack Benny" tome (and you're welcome to the assignment!)

By their very nature, the films referenced in this book have something to do with radio. But "something to do with radio" isn't always enough for inclusion when you're dealing with specifics. Films like *The Phantom Broadcast, Crooner, Larceny in the Air, The Great American Broadcast, Foreign Correspondent, Who Done It?, The Unsuspected, I'll Get By, The Great Man, Play Misty for Me, WUSA, Radio Days, Airheads, Talk Radio* and *Radioland Murders*

comedies for Vitaphone prior to his first important radio work, it was his feature-film debut in *The Big Broadcast of 1938,* one of several Paramount films spotlighting clusters of popular radio personalities, that earned him a lengthy contract with the studio. Hope quickly demonstrated that he could succeed in films even without his weekly radio program, and though there were inevitable references to radio in his movies (notably a few "inside" jokes in his *Road* pictures with Bing Crosby), Hope could easily have dropped out of the NBC lineup without any adverse affect on his film career. The same is true of Bing Crosby, Phil Harris, Orson Welles, Abbott & Costello, Glenn Miller and Red Skelton, all of whom undeniably owed a debt to radio (in Welles' case a *huge* debt, *vide* "War of the Worlds") but were perfectly capable of thriving professionally without it.

spend a lot of time in radio studios, but because most of these films don't feature actual radio personalities or refer to genuine programs, it would be pointless to include them here. For a comprehensive list of all radio-themed movies up to the year 2010, as well as in-depth thematic analyses of several of those films, refer to Laurence Etling's excellent *Radio in the Movies: A History and Filmography, 1926–2010* (McFarland, 2011).

In addition to feature films inspired by network radio, this book includes such multichapter serials as *The Lone Ranger* (1938 version), *Captain Midnight* and *Jack Armstrong*. But please don't look for the serialized adaptations of *Buck Rogers, Hop Harrigan, Don Winslow of the Navy* or *Terry and the Pirates* (among others) because they were not radio originals despite their popularity on the air.

Few things connected with the writing of this book caused me as much personal grief as the space-dictated decision to exclude individual entries for the dozens of short-subject adaptations of radio shows, and for the hundreds of one- and two-reelers featuring major radio personalities—including many of the nation's top band leaders, musicians and vocalists. These deserve a book of their own, and perhaps will have one someday. That said, I would be remiss not to reference at least *some* of the short-form films that owed their existence to radio.

One can hardly overlook the *Screen Songs* cartoon series produced by Max Fleischer for Paramount Pictures, with their famous "bouncing ball" singalongs. During the 1930s most of the *Screen Songs* featured live-action vignettes with such radio favorites as Kate Smith, Rudy Vallee, the Boswell Sisters, Cab Calloway, Vincent Lopez, Arthur "The Street Singer" Tracy and many others who would graduate to feature film appearances. In some cases, these little animated gems offered rare glimpses of radio artists who almost never stepped before a movie camera, notably Billy Jones and Ernie Hare ("The Happiness Boys") and Harry Frankel, aka "Singing Sam the Barbasol Man." This last-named personality echoed a policy that dated back to radio's earliest days, when the name of a musical group often included the sponsor's name so as to sidestep the government's short-lived ban on radio advertising. By the time these performers showed up on film, they faced another taboo imposed by movie exhibitors who objected to the "free advertising" of onscreen commercial plugs. Thus, the two Vitaphone one-reelers from the 1935–36 season featuring the A&P Gypsies and the Cliquot Club Eskimos were released theatrically as *Harry Horlick and His Gypsies* and *Harry Reser and His Eskimos*.

Just as all-star feature films were a popular method of highlighting numerous radio stars within a single picture, so too did the short subject field have its multistar offerings. One of the most successful of these was Vitaphone's *Ramblin' Round Radio Row* series (1933–1936), initially hosted by Jerry Wald, then a newspaper columnist and later a Warner Bros. scriptwriter-producer. Among the "radio row" personalities given brief chances to shine in this series were Frances Langford, Tito Guizar, George Jessel, Baby Rose Marie, the Pickens Sisters, Freddie Rich, Smith Ballew, Roy Atwell, Morton Downey, Sr. and kiddie show host "Uncle Don" Carney. (You all know what he supposedly said when he thought he was off the air, so we won't repeat it—and besides, he never said it.) Over at Universal, *I Know Everybody and Everybody's Racket* (1932) was emceed by columnist Walter Winchell and featured singers Donald Novis and Arthur Tracy, and bandleaders Don Reisman and Charles "Buddy" Rogers. This short was produced by Universal's Rowland-Brice unit, which was also responsible for the studio's imitation *Ramblin' Round Radio Row* miniseries *Nick Kenny's Radio Thrills*.

While the novice performers on radio's *Major Bowes and The Original Amateur Hour* didn't qualify as stars, Bowes featured quite a few of them in his two RKO musical shorts. The first of these, *Major Bowes' Amateur Theater of the Air* (1935) offered the youthful singing group "The Three Flashes," featuring a 19-year-old beanpole named Frank Sinatra. *Variety* reviewed the Bowes films as merely "tolerable"—as if that would prevent us from wanting to see them today. On the other hand, *Variety* said nothing about the scattered 1940s shorts based on the Armed Forces Radio Service's wartime variety series *Mail Call,* because it would have been unpatriotic to criticize the spectacle of high-priced film and radio entertainers donating their services gratis for the boys in uniform. Of the single-reel film adaptations of *Mail Call,* the one that is most often revived today features Abbott & Costello performing their classic "Who's on First"—and since the film was never intended to be shown to civilian audiences, Costello gets to utter his pre-radio punchline "I don't give a damn!"

Radio's many human interest series seemed to adapt themselves well to the one- and two-reel format. Ben K. Blake, a New York–based producer who released his short subjects through Columbia, enjoyed a measure of success with a 1935 group of one-reelers based on Marion Sayles Taylor's CBS advice series *The Voice of Experience.* Blake followed this small triumph with a 1936 package of shorts inspired by A.L. Alexander's *Court of Human Relations,* an NBC program tied in with *True Story* magazine. Then there was storyteller John Nesbitt's *The Passing Parade,* which began as a Mutual radio program in 1937 and evolved into an MGM short subject series which lasted from 1938 through 1949, *then* made the transition to television a little less than a decade later.

Other short subject series based on radio programs included RKO's *Information Please* (1940–41), transferred to the screen with the NBC radio panel (Clifton Fadiman, Franklin P. Adams, John Kieran, Oscar Levant) intact and with such guest panelists as Boris Karloff and Deems Taylor; Paramount's *The Quiz Kids* (1941–42), from the NBC game show hosted by Joe Kelly and featuring such child prodigies as Joel Kupperman; and Columbia's *Candid Microphone* (1948–51), based on Allen Funt's ABC radio precursor to *Candid Camera.* Another radio property, the comedy quiz *It Pays to Be Ignorant,* was obviously intended as the launching pad for a series of RKO one-reelers in 1948, but the first film in the series turned out to be the last. And we haven't even mentioned the group of mid–1930s shorts produced by Van Beuren for RKO release and starring radio humorists Goodman and Jane Ace ("The Easy Aces"), though several other comedy shorts featuring radio personalities like Jack Benny, Bergen & McCarthy and Fred Allen are referenced elsewhere in this the book.

Finally, a word about the scores of Hollywood animated cartoons featuring caricatured versions of radio favorites. Again, there's a whole separate book in this story, especially if you plan to write about the innumerable radio references in the output of Warner Bros.' animation unit. Randomly sampling these little masterpieces, one would think that Jerry Colonna and Joe Penner were the funniest comedians in radio—if not the *only* comedians in radio. But for all the ersatz radio stars popping up in animated form, only three cartoon shorts were directly based on radio properties. The first two, Van Beuren–RKO's *The Rasslin' Match* and *The Lion Tamer* (both 1934), featured the characters and voices heard on NBC's *Amos 'n' Andy.* The third entry came from Paramount's Famous Studios unit: *Land of the Lost* (1948), adapted from the ABC (and later Mutual) children's program of the same name. This 7½-minute cartoon adheres to the basic premise of the radio series, as youngsters Isabel and Billy take a fascinating underwater journey in search of Billy's missing jackknife, with the gentlemanly talking fish Red Lantern (voiced by Jackson Beck, replacing the radio version's Art Carney) as their guide. And just as in the radio show, the kids avoid drowning by latching onto the magic seaweed provided by their host. *Land of the Lost* is a charming and colorful diversion, but like most Paramount-Famous one-shots of the period it was a bit too lethargic to generate much enthusiasm, and no follow-ups were produced.

And in conclusion, I—

(SOUND: MUSIC CUE)

Thank you, Hal Erickson. And now, ladies and gentlemen, here's what you've all been waiting for: A historical overview of radio personalities and programs that Hollywood has tried, and sometimes succeeded, to transform into popular movie commodities.

But first, this brief word ...

The Personalities, the Programs, the Pictures

The following section focuses on Hollywood films that were either designed to showcase radio stars or were based on popular radio programs. The section covers the years 1926 to the present. Unless otherwise indicated, all films referenced are feature-length, with a running time of at least 55 minutes.

The entries are arranged in chronological order, based upon the release date of the first significant film mentioned in each entry. For example, you will find "The Shadow" listed chronologically in the year 1937, even though the films mentioned in the entry cover the years 1931 through 1994; and you will find Kay Kyser listed in 1939, the year of Kyser's first starring feature *That's Right—You're Wrong*.

In the entry headings, film titles are listed in italics (e.g., *It's a Joke, Son*). The titles of the radio programs and the names of radio characters are indicated with quotation marks (e.g. "Your Hit Parade" and "Baron Munchausen").

During the period covered in this book, there were four major radio networks. Three are still in existence: CBS (the Columbia Broadcasting System), ABC (The American Broadcasting Company) and NBC (the National Broadcasting Company), though the latter is currently a medium-scale sports network with little relation to its larger television counterpart. A fourth network, the Mutual Broadcasting System, was commonly known as MBS. Because this long-defunct network is not familiar to modern readers, I have avoided the acronym and referred to it in the text as either "Mutual" or "the Mutual network."

There might be some confusion involving NBC. In January 1927, this fledgling network was divided into two separate chains, NBC-Red and NBC-Blue, each with its own separate program lineup. Since the "Red" was the main network, it will be referenced in these pages simply as NBC; its sister network is listed as NBC-Blue.

In 1942 the FCC pressured NBC to divest itself of one of its chains, so that year the Blue Network became an independent operation. In 1943 the Blue was purchased by Edward J. Noble and renamed ABC, the name by which it is known today.

And now, back to our story ...

Ann Howe (the Radio Girl) (1926–1928)

Pointless though it may seem, the first radio personality to appear onscreen made her debut in silent films. That term "radio personality" is a bit misleading, however. Ann Howe did indeed rise to prominence because of radio—but not necessarily *on* the radio.

It was all explained in a newspaper article

syndicated by NEA on January 21, 1928. Don Meany, announcer for Los Angeles radio station KNX, felt that the broadcast industry needed a representative in the film industry, preferably an attractive female representative. Asking his audience for their reaction to this idea, Meany received thousands of letters encouraging KNX to run a contest to find the perfect "Radio Girl." Officially launched in early 1925, this contest was limited to young ladies who had not previously appeared in movies. The listeners were never permitted to see the contestants; their votes were based solely on verbal descriptions of the girls in question, as broadcast by Meany and the KNX staff.

The lucky winner was a pert brunette named Ann Howe, whose next goal was to get into movies as an actress. In the spirit of "what's good for one is good for all," KNX was assisted in its campaign to achieve stardom for Ann Howe by every other Los Angeles station. The "Radio Girl" was then sent on a nationwide tour, visiting the many regional radio outlets participating in the campaign. During her 18-month odyssey through the 48 contiguous states, Ann received 60,000 telegrams and 867,000 fan letters of support. It is not known whether Ann spoke over the radio at any time, but it's extremely likely that she did.

When Hollywood beckoned Ann to their hallowed studio halls (as if there was even a remote possibility that this wouldn't happen), the trades announced that her debut film would be the semi-autobiographical *Ann of Tin Pan Alley,* followed by four additional starring vehicles. Instead, her only known silent screen appearance was in the Hal Roach two-reel comedy *Mighty Like a Moose,* released July 18, 1926. The film is a typical Charley Chase farce in which Chase and Vivien Oakland play a married couple who fail to recognize each other after undergoing cosmetic surgery. Billed third in the cast as "Ann Howe (The Radio Girl)," the novice actress is consigned to the very small—almost infinitesimal—role of the couple's maid. Sporting a dutch bob, Ann appears for approximately 55 seconds and never has a close-up. Indeed, she spends most of her time being shoved out of camera range by the two leading players. A showcase it isn't.

The Ann Howe story was kept alive by the press for the next two years, by which time Hollywood was in the process of converting to talkies. Ann must have briefly relocated to New York during this period, since her next screen credit is the Vitaphone short *The Wild Westerner,* released on November 14, 1928. This peppy little one-reeler is dominated by vaudevillian Val Harris, in his established characterization as a decrepit old man with an eye for delectable young damsels. As an Eastern gal named "Remington" (a play on the cowboy portrait artist of the same name), Ann sings and dances two songs with the star, "The Grass Grows Greener" and "Wob-a-ly Walk," and also cracks a few jokes. Still not a showcase, but Ann is quite appealing.

And that, as they say, was that. Ann Howe the Radio Girl vanished into obscurity, her brief fling at filmmaking and the contest that brought her national renown lost in the sands of time. Suffice to say that this Ann Howe was not the "Anne Howe" who appeared *el buffo* in such 1990s porn epics as *Young and Anal 15* and *In Your Face 8.*

Rudy Vallee and *The Vagabond Lover* (1929)

Famed in American legend (to paraphrase the studio's later epic *Citizen Kane*) is the origin of RKO Radio Pictures. It was at a Manhattan oyster bar in October 1928 that David Sarnoff, president of Radio Corporation of American (RCA) and by extension the NBC radio network, conferred with Joseph P. Kennedy, whose many business concerns included the Film Booking Office (FBO) movie firm. Sarnoff had been looking for a customer to license his newly developed Photophone sound-on-film process, but the major Hollywood studios had already contracted with other companies for their transition to talkies. Kennedy had sold a considerable interest in FBO to RCA, so it was only logical that he would agree to showcase Photophone in all future productions. To secure coast-to-coast distribution for the talkie FBO efforts, RCA acquired a distributor: Keith-Albee-Orpheum, a fading vaudeville circuit that was anxious to break into motion pictures. With K-A-O's 100-plus theaters in their corporate clutches, Sarnoff and Kennedy named their new operation Radio-Keith-Orpheum (RKO)—and while RKO was the legal designation of the firm's distribution arm, Kennedy's FBO was officially rechristened Radio Pictures. With few exceptions, the acronym "RKO" would appear at the beginning of a film only in conjunction with another acquisition, Pathé Pictures, and in the cartoons produced by Van Beuren Productions, released through RKO; otherwise, the three letters were confined to the copyright listings in the opening credits. Until 1937, when "RKO Radio Pictures" became the blanket name for all of the company's subsidiaries, the studio's transmission-tower logo would beam out the words "A Radio Picture"—and nothing else.

With this in mind, and given the fact that it was in Sarnoff's best interest to promote his NBC radio chain as aggressively as possible, what better studio to begin courting radio personalities than RKO? Their inaugural release *Syncopation* (1929) featured singer Morton Downey and orchestra leader Fred Waring, both airwave favorites at the time. But Downey and Waring were major names *before* the emergence of radio: Sarnoff preferred to develop new movie stars whose chief claim to fame was their radio popularity—specifically, their popularity as NBC contractees.

Which brings us to Hubert Prior "Rudy" Vallee—or Vallée, as he was billed in fan magazines of the era. Born in Island Point, Vermont, in 1901, the wavy-haired, dreamy-eyed Vallee worked his way through Maine College and Yale as a bandleader, doubling in saxophone, banjo and piano. Though he felt his voice was too thin and nasal to gain audience acceptance, Vallee added "singer" to his résumé in order to impress potential employers with his versatility. His intimate, natural singing style, popularly (and sometimes derisively) known as crooning, was in marked contrast with the leather-lunged tenors and baritones then in vogue. To amplify his voice, Vallee used a megaphone, which soon became his trademark. When microphones came into common usage, Rudy enhanced his already acknowledged appeal with the ladies in the crowd by appearing to embrace and caress the microphone column.

Forming a new band called the Connecticut Yankees in 1928, Vallee was headlining at New York's Heigh-Ho Club (which would provide him with his familiar greeting "Heigh-ho, everybody") when he was hired by NBC flagship station WEAF to star in a weekly musical program. With WEAF's powerful signal blanketing the East Coast and much of the Midwest, Rudy's following increased dramatically, whereupon NBC programming head Bertha Brainard persuaded the network to promote Vallee to a coast-to-coast slot, stifling protests from her male colleagues by arguing that only a woman could fully appreciate the "hypnotic" power of Rudy's voice. On October 24, 1929, *The Fleischmann Yeast Hour* signed on the air with Rudy Vallee as host—and within what seemed like a few seconds, the NBC chieftains were forced to admit that Bertha Brainard had hit the nail on the head. Much to the chagrin of fire-breathing newspaper reporters and other self-appointed guardians of musclebound manhood, Rudy's female fans went bonkers whenever he made a personal appearance, a screaming-throng mania unsurpassed until the advent of Frank Sinatra in the 1940s.

Aware of Vallee's catnip effect on the ladies long before the singer's full-network bow, Sarnoff prodded RKO production chief William Le Baron to bring Rudy and his orchestra to Hollywood in the early autumn of 1929. Contrary to studio publicity, this was not Vallee's first foray into filmmaking. While still in New York in the spring and summer of that year, he and the Connecticut Yankees had appeared in an eponymously titled Vitaphone short, as well as the one-reel *Radio Rhythm,* somewhat clumsily photographed at Paramount's Astoria studio, in which Rudy interrupted a flow of characteristic tunes with an amusing takeoff on fellow bandleader Ted Lewis.

Neither of these shorts required Vallee to be an actor, merely to trot out the talents he'd already displayed on radio. But RKO had a feature-length film in mind, and people are generally expected to act in feature-length films, especially stars. The fact that Rudy had never played a character other than himself, nor had even done much talking on radio other than introducing the next number, wasn't important to Bill LeBaron and his associate producer Barney Sarecky, who assigned Hollywood scrivener James Creelman, Jr., to fashion a screen story into which Vallee and the Connecticut Yankees could logically be inserted. In a serialized "autobiography" which received national newspaper syndication in April 1930, Vallee (or his studio-appointed ghost) touched upon this: "In the choice of a story it was necessary to have one that would bring the seven boys [in the orchestra] into the picture and give them a logical reason for being there, but yet we wanted to avoid the hackneyed night club, backstage and college campus idea." Creelman lifted a few tidbits from Rudy's own career—the student kappellmeister who rises to radio renown—and then fleshed things out with an extended mistaken identity-innocent deception conceit.

Its title taken from one of Vallee's best-known songs, *The Vagabond Lover* revolves around aspiring musician Rudy Bronson. After months of taking mail-order lessons from star saxaphonist Ted Grant, he brings his college band along when he pays a visit to Grant's Long Island estate. The swell-headed sax player kicks Rudy and the boys out on their keesters, then leaves for an extended tour. Making a desperate attempt to storm the estate, Rudy is caught in the act by Grant's wealthy neighbor Mrs. Whitehall and her comely niece Jean. To prevent the boys from being arrested as burglars, band member "Sport" allows Mrs. Whitehall to assume that Rudy is really Ted Grant, whereupon the flustered hero is invited to perform at an orphan's benefit. Having fallen in love with Jean and not wishing to disillusion her, Rudy decides to bluff his way through the performance—and then the truth comes out at the worst possible moment. But by the time the benefit takes place, NBC microphones and announcers have somehow made their way to the Whitehall mansion and Rudy is besieged with lucrative of-

Rudy Vallee with his trusty megaphone in 1929, the year of his first starring picture *Vagabond Lover*.

fers. All this may seem old hat to film fans who've seen the same plot trotted out for other singers-turned-movie stars, but in 1929 it was a relatively new set of contrivances, and an inoffensive method of linking several musical numbers together into a semblance of continuity.

Vallee's 1930 newspaper autobiography indicated that he himself had chosen to play "a shy, embarrassed boy ... whose high idealistic principles caused him to be conscience-stricken throughout the entire picture due to the deception which he was practicing." Rudy would sing a different tune in interviews printed only a few years later, claiming he'd wanted "Rudy Bronson" to be a virile man of action, the better to discredit the prevailing critical consensus that all crooners were creampuffs. And since screenwriter Creelman had previously excelled in such raw-meat melodramas as *The Coming of Amos, Aloma of the South Seas* and *The Red Dance*, Vallee very likely believed at the time that this was the image he would project onscreen. But with the plotline at hand, Rudy has little to do but react in bewilderment to the aggressiveness of other characters: Besides the irascible Ted Grant and the effusive Mrs. Whitehall, he also tangles with an unpleasantly inquisitive town constable. He was also required to hem, haw and stammer uncomfortably as he tries to pass himself off as someone he's not.

As for the love scenes with leading lady Sally Blane (described in the publicity as "RKO's baby starlet," though she was 19), in 1930 Rudy was telling the world that he wanted to convey "a daze of puppy love from the moment I met the heroine of the story." What we see on screen is an inarticulate clod who spends most of his time moping like a moonstruck calf; he appears to be suffering less from puppy love than a bad case of heartburn. In an insightful moment from his newspaper autobiography, Rudy admitted, "There was little opportunity on my part for very much animation or life, and hardly a chance to smile.... The part was practically 'personality-less.'" Remove the modifier "practically" and you've said it all. There are manhole covers with more animation and personality than Rudy Vallee in *The Vagabond Lover*.

Nor is Vallee helped in the slightest by the stilted dialogue he is given to speak. In fact, the rest of the cast, though populated by such Broadway and Hollywood veterans as Charles Sellon, Nella Walker and Malcolm Waite, is often as much at sea as the novice star. Sally Blane, who'd been acting since age seven, is forced to mouth such inanities as "That's Mrs. Todhunter, my aunt's hated social rival"—a line that not even Katharine Hepburn could have delivered without sounding like the lead daffodil in a third-grade spring pageant.

Even with a non-actor as star and a strictly-from-hunger script, it might still have been possible to salvage the film with a skilled and supportive director at the helm. Too bad *The Vagabond Lover* didn't have one. Marshall Neilan had been one of Hollywood's golden boys in the silent days, turning out hit after hit and beloved by filmgoers and critics alike; at one time, he was the favorite director of Mary Pickford. Unfortunately, Neilan was a slave to those three malevolent mistresses known as Wine, Women, and Song. His public displays of drunkenness, his frequent and lengthy absences from his own movie sets, and his perverse cultivation of such powerful enemies as MGM mogul L.B. Mayer—whom Neilan disparaged as "Lousy Bastard Mayer"—had all but destroyed his career by the end of the silent era.

Through the kindness of the few friends he had left, Neilan was given a chance to redeem himself at RKO in 1929. Thrown off balance by the switchover to sound—he'd already made four talkies under horrendous conditions—and embroiled in a messy divorce from actress Blanche Sweet, Neilan was hardly prepared to face the challenge of transforming Rudy Vallee into John Barrymore when he staggered onto the set of *The Vagabond Lover*. Vallee later recalled that Neilan was not only uncommunicative but downright hostile: Whenever Rudy asked advice on how to deliver a line or perform a bit of business, the bleary-eyed director told him to shut up and sing.

Once hosannaed for his directorial innovations and brilliant on-set improvisations, Neilan clearly regarded this film as something to get over with quickly and to hell with what the end product looked like. Most early talkies seem primitive when seen today: *The Vagabond Lover* looks positively prehistoric. The only sequence with even a scintilla of cinematic flair is the lavish third-act production number, utilizing an entire RKO sound stage and enhanced by intricate lighting effects, in which 40 young girls in diaphanous costumes dance to the tune of the title song, their ballet-like terpsichore deftly morphing into a Charleston. The success of this sequence had absolutely nothing to do with Marshall Neilan: Covered by six cameras and twelve microphones, the dance number was timed and paced by the choreographer, the editing staff and the sound technicians.

In fairness, *The Vagabond Lover* isn't a total loss. Vallee's singing, which after all was the film's main selling angle, is pleasant and persuasive, though his much-publicized sexual magnetism ("NO DON JUAN ... NO CASANOVA ... NO VILLON EVER THRILLED THE WORLD TO THE DEPTHS OF ITS ROMANTIC HEART AS DOES THIS BLONDE BOY SINGER") is diluted by Neilan's insistence upon confining the star to long and medium shots. The scenes involving Rudy's band members—with professional actors Eddie Nugent and Danny O'Shea added to the mix—are enlivened by some adroitly handled overlapping dialogue. An exterior sequence in which Rudy bids an awkward goodbye to Blane is effectively counterpointed by the sound of a genuine train pulling into and out of a depot, unobtrusively demonstrating the superiority of RCA's Photophone over other sound systems. And despite the stagnant direction and scripting, a few moments of spontaneity manage to creep in, notably Vallee's joshing interplay with the Connecticut Yankees during a bouncy rehearsal session, and a charmingly disheveled recitation of "Georgie Porgie" performed by a group of little orphan girls.

The highlight is the gloriously *outré* damn-the-torpedoes performance by the magnificent Marie Dressler as the social-climbing Mrs. Whitehall. The lack of strong direction and adequate acting support didn't mean a blessed thing to Miss Dressler, who here as in all her talkie appearances is (in the words of director George Cukor) "a law unto herself." Bellowing her lines with a resonance that would have filled Madison Square Garden, waving her arms as if she's about to take flight, all but tearing her prop handkerchief to shreds and performing double and triple takes at the slightest provocation (and sometimes no provocation at all), Marie Dressler doesn't merely steal *The Vagabond Lover*: She bushwhacks, ropes and hogties the film.

If RKO's pre-release publicity can be believed, *The Vagabond Lover* was planned as a long, lavish super-spectacular with Technicolor highlights, just like the studio's previous musical blockbuster *Rio Rita*. There was even talk among RKO executives that the film would be shown on a reserved-seat, limited-release roadshow basis. But the studio dumped this strategy and elected to complete *The Vagabond Lover* quickly and economically, then give it a wide popular-price distribution, in order to capitalize on Vallee's radio fame before it (theoretically) peaked—and to beat the time of Paramount's *Glorifying the American Girl*, which showcased Vallee in a guest spot. The 67-minute RKO musical opened at New York's Globe Theater on November 24, 1929, with Rudy interrupting a live engagement at the Paramount Theater to make a personal appearance. The Globe was filled to overflowing with delighted fans (mostly female), and throughout the U.S. the crowds remained undiminished until well past New Year's Day. *The Vagabond Lover* closed out 1929 as one of RKO's three biggest moneymakers of the year.

Walter R. Greene of *Motion Picture News* had predicted on November 15 that the film would be a smash, but with a caveat: "As a production exploiting Vallee and his music, this can be billed heavily for substantial business. Little should be said about Rudy as a screen actor—he just isn't." This was the tone of the other reviews: As an actor, the star was a swell singer. Some critics were unduly nasty in their assessment of Vallee's screen presence: "Buck teeth weren't made as an aid to heart throbs and a wooden expression is seldom conducive to emotional fervor," sneered *Exhibitor's Herald-World*. But most observers came for the music and were willing to overlook Rudy's histrionic shortcomings, echoing the words of *Photoplay*: "Rudy goes through the whole gamut of emotions without moving a muscle. But when he sings—ah, that's another story. (A better one, too.) Vallee fans will be pleased."

Only in later years did *The Vagabond Lover* earn its not entirely warranted reputation as a dismal box-office flop. This began as early as 1933, when a newspaper article about Sally Blane stated bluntly that the Vallee film was unsuccessful. It's possible that the author of this piece was not referring to profitability, but simply judging a 1929 picture by 1933 standards: Many films that had been hits in the first full year of talkies—*In Old Arizona, Broadway Melody, The Cock-Eyed World*—were being written off as virtually unwatchable by the early 1930s. Nonetheless, the "failure" rep stuck, further fueled in the 1960s when Vallee himself would characterize *The Vagabond Lover* as a mega-bomb, complaining that the studio had sabotaged and double-crossed him by editing out all his good scenes and leaving only the dregs. His sour attitude might have been exacerbated by RKO's decision not to exercise the option on his contract after the film was completed, as articulated in a interoffice studio memo: "[A]lthough our picture proved to be a commercial success it was not in our opinion a good picture, nor was it in the opinion of the public. We did not deem Vallee a suitable motion picture personality.... It would appear that others in the industry shared our opinions for no other company undertook to make a picture starring Mr. Vallee."

Well, that's hardly the *whole* story. Rudy continued appearing in short subjects, made another guest appearance in Paramount's *International House,* and after a few Broadway successes returned to starring features at Fox and Warner Bros. in 1934. However, Vallee would not truly click as a film actor until his role as a stuffy middle-aged millionaire in Preston Sturges' *The Palm Beach Story* (1942) established him as one of Hollywood's most reliable character comedians. And of course he enjoyed steady success in radio, television, theater and nightclubs for the next four decades. Two years before his death in 1986, Rudy Vallee was able to chuckle benignly at the memory of *The Vagabond Lover* in a British TV interview—though he hastened to add, "It's a picture we never mention in our family. They're still fumigating theaters where it was shown."

"Amos 'n' Andy" and *Check and Double Check* (1930)

Despite their disappointment with Rudy Vallee (q.v.), William LeBaron and his fellow RKO executives continued pursuing the policy of constructing feature films around stellar NBC radio personalities. RKO's next candidate for film immortality was not only the most successful broadcast property of its time, but the most successful radio series of *all* time.

Freeman F. Gosden (1899–1982) and Charles C. Correll (1890–1972) had been partners since 1919, first as theatrical managers and then as a close-harmony singing duo. In 1923 they first stepped before a microphone at a small Chicago radio station. Two years later, the *Chicago Tribune*'s radio outlet WGN offered them $250 per week to develop a daily 15-minute radio serial based on one of the *Tribune*'s popular comic strips. Instead, the team chose to develop their own characters, dipping into their Southern roots by speaking their lines in a broad African American dialect. "We chose black characters," Gosden explained decades later, "because blackface could tell funnier stories than whiteface comics."

Debuting on January 12, 1926, *Sam 'n' Henry* was the story of a pair of penniless Southern black "boys" who had migrated North in hopes of improving their lot in life, a not unusual situation for the period. Gosden played the industrious, mild-mannered Sam Smith, while Correll was cast as the lazy, braggadocio Henry Johnson. The series struck a responsive chord with black and white listeners alike, emboldening Gosden and Correll to ask WGN to record the series on discs and distribute them to stations outside Chicago. When WGN vetoed the idea, the team moved to WMAQ, owned by the *Tribune*'s rival paper the *Daily News*. The legal ramifications of this move compelled the partners to change the names of their characters to Amos Jones and Andrew Brown, and thus on March 19, 1928, *Amos 'n' Andy* was born. The "chainless chain" of radio affiliates arising from the syndication of the show's transcription discs led to a nationwide NBC hookup beginning August 19, 1929, sponsored by Pepsodent. With various changes of format, *Amos 'n' Andy* spanned the entire history of big-time network radio, remaining on the air until November 25, 1960.

Before going any further, we must kill the elephant in the room. Although Gosden and Correll were meticulous in removing all overt racism in their series, purging the scripts of such trigger words as "darkie" and "colored" and avoiding references to watermelon, dice and razors, Amos 'n' Andy still conversed in an exaggerated dialect derived from the world of the blackface minstrel show, with malaprops and mispronunciations abounding. While the main characters were depicted as warm-hearted, multidimensional human beings, neither character was the brightest bulb, seemingly incapable of writing the simplest letter or calculating the most elementary math problem. From its first episode onward, *Amos 'n' Andy* was hotly debated among genuine African Americans: Some prominent black periodicals like the *Chicago Defender* were willing to accept the show for its good intentions and entertainment value; others like the *Pittsburgh Courier* condemned it as demeaning and detrimental to all black people and regularly organized campaigns in hopes of forcing it off the air. Scores of books and articles have been written about the series' sociopolitical significance, with one particular essay managing to find more hidden messages and meanings in *Amos 'n' Andy* than in the collected works of James Joyce. Nothing will be accomplished by hashing out the controversy any further here. Freeman Gosden and Charles Correll were two white men who became rich and famous portraying two black men. Enough said.

"Phenomenal" is the adjective usually used to describe the immense and unprecedented popularity of *Amos 'n' Andy* during its first three years on NBC. In its heyday, the show boasted 50,000,000 listeners at any given time. We've all heard the stories of how people could stroll through their neighborhood between 7 and 7:15 p.m. each evening and hear the entire program through the open windows of the houses along the street; of how movie theaters would stop the picture in progress to pipe in the program over the loudspeakers; of how businesses would change their work hours so that employees could get home in time to tune in the show and not miss anything; of how distinguished men of letters and wealthy captains of industry would refuse to see or talk to anyone during the 15 minutes that *Amos 'n' Andy* was wafting through the ether. Explanations for this spectacular response have ranged from the newness and novelty of radio itself, to the universal chord that the two struggling-but-optimistic characters struck with audiences in the early years of the Depression. A contributing factor was the series' deployment of the cliffhanger format to keep listener interest piqued from one episode to the next. Then there was critic Robert E. Sherwood's attribution of the show's success to the "humility" of stars Gosden and Correll, who by not being billed by their real names on the air enabled listeners to accept *Amos 'n' Andy* as "real people" and not merely actors. (Sherwood had no way of knowing that the stars had initially chosen to remain anonymous so as not to be typecast as blackface comedians.) Whatever the reason, in 1930 *Amos 'n' Andy* was the biggest thing ever to hit the entertainment industry—and RKO Radio Pictures couldn't ignore the phenomenon.

In the months leading up to the filming of the inaugural Gosden-Correll starring vehicle, RKO's publicity department insisted that the picture was being produced in answer to "millions of letters" from fans. In truth, it was the nucleus of a wide-range merchandising convergence involving RCA's radio and movie divisions, along with the individual licensees of Amos 'n' Andy phonograph records, souvenirs, toys, games, picture books and candy products. These interrelated entities received coast-to-coast newspaper saturation with an explosion of pre-film articles and two-page advertising splashes at the time of the film's nationwide release, which took place in 300 theaters simultaneously. The mammoth *Amos 'n' Andy* campaign of 1930 stands as the first true show business example of synergistic marketing.

The film went into development under the title *Amos 'n' Andy* before it was decided to rename it with one of the radio version's many popular catchphrases. There was certainly a huge selection to choose from: "Ain't dat sumpin'," "I'se regusted," "I ain't gonna do it," Amos' anguished moan "Ah-wah, ah-wah," and so on. The *bon mot* chosen was "Check and Double Check," a phrase used whenever Andy was taking inventory. To avoid a replay of their headaches with the mercurial Marshall Neilan in *The Vagabond Lover,* RKO selected pliable contract director Melville Brown to helm the Amos 'n' Andy vehicle.

Gosden and Correll were paid $250,000 for their participation in *Check and Double Check,* plus 50 percent of the film's profits. So that the team could continue their two daily broadcasts (for different time zones) without interruption during the three-month shooting period, a small radio studio was set up on the RKO lot, with the movie company shelling out the exorbitant costs required for an NBC telephone-line hookup from California to the East Coast. The two stars liked this setup so much that they would permanently move their base of operation from Chicago to Hollywood not long after filming wrapped.

Inasmuch as Gosden and Correll did all the writing on the radio version, by rights they should have handled the screenplay themselves. Since the series ran a scant 15 minutes per night, this would probably have resulted in a film running a little over an hour, a perfectly respectable length for a 1930 comedy feature. But RKO demanded a longer effort to secure "A" bookings; plus, the studio had planned *Check and Double Check* as a splashy musical comedy along the line of their recent 98-minute Wheeler & Woolsey picture *The Cuckoos*. To that end, RKO retained the services of Broadway's Bert Kalmar and Harry Ruby, who'd been brought West to adapt *The Cuckoos* from their own stage hit *The Ramblers*. Songwriters by trade, Kalmar and Ruby were also skilled story constructionists and gag writers, as witness their celebrated collaborations with the Marx Brothers. In keeping with established musical-comedy tradition, the writers concocted a scenario whereby the star comedians would be left alone to make funny while a "straight" subplot was propelled forward by the romantic leads.

In *Check and Double Check*, Amos 'n' Andy operate within their own plotline involving an annual ritual performed by the duo's fraternal lodge, the Mystic Knights of the Sea. Our heroes are chosen to venture into the "haunted" Williams mansion in the dead of night to retrieve a piece of paper bearing the words "Check and Double Check," left there by two other lodge members the previous year. The romantic subplot concerns a white couple, Jean Blair (Sue Carol) and Richard Williams (Charles Morton). The scion of a once prominent but now impoverished Southern family, Richard wants to marry the wealthy Jean, but hesitates until he can locate a deed which will enable him to sell his family estate and set himself up in business. The two storylines converge when it is revealed that Amos 'n' Andy had once worked for Richard's late and beloved father—who also was the owner of the very mansion which they must enter in order to retrieve that paper for their lodge. As expected, the paper gets mixed up with the deed, leading to many complications before Amos 'n' Andy can restore the crucial document to Richard and secure the boy's future happiness with Jean.

In a garden-variety musical comedy, the lead comics are permitted to freely associate with the young lovers. But in *Check and Double Check*, Kalmar and Ruby were confronted with a formidable social barrier. A previous Paramount feature starring blackface comedians Moran & Mack had been heavily criticized by Southern film patrons and exhibitors for the "familiarity" between the team and their white co-stars. Though by 1930 only the most obtuse radio fan was unaware that Freeman Gosden and Charles Correll were Caucasian, the mere fact that they were portraying African Americans barred their characters from any sort of casual socializing with the lily-white supporting cast. The only extended instance in which Amos 'n' Andy share the same frame with a white character is a key exposition scene with their former boss' son Richard—and throughout this dialogue exchange, the comedians are forced to behave in a manner so deferential that they might as well be the house slaves in *Gone with the Wind*. Gosden and Correll's radio series may have been praised for its "progressive" attitude towards race, but this was not commercially viable in the world of 1930s Hollywood, where studio executives were compelled to pussyfoot around lest they run afoul of Southern censorship boards.

For the first time in the history of movies, RKO was faced with the challenge of visualizing a set of radio characters and circumstances that had previously been left to the listeners' imagination. Thanks to the word pictures painted on the air by Gosden and Correll, together with the publicity photos, toys and storybooks already in circulation, it was no trick to bring Amos 'n' Andy's Harlem-based business enterprise, the Fresh Air Taxi Cab Company of America "Incorpulated," to full bloom on screen. The whole country knew that the "corpulation" consisted of a single broken-down Model T with no top and no windshield—hence the "Fresh Air" appellation. As for the their own on-camera appearance, the stars wanted a semblance of authenticity that would not have been possible had they used the traditional minstrel makeup—jet-black facial pigmentation, huge white lips—they'd previously worn for personal appearances. The RKO cosmeticians developed a more "realistic" makeup for the team, similar to that used by white actors when playing Othello. As part of a strategy to keep audience interest piqued until the film's release, the stars refused to issue any studio portraits of themselves in character makeup to the press, nor were reporters allowed on the set.

There was one aspect of the actors' characterizations that could not be dealt with by makeup alone. On radio, the blustering Andy gave the impression of being physically larger than the supplicative Amos—but in real life, Freeman Gosden stood a head taller than Charles Correll. In a *Pittsburgh Press* article written six years after the film's completion, Si Steinhauser explained how Correll appeared to tower over Gosden in front of the camera: "In *Check and Double Check* ... the illusion was carried out by special chairs, heavy shoe soles and out-of-proportion furniture made for Andy's use. And when they walked up stairs, in the picture Andy was always ahead of Amos."

In the interest of visual uniformity, virtually every other African American in the film was played by a white man in blackface, including the 200 or so extras in the lodge-hall scene. Likewise, the one major black character outside of Amos 'n' Andy was cast with a white actor. On radio, Gosden and Correll played *all* the roles, with Gosden doubling as Amos and as the series' most popular supporting character, that lovably larcenous potentate of the Mystic Knights of the Sea known as the Kingfish (his "real" name, George Stevens, was at the time unmentioned). Obviously Gosden couldn't play two parts simultaneously on screen, so it was necessary to find an actor who could approximate the Kingfish's radio voice and personality. Surprisingly, Gosden's first choice was a *non*-actor, NBC executive Alex Robb. But when Robb was called away to New York on business, the stars conducted a series of auditions, finally settling upon Russell Powell, a portly slapstick comedian who'd enjoyed some film prominence in the World War I era but had latterly been confined to bit parts. Powell's peculiar talent for making weird and somewhat disgusting vocal sound effects was not exploited by *Check and Double Check,* in which his characterization was confined to the established Kingfish radio image.

As it turned out, the Kingfish was the only other character from the radio version to appear in the film. RKO publicity flacks suggested that stuttering comedian

Amos (Freeman Gosden) and Andy (Charles Correll) ruminate over their taxi business in the team's 1930 film debut *Check and Double Check.*

Roscoe Ates would show up in blackface as "Lightnin," the lodge hall's slow-witted janitor; instead, the prominently billed Ates appears in a one-scene cameo as Brother Arthur. And in emulation of the radio version, Amos' sweetheart Ruby Taylor and Andy's gold-digging nemesis Madame Queen are spoken of but never seen. Gosden and Correll stopped short of doing female voices on the air, and the prospect of casting white women in blackface was something RKO just didn't want to deal with.

Beyond a few street extras in the exterior Harlem scenes, the only authentic black performers in *Check and Double Check* are Duke Ellington and his Cotton Club Orchestra, making their screen debut as entertainers at the heroine's Long Island estate. A personal friend of Gosden and Correll, Ellington would always credit this film as a major stepping stone in his career, despite a couple of awkward studio impositions. When it was decided not to film *Check and Double Check* as a musical, the Kalmar-Ruby song hit "Three Little Words," originally written for the romantic leads, was given to Duke's vocalist Sonny Greer. Unfortunately Greer developed a severe case of mike fright, so director Brown dubbed in the voice of his friend Bing Crosby—which led to hiring Crosby and his fellow Rhythm Boys, Harry Barris and Al Rinker, to sing "Three Little Words" while a trio of Ellington men merely mouthed the words. Additionally, two of the lighter-skinned members of Duke's aggregation, Barney Bigard and Juan Tizol, were ordered to wear darker makeup, just so the audience wouldn't think that the Cotton Club Orchestra was integrated!

"A RED LETTER EVENT IN HISTORY" was the hyperbolic herald for the nationwide release of *Check and Double Check* on October 25, 1930. Maybe such ad slogans as "A HUNDRED MILLION EAGER HEARTS AWAIT THEIR COMING TO THE SCREEN!" were true, or maybe it was just the hype itself that drew in the crowds, but whatever the case, the film's opening business was nothing short of spectacular. Chosen as the inaugural attraction at New York City's 2300-seat Mayfair Theater, *Check and Double Check* grossed a whopping $51,000 its first week. The picture broke house records in Chicago, Boston, Minneapolis, Cincinnati, Providence and elsewhere, and was held over in 125 cities. Budgeted at $967,000, *Check and Double Check* cleared a profit of $260,000, RKO's biggest haul until *King Kong* three years later.

When seen today, the film may disappoint those viewers primed to be outraged by the racial stereotypes, which for the most part are rather mild and harmless. Viewers familiar with the TV sitcom version of *Amos 'n' Andy,* which ran on CBS from 1951 to 1953 with black actors playing the classic radio roles, might be surprised that the combative relationship between Amos 'n' Andy in the film bears scant resemblance to what was depicted on television, and that the Kingfish is nowhere near as prominent as he would become by the 1950s. And casual viewers with no knowledge of either the radio or TV version will likely be bored to tears by this miserable excuse for a film.

Though released the same year as such cinematically fluid efforts as *All Quiet on the Western Front* and *Monte Carlo,* its plodding pace and dull direction make *Check and Double Check* look as if it was shot the day after talkies were invented. The wit, warmth and charm that Amos 'n' Andy conveyed on radio is completely scuttled by the film's hackneyed plotline and monotonous dialogue stretches. Such comedy "highlights" as the boys ineptly changing a tire and wandering warily around a haunted house are protracted far beyond their already negligible worth. In fact, except for a short sequence in which Amos tries to carry on a phone conversation with his girlfriend while Andy makes disparaging remarks, the film has no laughs at all.

Incredibly, the reviews for *Check and Double Check* were largely laudatory. While some of this effusion can be attributed to the number of local newspapers who merely reprinted the RKO publicity handouts, that doesn't explain how the critic for *Photoplay* could with a straight face report, "Situations and dialogue are hilariously funny, and there are two or three gags that are masterpieces." Many reporters did little more than review the opening-night audiences, who'd been preconditioned to laugh hysterically by their devotion to the radio show. One of the few dissenting voices was Harold W. Cohen, critic for the *Pittsburgh Post-Gazette*, who held a dim view of *all* comedy teams from Laurel & Hardy to the Ritz Brothers, and wasn't about to cut Amos 'n' Andy any slack. Describing the picture as "a freak attraction, manufactured primarily for the great radio public and only incidentally for those who take their movies seriously," Cohen added that "it would be both folly and futile to tell the man, woman or child who sleeps and eats Amos 'n' Andy that *Check and Double Check* is a pretty bad picture, sadly lacking in humor and imagination, and composed entirely of a series of flimsy situations strung together by the thinnest excuse for a plot.... On the air, they have at times managed to strike an individuality and a personality distinctly their own. Here, however, they appear to be just a couple of burnt-cork comics, with only their voices to distinguish them from the countless other blackface teams of considerably superior ability." Cohen concluded that despite the film's opening rush of popularity, the law of diminishing returns would kick in very soon.

RKO ultimately reached the same conclusion. The film's huge initial grosses notwithstanding, the studio accountants noticed a dramatic drop-off in business as time rolled on. The weekly box-office tallies printed in *Motion Picture News* told the sad story: During its second week in release, the film "wobbled badly" in New York, "tumbled" in Cincinnati and "dropped with a thud" in San Antonio. Those theaters that picked up the film in the months after its national premiere reported even worse news: "Apparently Montreal people do not know who Amos 'n' Andy are," sighed *Motion Picture News* on December 8, 1930. Research at the time indicated that most fans had seen the picture once, and with their curiosity satisfied had no desire to see it again. Others may have laughed their heads off, but the time they got home they'd forgotten what they laughed at. Still others advised their friends that *Check and Double Check* really wasn't all it was cracked up to be. Despite gossip-column scuttlebutt that Gosden and Correll were preparing to launch a second film in April 1931, RKO had already shown the boys the door. They would never make another picture for the studio.

Though Freeman Gosden and Charles Correll provided voices for a brace of Amos 'n' Andy cartoons made by Van Beuren Productions in 1934, and despite a brief blackface appearance in Paramount's *The Big Broadcast of 1936*, the team had pretty much concluded that their beloved radio characters were better heard than seen. Quoted in an October 1961 *Ebony* magazine article, Gosden and Correll stated simply that Amos 'n' Andy "didn't look the way that people imagined them." Never throughout their long careers would they admit that *Check and Double Check* was just plain awful.

"Seth Parker" and *Way Back Home* (1931)

In what seemed to be evolving into an annual event, RKO Radio released their third consecutive feature film based on a popular radio property just in time for the Thanksgiving trade of 1931. From the vantage point of eight decades, RKO's *Way Back Home* is hands-down the best of the three films, both in terms of acting and production expertise. It is also the film that requires the most explanation to a contemporary audience. Even those born years after the heyday of Rudy Vallee and Amos 'n' Andy (both q.v.) have at least *heard* of those personalities ... but who in blazes is this "Seth Parker" guy in *Way Back Home*?

Seth Parker was the *nom de radio* of Phillips H. Lord (1902–1975), a minister's son born in Vermont (some sources say Connecticut) and raised in Maine. After graduating from Bowdoin College, Lord worked as principal of the grammar school where his new wife Sophia was a teacher. In 1927 the couple moved to New York, where Lord unsuccessfully pursued a writing career while holding down two day jobs. Visiting a friend in Hartford, Connecticut, one evening in 1929, the Lords happened to hear a radio program ostensibly set in a small farming community. Two years later, he recalled the experience to Grace Kingsley of *New Movie Magazine*: "My wife and I heard one of these so-called rural sketches and we didn't think it was very good, the characters didn't seem true to life. We felt that justice wasn't being done to our New England countryside." Lord phoned the radio station to complain, citing the many inaccuracies in characterization and dialogue; the station manager challenged him to come up with a better program. Thus it was that 27-year-old Phillips H. Lord, whose prior performing experience had been confined to singing in his church choir, developed a daily radio sketch with his wife in which he cast himself as Seth Parker, elderly sage and spiritual leader of the mythical village of Jonesport, "way up on the coast of Maine." Basing the character on his own grandfather, Lord wore a full set of crepe whiskers when portraying Seth before the microphone, while Sophia Lord likewise donned age makeup for her portrayal of Seth's highstrung neighbor Lizzie Peters.

By the time *Sunday Evening at Seth Parker's* was picked up by the full NBC network on March 3, 1929, other actors and characters had been established: Effie Palmer as Seth's wife "Mother" Parker (also known as "Ma"); Raymond Hunter as "the ferocious and lovable" Captain Bang; Joy Hathaway and later Erva Giles as young newlywed Jane; and Bennett Kilpack as Lizzie's brother Cephus. Kilpack, the only member of the regular cast with professional theatrical experience, also played sentimental villager Lance Pettingal, allowing the actor to exercise his versatility whenever Cephus and Lance exchanged dialogue. Other characters appeared from time to time, while still others were seldom heard but only spoken of, notably town curmudgeon Wobbling Duffy.

The show ran each Sunday from 10:45 to 11 p.m. EST. In each episode, the regulars would congregate at Seth Parker's home, described by the announcer as "a little old farmhouse sitting high upon a hill and looking out over the Bay of Fundy," there to indulge in friendly conversation and "sing the old-fashioned hymns in the old-fashioned way." A typical episode began with Seth and his neighbors exchanging small talk, whereupon Ma Parker or one of the others chose the musical theme for the evening's "githerin.'" The songs ranged from church pieces like "O Happy Day" to the tunes of Stephen Foster, with Ma accompanying the singers on reed organ. Between songs, Seth gently ribbed his friends about their eccentricities and recalled humorous anecdotes about friends past; read letters, poetry and newspaper items out loud, with comic interpolations; and occasionally performed lay-minister duties by solving the problems and assuaging the fears of his companions. The spiritual overtones of *Sunday Evening at Seth Parker's* discouraged NBC from seeking out sponsors for fear of being accused of merchandising religion, but the series' wholesome, life-affirming values made it a huge success above and beyond the standard sustainer, especially for listeners whose efforts to "keep the faith" were being sorely tested by the Depression. Phillips H. Lord and his ensemble were soon supplementing their radio salaries with profits from *Seth Parker* books and magazine articles, phonograph records and personal appearances.

Despite the *Check and Double Check* box-office droop of the previous year, RKO executives were still dedicated to promoting the NBC-network division of parent company RCA. With a listening audience of 30,000,000 (second only to *Amos 'n' Andy* in popularity) and an average of 600 fan letters per day pouring into Phillips H. Lord's mailbox, *Sunday Evening at Seth Parker*'s seemed an excellent candidate for a film translation. Playwright Jane Murfin, a specialist in homey, sentimental drama, was assigned to adapt the property into a screenplay, initially titled *Other People's Business*. As with RKO's previous radio-to-movie translations, the radio version's original star was brought to Hollywood to recreate his role on screen. Lord was accompanied by his wife Sophia, Effie Palmer, Raymond Hunter and Bennett Kilpack, all of whom were cast as the same characters that had won the hearts of their radio fans (though Kilpack was confined to the single role of Cephus).

Murfin worked hand in glove with Lord to closely replicate the tone and atmosphere of the radio version. The star's first move was to purge the script of any colloquialisms that were not authentically New England-ish. "By cracky," "Land o' Goshen" and "I swan" were out; "Land sakes," "My soul and body" and "Madder than snakes at haying time" were in. Lord also oversaw such details as dialects, costumes and settings. When the studio location scout found a genuine farmhouse in Santa Cruz, California, that could stand in as the exterior of the Parker residence, Lord's reaction was "Okay, okay, but ... tain't neat enough. It would be painted and mended up." With the farmer's permission, the RKO staff gave the old house a complete makeover in a single day.

The fatal flaw of *Check and Double Check*—insubstantial storyline coupled with skimpy subplot—was averted by interweaving Seth Parker's weekly hymn sessions with two sturdy plot threads. The first of these involves Seth's beloved foster son Robbie, who'd been taken in by the Parkers after his drunken, abusive father dropped out of sight. The other storyline involves the secret romance between Mary Lucy Duffy and hired hand David Clark, illegitimate son of Jonesport's resident fallen woman "Runaway" Rose. When Mary Lucy defies her bigoted father Wobbling Duffy by becoming engaged to David, the old man throws her out of his house, whereupon the kindly Parkers offer the girl the hospitality and shelter of their home. Duffy gets even by informing Robbie's father Rufe Turner—who has turned up like the proverbial bad penny—that the Parkers never legally adopted the boy. A kidnapping, a hectic chase through the countryside, a court hearing and Seth's impassioned curtain speech on tolerance and forgiveness all lead to the inevitable happy ending.

Lord went along with Murfin's newly minted characters and melodramatic convolutions so long as he was allowed to retain the hymnfests that were at the core of the radio series. Figuring that the repetition of this weekly ritual might become monotonous on screen, Lord and Murfin contrived to stage Seth's "githerin's" not only at his own home, but also at a barn dance and a taffy pull, allowing for plenty of physical action to augment the dialogue and downhome philosophy. Taking this a step further, *Other People's Business* steered clear of the starchy, attenuated dialogue exchanges that had weighed down the Rudy Vallee and Amos 'n' Andy pictures by injecting as much visual excitement as possible, especially in the climactic chase. This sequence, incidentally, is an excellent example of how Lord was able to invest the film with the religiosity of his radio series in an entertaining and amusing fashion. In the original script, the evil Rufe Turner, racing away from Jonesport by horse and buggy with a reluctant Robbie in tow and Seth Parker in hot pursuit, was to have been struck and killed by a speeding train. In the finished film Turner survives, but is ultimately overtaken by Seth, who symbolically uses a heavy Bible to cold-cock the bad guy!

The director chosen for *Other People's Business* was a jovial, easygoing gentleman who was equally skilled at wordplay and physical dynamics. William A. Seiter had built his reputation on a series of sprightly Reginald Denny domestic comedies in the 1920s, and in the talkie era was renowned for his ability to bring out the best in such diverse performers as Laurel & Hardy, Nancy Carroll, Wheeler & Woolsey, Fred Astaire, Ginger Rogers and Deanna Durbin, simply by allowing them to behave like human beings instead of mere shadow players, and preventing them from "milking" any of their big scenes beyond their worth. Seiter was also adept at sustaining a satisfying pace for his films, be they comedy, musical or drama, and to bring his storylines to an entertaining climax with exciting—but never frenetic—action sequences. Only occasionally did Seiter falter, usually when working with actors who were unresponsive or resistant to his technique (Lou Costello in *Little Giant,* for example). But there was no danger of this happening with *Other People's Business*: Lord liked and trusted Seiter, and the director was virtually the only Hollywood luminary with whom Lord and his wife regularly socialized.

With the *Seth Parker* radio players in their traditional roles, RKO cast the other characters with Hollywood people. Fourteen-year-old Frankie Darro, in films since 1924, was chosen to play the troubled Robbie Turner. It was one

Standing on a platform in full "Seth Parker" makeup, Phillips H. Lord blesses the romance between dancers Bette Davis (in white dress) and Frank Albertson in *Way Back Home* (1931).

of the most emotionally challenging assignments in Darro's long movie career, which with such noteworthy exceptions as *Wild Boys of the Road* and *No Greater Glory* was largely confined to two-dimensional leads in B pictures. Robbie's despicable father Rufe was played by gravel-voiced ex-boxer and ex-vaudevillian Stanley Fields; Oscar Apfel, a jack of all trades during the early years of the movie industry (he'd co-directed Cecil B. DeMille's first feature *The Squaw Man*), was in his element as the overbearingly self-righteous Wobbling Duffy; "Runaway" Rose was another tear-stained turn for Dorothy Peterson, the talkies' archetypal long-suffering mother; and Frank Albertson, borrowed from Fox Studios, added another callow juvenile to his résumé in the role of the misunderstood David Clark (originally slated for RKO contractee Eric Linden).

Listed fourth in the cast is the film's 23-year-old ingénue Bette Davis, who'd been borrowed from Universal at a weekly salary of $300 to replace first-choice actress Anita Louise as sweet Mary Lucy Duffy. Viewers familiar with the later Bette Davis will likely be amazed that she doesn't take one furtive glance at Seth Parker's modest living room and bellow "What—a—*dump!*" But in truth, Davis would always regard this film as one of her best and most rewarding early efforts. Seiter, who selected Bette because he liked the "Yankee twang" in her voice, treated her with far more respect and consideration than anyone she'd worked with at Universal; Bette later insisted that Seiter was the first director to truly showcase her talents. Also, RKO makeup artist Ern Westmore greatly improved upon the garish cosmetic treatment the actress had been saddled with at Universal, de-emphasizing the lines of her mouth so that those legendary Bette Davis Eyes would blaze forth in all their glory.

Other People's Business began production in the late summer of 1931 despite the trepidations of a reader in RKO's story department, who complained that the plotline was dated and warned that potential audiences might be limited only to "those people who are interested in the singing of hymns, old folk songs and a very simple brand of humor." The reader added that "average young persons between the ages of fifteen and thirty, who form a very large percentage of the movie audience, do not listen to the broadcast." There was also the concern that a popular radio series does not a good picture make, as witness *Check and Double Check*.

The film wrapped on time and on budget, and was ready for shipment on November 13, 1931. By the time the 81-minute picture opened nationally in December, it had been rechristened *Way Back Home*—a title that, in the opinion of movie historian William K. Everson, was chosen to underline its similarity in plot to the old theatrical barnstormer (and phenomenally successful D.W. Griffith silent) *Way Down East*. Inasmuch as in *Way Back Home* one of the characters blatantly compares the film's events to the histrionics in *Way Down East,* Everson was probably right. Certainly the resemblance did not go unnoticed by *Film Daily*: "A modern version of *Way Down East* and that type of backwoods tear-jerker that will no doubt register heavy with the older folks, and with the small town crowds."

Variety was less generous than *Film Daily,* sneering that the $400,000 negative cost was "a lot of coin for a camp meeting on screen. As entertainment, the film is unbelievably bad." In contrast, *Photoplay* opined, "If you follow Seth Parker on the radio, you'll enjoy seeing as well as hearing him. He uses all his radio stuff." *Photoplay's* "If" was a big one, especially since prevailing movie tastes leaned heavily in the direction of hard-boiled gangster pictures. Hoping to turn a potential liability into an asset, RKO advertised *Way Back Home* as "something different," an alternative to (or antidote for) the crime melodramas "that are now fading," a film with "no pretense or hypocrisy" that the whole family could enjoy, featuring the "melodious old songs that the jazz age cannot obliterate."

If RKO was worried about tapping into an appropriate demographic for *Way Back Home* way back in 1931, the studio would have likely thrown in the towel even before attempting to seek out a similar demographic in the second decade of the 21st century. With absolutely no frame of reference, an average modern audience will likely find no entertainment value in such an antiquated property, despite its impressive production values and skilled direction. Again the question would arise: Who the blazes *is* this Seth Parker? Beyond that, why should a young contemporary filmgoer care anything about a corny old geezer and his psalm-singing neighbors? Why should any intelligent adult get into a lather over a child born out of wedlock? And where are the teenage vampires and zombies? About all a present-day film society can hope for in scheduling a screening of *Way Back Home* is that the hardcore Bette Davis fans will show up out of curiosity.

All of which is a tough break for the film,

which if given half a chance would prove quite enjoyable and even moving at times. With the possible exception of Sophia Lord's strident portrayal of Lizzie (the sort of role that Margaret Hamilton could play in her sleep), the radio actors and their characters make a smooth transition to the screen, with none of Rudy Vallee's awkwardness in *The Vagabond Lover* nor the inherent phoniness of whites playing blacks in *Check and Double Check*. As for Lord, the actor rarely betrays the fact that he is only 29 years old. His age makeup is most convincing (though it's a bit distracting to see the studio lights shining through his chin whiskers), and his body language is perfect for his superannuated character. Our only clues that Lord is considerably younger than Seth Parker are the actor's occasional lapses into his normal deep, resonant voice—ironic, considering that Seth was after all a radio invention.

RKO's fears that they'd be unable to attract an audience for *Way Back Home* proved mostly unfounded. The film didn't exactly break attendance records in the "sophisticated" big-city houses, but it successfully tapped into the small-town and rural audience pool that had made Will Rogers a box-office magnet in the early 1930s, and would perform the same magic for Gene Autry and Judy Canova in the next decade. The returns for *Way Back Home* indicated that a radio adaptation didn't *have* to crash and burn like the studio's two earlier attempts, and unlike *Check and Double Check* could even have staying power beyond its initial release. This did not, however, result in a steady stream of follow-ups. Despite such reasonably popular efforts as *Way Back Home,* RKO Radio closed out 1931 with the biggest revenue losses in its three-year history. In early 1932 the studio's management was completely overhauled, with young tyro David O. Selznick moving into the driver's seat. As we shall see in our notes on *Meet the Baron* and *The Chief,* there were few things on earth that Selznick hated more than attempting to make movie stars out of radio personalities.

And what of Phillips H. Lord and the radio version of *Seth Parker?* Well, things rolled along smoothly until 1936, when Lord got the brilliant idea of freshening up the series by having ol' Seth sail around the world and deliver his message to the home folks via short-wave radio. Plunking down $200,000, Lord purchased a three-masted schooner which he christened (what else?) *The Seth Parker* and cast off for the South Pacific. What resulted was a veritable tsunami of negative publicity when reports began trickling back to the States about nightly drunken orgies on board the schooner, and when certain American journalists suggested that bulletins about the *Seth Parker* nearly foundering in a brace of tropical storms were merely a publicity stunt. Returning home with his reputation as a squeaky-clean New England parson considerably tarnished, Lord reinvented himself as a producer of two-fisted crime melodramas, developing such popular radio properties as *Gang Busters, Mr. District Attorney* and *Counterspy* (all q.v.). These programs would, like *Seth Parker,* eventually make their way to the movie screen—albeit without a heavily made-up Phillips H. Lord in any of the starring roles.

Chandu the Magician and other "tie-in" films (1932)

Released by the Fox Film Corporation in September 1932, *Chandu the Magician* is the best known and best remembered byproduct of a brief but lively synergetic experiment in the first years of the 1930s. But before we get to *Chandu,* let's spend a little time with its two companion pieces.

Our tale begins in the fall of 1930 when Edmund D. Coblentz, editor of the daily *New York American,* received word of the radio broadcast of an actual courtroom trial in Denmark. Recognizing a good circulation-building gimmick when he heard one, Coblentz entered into negotiations for the *American* to sponsor a fictional serialized murder trial over New York's NBC-Blue affiliate WJZ. Written by Kenneth M. Ellis, *The Trial of Vivienne Ware* began its six-night run on November 23, 1930. Heavily influenced by the Thaw-White murder case of 1906, the narrative found Vivienne Ware accused of killing her architect lover Damon Fenwicke, with brassy showgirl Dolores Divine as chief prosecution witness. Several real-life jurists were featured in the cast, among them Senator Robert F. Wagner as the judge, New York Stock Exchange lawyer George Gordon Battle as counsel for the defense, and former New York Assistant District Attorney Ferdinand Pecora as the prosecutor. There was also a studio audience, who served as the "jury." (Anticipating Ayn Rand's *Night of January Sixteenth,* two endings were prepared in advance.) The morning after each broadcast, the *American* reported on the trial's progress, all the while con-

A double-purpose ad in a 1932 *Photoplay* magazine ballyhooing both the radio and film versions of the limited-run NBC serial *The Phantom of Crestwood.*

ducting a contest offering big cash prizes to the reader who came up with the best resolution for the serial.

The stunt worked well enough for Kenneth M. Ellis to rewrite *The Trial of Vivienne Ware* as a novel in 1931. That same year, several other NBC-Blue affiliates throughout the country were given the choice of broadcasting transcriptions of the original WJZ episodes, or staging their own in-house productions of Ellis' script, using local lawmakers in the cast. Station KRLA in Little Rock, Arkansas, chose the latter option, calling upon real-life Arkansas jurist Marvin Ellis—coincidentally the brother of the author—to portray the judge. KRLA was also one of several regional affiliates to dramatize the follow-up novel to *Vivienne Ware*, this one titled *Dolores Divine, Guilty or Innocent*. Especially with *Dolores Divine*, local newspaper editors who were in on the stunt played it to the hilt, printing daily recaps as if the trial was really taking place and even suggesting that the legal experts appearing in the broadcasts were under threat of death from sinister forces who were trying to "fix" the verdict!

All this was prologue for Fox Films' motion picture adaptation of *The Trial of Vivienne Ware*, directed by William K. Howard and released on April 29, 1932. Lifting elements from both of his novels, Kenneth Ellis collaborated on the script with Philip Klein and Barry Conners. The result is one of the most exhilarating murder mysteries ever made, its 56-minute running time packed with enough material for at least three movies. Joan Bennett stars as Vivienne, with Donald Cook as her defense attorney (and loyal sweetheart) John Sutherland, Jameson Thomas as the ill-fated Fenwicke, and Lillian Bond as Dolores Divine. In the opinion of most reviewers, the film's high point occurs as Dolores prepares to deliver her testimony, only to be stopped short when a mysterious assailant flings a knife at the witness chair. The film's radio roots are manifested in the character of Gladys Fairweather (ZaSu Pitts), a sob-sister journalist who sits at a microphone throughout the story to give her listeners a blow-by-blow description of the trial—and, to fill the ladies in on the *haute couture* outfits worn by the dazzling defendant. (Minus any sort of radio tie-in, *The Trial of Vivienne Ware* was unofficially remade by 20th Century–Fox as the 1942 "Michael Shayne" mystery *Just Off Broadway*. Apparently enough changes were made—from the victim of the knife-thrower to the identity of the murderer—for Fox to feel justified in omitting the names of the *Vivienne Ware* screenwriters in the opening credits, though Brett Halliday gets his usual token acknowledgment for creating the Michael Shayne character.)

RKO Radio reversed the *Trial of Vivienne Ware* procedure with its 1932 mystery melodrama *The Phantom of Crestwood*. A few weeks before production got underway, the studio publicly announced their intention of adapting Bartlett Cormack's screenplay as a six-part radio serial, to be nationally broadcast just prior to the film's release. Titled simply *The Phantom*, this weekly serial was heard from August 26 through October 1, 1932, as a "Radio Pictures Broadcast Special" segment on NBC's *Hollywood on the Air*. Once again, fans of the program were allowed to participate in its outcome: As stated by RKO's promotional campaign, "Tens of millions [are] invited to write their own original endings. 100 cash prizes will be distributed." The freshest wrinkle in this gimmick was RKO's decision *not* to broadcast the solution of the mystery in the final episode. Instead, listeners were urged to head down to the local Bijou on or around October 14, 1932—ten days after the contest ended—to enjoy the movie version of *The Phantom of Crestwood* and find out "who done it." *Motion Picture Herald* rightly predicted, "The ramifications of this campaign will be enormous."

The 71-minute film begins with a pre-credits prologue—a rarity in 1932—as NBC announcer Graham McNamee, backed up by a studio orchestra and a team of sound technicians, assures the moviegoers that what they are about to see is the long-awaited denouement of the radio serial that has kept them on the edges of their seats for the past several weeks (This remarkable sequence was removed from the syndicated TV prints prepared by C&C Films in 1956, though it has since been restored.) After such a mouth-watering buildup, it's a bit of a letdown when *The Phantom of Crestwood* turns out to be that old bromide about a beautiful but bitchy blackmailer (Karen Morley) who invites all of her victims to the same mansion on the same evening for one last, enormous payoff—and just guess what happens to her in the next reel. Timeworn though it may be, the story material is enlivened by the clever use of multiple flashbacks (far more than was customary in the pre–*Citizen Kane* era) and the unexpected introduction of a fugitive criminal (Ricardo Cortez) who is forced to turn amateur sleuth and solve the mystery to save himself from the hot seat. Because the film had to be completed before the radio program had run its course, the "surprise" murderer is not the same person as the one chosen in the cash-prize contest—and while there are enough false leads and red herrings to keep one guessing, experienced mystery buffs will probably tumble to the culprit's identity long before fadeout time. Directed and co-scripted by J. Walter Ruben, *The Phantom of Crestwood* earned a tidy $100,000 profit, yet another testament to the ever-increasing sales power of network radio.

Which brings us to *Chandu the Magician*, introduced as a radio series in the period between the serialized versions of *The Trial of Vivienne Ware* and *The Phantom of Crestwood*. *Chandu* logically belongs in this section as a movie screenplay that was heavily dependent upon the original radio continuity, and was ballyhooed as such by Fox. However, it differs from *Vivienne Ware* and *Phantom* in that it was not initially created with a newspaper promotion or a film sale in mind, but rather as one of the many West Coast radio programs designed to fill the scheduling gaps left open by the four-hour time difference between New York and Los Angeles.

In early 1931, L.A. radio producers Raymond R. Morgan and Harry A. Earnshaw decided to capitalize on the public's ongoing interest in magic. The idea was to build a radio serial around a magician hero, one who did not confine himself to parlor tricks or stage illusions, difficult to convey on radio, but specialized in hypnotism and the occult, which *could* be conveyed via dialogue and sound effects. Their protagonist was Frank Chandler, an American who while living in India had perfected his awesome powers of mass mind control—including the ability to render himself invisible—under the tutelage of a Hindu yogi. For the purpose of battling the forces of evil, Chandler adopted the secret identity of Chandu the Magician, a name that may have been chosen at random by the producers, or may have been a private joke on the radio censors: Chandu, it seems, was 1920s street slang for opium (a point not lost on such cosmopolitan wiseguys as columnist Walter Winchell). The scripts for the 15-minute episodes were written by Morgan and Earnshaw's office assistant Vera Oldham, who parlayed this early assignment into a long and fruitful career on such big network programs as *The Maxwell House Show Boat*.

All we really needed to know about *Chandu the Magician* was established in the first 68 episodes, in which Frank "Chandu" Chandler assisted his sister Dorothy and her children Bob and Betty in their globetrotting search for Dorothy's scientist husband Robert Regent. At the same time, "Uncle Frank" was on a mission of his own, using his hypnotic powers to rid the world of evil in general and the megalomaniac villain Roxor in particular. The various subplots came together when it developed that Regent had created a death ray "for the good of mankind" (huh?) and that he was being held captive by Roxor, who intended to use the demon machine to conquer the world. Along the way, Chandler found a loyal ally and alluring love interest in the slender form of Egyptian princess Nadji, who was herself ardently pursued by Roxor's minion Abdulah. It was pure unadulterated chop-licking melodrama, written to appeal primarily to youngsters who went in for that sort of blood-and-thunder folderol—though it turned out that the series' biggest audience was well above the age of consent.

First heard over Los Angeles' KHJ in August 1931 with Gayne Whitman in the title role, *Chandu the Magician* was simultaneously transcribed for syndication throughout the West. One of its earliest sponsors was Beech-Nut gum, then a regional operation running a distant second to Wrigley's Chicle concern. Beech-

Nut did so well with *Chandu* on a limited basis that the company opted to distributed the *Chandu* recordings to the East and Midwest, duplicating their West Coast success many times over. Other, larger sponsors now became interested in the property, especially since the story content contained no plugs for Beech-Nut and was thus flexible enough to accommodate any sort of advertising. Ultimately *Chandu the Magician* was awarded a live multistate hookup by California's Don Lee Network (later absorbed by Mutual) beginning October 10, 1932, a little less than a month after Fox's film version of the property went into release.

The studio pulled out its biggest artillery in promoting *Chandu the Magician* to film exhibitors throughout the nation: "Mightiest of radio names. Outstanding symbol of mystery and enchanted entertainment. Nightly, through the loudspeakers of the nation, he holds thrilling, throbbing millions in his spell. They're YOUR READY-MADE AUDIENCE, when you play this picture." The promo copy included a impressive list of local stations then carrying the radio show, all of whom were expected to come up with their own merchandising gimmicks, including magic-trick premiums for the kiddies. Fox also emphasized the showmanship inherent in their main casting choices. As Chandu, Edmund Lowe had already scored a hit playing a crime-busting magician in the studio's 1931 feature *The Spider*; and as Roxor, Bela Lugosi was certain to attract the huge following he'd cultivated as the title character in *Dracula*. In the role of Nadji, Irene Ware had no previous cinematic experience in the supernatural, but she could be relied upon to exude the same smoldering sex appeal she'd brought to her Broadway appearances in *Earl Carroll's Vanities*.

As scripted by the *Trial of Vivienne Ware* team of Barry Conners and Philip Klein, the movie edition of *Chandu* remains faithful to the Gospel According to Vera Oldham (given an onscreen "from the radio drama by" credit along with producers Harry Earnshaw and R.R. Morgan), avoiding the pitfall of excessive dialogue by translating virtually all of the series' cliffhanging thrills into purely visual terms.

Credit for maintaining an exhausting pace throughout the film's 72 minutes must be evenly divided between co-directors Marcel Varnel and William Cameron Menzies—though it is Menzies, Hollywood's premier art director and production designer (*Gone with the Wind* was but one of his later credits), who takes full honors for the overall "look" of the film, seamlessly combining miniatures with lavish forced-perspective sets and keeping things crackling with a full complement of special effects, process shots, double exposures, conjuring tricks, explosions, screaming natives, spectacular death traps, mass-destruction panoramas and spark-spewing lab equipment. The film's momentum is propelled ever forward by Louis De Francesco's nonstop musical score, combining the familiar *Chandu the Magician* radio theme with a wealth of evocative stock music leitmotifs, many of which would resurface in such later Fox features such as *Charlie Chan in Egypt*.

Spectacle of this nature was fairly commonplace in the early talkie era, and critics were generally blasé regarding *Chandu the Magician*, though not all were as demeaning as the correspondent for Scotland's *Glasgow Herald*: "Marvelous camera work wasted on a story that might have been amusing with less serious treatment." The most common complaint lodged back then was one that, alas, holds true when one sees *Chandu* today: As observed in *The New Yorker*, the film was "about yogis and death rays and the Nile, but none of the atrocities described seems as fearful as the acting." Not unexpectedly, the ripest thesping comes from Bela Lugosi, though in fairness his bravura performance was altogether appropriate to the story and dialogue at hand. But only a Bela Lugosi can pull off this type of barnstorming without embarrassment; when the rest of the cast indulges in Lugosi-like histrionics, the results are horrendous, especially the downright amateurish performances by Nestor Aber and June Vlasek as Bob and Betty Regent. (The two young actors later changed their names to Michael Stuart and June Lang, but it didn't matter: They still couldn't act worth beans.) *Chandu* is also bogged down with the pointless and pathetically unfunny comic relief by supporting player

Herbert Mundin, though at least his character opens the door for one of the film's most appealing special effects: a miniaturized lookalike that bedevils Mundin whenever he takes a swig of liquor.

Neither Mundin nor the other substandard performances prevented *Chandu the Magician* from earning a respectable $52,441 profit, nor from inspiring a 1934 follow-up, this time with Lugosi temporarily forsaking villainy to step into the role of Frank Chandler himself—though as noted by William K. Everson, Bela acts "as though he were not convinced that he wouldn't turn out to be the villain after all." As-

Edmund Lowe dominates this *Movie Classic* magazine ad for 1932's *Chandu the Magician*.

sembled by independent producer Sol Lesser for his own Principal Distributing Corporation, *The Return of Chandu* is a 12-episode serial adapted by Barry Baringer from characters and incidents created by the radio team of Earnshaw, Morgan and Oldham in the months following the "Roxor" continuity. Cyril Armbrister, director of radio's *Chandu the Magician,* was hired as the serial's dialogue director, and also played the role of swarthy minor villain Sutra. The storyline reunites Chandler-Chandu with sister Dorothy and her youngsters Bob and Betty, plus Princess Nadji, who this time around can't stick her head outside her door without getting kidnapped. It seems that Nadji has been slated as a human sacrifice by the Sect of Ubatsi, headquartered on the magic island of Lemuria. The feline-worshipping cult is dedicated to restoring their high priestess Ossana to life, which is where Princess Nadji comes in.

Many of the elements that had clicked in Fox's *Chandu the Magician* (and on radio prior to that) were carried over to *The Return of Chandu*: an exotic setting, a quasi-oriental super villain, Frank Chandler's perpetually imperiled loved ones, ominous sound effects whenever the hero senses danger approaching, periodic communications with the High Yogi via crystal ball, larger-than-life thrills and spills, invisibility and illusion, mass mesmerism, and an elaborate and intricate musical score, this last a specialty of producer Sol Lesser at a time when the soundtracks of most independent films were barren. Throughout the production's 208 minutes, the cagey Lesser demonstrates his prowess for squeezing a dollar until the eagle screamed. Though the serial is very economically produced, director Ray Taylor, cinematographer John Hickson and art director Robert Ellis exhibit a positively Chandu-like genius for sustaining the illusion of a million-dollar production. They are aided in this endeavor by Lesser's decision to rent space on the RKO-Pathé backlot, utilizing gigantic standing sets from such previous productions as *The King of Kings* and *King Kong*. Take a look at that towering wooden gate on the isle of Lemuria; it's the same fortification that prevented the mighty Kong from trampling down the natives of Skull Island.

The producer also knew how to get value for money once the serial was in distribution by adopting the credo of the Farmer to use everything twice. You'll notice that the first four episodes of *Return of Chandu* are essentially a self-contained story, with the hero repeatedly rescuing Nadji from the clutches of Ubasti's chief minion Vindyhan. Once this villain plunges to his death, the story goes off on a new tangent, with Chandu et al. avoiding capture, death, or both at the hands of Ubasti's second-in-command Vitras, with the added complication of Chandu temporarily losing his occult powers and being obliged to rely upon assistance from the kindly, all-knowing "white magic" practitioner Tyba. While this switched-gears continuity is in keeping with the radio original, it also enabled Lesser to prepare two separate feature film versions of his serial, each approximately 65 minutes in length. The first feature adaptation, also titled *Return of Chandu,* covers Chapters 1 through 4, while *Chandu on the Magic Island* is made up of footage from Chapters 5 through 12. Because most of the action highlights are concentrated in the second feature, it comes off as the more entertaining of the two. Just as he'd done with his previous serial-feature hybrid *Tarzan the Fearless,* Lesser filmed the individual chapters' cliffhanger endings while simultaneously shooting cover footage allowing the continuity to flow more smoothly in the feature versions.

Though Fox's *Chandu the Magician* is overall the better effort, *Return of Chandu* is the more satisfying adaptation in terms of fidelity to the radio series. Also, with the exception of the flat performance by the usually vivacious Maria Alba as Nadji, the acting in the serial is markedly superior to that in the Fox feature. Though *Variety* complained that Bela Lugosi is "wasted" in the serial but that "he stands shoulders above the rest," *Return of Chandu* benefits from the solid supporting performances by former silent star Clara Kimball Young as Dorothy Regent, Erich von Stroheim lookalike Lucien Prival as Vindyhan, and that grand old trouper Josef Swickard as Tyba.

Soon after *Chandu on the Magic Island* went into general release in January 1935, the radio

Chandu moved its base of operations from KHJ-Los Angeles to WGN-Chicago, with a brand-new cast headed by Howard Hoffman as Chandu. Broadcast over the entire Mutual network, this version lasted until mid–1936. The property then went into the storage bin for twelve years, during which time the airwaves were filled with *Chandu* derivations like *Mandrake the Magician, The Shadow* and *The Avenger,* as well as programs starring such real-life illusionists as Harry Blackstone and Joseph Dunninger. On January 28, 1948, producers Raymond R. Morgan and Harry A. Earnshaw dusted off the old Vera Oldham scripts and launched the *Chandu the Magician* saga all over again in a New York–based revival once more directed by Cyril Armbrister, with Tom Collins as Chandu, Irene Tedrow as Dorothy, Veola Vonn as Nadji and Luis Van Rooten as Roxor. The original series' eerie theme music was thumped out on the organ by that turbaned, sparkly-eyed idol of early television Korla Pandit. Ending its second serialized Mutual run on January 28, 1949, *Chandu the Magician* was given a final go-round as a weekly 30-minute series on both Mutual–Don Lee and ABC from February 3, 1949, through September 6, 1950, closing out its lengthy radio history just as the movie serial *Return of Chandu* was receiving its first TV airplay.

The *Big Broadcast* Films—and a few smaller ones (1932–1945)

Two lessons were learned from the spate of radio-related features released by RKO between 1929 and 1932. First, there was a great deal of money to be earned by allowing radio fans to see such favorites as Rudy Vallee, Amos 'n' Andy and Seth Parker on screen. Second, this financial boom was ephemeral at best: Once filmgoers knew what the top radio personalities looked like, they seemed uninterested in seeing those personalities on a repeat basis. It was impossible for Hollywood to ignore the initial box-office success of *The Vagabond Lover, Check and Double Check* and *Way Back Home* (all q.v.); but if the marriage between radio and film was to be a lasting one, what was needed was something different than the limited-appeal formula of visualizing one single star or program at a time.

A potentially viable approach was the "all-star" film, a genre that had worked quite well at the very beginning of the talkie era. Taking their cue from the expensive Broadway extravaganzas of Flo Ziegfeld, the major Hollywood studios capitalized on the novelty of sound by throwing together spectacular musical-comedy revues featuring as many major names as could be crammed into a two-hour timeframe. MGM's *Hollywood Revue of 1929,* Warner Bros.' *The Show of Shows* and Paramount's *Paramount on Parade* featured all their studios' biggest stars (with a few holdouts like MGM's Garbo and Warners' George Arliss), and each film was a moneymaker. But by 1930 the bloom was off the rose for the plotless all-star revue, as Universal learned to their chagrin when their expensive, full-color *The King of Jazz* failed to earn back its cost. This drop-off in audience interest not only brought production of these vaudeville-style efforts to an end, but also scotched plans of making them annual events. Only Fox attempted a yearly edition of its *Movietone Follies,* but this project lasted only two films. And while RKO had in 1929 announced plans to produce an annual all-star opus under the umbrella title *Radio Revels,* the idea was quietly dropped before the cameras started turning.

By 1932, however, Paramount was reconsidering the all-star format as a means of showcasing radio personalities. Like the other studios, Paramount had since 1929 been featuring radio attractions in their short-subject product with considerable success. Audience and exhibitor response to Paramount's one-reelers and "bouncing ball" cartoons featuring Rudy Vallee, Burns & Allen, the Mills Brothers and others had been positive enough for the studio to think in terms of feature-film appearances for these stars; and there was also considerable interest stirred up by the profitable Bing Crosby two-reelers produced by Mack Sennett for Educational Pictures release. Rather than risk highlighting any one of these stars as the solo attraction of a costly feature film, Paramount opted to gather several of them together, so that if the audience got tired of watching, say, Bing Crosby, there was always Burns & Allen or someone else to take up the slack for a reel or two, and still another star waiting in the wings to hold the viewer's interest until fadeout time. Moreover, an all-star film offered something that no single radio show of the 1930s could ever hope to afford—at least not on a weekly basis. And rather than lump all these radio favorites into a no-plot revue, why not offer a coherent plotline to satisfy those fans who actually came to the movies to watch stories rather than personalities?

The property chosen for Paramount's initial foray into their "all-radio-star" policy was adapted from a stage play in which the studio had heavily invested: *Wild Waves,* written by William Ford Manley. Having worked in the production end of radio for several years, Manley had fashioned a devastating comic attack on the broadcast industry, in the manner of Kaufman and Hart's recent theatrical Hollywood satire *Once in a Lifetime. Wild Waves* is set in the studios of struggling radio station WWVW, which faces bankruptcy unless it can hold onto its star attraction, handsome crooner Roy Denny. What his adoring public doesn't know is that Denny is an irresponsible rotter, presently being sued for desertion and child support. He doesn't even do his own singing, having been hired merely to pose for WWVW's publicity photos. In truth, Denny's voice is ghosted by John Duffy, a bashful lad who toils away in the lowly position of chime-ringer for the station's hourly time signal. When WWVW's ambitious programmer Nancy Hodson and long-suffering station manager Mitch Gratwick urge Duffy to come out of his shell and become a radio singer in his own right, the despicable Denny has all three of them fired. This precursor of *Singin' in the Rain* ends much the same way as that classic 1952 movie musical, with Denny exposed as a fraud and Duffy skyrocketing to stardom. Starring Bruce MacFarlane as Denny, John Beal as Duffy, Betty Starbuck as Nancy and Osgood Perkins as Gratwick, *Wild Waves* received excellent revues and positive word-of-mouth during its out-of-town tryouts, but laid an egg when it finally hit Broadway on February 19, 1932.

Even so, screenwriter George Marion, Jr., used Manley's play as the bare bones for Paramount's new musical comedy *The Big Broadcast.* Marion retained such plot points as the financially strapped radio station, the harried station manager and the unreliable singing star; in the process, the play's satirical elements were muted, the singer was de-vilified and made more sympathetic, a romantic triangle was added, and the whole thing was wrapped up with a splendiferous international-broadcast finale. The film's foundation on a sturdy plotline was heavily promoted by the Paramount publicists to assure moviegoers that they weren't in for merely another shapeless star parade of the sort that had wasted too much celluloid a few years earlier: "It is not to be supposed ... that *The Big Broadcast* is merely a glorification of the personalities of the various stars, for their songs and nonsense are all incidental to a straightforward, believable and amusing story ..." Well, straightforward and amusing, anyway.

While the previous radio-based films from RKO drew heavily from the NBC talent roster, *The Big Broadcast* focused on stars from rival chain CBS, beginning with Bing Crosby (1903–1977), who had joined the network as a solo performer in 1931 after breaking away from the Rhythm Boys and bandleader Paul Whiteman. Signing Crosby to a one-feature contract, Paramount bowed to the singer's request that he not be forced to carry the entire picture by himself, nor would he be top-billed as the only star. In this way, Crosby reasoned, he would not have to shoulder all the blame if the film flopped. (In contrast, bandleader Guy Lombardo, originally slated to make an appearance in the film, dropped out because he refused to accept anything less than preferential billing.) Throughout the rest of his movie career, Bing held fast to this policy, insisting that at least one other star share over-the-title billing with him. In the case of *The Big Broadcast* Crosby went one step farther: Inasmuch as he was a virtual newcomer to feature films, Bing didn't feel comfortable winning the heroine at fadeout time, and asked

The all-inclusive sheet music cover for "Please," one of Bing Crosby's two big hits from *The Big Broadcast* (1932).

that his co-star Stu Erwin receive this honor—which Erwin, a character comic who'd never thought of himself a romantic lead, would ever after regard as ridiculous.

Since in essence Crosby was playing the screen counterpart of *Wild Waves'* Roy Denny, Paramount had no problem denying him the fadeout embrace with leading lady Leila Hyams. The studio had already chosen not to depict Crosby's character "Bing Hornsby" as the paragon of virtue portrayed by Rudy Vallee in *The Vagabond Lover*, dwelling instead on a few of Bing's real-life personality flaws, including his checkered romantic life, his chronic overdrinking (one could not help but notice his excess *avoirdupois* in the film), his frightening mood swings, and his larkish attitude towards his radio career. These peccadilloes were well-known to the public in 1932: It was only after Bing Crosby became an American Institution that his less admirable character traits were downplayed by the press.

Still, Paramount was anxious to build up Crosby as a feature film favorite, so his movie character is nowhere near the phony-baloney louse personified by Roy Denny in *Wild Waves*. If the onscreen Bing is habitually late for his broadcasts, it isn't ego-tripping but a consequence of his love for temptress Mona Lowe (Sharon Lynn). If Bing shifts from his customarily jaunty self to a potential suicide (a sequence as hilarious as it is disturbing), it is because Mona has callously thrown him over for a millionaire. And if it appears that Bing is going on a drunken binge that will financially destroy the radio station's new owner Leslie McWhinney (Stu Erwin), in fact he is doing nothing of the sort, but simply and deliberately making himself look bad in the eyes of star struck Anita Rogers (Leila Hyams) so that Anita will realize that Leslie and not Bing is the man for her. The strongest link between the film's likable "Bing Hornsby" and *Wild Waves'* detestable Roy Denny—not to mention *Wild Waves* itself—occurs in the final scene, when in a last-ditch effort to salvage the "Big Broadcast" upon which he has hinged all his hopes and dreams, tone-deaf Leslie McWhinney is forced to imitate Bing's crooning in front of the microphone (which suddenly sprouts a pair of crossed eyeballs!).

Though his character is identified as Bing Hornsby in all Paramount press releases, Crosby goes by the name of "Bing Crosby" in *The Big Broadcast*, the only occasion outside of later guest-star appearances that he would play "himself" on film. Similarly, though George Burns and Gracie Allen were to have been given character names in their respective roles as a frantic radio station manager and a dizzy receptionist, they retain their real names onscreen, albeit more formally billed in the credits as George N. Burns and "Grace" Allen. In other script-to-screen alterations, the call letters of the broadcast station in which most of the action transpires are changed from WHAM (the actual "calls" of a Rochester, New York, outlet) to WADX; and the character played by George Barbier, dyspeptic radio sponsor Mr. Aikenhead, emerges onscreen with the less pun-ny moniker Mr. Clapsaddle.

Paramount's publicity flacks would have had you believe that Burns & Allen were making their film debut in *The Big Broadcast*, though most moviegoers had already seen the team in their one-reel comedy skits (*Fit to be Tied, Walking the Baby, Once Over Light*, etc.) produced at the studio's facilities in Astoria, Long Island. Likewise movie veterans by virtue of prior short-subject appearances were the film's other "newcomers": radio singers Kate Smith, Arthur Tracy, the Boswell Sisters and the Mills Brothers (who at the time were even more popular than Bing Crosby), and orchestra leaders Cab Calloway and Vincent Lopez—the latter having made his first radio appearance in 1921 and his first film in 1928, predating everyone else in the picture. Also, tenor Donald Novis had already been featured in the 1929 Ronald Colman vehicle *Bulldog Drummond*, so he could hardly be considered a movie "virgin" either. (Novis' musical number "Trees" was cut from *Big Broadcast* during previews but restored just before the film's premiere, explaining why he is billed dead last in the closing credits.) The specialty numbers by Smith, Calloway, Novis, the Millses and the Boswells were filmed in Astoria rather than Hollywood, enabling the performers to fulfill their radio duties in New York without making a disruptive trip to California. For the benefit of those who had never before seen any of *The Big Broadcast*'s radio personalities in the flesh, all the above-mentioned artists except Novis are introduced in an inventive pre-credits sequence, their "frozen" portraits, encircled in a huge microphone, coming to life as the camera closes in on each individual face. Unbilled in the credits but identified on-screen with small desk placards are the regular radio announcers for several of these performers: Cab Calloway and Vincent Lopez's Jimmy Wallington, the Boswell Sisters' Norman Brokenshire, the Mills Brothers' Don Ball and Kate Smith's William Brenton.

In keeping with Paramount's policy of incorporating the radio stars into the main story rather than relegating them to unrelated cameos, Arthur Tracy is first seen in a speakeasy sequence singing the melancholy "Here Lies Love," later performing a reprise as a ghostly apparition during Bing Crosby's abortive suicide attempt. And while Vincent Lopez's big number (featuring drummer-vocalist Mike Riley of "The Music Goes 'Round and 'Round" fame) occurs during the climactic radio broadcast, he is introduced as the rooftop orchestra leader at the hotel where Crosby is staying—feeding into Bing's self-destructive urges by playing (you guessed it) "Here Lies Love." Most of the other guest performers are logically showcased during the "Big Broadcast" in the last two reels, wherein the WADX announcers stall for time while awaiting the arrival of Crosby by substituting the Boswell Sisters' antic harmonizing of "Crazy People," Cab Calloway tearing through the coke-sniffer's anthem "Kickin' the Gong Around," and so on. Also adroitly woven into the storyline are Crosby's two songs "Here Lies Love" (already cited) and "Please," written by Leo Robin and Ralph Rainger. "Please" is first heard as an *a capella* rehearsal piece with Bing warbling to Eddie Lang's guitar accompaniment, then as a 78-rpm recording that is variously warped and broken as Leslie McWhinney tries to rush it to the radio station, and finally as the musical resolution to the Bing-Anita-Leslie triangle—and an appropriate counterpoint for the fickle Mona Lowe's well-deserved comeuppance.

With a powerful lineup of radio talent, an inventory of great tunes and an entertaining screenplay already going for it, *The Big Broadcast* could have passed muster even with a pedestrian director at the helm; fortunately, Frank Tuttle was better than pedestrian. In addition to his sensitive handling of the nervous Crosby (giving the singer props and stage business to help him overcome his awkwardness), Tuttle displays his affection for the effervescent musical comedies of French director René Clair (*Sous les Toits de Paris, Le Million*) by investing the picture with a variety of delightful Clair-like touches, from the rhythmic dialogue recited by Burns & Allen and the singing trio Major, Sharp & Minor during a telephone montage, to a slapstick scrimmage in which Bing's rabid female fans descend upon him like a squad of football players. The director also pays homage to his own silent comedy-roots with an extended pantomime sequence, replete with exaggerated music effects and character bits by such two-reeler stalwarts as Eddie Dunn and Lyle Tayo, involving Stu Erwin's frantic efforts to snatch a phonograph record from a shuttered store in the dead of night.

The seventh top-grossing film of 1932, *The Big Broadcast* re-legitimized the all-star format (except perhaps for the *Variety* reviewer, who flipped off the picture as "a succession of talkie shorts"). It also proved the bankability of star Bing Crosby—much to the surprise of Paramount, who had initially wanted to hold out for a bigger name like Rudy Vallee in the lead. The film's success encouraged the studio to continue churning out musical comedies featuring clusters of radio stars, beginning in 1933 with the similarly structured *International House*. Carried over from *Big Broadcast* are film funster Stu Erwin (whose character's romantic entanglements are treated purely as a joke this time around) and radio headliners Burns & Allen, the latter provided with far more screen time and funnier material than in the first film—a sure sign that they, like Bing Crosby, had passed Paramount's smell test in *Big Broadcast* and were being groomed for bigger things. Also back from the earlier film is Cab Calloway, performing yet another *paean* to drug use, the outrageous "Reefer Man."

In addition to Burns, Allen and Calloway, *International House*'s assemblage of radio favorites includes Rudy Vallee, spoofing his own image by singing a love ballad to a megaphone—a gag he absolutely detested, by the way; ten-year-old jazz singer Baby Rose Marie, then starring in her own 15-minute musical series for NBC (and decades removed from her second coming as sharp-tongued Sally Rogers on TV's *The Dick Van Dyke Show*); and the CBS comedy team of Col. Lemuel Q. Stoopnagle (F. Chase Taylor) and Budd Hulick. Most of the radio performers' connection with the storyline is tenuous, coming by way of their appearances on the "Radioscope," an elaborate television device that has attracted potential investors from around the world to a luxury hotel in the Chinese city of Wu-Hu. The only active participants in the plot intrigues are Burns & Allen, cast as the hotel's caustic doctor and nutty nurse. George and Gracie carry the film's comic burden until the arrival of W.C. Fields as bibulous aviator Professor Quail, who immediately takes charge by giving garrulous Gracie the evil eye and muttering, "What's the penalty for murder in China?"

Top billing in *International House* somewhat unfairly goes to Peggy Hopkins Joyce, a "famous for being famous" Ziegfeld showgirl who had been making headlines for two decades with her endless marital escapades; she had in fact been the inspiration for the character of Mona Lowe in *The Big Broadcast*. The hilarious double-entendre byplay between Ms. Joyce and Fields (Peggy: "I'm sitting on something"; Fields: "I lost mine in the stock market!") so totally dominates the film's climax that it is quite possible for one to completely forget all the formidable radio talent that has gone before.

Given the shortest of short shrifts in the picture are Stoopnagle and Budd, here confined to an unfunny vignette in which they advocate "Stoopnocracy" (a takeoff of the then-trendy theory of technocracy) by demonstrating their latest inventions. Twenty-first-century audiences would never guess from *International House* that Stoopnagle and Budd were radio satirists of the first order, the Bob & Ray of their day. The comedians were seen to better advantage in their short subjects of the 1930s, especially F. Chase "Stoopnagle" Taylor in a brace of faux newsreels released by Educational Pictures in 1938 under the title *Cavalcade of Stuff*. Produced by cinematographer Don Malkames, previously responsible for Universal's similarly lampoonish *Goofy Newsreel* series, the *Cavalcade of Stuff* one-reelers feature the poker-faced Col. Stoopnagle introducing a man who has solved the problem of crowded telephone booths by constructing a booth with the phone on the outside; a fatuous politician who hands the colonel a testimonial check while cautioning him not to cash it until Monday; a child prodigy who sings backwards; and home-improvement expert Madame Fennessy, who recites the same instructions over and over like a broken record: "You take a small bottle—you can't do it with a big one—and you break it up into small pieces. You shellac them, and wait 24 hours, and shellac them again. And when you get through, they look just like fish scales." Alas, Stoopnagle and Budd are never given a similar chance to shine in *International House*.

The *Big Broadcast* franchise was reactivated under its own name with *The Big Broadcast of 1936* (originally *The Big Broadcast of 1935*, but released too late in the year for that title to have any relevance). By now Paramount's top musical star Bing Crosby only has time to contribute a single number, "I Wished on the Moon" (with lyrics by Dorothy Parker!), staged in a disappointingly dreary manner by director Norman Taurog. Burns & Allen have also returned from the series' initial entry, playing the inventors of yet another television device called "The Radio Eye," which like *International House*'s Radioscope picks up sounds and images at random from throughout the world. Also as in *International House*, this invention enables the film to spotlight various specialty performers without fretting over such pesky details as logically integrating them into the plot. Amos 'n' Andy, in their first film appearance since 1930's *Check and Double Check* (q.v.), recreate a radio sketch in which they assume control of a Harlem grocery store; Jessica Dragonette, the incredibly popular singing star of NBC's *Cities Service Concerts* who had hitherto resisted all entreaties to appear on film, honors her fans with an uncredited guest spot; and Ray Noble and His Orchestra (featuring trumpeter Charlie Spivak) take time off from radio's *The Coty Program* to perform Noble's own composition "Why Stars Come Out at Night."

The plot of *Big Broadcast of 1936* is less cohesive than its 1932 forerunner. Paramount contractees Jack Oakie and Henry Wadsworth play Spud and Smiley, who as the entire staff of tinker-toy radio station WHY have combined their speaking and singing talents to impersonate a fictional crooner named Lochinvar. (The role of Smiley was to have gone to tenor Joe Morrison, then riding high with his hit tune "Headin' for the Last Roundup," but Morrison had struck out in his previous film appearances and was replaced by Wadsworth—whose voice was dubbed by radio's Kenny Baker.) Fascinated by the potential of the Radio Eye, Spud and Smiley hopscotch all over the world exploiting the invention without making proper compensation to Burns & Allen. Somewhere along the line the story evolves into a dry run for Paramount's later Hope-Crosby "Road" pictures, with the protagonists facing certain death at the hands of two South American assassins (C. Henry Gordon and Akim Tamiroff), all because Spud has tickled the fancy of predatory Countess Ysobel (Lyda Roberti). The climactic chase scene halfheartedly returns to the "Big Broadcast" motif as the fleeing Spud pleads for help over a short-wave hookup, his entreaties ignored by a group of broadcast executives who assume that the beleaguered fugitive is merely trying to win a radio contest of his own invention. And in case you're wondering how the film's official leading lady Wendy Barrie figures into all this, so am I ... and I've seen the picture.

While the first *Big Broadcast* was tipped in favor of its radio stars, the 1936 edition is top-heavy with movie, stage, nightclub and vaudeville personalities. Among the renegade telecasts picked up by the Radio Eye are Ethel Merman's rendition of "It's the Animal with Me" (backed up by a chorus line of elephants), which was actually filmed for but dropped from the 1934 Bing Crosby musical *We're Not Dressing*; a dramatic vignette involving a doctor (Sir Guy Standing), a nurse (Gail Patrick), a seriously ill child (Virginia Weidler) and her anxious brother (David Holt), which grinds the picture to a dead halt before it's even half over; a lighter domestic sketch with the ever-reliable Charlie Ruggles and Mary Boland; Bill Robinson, the Nicholas Brothers and the Dandridge Sisters (including Dorothy) in the boisterous production number "Miss Brown to You"; a somber performance by the Vienna Boys' Choir; and best of all, the classic house-building routine by vaudevillians Willie, West and McGinty, which is sprinkled throughout the picture. A few specialties filmed for *Big Broadcast of 1936* were dropped from the release print, notably a number by Ina Ray Hutton and the Melodears which later showed up in the 1936 Paramount short *Star Reporter*. Another casualty in every sense of the word was the great Argentine tango singer Carlos Gardel, known to his millions of followers as El Zorzal Criollo ("the Song Thrush"). Gardel's death in an airplane accident on April 24, 1935, moved Paramount to cut his two numbers from *Big Broadcast of 1936* out of respect; but popular demand in Latin America was so overwhelming that his scenes were retained for the Spanish-language version of the film (*Cazadores de Estrella*), and have since been restored to some English-language prints.

Released in the fall of 1936, *The Big Broadcast of 1937* avoids the previous edition's overemphasis on film stars like Jack Oakie and Lyda Roberti. Instead, the film harks back to the original *Big Broadcast* by devoting ample screen time to its lineup of radio and recording favorites, beginning with top-billed Jack Benny in his first Paramount feature. Jack plays a shoestring radio station manager who must curry favor with wacky sponsors Burns & Allen, here making a rare film appearance as the married couple they really were. Radio tenor Frank Forest, whose days of glory as resident vocalist on the Mutual network quiz program *Double or Nothing* were still ahead of him, plays the station's star attraction, who threatens to walk out unless a female disc jockey on a small-town radio outlet stops making fun of him during her all-night program. The lady "jock" is played by band singer Shirley Ross, recently rescued by Paramount from a desultory MGM contract and a frequent visitor to network radio, notably during the 1937–38 season of Burns & Allen's show. Hotshot talent agent Ray Milland (replacing Paramount's first choice Randolph Scott) builds the Forest-Ross competition into a phony romance, culminating with Forest's marriage proposal to Ross during a coast-to-coast broadcast sponsored by George and Gracie's product, Platt's Airflow Golf Balls. The fact that by now Milland himself has fallen for Ross leads to a twist ending that surprises everyone but the audience.

Wending their way through the storyline were two relatively new radio personalities, novelty singer Martha Raye and Arkansas humorist Bob Burns. Raye was then appearing weekly on Al Jolson's program, while Burns had spent most of the previous year cementing his radio reputation on Bing Crosby's *Kraft Music Hall*. The two performers had also been teamed onscreen in the 1936 Crosby vehicle *Rhythm on the Range,* which represented Martha's movie debut. Playing Benny's accident-prone secretary in *Big Broadcast of 1937,* Martha is held in reserve until the film's broadcast climax, when sponsor Gracie

This *Film Daily* ad for *The Big Broadcast of 1937* showcases the three principal reasons for attending the picture.

Allen impulsively gives her a chance to belt out a sizzling scat number. In a larger role, Bob Burns wanders around the studio in search of celebrated conductor Leopold Stokowski, hoping that the Great Leopold will find a place in the Philadelphia Symphony Orchestra for Burns' beloved "bazooka," a weird trombone-like instrument fashioned from a whiskey funnel and two gas pipes. (Though Stokowski would not take charge of the NBC Symphony Orchestra until 1941, his many guest conductor appearances on both NBC and CBS during the

1930s qualified him as a radio star for the purposes of this film.)

Other radio luminaries appearing in *Big Broadcast of 1937* are Benny Goodman and His Orchestra (featuring Gene Krupa), harmonica virtuoso Larry Adler, dialect comedian Sam "Schlepperman" Hearn—then a regular on Jack Benny's show, famous for his Yiddish-flavored salutation "Hello, stranger!"—and venerable vaudevillian Benny Fields, whose career had recently been jump-started on CBS' *Ziegfeld Follies of the Air*. It would be nice to report that all these entertainers are seen to fullest advantage in the film—nice, but inaccurate. Director Mitchell Leisen seems more interested in the costumes and décor than the story, songs and comedy. As a result the 102-minute *Big Broadcast of 1937* is the dullest, lumpiest series entry to date—and except for a stunningly photographed concert piece with Stokowski, in which only the conductor's hands are illuminated, this edition is the least cinematic *Big Broadcast* of all.

Still, it was beneficial in furthering the movie careers of Jack Benny, Martha Raye and especially Bob "Bazooka" Burns, who after 20 years' obscurity in the farthest fringes of show business had broken into the big time with a 1935 guest appearance on Rudy Vallee's radio program. Burns' rambling reminiscences about life in his Arkansas home town of Van Buren were incentive enough for Paramount to start building up the comedian as the logical successor to the late cowboy philosopher Will Rogers. Burns' subsequent studio vehicles—*The Arkansas Traveller*, *I'm from Missouri* and *Our Leading Citizen*—adhered faithfully to the folksy Rogers formula, enabling bucolic old "Bazooka" to develop a strong fan following in rural communities. The failure of 1940's *Alias the Deacon* led to a parting of the ways between Paramount and Burns, who nonetheless continued to prosper on radio until 1947, and in private life as a wealthy San Fernando Valley rancher until his death at age 65 in 1956. Burns' legacy has lived on in the form of the U.S. Army's specially designed M-1 rocket launcher, which in tribute to the comedian's musical instrument of choice is also known as the Bazooka.

Paramount had originally planned to reunite stars Jack Benny, Burns & Allen and Martha Raye with director Mitchell Leisen in the final series entry *The Big Broadcast of 1938* (released early that year), but the studio's decision to cast the very expensive W.C. Fields led to the elimination of all but Raye and Leisen. At first glance it may seem that Fields' inclusion was intended to attract filmgoers who weren't necessarily radio fans, as had been the case with *International House*. In fact, at this point in time the comedian was himself regarded as a major radio star. Having been absent from films for over a year due to a near-fatal illness, Fields had radio to thank for keeping him alive—professionally and otherwise—during his lengthy convalescence. Not yet physically strong enough to return to movies, Fields was nonetheless in splendid shape vocally, and was a welcome guest performer on network radio during the 1936–37 season. NBC's *The Chase and Sanborn Hour* became what the comedian's biographer Simon Louvish has described as "a life-raft for Fields," due in no small part to the ongoing war of insults between Fields and ventriloquist Edgar Bergen's dummy Charlie McCarthy (see separate entry). Though rumors persist that the temperamental Fields hated sharing the spotlight with his wooden nemesis, there is a considerable body of evidence that W.C. himself wrote many of Charlie's best comeback lines. Whatever the case, by mid–1937 a whole new generation of fans had "discovered" Fields, and his star was again on the ascendancy.

Having landed the *Big Broadcast of 1938* assignment on the strength of his recent radio appearances, Fields wanted to keep up the momentum by co-starring opposite Bergen & McCarthy onscreen. But producer Samuel Goldwyn had first dibs on the ventriloquist's services, so Fields ended up receiving sole over-the-title billing, the only performer accorded this honor in the entire *Big Broadcast* franchise. The character planned for Jack Benny, that of an alimony-dodging radio announcer, went to new Paramount contractee Bob Hope, billed sixth in his first feature film appearance. Like Fields, Hope was being spotlighted to cash in on his ever-increasing radio prominence. At the time of filming, Bob was co-starring on NBC-Blue's *Rippling Rhythm Revue* with orchestra leader Shep Fields, who likewise appears in *The Big Broadcast of 1938* along with Hope's vaudeville and radio straight woman Patricia "Honey Chile" Wilder (see **The Bob Hope Connection**). Also in the cast is another member of the Paramount family, Dorothy Lamour, then currently co-starring with W.C. Fields on *The Chase and Sanborn Hour* and thus a handy woman to have around for publicity photo purposes. Billed just below Fields and just above Lamour, Martha Raye is seen as W.C.'s hard-luck daughter, who has become a permanent jinx by crashing her plane into a shipload of mirrors. Another holdover from *Big Broadcast of 1937*, Shirley Ross, is cast as the first of Bob Hope's three ex-wives, and the one who wins him back at fadeout time.

The "Big Broadcast" in this outing is a shipboard affair, staged in the midst of a transatlantic race between two humongous ocean liners, the *Gigantic* and the *Colossal*. In addition to the abovementioned performers, the film's manifest of radio talent includes Mexican singing sensation Tito Guizar (then appearing on several American variety shows) and Metropolitan Opera soprano Kirsten Flagstad (a regular on NBC's *General Motors Promenade Concerts*); accompanied by Met conductor Wilfred Pelletier, she performs "Brunhilde's Battle Cry" from Wagner's *Die Walkure*. While Guizar is permitted two numbers, Flagstad's second aria was cut from the final release print, though an excerpt was retained for the coming-attractions trailer.

To say that director Mitchell Leisen does a better job holding things together here than in *The Big Broadcast of 1937* would be only half-true, since Leisen had nothing to do with the comedy sequences involving W.C. Fields, inarguably the highlights of the show. Unable to get along with the notoriously obstinate Fields, Leisen gave up the ghost and handed the comedian over to Theodore Luther Reed, who helmed virtually all of the Great Man's self-scripted routines. Though Fields remains the premier attraction when *The Big Broadcast of 1938* is seen today, it isn't fair to sell the other performers short. In particular, the film gave Bob Hope the boost he needed to add motion pictures to his list of professional triumphs, most memorably in his bittersweet duet with Shirley Ross, "Thanks for the Memory"—which, need we add, instantly became Bob's signature tune for radio, television, and forever.

The popularity of Paramount's *Big Broadcast* films led to the inevitable imitations, even from Paramount. While the studio's "College" musical series was not as radio-centric as the *Big Broadcast* franchise, each series entry features one or more big radio names. And although the first three titles—*College Humor* (1933), *College Rhythm* (1934) and *Collegiate* (1936)—are dominated by the antics of comedy lead Jack Oakie, top billing in all three goes to a popular radio attraction.

Bing Crosby heads the cast of *College Humor* as a professor of dramatics with a fondness for conducting his classes in song. The romantic triangle involving Crosby, co-ed Mary Carlisle and football hero Richard Arlen differs from the similar setup in *Big Broadcast* in that this time Bing is the stalwart, reliable suitor and Arlen is the irresponsible drinker—and thus it is Bing who wins the heroine. Though he has less screen time than in *Big Broadcast*, Crosby has the advantage of superior material. His first big number "Learn to Croon" makes excellent use of the rhythmic-dialogue device as Bing dispenses romance tips to his students with a medley of his past hits. Later on, an amusing progression of song, dance and dialogue fragments featuring practically everyone else in the cast provides a lively prologue to Bing's laid-back rendition of "The Old Ox Road." Also recruited from *The Big Broadcast* are Burns & Allen, in what amounts to a cameo appearance as a pair of campus caterers.

The next two series entries, *College Rhythm* and *Collegiate*, are detailed in the separate entry on radio funnyman Joe Penner. Burns & Allen are back in 1936's *College Holiday* (also discussed elsewhere), billed second and third after star Jack Benny, with Martha Raye billed fifth and nominal romantic leads Marsha Hunt and Leif Erickson relegated to seventh and eighth place.

For the final entry *College Swing* (1938), top billing at last goes to Burns & Allen, who certainly deserve it. Or at least Gracie deserves it, since she has the biggest part in the picture as a habitually failing college student who stands to inherit a staid old university if she can only pass her final exams. Once this hurdle is cleared, Gracie begins hiring comedians, singers and dancers for the new faculty while installing herself as "Dean of Men" (it's Gracie Allen, remember?). Fourth-billed Bob Hope plays a silver-tongued tutor who is hired to help Gracie bluff her way through her finals. This was supposed to be a minor role, but Hope was feeling his oats after his strong showing in *Big Broadcast of 1938*, demanding and receiving a major buildup in the script. As a result, though George Burns is contractually billed first in the cast he is reduced to grunting and glowering at Gracie's stupidity while Hope gets all the best setup lines and comebacks. And since the script also contrives to have Gracie fall in love with stuffy college regent Edward Everett Horton (a last-minute replacement for Charles Butterworth), poor George must have really felt like a fifth wheel in this picture. The inescapable Martha Raye is on hand as the college's professor of psychology (sure, why not?), while other radio performers in the cast include orchestra leader Skinnay Ennis and longtime *Kraft Music Hall* comedy foil Jerry Colonna, both of whom were subsequently hired for Bob Hope's new Pepsodent radio program.

Other Hollywood studios attempted to launch film series emulating the radio-related Paramount offerings, with generally indifferent results. (MGM's *Broadway Melody* films are a breed apart, though radio's Jack Benny and Frances Langford are prominently cast in *Broadway Melody of 1936*.) As mentioned at the beginning of this entry, RKO Radio had drawn up plans in 1929 for an all-star mélange titled *Radio Revels*, but they were scotched. Five years later the project was again announced in the trades, now

George Burns and Gracie Allen, enduring radio favorites and perennial attractions of Paramount's *Big Broadcast* and *College* movie series.

titled *Radio City Revels* in honor of the first anniversary of New York's Radio City Music Hall, which had a corporate tie-in with RKO. Like the abortive 1929 effort, *Radio City Revels* was trumpeted as the first film in an annual series, with Fred Astaire and Ginger Rogers heading a cast featuring studio contractees Irene Dunne and Wheeler & Woolsey, plus radio commentator Walter Winchell as himself.

This too came to naught, but RKO didn't entirely abandon the idea. Though not bearing the *Radio City Revels* imprimatur, the studio's *New Faces of 1937* was born of the same concept. The plot of *New Faces of 1937* is set in motion by fly-by-night Broadway producer Jerome Cowan, who has amassed a fortune by deliberately producing flops and pocketing all of the investors' money without having to pay them a percentage. Yes, it's the same hoary old backstage legend that would serve as the basis for Mel Brooks' *The Producers* (1968). The major difference between *New Faces of 1937* and *The Producers* is that *The Producers* is good.

Technically the film's "new faces" consist of the unknowns who appear in a lengthy audition sequence, including such stars-in-incubation as Ann Miller and the Chocolateers dance trio. If you squint a bit, the title might also extend to second-billed Milton Berle, whom RKO promoted as a movie newcomer even though he'd been in films since the silent era and had starred in the above-average 1934 Educational Pictures short *Poppin' the Cork*. A vaudeville and Broadway headliner of long standing, Berle had made a major foray into radio as resident comedian of CBS's *Community Sing* (parodied in the 1937 "all-star" Warner Bros. cartoon *The Woods Are Full of Cuckoos*). Inasmuch as two other regulars from the CBS program, Bert Gordon ("Count Mischa Moody") and Tommy Mack ("Judge Hugo Straight"), are also in the RKO picture, it is very likely that Berle's participation was due more to the popularity of *Community Sing* than his past theatrical credits.

Irving Brecher, then writing for Berle's radio program, later told interviewer Lee Server that *Community Sing* was moved from New York to Hollywood to accommodate the star's shooting schedule. When producers Edward Small and Sam Briskin decreed that the first script for *New Faces of 1937* was inadequate, Berle recommended Brecher for the rewrite, which he did in collaboration with Nat Perrin and Philip Epstein. Perhaps because one of his own boys was now on the RKO staff, Berle ends up with the film's funniest scene, a stockbroker sketch with Richard Lane that had originally been written by David Friedman (*The Eddie Cantor Show*) for the 1934 Broadway revue *Life Begins at 8:40*. Overall, Berle comes off better than the film's other radio recruits Joe Penner, Harriet Hilliard, Harry "Parkyakarkus" Einstein and Patricia "Honey Chile" Wilder—and frankly, Uncle Miltie is of the few reasons to sit through *New Faces of 1937* today. The reviewer for the *Fox West Coast Bulletin* groused over the "unfortunate exploitation of prominent radio artists from their natural field to the screen in keeping with the new demand to see as well as hear these favorites," describing the picture as "a flopping morsel of the hodge-podge variety, reverting back to the custard pie-slinging days hardly redeemed with a few pretty dance sets."

The box-office failure of *New Faces of 1937* should have scuttled RKO's plans for an annual all-star revue. Yet the studio inexplicably held onto the delusion that they could formulate a radio-based attraction that would stir up popular demand for more of the same on a yearly basis. In 1938 the title *Radio City Revels* was finally affixed to a piece of musical nonsense predominated by performers who had either made their names in radio or were currently featured on network programs. Berle is back, this time teamed with Jack Oakie (then starring on the CBS variety hour *Jack Oakie's College*) as a pair of unsuccessful songwriters who stumble upon a natural-born tunesmith in the person of Bob "Bazooka" Burns (on loan from Paramount). Trouble is, Burns can only compose songs while he's asleep. RKO honestly expected this contrivance to keep audiences glued to their seats for 90 minutes.

Berle, Oakie and Burns' radio confreres include *The Jack Benny Program*'s vocalist Kenny Baker and announcer Don Wilson, singers Jane Froman and the Vass Sisters, and orchestra leader Hal Kemp. Veteran Broadway and Hollywood comedians Helen Broderick and Victor Moore may have been cast because of their previous triumphs in RKO's Astaire-Rogers pictures, but more likely because they had just finished appearing in tandem as CBS radio's summer replacements for Nelson Eddy. About the only participants who *weren't* making regular radio appearances at the time are ingénue Ann Miller, late of *New Faces of 1937,* and eccentric dancers Buster West and Melissa Mason, who'd just come off the Broadway musical *White Horse Inn.*

Curiously, *Radio City Revels* did not open at Radio City Music Hall, but was instead unveiled at New York's Globe Theater. As it turned out, the Music Hall's loss was the Globe's loss: *Radio City Revels* bore the distinction of being an even bigger bomb than *New Faces of 1937,* posting a $510,000 deficit—and for the second time RKO's hopes for an annual series were dashed.

Please note I didn't say those hopes were *forever* dashed. In 1945 RKO tried, tried again with *Radio Stars on Parade.* Marching in *this* parade are vocalist Frances Langford and bandleader Skinnay Ennis from NBC's *The Pepsodent Show Starring Bob Hope,* Ralph Edwards and his *Truth or Consequences* radio troupe, guitarist Tony Romano, rustic impressionist Rufe Davis, Kay Kyser's singing group The Town Criers, and (again) announcer Don Wilson. The "two-bit impresario" gimmick is hauled out once more as lead comedians Wally Brown and Alan Carney—the starving man's Abbott & Costello—try to promote Frances Langford to stardom, mainly by laying waste to a radio studio while being pursued by Frances' sinister suitor Sheldon Leonard. Some sporadic fun is to be had in the *Truth or Consequences* segments, recreating that NBC program's hilariously humiliating audience-participation stunts with reasonable accuracy; but even here Brown & Carney insert themselves where they're not wanted by showing up in drag. (The team also spoils a terrific number by the Cappy Bara Boys harmonica trio.) At least Langford and Tony Romano emerge from the picture unscathed, performing "Don't Believe Everything You Dream" with the same effortless charm they'd projected in their appearances with Bob Hope's USO troupe during World War II. Admittedly, *Radio Stars on Parade* did better at the box office than either *New Faces of 1937* or *Radio City Revels,* but only because it was produced at one-fourth the cost. When no sequel resulted from this effort, RKO finally got the hint and permanently dropped their plans for a yearly series.

Outside of 1938's *Goldwyn Follies* (see **Edgar Bergen and Charlie McCarthy**) and Monogram's one-off *Swing Parade of 1946,* which features Phil Regan, Connee Boswell, Louis Jordan and the Will Osborne Orchestra, it doesn't appear as though the radio-connected musicals from the other Hollywood studios were planned as continuing series. Over at Columbia, *Start Cheering* (1938) spotlights radio's Professor Quiz, Louis Prima, Gertrude Niessen, Johnny Green and Jimmy Wallington; *Time Out for Rhythm* showcases Rudy Vallee, Glen Gray's Orchestra and Bob Hope stooges Brenda & Cobina; 1943's *Reveille with Beverly* (see separate entry) uses an actual radio disc jockey program of the period to link together several unrelated star specialties; and *Jam Session* (1944) lives up to its title by featuring the orchestras of Charlie Barnet, Louis Armstrong, Alvino Rey, Jan Garber, Glen Gray and Teddy Powell, as well as singers Nan Wynn and the Pied Pipers (with Jo Stafford). But beyond sharing the same studio facilities and many of the same plot devices, these Columbia efforts are otherwise independent of one another.

Warner Bros' *Gold Diggers* series was chiefly designed to show off the studio's own contractees and thus didn't bother much with radio-generated stars. Other than 1937's *Hollywood Hotel* (q.v.) and the conglomeration of broadcast and film favorites in the wartime musicals *Thank Your Lucky Stars* (1943) and *Hollywood Canteen* (1944), the closest Warners came to an "all-star" radio festival was the 1934 Dick Powell vehicle *Twenty Million Sweethearts,* which opens with a marvelous montage of art-deco radio sets featuring the vocal talents of Bing Crosby, Morton Downey, Rudy Vallee, Ben Bernie, Arthur Tracy, Joe Penner, Kate Smith and Amos 'n' Andy. Or *does* it? You might have been fooled into thinking you were hearing the actual above-mentioned stars had you not taken notice of the film's opening credits, where it is stated outright that all those airwave luminaries are being impersonated by a novelty trio called the Radio Rogues (Jimmy Hollingwood, Eddie Bartell and Henry Taylor), who perpetrated the same harmless deception in several other features (notably *Reveille with Beverly*) as well as a brief series of Columbia two-reelers.

An intriguing byproduct of Paramount's *Big Broadcast* series is a one-shot from Universal, 1934's *Gift of Gab*. Long unavailable for reappraisal, this film was for many years a much coveted item by devotees of the Three Stooges, since the Universal publicity handouts indicated that the threesome made a guest appearance in the film. But once *Gift of Gab* was rediscovered, it was revealed that the film features another trio of comedians—John "Skins" Miller, Jack Harling and Sid Walker—who billed themselves as "The Three Stooges" just this once and never again. Moreover, these "Stooges" don't even receive an onscreen credit for their thirty-second bit, which is more influenced by the Ritz Brothers than the antics of Curly, Larry and Moe.

The "multicolossal!" *Gift of Gab* utilizes a radio station setting (mythical outlet WGAB) and a sappy storyline involving an egotistical broadcast celebrity (Edmund Lowe) and the women in his life (Gloria Stuart, Alice White) to justify its kaleidoscopic presentation of radio and movie guest performers. Though these highlights are ostensibly being broadcast to a nationwide audience, only a handful actually feature such necessities as microphones and sound engineers. These include the musical specialties by Gus Arnheim and His Orchestra, Gene Austin, Ruth Etting, Ethel Waters and the Downey Sisters—not to mention the Beale Street Boys, who are afforded more screen time than any of their better-known colleagues with a series of satirical singing commercials for sponsor Victor Moore. While most of the picture was lensed at Universal City, some of the musical selections were filmed in New York, as was a next-to-closing cameo by fabled critic-raconteur Alexander Woollcott, apparently reading his own material during what is supposed to be a broadcast of his *Town Crier* program for CBS.

Unlike the film's musical numbers, *Gift of Gab*'s comedy sketches make absolutely no effort to convince the audience that they're being staged in a radio studio. Not only is there no microphone in sight, but most of the humor relies upon physical gags, double takes and the shock of recognizing several famous faces in bit parts. Identified by his radio soubriquet "The Armour Star Jester," Phil Baker walks through a prop-laden doctor sketch with Hugh O'Connell and Helen Vinson, struggling to elicit chuckles with silly non sequiturs and abysmal puns. Slightly better if only because of its audacity is a prolonged murder-mystery sketch featuring Roger Pryor and Chester Morris as mentally challenged detectives, Binnie Barnes and June Knight as addlepated witnesses, Paul Lukas as the urbane and not-quite-dead murder victim, and—hold on to your hats—Bela Lugosi and Boris Karloff, the former hiding in a closet and asking what time it is, the latter making an impressive entrance in full "Mr. Hyde" regalia only to bum a match from the detectives. Neither of these sketches is anywhere near as funny as Woollcott's sly wink to the camera, as if to say "So you poltroons out there think this is what a radio broadcast *really* looks like, do you?"

And if any of *you* poltroons—er, gentle readers—out there think that I've forgotten to mention the only truly successful non–Paramount derivation of the *Big Broadcast* series, please refer to the separate entry on Republic's *Hit Parade* films of the 1930s, 1940s and 1950s.

Kate Smith and *Hello, Everybody!* (1933)

The overwhelmingly positive response to Kate Smith's cameo appearance in *The Big Broadcast*, combined with her enormous popularity as a CBS radio star, prompted Paramount Pictures to temporarily set aside their policy of showcasing several radio personalities in a single picture, and to serve up a separate starring vehicle for the "Songbird of the South."

Born in Greenville, Virginia, in 1907, Kathryn Elizabeth "Kate" Smith was still a teenager when she entered vaudeville as a singer and straight woman for a variety of comedians, most of whom made cruel and artless "fat" jokes at the girl's expense (she weighed between 210 and 235 pounds for most of her adult life). Kate debuted on Broadway in 1927, appearing in *Harmony Lane* and *Hit the Deck* before joining the cast of the musical *Flying High* in the role of Big Tiny Little, stopping the show each night with her "hotcha" Charleston dance routine. Unfortunately, the show's lead comic Bert Lahr not only persisted in ad libbing about Kate's poundage in front of the audience, but continued to hector the poor girl backstage, at one point quipping that if the show ever folded she could always get a job in a circus. Humiliations of this nature convinced Kate to quit the theater, and possibly even give up show business. But salvation was at hand in the form of Columbia Records executive Ted Collins, who assured her that if she stayed the course she would never again have to put up with jokes about her weight, and that she would always be showcased in as attractive and tasteful manner as possible. Within the next few years Collins would resign from Columbia to serve as Kate's manager, mentor, business partner and closest friend, all of which he remained until his death in 1964.

Kate gathered further momentum with a starring series for CBS radio beginning April 26, 1931. Heard several days per week, the 15-minute *Kate Smith and Her Swanee Music* was sponsored by La Palina Cigars and featured Jack Miller (later Ms. Smith's orchestra leader) on piano. Budgeted at $1,500 per

Kate Smith, singing star of CBS radio and Paramount's *Hello, Everybody* (1933), shares billing with her manager-mentor Ted Collins in this *Radio Annual* ad from 1941.

show, the series netted millions for the network, the sponsor and Kate Smith herself, who always split her share 50–50 with Ted Collins. Listeners nationwide were captivated by Kate's chipper greeting "Hello, everybody," her familiar sign-off "Thanks for listenin'," and her repertoire of sweet, languid Southern ballads, most memorably her theme song "When the Moon Comes Over the Mountain." As Kate's listenership soared with each passing month, a major motion picture for the star was a foregone conclusion.

The fact that Kate had made her first feature film appearance in *The Big Broadcast* did not make a subsequent Paramount contract a *fait accompli*. Taking full advantage of his client's drawing power, Collins pitted all the Hollywood studios against each other in a bidding war for Kate's services. Paramount won the battle, but only after promising Smith and Collins what one observer described as "a bucketful of money" and full creative control. Next came the matter of finding a suitable vehicle for the singer. Though Kate's fans demanded very little beyond her presence and several of her best songs, the studio could not realistically expect to hold the average audience's attention for seven or eight reels with singing alone.

Fannie Hurst's short story "Nice Girl," allegedly written with Kate in mind, served as the foundation for *Queen of the Air,* the working title for the screenplay concocted by Dorothy Yost and Lawrence Hazard. In the tradition of *The Vagabond Lover* (q.v.), the storyline fictionalizes the events leading up to Kate's ultimate triumph on the airwaves. In the film, the heroine is a big-hearted Colorado farm owner, beloved by everyone in her community and the sole support of her many relatives. A big-city trust called the Power and Water Company, planning to build a hydroelectric dam that will flood the valley, tries to force the neighboring farms to sell their property. The sole holdout is Our Gal Katie, who uses her God-given singing talent—first heard at a town debate which is broadcast to the nation—to become a highly paid network radio star. This enables Kate to settle her neighbors' legal fees, and also places her in the financial position to persuade the Power and Water Company to reroute the dam's pipeline.

Now that the plot was in place, what was needed (according to Paramount) was the traditional Hollywood love story. Under average circumstances, the romance in *Queen of the Air* would involve the star and a studio-selected leading man. Two stumbling blocks here: First of all, Kate Smith and Ted Collins didn't really feel the need for a love story, citing the fact that the major appeal of the singer's radio show was its simplicity, unencumbered by clichéd storytelling gimmicks. Secondly, the likelihood of finding a box-office–proven leading man for a woman of Kate Smith's girth was, if not impossible, certainly remote. Perhaps if Wallace Beery or Oliver Hardy had been under contract to Paramount, the writers might have circumvented this problem by creating a pair of rotund, semi-comic sweethearts. (This device would work beautifully five decades later on TV's *Roseanne*.) Instead, it was decided to develop a secondary romance between a handsome troubleshooter for the Power and Water Company, played by Paramount's own Randolph Scott, and Kate's attractive younger sister, played by freelancer Sally Blane (previously Rudy Vallee's honey in *The Vagabond Lover*). Kate's character would have to settle for the farm and the fame, while Sis landed the hero.

There was still another scripting problem, one unique to this film. Not only had Collins signed onto the project at a hefty fee as Smith's on-set advisor, but at Kate's insistence the studio would have to cast *him* in the picture as well. He was assigned the role of the "Nationwide Broadcasting System" representative who hires the heroine to sing on the air. In a moment of divine inspiration, it was decided to name this character "Ted Collins." The star herself had been given the fictional name "Kate Beverly" in the script, but by the time the cameras rolled her character had been rechristened "Kate Smith," the same sort of eleventh-hour decision that permitted Bing Crosby to play "himself" and not Bing Hornsby in *The Big Broadcast*.

In her 1960 memoir *Upon My Lips a Song,* Kate devotes all of two sentences to her first and only starring film, allowing that while she enjoyed her visit to California, "I didn't much like the movie capital." Judging by most other accounts, the feeling was mutual. Fifty years later, Kate's co-star Sally Blane recalled that the singer descended upon Tinseltown with her entire entourage in tow, then proceeded to assume the role of condescending grande dame with her Paramount co-workers. "You got the feeling that she didn't approve of Hollywood; she just wanted to take their money. It felt to us like an intrusion." Previous radio stars who'd made the trek to Hollywood would at least try to meet the moviemakers halfway. But according to Blane, "here we had this big stout woman who just had nothing to do with us."

Director William A. Seiter, who had managed to strike a happy medium with Phillips H. Lord and his "Seth Parker" cast in *Way Back Home* (q.v.), was unable to establish any sort of rapport with Kate Smith. She reportedly put up resistance to virtually all his directorial suggestions and nitpicked every line and gesture, forcing even the simplest scene to be taken and retaken endlessly. Though in time Smith would earn the industry's respect for her near-dictatorial perfectionism in all aspects of her career, it would seem that she hadn't yet developed a talent for diplomacy during her first visit to Hollywood. In desperation, Bill Seiter ended up doing what he always did when confronted with a recalcitrant star: He dug in his heels and grimly filmed every one of Kate's scenes *exactly* as written, making no effort to breathe any life or spontaneity into what had already been set down on paper.

Kate further demanded that her set be closed to all other Paramount personnel, which some observers attributed to her dislike of Mae West, whose own starring vehicle *She Done Him Wrong* was in production on a neighboring soundstage. While stories of this nature are usually told against Smith, one might take a moment to consider her viewpoint. As a Hollywood newcomer with minimal acting experience, she was understandably jittery and self-conscious, and a closed set was nothing unusual even for seasoned film stars like Garbo. Also, remember the pain Kate had endured when subjected to "fat" jokes by her vaudeville and Broadway co-stars; the last thing she needed was a wisecracker like Mae West (no sylph herself) within earshot. Finally, according to a December 1932 *Radio Digest* article by Mildred Miller, at the time *Queen of the Air* was in production Kate was being targeted by certain Hollywood columnists because of her many benefit performances for disabled ex-servicemen, and her generous showering of expensive gifts upon these wounded warriors. The fact that Kate had been giving free musical shows for World War I veterans ever since childhood meant nothing to the professional gossipmongers, who questioned her sincerity and snarkily suggested that she was merely trying to generate publicity for herself. This was flagrantly unfair, and Kate had every right to feel under siege. With this in mind, it's just possible that her imperious attitude and insistence upon a locked set were as much a defense mechanism as an ego trip.

Two months prior to its New York opening in January 1933, the film's title was changed to *Hello, Everybody!*, thereby preventing anyone from mistaking *Queen of the Air* for an aviation epic. According to Paramount publicist Arthur Mayer, its final budget was $2,000,000. While this figure seems a tad exaggerated in light of the film's very modest-looking production values, it is a fact that the Kate Smith "special" was the studio's most expensive musical to date. Paramount likewise spared no expense giving the film one of the biggest promotional blitzes since RKO's *Check and Double Check*. Not only did billboards and posters blanket every city and town where the film played, but the studio also bought up entire newspaper pages in many markets, filling them with ads, biographical sketches of Smith and Fannie Hurst, and announcements for such promotional stunts as a Kate Smith "Sing-alike" contest. Movie houses throughout North America reported turn-away business for the film's premiere: In New York City, the Paramount Theater posted its first weekend profit in months.

And yet, within six days of the gala opening, the Paramount dropped *Hello, Everybody!* like a stone, hastily substituting another film from its parent studio, *Luxury Liner*. With very rare exceptions, the story was the same everywhere else: Packed crowds for the first few showings, empty houses thereafter. So far as theater managers were concerned, *Hello, Everybody!* should have been titled *Hello, Anybody?*

The studio's post-mortem sessions brought forth several excuses for the film's box-office failure. It was too expensive to make a profit at popular prices; people think twice about plunking down money for entertainment they can get at home for free; once the film was seen, everyone's curiosity was satisfied and there was no return business; Kate's fans were disappointed by her phlegmatic acting style; there wasn't enough story; there was too much story; rural and Midwestern audiences were sidetracked by the concurrently released Will Rogers vehicle *State Fair*; reviews of the film were terrible; the picture was worse.

Rather than take on the above excuses one on one, let's examine the last two. In truth, reviewers did not universally pan the picture. Many critics liked it, echoing the words of *The Hollywood Reporter*: "In spots where the warbling Kate Smith is popular (and that's just about everywhere in the USA) *Hello, Everybody!* should be a mop-up." Of those who disliked it, several held the picture and not Kate responsible: "Miss Smith sings with her usual pleasing charm, but the illusion is destroyed that puts her over on the radio," grumbled *Film Daily*. The only "constant" in the reviews was the tendency to joke about Smith's weight. Even those commentators who were politely inclined towards the singer could not resist using such pejoratives as "singing pachyderm" and "400 pounds of pathos." Here was the one aspect of the film that the overprotective Ted Collins could not control.

There is more substance to the argument that *Hello, Everybody!* was a poor picture—at least for the first 25 minutes or so, during which Kate does a lot more talking than singing. A mortal blow was struck the early portions of the film by the screenwriters' determination to force the audience to feel sorry for Kate as she watches hero Randolph Scott, for whom she harbors a crush, billing and cooing with her kid sister Sally Blane. While Kate performs most of her musical numbers in a radio-show setting, the film includes one "character" song: the lachrymose Sam Coslow-Arthur Johnston composition "Moon Song" (aka "That Wasn't Meant for Me"), the lyrics of which tell us in so many words "Nobody loves a fat lady." The average movie audience doesn't like having the scriptwriters wheedle their sympathy, and has seldom if ever taken a self-pitying protagonist to its heart, preferring instead those "smilin' through" souls who are able to get past their personal woes without drowning in bathos. Worse still, the scripters were sending out precisely the wrong message to those thousands of chubby young girls who looked upon Kate Smith as a role model.

But once Kate calls off her pity party and hunkers down to the job of saving her neighbors' farms, *Hello, Everybody!* comes to life, steadily improving as it goes along. Though director Seiter can't do much to overcome his star's by-rote line readings, he is more successful fleshing out the other characters, notably the always delightful Charley Grapewin as Kate's chief cook and bottle washer. Better yet, the last half of the film, which mostly takes place in a radio studio, showcases Smith doing what she does best: singing warmly, sincerely and enthusiastically to an adoring radio public. Especially delightful (to this observer at least) is a totally unanticipated moment during Kate's rendition of "Dinah" when she suddenly breaks into the Charleston routine she'd made famous in the Broadway show *Flying High*. Admittedly, this vignette initially draws howls of laughter (the *Variety* review said as much), and one is worried that the floor will not be able to withstand the assault. But Kate is astonishingly light on her feet, and the entire number is performed with such ebullience that you gotta love the girl as she takes it home with a twinkle and a grin to the sounds of a cheering audience.

Another of Kate's big numbers is the principal reason that *Hello, Everybody!* is seldom revived on TV today. Stepping up to the microphone, Kate announces that her next selection is "for all the little colored children in orphanages." We are then treated to the gloriously tasteless "Pickaninnies' Heaven," in which Kate lovingly paints word pictures of the stereotypical delights awaiting black youngsters once they pass the Pearly Gates: watermelon vines, pork chop bushes, and need we go on? For those who can get past the outrageousness of the lyrics (to say nothing of the title), "Pickaninnies' Heaven" offers one of the film's biggest unintentional laughs. Once Kate launches into her song, the picture dissolves to a group of black orphans in pajamas, listening to the radio. As the camera pans across their faces, we briefly pause for a close-up of one gimlet-eyed urchin whose "Are you *jivin'* me, sister?" expression practically stops the picture cold!

Though *Hello, Everybody!* stands the test of time better than expected, the fact remains that the picture tanked in 1933. And while a few studio-sponsored columnists of the period insisted that the star had so much fun making the film that she was looking forward to appearing in as many as two more vehicles, a bitter Kate Smith had this to say in 1934: "If you like living in glass houses, if you have nerves that can stand the wear and tear of fighting directors and picture-stealers and makeup men and costumers, then you're the stuff a movie star is made of. If you're not, you'd better stick to your nice quiet job in a radio studio."

Except for a handful of musical short subjects, Kate would not appear before the movie cameras again until 1943. That was the year of her brilliant and untoppable rendition of what had been her signature tune since 1938, Irving Berlin's "God Bless America," in Warner Bros.' Technicolor flag-waver *This Is the Army*. By that time, she had assumed the mantle of National Institution, and as such was beyond criticism—even from those who could not help but notice that practically *every* song Kate Smith performed after 1943, be it written by Maurice Jarre or the Beatles, sounded exactly like "God Bless America."

"Baron Munchausen" and *Meet the Baron* (1933)

When in 1933 Metro-Goldwyn-Mayer elected to follow the lead of rival studios RKO and Paramount by building feature films around radio stars, no one could have been less enthusiastic about the decision than new MGM vice-president David O. Selznick. As head of production at RKO in 1932, Selznick had successfully put down all efforts to perpetuate the studio's radio-to-movie policy as exemplified by *The Vagabond Lover, Check* and *Double Check* and *Way Back Home* (all q.v.). But no sooner had he pitched camp at MGM (where he'd previously worked in the late 1920s) than he had to fight the same battle all over again.

As Selznick recorded in a letter quoted by his biographer Rudy Behlmer in 1972: "MGM had decided to capitalize on the popularity of radio stars, and at the suggestion of [producer] Harry Rapf, signed Ed Wynn and Jack Pearl. I have never been a devotee of radio comics. I had never heard either Wynn or Pearl on the radio… . Rapf had been my benefactor in the early days at Metro, and when he appealed to me to take one of them over (because he had initiated both, had felt responsibility for both, and felt he could only handle one at a time), I agreed and he gave me Pearl. I made the picture with a loathing for it, and it was a terrible flop." To the end of his days, Selznick would describe the Jack Pearl vehicle *Meet the Baron* as "a horror."

A New York City native who came into the world as Jack Perlman in 1894, Pearl was among the many Broadway entertainers who started his career in Gus Edwards' *School Days* vaudeville act. When the German-dialect comic playing the schoolteacher fell ill, Jack stepped into the role, teaching himself a Teutonic accent that in later years was praised for its authenticity by fellow performers. Graduating to Broadway revues, Pearl appeared in several editions of *The Ziegfeld Follies,* where he was occasionally teamed with straight man Cliff Hall. In 1932, comedy writer Billy Wells hired Pearl and Hall for an hour-long NBC radio variety series sponsored by Lucky Strike cigarettes. It was Wells who suggested that Pearl portray a spinner of tall tales, relating his imaginary adventures in fractured English to the increasingly skeptical Hall. One of the Lucky Strike ad men came up with the character name "Baron Munchausen," inspired by the actual 18th century German nobleman Von Münchhausen who was legendary for his farfetched reminiscences of battlefield heroics. While writing the routines, Wells persistently called Pearl's partner "Charlie" because he couldn't remember Hall's real name: Pearl in turn referred to his stooge as "Sharlie." The Baron Munchausen routines invariably built up to the moment when Charlie would have the audacity to question Munchausen's credibility, whereupon the Baron would giggle and shoot back, "Vass *you* dere, Sharlie?"

Playing to a radio public conditioned to laugh automatically at popular catchphrases, "Vass *you* dere, Sharlie?" caught on like wildfire in schoolrooms, smokers and speakeasies everywhere: It was even heard as a fadeout punchline in the 1933 James Cagney film *Picture Snatcher*. Those four little words propelled Pearl to stardom, and within a few months of its September 8, 1932, premiere, *The Jack Pearl Show* was second only to Eddie Cantor in the ratings. Movie offers began pouring in, with MGM's Harry Rapf snaring Pearl for a picture contract.

Listening to old recordings of Pearl's radio

Jack Pearl in character as Baron Munchausen, albeit without the beard he wore in his MGM screen appearances (courtesy Tim Hollis).

show, one is impressed by his energy, consistency of characterization and razor-sharp comic timing. But one cannot imagine wanting to spend more than ten or fifteen minutes in the man's company. This didn't seem to bother Rapf, who engaged Pearl's services for not one but *two* starring films. The first trade-paper announcement for MGM's upcoming "Jack Pearl All-Star Comedy" appeared in May of 1933, promising exhibitors "something different": a musical extravaganza directed by Sam Wood, in which Pearl would share screen space with such established favorites as Jimmy Durante and cartoon icon Mickey Mouse! Of this, more later.

Once Selznick took over the project, the trades were informed that Pearl's initial effort would be titled *The Big Liar,* with Stu Erwin, borrowed from Paramount, in support. Over the next few months, six highly paid writers labored on the script and dialogue, including Herman J. Mankiewicz, Norman Krasna, Allen Rifkin, P.J. Wolfson, Arthur Kober and Baron Munchausen's "father" Billy Wells. Somewhere along the line, Erwin was dropped from the cast and Jimmy Durante was brought into the fold. Other players included MGM contractees Ted Healy and his Stooges (Moe Howard, Curly Howard, Larry Fine), RKO's Edna May Oliver, and freelancer ZaSu Pitts. The film's songs were to be supplied by Richard Rodgers and Lorenz Hart, but the team had only written a few fragmentary tunes when they were replaced by Jimmy McHugh and Dorothy Fields. (One of the abandoned Rodgers-Hart compositions, "Give a Man a Job," was recycled as a Jimmy Durante specialty for a 1934 MGM short promoting the National Recovery Act.)

The plot for *The Big Liar*—retitled *Meet the Baron* prior to its October 20, 1933, release—expands upon the title character's fondness for stretching the truth by casting Pearl, billed in the opening credits as "The Famous Baron Munchausen of the Air," as a man who is merely *pretending* to be Munchausen. The real Baron (Henry Kolker) is an unscrupulous explorer who, to cover up his various villainies, leaves his two incompetent guides, Julius (Pearl) and Joe (Jimmy Durante, billed as "The Favorite

'Schnozzle' of the Screen"), to perish in the African jungle. The boys are found by a rescue party who mistake Julius for the Baron, whereupon Joe tells him to keep up the pretense so that they can return to America. Whisked off to a hero's welcome in New York City, the "Baron" makes a network radio appearance in which he boasts about his faux exploits for the benefit of announcer Charlie Montague (played by Ben Bard, previously teamed with Pearl on stage and in a 1926 Vitaphone short). When Dean Primrose (Oliver) of the all-girl Cuddle College hires the "Baron" to give a lecture for the student body, a reluctant Julius is forced to continue his charade, even if it means lying to the woman he loves (Pitts). The reappearance of the real Munchausen exposes Julius as a fraud, but his tall tales on radio have proven so popular with the public that he is signed to a big network contract—and as if this wasn't gratification enough, his sweetheart declares that she loves him for himself instead of the man he is not.

Only about 40 of the film's 66 minutes are needed to dwell upon the above narrative, compelling Selznick to fill the rest of the picture with ostentatious production numbers, comic turns with Ted Healy and his Stooges, and pulchritude aplenty courtesy of the "Metro-Goldwyn-Mayer Girls." Early on, the audience is treated to the surrealistic ensemble number "Hail to the Baron Munchausen," featuring snatches of song from city officials, tour guides, cops, Chinese laundrymen, Irish washerwomen, a group of Mae West–style hookers, and even the Statue of Liberty, who moans "I've gotta sing a torch song" for the celebrated Baron. This is followed by the Busby Berkeleyesque girlie show "Clean as a Whistle," focusing on the implicitly *au naturel* students of Cuddle College as they sing in the shower. For reasons that must have made sense at the time, this last musical spectacle is combined with the antics of Healy and the Stooges as they spend a whole reel running through a litany of plumbing gags, attempting to fix the pipes while making their way blindfolded through a gauntlet of dripping female flesh. With all this going on, who needs Baron Munchausen?

Well, it *is* his movie, so I guess we have to let him play. Sporting a beard that he never wore in any of his radio publicity photos, Pearl is allowed about five minutes to shine in a give-and-take gab session with Ben "Charlie" Bard, an admittedly hilarious sequence even for those who dislike the whole idea of Baron Munchausen. Otherwise, Selznick displays his contempt for Pearl by keeping the actor off-screen for most of the first three reels. When Jack finally does takes center stage, he comes off a distant runner-up to the powerhouse lineup of supporting comics—especially the Three Stooges, who are at the top of their pre-stardom form. The review of *Meet the Baron* in the *Rochester* (New York) *Evening Journal* said it best: "Its amusement value is based not so much on Jack Pearl as it is on the work of the other comedians. As a film actor, Pearl is still a good radio comedian."

Once Selznick discharged his duties on *Meet the Baron,* he wanted nothing to do with the second Pearl vehicle that the contract called for. But another film *had* to be made—and now is as good a time as any to hark back to that May 1933 studio announcement concerning the "Jack Pearl All-Star Comedy" with Jimmy Durante and Mickey Mouse. This was in fact an old Harry Rapf daydream that had been knocking around MGM since June 1932, when the producer first proposed a *Grand Hotel*–style farce featuring top comedians from all the studios. The project was shelved until February 1933, when it was announced that Buster Keaton was developing a parody titled *Gland Hotel,* featuring himself, Marie Dressler, Polly Moran, Jimmy Durante and Laurel & Hardy, among many others. Keaton's dismissal from MGM scotched *this* idea, but Harry Rapf still wanted to resuscitate the original project under the title *The Hollywood Revue of 1933*. In April of that year, production began with Durante and Mickey Mouse "locked," and with a proposed guest star roster featuring everyone on the MGM lot from Clark Gable to Johnny Weissmuller. One month later came the announcement that Jack Pearl had been thrown into the goulash, a move intended to solve a problem that had vexed everyone concerned with *Hollywood Revue of 1933*: Despite its enormous cast, the film had no "central" star.

One by one, the announced guest stars dropped out; also disposed of were most of the songs by (again) Rodgers & Hart, with the noteworthy exception of "Hollywood Party"—which in turn became the film's new title. At least eight writers came and went, as did several directors, including Sam Wood (remember him?), Richard Boleslawski and Edmund Goulding. Charles Reisner directed what was left of the "all-star" cast with the help of Richard Rowland and George Stevens, the latter spending a few days improvising a terrific egg-breaking routine with Laurel & Hardy and Lupe Velez. Allan Dwan knotted up the loose ends, tacking on a coda featuring Durante and his real-life spouse Jean that was intended to make sense of the hopelessly chaotic scenario.

Released without any directorial credit on June 1, 1934, *Hollywood Party* can be regarded as a "Jack Pearl vehicle" only in the sense that its threadbare plot is motivated by Baron Munchausen's appearance at a lavish soirée in the home of Durante, who as moviedom's jungle monarch "Schnarzan" wants to purchase the Baron's pride of lions to appear in his next picture. Billed fourth in the opening credits and still sporting his *Meet the Baron* chin spinach, Pearl appears very briefly and is never permitted to tell a single fib. The comedian makes his first appearance as Durante stage-manages a Ziegfeldesque "Welcome" musical number featuring nearly naked chorines, black Zulu dancers, and an effeminate gorilla whom the Baron identifies as "Ping Pong." That's about as good as it gets.

Ending one of the shortest movie careers in history, Pearl returned to his radio gig, still coasting on the popularity of "Vass *you* dere, Sharlie?" Ignoring friendly warnings by his colleagues that audiences would eventually tire of the same old *schtick* week after week, Pearl resisted varying his style in the slightest, and by 1935 he had pretty much worn out his welcome. Staging several comebacks over the next 15 years, Pearl would invariably promise the public something new and novel—but somehow he always retreated to Baron Munchausen. By the time he wrapped up his final radio series in 1951, many of his fellow performers spoke of Pearl in the past tense, and only as a cautionary example of what can happen when a comedian becomes trapped in his own catchphrase. Pearl may have never known how right he was when he said in a 1930s interview, "This business of being funny is not be laughed at."

Ed Wynn and *The Chief* (1933)

When David Selznick agreed to take over production of Jack Pearl's *Meet the Baron* in early 1933 (see separate entry), producer Harry Rapf was left with the other radio-inspired MGM film then in the works. Rapf probably thought he'd gotten the best of the bargain, inasmuch as *his* star was Ed Wynn. While Selznick was saddled with the job of introducing Pearl to moviegoers unfamiliar with the comedian's radio work, there was hardly an American showbiz fan alive who didn't know Ed Wynn.

Born Isaiah Edwin Leopold in Philadelphia in 1886, Wynn was 15 years old when he ran away from home to join a traveling theatrical troupe; he was still entertaining audiences at the time of his death, 65 years later. Following extensive vaudeville experience, Ed made the first of several annual appearances with the *Ziegfeld Follies* in 1914. Boycotted on Broadway for his courageous support of the 1919 Actor's Equity strike, he began writing and producing his own revues, scoring his biggest success to date as the title character in the 1922 musical *The Perfect Fool*. In cold print, an inventory of Wynn's specialties hardly seems to add up to enduring stardom. He lisped his dialogue in a high-pitched falsetto, giggled at his own jokes, trafficked in wheezy one-liners and deliberately horrendous puns, wore silly costumes, hats and makeup, and surrounded himself with wacky props and zany "inventions." So did a lot of dime-a-dozen comics at the time. But Wynn possessed that special, indefinable magic which held an audience spellbound, leaving them limp with laughter and demanding encores as the curtain fell. Wynn once famously noted that while a comic says funny things, a comedian says things funny. Combing through the man's unfailingly positive newspaper reviews throughout his stage career, and hearing of such disparate performers as Stan Laurel, Red Skelton and Groucho Marx proclaiming him as "the master," one could easily conclude that Ed Wynn was the greatest comedian of the 20th century.

As big a star as anyone could ever hope to be in 1922, Ed added to his accomplishments with a historic radio appearance on June 12 of that year over New York's WJZ, becoming the first actor ever to present a complete Broadway show (*The Perfect Fool,* of course) over the airwaves. But according to the comedian, "in its present state" radio was not yet ready to support performers of his caliber on a regular basis, an opinion to which he still held firm in early 1932 as he resisted all entreaties to star in a weekly radio show. After one such offer from Texaco Gasoline, Ed flippantly responded that he'd have to be paid $5,000 a week to even consider such an idea. To his amazement, Texaco met his price, and on Tuesday, April 26, 1932, he stepped before an NBC microphone at 9:30 p.m. EST to assume the title role on the weekly, 30-minute *Texaco Fire Chief* variety series.

With popular announcer Graham McNamee as his stooge, Ed ran through 30 years' worth of tried-and-true material, introducing such new ideas as a weekly "advice" segment in which he gave foolish answers to fans who had allegedly written in. (Actually, this bit wasn't all that new: Ed had gone through the same paces with his own newspaper column in the 1920s.) And like practically every other radio comedian, Wynn appreciated the value of running gags and catchphrases, beginning each broadcast with "Tonight the program's gonna be different, Graham," forever threatening to present his own "three-act opera," and punctuating his rambling anecdotes with a long, drawn-out "Sooo-ooo-ooo." Except for the straight lines and commercials from McNamee and periodic musical interruptions from the orchestra (led first by Don Vorhees, then by Eddy Duchin), Ed Wynn was the whole show—and just as he'd done on stage, Wynn always appeared before the studio audience in full costume and makeup,

an oversized fireman's helmet atop his head. Existing transcriptions reveal that the radio series was relentlessly corny even by 1932 standards, but Wynn's high spirits were infectious and his sheer energy overwhelming. *The Texaco Fire Chief* won Ed millions of new fans who had never seen him on stage—and more importantly, sales of Texaco's fuel products soared, moving *Variety* to describe the program as "a model upon which future advertising broadcasts will be based."

It was a tough and demanding assignment even for a workaholic like Wynn, who after spending years taking pride in the fact that he created all his own stage material was forced to hire a writing staff to sustain the pace of 55 jokes per week. Having to rely upon "outside help" was one of the reasons that Ed had shied away from movie work in the past. His 1927 screen debut in the silent feature *Rubber Heels,* filmed at Paramount's Long Island studio, had been an unpleasant experience for the comedian, who complained that he'd been "de-Ed Wynnized" by a director who shoehorned him into an unsuitable character; in fact, Wynn so hated the film that he offered to buy the negative and destroy it. Ed's first talkie *Follow the Leader* (1930), also filmed in Long Island, was more satisfying because it had been adapted from his own Broadway hit *Manhattan Mary,* allowing him to repeat his best stage business rather than conform to the dictates of others. But *Follow the Leader* played to tepid box-office and critical response, discouraging Wynn from pursuing future film projects.

With *The Texaco Fire Chief* playing to spectacular ratings during the 1932–33 season, studio heads who'd previously written Wynn off as just another stage attraction unsuited to the screen quickly changed their minds. MGM's Harry Rapf was the executive who made the offer that Ed couldn't refuse, and for the first time the "Perfect Fool" would be making a feature picture in Hollywood. Tentatively titled *The Fire Chief* to thoroughly exploit the comedian's radio renown, the film would be directed by former Chaplin associate Charles Reisner and scripted by Bert Kalmar and Harry Ruby, who since their disastrous collaboration with

Amos 'n' Andy on *Check and Double Check* (q.v.) had redeemed themselves with sublime gag-filled screenplays perfectly attuned to the talents of the Marx Brothers and Eddie Cantor, among others. But Kalmar and Ruby were called away to work on the Marxes' *Duck Soup*, leaving *The Fire Chief* in the hands of Arthur Caesar and Robert E. Hopkins, admittedly talented gagsmiths who nonetheless couldn't seem to get a handle on Ed Wynn. The main problem was that despite the title, Ed was in the wrong picture.

Set in the Bowery of the Gay '90s, the story concerns Henry Summers (Wynn), the bungling son of a legendary fire chief who'd been killed in the line of duty. Henry is unable to live up to his dad's reputation until he accidentally saves a woman from a burning building and becomes a hero. His shady employer Morgan (Purnell Pratt), in league with gambling boss O'Rourke (William "Stage" Boyd), runs Henry for alderman against crooked incumbent Clayton (C. Henry Gordon). To keep our hero from dropping out of the race—and from figuring out that he's merely a dupe to further O'Rourke's criminal activities—entertainer Dixie Dean (Dorothy Mackaill) is dispatched to vamp Henry into compliance. Meanwhile, Clayton's henchman Big Mike (Nat Pendleton) puts pressure on Summers to withdraw his name from the ballot, going so far as to kidnap Henry's mother (Effie Ellsler). To simultaneously rescue his mom and scare people off from voting for Clayton, Ed scampers wildly around town wearing a lampshade on his head and pretending to be crazy (not much of a stretch).

Co-writer Caesar had previous worked on several Joe E. Brown vehicles, and one can envision Joe E. sailing effortlessly through the plot contrivances and comic set pieces of *The Fire Chief* without damaging his established character. But the film is all wrong for Wynn, who is not only miscast as the guileless and hopelessly naïve Henry Summers but is also far too old for the part. And while it is true enough that Wynn was a visual comedian, he was *not* a slapstick comedian. The film's Sennett-style comic "highlights" are not only clumsy but embarrassingly artificial. Describing his Hollywood experience in a December 1933 newspaper interview, Ed recounted: "They made me hang out the window of a burning building four floors above the street. They made me run through smoke-filled halls with the flames licking my coat tails, they made me hang onto the rear platform of a fire engine pulled by a couple of runaway horses, and, worst of all, they made me wrestle a 300-pound bear named Samson." One is surprised the Fire Chief's pants didn't suddenly ignite while he was saying this: In the film, it is distressingly obvious that virtually all of the heavy slapstick duty is performed by Ed's stunt double—and that "Samson" is just a fat guy in a bear costume.

Inasmuch as the writers seemed bent upon

Even if this undated studio still of Ed Wynn isn't from his 1933 starring film *The Chief*, it may as well be.

turning Wynn into Joe E. Brown, it is no surprise that the comedian is barely permitted to do any of his own characteristic material; he doesn't even get to trot out his trademarked inventions, though his muddling-misfit character is just the sort of fellow who'd be tinkering away on useless machinery in his basement. Only rarely does a good line or bit of business emerge: When a gun-wielding hoodlum shouts, "Don't move or I'll shoot!" Ed shouts back "Don't shoot or I'll move!" One of the film's few genuine "Ed Wynn" scenes occurs near the end, as he races all over the Bowery grabbing people by the lapels and shrieking "*I'm crazy! I'm crazy!*" Unfortunately, this scene illustrates Wynn's major flaw as a screen actor, at least in 1933: Ed has not yet learned how to tone himself down for the camera. Instead of coming off as the lovable eccentric he played on radio, he is strident, crass, annoying and utterly unappealing.

The weirdest moment takes place a few minutes before the fadeout. No sooner has the plot come to a resolution of sorts than we dissolve to Wynn as "himself," wearing his Texaco Fire Chief outfit and standing at an NBC microphone before a studio audience. He proceeds to tell announcer Graham McNamee the *real* outcome of the story in the manner of one of his "three-act operas," with goofy verbal gags and groan-worthy puns abounding. Once that's over with, he answers letters from his listeners, just like he did on radio every Tuesday night. The familiar *Texaco Fire Chief* siren is sounded, Ed and Graham sign off the air ... and that's it.

No one back in 1933 was quite sure why the film arrived at this Pirandellian epilogue, though a few critics suggested that the filmmakers knew the rest of the movie was hopeless and opted to haul in the "real" Wynn so the audience would leave happy. Some reviews cited the closing gag as the best thing in the picture! MGM studio records reveal that the film as initially conceived was to have opened during a *Texaco Fire Chief* broadcast, with Ed launching into the description of the film he'd just completed, at which point the picture would dissolve to the plot proper, returning to the radio show for the climax. At the last moment MGM decided to remove the prologue and cut "flat" to the story, rendering the final scene pointless. As confusing as this must have been to filmgoers familiar with Wynn's radio show in 1933, imagine the reaction of 21st century TV addicts who, knowing squat about *The Texaco Fire Chief,* chance upon on the film during an early-morning TCM telecast. If you ever happen to hear several neighborhood voices rising as one and screaming "What the hell was *that*?" you'll know what they've just seen.

Minus the original opening, the film—retitled simply *The Chief* just prior to its release on November 3, 1933—ran about 62 minutes. With Wynn refusing to return to Hollywood for retakes, short-subject specialist Jules White and a few other house directors shot a handful of "pickup" scenes to bring the running time up to 65 minutes, just barely qualifying *The Chief* as an "A" picture (and aggravating theater owners who had to rent several expensive short subjects to pad out the length of the program, a grievance also leveled at the Marx Bros.' 69-minute *Duck Soup* around the same time). Neither audiences nor critics were pleased, with the *New York Times* speaking for everyone: "What it all comes down to is that Mr. Wynn is genuinely funny and *The Chief* is not." Allen Saunders of the *Toledo News-Bee* forsook the *Times*' restraint: "If *The Chief* was intended to be a good picture, well, MGM can rise and take a bow for first honors as the occupational center of American stupidity."

Except for a *gratis* guest appearance in the morale-boosting musical *Stage Door Canteen* (1943), Wynn would not appear in another feature film until 1956's *The Great Man,* by which time he had reinvented himself as a dramatic actor. He went on to deliver a poignant Oscar-nominated performance in *The Diary of Anne Frank* (1959), then spent the last years of his life contributing lighthearted support to such Disney films as *The Absent Minded Professor, Babes in Toyland* and *Those Calloways.* His best Disney showing was as the jovial Uncle Albert in 1964's *Mary Poppins*: The irresistible image of 77-year-old Ed Wynn floating to the ceiling while laughing uncontrollably is a far more fitting testament to his talents than that misbegotten mélange known as *The Chief.*

Myrt and Marge (1933)

With the comedy series *Amos 'n' Andy* and *The Goldbergs* (both q.v.) blazing trail for serialized network radio programs, the first important *dramatic* example of what would later be designated as "soap operas" premiered on November 2, 1931, on CBS, after a successful local run in Chicago. Though scheduled opposite NBC's *Amos 'n' Andy* from 7:00 to 7:15 p.m. EST, *Myrt and Marge* nonetheless rapidly built up a very sizable nationwide audience, and before long it was regularly listed in radio's Top Ten. Created by former vaudeville dancer Myrtle Vail, the series was the backstage saga of the Chic-Chicks, the 24-girl dancing chorus in "that most glittering of all Broadway extravaganzas, *Hayfield's Pleasures*." When aspiring 16-year-old hoofer Margie, played by Vail's real-life daughter Donna Damerel, collapsed from hunger during rehearsal, worldly Myrtle (Vail retained her actual first name), a 32-year-old Broadway veteran, took the youngster under her wing, appointing herself Marge's mentor and doing her darnedest to shield the green kid from the predatory males who trolled the Great White Way. Pitching *Myrt and Marge* to Chicago-based Wrigley's Gum, Vail won the potential sponsor over by naming her principal characters Myrtle *Spear* and Margie *Minter* (figure it out yourself).

Just as *Amos 'n' Andy* was considered a groundbreaker for treating its black characters as sympathetic human beings rather than mere comic buffoons, *Myrt and Marge* was regarded as quite advanced and innovative for its time. A *Variety* review from October 1931, *before* the series launched its network run, tallied a list of radio "firsts" on *Myrt and Marge*. It was the first program to deglamorize show business with the frankness and "rough" quality of its dialogue (though tame by contemporary standards, the repartee was loaded with Depression-era double entendres); it was the first network series to feature a drug addict (Marge's scapegrace brother) as a recurring character; and it was the first to include an openly gay character in its regular cast. (*Variety* wasn't quite as progressive as the series, using the word "pansy.")

Network publicity photograph of Myrt (Myrtle Vail, left) and Marge (Donna Damerel).

This last point may need some elucidation. Played by Ray Hedges, Clarence Tiffingtuffer was the fluttery costume designer for *Hayfield's Pleasures,* and in keeping with the then-prevalent stereotype of this sort of character he was decidedly epicene in his vocal inflections. Though not quite the "thithy" described by *Radioland* (he never lisped), Clarence was clearly homosexual in both word and attitude. Originally intended as comic relief, he would over the years emerge as one of the series' strongest and most positive characters. As the archetypal Gay Best Friend of the two heroines, Clarence stood ready to put his reputation, his career and even his life on the line to protect the girls from harm.

With the second wave of radio-to-movie adaptations well underway in 1933, Universal Pictures entered into negotiations with Myrtle Vail, Wrigley's and CBS to transfer *Myrt and Marge* to the screen. Venerable playwright-director-actor Willard Mack, an acknowledged master of florid melodramas, was the studio's choice to pen the screenplay, but Mack handed his duties over to his wife Beatrice Banyard. To sidestep the pitfalls of adapting an ongoing radio continuity to a self-contained film—characters and plot developments in play at the time of filming ran the risk of being outdated or nonexistent when the picture was finally released—Banyard completely jettisoned the radio version's setting, backstory, and even its theme music ("Poor Butterfly"), salvaging only the characters of Myrt, Marge and Clarence.

Originally titled *The New Deal,* the film's story had nothing to do with politics but instead concentrated on a broken-down musical revue titled *My Lady's Legs.* The withdrawal of the show's backer threatens to throw the troupe out of work, but lead dancer Myrtle Spear takes over management, at the same time dropping out of the cast to give younger talent a chance. With small-time vaudevillian Eddie Hanley as star, the performers stop over at a theatrical boarding house run by the formidable Mrs. Minter, whose pretty and talented daughter Margie not only catches the eye of Eddie but also the show's new "angel" (played in the film by Thomas Jackson, usually seen in detective roles), a middle-aged lech who agrees to bankroll *My Lady's Legs* only so that he can get his grimy paws on the ingénue. Once Margie joins the show, Myrtle must deploy several evasive maneuvers to keep the kid from being despoiled by the rapacious financier. After a violent confrontation with Eddie, the un-angelic angel withdraws his cash and arranges to have the show impounded and the cast thrown in jail. But all turns out for the best when Margie's mom shows up out of nowhere and agrees to finance the Broadway bow of *My Lady's Legs.* (By introducing the character of Mrs. Minter, Beatrice Banyard unwittingly contradicted a future plot point on radio's *Myrt and Marge,* in which it was revealed that Myrt was really Margie's long-lost mother.)

Virtually indistinguishable from the myriad of backstage tearjerkers ground out by Hollywood in the first five years of the talkies, Banyard's script for *The New Deal* was far more maudlin than anything heard on the radio version of *Myrt and Marge,* and it is to the everlasting credit of producer Bryan Foy that he hired the incomparable Al Boasberg to infuse the picture with some much-needed comedy. Since moving to Manhattan from his native Buffalo in 1923, the corpulent, gregarious Boasberg had established himself as one of the best and highest-paid gag writers in America. He was so busy supplying one-liners and special material to vaudevillians like Burns & Allen and Jack Benny that he had to set up a weekly wire service, telegraphing jokes to his clients; it was said that virtually half the acts playing the Loews Circuit were subsisting on Boasberg's material. He also worked extensively in silent films, traveling to Hollywood in 1926 to contribute gags for the Buster Keaton classics *The General* and *College.* In talkies, Boasberg was essentially a script doctor, punching up the work of other writers with wisecracks, sight gags and punchlines. If Boasberg had never done anything else in Hollywood, he would be immortalized for dreaming up the celebrated "stateroom scene" in the Marx Bros.' *A Night at the Opera* (1935).

Boasberg preferred working at home, sitting

in a huge bathtub and firing off jokes into a dictaphone. Every so often, however, he hauled his carcass down to the studio to dabble in direction, concentrating mainly on comedy shorts. His first feature film directorial assignment was *The New Deal*. By the time he signed onto the project, it had been retitled *Myrt and Marge*. In concert with producer Bryan Foy, an old pal from vaudeville, Boasberg filled the supporting cast with tried-and-true variety performers. The role of hero-by-default Eddie Hanley went straight to Bryan's brother Eddie Foy, Jr., who performs some remarkably complex tap dance routines. Two of Broadway's greatest *grande dames*, nightclub chanteuse Grace Hayes and musical-comedy headliner Trixie Friganza, were cast as earthy touring actress Gracie and the fearsome Mrs. Minter, respectively. Birdlike Jimmy Conlin, formerly teamed with his wife Myrtle Glass in one of vaudeville's loosest and loopiest double acts, appears briefly as a seedy comic. And just as they'd practically stolen the show in the Jack Pearl vehicle *Meet the Baron* (q.v.), Ted Healy and his Stooges (Moe, Larry and Curly), on loan from MGM, dominate every scene they're in as the theatrical troupe's chief electrician Mullins and his three roughneck assistants. The Healy-Stooge routines are even funnier here than in *Baron*, with such gems as Ted's imitation of Al Jolson and a literal running gag involving "Stoogette" Bonnie Bonnell as a lamebrained hanger-on.

As for the three transplants from radio's *Myrt and Marge*, Myrtle Vail and Donna Damerel perform with such casual expertise that it's hard to believe they'd never appeared in a film before. Though she gets off to a shaky start in her first big scene, working so hard to be "spontaneous" that she sounds as if she's going up in her lines, Vail improves steadily as the film goes on, and is particularly effective in the scene where she has a heart-to-heart talk with Margie about the unsavory would-be Romeos who always lurk at the stage door waiting to pounce. The film makes allowances for the fact that Vail is a decade older than the radio version of Myrt with a nastily amusing dance number showing the stocky actress vainly struggling to keep up with the younger chorines. Likewise, Donna Damerel is obviously several years removed from the "sweet 16" Margie of the airwaves, but the script doesn't even try to pass her off as a teenager. A comely young woman made all the more appealing by a pronounced overbite, Damerel proves to be a better-than-average singer-dancer, though the dreadful songs by M.K. Jerome and Joan Jasmyn don't give her much to work with.

The most fascinating of the three radio carryovers is Ray Hedges, billed onscreen only by his character name "Clarence," just as Vail and Damerel are billed only as "Myrt and Marge (Radio's Sweethearts)." If anything, Hedges' sly, knowing portrayal of Clarence is even more effective on screen than on radio, enhanced by some magnificently bitchy put-down lines. Dismissing woebegone comic Jimmy Conlin, Clarence sneers, "Why don't you look in the mirror and get your first laugh?" Finding a tear in the ladies' lingerie, he moans, "This looks like King Kong wore it to a masquerade!" And when the troupe runs out of train fare, a randy-looking chorine asks, "Can we walk back?" giving Clarence the golden opportunity to hiss, "That'd be the first time *you* ever walked back." So convincing was Hedges' performance, both on film and on the air, that it caused him no little discomfort when confronted by fans who refused to separate character from actor. In a June 1935 *Radio Mirror* article, Ray Hedges begged interviewer Charles J. Gilchrest to assure the public that, honor bright, he wasn't really the sissy he played so persuasively. "Please tell them about the real me ... about the he-man who goes mountain climbing, who thoroughly enjoys horse riding and deep sea fishing and fencing and tennis." Okay, Ray. Sure. Right. But he *was* awfully good as Clarence, wasn't he?

The last minute or so of *Myrt and Marge* invokes memories of Ed Wynn's *The Chief* (q.v.), with all the actors appearing as "themselves" at a radio broadcast of the program on station OKOG. This gimmick is more effective here than in the Wynn film because it is short and not overplayed, serving its purpose of satisfying the curiosity of radio fans who wondered what their favorite characters *really* looked like. And besides, how often do we get to see the Three

Stooges without their traditional hairstyles, wearing clean clothes that actually fit?

Released November 25, 1933, *Myrt and Marge* had the bad fortune to follow on the heels of MGM's two misfire radio-driven features *Meet the Baron* and *The Chief* (q.v.). It was a better film than either of its predecessors, but movie fans were growing weary of such parasitic fare, while devotees of the radio series didn't approve of having Myrt and Marge yanked from their familiar environs and plunked into a less compelling storyline; nor did they find the increased comedy content appropriate to a show that had built its following as a drama. Trade reviewers were generally supportive, though most felt that the film's main attraction was the strong Hollywood supporting cast rather than the two radio stars. Describing the picture as "first class entertainment" with an abundance of "spicy" laughs, *Motion Picture Daily* qualified these compliments: "Actually, Ted Healy and his gang furnish all the laughs with Eddie Foy, Jr. assisting with his neat routine of dance and song."

A box-office bust, *Myrt and Marge* fell into obscurity after its initial release, never to be reissued theatrically or shown on commercial television. So little was known about the picture that as late as the mid–1970s, otherwise knowledgeable historians were insisting that the Three Stooges weren't even in it! Finally the film resurfaced in the 1980s, allowing contemporary viewers to judge it for themselves. Admittedly the picture is no lost treasure, looking mighty ragged for a major-studio release (the one big production number, a bizarre affair with chorus girls emerging from a giant coiled snake, seems to belong to another movie). But as a filmed record of the vast array of entertainment choices Americans had in 1933, *Myrt and Marge* is invaluable.

The CBS radio edition of *Myrt and Marge* continued unabated until March 27, 1942, managing to survive the sudden death of co-star Donna Damerel by a full year (she was replaced by Helen Mack). A syndicated version, using updates of the original scripts, made the rounds in 1946 and 1947; produced by Myrtle Vail, this revival starred Alice Yourman as Myrt, Alice Goodkin as Marge, and Ray Hedges in his original role as Clarence. Living to the age of 90, Myrtle Vail spent her last 20 years in retirement save for a handful of film roles landed through the auspices of her actor-writer grandson Charles B. Griffith, most memorably Mrs. Krelboyne in Roger Corman's *Little Shop of Horrors* (1960).

Jack Benny and Fred Allen (1934–1945)

Few things are more irritating to pop-culture aficionados than people who claim to be "movie freaks" or "old-time radio buffs" on the basis of having seen a handful of classic films or heard a dozen or so vintage radio recordings. These are the people who list among their favorite "comedy teams" Mae West and W.C. Fields (who made one whole picture together); who stubbornly insist that the closing tag of *The Burns and Allen Show* was George's "Say goodnight, Gracie" and Gracie's "Goodnight, Gracie"; and who invoke the name of the great Fred Allen *only* when referring to his radio feud with Jack Benny. Think a moment: Here is the man of whom James Thurber once said, "You can count on the thumb of one hand the American who is at once a comedian, a humorist, a wit and a satirist, and his name is Fred Allen." Here is the man who fearlessly fought endless battles with networks, sponsors and censors to secure the right for himself and his fellow comedians to tell jokes about what they wanted to, when they wanted to, without the threat of being cut off the air or banished entirely. And yet, in all too many instances he is mentioned only as a footnote in the career of Jack Benny, on the basis of a patently phony feud that didn't begin until 1936—at which time both participants had been in show business for over two decades— and was already old news less than a year later.

Excuse us a moment while we go out on a limb. Part of the reason Fred Allen has not lingered in the memory as long as Jack Benny is Fred Allen himself. Until very recently—if the past forty years can be regarded as "recent" in the grander scheme of things—Allen's body of work has been largely represented by the six feature films in which he appeared. And if he'd had more to say about the situation, he wouldn't have even made *those* six films.

Up until 1936, the names "Jack Benny" and "Fred Allen" were seldom spoken in the same breath, even though their career paths were remarkably similar. Both men were born the same year (1894), Benny in Waukegan, Illinois, and Allen in Boston. Both came into the world with different names—Benny as Benjamin Kubelsky, Allen as John F. Sullivan—and both went through a dizzying array of stage names before settling on their most famous appellations. Both started in show business at an early age, and both originally aspired to excel in areas other than comedy: Allen as a juggler and ventriloquist, Benny as a violinist. Once they both realized that comedy was their forte, they began to prosper in vaudeville, often in the role of "master of ceremonies," a fancy designation for the guy who tells jokes in front of the curtain while the sets are being changed. Both enjoyed considerable success on Broadway, and both began appearing in one- and two-reel films long before they'd even given radio a thought. Both had onstage partners who happened to be married to them: Fred's lifelong bride was Portland Hoffa, while Jack's spouse was Mary Livingstone (*née* Sadie Marks). And both emerged as radio stars within six months of one another, Benny on NBC-Blue's *The Canada Dry Program* beginning May 2, 1932, Allen on CBS's *The Linit Bath Club Revue* starting October 23, 1932.

Stylistically the two men were as different as night and day. In emulation of his role model Frank Fay, Benny originally performed his act by speaking in a casual, conversational tone, delivering jokes and punchlines as if they were throwaways. A strikingly handsome man, he played the part of a nattily attired *bon vivant* who amused himself by mocking the conventions of romance and social propriety—at the same time reserving his harshest mockery for himself, usually by commenting on his own amorous disappointments or his unwillingness to ever pay his own way. (The character of the elegant boulevardier without a penny in his pocket was common in the 1920s.) To those familiar with Benny's outrageously exaggerated "cheap" jokes on his later radio program, these early jokes are somewhat mild ("I took my girl out to dinner, and when I proposed she was so surprised that she dropped her tray") and occasionally a bit rakish, as in the 1931 Paramount short subject *A Broadway Romeo* in which Benny generously offers to stake an impoverished man to a meal, only to trick the poor fellow into paying Jack's tab! Having learned through trial and error that he got his biggest laughs by putting himself down, Benny was perfectly in character when, for his inaugural radio appearance on Ed Sullivan's program in 1931, he introduced himself with, "This is Jack Benny. There will be a slight pause for everyone to say, 'Who cares?'"

Born with a face made for radio, the sour-persimmon–visaged Fred Allen could also tell jokes at his own expense, but was most effective when using his pinched nasal voice to skewer the pretensions of others. No one was spared his satiric and sarcastic barbs, neither pompous big-city politicians nor obnoxious small-town wiseacres. Confronted by the humorless title character in his 1929 Paramount one-reeler *The Installment Collector,* Allen immediately sizes the other man up and deadpans, "Some forty years ago your parents should have taken birth control more seriously." He even made sport of his audience, lampooning the typical Broadway playgoer's fondness for timeworn gags by creating a stage backdrop depicting a cemetery, each tombstone engraved with a tired old joke and its equally rheumatic punchline. In essence, Fred Allen was Will Rogers minus the bucolic charm, and audiences loved his acidulous delivery and mock-imperious fondness for ten-dollar words (Returning to *The Installment Collector,* Fred reacts to the unwarranted laughter of a secondary character by muttering "What causes your hyena gland to function without encouragement?")

Their divergent styles notwithstanding, Benny and Allen shared the opinion that to enjoy lasting success in radio, a comedian could not continue relying on the jokes and routines he'd done to death in vaudeville and on Broadway (the name Ed Wynn comes to mind). The two men also had an aversion to the "anything for a cheap laugh" policy of certain other radio comics, who would perform sight gags and wear ridiculous costumes to get a rise out of the studio audience while ignoring the home folks huddled around their consoles. Both Jack and Fred carefully attuned their programs to the new medium by experimenting with innovational formats, clever sound effects and other elements that would have their strongest impact on radio. Allen forsook the standard weekly gagfests of his peers by presenting "theme" shows, self-contained playlets in which a single topic or situation was explored comedically and his character was adjusted to fit the evening's topic. Benny on the other hand preferred consistency of characterization, but agreed with Allen that the standard format of network variety programs in the 1930s was not carved in stone. Whereas comedians like Eddie Cantor used their announcers and orchestra leaders as straight men and stooges (a word both Benny and Allen disliked), Jack saw nothing wrong with allowing his announcers, conductors, vocalists and supporting players to share the jokes and even deliver the punchlines. Jack subscribed to the theory that allowing everyone in the cast to get laughs made the overall program all the funnier.

While Allen remained the master of his radio domain, permitting others to get laughs so long as he was allowed to exercise that mastery with a devastating punchline or withering ad lib (unlike most of his contemporaries Allen wrote practically all his own material), Benny's popularity increased the more he allowed himself to be everyone else's straight man, and the butt rather than instigator of the jokes. (Jack not only had a large retinue of writers but openly and proudly acknowledged that fact.) Though both approaches to comedy were viable and both attracted big audiences and major sponsors, Benny would enjoy wider popularity than Allen throughout the 1930s, ending the decade as the highest-paid and highest-rated comedian on radio.

For all their success in other show business endeavors, neither Benny nor Allen made much of an impression in movies during the first half of the 1930s. Jack's initial feature film appearances for MGM in the early-talkie era were unsatisfying enough for the comedian to break his contract with the studio, while Allen's intense dislike for Hollywood ("a great place to live if you happen to be an orange") precluded any desire to pursue film stardom. By 1934, however, Benny's radio popularity was encouraging enough for him to give movies another chance. Nineteen thirty-four has also been chosen as the starting date for this entry on Benny and Allen because it was the first year that Jack's radio career had a significant influence on his movie work. Produced by Edward Small for United Artists release, *Transatlantic Merry-Go-Round* was the first film to capitalize on Benny's radio fame; accordingly, his material was written by his radio collaborator Harry Conn. One of the many "*Grand Hotel*-at-sea" conglomerations of the era, *Transatlantic Merry-Go-Round* introduces several seemingly unrelated characters and situations before bringing them all together in a moment of extreme duress, in this case the murder of a crooked gambler (Sidney Blackmer) aboard a luxury liner. As Chad Denby, emcee of the ship's combination radio show and musical revue, Benny is connected to the main plot by virtue of the fact that his star vocalist Sally Marsh (Nancy Carroll) is one of the murder suspects—and, incidentally, the girl Chad secretly loves. Benny plays several of his scenes straight, albeit with a touch of sly humor even in such somber moments as Denby's gallant exit from Sally's life when she falls for reformed jewel thief Jimmy Brett (Gene Raymond).

Having not quite established the Jack Benny character that we are now familiar with (he even picks up a check in one scene!), the comedian is nonetheless quite appealing as a suave and cynical sidelines observer. The film directly references Benny's radio show with a comedy skit his troupe performs for the passengers, a parody of the movie *Grand Hotel* ("Grind Hotel") that Jack had previously done on the air. In the original version Benny played the John Barrymore part of "The Baron" while Mary Livingstone was heard as Joan Crawford's character Flaemmchen, rechristened "Flim Flam." In the film, Jack again subs for Barrymore while Nancy Carroll imitates Greta Garbo, former child star Mitzi Green impersonates ZaSu Pitts, and comedienne Patsy Kelly plays a telephone operator. Another carryover from Benny's radio series is singer Frank Parker, spotlighted in the Busby Berkeley–style production number "It Was Sweet of You." In addition to Benny, *Transatlantic Merry-Go-Round* features radio's Boswell Sisters at their very best in the energetic ensemble number "Rock and Roll" (sic!), bobbing up and down in a prop rowboat while a line of chorus girls feigns seasickness. Like most other film appearances by the Boswells, this sequence tastefully camouflages the fact that Connee Boswell was paralyzed from the waist down.

Some of Benny's other films from this period touched upon his radio prominence. In MGM's *The Broadway Melody of 1936* (1935) he was atypically cast as a Winchellesque gossip reporter; and in his first Paramount film *The Big Broadcast of 1937*, he plays the owner of a mortgage-laden radio station, with fellow airwave stars Burns & Allen as his new sponsors, the owners of Platt's Airflow Golf Balls. Jack's comic style in these films is dictated more by what he was doing on radio than what he'd done on stage, though vestiges of his old master-of-ceremonies wryness can still be glimpsed. At the end of *Big Broadcast of 1937*, he breaks down the fourth wall and informs the movie audience that the entertainment they've just seen has been "presented through the courtesy of Providence, Paramount and Platt's Golf Balls." And in his next picture *College Holiday* (1936), a double satire of campus theatricals and the controversial eugenics movement, the climactic stage show concludes with Jack descending from the flies on a huge cardboard valentine, directly addressing the moviegoers: "Ladies and gents, I hope you've noticed our attempt in this picture to maintain the spirit of classic Greek tragedy throughout. Whenever the story interfered with art, we did not compromise. We gave up both.... Good night, folks."

Around the same time that Benny was revitalizing his movie career, Fred Allen finally accepted a call from Hollywood to make his feature film debut. Having recently launched NBC's *Town Hall Tonight*, his most successful radio project to date, Fred was now being courted by the same Hollywood moguls who'd previously considered him too unphotogenic for the movies. (The only producer who had anything nice to say about Fred's disastrous 1931 Paramount screen test was comedy maven Mack Sennett.) In 1935 Allen made the long-avoided trek westward with his top writer Harry Tugend in tow to start work on the 20th Century–Fox musical comedy *Thanks a Million*; sweetening the project was the script by Allen's good friend Nunnally Johnson. It was a satirical swipe at the political-hack tendency to nominate candidates who look nice and speak well rather than those actually qualified to hold office. Originally titled *Sing, Governor, Sing,* the film concerns a ragtag musical troupe stranded in a small town where a political rally is about to be held on behalf of corrupt and incredibly boring gubernatorial candidate A. Darrius Cullman (Raymond Walburn). Noting the lack of interest in the event, the troupe's quick-witted manager Ned Lyman (Allen) suggests that his entertainers perform outside the rally to stir up an audience. Cullman comes to regret giving the go-ahead to this idea when Ned's star singer Eric Land (Dick Powell) captivates the crowd with his dazzling appearance and extemporaneous charm. Before long Eric himself is being promoted as a candidate for governor, with Ned as the boy's campaign manager. Along the way, Ned makes the Fred Allenesque crack that if the leader of a jazz band can be elected to political office, *anyone* can—a remark that offended Washington State's bandleader-turned-lieutenant governor Victor Aloysius Meyers to the extent that he sued 20th Century–Fox for $25,000. (Its satiric sting surgically removed, *Thanks a Million* was remade in 1945 as *If I'm Lucky*, with Perry Como as the singing candidate and Phil Silvers in Allen's role.)

As much as he hated Hollywood, Allen had a wonderful time making *Thanks a Million* and was quite convivial with his co-stars: Raymond Walburn would always refer to him as "Dear Fred Allen." The comedian's first important film appearance also pleased fans and critics, with the *New York Times* lauding Fred as "a happy success." In September 1936, Louella Parsons reported that 20th Century–Fox's Darryl F. Zanuck had signed Allen to a long-term contract and planned to make a film version of *Town Hall Tonight* co-starring Fred's wife Portland Hoffa. But this news item was dwarfed by an event that occurred on Allen's radio broadcast of December 30, 1936.

Whenever the topic of the Benny-Allen feud comes up, people hasten to add that in reality Jack and Fred were close friends. Existing evidence indicates that they were friends, but not all that close. Each man admired the other's work, Benny praising Allen for his wit and Allen congratulating Benny for developing the "ensemble" format that made his program so popular. The two men were always on excellent terms professionally, but beyond that they travelled in different circles and didn't see much of each other socially. Seldom did one mention the other on radio, and then never disparagingly: Benny's April 4, 1936, radio sketch "Clown Hall Tonight" was indeed a takeoff of Allen's show, but with no malice. Benny probably wouldn't have been singled out by Allen on the night of December 30, 1936, were it not for a conspicuous running gag on Jack's program. At that time his character was well established as a self-styled big shot who bragged about his prowess in just about everything, the better for his co-stars—Mary Livingstone, orchestra leader Phil Harris and the rest—to burst his bubble with a few well-aimed barbs. Among Jack's supposed accomplishments was his virtuosity on the violin, and on several programs he would show up prepared to perform a selection, only to be interrupted just as he was scratching out the first few notes or even before he touched bow to fiddle. In *College Holiday* this recurring gag was recreated on film, and critics commented that Jack was no more successful proving that he was the second Paganini in the movies than he was on radio. The gag at this point was not so much that he played the violin poorly, but that for all his bluster he barely played it at all.

So when on *Town Hall Tonight* ten-year-old violin prodigy Stuart Canin gave a flawless rendition of Schubert's "The Bee," it was only natural for Fred Allen to make a biting reference to Benny. Since this broadcast no longer exists, we cannot be certain precisely what Allen said, but it was along the lines of "Jack Benny should be ashamed of himself." We also don't know if Jack heard this broadcast, or if one of his writers told him about it. Whatever the case, Jack found Fred's insult hilarious and responded in kind with a slurring riposte on his program of January 3, 1937. Allen was not only pleased but amazed by this reaction, since Benny's program drew a far larger audience than his, and any sort of on-air recognition by Jack could only be beneficial. With neither comedian consulting the other at first, both kept up a war of words on their respective programs, Allen dispensing most of the insults while Benny sulked over the fact that his co-stars admired Fred and didn't think Jack had the nerve to show him up by playing "The Bee" himself. This was part and parcel of the Benny radio character, who always put up a big bluff but tended to back down when challenged. Finally on February 28, 1937, Jack did play "The Bee," and not at all badly, but he knew that Fred would keep the gag going by making a snarky comment about the performance on his own show. At this juncture each comedian was verbally assaulting the other with impunity, most of the cutting remarks referring to talent (or lack thereof) and physical appearance. Jack later insisted that if he and Fred had actually gotten together before the Stuart Canin appearance and mapped out a mock feud *a la* Walter Winchell and Ben Bernie (q.v.), it would not have been nearly as funny or effective as allowing the gag to blossom naturally.

The brouhaha reached its climax on the March 7, 1937, *Jack Benny Program*, on which Fred Allen was slated to appear. So many tickets were sold for what was anticipated as "the fight of the century" that the broadcast had to be relocated to the grand ballroom of New York's Hotel Pierre. The program lived up to its hype, though Allen later remarked that no matter what he and Jack did or said that night it would be anticlimactic. From that moment on, the feud simmered rather than boiled over the airwaves: As far as Benny and Allen were concerned, the routine was now a secondary running gag, something to fall back on whenever there weren't enough other jokes on a particular broadcast.

Meanwhile, 20th Century–Fox changed their minds about a film adaptation of *Town Hall Tonight* and assigned Allen to the role of two-bit theatrical producer Gabby Green in their 1938 musical remake of the 1925 silent *Sally, Irene and Mary*. According to Jimmy Fidler's column of December 23, 1937, Fred startled Hollywood by refusing any salary until shooting began because "no pay should be forthcoming until the start of production." To the dismay of fans who hoped he would relocate his radio show to California and continue making pictures, Fred insisted that comedians who did movies by day and radio by night were insane. "What does it get them? A nervous breakdown, an enforced vacation in the desert—and, about April First, a little pep note from [Treasury Secretary] Morgenthau, thanking them for doing a swell job." Another burr in Allen's backside was the fact that he'd carefully arranged to take four weeks off his radio show to do *Sally, Irene and Mary* but the studio delayed the movie's start date.

Two things promised to make this experience tolerable for Allen. During his Hollywood stay he would lodge comfortably at the Beverly Hills home of Jack Benny (who had gone off on vacation); and the studio intended to cast Portland Hoffa as either Irene or Mary. Many was the time that Fred was prepared to walk off his radio show, only to be mollified by the knowledge that Portland would be on stage with him to provide moral support; surely this would also be the case during filming. Exactly what happened next is unclear, but the studio publicity department insisted that Portland had pulled out because she felt she didn't photograph well. While Fred encountered no problems with his female co-stars Alice Faye, Joan Davis and Marjorie Weaver, it just wasn't the same without Portland's comforting presence. And while Allen was allowed to provide much of his own dialogue, the overall experience of *Sally, Irene and Mary* moved him to refer to the film ever afterward as "Sally, Irene and Lousy." He swore he'd never return to Hollywood, and he meant it. For a while.

Meanwhile more and more of Jack Benny's radio persona was creeping into his film work, though his character's name and profession changed from picture to picture. Audiences didn't seem to mind as much as the critics: In his review for Paramount's *Artists and Models Abroad* (1938), the *New York Times'* Frank Nugent carped that while Benny's character "has a score of funny lines," the comedian "airs them as though he were rehearsing a radio script. We resent being treated as 'the vast unseen radio audience.'" Comments like this vexed Jack, who wanted to be accepted as a light leading man without relying upon his radio work to bring in customers. Years later he complained to writer Milt Josefsberg, "They always cast me as the Jack Benny character I portrayed in vaudeville and radio, and that isn't me. Hell, if only once they had cast me as Benny Kubelsky, I might at least have had a character part to play that would have let me act."

In 1939 he signed a new Paramount contract for two pictures per year, still hoping that he'd be allowed to play something other than his familiar character. In *Man About Town* (1939), the first of three consecutive Benny vehicles directed by Mark Sandrich, Jack's role as theatrical producer Bob Temple is superficially different from what his fans expected. But the farcical storyline, which found Bob trying to impress his star Diana Wilson (Dorothy Lamour) with his romantic prowess by pretending to have affairs with two very married noblewomen, is in lock-step with the radio Jack Benny who always got in trouble by pretending to be something he wasn't. And just so his radio fans wouldn't think Benny was abandoning them, the supporting cast features two *Jack Benny Program* regulars, Phil Harris and Eddie "Rochester" Anderson. The repartee between Jack and Rochester is easily the best thing in the picture, a fact not lost on Paramount when the studio began seeking out future properties for the comedian.

"After ten years of making movies, I was back to playing Jack Benny again in name as well as character." This was Benny's lament to Milt

Josefsberg concerning the remaining two pictures on his Paramount contract—though Jack admitted that he had only himself to blame because he loved to act and the money was great. Following the critical and financial success of *Man About Town,* Paramount dished up a musical comedy that not only extensively referenced Jack's radio program, but was entirely dependent on audience familiarity with that program for its full entertainment value. Co-scripted by Jack's ace radio writers Bill Morrow and Ed Beloin, *Buck Benny Rides Again* (1940) was inspired by a recurring sketch on Jack's show in which he adopted a faux he-man voice to impersonate a cowboy hero. Cast in the film as famous radio star Jack Benny, our hero goes to epic lengths to convince heroine Joan Cameron (Ellen Drew) that he's no mere city dude but a gen-u-wine, rootin' tootin' westerner. This deception leads to numerous slapstick complications at a posh dude ranch, culminating in Jack having heroism thrust upon him when a "phony" robbery turns out to be the real thing.

Phil Harris is back in *Buck Benny Rides Again,* likewise playing himself, and so is Eddie "Rochester" Anderson, whose exchanges with Jack are funnier than ever. At a period in history when opportunities for black actors to excel in Hollywood were slim to none, Jack and his writers were generous beyond measure with Rochester, providing him ample screen time, sidesplitting dialogue (including the film's closing gag) and even a romance of his own with Joan Cameron's saucy maid Josephine (Theresa Harris). He also gets to perform one of the film's two big Jimmy McHugh-Frank Loesser song hits, "My My" (the other hit was "Say It [Over and Over Again]"), dazzling Josephine with some fancy footwork; and just before the final reel, Rochester has the camera all to himself with a pantomime routine in which he portrays an Indian (talk about culture clash!). Other *Jack Benny Program* stalwarts appearing herein are Andy Devine, who'd been featured in the "Buck Benny" radio skits, and 21-year-old Dennis Day, hired as Jack's resident tenor only days before shooting started. Jack's announcer Don Wilson also shows up at the beginning to read the credits, while Mary Livingstone, who'd sworn off moviemaking after 1937's *This Way Please* (see **Fibber McGee and Molly**), is heard but not seen in a handful of broadcast recreations. And for the first time in a Jack Benny picture, the Benny-Allen feud is invoked as the onscreen Jack is goaded into carrying out his cowboy masquerade by the snide radio commentary of Fred Allen, who like Mary Livingstone is represented by his voice alone.

The self-referentialism in *Buck Benny Rides Again* gets a bit too thick at times, and not all of it works. One radio carryover that falls flat when visualized is Jack's ancient Maxwell automobile, which is frankly much funnier heard (courtesy of the sputtering, wheezing Mel Blanc) than seen. Also not entirely coming off as a visible presence is Benny's pet polar bear Carmichael—you know, the one that supposedly ate the iceman in Jack's basement—though *Photoplay* thought that the big bruin was "cute." *Photoplay* also spoke for most critics and fans by describing *Buck Benny Rides Again* as "the best adaptation of radio personalities to the screen so far done by Hollywood." When the film ended up one of the ten top moneymakers of 1940, Paramount wasn't about to be dissuaded from delivering more of the same.

Although the Benny-Allen feud had by 1940 lost its topicality, the gag was still part of the repertoire of both comedians, inspiring producer-director Mark Sandrich to use the feud as the basis for Paramount's next Jack Benny vehicle *Love Thy Neighbor* (1940). As in *Buck Benny Rides Again,* Jack would play "himself," this time teamed (in a manner of speaking) with Fred Allen, also cast as himself. Still not keen about working in Hollywood, Allen put up a fight when approached by Sandrich, but finally his resistance wore down and he signed a one-picture contract. Fred agreed to appear in *Love Thy Neighbor* on condition that he receive over-the-title billing (Benny's contract stipulated that his name would come first) and that his role was of equal importance to Jack's. If Benny was permitted to feature Rochester again, Fred was allowed to bring along the singing group The Merry Macs, who until recently had been regulars on his radio show. And

Mary Martin (center) vainly tries to arbitrate a difference of opinion between Fred Allen (left) and Jack Benny in this posed shot from Paramount's *Love Thy Neighbor* (1941).

if Jack could have his radio writers Bill Morrow and Ed Beloin at his beck and call, Fred could have his agents Howard Reilly and Walter Batchelor on the set to protect his interests.

The plot of *Love Thy Neighbor* is (like its predecessor) motivated by Benny's love life (as on radio, the film perpetuates the fallacy that Jack and Mary Livingstone were merely co-workers instead of husband and wife). This time his leading lady is Mary Martin as Mary, whom Jack hires as a singer in his new musical revue, then pursues romantically. What Jack doesn't know is that Mary is Fred Allen's niece, and once the truth is out, Mary works like a galley slave to bring Jack and Fred's silly feud to an end, even though she's dealing with a pair of overgrown and very petulant children. With barrages of insults hurled by both stars at every opportunity, the storyline stops, starts and stops again so often that you feel like you're on a commuter bus.

Some show business journalists aren't happy unless they can report discord even where none exists, and such was the case with Kay Proctor, who in the January 4, 1941, issue of *Movie-Radio Guide* suggested that *Love Thy Neighbor* was "an unexploded bomb"—not because it threatened to be a lousy movie, but because of the supposed friction between its two stars. Casting doubt on Benny and Allen's protestations of friendship, Proctor states, "The truth is the feud started as a gag, but somewhere along the line it got out of hand," and now Jack and Fred were "kidding on the square." As evidence, the writer notes that the studio prop crew painted a white line between the two stars' dressing rooms, and had strict orders to give Fred anything Jack asked for, from a glass of water to a cigar. The stars are depicted as sitting in their dressing rooms diligently counting the number of lines each one spoke and the number of scenes each one appeared in to make sure everything was even-steven. The film's opening title sequence, in which animated versions of the two stars' names bump each other off the screen and chase one another around the rest of the credits (a gag contributed by the Leon Schlesinger cartoon studio), was allegedly the result of both men demanding preferred billing. And when during rehearsals Fred quipped that Jack should be happy to be billed second because all his relatives read from right to left anyway, Jack is supposed to have angrily turned to his writers Beloin and Morrow and barked, "Top that gag—or else!"

All of this might have happened, but none of it points to hostility between the two leads. The policy of the crew treating stars equally and pulling "inside" jokes was standard procedure at all studios. The ritual of counting lines, estimating screen time and fretting over billing is something that every major star with an ounce of competitive drive does on the set; Cary Grant and Myrna Loy went through the same rigmarole during production of *The Bachelor and the Bobby Soxer*, and no one has ever suggested *they* hated each other. And while we're sure Benny made some sort of crack to his writers when Fred zapped out a good ad lib, it's a matter of record that Jack always treated his writing staff with decency and respect, and would never fire anyone over trivialities (moreover, Ed Beloin had been recommended to Jack by Fred Allen).

We know for certain that Jack and Fred didn't socialize much at the studio, but that was nothing unusual. We also know that both comedians were unhappy with the finished script, but while Jack tended to be sullen and withdrawn, Fred made the best of things by joking around with his co-workers and making himself available to journalists. One can't help noting, however, that when interviewed by Robin Coons, Fred seemed to be going out of his way not to be funny, greeting the reporter with, "Say, what do you fellows find to write about the on a set like this? Nothing ever happens, far as I can see." And when asked by Coons to comment on Jack Benny, the best Fred could come up with was that Jack never ate hot dogs because they made him sick.

Though by rights *Love Thy Neighbor* should have been the last and most hilarious word on the celebrated Benny-Allen feud, it is more like the little girl with the curl: When it's good it's very very good, but when it's bad it's horrid. There was a lot of corny comedy in *Buck Benny Rides Again,* but at least it was consistent with Benny's character and the western setting. The hokey humor in *Love Thy Neighbor*—an artificial-looking speedboat chase with cartoon sound effects, Jack and Fred dressed as babies in the final shot—could have been performed by any second-rate comic, and seems to be wedged in willy-nilly. And let's for a moment go back to the word "character." Benny plays the same guy he did on radio, and we can live with that; but Allen never *had* a radio character, nor did he need one so long as his fans enjoyed his amiably aloof "commentator" role on *Town Hall Tonight* and its successor shows. Thus, *Love Thy Neighbor* has to impose a character upon Fred Allen, and the choice couldn't be more unfortunate. Allen's hatred of Benny in the film is so over-the-top vitriolic that he can't help but come off as the aggressor in the feud, a neurotic—nay, psychotic—villain who actually stalks around wielding a rifle and threatening to shoot Jack on sight! As a result, the film's overall treatment of the famous feud is about as funny as the Gunfight at the OK Corral. And while we may laugh at Fred Allen in *Love Thy Neighbor,* it is virtually impossible to *like* him.

So what's good about the picture? Well, most of the Benny-Allen verbal exchanges are nimbly handled by director Sandrich, especially the scene in which the two combatants repeatedly interrupt a nasty argument to politely sign autographs for their fans. Mary Martin is just plain wonderful as the heroine, reprising her starmaking song "My Heart Belongs to Daddy" from the Cole Porter stage musical *Leave It to Me* (though alas, she is not permitted to perform her Broadway striptease). Best of all, *Love Thy Neighbor* represents the finest cinematic pairing to date of Jack Benny and Rochester, with the latter hitting a musical bullseye in the charming duet "Dearest, Darest I" with his *Buck Benny Rides Again* vis-à-vis Theresa Harris. (This scene takes place at a Harlem New Year's party, staged in an elegant ballroom with immaculately dressed revelers and hosted by a portly black man who speaks impeccable English—a far cry from the minstrel-show treatment forced upon African Americans in most musicals of the period.)

Though it received quite a drubbing from the critics, *Love Thy Neighbor* was a another box-office success for Jack Benny, who nonetheless promised himself that he'd avoid playing his radio character in future films. These subsequent efforts included his two favorite pictures, *Charley's Aunt* (20th Century–Fox, 1941) and Ernst Lubitsch's brilliant black comedy *To Be or Not to Be* (UA, 1942), with Benny giving the performance of his career as "that great, great Polish actor Joseph Tura." (In 1944, Jack backtracked a bit with an amusing guest appearance as himself in Warner Bros.' all-star flagwaver *Hollywood Canteen*.) While Benny's film output never attained the heights of his radio career, most of his pictures made money, even the much-maligned *The Horn Blows at Midnight* (Warners, 1945).

Once Fred Allen had fulfilled his duties in *Love Thy Neighbor*, he again announced that under no circumstances would he ever, *ever* appear in another Hollywood picture. By this time radio was not only his life's work, it was his life. He would write and rewrite his weekly scripts into the wee hours, changing jokes and entire routines right up to air time for the sake of topicality, driving himself mercilessly and at risk to his already precarious health. At the end of the 1943–44 season a severe case of hypertension forced him off the air for an entire year, yet even in this period he could not remain idle. The enticing prospect of earning a fortune in a capital-gains arrangement brought him back before the movie cameras in the fall of 1944. Produced by Jack Skirball for United Artists release, *It's in the Bag* (working titles: *Fickle Fortune* and *The Fifth Chair*) would be the first feature to star Fred Allen and Fred Allen alone. Working on a tight budget, Fred agreed to waive his usual high salary and accept a percentage of the profits, persuading several of his celebrity friends to make guest-star appearances under a similar financial arrangement. But the money was secondary to the promise of artistic satisfaction held out by this project: With Allen collaborating extensively on the screen treatment, the comedian was able to guarantee himself a great deal more creative input than in any of his previous films.

Of course, a curmudgeonly Fred Allen was always good copy for journalists, and he didn't disappoint the reporters visiting the set, making his standard complaints about getting up at 6 a.m. and shooting scenes out of sequence. In an interview with Erskine Johnson, Fred kvetched, "You can't move around in front of the camera. You have to stay in focus and you can't spoil the lighting. The perfect actor in Hollywood is one with rigor mortis in his body and a neon head." But in the final analysis the comedian could take pride in the fact that *It's in the Bag* was (and is) the finest sustained example of Fred Allen's special brand of humor ever captured on celluloid.

Directed by Richard Wallace and co-written by Alma Reville—yes, Mrs. Alfred Hitchcock—the 1945 film is adapted from the same Russian fable by Ilya Ilf and Yevgeni Petrov that later served as the basis for Mel Brooks' *The Twelve Chairs* (1970). The first several reels are an agreeable mixture of plot and comedy, with flea circus owner Fred Floogle (Allen) inheriting his late uncle's vast fortune, only to discover that the reputed $12 million legacy has been hidden in five chairs—which Fred has unwittingly sold for auction. Despite the mass of plottage in the early scenes, there is plenty of breathing space for the stellar supporting cast, including Binnie Barnes as Fred's high-strung wife, John Carradine as a slimy lawyer, Robert Benchley as Fred's potential in-law (delivering a uniquely Benchleyesque lecture about a mousetrap), and Jerry Colonna as a sponging pediatrician. But once the search for the elusive chairs gets underway, plot and coherence are thrown out the window and the film becomes a string of self-contained comedy sketches in the tradition of Fred's radio show, including an entirely gratuitous but screamingly funny episode, written by Morrie Ryskind, in which Fred and his missus encounter no end of frustration trying to see a movie in an overcrowded theater.

The film's treatment of its guest stars is likewise in the spirit of Fred's radio work, with the script lampooning and exaggerating their public images to the *nth* degree. In recognition of the many hoodlum roles played by William Bendix, the actor is cast as the head of the dreaded "Bill Bendix Mob," conducting his criminal empire in the manner of a stuffy stockholders' meeting. When his disloyal henchmen prepare to rub him out, Bendix is actually relieved: He'd never wanted to be a crook in the first place, and had taken charge of his mob only to please his mother. Elsewhere, Don Ameche, Rudy Vallee and Victor Moore are reduced to working as singing waiters in a Gay '90s nightclub. When Fred expresses surprise that the man who played Alexander Graham Bell (Don), the king of the crooners (Rudy) and the matinee idol of the gaslight era (Victor) have fallen so low, Ameche sadly explains that he ran out of inventions, Vallee that he ran out of megaphones, and Moore that he ran out of breath.

Jack Benny has also been tapped for a guest-star appearance, and while critics felt that his sequence was one of the film's highlights, it inevitably disappoints a little when seen today. Discovering that Benny has purchased one of the chairs, Fred shows up at his doorstep posing as the president of the Jack Benny Fan Club. The encounter is surprisingly cordial, with Jack blithely ignoring Fred's veiled insults and offering his visitor the courtesy of the house ... as long as he pays for it. By 1945 the "cheap" jokes were flying fast and free on Jack's radio show; accordingly, Allen milks the comedian's stinginess and moneygrubbing for all their worth, with Benny posting a hat-check girl in his closet to take Fred's hat and coat for a price, offering Fred a cigarette by guiding him to the vending machine in his living room, and so on. While filming this sequence, Benny brooded that the excessive piling-on of stingy gags tended to beat the joke to death, but agreed to go through with the scene as a favor to Allen. Jack's instincts were right on target: There really *can* be too much of a good thing.

But the Benny-Allen routine is heaps better than the film's uncontested low point, when Fred pays a visit to his "Allen's Alley" radio regular Minerva Pious in her familiar role as Mrs. Pansy Nussbaum. The episode starts weak, gets weaker, and seems to go on forever. Possibly Allen sensed that the scene laid an egg, since halfway through the conversation with Mrs. Nussbaum, Fred's off-screen voice abruptly breaks in with, "While they are boring each other with some dull dialogue, I'll tell you folks who were buying candy and have just come in what has happened up to now." Throughout the picture Allen takes the audience into his confidence by delivering verbal asides directly to the camera, even allowing supporting players Binnie Barnes, Sidney Toler and John Miljan to also break down the Fourth Wall. His sporadic off-screen narration is an extension of this, beginning with the opening production credits in which he is heard explaining, "The associate producer is the only man who will associate with the producer" and that writer Morrie Ryskind's sole contribution to the script was "half a pound of butter so the bread in a dinner scene would look yellow." Again emulating his radio program, Allen often uses his narration to comment sarcastically on a misfire joke or an overused comedy cliché. During a brief scene in a jail cell, his disembodied voice remarks "You will notice that Floogle wears a convict suit. You have seen Floogle arrested. You have seen Floogle behind bars. This isn't enough. Floogle now wears stripes so that you will know that he is a prisoner. This director overdoes everything. He's been married six times."

Some of you out there may now be rising from your seats to shout, "Hey, I've just seen *It's in the Bag* on TV, and *I* didn't hear the off-screen commentary you're talking about!" That's because the film was released in two versions, one with narration, one without. Most currently available prints are narration-less, much to the chagrin of Allen purists like myself.

For all its faults, *It's in the Bag* holds up very nicely when seen today. Unfortunately it did only mediocre business, moving its star to comment ruefully that everybody made money off the picture but him. At the time of its release, both Allen and Jack Benny had pretty much decided to give up on the movies and concentrate on what they did best. Jack continued to prosper in radio and TV, and in personal appearances and charity benefits, for the next three decades. Having long confined his film activities to gag cameos, in 1974 he accepted his first starring movie assignment since *The Horn Blows at Midnight,* appearing with Walter Matthau in the adaptation of Neil Simon's *The Sunshine Boys*. After Jack's death on December 26, 1974, the role went to his lifelong friend George Burns.

Not long before the cancellation of his NBC radio program in 1949, Fred began an interview with journalist Bob Thomas by proudly boasting "I just talked a guy out of putting me in a movie," adding, "I'm no good in pictures. I proved that with the last one." Yet when his old pal Nunnally Johnson asked Allen to fill in for an indisposed Clifton Webb (Fred's co-star in the 1928 stage revue *The Little Show*) in the "Ransom of Red Chief" segment of Fox's multistory film *O. Henry's Full House* (1952), Fred accepted, even though he and his co-star Oscar Levant looked so much alike that it was kind of spooky. Fred contributed a funnier cameo to another Nunnally Johnson–scripted portmanteau picture, *We're Not Married!* (Fox, 1952), in which he and Ginger Rogers essentially recreated his radio sketch about a lovey-dovey radio couple who can't stand the sight of each other away from the microphone. Though Fred Allen made several live TV appearances in the 1950s, *We're Not Married* was the last time he was seen on film.

Once Allen was out of radio, he and Jack Benny quietly buried the bladeless hatchet and ended the feud that never was. Except for a memorable 1952 episode of Benny's TV show, the two men expressed nothing but affection and admiration for one another in public: Jack would continue showering praise on his former "nemesis" long after Allen's death in 1956. Today, after years of being represented only by six films and a smattering of recorded broadcasts, there are enough extant radio samples of the brilliance of Fred Allen for everyone to fully appreciate what the shouting was all about.

Joe Penner (1934–1940)

Media historians tend to lump Joe Penner together with his fellow radio comedian Jack Pearl (see **Baron Munchausen**), and there are similarities between their starring careers. Both men learned their trade in that school of hard knocks known as vaudeville, both graduated to specialty spots on Broadway, both became overnight radio sensations by virtue of a single comic catchphrase, both peaked relatively early, and both suffered a sharp eclipse a scant few years after achieving national prominence. But while Pearl stubbornly clung to the punchlines and gimmicks that had made him famous, Penner was forever endeavoring to transcend his established *schtick* and experiment with fresh ideas and material, albeit with negligible success. And while Pearl's movie career was over and done with after two years and two features, Penner managed to hang on in Hollywood for six years and ten pictures, five of them starring vehicles.

Born József Pintér in a small Hungarian (now Serbian) village in 1904, Joe Penner was eight years old when he emigrated to America. Though an unusually bright student in his native country, Joe had so much trouble learning English that he was demoted to a kindergarten class, a humiliation which fed into the insecurities that plagued him throughout his life. After a succession of low-level jobs, Penner cultivated a fondness for the stage, working his way slowly upward as a comedian and eccentric dancer. Using a half-smoked cigar as a prop and wearing a battered derby and checkered coat, the little comedian built upon his amusing physical appearance by exaggerating his naturally nasal voice and slight lisp, adding a moronic laugh ("Yuck-yuck-yuck") and a drawn-out whine for good measure. Shunning witty repartee, he found he could get laughs by shouting such admonitions and lamentations as "Don't ever *doooo* that," "*Wooooe* is me," and especially "You *nasss-ty man*!" Penner's most famous catchphrase came about after strenuous trial and error. Adapting an old "crossover" routine from burlesque, Joe would approach a straight man and attempt to make a ridiculous business transaction. Lines like "Wanna buy a cow?" or "Wanna buy a rhinoceros?" met with moderate chuckles, but when during a vaudeville appearance in Alabama he ad-libbed "Wanna buy a duck?" the audience howled. Penner would use this imbecilic query over and over to universal approval for the rest of his vaudeville career, and in such Broadway productions as *East Wind* and *The Vanderbilt Revue*.

Though he headlined a cluster of Vitaphone movie shorts in 1931, Penner was largely unknown to audiences outside of Manhattan until he was booked for a one-shot appearance on the July 13, 1933, edition of *The Rudy Vallee Hour*. Per his custom, Vallee introduced his guest star with a long-winded preamble: "One of the mysteries of show business, to me at least, is the comparative obscurity of Joe Penner. Somehow he has never had the big break. But I'm sure [he will rank] along with the Cantors, the Wynns and the Pearls. I think Joe is a really great comedian, and I'm sure you will soon agree with me. We welcome Joe Penner." Existing transcriptions of this momentous broadcast more than justify Vallee's confidence: Joe was not merely a hit, he was a smash. After a second appearance on the Vallee show, the J. Walter Thompson agency fashioned a weekly half-hour series around Penner, sponsored by Fleischmann's Yeast (who also underwrote Vallee) and featuring orchestra leader Ozzie Nelson and his vocalist Harriet Hilliard. Though bearing the name *The Baker's Broadcast* when it debuted over NBC-Blue on October 8, 1933, it was "The Joe Penner Show" all the way so far as the public was concerned. By January 1934 Penner was second only to Eddie Cantor as radio's most popular comedian, and his "Wanna buy a duck?" had become a national byword—not to mention "You *nasss-ty* man!," which was already being parroted in animated cartoons and would by the end of 1934 serve as the title for one of Alice Faye's songs in the movie *George White's Scandals*.

By that time Penner himself had matriculated to feature-length films at Paramount Pictures, a studio that hadn't forgotten their previous success with such broadcast attractions as Burns & Allen and Bing Crosby. In keeping with their policy of showcasing radio favorites along with proven film personalities in star-studded musicals, Paramount cast both Penner and singer Lanny Ross, then the premier vocalist on CBS's *Maxwell House Showboat,* in *College Rhythm* (1934), the latest entry in the studio's string of annual big-budget campus musicals. In addition to Joe and Lanny—who'd been signed by Paramount as a backup singer in case Bing Crosby started making trouble—the film's talent roster included Jack Oakie, Lyda Roberti, Mary Brian and Helen Mack.

Scripted by George Marion, Jr. (*The Big Broadcast*) from a story by Walter de Leon, Francis Martin and Joe McDermott, and directed by the famously even-tempered Norman Taurog (you *had* to be even-tempered when juggling a cast full of star egos), *College Rhythm* features Jack Oakie as Francis J. Finnegan, campus football star and self-styled "Cupid's gift to co-eds." The arrogant Finnegan delights in stealing the girlfriends of his scholarly rival Larry Stacey (Lanny Ross), with fickle Gloria (Mary Brian) his latest acquisition. Larry warns Francis that while he may be a B.M.O.C. now, that won't amount to a hill of beans in the outside world. Sure enough, upon graduation Finnegan can't

Cover art from a 1934 "Big Little Book" cashing in on the radio popularity of comedian Joe Penner (courtesy Milton Knight).

find a job until he scrounges up a lowly position at the deluxe department store owned by Larry's father ("Stacey's," based on guess what). The feud between Larry and Francis reignites when Stacey Sr. (George Barbier) insists upon promoting Finnegan to capitalize on his football fame. For its gala reopening, the store adopts a "college" theme, hiring cute coeds as countergirls and male scholars as floorwalkers, and staging mammoth musical rallies with cheerleaders and swing bands. This leads to a rivalry between Stacey's and its chief competitor Whimple's, whose employees challenge the Stacey's staff to a football game. After the expected last-minute-touchdown climax, Larry and Francis bury the hatchet, with Larry willingly giving up Gloria in favor of a new heart balm, his demure secretary June (Helen Mack). Along the way we are treated to several newly written tunes by Mack Gordon and Harry Revel, notably "Stay as Sweet as You Are" and "Take a Number from One to Ten"—both of which would become background music for Paramount's Max Fleischer cartoons.

Though given top billing, Penner is essentially the film's comedy relief, cast as the caretaker of the football team's mascot, a duck named Goo-Goo. From the moment the little mallard waddles onscreen, the audience eagerly primes itself to hear Joe's familiar "Wanna buy a duck?"—and hear it they do, almost to excess, with a whole farmload of "substitute" ducks adding to the hilarity. Joe's other catchphrases are also in play, with "You *nasss-ty* man" at one point quacked out by Goo-Goo! Even those filmgoers who were not enraptured with Penner had to admit that he was pretty darn funny here, especially in his scenes with zesty Lyda Roberti, who in the role of Stacey's pet-store proprietor goes into fits of orgasmic passion whenever Joe gives out with his trademarked "Yuck-yuck-yuck." And while Roberti and Lanny Ross shoulder most of the musical responsibilities in *College Rhythm,* Joe scores a bullseye with his own specialty number, "Goo-Goo I Go Ga-Ga Over You."

If Paramount had intended *College Rhythm* as a launching pad for the film careers of Lanny Ross and Joe Penner, they were halfway successful. *Variety* spoke for most of the trade reviewers when it declared, "Penner makes good, the first strictly radio comedian to do so in pictures," but Ross was not so lucky. The lanky lyric tenor had already been showcased in the studio's *Melody of Spring,* also directed by Norman Taurog, in which Lanny enjoyed the strong support of Ann Sothern, Charlie Ruggles and Mary Boland. Placing Ross in a college setting was not only well suited to his youthful good looks but also beneficial publicity-wise, since the singer's real-life athletic achievements at Yale (he'd been chosen for the 1928 U.S. Olympic team, but had to turn the opportunity down) were well known to the public. But when he was cast opposite W.C. Fields in the 1935 Paramount musical *Mississippi,* it became clear that Ross' acting skills were not up to the challenge of portraying a disgraced Southern gentleman who is mistaken for a murderer. At the request of *Mississippi*'s songwriters Richard Rodgers and Lorenz Hart, Ross was replaced by Bing Crosby, and his option was not picked up by the studio. Lanny cut his losses and returned to radio, later adding Broadway and television to his credits and retiring in prosperity long before his death in 1988.

While Lanny Ross was cleaning out his dressing room at Paramount, Penner was prepping himself for his second movie appearance at the studio, again in a campus musical. This assignment came around the same time that Joe had abruptly exited *The Baker's Broadcast,* upset over the sponsor's refusal to freshen up the writing and alter the format. Having seen Jack Pearl's radio career nosedive once the public was fed up with "Vass *you* dere, Sharlie?" Penner did not want to become permanently defined by "Wanna buy a duck?" and his other now-too-familiar catchphrases. When Fleischmann's ad agency J. Walter Thompson put up resistance to Joe's suggestions, he took a walk, remaining off the air for over a year. While some observers have cited his decision as just another example of an overnight success who became too full of himself to heed the advice of others, in fact Penner was one of the least egotistical comedians in the business—and also one of the nicest. Coworkers Ozzie Nelson and Mel Blanc (the radio voice of Goo-Goo the duck) have had nothing but kind things to say about the man, who was unfailingly generous with his praise, time and money (one of his pet causes was providing new medical equipment for children's hospitals). Penner's ruminations over the direction his radio show had taken arose out of his basic feelings of inadequacy and his constant, almost psychotic worrying. While in this vulnerable state he tended to accept bad advice from the wrong people, and suffered mightily as a result. But all that had not yet come to pass when *Collegiate* started production in the late summer of 1935.

Collegiate is a musical adaptation of the Alice Duer Miller novel *The Charm School*, previously filmed twice during the silent era. The film reunited Penner with scripters Walter de Leon and Francis Martin, tunesmiths Mack Gordon and Harry Revel (who also appear onscreen), and co-star Jack Oakie, the latter cast as the wastrel nephew of a wealthy woman. Upon his aunt's death, Jerry Craig (Oakie) inherits a girls' seminary, with the proviso that his inheritance will be null and void if he doesn't stop drinking (and this was long before Dudley Moore's *Arthur*). Heading off to the seminary in the company of his publicist Scoop (Ned Sparks)—whose job it is to keep his boss' name *out* of the papers—Jerry comes across a goofy amnesiac (who else but Penner?) who is convinced that he is a world-renowned Australian polo player with an unlimited bank account. With the amnesiac merrily issuing checks to cover expenses, Jerry transforms the moribund seminary into an art-deco charm school with a faculty that includes gorgeous ladies and professional entertainers, among them dancer Betty Jane Cooper and real-life swimming champ Georgia Coleman. He also wins the love of his prim-and-proper secretary (Frances Langford in a role slated for Ginger Rogers), who takes off her glasses and ... well, we all know the name of *that* tune. Disaster threatens when the genuine polo player shows up and Jerry goes off on a toot, but the amnesiac saves the day when a bump on the head reveals his true identity: wealthy radio comedian Joe Penner.

The Gordon-Revel songs in *Collegiate* include "You Hit the Spot" and "I Feel Like a Feather in the Breeze," along with another specialty number for Penner, "Who Am I?" As part of his campaign to shed his old catchphrases, Joe uses the picture to audition a new one, the plaintive cry "Policeman! Police*maaan*!" which should be familiar to anyone who's seen Tex Avery's ersatz Joe Penner in the 1937 Warner Bros. cartoon *Cinderella Meets Fella*. Joe is also given the opportunity for some soft-pedaled pathos as he falls in love with pert coed Dorothy (Betty Grable in her first Paramount feature), who empathizes with the amnesiac's identity crisis because she herself is an orphan. Reviews for Penner's performance were not quite as glowing as they'd been for *College Rhythm*, with Frank Nugent's *New York Times* commentary frequently quoted as an example of how the tide was beginning to turn against the comedian: "With or without his duck or rocking hat, he is a pantaloon and buffoon, not a humorist." Actually Nugent meant this as a compliment, but the rest of his review is often left out by film historians who have a low tolerance for Joe Penner: "That in itself is quite all right and no one—we least of all—has any right to say that he change his style." These worthies might have a better argument by quoting the terse critique from the National Council of Jewish Women: "This is a dubious musical farce."

Dubious or no, when *Collegiate* opened in January 1936, it rang up the best business that Los Angeles' Paramount Theater had enjoyed since the spring of 1935, and grosses were equally impressive all over the country. The success of Penner's first two films led to a three-year contract with RKO Radio, which announced that Joe would start his first RKO picture sometime in the spring of 1936. Proposed titles included *Convention in Cuba*, about which little is known, and *The Assassin*, which would have cast Penner in the unorthodox role of a hired killer with a heart of gold! As RKO sought the proper vehicle, the studio's publicity department trumpeted the addition of Penner to their contract roster: "The screen's perfect idiot ... throws his fiery genius at the feet of a hardened world ... and all they do is laugh!"

Penner's return to network radio on October 4, 1936, delayed the start of his RKO contract by a month or so. A longtime admirer of Jack Benny, Joe jumped at the chance to hire Benny's former head writer Harry Conn, who'd sweet-talked his way into the assignment with grandiose stories of how Jack owed all his success to him. Conn envisioned Joe as star of a weekly situation comedy rather than the comedy-variety series of his NBC-Blue days. The childlike comic was cast as a character named Joe Penner, the square-peg-in-a-round-hole black sheep of the wealthy "Park Avenue Penners." The star and writer had little trouble selling the project to a new network, CBS, and a new sponsor, Cocomalt. With the weekly half-hour *Joe Penner Show* getting off to a strong start (there's nothing like curiosity to draw a crowd), and with that fat RKO contract in his pocket, it appeared that Joe would soon be hotter than ever.

But Penner's first RKO assignment, *New Faces of 1937,* sent him right back to the starting gate as merely one of several stars hired to buoy up a large-scale musical. The situation was far more demeaning than at Paramount, where at least Joe had been the only professional comedian in the batch. *New Faces of 1937* headlined no fewer than four high-pressure radio funsters: In addition to top-billed Penner, the picture starred Milton Berle, Parkyakarkus and Bert Gordon, not to mention popular radio supporting comics Tommy Mack and Patricia "Honey Chile" Wilder. Poor Joe barely has a moment to himself in the film, and whenever he shares a scene with one of the other comedians he generally comes off second-best. As a final kick in the pants, with rare exceptions the material the comic has to work with is—well, to quote *The New Yorker*'s John Mosher, "One may say of the film that if vaudeville be dead, it's buried here." The only aspect of the film in which Penner could take any pride was his refusal to exhume one of his now-passé catchphrases: As originally scripted, Joe was to have made his first entrance leading a duck on a leash. (For more on *New Faces of 1937,* see **The *Big Broadcast* Films** and **The Eddie Cantor Connection**.)

The film was but the first of several setbacks endured by Penner in 1937; another was the ever-eroding ratings of his radio show, which turned out *not* to be the sure thing that Harry Conn had promised. Joe's second RKO film, *The Life of the Party,* again teamed him (sort of) with Parkyakarkus, with character comedians Victor Moore, Helen Broderick and Billy Gilbert in support. ("RADIO, STAGE AND SCREEN PLUNDERED TO GIVE YOU THE GREATEST COMEDY CAST EVER ASSEMBLED FOR ONE PICTURE!" bellowed the ad copy.) The knowledge that he'd be reunited with his old *Baker's Broadcast* friend Harriet Hilliard, who'd also appeared in *New Faces of 1937,* more than likely lifted Joe's spirits, at least temporarily.

Life of the Party was directed by comedian-friendly William A. Seiter and co-scripted by the normally dependable Bert Kalmar and Harry Ruby. Once again, Joe receives top billing in a comedy relief role, with the emphasis thrown to romantic leads Hilliard and Gene Raymond. The story is the old chestnut about the carefree young man—Barry Saunders, played by Raymond—who'll lose a million-dollar inheritance if he marries before the age of 30. In alignment with his then-current radio show, Joe is the scourge of the "Park Avenue Penners," in particular his long-suffering mother Mrs. Penner (played by the magnificent Margaret Dumont, on sabbatical from the Marx Brothers). Heroine Mitzi (Hilliard), the daughter of an impoverished countess (Ann Shoemaker), flatly rejects her mother's efforts to marry her off to Joe and Barry's offer to wed her once he's passed his 30th birthday. Mitzi declares defiantly that singing is her life, leaving her no time for romance. (Wait until Reel Eight, honey.) Penner's big scenes are in concert with Parkyakarkus, playing a hotel detective hired by Mrs. Penner to keep her dimwit son out of mischief, and with Billy Gilbert as an orchestra leader who nearly bursts a blood vessel as he suffers through Joe's torturous vocalizing.

The *New York Times* said of *Life of the Party* that outside of Harriet Hilliard's performance, the rest "will depend on your ability to adapt yourself to Penner and Parkyakarkus, to Mr. Raymond's dressing gowns and coyness, to a banal plot." *Stage* magazine was briefer and blunter: "Joe Penner and Parkyakarkus supply their own particular brand of tiresome humor." While *Life of the Party* wasn't the box-office disaster that *New Faces of 1937* had been, it performed poorly enough for RKO to make some adjustments in Penner's contract. Abandoning the fairly ambitious vehicles they had planned for the comedian, RKO palmed Joe off to their B-picture division.

Ironically, Penner was about to enter into his busiest period as a movie star just as his radio career was in its early death throes. Playing to only a quarter of his *Baker's Broadcast* audience, *The Joe Penner Show* expired after two years, and his follow-up series on CBS in 1938 and NBC in 1939 fared no better. At the same time, Joe headlined five modest features for RKO, all but the last film doing quite respectably at the box office. It has been well documented that most B-picture units of the late 1930s were tightly knit, mutually supportive operations, with cast and crew feeling as if they were part of a family. This congenial on-set atmosphere was very important to an emotionally needy entertainer like Penner, a chronic worry-wart even when things were going well (and despite an enduringly happy marriage to Eleanor May Vogt). He certainly must have drawn a measure of security from the fact that four of his five RKO vehicles utilized the same creative staff, producer Robert Sisk and co-writer Bert Granet; that three were directed by one individual, Leslie Goodwins; and that the supporting casts included several actors making repeat appearances, among them Tom Kennedy, Jack Carson, Fritz Feld, George Irving and Frank M. Thomas—not to mention Joe's *New Faces of 1937* vis-à-vis Lorraine Kreuger and his *Life of the Party* co-star Billy Gilbert.

And no matter how much inner turmoil he may have been suffering over his demotion to B pictures, Joe remained unflaggingly gregarious and generous. Given a choice of leading ladies for his first vehicle *Go Chase Yourself* (1938), Joe recommended RKO contractee Lucille Ball, who had impressed him with her work on Phil Baker's radio show, and who in this film was afforded her first screen opportunity to extensively exhibit her unique comic gifts. For his fourth starrer *The Day the Bookies Wept* (1938), Joe requested that his former *Collegiate* co-star Betty Grable be borrowed from Paramount for one of *her* best pre-superstardom assignments. And it was surely no accident that character actor Richard Lane, who'd appeared with Joe in the 1930 stage musical *Vanderbilt Revue,* was given prominent roles in four of Penner's RKO "B"s (a prior commitment kept him out of the fifth). Joe's largesse extended well beyond his fellow actors: He continued opening his pockets to a variety of worthwhile charitable causes; and after shooting wrapped on *Day the Bookies Wept,* in which he played a cab driver, Joe treated the many authentic cabbies who'd served as extras and technical advisors to a gala on-set party.

As a group, Penner's final five RKO pictures were no better than adequate, and often less than that. None of them is likely to spawn a latter-day cult following for the comedian or a worldwide Sons of the Desert–style fan club. Because of the presence of Lucille Ball, *Go Chase Yourself* is the one most often telecast today, and as such generally serves as the contemporary viewer's first exposure to Penner. Granted, the film did well at the box office and even earned some laudatory reviews: *Variety* gushed, "Joe Penner is here seen in his best and most amusing picture, a bright, brisk comedy guaranteed to keep any audiences chuckling and built on a coin-garnering pattern of entertainment ... [It's] a top piece of comedy writing studded with fresh and fancy gags and snappy lines." But despite a funny opening scene with Joe neglecting his duties as a bank clerk to practice his crooning skills (or lack thereof) and an exciting runaway-trailer finale, *Go Chase Yourself* comes a-cropper in its misguided effort to impose upon Penner a fey Harry Langdon–like characterization. This "new, improved" Penner is just too insubstantial to carry a 71-minute picture: Worse still, his usual comic eccentricities now seem more grotesque than funny.

For the remainder of the RKO series, critical response was virtually unanimous: "A matter of taste." Those who enjoyed Joe's antics would continue to do so, but these films were hardly calculated to win over those who couldn't bear the sight of the man. There is also a disturbing strain of retrogression throughout the series. *I'm from the City* (1938) makes a futile stab at recapturing Joe's early radio appeal by bringing back his beloved duck, whose wise-quacks are here provided by Clarence Nash, the voice of Disney's Donald. And both *Mr. Doodle Kicks Off* (1939) and *Millionaire Playboy* (1940) try to squeeze whatever value still existed from the "Park Avenue Penners" concept by casting Joe as a wealthy numbskull whose personal peculiarities cause nothing but embarrassment for friends and family alike. The one RKO feature that has the least wrong with it is *The Day the Bookies Wept*, a Runyonesque racetrack farce that for once allowed Joe to play a reasonable facsimile of a human being.

After he and RKO parted company, Penner swallowed his pride and accepted a third-billed role at Universal, where his co-star was another specialized comedian who'd been taken down a peg from top-billed stardom, Martha Raye. The first film packaged for Universal by Jules Levey's new Mayfair Productions, *The Boys from Syracuse* (1940) is a pedestrian adaptation of the Rodgers & Hart Broadway musical hit based on Shakespeare's *The Comedy of Errors*. The film had been intended as a vehicle for the Ritz Brothers, but when they dropped out over arguments about the inadequacy of their roles, Levey and director Eddie Sutherland approached Penner to fill the gap. The storyline, cleaned up by screenwriter Paul Girard Smith from George Abbott's racy libretto, is a mistaken-identity roundelay involving two sets of identical twins: Antipholus of Syracuse and Antipholus of Ephesus, both played by Allan Jones, and Antipholus' two lookalike slaves, both named Dromio and both impersonated by Joe Penner. Contributing to the confusion are Antipholus of Ephesus' jealous wife (Irene Hervey) and amorous sister-in-law (Rosemary Lane), and Dromio of Ephesus' overbearing spouse (Raye).

The movie was burdened with too many silly anachronisms (set in ancient Greece, the script is crammed with references to Hitler, Walter Winchell, streetcars, cocktail lounges, pinochle and the like), and an overall mishandling of the Rodgers-Hart score ("Falling in Love the Love" was as overplugged as "Sing for Your Supper" was rudely truncated). *The Boys from Syracuse* was generally regarded as a disappointment but to this observer, the film represents Joe Penner's finest hour-and-a-quarter on screen. Making surprisingly subtle differentiations between the two Dromios, Joe effectively suppresses his more irritating mannerisms and delivers a comedy performance (performances?) that can stand on its own merits rather than rest upon his radio fame. Worth the admission price in itself is Joe and Martha Raye's sprightly rendition of the risqué Rodgers-Hart duet "He and She," with the two seasoned pros making up for the heavily laundered lyrics with some beautifully timed byplay and a dash of refined slapstick.

Joe would never have the opportunity to build upon this personal triumph. While in Philadelphia with the touring company of the Broadway musical *Yokel Boy*, 36-year-old Joe Penner died in his sleep from heart failure on January 10, 1941.

The Eddie Cantor Connection: "Parkyakarkus" and "The Mad Russian" (1936–1945)

Long before shock-jock Howard Stern (q.v.) proclaimed himself "King of All Media," the unchallenged bearer of this title was diminutive "banjo-eyed" entertainer Eddie Cantor (1892–1964). Born Isadore Iskowicz on New York's Lower East Side, Cantor charmed and cajoled his way up the show business ladder to emerge as a *Ziegfeld Follies* headliner at the age of 25. Billed as "the apostle of pep," Eddie was never the world's greatest comedian, singer or dancer, but he put so much energy and enthusiasm into his work that you couldn't help but love him— or, failing that, admire his *chutzpah*. After 1917 everything Cantor touched turned to gold: His Broadway "book" shows (*Kid Boots, Whoopee*) were SRO hits; his film musicals for producer Sam Goldwyn (*The Kid from Spain, Roman Scandals*) were among the biggest box-office smashes of the 1930s; and his hour-long NBC radio program, debuting September 15, 1931,

Billed as "Parkyakarkus" even on this studio still, Harry Einstein (far left) poses with his *New Faces of 1937* co-stars Milton Berle, Harriet Hilliard and Joe Penner.

sent Chase and Sanborn's product flying off the grocery shelves, posting the highest ratings up to that time. (He'd later score a similar success on television, but that's a bit beyond the scope of this book.)

For his first couple of seasons on NBC, Eddie flew solo. Except for the occasional dialogue exchange with announcer Jimmy Wallington, the comedian held court over his program's comedy content all by himself. Not that the cheekily egotistical Cantor minded being the whole show, but after a while the strain got to him and he began adding other regulars to the program. Priding himself on being a great judge of talent, Cantor gave early media breaks to such major names as Burns & Allen, Deanna Durbin, Bobby Breen, Dinah Shore, Sammy Davis, Jr., and Eddie Fisher. While Cantor could claim with some justification to have discovered these worthies, and their exposure on his various programs and live stage shows certainly did them no harm, their subsequent show business success was due to their own talent and drive (even juvenile singers Durbin and Breen had already been signed to fat movie contracts by the time Eddie brought them before the microphone). But there were a couple of *Eddie Cantor Show* regulars who might never have gone any farther than a trivia question were it not for their radio association with the comedian—and coincidentally, both performers specialized in the now-vanished art of dialect humor.

The first of these gentlemen joined Cantor's entourage in 1934. Born in Boston in 1904, Harry Einstein was advertising director for the Kane Furniture Company when he began showing up on various local radio programs doing a comedy routine posing as a Greek politician named Nick Parkyakarkas (as in "park your carcass"), based on actual members of that ethnic group whom Einstein had met at his father's importing warehouse. Greek dialect comedians were nothing new, with Omaha-born George Givot ("Harr you like *dot?*") leading the pack in nightclubs, films and radio during this period. Nor was there anything innovative about Nick Parkyakarkas, who spoke in the fractured, convoluted, malaprop-laden manner common to the Greek imitators of vaudeville. But Einstein was funnier and cleverer than most of his competition, and an excellent comedy writer in the bargain. Enchanted by Harry's radio bits on Boston station WNAC, Cantor hired the beefy, cigar-chomping Einstein as both comedy foil and gag writer for his network program. While his first appearance on the Cantor show was reportedly a letdown (his voice level never varied and bordered on the monotonous), Einstein's character, now known as Parkyakarkus, rapidly grew on audiences. "Parky" remained with Cantor after the comedian switched sponsors from Chase and Sanborn to Pebeco Toothpaste in 1935, and also appeared in Eddie's traveling variety troupe, where his dialect act always seemed to go over better than on radio.

Also in 1935, Cantor increased the dialect-comic population on his program 100 percent when he hired a veteran stage comedian who had come into the world as Barney Gorodentsky in 1895 (some sources say 1900). Billed as Bert Gordon, the New York–born entertainer employed a variety of funny dialects in vaudeville, relying heavily upon his shock of unwashed hair and Dumbo-like ears to score his biggest laughs. He made his Broadway bow in *George White's Scandals of 1921* and was introduced to radio by Jack Benny in 1933, appearing in an ongoing "Sherlock Holmes" skit as a decidedly Hebraic Dr. Watson. Reportedly Gordon offered his services to Cantor after Parkyakarkus made it big, reasoning that two thick dialects were funnier than one. In his early appearances on Cantor's show, Gordon's character was undefined, but by 1936 he was firmly established as "The Mad Russian." Unlike Parkyakarkus, whose character was formally worked into Eddie's monologues and sketches, the Mad Russian was likely to materialize at any time, butting into the introduction of a distinguished guest star or the performance of a "straight" sketch with his breathless Slavic salutation "How do you *dooooo?*" On the off-chance that this or his other catchphrases ("Silly boy!" "Do you *mean* it?" "Shall I *tell* him?") didn't bring down the house, Gordon could always count upon his surefire visual gag of twisting the tops of his ears and stuffing them into his ear canals just before coming onstage, then having them suddenly pop out like a pair of unfurling flags as he approached the microphone.

While Cantor managed to keep his radio and film career separate entities in the minds of public by playing "himself" on radio and different characters on film, in 1936 he briefly closed the gap by engaging Harry Einstein as a supporting actor and co-scripter for his Goldwyn-produced musical *Strike Me Pink*. Generally conceded to be a disaster, *Strike Me Pink* nonetheless earned Einstein some positive critical commentary in the role of Eddie's erstwhile bodyguard Nick Parkyakarkus. This not only encouraged Einstein to pursue other film work, but also to try to have his name legally changed to Parkyakarkus (he failed). Signing a short-term contract with RKO Radio in 1937, Einstein appeared opposite fellow radio luminary Joe Penner (q.v.) in the all-star musical *New Faces of 1937*. RKO envisioned Penner and Parkyakarkus as a comedy team, but this didn't pan out when it became obvious that Parky overpowered Joe onscreen, endangering the studio's future plans for a solo Penner series. It was while making this film that Einstein fell in love with co-star Thelma Leeds, who would become his second wife. The couple's two sons grew up to be comedians Bob Einstein and Albert Brooks.

Also in *New Faces of 1937* was Einstein's *Eddie Cantor Show* confrere Bert Gordon—but *not* as the Mad Russian. Concurrent with his Cantor appearances, Gordon was featured as Mischa Moody on the CBS variety series *Community Sing*, hosted by Milton Berle and featuring comic Tommy Mack as the excitable Judge Hugo Straight. When Berle and Mack were signed for *New Faces of 1937*, Gordon went along to repeat his Mischa Moody characterization onscreen. Though billed as Gordon's film debut, the comedian had previously shown up in a Jewish characterization in Paramount's *Madison Square Garden* (1932) and in small roles in a pair of minor 1935 pictures. (He reportedly plays the frizzy-haired radio technician in the 1934 "Our Gang" comedy *Mike Fright,* but I don't think that's him.)

Despite the failure of *New Faces of 1937* RKO had faith in both Penner and Parkyakarkus, reteaming them in the 1937 musical comedy *Life of the Party,* where once again Parky towered over Penner both literally and figuratively. Parkyakarkus (as he was now officially billed in the credits) was then featured along with his *Life of the Party* co-stars Gene Raymond, Helen Broderick, Victor Moore and Billy Gilbert in RKO's Ann Sothern vehicle *She's Got Everything* (1938), He went on to receive top billing in the studio's hour-long programmer *Night Spot* (1938), where he was once again cast as an incompetent bodyguard. None of these films did anything to convince Hollywood that Parkyakarkus was star material, yet he was still emboldened to insist upon a raise from Eddie Cantor or demand release from his contract. Eddie chose the latter option, though there seems to have been no rancor between the two men.

Meanwhile, Bert Gordon landed one of his better screen roles in the 1938 Republic musical *Outside of Paradise.* Cast as the drummer in leading man Phil Regan's orchestra, Gordon performs the specialty number "I'm the Power Behind the Throne" and offers a compelling ethnic contrast with the picture's Irish village setting. His radio catchphrases are melded into the dialogue to the extent that they're spoken by practically everyone else in the cast; and in the final scene he dresses up like a leprechaun, *feh* and begorrah! Though a diverting trifle, *Outside of Paradise* was not the sort of picture that would encourage Gordon to sever ties with Eddie Cantor, so despite the two performers' frequent squabbles over material they remained together throughout the next decade. Their professional relationship even withstood a potentially volatile incident in 1939 when Gordon was accused of physically assaulting two *Eddie Cantor Show* audience members who complained after Eddie told a joke about Adolf Hitler. (The charges were dropped.)

Between 1938 and 1940 both Harry Einstein and Bert Gordon worked briefly with Al Jolson, Einstein on Jolie's radio show and Gordon in the Broadway musical *Hold on to Your Hats.* We wouldn't see either Parkyakarkus or the Mad Russian on screen again until the early 1940s, with Gordon getting the best of it at Columbia Pictures while Einstein—now billed onscreen as Harry Parke—was confined to the minor studios. All three of Gordon's Columbia films were directed by future Abbott & Costello associate Charles Barton, and none ran any longer than 66 minutes—wisely, since a little bit of Bert Gordon went a long way. The 1941 musical *Sing for Your Supper* (working title: *Ten Cents a Dance)* finds Gordon playing a character identified only as "The Mad Russian" in a light soufflé about society debutante Jinx Falkenberg posing as a dance hall hostess. Moving from fourth to second billing as phony Russian prince Boris Rascalnikoff in *Laugh Your Blues Away* (1942), Gordon again appears opposite Falkenberg; here she plays a blues singer posing as Boris' regal sister. Bert finally achieves star billing in *Let's Have Fun* (1943), which bore the title *Shall I Tell Them?* right up to the first preview and was described as "a monotonous little package" by critic Wayne Paulson of the *Portsmouth* (Ohio) *Times.* Traveling by the name of Boris Ras*kol*nikoff, Gordon plays an unemployed stage director who works as a taxi driver to help support an impoverished family, ending up as the guiding force behind a Broadway hit titled *The Road to Siberia.* At this juncture it should be noted that Gordon's popularity received a major boost when the U.S. and the Soviet Union became allies during World War II.

Gordon's modestly budgeted Columbia efforts look like the *Lord of the Rings* trilogy when compared to the threadbare quickies Parkyakarkus appeared in during the same period. PRC's *A Yank in Libya* (1942) is a salmagundi of badly staged backlot scenes and mottled stock footage, worth seeing only for Harry Einstein–Parke's offbeat characterization. Though hero Walter Woolf King immediately recognizes the newly bearded comedian as Parkyakarkus, he isn't a Greek at all but a Brooklyn-accented hustler posing as an Arab "grazoo," which is apparently local slang for horse thief. In contrast with his blundering bodyguards in *Strike Me Pink* and *Night Spot,* this Parkyakarkus is a handy man with his fists and possessed of more than his fair share of courage. It's an intriguing performance; too bad it couldn't have also been funny. In another PRC masterpiece, *The Yanks Are Coming* (1942), Parky provides faintly comic relief for a sluggish story about a conceited bandleader (played by real-life baton wielder Henry King, who couldn't act if his life depended on it) becoming a right guy after his brother is killed in the war. Sporting a mustache and chubbier than usual, the comedian plays his role with an accent that wavers uncertainly between Greek and Yiddish. Asked his name at one point, Parky replies with typical wartime flippancy "It used to be Parkyakarkus, but priorities made me shorten it." Only Monogram's *Sweethearts of the U.S.A.* (1944) gives him something better to work with; in this one, defense worker Una Merkel dreams that she has teamed with detective Parky to track down a gang of bank robbers, a pursuit that leads the pair to a haunted house. Elementary stuff, but funny—and as a bonus, the film allows us to find out whatever happened to singer Donald Novis after his burst of radio popularity in the 1930s.

Bert Gordon, alias "The Mad Russian," seems rather sedate (or maybe sedated) in this late–1930s NBC publicity shot (courtesy Thrilling Days of Yesteryear blog).

His Columbia contract at an end, Bert Gordon did an unbilled cameo in the all-star Warner Bros. musical *Thank Your Lucky Stars* (1943), his only picture with Eddie Cantor. This film was also the only occasion that Cantor directly referenced his radio program onscreen, with the plot revolving around an obstreperous Eddie withholding his vocalist Dinah Shore from a spectacular morale-boosting stage show. (Despite the positive vibes he received from his public and peers for his selfless efforts on behalf of the American Federation of Radio Artists and the March of Dimes, it was no secret that Cantor was not as lovable as he seemed on radio—and he didn't seem to mind satirizing his "real" self in *Thank Your Lucky Stars.*) According to contemporary sources, Gordon was also slated to appear in Cantor's RKO vehicle *Show Business* (1945), but this didn't happen.

While Harry "Parke" was doing box-office duty as Parkyakarkus in the 1945 musicals *Earl Carroll Vanities* (Republic) and *Out of This World* (Paramount), Gordon was putting paid to the movie-star phase of his career by visiting Parke's former home turf PRC. Long out of circulation, PRC's *How Doooo You Do!* (1945) has for decades been highly sought after by comedy buffs on the strength of its tantalizing synopsis, to wit: Vacationing from their radio show, Gordon and Harry Von Zell (then Eddie Cantor's announcer) repair to a resort hotel in Desert Springs, where they immediately become embroiled in a murder investigation. To help out the authorities, Bert contacts several Hollywood actors who specialize in detective roles: Keye Luke, James Burke, Fred Kelsey, Thomas Jackson and Leslie Denison, all playing "themselves." Unfortunately these Gower Gulch gumshoes are helpless without a script to guide them (one of them admits, "I couldn't even solve a crossword puzzle"), so Bert and Harry must take charge of things. As it turns out, there's been no murder at all, so everything ends happily—almost. As THE END is flashed onscreen, the camera pulls back to reveal the cast of *How Doooo You Do!* watching their own film in a studio projection room. When the producer complains that audiences won't accept a murder mystery without a murder, Bert calmly requests that the film's final scene be run again, whereupon he shoots a gun at the movie screen and the "victim" falls dead!

Alas, what could have been a delightful Poverty Row *Hellzapoppin'* is exposed as one long and laborious letdown whenever the recently rediscovered *How Doooo You Do!* is shown today. Under the ponderous direction of Ralph Murphy, the screenplay by Harry Sauber and Joseph Carole seems even flabbier than it is, with good lines like "You guys are taking a perfectly legitimate murder mystery and turning it into a screwball farce!" cast adrift in a sea of bad ones. The self-referential notion of featuring familiar movie detectives using their own names is inspired, but once the gag is established, it has nowhere to go. And as if the film's 80-minute running time wasn't padded enough, the currently available prints tack on a tiresome 6-minute "prologue" taken from an unrelated 1940s short subject featuring Harry Von Zell and fellow announcer Harlow Wilcox.

Some minor pleasures can be had in the film's opening radio-broadcast sequence featuring Gordon, Von Zell, singers Cheryl Walker and Ella Mae Morse, and silent-film star Claire Windsor, as charming and gorgeous as ever in her final screen appearance. More than one observer has pointed out that this sequence is basically *The Eddie Cantor Show* minus Eddie, with Von Zell pulling double duty as host and star while Gordon exercises his "Mad Russian" prerogative of popping up unannounced and uninvited, his "How do you *doooo?*" effectively squelching a straight interview with the elegant Miss Windsor. For the rest of the picture Ella Mae Morse makes like Cass Daley as she amorously pursues the highly resistant Mad Russian; Cheryl Walker romances reporter Frank Albertson (who like all the other stars introduces himself in the opening credits, in case the viewer might confuse him with Ella Mae Morse); and Claire Windsor doesn't seem to have any function other than sharing the same initials as Cheryl Walker, presumably an important plot point in the script's early drafts (nothing is made of it in the finished film). Of the other supporting players, Charles Middleton shakes loose from his usual Ming the Merciless menace with a marvelously deadpan comic turn as the local sheriff, who becomes so flustered by Gordon and Von Zell's cloddish efforts to deflect suspicion from Cheryl and Claire that he bellows, "All right! Is there anyone *else* here who wants to confess to the murder?"

As for top-billed Gordon, the film's emphasis on physical humor serves to reveal that the Mad Russian is funny only from the neck up. Far better represented is Harry Von Zell, whose unexpected flair for broad humor would serve him quite well in later years when he starred in an above-average series of Columbia two-reel comedies, and especially during his six-year stint as the long-suffering, frequently fired announcer on TV's *George Burns and Gracie Allen Show*.

With Gordon giving up films and resuming his duties on *The Eddie Cantor Show* as well as his recurring character on *Duffy's Tavern,* Harry "Parkyakarkus" Einstein ("Parke" no more) likewise forsook filmmaking to spend three seasons starring in his own NBC (and later Mutual) radio comedy series *Meet Me at Parky's.* A Greek-accented version of *Duffy's Tavern* (q.v.), the series was unremarkable save for the episode of March 23, 1947, in which the star devoted an entire half-hour to the Greek War Relief Association. *Meet Me at Parky's* might have hung on a bit longer were it not for Harry Einstein's ongoing health problems; fortunately he was able to take early retirement, having amassed great wealth through real estate transactions.

After leaving *The Eddie Cantor Show* in 1949, Gordon encountered difficulty securing radio and TV work, a situation that has been attributed to everything from a drop-off of interest in dialect comedy to Gordon's allegedly subversive political beliefs. He kept active on the Borscht belt theatrical circuit, appearing in solo venues and musical revues before older Jewish audiences who still cherished his special brand of ethnic humor. Virtually forgotten by the early 1960s, Gordon enjoyed a brief renaissance when producer Carl Reiner invited him to appear alongside fellow radio veterans Arlene "Chatterbox" Harris (see **Al Pearce and His Gang**) and Richard Haydn on the April 1, 1964, episode of *The Dick Van Dyke Show*. Though looking somewhat desiccated, "The Mad Russian" proved he still had the moxie to draw big laughs from an audience, and as a result he was booked for an engagement at Billy Gray's Band Box in Los Angeles. This would be his last professional appearance: Ten years later, 79-year-old Bert Gordon died of cancer in his Duarte, California, home.

It would be presumptuous and in questionable taste to suggest that Harry Einstein's exit was a more fulfilling one, but read on and judge for yourself. Comfortably settled throughout the 1950s, with rare exceptions Einstein limited his entertaining to private celebrity roasts at the Beverly Hills Friar's Club. On the evening of November 24, 1958, Harry was among the speakers at a roast honoring Lucille Ball and Desi Arnaz. To use a word that every professional comedian will understand, he "killed." Many of the 1,150 people in the audience would later insist that not only had Harry Einstein never been funnier, but also that they had never heard a funnier testimonial in Friar's Club history. Ending his speech to the sound of warm, enthusiastic applause, Harry took his seat and suddenly slumped sideways, his head resting in the lap of fellow Friar Milton Berle. "Please, somebody, a doctor!" cried Berle, and everyone thought he was kidding. He wasn't. On what might well have been the most triumphant evening of his life, Harry Einstein died of heart failure at the age of 54.

"The Air Adventures of Jimmie Allen" and *Sky Parade* (1936)

The granddaddy of all juvenile aviation serials, *The Air Adventures of Jimmie Allen* was created for radio by two World War I flying aces, Robert M. "Bob" Burtt and Wilfred G. "Bill" Moore. Picked up for sponsorship by the Skelly Oil Company, the daily 15-minute serial was first transcribed in 1933, then syndicated to local radio stations in Kansas City, Denver and Tulsa. Eventually the program's distribution spread east of the Mississippi, and the episodes could still be heard in regional re-broadcasts long after production ceased in 1937.

Played by middle-aged actor John Frank, 16-year-old Jimmie Allen—a "wide-awake, clear-eyed youth"—started out as a pilot trainee for National Airways. Under the tutelage of veteran war ace and Federal agent Speed Robertson (Robert Fiske), Jimmie obtained his pilot's license and was soon embarking upon a thrilling array of airborne escapades, from a daring nonstop transcontinental flight to a prolonged battle with crazed inventor Professor Proteus. Others in Jimmie's entourage included his girlfriend Barbara Croft and gabby mechanic Flash Lewis.

The serial's principal attraction for its youthful fans (not to mention Skelly Oil's advertising department) was its multitude of commercial tie-ins, giveaways and premiums: model planes, aviation maps, whistles, photo albums, franchised air races and membership emblems for the Jimmie Allen Flying Club (which numbered among its members such adolescent celebrities as Mickey Rooney and Shirley Temple). In addition, the character appeared in cartoon form in the "Big Little Book" *Jimmie Allen and the Air Mail Robbery*. Such was the popularity of the franchise that Kansas City ad man Russell C. Comer was able to saturate the entire country with transcriptions of the radio series without ever having to link up with any of the major networks. Comer's promotional acumen extended all the way to Hollywood in 1936, when Paramount Pictures assembled a feature film version of the serial titled *Sky Parade*.

Directed by Otto Lovering from a script by Byron Morgan, Bryan Marlowe, and Arthur G. Beckhard, *Sky Parade* followed the example of the radio serial by allowing audiences to believe that there really was a Jimmie Allen and that he was playing himself on the big screen. Because of his advanced age, the serial's star John Frank was never publicized by Skelly Oil or by the show's syndicator. Instead, teenager Murray McLean Jr. was hired to stand in for Frank during personal appearances and in publicity photos. Young McLean was also engaged to star in *Sky Parade*, for which he was billed as Jimmie Allen in the film's credits and all advertising.

A new and slightly disjointed backstory was developed for the film involving Jimmie's father, World War I flying hero Scottie Allen (played by Robert Fiske, the radio version's Speed Robertson). After the Armistice, Scottie joins a traveling air circus with his old pals Speed (William Gargan) and Tommy (Kent Taylor), backed up by loyal mechanic Flash (Sid Saylor). This allows the producers to insert a lot of stunt aerial footage into the early portions of the film, which *Pittsburgh Press* critic Sanford L. Cooper dismissed along with the dramatic passages as "dull and unexciting." (No one bothered to ask the cheering youngsters in the audience what *they* thought.) After Scottie is killed in a attempt to break a distance record, Speed takes full responsibility for the orphaned Jimmie, causing friction with Speed's stunt-parachutist sweetheart Geri (Katherine DeMille)—whose last name is Croft, the film's only vestige of Jimmie Allen's puppy love Barbara Croft. After several years we find Speed and Tommy running a commercial concern known as Continental Airlines (well before there really *was* one) and spending their spare time testing out an advanced automatic-pilot device, which their ex-friend Casey (Grant Withers) intends to steal on behalf of smuggler Gat Billings (Edgar Dearing). While flying to Washington to secure a patent for the device, several of the people we care about are waylaid by the villains, and it is up to rookie pilot Jimmie—heretofore relegated to the background—to grab the controls of the Aerona low-wing monoplane and save the day. (Incidentally, when actor William Gargan appears with a bandaged face in the film, he's not acting: During production, he suffered a lacerated chin in a minor traffic accident.)

Needless to say, *Sky Parade* was promoted like the Second Coming on radio's *The Air Adventures of Jimmie Allen*. It was hoped at the time that the film would generate enough interest and revenue to launch a whole series of Jimmie Allen pictures. Unfortunately, Paramount producer Harry Hoyt, who in order to make the film had forged a contract with Arthur F. Beck's Air Adventures Corporation, was sued along with Beck by one Sidney Marcus, who claimed that he had been promised a job and a percentage of the film's profits in exchange for lending Hoyt the money to get the project off the ground. Marcus lost the suit, but the negative publicity did nothing to advance the case for a stream of Jimmie Allen sequels, and also severely damaged *Sky Parade*'s box official potential. Too, the radio serial was in the process of closing down production: There was no discernable advantage in building a new film series on a failed picture and an apparently dormant radio property.

Ironically, radio's *Air Adventures of Jimmie Allen* enjoyed a longer life—or rather, after-life—than anyone expected. In addition to the well-circulated re-broadcasts from the 1930s, an updated adaptation was syndicated for sponsorship by the International Shoe Company in 1946. Starring Jack Schlickter as Jimmy, Shelby Storck as Speed and Twila Comer as Barbara Croft, this revival managed to hang in there for 400 quarter-hour episodes. As for the show's originators Bob Burtt and Bill Moore, they had long since retooled the *Jimmie Allen* formula, with Skelly Oil again footing the bills, as another aviation serial titled *Captain Midnight* (q.v.)

"Your Hit Parade" (1937–1951)

The popularity of Paramount's radio-related *Big Broadcast* films (see separate entry) encouraged rival studios to follow suit with their own star-studded musicals in hopes of generating yearly or semi-yearly series of their own. Most of these efforts were unsuccessful, with the noteworthy exception of a group of films cranked out by one of Hollywood's smallest studios—and one that wasn't even in existence when the first *Big Broadcast* picture was released in 1932.

A former executive with the American Tobacco Company, Herbert J. Yates went into the movie business in 1918 when he launched Republic Laboratories, supplying technical services to several of Hollywood's lesser film firms. Within the next decade Yates changed the name of his operation to Consolidated Laboratories, serving and financing such B-picture factories as Mascot, Monogram, Liberty, Majestic and Supreme. In 1935 he foreclosed on all these concerns and created his own production company,

Republic Pictures. Retaining the services of Mascot's CEO Nat Levine and acquiring the old Mack Sennett studio in the San Fernando Valley, Yates commenced producing a steady stream of inexpensive westerns, action pictures and serials under the Republic banner. By 1936 the studio had built up enough profits and public goodwill to branch out into more ambitious features, with Yates establishing the policy of assembling at least one "prestige" picture per year. Beginning with *Follow Your Heart* (1936), starring opera singer Marion Talley, the earliest of Republic's A-grade efforts were musicals.

Their second deluxe production was inspired by a radio variety series that had been unveiled by NBC in a 60-minute format on April 1, 1935. Sponsored from the very beginning by Lucky Strike cigarettes, *Your Hit Parade* based its weekly musical selections on public demand. "You've told us by your purchases of sheet music and records, by your requests to orchestra leaders in the places you've danced, by the tunes you've listened to on your favorite radio programs" was announcer Ben Grauer's explanation of the criteria used to determine the 15 top songs heard on each broadcast. At first, these songs were performed in a random manner, with a few older tunes—"Lucky Strike Extras"—thrown in for variety. By and by *Your Hit Parade* established its familiar format of offering the tunes in a countdown format, with the "Number One Song," heralded by trumpet and drum roll, showcased at the climax of each program. So popular that it was broadcast twice a week on NBC, *Your Hit Parade* moved to CBS on April 25, 1936, with Andre Baruch replacing Ben Grauer, while a half-hour version, also sponsored by Lucky Strike, aired over its original network beginning in November of that year.

The Republic version of the property went into production in December 1936 as *We're on the Air*, ultimately acquiring film rights to the title *The Hit Parade* in hopes of attracting the radio program's enormous following. Boasting a budget of $500,000 at a time when the average Republic feature came in at a fraction of that amount, the film was directed by Gus Meins, previously associated with Hal Roach's "Our Gang" comedies, and scripted by Samuel Ornitz (*Follow Your Heart*) and Bradford Ropes (author of the original novel *42nd Street*). The "book" portion of the show starred Phil Regan, former vocalist for the Guy Lombardo Orchestra who was often billed as "The Singing Cop" because of his previous vocation as a New York City policeman. In films since 1933, Regan had previously headlined the minor Republic musicals *Laughing Irish Eyes* and *Happy Go Lucky*, building a following with his pleasant Irish tenor and lightweight acting style. Republic's original choice for Regan's leading lady was popular singer Kay Thompson, a frequent guest star on radio's *Your Hit Parade*. No sooner had her casting been announced in the *Los Angeles Times* than Thompson was forced to bow out because of her commitment to the New York-based radio series *It's Chesterfield Time*. Her replacement was Frances Langford, then a regular on CBS' *Hollywood Hotel* and Thompson's top rival in radio popularity polls.

The plot is set in motion when singer Monica Barrett (Louise Henry) drops her agent-boyfriend Pete Garland (Regan) after he lands her an important radio gig sponsored by reformed slot-machine kingpin Mulrooney (Ed Brophy in one of his "If I had any hair I'd tear it out!" performances). Though Pete had plucked Monica from obscurity and made her a star, she now considers herself too good for him and prefers to travel in the company of such Park Avenue socialites as lawyer Teddy Leeds (Monroe Owsley). To get even with Monica, Pete vows to find another "nobody" to mold into stardom. At a cheap dive, he spots Ruth Allison (Langford) performing in a "sister" act with Eadie White (Pert Kelton). With Pete's input Ruth becomes a big attraction, but her rise to fame is threatened by a deep dark secret: She has served time in jail, and is currently being pursued by a diligent detective (William Demarest) for jumping bail. Jealous of Ruth's success, Monica manages to expose the girl's past to the newspapers, motivating Pete to stage an all-star radio testimonial to arouse public demand for Ruth's exoneration. All turns out for the best when the detective shows up with a

A trade magazine advertisement for Republic's initial *Hit Parade* film of 1937.

pardon for Ruth, the guilty party having confessed to her alleged (and unspecified) crime.

The film's tie-in with radio's *Your Hit Parade* includes the title, the opening-credits presentation of the program's theme song "Happy Days Are Here Again" (the more familiar sponsor-dictated theme "Lucky Day" had not yet been adopted), the presence of orchestra leader Carl Hoff and the Hit Parade Orchestra, and the appearance of the singing Tic Toc Girls in the closing medley. (Series announcer Ben Grauer was slated to appear, but didn't.) Adhering to the *Big Broadcast* formula, the film features a number of radio favorites, most of them carefully integrated into the storyline. Max Terhune, resident comedian of NBC's *National Barn Dance* (q.v.) and soon to be a regular in Republic westerns, plays Pete Garland's sidekick Rusty, providing Terhune ample opportunity to trot out his ventriloquism and his peculiar talent for imitating barnyard noises. While seeking a replacement for the fickle Monica and later endeavoring to get Ruth a decent singing job, Pete and Rusty drop in at the nightclubs where orchestra leaders Eddy Duchin and Duke Ellington are performing, with Ellington accompanied by the exquisitely voiced Ivy Anderson (best remembered for her appearance in the Marx Bros.' *A Day at the Races*); Duchin and the Duke will return during Ruth Allison's testimonial. For Ruth's first radio appearance, Pete calls in a favor from comedian Al Pearce (see **Al Pearce and His Gang**), who during his program performs an "Elmer Blurt" sketch with his radio cohorts Monroe "Lord Bilgewater" Upton and Arlene "Chatterbox" Harris. And in the climactic testimonial scene we see announcer Ed Thorgersen and Marion Sayles Taylor, billed on his own CBS radio-advice program as "The Voice of Experience," imploring the public to give Ruth a break (Thorgersen was then a commentator for 20th Century–Fox's *Movietone News*, while Taylor had starred in his own series of short subjects produced by Ben K. Blake for Columbia Pictures, so both were familiar faces to moviegoers.) Also pitching in on Ruth's behalf is the minstrel team of Pick (Malone) and Pat (Padgett), network radio stalwarts since 1934. In fact, Pick and Pat are billed twice in the credits, first under their own names, then as their blackface alter egos Molasses and January.

Also afforded guest-star billing are a few performers not usually associated with radio. Greek-dialect comedian George Givot portrays a seedy cabaret manager (Givot did have his own radio show from time to time, but was better known for his stage and screen work); rustic novelty singers Oscar and Elmer (Ed Platt, Lou Fulton) appear as Max Terhune's kinfolk; and three ex-stooges of comedian Ted Healy—not Curly, Larry and Moe, but the Gentle Maniacs (Paul "Mousie" Garner, Sam Wolf, Dick Hakins)—show up as nightclub comics performing a rather messy musical spoof. In order to accommodate those Manhattan-based performers who were unable to make the trip to Hollywood, some of the specialties and guest turns in *Hit Parade* were filmed at the Biograph studios in the Bronx under the supervision of Ralph Staub. Republic did nothing to hide the fact that not all of the picture was produced in their own California facilities. Indeed, the studio's publicists pointed with pride to the scene in which a New York–filmed number with Eddy Duchin is seamlessly matched with a California-filmed medium shot of Frances Langford, using a double for the actress to sustain the illusion.

Most currently available public-domain prints of the 83-minute *The Hit Parade* are struck from the 67-minute reissue version titled *I'll Reach for a Star,* with some of the featured performers showing up only fleetingly and a few (like Arlene Harris) not appearing at all. Even in this truncated form the quality and polish of the production shines through, fully justifying the rave review from *Independent Exhibitors' Film Bulletin*: "Major studios may well have to look to their laurels! This Republic musical is exactly what the title conveys, a hit, in every sense of the word.... The radio background provides a natural device for introducing the acts, and serves to keep the film paced at a smart tempo." In the spirit of its radio-show inspiration, the film yielded two hit songs which received plenty of airplay in the months to come, "Was It Rain?" by Lou Handman and Walter Hirsch and "Love Is Good for Anything That Ails You" by Cliff Friend and Matty Melnick. The success of these tunes further increased the impressive box-office take of *Hit Parade*, which did so well that it barely needed the hyperbole of its ad campaign: "ALL your radio favorites join with the screen's brightest names to bring you a sparkling entertainment of high-powered humor, gorgeous girls, tantalizing tunes. And STARS! STARS! STARS!"

Another of the film's advertising tags was "IT'S DIFFERENT! NEW AS TELEVISION!" Actually, the concept of television was nothing new for Republic, where throughout the 1930s the still-experimental medium was treated as an established and commercially viable source of popular entertainment in such films as *The Singing Cowboy, Exiled to Shanghai, S.O.S. Tidal Wave* and *Manhattan Merry-Go-Round* (q.v.) Television also plays a major role in the first of Republic's four follow-ups to *The Hit*

Parade, 1940's *The Hit Parade of 1941* (reissue title: *Romance and Rhythm*), directed by John H. Auer and again co-scripted by Bradford Ropes. The film was to have been made as an immediate follow-up to the first series entry, but production was delayed for nearly three years as Republic focused on other big-budgeters like *Man of Conquest* and *Dark Command.*

Kenny Baker, house tenor on the Jack Benny and Fred Allen radio programs, stars in *Hit Parade of 1941* as radio manager David Farraday, whose station WPX is so cash-poor that his pal Charlie Moore (Phil Silvers in his screen debut) resorts to sidewalk-pitchman tactics to scare up listeners. As if this wasn't bad enough, television is now on the horizon, threatening to make all radio stations obsolete. Enter potential backer Mrs. Emily Potter (Mary Boland), who agrees to pump money into WPX and finance new TV equipment providing that David build a program around her daughter Annabelle (Ann Miller), a talented dancer. Unfortunately Mrs. Potter wants Annabelle to sing on the air, a tricky proposition in that the girl can't carry a tune in a wash bucket. By accident, the voice of David's star vocalist Pat Moore (welcome back, Frances Langford) is piped out over the ether during Annabelle's broadcast. Because she loves David, Pat is willing to remain Annabelle's "ghost" voice when WPX converts to television, standing by a microphone and matching Annabelle's lip movements on the TV monitor (sound familiar, Gene Kelly fans?). The ruse is revealed when Pat's sister Judy (Patsy Kelly) flips a switch in the control room during a telecast. But instead of ruining WPX, this moment of truth bestows stardom upon Pat—while Annabelle, who prefers dancing anyway, happily remains on the station's payroll as the resident toe-tapper.

With such visual highlights as a "challenge" number pitting Frances Langford's voice against Ann Miller's dancing feet (choreographed by Danny Dare with the uncredited assistance of Hermes Pan), and the musical-satire specialties featuring Borrah Minnevitch and His Harmonica Rascals, *Hit Parade of 1941* has very little to do with its radio-series "inspiration"—or with radio, for that matter. The presence of network-broadcast favorites Baker, Langford, orchestra leader Jan Garber and the singing group Six Hits and a Miss are about all the film can offer to warrant its radio-based title. At least the original *Your Hit Parade* network series was able to cash in on its repeated exposure of *Hit Parade of 1941*'s one hit tune, "Who Am I?" (Jule Styne, Walter Bullock), which also earned an Oscar nomination.

Now known by its reissue title *Change of Heart,* the third series entry *Hit Parade of 1943,* directed by Albert S. Rogell, rehashes an oft-used Republic plotline: a burned-out songwriter taking credit for tunes written by a talented newcomer. John Carroll (replacing Milton Berle) heads the cast as Rick Farrell, a fly-by-night composer and music publisher who steals some songs written by heroine Jill Wright (a pre-superstardom Susan Hayward). After an hour of double-crosses and double-double-crosses, Rick and Jill fall in love and her authorship is acknowledged. Along the way, comedy is provided by the always welcome Eve Arden and by short-subject perennial Tom Kennedy, whose recitation of the dreadful lyrics to "Autumn Leaves in the Gutter" was designed as the payoff to a nationwide "worst song" contest, a publicity stunt concocted by Republic in conjunction with the film.

The "broadcast" aspect of the story occurs at the beginning and end of the picture, with orchestra leader Freddie Martin first rehearsing in the studios of the "UBC" network, then performing full-blast during a climactic War Bond rally (the 82-minute film's more overt wartime references are missing from the 69-minute reissue prints). Other specialty numbers are presented in the various nightclubs owned by secondary character Bradley Cole (Melville Cooper). Drawn from the radio ranks are guest stars Ray McKinley and His Orchestra, the Three Cheers, the Music Maids, and Count Basie. This last-named artist is among the preponderance of African American talent appearing in *Hit Parade of 1943,* including Dorothy Dandridge, the Golden Gate Quartet, and uncredited but well-represented performers Ernie Morrison, Dorothea Dunham, Neva Peoples and Ruth Scott. The film's highlight is the lavish "Harlem Sandman" number, featuring a lavish taxi-shaped cloud floating to the stage, a snatch of 1940s-style rap talk, and a superb ensemble dance choreographed by Nick Castle. Representing another ethnic base is specialty dancer Chinita Marin, who went on to steal the show in RKO's hands-across-the-border musical *Pan-Americana* (1945). Oscar nominations for *Hit Parade of 1943* went to the Jule Styne-Harold Adamson song "Change of Heart" and the musical direction by Walter Scharf.

Produced and directed by Frank McDonald, entry #4 *The Hit Parade of 1947* (reissued as *High and Happy*) was the first of the Republic series since the original *Hit Parade* to boast a direct link to its radio source. Making her movie debut in this picture is singer Joan Edwards, a *Your Hit Parade* regular from 1941 through 1946 whose presence inspired a nationwide "Moan-and-Groan-for-Joan" fan club comprised of homesick servicemen. Here she is cast as "herself," one-fourth of a nightclub singing act called the Tune Toppers, which also features Kip Walker (Eddie Albert), Ellen Baker (Constance Moore) and Eddie Paige (Gil Lamb). The latter-day theory that the Tune Toppers were based on the real-life cabaret quartet The Revuers would seem to be supported by the film's spin on 20th Century–Fox's callous dismissal of "Revuers" Betty Comden, Adolph Green and Alvin Hammer when the studio signed only the fourth member, Judy Holliday, to a movie contract. In *Hit Parade of 1947,* arrogant Kip Walker breaks up the Tune Toppers to go solo, only to bomb with his abrasive "satirical" routines while former partner Ellen Barker soars to stardom under the patronage of movie executive Rodney Huntley (Bill Goodwin). Though no Oscar nominations were earned by this edition of *Hit Parade, Film Bulletin* assured exhibitors that the presence of Joan Edwards and Bill Goodwin would draw the "radio addicts," while the film's musical guests Woody Herman, Roy Rogers, Bob Nolan and the Sons of the Pioneers would attract "jive-minded filmgoers" and western fans.

Like its predecessors, the fifth and last of Republic's *Hit Parade* series was given a different reissue title to avoid paying licensing fees in perpetuity: That's why *The Hit Parade of 1951* (1950) is now seen on television as *Song Parade*. Directed by John H. Auer, the film stars John Carroll, who'd previously headlined the 1943 edition, in the dual role of heavily-in-debt Las Vegas gambler Joe Blake and his exact lookalike, clean-living radio baritone Eddie Paul. In a plot device lifted from the earlier Republic radio-related comedy *Here Comes Elmer* (see **Al Pearce and His Gang**), Joe is conked on the casaba and awakens with the delusion that he's really Eddie, confusing Joe's nightclub-dancer girlfriend Chicquita (Estelita Rodriguez, Republic's resident Latin bombshell). No mention of radio's *Your Hit Parade* is uttered throughout the film's 84 minutes, nor could supporting players Marie "The Body" McDonald and Frank "Crazy Guggenheim" Fontaine qualify as radio favorites. Even the specialty performers, Bobby Ramos and His Band and the Firehouse Five Plus Two (comprised of seven Walt Disney Studio animators), are essentially visual attractions.

While *Hit Parade of 1951* was playing its final theatrical dates in the boonies, the NBC radio version was beginning the slow decline that culminated in its cancellation on January 16, 1953. The property was now most closely associated with the weekly NBC (and later CBS) television version, sponsored as ever by Lucky Strike. Starring singers Snooky Lanson, Dorothy Collins and Gisele MacKenzie and orchestra leader Raymond Scott, TV's *Your Hit Parade* (occasionally simulcast on radio) was among the first variety programs to be regularly telecast in color, and *the* first to be introduced by the animated NBC peacock. Gradually becoming an anachronism as popular music transitioned from big bands and ballads to rock 'n' roll, *Your Hit Parade* nonetheless kept afloat for nine seasons, the Hit Parade Singers performing their final "So long for a while" on April 24, 1959.

The Winchell-Bernie "Feud": *Wake Up and Live* (1937) and *Love and Hisses* (1937)

From the Hatfields vs. the McCoys to cable-TV pundits Bill O'Reilly vs. Stephen Colbert, feuds have always been good copy. It hardly matters that many of these "bitter rivalries" have been entirely fabricated for publicity purposes: Few things bring the roses to the cheeks of the public more than witnessing a pair of famous, wealthy and presumably mature human beings exchanging childish insults for the benefit of the cameras and microphones.

The advent of big-time radio in the 1930s fostered several feuds both large and small in full dudgeon—a few of them genuine, but most of them mere publicity stunts. The most famous of these rivalries, Jack Benny vs. Fred Allen and W.C. Fields vs. Charlie McCarthy, are dealt with elsewhere in this book. Less well known to contemporary showbiz fans is the father of all radio feuds. So here we are, ladies and gentlemen: In this corner, Walter Winchell; and in *this* corner, Ben Bernie.

It would be hard to overstate the power and influence wielded by newspaper columnist Walter Winchell (born Walter Weinschel in 1897) at the height of his glory. A product of the meanest of New York's mean streets, Winchell quit school in the sixth grade to pursue the life of a vaudeville singer and hoofer. His journalistic career was launched in 1920 when he began contributing backstage gossip to *The Vaudeville News,* and within four years he was on the staff of the infamous tabloid *The New York Graphic.* By the time he signed with Hearst's *New York Daily Mirror* in 1929, he was pulling down $500 a week as the nation's foremost gossip columnist—and if he did not invent this genre as has often been stated, for many years he made it his own personal fiefdom. Rubbing shoulders with stage producers, nightclub owners, social arbiters, politicians, policemen and racketeers, Winchell dispensed hundreds of thousands of words in terse, fragmentary sentences in his daily column *On-Broadway,* drawing upon a vast array of sources to spread both rumor and fact about the rich and powerful and breaking big stories before anyone else had a hint of what was going on. It is said that he once reported a gangland slaying before it had even taken place. A fearless crusader against political corruption and organized crime, he was among the first to openly attack the Nazi regime in Germany at a time when most journalists remained silent, and he also arranged to turn over more than one fugitive mobster to the Feds when the "official" authorities seemed unable to do so. But Winchell's fan base was far more interested in his spicy and scandalous tidbits about the lives and loves of showbiz celebrities, which he doled out generously—and just this side of libel. To skirt the self-censorship then prevalent in the Fourth Estate, he avoided frankness in matters of pregnancy and childbirth with "Winchellisms" like "infanticipating" and "blessed event." This sort of Winchell-bred "slanguage" contributed such colorful words to the English language as "scram," "pushover," "giggle water," "swelegant," and "sassiety," and such code phrases as "that way" for a secret romance, "middle-aisling it" for an impending marriage and "Reno-vated" for an impending divorce. By the late 1930s Winchell enjoyed a worldwide circulation of 2000 newspapers representing 50,000,000 readers. Even the smallest item in his column could make or break a career, and "Mrs. Winchell's little boy Walter" was neither reluctant nor hesitant to use his power as a scythe to lop off the heads of anyone who annoyed or offended him.

But being the crown prince of newsprint wasn't enough for W.W., who aspired to conquer every form of media. He launched his radio career in 1930, first under the sponsorship of Saks Fifth Avenue on CBS, and beginning December 4, 1932, as star of the weekly 15-minute *Walter Winchell's Jergens Journal,* sponsored by Jergens Lotion and heard over NBC-Blue. Winchell's radio style was exactly the same rat-a-tat yellow journalism he'd popularized in his newspaper column, only more so. In a high-pitched nasal voice he barked out headlines and gossip bites in a breathless, 197-word-per-minute staccato, as if he'd just rushed from the copy room and was anxious to burst out of the studio and pick up another late-breaking scoop on the street ("Good evening Mr. and Mrs. America and all the ships at sea! Let's go to press!") There was no dead air on a Winchell broadcast: Between news flashes he pounded out an incomprehensible stream of Morse code on a telegraph key, a master stroke of showmanship. Even years after he'd abandoned vaudeville, Winchell was still a ham at heart, and audiences loved it. Not everybody loved *him*, however, and despite a long list of friends at his beck and call, Winchell seemed to revel in cultivating an even longer list of enemies.

In contrast, it was extraordinarily difficult to find anyone who *didn't* like Ben Bernie. Born in Philadelphia as Bernard Anzlevitz in 1891, he was a violin prodigy who grew tired of the instrument while earning money as a music teacher at the age of 15. Entering vaudeville in 1910, Bernie teamed with accordion player Phil Baker five years later in a musical act which went nowhere until the two men began incorporating comedy in their repertoire. After Baker enlisted in the Navy, Bernie soloed for several years, along the way coming to the conclusion that the public was more interested in the personality of a musician than the music itself, adjusting his act to de-emphasize the violin and emphasize light humor and off-the-cuff witticisms. In 1922 he purchased a jazz band from Don Juelle, renaming the aggregation Ben Bernie and All the Lads. Though he went through the motions of conducting, Bernie was content to leave that responsibility to his first violinist Mickey Garlock, confining himself to a steady stream of jocular commentary between numbers. Referring to himself as "The Old Maestro" (at age 31!), Bernie addressed the audience as "Youse guys and youse gals," ended his set with "*Au revoir,* pleasant dreams," and throughout the performance peppered his drawling intros, outros and in-betweens with a casual "Yowsah, yowsah." The affable, cigar-smoking Bernie treated his audience as friends and intimates rather than a faceless crowd, and it was only a matter of time before his success with this approach would extend beyond his nightly gig at Manhattan's Roosevelt Hotel.

In 1923 Bernie made his first radio appearance on New York's WJZ, and the following year he was among a handful of entertainers to appear in experimental talking short subjects for DeForest Phonofilm. His one-reel *Ben Bernie and All the Lads* features Oscar Levant on piano and tenor saxophonist Don Pettis performing the first sax solo ever filmed during a rendition of Bernie's signature tune "Sweet Georgia Brown." Returning to WJZ in 1930, Bernie began his radio career in earnest, and on September 13, 1932, *Ben Bernie, The Old Maestro* settled in for a long weekly run on NBC under the sponsorship of Blue Ribbon Malt Extract, which during Prohibition was legally sold as an ingredient for homemade beer. Bernie became even more closely associated with his sponsor when Blue Ribbon merged with the Pabst Brewing Company after Repeal in 1933.

Despite their diametrically opposite personalities, Bernie and Winchell were good friends while they were starring on separate branches of the NBC tree, each man greatly admiring the other's work. Already leaders in their chosen fields, Bernie and Winchell hardly needed to exchange compliments to increase their respective audiences, but still felt that they owed one another a little public attention. It will probably never be known which of the two men came up with the idea of using reverse psychology in their mutual-promotion campaign, but my money is on Winchell. Some time around 1932, the columnist began printing and broadcasting items casting aspersions on Bernie's talent and intellect, with such snide comments as "Ben Bernie could never be president because his head is too big to put on a three-cent stamp." The jibes were never as vicious as the insults he bestowed upon people he truly disliked such as Ed Sullivan and Jack Paar, but Winchell's jabs at the bandleader were pointed, rather like the putdowns between old school chums: "Ben Bernie is the poor man's Toscanini. The very, very poor man's"; "Ben Bernie—Little Boy Blah"; "[Playwright] Henri Bernstein in the Tavern at one table and Ben Bernie at another—poet and peasant," and on into infinity. For his part, Bernie tossed soft-edged harpoons in Winchell's direction in his radio broadcasts and nightclub appearances, and during occasional joint stage appearances and charity fundraisers with his "enemy" Walter. This bloodless war of words served its purpose of boosting both combatants' radio listenership and enhancing interest in their non-radio activities—and only a total doofus could have taken the whole farrago seriously.

The Winchell-Bernie feud spilled over into motion pictures of the period, directly and indirectly. The 1932 Broadway and Hollywood comedy *Blessed Event* starred Lee Tracy in the first of his many Winchellesque roles as a vituperative gossip columnist who carried on a public battle with an equally fictional bandleader (played in the movie version by Dick Powell). References to Ben Bernie or characters based on Bernie were also included in other films inspired by Winchell's success, a few of them— *Okay America!* and *Is My Face Red?*—drawing their titles from well-known WW catchphrases. (The columnist was to have played his screen counterpart in *Okay America!*, but prior commitments got in the way and the role went to a miscast Lew Ayres.) Winchell himself got a few digs in at the Old Maestro in his starring short subjects for Vitaphone and Universal, as well as in his screen story for Darryl F. Zanuck's *Broadway Through a Keyhole* (1933), a bountifully entertaining *a clef* version of the real-life romantic triangle involving mobster Larry Fay, dancer Ruby Keeler and entertainer Al Jolson (earning Mr. Winchell a punch in the nose from Mr. Jolson when the two ran into each other at Hollywood Legion Stadium). Elsewhere, Bernie made his film acting debut in Paramount's *Shoot the Works* (1934), cast as—what else?—a bandleader (named Joe Davis) embroiled in a feud with—what else?—a gossip columnist (named Larry Kane and played by William Frawley). And through the facilities of "Termite Terrace," anthropomorphic-animal caricatures of Winchell and Bernie shot invective at each other in the Warner Bros. cartoons *The CooCoo Nut Grove* (1936) and *The Woods Are Full of Cuckoos* (1937).

Splendid showmen that they were, Walter and Ben would have been fools not to jump at the chance of exploiting their feud in their own starring film—and producer Darryl F. Zanuck was just the right man to handle the details. Since merging his independent 20th Century Pictures with the Fox Film Corporation in 1935, Zanuck had been dedicated to carrying on his policy, established during his Warner Bros. years, of making films "Drawn from Today's Headlines." Now with the combined 20th Century–Fox facilities behind him, Zanuck could extend this policy beyond dramas and adventure films and include musical comedies inspired by current events. Nineteen thirty-five's *Thanks a Million* (see entry on Fred Allen) is a lighthearted commentary on recent efforts by professional entertainers to enter politics; *Sing Baby Sing* (1936) is a takeoff of the cross-country romance between stage legend John Barrymore and his teenage tootsie Elaine Barrie; *Pigskin Parade* (1936) lampoons the practice of granting college scholarships to less-than-brilliant students in order to beef up collegiate football teams; and *One in a Million* (1937) is built around the 1936 Winter Olympics, to the extent of starring three-time Olympic skating champion Sonja Henie.

In every instance, Zanuck saw to it that the central gimmick was supported by solid story values, and that the star players got back-up from a cast of gifted entertainers, any one of whom could have headlined a picture on his or her own. Such was case with 20th Century–Fox's first pairing of Winchell and Bernie: *Wake Up and Live,* directed by Sidney Lanfield. The film's title came from an unlikely source, a best-selling non-fiction book by Chicago journalist Dorothea Brande. A major figure in the field of motivational literature, Brande used her book to set forth a eight-word formula that if applied properly would forever change the life of the reader: "Act As If It Were Impossible to Fail." This sort of advice was hardly necessary for the successful-beyond-imagination Winchell and Bernie, so screenwriters Harry Tugend, Jack Yellen and Curtis Kenyon came up with a couple of secondary characters who might benefit from Brande's advise. For this purpose, the writers harked back to a premise that had already done service in such earlier films as *Crooner* and *Twenty Million Sweethearts*: the phenomenon of "overnight" stardom bestowed upon radio singers.

In the early scenes of the 92-minute *Wake Up and Live,* vaudeville singer Eddie Kane acts as if it were impossible to succeed. Getting his first big break with a network radio audition, Eddie suddenly comes down with a paralyzing case of mike fright, hilariously visualized by an animated microphone that morphs into a fire-breathing demon. Unable to get any sort of radio job other than a studio page, Eddie overhears a broadcast by motivational singer Alice Huntley, whose radio show's theme song is "Wake Up and Live." Alas, despite her daily self-help advice Alice is unable to help herself, and her program is cancelled because it lacks audience appeal. When she finds out that Eddie is possessed of a beautiful singing voice but is unable to perform before a microphone without fainting, Alice takes him under her wing and preaches her philosophy of acting as if it were impossible to fail. So how does this fit in with the "overnight stardom" plot peg? Well, while fooling around in front of what he thinks is a dead microphone, Eddie starts to sing, unaware that his voice is being piped out to a nationwide audience. Before long Eddie has earned renown as the Phantom Troubadour, a spoof of radio's once-popular "Silver Masked Tenor" Joseph M. White. Alice meanwhile has figured out that Eddie and the Phantom Troubadour are one and the same, even though *he* hasn't yet. While giving him nightly confidence-building lessons in her apartment, Alice covertly broadcasts his voice to the nation, intending to save her own radio career by exploiting Eddie's—though she eventually falls in love with the poor sap and ends up acting in his best interest rather than her own.

So far so good. Now let's add the Winchell-Bernie feud to the equation. When Walter Winchell finds out that his secretary Patsy Kane's brother Eddie has just come off a vaudeville tour, Walter decides to play a prank on shady talent agent Gus Avery by writing up a favorable notice for Eddie, even though he's never seen the boy. After his failed audition, Eddie gets a page job with the same radio network carrying both Winchell and Ben Bernie. Our hero's impulsive "dead mike" broadcast is heard during a remote from the Hi-Hat Club, where Bernie and All the Lads are appearing. With the other Broadway columnists speculating over the Phantom Troubadour's identity, Winchell schemes to simultaneously scoop his rivals and make Bernie look ridiculous by hiring a famous singer to unmask himself as the Troubadour, but this ploy fails when Eddie's voice is fed over the club's P.A. system once more. The rest of the picture is a prolonged game of one-upsmanship, as Winchell and Bernie scramble to trump one another by being the first to reveal the name of the Phantom Troubadour. The story and the feud are resolved at the gala opening of the Manila Club, when Eddie finds out for the first time that he himself is the elusive Troubadour. Touched by the sight of Eddie conquering his mike fright, Winchell and Bernie publicly shake hands and make up, exchanging orchids (Winchell's traditional gesture of congratulation) to prove that they're now bosom buddies—at least until next time.

There's a lot more to the film of course, including a phony kidnapping engineered by the four-flushing Gus Avery on behalf of his new client (and Eddie's former stage partner) Jean Roberts, as well as musical specialties by Joan Davis, the Condos Brothers and the Brewster Twins, and even a surprise cameo by black comedian Eddie Anderson referencing his recent ascendancy to fame as "Rochester" on *The Jack Benny Program*. (Anderson gets the names Jack Benny and Ben Bernie mixed up, a gag based on Jack's actual early-career decision to alter his professional name "Ben Benny" to avoid confusion with the bandleader.) Adding spice to the stew are some amusing deviations from the well-known facts: So that Fox could avoid paying a fee to the two stars' real-life radio sponsors, Winchell signs off his broadcast with "lotion of love" from Peachbloom Beauty Lotion, while Bernie's advertising checks are signed by Red Seal Malt.

Secure in the knowledge that the Winchell-Bernie combination would automatically draw crowds—which it did, breaking the one-day attendance record when the film premiered at New York's Roxy Theater—Darryl Zanuck was able to use *Wake Up and Live* as an opportunity to spotlight his new contact player Alice Faye, who hadn't yet broken through to full stardom, in the role of the "Wake Up and Live" girl. Another Fox contractee was brought in when negotiations fell through for Eddie Cantor to star as the mike-shy singer. Jack Haley ended up with his best screen role to date as the clueless

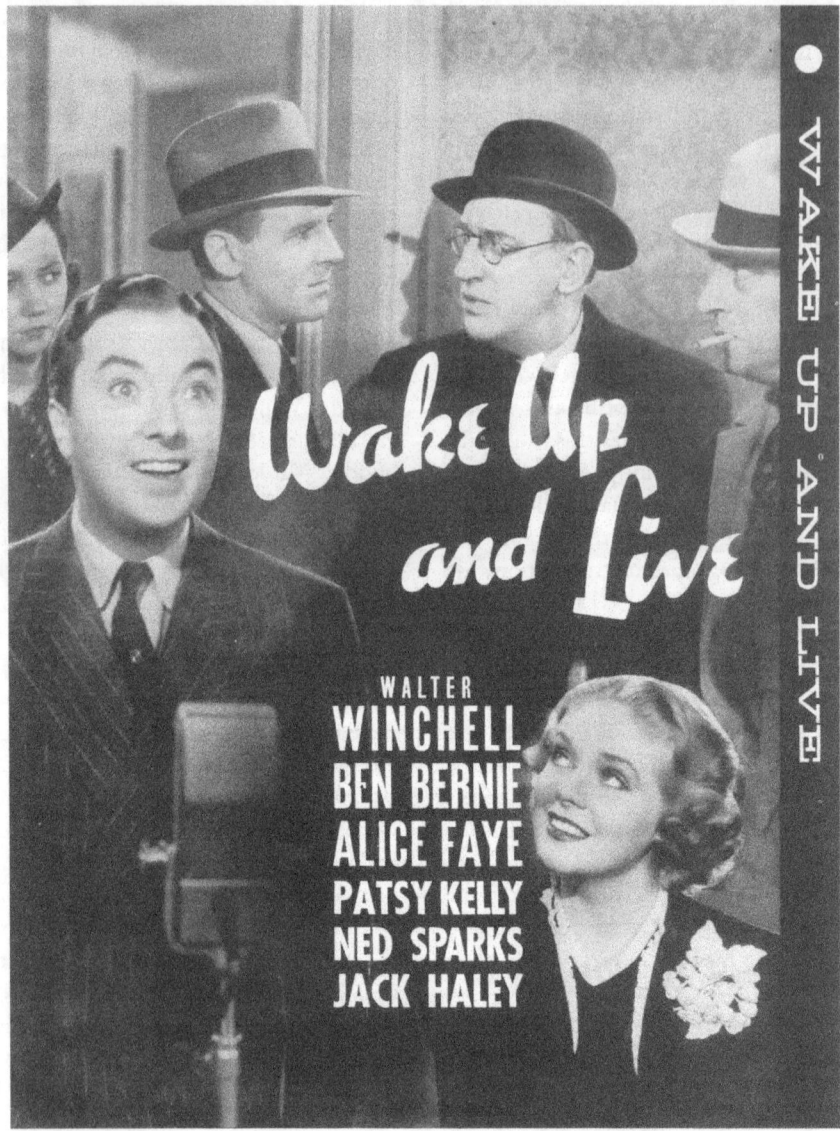

Twenty years after its theatrical release, the Winchell-Bernie vehicle *Wake Up and Live* was syndicated to local television stations. Here's the cover photograph from the TV pressbook—but pay no attention to the billing. Featured are (from top left) Patsy Kelly, Jack Haley, Walter Winchell, supporting player Walter Catlett, and Ned Sparks, with Alice Faye at bottom right ... and no Ben Bernie.

Masked Troubadour, whose character is named Eddie just as if Cantor had played the part after all (Similarly, Alice Faye is Alice and supporting player Patsy Kelly is Patsy). Haley's dulcet Troubadour tones are dubbed in by Ben Bernie's regular vocalist Buddy Clark, a "secret" that everyone who could read a newspaper knew about long before the film's April 22, 1937, release. As for Winchell and Bernie themselves, both men prove to be skilled and engaging actors, with a keen sense of comic timing and a good-sport willingness to kid themselves and their public images. As a bonus, in the final scene Winchell demonstrates that his singing voice was just as tolerable and on-key in 1937 as it had been back in his vaudeville days.

Beyond its comedy content, posh production values and sprightly songs by Mack Gordon and

Harry Revel (including Alice Faye's big hit "There's a Lull in My Life"), the reason *Wake Up and Live* retains its entertainment value today is that, for all of the inside jokes and dated byplay attending the feud between the two stars, it does not totally rely upon audience foreknowledge of the Winchell-Bernie dynamic for its full effectiveness. The 1940 Jack Benny-Fred Allen vehicle *Love Thy Neighbor* (discussed elsewhere) has a tendency to fall flat when shown to contemporary audiences unfamiliar with its radio-feud premise. Conversely, proof that *Wake Up and Live* has a strong enough foundation to stand on its own even without the presence of Walter and Ben can be heard in the February 21, 1944, *Lux Radio Theater* adaptation of the Fox film, refashioned as a showcase for singing sensation Frank Sinatra. Neither Bernie (who had died the previous year) nor Winchell appear in this version: Instead, their characters are renamed Charlie Stanton and Marty Hackett, played respectively by bandleader Bob Crosby and comic actor James Gleason. And behold, the story and dialogue are just as funny and potent as ever, capable of generating positive response even from modern-day listeners who've never heard of Walter Winchell and Ben Bernie.

Unfortunately this is not the case with Fox's follow-up Winchell-Bernie picture *Love and Hisses,* again directed by Sidney Lanfield and released December 21, 1937. So heavily does this film depend upon the audience's familiarity not only with the two stars' feud but also with the then-current welter of publicity surrounding leading lady Simone Simon that it holds about as much relevance for 21st century viewers as the Dead Sea Scrolls. The overbearingly self-referential tone of Art Arthur and Curtis Kenyon's screenplay extends to the Mack Gordon-Harry Revel songs, especially the "slanguage"-laden ditty "I Want to Be in Winchell's Column."

Love and Hisses cuts to the chase in the very first scene when Bernie tricks Winchell into paying for their lunch at Lindy's restaurant (a shameless plug for a familiar Winchell hangout in New York). To get even, Winchell uses his radio pulpit to attack a new French songbird named Eugenie who is being promoted by Bernie, calling the girl an untalented phony despite never having heard her sing. Not long afterward, Winchell makes the acquaintance of Yvette Guerin (Simone Simon), the daughter of a French nobleman. Impressed by Yvette's singing voice, Winchell offers her services to Bernie, who huffily insists he is not interested in any protégé of Winchell's—prompting W.W. to ballyhoo his new discovery over the radio. What the columnist doesn't know is that Yvette and Eugenie are both the same girl, and that Ben Bernie has stage-managed this subterfuge so that Winchell will transform Yvette into a star despite her association with Bernie. In a comedy setpiece referencing 20th Century–Fox's gargantuan publicity campaign to thrust Simon into Hollywood stardom, part of which involved pummeling the public with the fact that the actress' name was pronounced "See-MOAN See-MOAN," the heroine is persuaded by Winchell to adopt the professional moniker Yvette Yvette—which she immediately dismisses as silly. A guaranteed howler back in 1937, this bit is lucky to get a polite snicker today.

And so it goes for 82 minutes, reprising several of the ingredients that had flavored *Wake Up and Live,* including another phony kidnapping (this time with Bernie as the victim), the return of Joan Davis and the Brewster Twins, and an encore appearance by the tabernacle-like Manila Club set. Reviewing the finished product, *Film Bulletin* said, "The difference between *Love and Hisses* and its Winchell-Bernie predecessor, *Wake Up and Live,* is the difference between Alice Faye and Simone Simon as musical comedy stars. That is why *Wake Up and Live* was better. Nevertheless, the new effort is a snappy comedy that carries on the feud between the 'rivals' with good humor and plenty of action." *Love and Hisses* also gets by on the specialty turns from the Raymond Scott Quintet, who perform the pulsating "Powerhouse" (instantly recognizable to anyone who's ever seen a Warner Bros. cartoon of the 1940s), and from supporting comic Bert Lahr, who brings down the house with a baby-talk love scene. Another Lahr routine, totally ad libbed and bizarre in the extreme, was cut from the film but exhumed for the 1999 cable TV special *Hidden Hollywood II*.

Love and Hisses represented Ben Bernie's *au revoir* to the screen, and the last "dramatic" film appearance by Walter Winchell, who thereafter limited himself to guest spots and narration assignments. Both men continued to thrive on radio, keeping the fires of their faux feud stoked until the early months of World War II, when Bernie called a truce after being chastised by a female fan who was insulted that Ben would speak ill of such a great patriot as Walter. (This lady may have been the only person still standing who wasn't in on the gag.) Winchell toned down his ribbing when Bernie became seriously ill in 1942, and couldn't say enough kind things about his old sparring partner after Bernie's death from a pulmonary embolism on October 23, 1943. The many friends and professional associates who adored the generous, golden-hearted Old Maestro could at least take solace in the knowledge that Bernie left this world while he was still on top. In contrast, Walter Winchell would ultimately outlive his popularity, his power and his celebrity status, with his legions of enemies feeling more pity than scorn for the shriveled husk who passed away embittered and half-forgotten on February 20, 1972.

"Fibber McGee and Molly" (1937–1944)

Fibber McGee and Molly was a radical departure from the plethora of network comedy-variety series permeating the airwaves in the mid–1930s. Instead of headlining a proven Broadway favorite like Eddie Cantor, Jack Benny or Phil Baker, the weekly, half-hour series starred a pair of hitherto obscure vaudevillians who didn't even appear under their own names. But within a few years after its NBC debut on April 16, 1935, *Fibber McGee and Molly* was every bit as popular as any "big name" program—and its two stars were, for the first time in their lives, genuine 14-karat celebrities.

Their real names were Jim and Marian Jordan. Both were born in Peoria, Illinois, Jim in 1896 and Marian (*née* Driscoll) in 1898. They met as teenagers while singing in the same church choir, both sharing a love for performing in public. During Jim's first foray into professional singing with a touring revue, Marian stayed behind as a voice teacher. In 1918 they were married, and before long they had hit the road as a musical team. Time and again they would leave Peoria with trunks packed and hope in their hearts, and time and again they would return to Peoria, broke and dispirited.

With two children to support, the Jordans were on the verge of packing it in and getting permanent "civilian" jobs when, on a dare, they made their first radio appearance over Chicago station WIBO in 1924. Scoring a surprise hit with a six-minute medley of comic songs, they were offered a contract to appear as "The O'Henry Twins" in a musical program sponsored by the titular candy company. Other radio jobs followed, with Jim and Marian adding a variety of character voices to their repertoire. It was in 1929 that the couple met a young aspiring cartoonist named Don Quinn, then trying to crack radio as a writer. Born with a gift for absurdity and clever wordplay, Quinn contributed material to the Jordans' various radio gigs, and in 1931 all three collaborated on a daily 15-minute comedy serial for Chicago's WMAQ titled *Smackout*, which was picked up by CBS and later NBC. It was on this seminal project that the trio developed a number of sharply defined characters, notably an elderly windbag who liked to spin tall tales. While *Smackout* was still running, the Johnson's Wax company of Racine, Wisconsin, sent out a call for "unknown" performers to take over a weekly 30-minute NBC variety program. Johnson's previous experience with a "name" star, singer Tony Wons, hadn't worked out as expected, and the company had decided to cultivate a star commodity and watch it grow as the show caught on with the public (they hoped). Don Quinn came up with *Fibber McGee and Molly*, with of course Jim and Marian as the leading characters. When *Smackout* folded in August of 1935, the Jordans literally made *Fibber McGee and Molly* their life's work.

The series was forged from the Jack Benny

template of featuring a weekly comedy throughline to string the jokes together, periodically interrupted by musical numbers from a prominent orchestra (Rico Marcelli's during the first season) and including an "integrated" commercial in which the announcer—here Harlow Wilcox—traded quips with the stars. As the series was originally conceived, Fibber McGee and Molly travelled along U.S. Route 42 in their ancient roadster, having assorted misadventures at every pit stop. The stars' basic characterizations were already in place—Fibber as a garrulous spinner of exaggerated stories about his life experiences, Molly as his pragmatic, long-suffering wife—but there were still a few rough edges, notably Fibber's pugnacious attitude toward strangers and Molly's shrewish determination to burst her spouse's bubble at every opportunity. The characterizations began to mellow some five months into the series when Fibber won a house in a raffle and settled down at 79 Wistful Vista. Now each episode revolved around a minor crisis in the McGee household, usually Fibber's disastrous efforts at home repair. While Marian Jordan continued playing a number of supporting roles (most prominently a precocious little girl named Teeny, who drove Fibber crazy with her endless questions), Jim Jordan more or less limited himself to Fibber, and a pair of gifted supporting players, Isabel Randolph and Bill Thompson, were added to the cast as various residents of Wistful Vista. As the series grew in popularity, so too did the universal distribution of its catchphrases: Molly's "T'aint funny, McGee," as her husband chortled at his own bum jokes; Teeny's "Whatcha doin', mister, huh, whatcha doin'?"; and Bill Thompson's "Old Timer" responding to Fibber's dubious reminiscences by wheezing, "That's pretty good, Johnny, but that ain't the way *I* heerd it."

Also in the Jack Benny tradition, actual events in the lives of the Jordans were woven into the *Fibber McGee and Molly* scripts. The broadcast of April 26, 1937, found the McGees bidding a temporary farewell to orchestra leader Ted Weems and his vocalist Perry Como and hurriedly packing their suitcases in preparation for heading to Hollywood to appear in their first film, Paramount's *This Way Please*—and indeed, the next few months' programs featured the Jordans broadcasting from Los Angeles rather than Chicago, with the Jimmy Grier Orchestra and singer Tommy Harris spelling Weems and Como. During that period, not only did Jim and Marian Jordan appear before the cameras "in character" for the

A charming formal portrait of Fibber McGee and Molly (Jim and Marian Jordan), from the 1943 *Radio Annual.*

first time, but so did another NBC radio attraction, *The Jack Benny Program*'s Mary Livingstone. This was standard operating procedure for Paramount, who had previously inserted such airwave favorites as Burns & Allen and Joe Penner into their "all-star" musicals. *This Way Please* was more of an "all-supporting player" confection, built around one acknowledged movie star: Charles "Buddy" Rogers, "America's Boy Friend" of the early talkie era, here making his movie comeback after a year of live appearances fronting his own jazz band.

Accustomed to the relaxed and hospitable atmosphere of their radio show, Jim and Marian Jordan were no doubt unprepared for the backstage intrigue brewing on the set of *This Way Please*. In their last broadcast before relocating to L.A., they had announced that new Paramount sensation Shirley Ross would be costarring in the film with Buddy Rogers. Alas, Ms. Ross was then suffering from that dread disease which often infects overnight movie stars, Swell-Head-Itis. The actress went into full diva mode three days into production when she began working with Mary Livingstone. Convinced that Mary's part was being built up at her expense, Shirley stormed off the set—reportedly in the middle of a scene. Faced with a tight schedule and no leading lady, Paramount summoned a 20-year-old starlet recently signed to a stock studio contract: Betty Grable, who'd previously appeared in Buddy Rogers' RKO vehicle *Old Man Rhythm* (though not as his leading lady) and had just finished working with Joe Penner (q.v.) in the campus musical *Collegiate*. No great shakes as an actress at this point in her career, Grable nonetheless adequately filled the role's musical requirements, especially an energetic tap-dance routine in which the camera concentrates on her soon-to-be-famous legs. And unlike the temperamental Shirley Ross, Betty evidently got along just fine with Mary Livingstone, else she wouldn't have later co-starred with Mary's husband Jack Benny in 1939's *Man About Town*.

Whipped up by no fewer than five credited writers including silent movie queen Seena Owen, *This Way Please* is largely set in a palatial Hollywood movie theater called the Occident (a play on Grauman's Chinese), in those wonderful bygone days when first-run houses featured live entertainers and regiments of pretty usherettes. Rogers plays the Occident's star attraction, egotistical singer Brad Morgan, who has the Rudy Vallee–like habit of forcing his female "protégées" onto theater manager Crawford (Porter Hall). When Morgan demands that novice usherette Jane Morrow (Grable) be given a tryout in the theater's stage revue, the fed-up Crawford fires both Brad and Jane. But after innocent little Janie impresses Crawford in an open audition, the Occident's publicity man Inky Wells (Ned Sparks) cooks up a campaign promoting the young aspiring dancer as "The Girl Who Broke Brad Morgan's Heart," carrying this a step farther by arranging for Brad and Jane to be married on the stage of the Occident. Convinced that Jane is complicit in a cynical ploy to sell tickets, Brad intends to desert the girl at the altar and invites the press to watch her humiliation. Realizing at the last moment that he and Jane are truly in love, he whisks her away from substitute groom Stu Randall (Lee Bowman doing a "Ralph Bellamy").

If you're wondering how Fibber and Molly fit into all this, the answer is "just barely." The couple shows up early in the proceedings driving a recreational trailer with their names painted on the side, explaining to a glowering cop (played by perennial Laurel & Hardy foil James Finlayson) that they're on a motoring vacation to California. Since the cop turns out to be an old beau of Molly's, he allows them to park illegally in front of the Occident, which Molly has insisted upon entering because she wants more than anything to see Brad Morgan (but not for the reason you'd expect). Jumping to the conclusion that the McGees have driven all the way from Wistful Vista for the sole purpose of taking in Brad's stage act, Inky Wells figures that this is an excellent publicity angle and invites the couple into the manager's office, where they end up spending most of their screen time. The Fibber McGee & Molly of *This Way Please* aren't quite as relaxed and natural as in their later screen appearances, coming off more like the earlier, rough-edged versions of the characters. Both are costumed to look like rubes, with

Fibber wearing an owlish pair of spectacles and Molly in a dowdy print dress. Fibber shouts his lines in an artificially high-pitched voice, while Molly has a pronounced Irish brogue. Also, their relationship is more combative than we're accustomed to: When Molly complains that a man is winking at her, Fibber mutters, "Well, anyone can make a mistake."

Only in a brief backstage sequence do Fibber and Molly exhibit the warmth and mutual affection that we now associate with the characters. Breezing their way through some rather intricate dialogue that was obviously penned by Don Quinn (though he receives no billing), the couple fondly harks back to their honeymoon in Niagara Falls, with Molly adopting a couple of alternate voices (one of them Teeny) as she remembers the people they met along the way. But no sooner have we grown genuinely fond of this charming couple than they drop out of sight—literally, into an orchestra pit, where they remain until the picture is practically over.

Mary Livingstone, the show's other radio recruit, has a more integral role as Maxine, the niece of theater owner Crandall and erstwhile girlfriend of Inky Wells. Introduced off-camera with her familiar *Jack Benny Program* laugh, Mary recites one of the nonsensical poems that were the trademark of her radio character and then assumes her assigned place in the storyline as a wisecracking Patsy Kelly type. Just as Fibber and Molly aren't completely at ease in front of the camera, Livingstone, who was known to suffer from severe stage fright, seems extremely nervous throughout the film, rigidly planting herself in a chair for many of her scenes and tightly clutching her bonnet as if terrified to let go during her one musical number. *This Way Please* was her first and last film.

An unpretentious and very economical production, *This Way Please* contains the usual quota of musical-comedy clichés that are nonetheless transcended by the stylish direction of Robert Florey. For all of its familiar plot devices, it manages to spring a few delightful surprises, notably the casual, off-the-cuff insertions of the specialty numbers by seasoned funsters Rufe Davis, Romo Vincent and Jerry Bergen. And in anticipation of the later Crosby-Hope "Road" pictures, the film engagingly ribs its home turf Paramount with an extended "mixed-up soundtrack" spoof of the studio's recent espionage melodrama *The General Died at Dawn* (with an unbilled Akim Tamiroff repeating his role), and the hilariously inappropriate insertion of a loud and boisterous edition of the *Paramount Newsreel* during the climactic wedding.

Critical consensus for *This Way Please* was straightforward: If you like the stars, you'll like the film (*Variety* and *Box Office* did, others didn't). Neglecting to mention Fibber and Molly at all, *Independent Exhibitors Film Bulletin* predicted, "What results this will have at the box office depends solely on what exploitation possibilities can be milked from the dubious names of Buddy Rogers and Mary Livingstone." The film's novelty value, together with the force of the Paramount promotional machine, assured a respectable profit. But whether or not *This Way Please* was a critical and financial success mattered little to Jim and Marian Jordan, who couldn't have rushed into a second picture even if they wanted. On November 15, 1937, Marian abruptly left the radio series, citing serious health issues. Her absence turned out to be longer than expected, forcing Jim Jordan to go it alone for 18 months on what was now titled *Fibber McGee and Company*.

The show reverted to its original title with Marian's return on April 18, 1939. It soon became apparent that her comeback—or perhaps her long regenerative hiatus—had had a galvanizing effect on the series. The Jordans were now shorn of their old vaudeville affectations, with both actors speaking in their normal voices and the down-to-earth "folks next door" quality of their personalities shining brighter than ever. The writing became sharper and more consistent; a whole new array of topnotch supporting actors, colorful recurring characters and eminently quotable catchphrases were brought into play; the long search for a permanent orchestra leader came to an end with the signing of Billy Mills; and the very important sound-effect gag of Fibber McGee's overstocked front hall closet was introduced in 1940, almost immediately entering the realm of folklore. Their show's ratings soared to the point that Fibber and Molly spent the lion's share of the 1940s on the same lofty plane as Benny, Hope and all the other radio heavyweights.

Also during this period, *Fibber McGee and Molly* moved permanently to NBC's Hollywood studios, making it easier for the stars to commute in case another movie deal dropped in their laps. Which is just what happened in 1941, when a package deal formulated by RKO Radio Pictures and the MCA talent agency resulted in a lucrative two-picture starring contract for Jim and Marian Jordan. They'd come a long way from the O'Henry Twins.

For a more thorough analysis of *Look Who's Laughing* (1941) and *Here We Go Again* (1942), we refer you to the entry on the two films' costars Edgar Bergen and Charlie McCarthy. It can be noted here that both Marian and Jim were far more natural and self-assured before the cameras than they'd been in *This Way Please,* their characters' rapport so casual and effortless that they seem to have been acting in films for years. Gone are the artificial yokel vernacular and country-bumpkin costumes of the earlier picture. The McGees converse in the unaffected patois of middle America, Fibber has shed those stupid horn-rimmed glasses, and Molly is much more attractively outfitted and coiffed. The prickly relationship between the McGees in their first movie has mellowed into gentle tolerance for each other's foibles, particularly on the part of Molly, who unflaggingly supports and defends her husband no matter how big a fool he makes of himself. Best of all, the characters' genuine warmth and sentiment, qualities largely missing from *This Way Please,* have been restored. In *Look Who's Laughing,* Molly stops being funny for a moment to explain why she loves Fibber so much. This solid piece of thesping might have been award-worthy in a more prestigious picture.

In both of these RKO films, the team's radio writers Don Quinn and Leonard L. Levinson provided special material for Fibber and Molly, so naturally many of the best bits of business from the NBC version are transferred to the screen. Some of the more enjoyable vignettes included Fibber's brain-bending conversations with Wistful Vista's never-seen telephone operator ("Oh, is that you, Myrt? How's every little thing?"), his throwaway one-liners ("It's just like eatin' lettuce. There's nothin' to it"), and especially his rapid-fire, tongue-twisting tall tales, an aspect of his character handled rather prosaically in *This Way Please.* About to show off one of his self-made home appliances in *Look Who's Laughing,* Fibber nostalgically recalls his days at the Biggs Machine Company. "You shoulda seen the special shop old man Biggs set up for me, just to tinker around in." (Pause for effect, then the deluge.) "BIGGS' TINKER McGEE, I was known as in them days. Bigg's Tinker McGee, the brawny and brainy Bonaparte of the benzine buggy blacksmiths, busy as a beaver and bright as a beacon at boltin' bumper brackets on big bus bodies, bringin' back the bacon as the boss of the break-band, bumblebee of the brace 'n' bits and big bullfrog of the brass bicycle bell-boggers, a brilliant breezy bozo for the beginning boy to copy—but *here*'s my pride and joy, a dishwashing jalopy!"

As part of the package arrangement with RKO, the Jordans brought along a few of the radio series' best supporting players. Harold Peary had first played Fibber's bombastic neighbor Throckmorton P. Gildersleeve in September of 1939, becoming so popular that he began making film appearances as Gildersleeve in 1940. In *Look Who's Laughing,* "Gildy" is something of a comic villain, though he reforms by the final reel; and in *Here We Go Again,* his friendly-enemy relationship with Fibber reaches hitherto unscaled heights, especially during a riotous game of pool. (See the separate entry on *The Great Gildersleeve* for information on the character's own starring series.) Likewise appearing to good advantage in both films is Isabel Randolph as Wistful Vista's self-anointed social leader Mrs. Abigail Uppington. In *Here We Go Again,* "Uppy" leads a group of Girl Guides in a portentous recitation of "Hiawatha," a scene anticipating Eulalie Mackecknie Shinn's "Wa Tan Yee Girls of the Local Wigwam of Heeawatha" in the Broadway hit *The Music Man.*

Another *Fibber McGee and Molly* regular, the multifaceted Bill Thompson, was slated to recreate his role as "The Old Timer" in *Look Who's Laughing*, but RKO evidently felt that the boyish Thompson was too much the Young Timer to be convincing (something that apparently didn't bother Paramount Pictures the previous year when they cast Thompson in his familiar characterization in *Comin' Round the Mountain*). Thus, grizzled character actor George Cleveland plays a deaf-as-a-post senior citizen who is the Old Timer in everything but name, first in a fleeting bit in *Look Who's Laughing*, then in a more sizable role as the decrepit manager of a ramshackle hotel in *Here We Go Again*. Bill Thompson himself is compensated with an onscreen appearance in *Here We Go Again* as the henpecked, mush-mouthed Wallace Wimple, a character first heard on radio in 1941. Though still too young-looking for the part, Thompson's priceless vocal inflections are a surefire laugh magnet. (The actor later reprised his Wimple voice for Tex Avery's "Droopy" and Hanna-Barbera's "Touché Turtle" cartoons.) A third Bill Thompson radio character, the W.C. Fields–like Horatio K. Boomer, was never seen in films, though his most famous catchphrase is referenced in *Look Who's Laughing* when Fibber McGee comes across a "check for a short beer."

Still another *Fibber McGee and Molly* supporting player who made the transition to film was Gale Gordon, though not in his familiar radio role as the easily flustered Mayor LaTrivia. Gordon is seen in *Here We Go Again* as Molly's oft-discussed former boyfriend Otis Cadwalder, who in the film recognizes his old flame as "Molly Driscoll," an inside reference to Marian Jordan's maiden name. The scene in which Otis and Molly dance together to the bouncy rhythms of the Ray Noble Orchestra is one of the many small delights in the generally uneven *Here We Go Again*.

Finally, the radio series' announcer Harlow Wilcox, his black hair streaked with gray and his face lined with age makeup, has a couple of good scenes in *Look Who's Laughing* as the McGees' friendly neighborhood banker, who offers a heartfelt apology as he forecloses on their home. And as a bonus, *Look Who's Laughing* also features a bit of prescient casting: Seen as a member of the Wistful Vista Chamber of Commerce is Arthur Q. Bryan (aka the voice of Warner Bros.' Elmer Fudd), who in 1943 joined the radio cast as Fibber McGee's eternal nemesis Doc Gamble.

The one carryover from the radio version that doesn't play at all well on film is Fibber McGee's hopelessly cluttered hall closet. There was simply no way that the visual literalization of a bunch of boxes, brooms, old shoes, forgotten overcoats, dusty mandolins and empty Johnson's Wax bottles cascading out of that closet could ever measure up to the images conjured in the mind's eye by the radio show's team of sound-effects wizards. Perhaps this is the reason that, when *Fibber McGee and Molly* was reborn as a short-lived TV sitcom (with different actors) in 1959, the fabled closet was kept sacred—and well off camera.

Both *Look Who's Laughing* and *Here We Go Again* were fantastic moneymakers for RKO, prompting the studio to negotiate a new exclusive two-year contract with the Jordans in 1943, the year that *Fibber McGee and Molly* was the nation's highest-rated radio show. Politely but firmly taking advantage of their new clout, Jim and Marian stipulated that they not be required to share screen time with another star name of equal stature as they had with Edgar Bergen in their first two RKO films, but instead be allowed to carry their third effort by themselves. The Jordans would probably have preferred that Allan Dwan, producer-director of their earlier films for the studio, be involved in their new project, but Dwan was now contractually obligated to Edward Small Productions. Actor-turned-scriptwriter Howard Estabrook, whose writing credits included the MGM "home-front" drama *The Human Comedy,* assumed producing duties for the new film, sharing script responsibilities with old reliable Don Quinn. Titled *Heavenly Days* after one of Molly's many radio catchphrases, the film was to have been directed by comedy specialist Richard Wallace; when Wallace accepted an assignment at Columbia he was replaced by Ray Enright. Ultimately Enright also proved unavailable, so when filming began in December 1943 it was Howard Estabrook who was calling the shots for his first credited directorial assignment since 1916.

The names "Jim and Marian Jordan" never appear on-screen in *Heavenly Days*: They are billed only as Fibber McGee and Molly, a precedent establish in *Here We Go Again*. This was at the Jordans' insistence. No one was more aware than Jim and Marian that, as far as the public was concerned, they *were* Fibber and Molly and not just a pair of play-acting entertainers. The team signed all their fan mail and autographs "in character," made guest appearances exclusively as the McGees, and even withdrew themselves from consideration for a star on the Hollywood Walk of Fame when the nominating committee refused to use "Fibber McGee and Molly" as their designation, arguing that it was against committee policy to award stars to fictional characters. The team's reaction was a flustered, "Well, who the hell has ever heard of Jim and Marian Jordan?," though they could just as easily have challenged the decision by noting that 90 percent of Hollywood's luminaries were using professional aliases: That star for "Robert Taylor" on the Walk of Fame doesn't say "Spangler Arlington Brugh," does it now?

But back to *Heavenly Days*. In contrast with the grab-bag storylines in their initial RKO starrers, the team had an actual coherent plot to work with this time. Invited to Washington DC by Molly's wealthy cousin Ettie Clark (Frieda Inescort), the McGees aren't entirely sure why, though Fibber is convinced that he's on the ground floor of a top secret project (now he's fibbing to *himself*!). En route to the nation's capital, a running gag is established wherein Fibber insists that he could never be labeled as an "Average Man" because he's well above average—an attitude shared by every other "Average Man" he comes across. The McGees' chance encounter with famous pollster Dr. George Gallup (played not by the real Gallup but by Don Douglas) leads to a nationwide poll to find the one person who perfectly fits the designation "Mr. Average Man." Once in Washington, Fibber and Molly are briefly placed in charge of a group of war orphans (each child conveniently representing a different country) by Senator Bagby (Eugene Pallette), who gives the McGees a pass to the Senate gallery. Having seen firsthand the tragic consequences of a world where democracy has been crushed under the heel of dictatorship, Fibber marches into the gallery and makes a patriotic speech about the responsibility of every citizen to cast a vote at election time, but since his outburst is utterly against protocol he is unceremoniously escorted out, infuriating Bagby and embarrassing Cousin Effie's politically ambitious husband Alvin (Charles Trowbridge) in one fell swoop. Though Molly is proud of Fibber, he feels he has made a jackass of himself and returns to Wistful Vista in defeat. But a pair of clever newspaper reporters (Barbara Hale and Gordon Oliver) have picked up on Fibber's tirade and turn him into a national hero for raising the public's awareness of their fundamental civic duties. Upon returning home, Fibber is met by Dr. Gallup, who hands McGee an award for being unanimously chosen as—do we have to say it?—"Mr. Average Man."

If none of this seems terribly funny, that's because it isn't. *Heavenly Days* is little more than a 71-minute civics lesson, the sort of stuff that the Disney cartoons used to handle in seven minutes flat, and in Technicolor. Most wartime propaganda films are inherently dated, but the best of them—Disney's *Victory Through Air Power*, Capra's *Why We Fight* series—have the saving grace of solid entertainment values. This cannot be said of *Heavenly Days*, in which the "Get Out the Vote" and "Political Responsibility Is a Two-Way Street" messages are drilled into the viewer's brain with a ball-peen hammer. Outside of Fibber McGee & Molly, all the characters are agit-prop stereotypes: Pallette as the fatuous liberal who'd rather talk than act, Trowbridge as the stuffy conservative who is more concerned with his image than the Greater Good, Raymond Walburn as the small-town Babbitt who gets away with isolationism and war profiteering because good people do nothing, and so it goes. Even the film's throwaway jokes, normally highlights in the Fibber McGee and Molly pictures, are depressingly heavy-handed. Observing Washington's rows of Japanese cherry blossoms, Fibber quips, "When do they bloom? Every December 7th?" The film hits rock bottom when the central-casting war orphans show up. Such treacly lines as "How much I feel my heart full of joy" and "Why is war?" sound even more maudlin when recited in patently phony foreign accents. Mercifully, Molly closes this sequence by singing a lullaby in her "Teeny" voice, which might have been more effective had not the audience been put to sleep long before the youngsters.

There are some good moments in *Heavenly Days,* but you may have to sand-blast for them. A scene with the singing group The King's Men (the only *Fibber McGee and Molly* regulars to appear in the film outside of the stars), in which train passenger Fibber joins a quartet of lonely G.I.s in a soulful rendition of the World War I–era ballad "I'm Always Chasing Rainbows," is sweetly handled, retaining much of the same emotional impact it had on wartime audiences. Also of merit are the film's occasional forays into fantasy. In the opening scene Fibber imagines a conversation with his ghostly lookalike, the fife player from the "Spirit of '76," who arouses both his patriotism and ours. A later Gilbert & Sullivan–style dream sequence finds Fibber floating into the Senate chamber on a cloud, warning the assemblage that they must cast off the shackles of indifference to those who would undermine the American Way— only to be suppressed by Raymond Walburn, who binds Fibber with a symbolic ball and chain. It's blatant, but it works.

Two months before its release, *Heavenly Days* rather incredibly found itself at the center of a controversy because of a new piece of legislation. Drafted by Senator Robert A. Taft, the Soldier Voting Act allowed American military personnel overseas to cast ballots in national elections for the first time in history. At the same time, the Act denied the military access to any publications or movies that might be construed as influencing an election's outcome. Before long, a list of banned films was released to the public. Topping the tally was the expensive biopic *Wilson,* regarded by many as a commercial for the Democratic party. The next title on the list was poor little *Heavenly Days*—and all because of that dream sequence in which Fibber exhorts his fellow citizens to go out and vote. No specific political party is mentioned in the film, but the Soldier Voting Act was vague enough to render *Heavenly Days* "possibly objectionable." A public-relations nightmare ensued, and within three days several "cautiously worded" official statements were in circulation, variously claiming that no such ban was yet in effect, no such ban had ever been considered, and even if there *was* a ban there wouldn't be soon. Some historians have suggested that the whole affair was blown out of proportion by enemies of Taft, while others cite the *Heavenly Days* brouhaha as yet another example of blind bureaucracy and political doublespeak run amok. Whatever the case, Walter Winchell was still reporting the "military ban" story as fact when the film was released in October 1944.

No one can say for sure how many of our boys in uniform ultimately got to see *Heavenly Days,* but we can venture a rough guess as to how many civilians enjoyed the picture: not many. Unlike its two moneyspinning predecessors, the film posted a loss of $205,000. The two-year contract between RKO and the Jordans was quietly nullified and the team returned to what they did best and where they felt most welcome. Except for an amusing appearance in the 1945 short subject *All-Star Bond Rally,* produced at 20th Century–Fox on behalf of the U.S. Department of the Treasury (it has been said that the Jordans raised more money for the War effort than even Bob Hope), Fibber McGee and Molly would stuff their movie career into the front hall closet along with all the rest of their memorabilia. The NBC radio series continued going strong until 1955; two years later the team returned to record a batch of four-minute comedy segments for their old network's weekend radio potpourri *Monitor,* an arrangement that ended with Marian Jordan's death in 1961. Outliving Marian by 27 years, Jim Jordan settled into happy and wealthy retirement with his second wife Gretchen Stewart, briefly re-emerging to make a guest appearance on the TV sitcom *Chico and the Man* and to provide the voice of the befuddled albatross Orville in the 1977 Disney animated feature *The Rescuers.*

"The Shadow" (1937–1946, 1994)

The Shadow, mysterious character who aids the forces of law and order, is in reality Lamont Cranston, wealthy young man about town. Years ago in the Orient, Cranston learned a strange and mysterious secret: the hypnotic power to cloud men's minds so they cannot see him. Cranston's friend and companion, the lovely Margot Lane, is the only person who knows to whom the voice of the invisible Shadow belongs.

With variations, this was the introduction heard throughout the 1940s on the classic radio melodrama *The Shadow*. And it is entirely accurate—within limits. The full history of *The Shadow* as a literary, radio and motion picture property is a wee bit more complex—and lest it become a book in itself within these pages, we will touch upon the highlights while advising the reader to scare up a copy of the excellent and very thorough *The Shadow Scrapbook* (Harcourt, Brace Jovanovich, 1979).

Briefly: In 1930, the prolific publishing firm Street & Smith wanted to dip their toes into that there newfangled radio machine in hopes of boosting their print circulation. The company decided to unveil a weekly dramatic anthology culled from its own *Detective Story Magazine*. Beginning on July 31, 1930, the CBS network's *Detective Story Hour* (actually a half-hour) showcased stories that were either appearing in the latest issue of the same-named magazine, or were slated to appear soon. Radio writer Harry Engman Charlot added the character of a mysterious narrator, originally played by James LeCurto and known only as the Shadow. Never participating in the story, the Shadow merely provided a running commentary in the traditional "all-seeing host" manner. Before long, listeners were besieging local newsstands with requests—not for *Detective Story Magazine*, but for "that magazine about the Shadow." Since Street & Smith was already planning a contest in which their readers would be invited to submit a physical description of the Shadow, it was no quantum leap to begin publication of a quarterly (and later bi-weekly) *Shadow* magazine, with a novel-length "Shadow" tale in each issue, beginning in April 1931.

The introductory story "The Living Shadow" was the handiwork of Walter B. Gibson (1897–1985), a pulp writer of vast and varied experience. Formerly a stage magician who had ghosted magazine articles for such prominent prestidigitators as Houdini and Blackstone, Gibson reveled in the art of illusion and misdirection. His version of the Shadow was so named because of the character's uncanny, almost mystical ability to move around unobtrusively in the shadows and show up just when he was needed. No actual invisibility was involved at this early juncture, though as an accomplished hypnotist the Shadow probably could have clouded men's minds had he so desired.

Gibson loved to play around with the vagaries of identity, beginning with own his *nom de plume* Maxwell Grant, which he used for all his "Shadow" stories. The Shadow himself was given the alter ego of wealthy playboy Lamont Cranston early on—but in Gibson-Grant's third published story "The Shadow Laughs," it turned out the character wasn't Lamont Cranston at all, but instead a crimefighting adventurer who just happened to *look* like Cranston. In subsequent stories the Shadow assumed several identities and disguises, finally revealing himself to be a famous aviator named Kent Allard. But since his favorite guise was Lamont Cranston, the reading public at large accepted Allard in that role—as did the writers of the *Shadow* radio series, who pegged the character's true identity as Lamont Cranston and no one else from 1937 onward.

That series wasn't called *The Shadow* during its first few seasons on the air, instead going by such "aliases" as *Blue Coal Radio Revue* (in deference to its longtime anthracite sponsor) and *Love Story Dramas*. While the magazine version of the Shadow had become very proactive, headquartered in a gadget-filled mansion and maintaining a large retinue of loyal lieutenants to assist him in his war against crime, during the early 1930s the radio Shadow remained exclusively a narrator, commenting on the action and providing a "crime does not pay" coda without participating in the story or its outcome. This "disengaged observer" status was carried over to the first film adaptation of the character in a group of six two-reelers produced by Universal Pictures and released under the blanket title *Shadow Detective Series*. Based on stories published in *Detective Story Magazine*, the Universal shorts were for many years considered lost, but recently three have been located and released on DVD, including the series debut *A Burglar to the Rescue* (1931). Though not technically invisible, the title character is an essentially unseen presence, depicted only as a shadow projected on a blank wall; and as on radio, he narrates but never intervenes. (This formula was later adopted for Columbia's *Whistler* film series, likewise inspired by a radio program.) The voice of the Shadow in these seminal two-reelers is provided by Frank Readick, who had succeeded James LeCurto in the radio version.

A Burglar to the Rescue is a tidy "hoist on his own petard" yarn about an embezzling banker (Thurston Hall) who outsmarts himself when he tries to buy off a disgruntled ex-employee (Frank Shannon). The next available "Shadow" entry *The House of Mystery* (1931) involves the apparent murder of a gold-digger (Geneva Mitchell) and the futile efforts by an anxious father (James Durkin) to protect his errant son (Bernard Stone). The last known surviving short, *The Circus Show-Up* (1932), is the most fascinating of the bunch thanks to an offbeat bit of casting: Sally Blane stars as a circus employee accused of murdering a trapeze artist—played by Blane's real-life sister Polly Ann Young. The search goes on for the three missing films in the *Shadow Detective Series: Trapped* (1931), *Sealed Lips* (1931) and *The Red Scare* (1932).

If you're wondering why this entry has been placed chronologically in 1937 rather than the 1931–32 timeframe of Universal shorts, it's because the "true" radio Shadow did not show up either on the air or onscreen until that year. Dissatisfied with the radio character's passive nature, Street & Smith urged sponsor Blue Coal to drop the anthology format and allow the Shadow to actively participate in the stories; when Blue Coal refused, Street & Smith pulled the plug on the series effective March 27, 1935. It would be two years before the publisher and the sponsor forged an agreement to depict the radio character in the same manner as the print version. Switching networks from CBS to Mutual, the "new" *Shadow* was unveiled on September 26, 1937, with 22-year-old Orson Welles as radio's first Lamont Cranston.

Carried over from the earlier radio incarnations was the Shadow's opening query "Who knows what evil lurks in the hearts of men? *The Shadow knows!*"—followed by a sinister, drawn-out laugh. The magazine version provided the series' secondary characters Commissioner Weston and Inspector Cardona, but with the exception of the versatile Harry Vincent in the first Mutual episode "The Death House Rescue" and garrulous cab driver Moe "Shrevvy" Shrevnitz throughout the rest of the series, none of the Shadow's other faithful assistants—reporter Clyde Burke, secret service agent Vic Marquette, wireless operator Burbank, underworld contact Cliff Marsland et al.—made the cut in the radio version. In their place was Lamont Cranston's "constant friend and aide," the lovely Margot (pronounced Margo) Lane, adding a dash of glamor and romance to the proceedings. (The first actress to play Margot was Orson Welles' Mercury Theater colleague Agnes Moorehead.) Obligingly, Walter B. Gibson began including Margot in the magazine stories.

As noted by comic book historian Ron Goulart, prior to the character's radio resurrection in 1937 the Shadow of the pulps "never appeared before the reader undisguised ... he hung out in dark and shadowy places and behaved as a first-class mystery man, but never, not once, did he exhibit the slightest tendency to become invisible." The new Mutual radio version introduced his hypnotic powers of invisibility, a device conveyed over the air by having Cranston's voice filtered whenever he morphed into the Shadow. Anthony Tollin, contributing editor of *The Shadow Scrapbook*, applauded this new character dimension: "How could there be a more perfect radio hero than an invisible man, as ethereal as the airwaves themselves?" During the Orson Welles era, the Shadow could read minds as well as cloud them, and in the manner of Chandu the Magician (q.v.) he was able to hypnotize people who were miles away. These powers would gradually diminish as the character became less omnipotent and more human.

While the Mutual radio revival was being prepared, the Shadow made his feature film debut in *The Shadow Strikes,* produced by independent Colony Pictures and released by Grand National on October 29, 1937. The 62-minute film was advertised as the "return" of silent-movie matinee idol Rod La Rocque, though in fact he'd been making pictures all through the talkie era. Four films were planned for the new Colony series (described by publicists as "Americanized Charlie Chan yarns"), all to be adapted by Al Martin from stories that had appeared in *The Shadow Magazine. The Shadow Strikes* was inspired by Walter Gibson-Maxwell Grant's "The Ghost of the Manor," first published on June 15, 1933, with most of the character names retained.

The "Kent Allard" intrigue is disposed of and the hero is firmly identified as Lamont Cranston, though his name is misspelled "Granston" in the opening cast list. As before, Cranston is a wealthy amateur sleuth, with the newly minted motivation of avenging his father's murder. In line with Cranston's habit of assuming different identities whenever the need arises, he spends most of the picture posing as a lawyer named Randall, initially to avoid arrest and later to allow him a free hand to investigate the murder of one of Randall's clients. Despite assurances in *The Shadow Magazine* that the character's many assistants would make their film bow in *The Shadow Strikes,* none of the literary Shadow's agents appear in the film, wherein Cranston is aided by a heretofore unmentioned valet named Hendricks (Norman Ainsley). And since the film was in pre-production before the revised radio program, there is no Margot Lane: Instead, the heroine is Marcia Delthern (Lynn Anders), the murder victim's niece.

Further indication that *The Shadow Strikes* was inspired by the "Famous Shadow Stories" referenced in the ad posters and not by the still-in-transition radio program is the fact that invisibility plays no part whatsoever in the picture. Emulating the cover art displayed in *The Shadow Magazine,* Cranston's disguise consists of a trenchcoat, a wide-brimmed hat and a face-obscuring muffler. He does indeed seem to emerge from the shadows to dispense justice, but remains in full view of the audience when doing so and visible to everyone onscreen. He doesn't even bother to disguise his voice, making it extremely difficult to accept that no one connects the Shadow with Cranston until the final reel.

Directed by Lynn Shores with all the mobility of a fire hydrant in winter, *The Shadow Strikes* is a molasses-slow effort dragged down further by La Rocque's lethargic performance. *Variety* dissed the picture as "marred by stupid dialog, feeble acting, misdirection and dangling continuity." But thanks to the popularity of the radio show, the film performed well in neighborhood houses and small towns, enabling Colony–Grand National to continue their proposed series with the April 22, 1938, release *International Crime* (working titles: *The Shadow Speaks, The Shadow Murder Case*). The source for this 64-minute effort was "Foxhound," written by Ted Tinsley for the January 15, 1937, edition of *The Shadow Magazine.* Apparently in response to reader demand, several of the Shadow's pulp-novel supporting players are in attendance, with Thomas Jackson as Commissioner Weston, Lou Hearn as hackie Moe Shrevnitz, and future *Juke Box Jury* host Peter Potter (here billed as William Moore) as moviedom's first—and last—incarnation of newshound Clyde Burke. The influence of the Mutual radio version is finally felt on screen, with Cranston (La Rocque again) reconfigured as a radio crime reporter, assisted by his sponsor's niece Miss Lane (Astrid Allwyn), whose first name is Phoebe rather than Margot—and who is also a birdbrain, in marked contrast to her radio counterpart. Despite the heaviness of its plotline involving enemy spies, as directed by comedy specialist Charles Lamont *International Crime* is played as much for laughs as for thrills. Enlivened by this tongue-in-cheek approach, La Rocque delivers a jauntier and more spirited performance here than in *The Shadow Strikes,* gently mocking his character—who *never* appears in disguise and calls himself the Shadow only during his broadcasts—with such self-referential lines as "The Shadow doesn't know." With this is mind, one need hardly add that there is no invisibility or hypnotism present in *International Crime.*

The decline and fall of Grand National during the 1938-39 movie season brought an end to the *Shadow* film series, though the radio program remained healthy into the 1940s. Orson Welles and Agnes Moorehead were respectively succeeded by Bill Johnstone and Marjorie Anderson as Lamont and Margot, who in turn were replaced by Brett Morrison and Grace Matthews, the actors who held down the roles for the longest period. The grimness of the earliest Mutual episodes—full of demented scientists and Napoleonic gangsters committing mass murder with booby-trapped light bulbs, poisoned reservoirs, lethal fog machines and other ingenious methods of destruction—gradually gave way to a lighter approach, with Lamont and Margot exchanging witty banter after narrowly escaping from their latest harrowing adventure. There was still madness and mayhem aplenty on radio's *Shadow,* but the seriousness and sobriety of the magazine version was not always to be heard over the air. Whether or not Walter B. Gibson approved of this approach, it is known that he considered the next film version of the property, the 15-chapter Columbia serial *The Shadow* (1940), to be the best of all the cinematic adaptations. Adapted from Gibson's "The Lone Tiger" (published February 15, 1939), the serial was an unabashed return to the *sturm und drang* of the pulp novels, complete with a death ray–wielding criminal mastermind known as the Black Tiger.

Among the reasons Gibson enjoyed the serial was that he regarded Victor Jory's dual portrayal of Lamont Cranston and the Shadow to be the most faithful screen interpretation of either character. Looking like a *Shadow Magazine* cover come to life, the saturnine Jory possesses a rich theatrical voice ideally suited to both of his identities—not to mention a demonic laugh that could curdle one's blood. In fine "Maxwell Grant" tradition, the serial's Cranston occasionally dons the alternate disguise of wily Oriental Lin Chang, the better to gather information in those less fashionable parts of town where a wealthy socialite would be too conspicuous. And in keeping with Columbia's ad campaign declamation that *The Shadow* was "right out of the airwaves and magazine stories," the serial's secondary characters were lifted from both the print and the radio adaptations: Commissioner Weston (Frank LaRue), Inspector Cardona (Edward Peil Sr.), and, for the first time in films, Margot Lane (played along more brittle lines than radio's Margot by Veda Ann Borg). As a bonus, the Shadow's oldest and most trusted assistant Harry Vincent makes his one and only screen appearance, played by Roger Moore (no, not *that* Roger Moore). For the purposes of the storyline, Vincent is not only Cranston's right hand man but also his chauffeur, eliminating the need for Moe "Shrevvy" Shrevnitz.

Yet again, invisibility is not among the screen Shadow's talents, forcing Cranston to don a mask whenever taking up his crimefighting guise. This didn't prevent the serial's *villain* from becoming invisible at various moments to conceal his identity from both the authorities and his own henchmen. That the mysterious Black Tiger turns out in the last episode to be a member of the same Citizen's Committee that has demanded the scoundrel's capture for the past fourteen weeks is a typical chapter play device, as is having the Black Tiger's voice dubbed by Richard Cramer, an actor not otherwise in the serial. Perhaps out of respect for the source material, James W. Horne does not direct *The Shadow* in the same derisive, self-satirical manner as his other Columbia serials, and the results are most satisfactory. This viewer's only complaint is that the *film noir* ambience of the radio *Shadow* is missing from the serial, where most of the action takes place in broad daylight.

The same year that Columbia's *Shadow* was released theatrically, a comic book and newspaper strip version of the property appeared, both drawn by Vernon Greene—and both, like the previous movie adaptations, keeping the Shadow in plain sight at all times. Eventually the various literary versions of the character incorporated his gift for making himself invisible, proof positive of the radio version's ever-growing popularity. (In 1943 the program boasted a 39 percent share of the crucial New York audience.)

We next saw the Shadow onscreen courtesy of Monogram Pictures. Filmed between 1945 and 1946, Monogram's three *Shadow* features starred Kane Richmond as Lamont Cranston and Barbara Reed as Margot Lane, and all three were produced by Joseph Kaufman and written by George Callahan. None of the pictures was based on an original pulp magazine story, but instead more closely resembled the gimmicky whodunnits Callahan had been churning out for Monogram's *Charlie Chan* series. The writer also drew inspiration from Paramount's *Bulldog Drummond* films by making a running gag out of the delayed marriage of Lamont and Margot (who never even broached the subject of matrimony on radio or in print).

A casual viewing of the three Monogram efforts—*The Shadow Returns* (1945), *Behind the Mask* (1946) and *The Missing Lady* (1946)—might lead the viewer to conclude that at long last, the character's power of invisibility has been brought into play. Certainly it appears that whenever Cranston becomes the Shadow, the people around him are unable to see him. Directors Phil Rosen (*The Shadow Returns*), Phil Karlson (*Behind the Mask*) and Joseph Kaufman (*The Missing Lady*) enhance the illusion with extended scenes in which the other actors directly address the camera while the Shadow is represented by an off-screen voice; and on some occasions, the only glimpse the audience gets of the character is a dark silhouette. But a closer examination reveals that the films tend to tap-dance around the issue of invisibility, depicting the character as a fully visible cloaked-and-masked figure in many scenes and never showing him actually dematerializing. One is reminded of all those cinematic ghost stories in which *we* can see the spirits but the onscreen characters can't. Was this the effect that Monogram was aiming for—or can it be that all the supporting characters in the *Shadow* movies suffered from myopia and night-blindness?

Admirably enacted by serial veteran Kane Richmond, the Monogram version of Cranston is a professional rather than amateur criminologist, who in the opening entry *The Shadow Returns* has given up crimefighting at the request of fiancée Margot and settled down to a mundane job as an attorney—but not for long, of course. Commissioner Weston (Pierre Watkin in all three films)

Poster art for Monogram's *The Shadow Returns* (1945).

has somehow become Lamont's uncle, while gabby cabbie Shrevvie (Tom Dugan in the first film, George Chandler thereafter) has been dumbed down from a loyal legman to the 20th century equivalent of a comical western sidekick. "Dumb" is also the operative word for Inspector Cardona (Joseph Crehan in *The Shadow Returns* and *Behind the Mask,* James Flavin in *The Missing Lady*), who is forever rejecting vital clues out of hand or overlooking them entirely—a far cry from the intelligent and efficient ace detective of the pulps. But both Shrevvie and Cardona are Rhodes scholars compared to Monogram's Margot Lane. As (over)played by Barbara Reed, Margot is not only stupid but also strident, dangerously impulsive and childishly petulant, eternally bollixing up Lamont's investigations with her indiscreet verbal outbursts, bumbling "assistance" and unfounded jealousies. The character reaches heretofore unscaled heights of obnoxiousness in *Behind the Mask,* her moronic behavior matched only by Shrevvie's dumb-blonde girlfriend Jennie (Dorothea Kent). At the end of the picture, Lamont and Shrevvie settle with their respective sweeties by turning them over their knees and administering a spanking (you could get away with that in 1946).

Despite too much emphasis on comedy of this nature, the Monogram *Shadow*s are entertaining, compact little mystery melodramas. *The Shadow Returns* features a killer who uses a bullwhip to yank his victims off a high terrace to their doom. *Behind the Mask* involves a blackmailing reporter who is bumped off by someone posing as the Shadow, forcing our hero to keep one step ahead of the police while piecing the clues together. (Don't look for the "signature" of cult director Phil Karlson in this one; much of the film was helmed by William Beaudine while Karlson was laid low with ptomaine poisoning.) And *The Missing Lady* concerns a valuable statuette which becomes the key to solving the murder of an art dealer. Because it was directed by series producer Joseph Kaufman, an avowed devotee of the Shadow who treated the character with the respect due him, *The Missing Lady* might well have been the best of the three films were it not for the ramped-up interference of the ever-annoying Margot Lane.

After the cessation of the Monogram series, *The Shadow* gradually faded from public view, with *The Shadow Magazine* publishing its last issue in the summer of 1949 and the comic-book version following suit the same year. (The newspaper strip had long since folded.) The collapse of the anthracite industry in the postwar era lost the radio *Shadow* its longtime sponsor Blue Coal, but the series continued to run with other advertisers, becoming a sustaining program during its final season; the terminal episode, "Murder by the Sea," aired December 26, 1954.

Earlier that year an attempt was made to transfer *The Shadow* to television. Meridian Productions, then busy with the CBS anthology *Schlitz Playhouse of Stars,* assembled a 30-minute *Shadow* pilot starring British actor Tom Helmore as Lamont Cranston (now identified as a psychiatrist) and Paula Raymond as Margot Lane. Written by Pete Barry and directed by Charles Haas, the pilot episode "The Case of the Cotton Kimono" represents the first time that Lamont Cranston's hypnosis-induced disappearing act was shown on film. As Cranston changes into the Shadow, we see a superimposed flash of light, then hear a disembodied voice. Though a clever and well-handled effect, one has trouble imagining it holding up for a full 39-week series. Too, Helmore's "Shadow laugh" is completely bereft of menace, sounding more like Bozo the Clown. While the *Shadow* pilot didn't sell, a good-quality print is currently available in several DVD collections.

Another stab at launching a *Shadow* TV series occurred in 1958. Produced and co-directed by legendary cinematographer James Wong Howe, the 57-minute pilot was filmed on location in New Orleans, and as a result fairly oozes with atmosphere, intrigue and near-nonstop Dixieland jazz. Richard Derr stars as Lamont Cranston, who is brought into the story when his musician friend is murdered just after delivering an ominously abrupt message. While investigating his friend's death, Cranston becomes entangled in a South American revolution. Though there are two leading ladies—one of them a nightclub owner played by Helen Westcott, who was evidently slated to be a regular on the new *Shadow* series—neither of them is Margot Lane. Cranston's "constant friend and companion" for this excursion is his spiritual mentor Jogendra, played by Marc Daniels. The Zen-like Jogendra has instructed Lamont in the finer points of mesmerism and mind control, including the capability of transmitting telepathic warnings from great distances. The dialogue between Cranston and Jogendra is rife with metaphors and double meanings—and this, coupled with Jogendra's bemused reaction whenever Lamont brings up the topic of women, ever so discreetly suggests that the relationship between the two men goes way beyond Teacher and Student.

As in the 1954 *Shadow* pilot, the 1958 film matter-of-factly visualizes Cranston's ability to vanish from sight at will. The special effects are generally unremarkable—a dissolve, a shadow without a body, etc.—but on two occasions Lamont's dematerialization is accomplished with a convincingly animated "fog" effect. There are a few other stylish directorial touches here and there, notably a car chase through one of New Orleans' cemeteries; but for the most part this unsold *Shadow* pilot never quite rises above its cheapness, which must have been all the more glaring when in late 1958 the film was released theatrically by Republic as *The Invisible Avenger*.

In 1962 *Invisible Avenger* was reissued as *Bourbon Street Shadows,* with new "adult" footage added. This was most likely in response to a general renewal of interest in the Shadow, spearheaded by radio packager Charles B. Michelson's decision to syndicate 52 episodes of the original radio series (harvested from the period between 1938 and 1948) to over 100 local stations throughout the country. Though several of the transcriptions were of substandard quality, the *Shadow* revival was a great success, with the program still playing nationally well into the next decade. Also, many of Walter B. Gibson's vintage Shadow novels were reprinted in paperback form, with several new titles added to the manifest written by Gibson himself and by Dennis Lynch using Gibson's old pen name Maxwell Grant.

In 1975, a third *Shadow* TV pilot was announced in the trades, though it never got past the planning stage. However, the property was still attractive enough in 1982 for producer Martin Bregman to purchase the motion picture rights. Nothing much happened until 1987, when director Sam Raimi evinced interest in directing a *Shadow* feature film, with English actor Ben Cross (*Chariots of Fire*) as Lamont Cranston. When these plans fell through, Raimi elected to create his own masked superhero character, and that's how *Darkman* was born. Then in 1990 screenwriter David Koepp (*Jurassic Park, Mission: Impossible*), a lifelong fan of radio's *Shadow,* was hired to write a new draft for Bregman's project, with the action taking place in the late 1930s. Doing his homework, Koepp cherry-picked elements from all previous print, film and broadcast versions of the Shadow, adroitly weaving the character's celebrated "Who knows what evil lurks ..." intro and "The weed of crime bears bitter fruit" outro into the dialogue and including a number of Walter Gibson–created characters who hadn't seen the light of day for decades.

Resurrected from the pulps was the screenplay's principal villain Shiwan Khan, last surviving descendant of Genghis Khan, who desires to rule the world through force, violence and black magic. Like his literary counterpart, Shiwan Khan's formidability as an adversary is due to his mastery of hypnotic and mystical powers as great as Cranston's. On the side of the hero are old reliable Moe "Shrevvy" Shrevnitz and another long-forgotten pulp character, Chinese scientist Dr. Roy Tam, who appropriates the backstory of Harry Vincent (not in the film) when the Shadow rescues him from a watery grave. In place of Police Commissioner Weston is oafish Commissioner Wainwright Barth, who in the pulps had indeed briefly succeeded Weston and was every bit the incompetent dolt portrayed in the film. And in a likely homage to the 1946 Monogram film *The Shadow Returns,* Commissioner Barth happens to be Cranston's uncle.

Lifted from the radio version is heroine Margot Lane, here the daughter of an altruistic scientist whom Shiwan Khan has hypnotized for the purpose of creating a "beryllium sphere," pre–Hiroshima code for an atomic bomb. Also taken from radio is the Shadow's own backstory, as articulated in the October 24, 1937, episode "The Temple Bells of Neban." On this broadcast, Cranston reveals to Margot, "Years ago in India, a yogi priest, keeper of the Cobras at Delhi, taught me the ancient mysteries. He taught me the mesmeric trick that the underworld calls invisibility." Koepp's screenplay adds a new twist to the old story by introducing the good guy as a *bad* guy: homicidal drug lord Ying Ko, "the butcher of Llhasa." After cutting a murderous swath through Tibet, Ying Ko is abducted by beneficent wise man Tulku, who over a period of years rechannels the villain into the hero that we know and love, instructing the ex-baddie in those "ancient mysteries" and enabling him to become invisible and to transmit telepathic messages. Before sending him back to the outer world, Tulku tells the reformed Ying Ko, "You know what evil lurks in the hearts of men, for you have seen that evil in your own heart."

At this point Koepp references the Kent Allard-Lamont Cranston confusion by revealing that Ying Ko's subsequent guise as dilettante detective Lamont Cranston isn't really a guise since he's been Lamont Cranston all along—and that Ying Ko was the alias. Relocating to "that most wretched lair of villainy we know as New York City," Cranston poses as an indolent playboy by day and assumes the identity of the invisible Shadow by night to thwart all sorts of illegality, with no one aware of his own criminal past—no one, that is, except Shiwan Khan, himself a former pupil of Tulku, who has murdered the ancient yogi and gone over to the Dark Side.

The ongoing success of Warner Bros.' *Batman* movie franchise in the early 1990s accelerated Universal Studios' determination to get *The Shadow* into production, hoping not only to precipitate a series of profitable sequels but also to cash in with ancillary merchandising campaigns. The latter motivation was made obvious by the film's excess emphasis on Moe Shrevnitz' tricked-up taxicab, which looks and functions more like a tank, and especially a peculiar weapon called the Phurba, a triple-edged dagger with a mind of its own (and also a voice, supplied by Frank Welker). The Phurba certainly would have made a swell plaything, though one cannot imagine any child being allowed to bring a toy dagger to show-and-tell.

Released for the summer-blockbuster trade in 1994, *The Shadow* is visually beyond praise, a testament to the talents of cinematographer Steven H. Burum, art directors Jack Johnson, Dan Olexiewicz and Steven Wolff, production designer Joseph C. Nemec III, and ten different special effects shops including Industrial Light and Magic. The huge Manhattan exterior set, taking up five Universal soundstages, is a masterful blend of reality and nostalgia, especially the affectionate recreation of the fabled "living billboards" created in the 1930s and 1940s by Douglas Leigh. The Shadow's invisibility is marvelously conveyed via swirling anthropomorphic vapors, allowing us to see and not see the character all at once. And certain individual effects are dazzling, notably the sudden materialization of a towering downtown hotel which Shiwan Khan has rendered invisible through mass hypnosis; and a bravura sequence, driven by Jerry Goldsmith's pulsating musical score, in which a written message from one of the Shadow's associates is shown racing its way through a spaghetti-like network of pneumatic tubes.

The fact that this scene is the most memorable moment of *The Shadow* unfortunately does not speak well for the rest of the film. As much as one wants to heap praise on screenwriter Koepp for all his hard work and research, it must be noted that the film falls flat whenever it lapses into campy comedy, which is much too often. Director Russell Mulcahy (*Highlander*) seems unable to establish a consistent pace or tone for the film, which comes across like several short subjects haphazardly stitched together. As for the performances, Alec Baldwin is a cold fish as Lamont Cranston and the Shadow, Penelope Ann Miller is an anemic Margot Lane, and John Lone is downright boring as Shiwan Khan. The stellar supporting cast is given practically nothing to do, but at least they do it very well. Especially noteworthy are Peter Boyle, who plays Moe Shrevnitz like a

PG-13 variation of his character in *Taxi Driver*; Jonathan Winters, appropriately beetle-browed as Commissioner Barth; Sab Shimono, cagily inscrutable as Dr. Tam; Ian McKellen, somewhat anticipating his Gandalf in the *Lord of the Rings* trilogy as well-meaning Dr. Reinhardt Lane; and Tim Curry, goggle-eyed and over the top as ever in the role of Lane's less honorable associate Farley Claymore. (McKellen and Curry had previous co-starred onstage in *Amadeus*. This isn't *Amadeus*.)

Despite a strong opening week, *The Shadow* withered on the box-office vine, ultimately posting a $48,000,000 worldwide gross on a $40,000,000 investment. Since a picture must earn at least two and a half times its cost to break even, you do the math. Its failure has not dissuaded Sam Raimi from pursuing his dream, previously thwarted back in the 1980s, to produce and direct a definitive screen version of *The Shadow*; as of this writing, his on-and-off project is "on" again, though no camera has yet turned. Meanwhile, recordings of the original *Shadow* radio show continue to play on public radio stations throughout the U.S., and sales of *Shadow* CD collections remain hot amongst Old Time Radio buffs, who should know darn well by now What Evil Lurks in the Hearts of Men.

Manhattan Merry-Go-Round (1937)

Maintaining a policy of augmenting their annual quota of B-westerns and inexpensive programmers with at least two "prestige" films per year, Republic Pictures followed up its 1937 success *The Hit Parade* (q.v.) with another lavish, star-studded $500,000 musical, *Manhattan Merry-Go-Round*. Released on November 16, 1937, this latest extravaganza was, like *Hit Parade*, inspired by a popular radio series; and also like *Hit Parade*, the new film took considerable liberties with its source material.

First heard over NBC-Blue on November 6, 1932, the weekly half-hour *Manhattan Merry-Go-Round* was essentially *Your Hit Parade* as filtered through the sensibilities of those phenomenally prolific radio-program packagers Frank and Anne Hummert. Responsible for such daytime serials as *Stella Dallas,* such detective dramas as *Mr. Keen, Tracer of Lost Persons* and such kiddie fare as *Little Orphan Annie,* the Hummerts had definite and unwavering ideas of what made a successful radio series tick. Put bluntly, Frank and Anne appealed to the lowest common denominator. There was nothing on a Hummert program that wasn't instantly graspable for the stupidest audience member. Program formats were simple, direct, and uncluttered, with no room for doubt as to what show one was hearing. Plotlines on dramatic programs never contained any "artistic" grace notes or digressions that might confuse or distract the listener. Important story or continuity points were repeated ad infinitum so that nothing could possibly be missed. And characters were clearly defined by the incessant use of full names, professions, personality traits and relationship to the plot at hand. No one was introduced merely as "Dr. Jones" on a Hummert show, but instead was laboriously pigeonholed as "Dr. Samuel Jones, the eccentric personal physician to beautiful young socialite Mrs. Edna Van Rensseller, the principal suspect in the murder of her wealthy financier husband Mr. Charles Van Rensseller." While it may seem as if the Hummerts were using crayons instead of typewriters, their formula remained immensely profitable throughout the length and breadth of radio's Golden Age.

Manhattan Merry-Go-Round upheld this spell-it-out tradition by sustaining the illusion of a weekly excursion to "all the big night spots of New York town," the listener being whisked along with a group of sophisticated revelers from one location to another, all within a glamour-packed 30 minutes. Announcers like Ford Bond and Roger Krupp would identify each cabaret and supper club by name to convince us that we were actually taking in the floor show at the Stork Club, the Zanzibar or the Copa, when in fact the performers never set foot outside the radio studio. While the series briefly flirted with guest stars in the mid–1930s, for the most part the performers were limited to such house singers as "beloved star of stage and radio" Thomas L. Thomas, the team of

Marion McManus and Nick O'Connor, or that sultry specialist in "French ditties" Rachel Carlay and the latest of her handsome young protégés (all of whom went by the *nom de microphone* "Pierre Le Kruen"). The only fluid and changeable element of the series was its roster of "the top songs of the week," as determined by record and sheet-music sales. Even with these up-to-date tunes, *Manhattan Merry-Go-Round* slavishly adhered to the time-honored Hummert policy of eliminating all potential listener confusion, with the announcer's opening assurance that the songs would be "sung so clearly that you can understand every word and sing them yourself." (This weekly mantra would later be wickedly lampooned by radio humorist Gary Owens and his frequent promises of "songs sung so clearly that you can understand every worrvvxzzz.")

Way back in 1935 Republic had announced its intention to film something called *Metropolitan Merry-Go-Round* with Roger Pryor and Pinky Tomlin heading the cast, but the studio decided that a tie-in with a successful radio show would be a better box-office enticement. The film version of *Manhattan Merry-Go-Round* (British title: *Manhattan Music Box*) provided Frank Hummert with a "created by" credit which, sweetened by the oodles of money he received for the film, was apparently incentive enough for Hummert to cede the dictatorial control he wielded over his radio properties and allow Republic to do whatever they wanted in the picture.

Leo Carrillo heads the cast in one of his patented soft-hearted gangster roles as Tony Gordoni. With the collapse of Prohibition, he has gone into a legitimate racket: providing loans to failing businesses at exorbitant interest, then taking over those businesses when the owners default. As he swoops down on his hapless debtors, Tony proclaims, "I am a man of few words—and when I talk I say a lot." (He says this a lot.) Gordoni's latest acquisition is the Associated Record Company, which has been on its uppers ever since severing ties with hotheaded singing star Jerry Hart (played by *Hit Parade* leading man Phil Regan). To build up Associated's talent pool, Tony sends his torpedo Danny the Duck (James Gleason) to round up the biggest musical names from New York's swellest niteries, meaning not only Jerry Hart but also the likes of Ted Lewis and Cab Calloway (whom Danny corrals at the "Cottonpickers' Club!"). Tony also raids radio station WXXZ, sponsored by fellow Italian Spadoni (Henry Armetta), where the Kay Thompson Singers hold court each evening. The main plotline of Harry Sauber's screenplay rears its ugly head when Tony's virago of a mother (Nellie V. Nichols) orders her son to sign up a singer from the "home country"—namely, the tempestuous and slightly birdbrained opera diva Charlizzini (wonderfully portrayed by the brilliant Russian-born *premiere danseuse* and choreographer Tamara Geva, best known today as the wife of George Balanchine). To persuade the prima donna to cut her first-ever recording, Tony exhorts Jerry to make love to Charlizzini or lose the use of his life, leaving our hero's oft-jilted fiancée Ann Rogers (Ann Dvorak, in a refreshing break from her usual tragic roles) waiting in the lurch once more. Also appearing in the film as the diva's manager is Luis Alberni, who in combination with Carrillo, Tamara Geva, Henry Armetta and Nellie V. Nichols spews out so much broken English that it's a wonder the film wasn't closed down by the Anti-Defamation League.

Manhattan Merry-Go-Round has frequently been sloughed off as a "hodgepodge," but thanks to director Charles F. Reisner and musical supervisor Harry Grey it actually holds together nicely, especially when compared to similar "monster" musicals from the major studios (MGM's *Broadway Melody of 1938* immediately comes to mind). Its relationship to the same-name radio program doesn't extend much further than the use of the show's well-remembered theme song during the opening credits, and the brief nightclub-hopping sequence as Danny the Duck scouts out talent for his boss. Early in the film the titular "Manhattan Merry-Go-Round" appears onscreen, no longer merely a metaphor but a fictional New York nightspot where Jerry Hart and the Louis Prima Band perform on a carousel in the middle of a gigantic revolving stage. The overall effect is most impressive (the film received an Oscar nomination for its art direction), though more sensitive viewers might end up with a touch of vertigo. And as was the case with *Hit Parade,* the tunes heard in *Manhattan Merry-Go-Round* are not "the top songs of the week," but were specially composed for the film by Sammy Cahn and Saul Chaplin, among many others.

Also in the *Hit Parade* tradition, some of the specialty numbers in *Manhattan Merry-Go-Round* were filmed at New York's Biograph studios by uncredited director John H. Auer. Among those performers who took a pass on trekking out to Hollywood were the Kay Thompson Singers, whose presence in this film was Republic's compensation for Thompson having lost the female lead in *Hit Parade* to Frances Langford. To sidestep the intricacies of matching Kay's New York–filmed scenes with those lensed in Hollywood, one of her numbers is presented on the screen of a "short-distance" television receiver—one of many examples of Republic's ongoing fascination with this still-embryonic entertainment medium. Thompson might not have made this primitive TV appearance, nor even her other big scene in the picture, if the studio had gone through with its plan to use her singers as back-up for the feature film debut of New York Yankees slugger Joe DiMaggio. "I want to look like a star in this movie!" screamed Kay at the prospect of sharing her space with Joltin' Joe, so the brief DiMaggio scene—which includes precious little acting or singing (thank Heaven for small favors), but lots of stock footage from the 1936 World Series—was instead backed up by Hugh Martin's orchestra. Joe was so nervous that it took 12 takes to nail the scene, but he could take comfort in the fact that the ordeal enabled him to meet his future wife Dorothy Arnold, one of the film's singers. (Note how I didn't say "his first wife." If you don't know this already, you've been on the planet Neptune for the past six decades.)

Among the performers whose numbers were filmed in Hollywood was Republic's very own singing cowboy Gene Autry, given an "introducing" credit in the opening titles even though he had been keeping the studio solvent with his turnstile-clicking B westerns ever since 1935 (Gene's sidekicks Max Terhune and Smiley Burnette also show up for a couple of seconds). It is Autry who delivers the film's biggest unintentional (?) laugh during a record studio scene in which he seems not to understand the mechanics of transcribing a song, expressing gape-mouthed amazement upon hearing his own voice played back!

Premiering in San Francisco, *Manhattan Merry-Go-Round* grossed a veritable mint by Republic's or anyone else's standards. The *San Francisco Examiner* congratulated the little studio for its leap into the A-picture class with a production that was "more entertaining than some widely heralded, highly financed films with music." The film was reissued several times over the next two decades, its 87-minute running time trimmed to 82 and then 78 minutes to accommodate double bills. A few currently available prints are taken from one of these shortened versions, with Louis Prima's appearance reduced to practically nothing and Virginia Dabney's role as James Gleason's Southern dumbbell girlfriend so abbreviated that some research sources claim she doesn't appear at all. Even in this abridged form, *Manhattan Merry-Go-Round* remains one of the better radio-derived musicals of its era—and thanks to the novelty appearance by Joe DiMaggio, the film has kept the name of the radio series alive well beyond the show's final broadcast on April 17, 1949.

Hollywood Hotel (1937)

Conceived by visionary Los Angeles land developer Hobart Johnstone Whitley and erected in 1902 on a strawberry patch fronting Hollywood Boulevard, the original Hollywood Hotel evolved from a small stucco building into one of Southern California's largest and most fashionable hostelries. In its glory, the three-acre structure boasted 125 guest rooms, a lavish ballroom, a separate music room, a chapel and an expansive lawn with many beautiful gardens. The growth of Los Angeles' motion picture industry greatly increased the hotel's business, with most of the top movie stars, producers and directors gathering in the ballroom every Thursday night, as much to be seen as to enjoy themselves. Its luster slowly began to fade in the mid-1930s with trendier establishments like Ciro's and the Beverly Wilshire becoming the new "in" places, and by 1956 the Hollywood Hotel was a rundown shell of its former self. The building was razed that year to make way for a multi-million-dollar business development: The Hollywood and Highland Center, as of this writing the home of the Academy Awards ceremonies, now stands where the Hollywood Hotel once towered over Highland and Orchid Avenues.

Debuting October 5, 1934, on CBS with the sponsorship of Campbell's soups, the weekly, 60-minute *Hollywood Hotel* was the first important network variety series to emanate from the West Coast. At that time the exorbitant cost of transmitting Los Angeles–based radio programs via telephone wire to the East Coast—reversing the established New York-to-Hollywood hookup—was too prohibitive for most producers. Louella Parsons, Tinseltown's most powerful and influential columnist, circumvented this expense by persuading (and occasionally strong-arming) many of the industry's biggest stars to appear on *Hollywood Hotel* for free, except for a complimentary case of soup from the sponsor. Only the series' regulars, including hostess Parsons, the emcees and announcers, the orchestras and their vocalists, and a cluster of stalwart radio actors who appeared in various supporting and minor roles, received financial remuneration for their efforts, and not all that much. Eventually the telephone charges were lowered (the circuits were reversed in 1937), and the newly strengthened Radio Guild demanded that everyone on the program be paid more than a few cans of vegetarian vegetable and chicken noodle. No longer the comparatively low-cost novelty it had once been, *Hollywood Hotel*—now minus the participation of Louella Parsons—ended its run on December 2, 1938.

At first glance, the information in the two previous paragraphs would seem to have more than a nominal connection. Virtually every article or book written about the history of Los Angeles has either inferred, or stated outright, that the radio series *Hollywood Hotel* was broadcast from the fabulous Orchid Room of the real Hollywood Hotel. In truth, there never was a fabulous Orchid Room. More to the point, the radio series never even got as far as the hotel's parking lot. *Hollywood Hotel* was initially staged in the studios of radio station KHJ, later moving to the larger facilities of the Figueroa Playhouse to accommodate a studio audience. The illusion of a glamorous hotel ballroom bustling with celebrities was sustained by such underpaid radio performers as Ted Osborne and Mary Jane Higby, breathlessly ad libbing as they pretended to recognize such luminaries as Myrna Loy and Bette Davis milling through the crowd. Parsons would wholeheartedly participate in the charade, interrupting her introductory comments with mock-surprise exclamations like, "Why, Tyrone Power! I haven't seen you since last week!"

According to her biographer Samantha Barbas, Parsons was approached by Warner Bros. in late 1936 to star in a film version of *Hollywood Hotel* as a strategy by Jack Warner to get on the good side of Louella's publisher boss William Randolph Hearst, who felt that the studio had mishandled his paramour Marion Davies by casting her in three consecutive flops. Other sources indicate that it was actually Parsons who approached Warner through her agent Jules Stein, offering the entire *Hollywood Hotel* radio package, regular performers and all, with the proviso that no one else in the film would receive on-screen billing more than "75 percent large as type used for Miss Parsons." Of course, Louella would play herself—much more benignly than the real Louella—while in tables-are-turned fashion the review for *Hollywood Hotel* in the Hearst papers would be written by actress Mary Pickford.

Included in this arrangement were *Hollywood Hotel*'s announcer Ken Niles, singing emcee Jerry Cooper, and orchestra leader Raymond Paige, appearing in the film under their own names; Paige's vocalist Frances Langford, who for the purposes of the storyline was cast as fictional songstress Alice Crayne; and Duane

Thompson, recreating her radio role as the switchboard operator who opened every broadcast with a chipper "Hollywood Hotel ... one moment, please, I'll connect you ..." Finally, Dick Powell, who had been emcee and lead vocalist of radio's *Hollywood Hotel* during its first three seasons, returned to the fold in the "book" portion of the film scripted by Jerry Wald, Maurice Leo and Richard Macauley. Powell is cast as Ronnie Bowers, saxophone player with the Benny Goodman Orchestra (as "themselves"), who leaves his home town upon receiving a ten-week movie contract with Hollywood's "All-Star Studios."

The film was directed by choreographer Busby Berkeley, and it isn't unusual to find it written off as a lesser entry in Berkeley's impressive list of credits. While it is true that *Hollywood Hotel* lacks the spectacular geometrically choreographed production numbers normally associated with the director, Berkeley nonetheless infuses its 107 minutes with a satisfying quota of distinctive musical touches. The opening number "Hooray for Hollywood" (the first presentation of this iconic Johnny Mercer–Richard A. Whiting composition, though definitely not the last) is a minor masterpiece of perpetual motion, boasting a flotilla of gleaming white automobiles decorated with signs bearing the names of then-current film favorites, as Dick Powell, Benny Goodman et al., Frances Langford and singer-trumpeter Johnnie "Scat" Davis (formerly with bandleader Fred Waring and previously featured along with Waring in *Varsity Show*) manage the neat trick of being ensemble players and sharply defined individuals all at once. "I'm Like a Fish Out of Water" transcends the comic-opera format of a ballad performed "straight" by the romantic leads and then "funny" by the secondary comedians with some attractive compositions involving a huge water fountain. "Silhouetted in the Moonlight" represents the first love song ever filmed at the Hollywood Bowl, enhanced by Berkeley's cunning spatial and acoustic innovations. "Let That Be a Lesson to You," staged in a drive-in restaurant based on an actual Hollywood outdoor eatery known as Carpenter's, is a typically expansive Berkeley confection beginning with a simple Dick Powell solo and progressively blossoming into a full ensemble number with isolated snatches of song from various supporting actors, bit players and seemingly impromptu trios and quartets. (Any sequence featuring a tight close-up of plug-ugly character actor Constantine Romanoff singing falsetto is a thing of beauty and a joy forever.) And in a climactic mood piece built around Raymond Paige's haunting signature tune "Dark Eyes," all the "acting" is performed by cinematographer George Barnes' fleet of roving cameras.

Just as *Hollywood Hotel* is regarded as a minor Berkeley film, the storyline has been described as everything from slight to nonexistent. Wanna bet? The main plot of hero Ronnie Bowers (Powell) trying to achieve Hollywood fame and fortune only to be relegated to obscurity as the off-screen singing voice of pompous screen idol Alexander DuPre, is melded with the travails of wannabe actress Virginia Stanton, whose chances for success are all but destroyed when she is hired as a stand-in for her lookalike, tempestuous movie queen Mona Marshall. A string of comic conspiracies, devised by Ronnie's two-bit agent Fuzzy in league with Mona's zany sister Dot and addlepated father Chester, catapult Ronnie to overnight stardom when he subs for DuPre during the film's climactic *Hollywood Hotel* broadcast. Drawing inspiration from the recent "Hollywood-laid-bare" dramatic feature *A Star Is Born*, *Hollywood Hotel* thrusts several daggers in the direction of the motion picture industry, with trenchant commentary on the cluelessness of producers, the brusque and insensitive treatment of the "little people" in the business, and the limited intellectual capacities of movie stars who have come to believe their own publicity. And in a satirical swipe that was thoroughly up-to-date in 1937, the film spoofs the nationwide hysteria surrounding the best-selling novel *Gone with the Wind* by casting Mona Marshall and Alexander DuPre as Lucy O'Mara and Bob Cutler in a saccharine Civil War musical.

Both Ginger Rogers and Bette Davis had been offered the dual role of Virginia Stanton and Mona Marshall, and both turned it down. The role was then split in two and played by real-life sisters Rosemary Lane (Virginia) and Lola Lane (Mona), who weren't exactly identical but could pass as such with the right lighting and makeup. Bette Davis also balked at playing Mona's wisecracking secretary Jonesy, insisting the part was too small for an actress of her stature. Evidently Glenda Farrell didn't have such qualms, and her performance as Jonesy is one of the film's highlights. Contributing to the overall frivolity are Alan Mowbray as the vainglorious Dupre, Ted Healy in his final screen role as roughneck agent Fuzzy (Healy died as a result of injuries received in a brawl shortly before the film's release), and Mabel Todd, previously a regular on the radio variety series *Al Pearce and His Gang* (q.v.), channeling Martha Raye as Mona's scatterbrained kid sister. Additionally, Edgar Kennedy as a scowling restaurant owner provides a superb self-referential gag when, on the verge of performing his famous face-wiping slow burn, he is beaten to the punch by Dick Powell and Ted Healy. The one sour note is struck by the usually reliable Hugh Herbert, whose performance as Mona's daffy father is too much of a bad thing, especially when he pops up disguised in blackface amongst a group of African American extras.

This embarrassing moment is to a great extent expunged by the presence of the Benny Goodman band, who during what is supposed to be a rehearsal session give out with what might be the definitive performance of "Sing Sing Sing." This landmark piece was originally written to include a vocal, but Benny was so pleased with the filmed results that it would remain strictly instrumental ever afterward. But we mentioned that Goodman made up for that stupid blackface scene, didn't we? No sooner has "Sing Sing Sing" ended than we're treated to a knockout rendition of "I've Got a Heartful of Music" performed by the Benny Goodman Quartet: Benny on clarinet, Gene Krupa on drums, Lionel Hampton on vibraphone and Teddy Wilson on piano. This represented the first time that a racially mixed musical group was shown onscreen in a major motion picture—and while there's no record of Goodman having to do battle with studio executives over featuring black and white musicians performing together, you can be damn sure that Benny would have fought tooth and nail on behalf of Hampton and Wilson if any objections arose. We *do* know that Goodman threatened to quit the movie cold if the studio went through with its plans to cut out close-ups of his trumpet player Harry James and insert Johnnie "Scat" Davis instead.

The film's closing *Hollywood Hotel* recreation is entertaining but highly fanciful. Since as mentioned no Orchid Room actually existed in the real hotel, the Orchid Room seen herein was wholly the product of art director Robert M. Haas' imagination, right down to the individual microphones at every table so that the show's performers never have to walk all the way to the main stage. Also, though Jerry Cooper was both master of ceremonies and lead vocalist on the concurrent radio series, here he is solely the singer, while the show's announcer Ken Niles has been promoted to emcee. Finally, this filmed broadcast represents a remarkable technological advance in the world of network radio: a variety program that does without the services of a director or a sound engineer.

At least the closing portion of the broadcast scene is fairly faithful to the radio original, as Louella Parsons introduces dramatic highlights from the upcoming Mona Marshall-Alexander DuPre Civil War epic. This sort of sneak preview was a regular feature of the CBS version, so what we see here is not too far removed from reality. But even *this* scene is compromised by an inaccuracy that was probably picked up only by the actors who'd appeared on radio's *Hollywood Hotel*. When Ronnie Bowers shows up as a substitute singer for Alexander DuPre, he is not only identified by his own name but is offered a $2,000 payment for his voice work. As everyone who worked on the real show could have told you, any non-celebrity actor who traded anonymity for on-the-air billing would have automatically sacrificed his or her $20 paycheck. Thus, Ronnie Bowers would have left the studio with naught but a boxful of Campbell's Soups—or maybe not, given the fact that after the December 1937 release of *Hollywood Hotel,* Campbell's sued Warner Bros. for unauthorized use of the radio show's title.

Edgar Bergen and Charlie McCarthy (1938–1947, 1979)

Why—people have been asking me for the last two days—why put a ventriloquist on the air? The answer is, "Why not?" True, our ventriloquist, Edgar Bergen, is an unusual one—a sort of Noël Coward or perhaps Fred Allen among ventriloquists, a dexterous fellow who depends more on the cleverness and wit of the material than upon the believe-it-or-not nature of his delivery. Mr. Bergen works with a dummy—several of them, in fact—but this one is a typical ventriloquist's dummy except that is arrayed with top hat and tails. Just imagine a dummy and take my word for it that both voices you will hear are owned and operated by just one man—Edgar Bergen.

These words were delivered by Rudy Vallee as he introduced a ventriloquism act on the December 17, 1936, edition of *The Royal Gelatin Hour*. Earlier in the broadcast, Vallee had said, "If you wonder what in the name of all that's holy can be done with a ventriloquist on the air, stick around and we'll show you." For many of Vallee's listeners, this would be their first exposure to Bergen and his wooden partner Charlie McCarthy. But for those familiar with the act's appearances in vaudeville and single-reel film comedies, there was little doubt that Bergen would go over big on radio. Those "in the know" were aware that the act's primary attraction was not the gimmick of ventriloquism but the quality of the material—and of more importance, the inescapable illusion that Charlie McCarthy was no ordinary dummy, no mere appendage of Bergen's talent, but a living, breathing entity unto himself. If the laws of nature and logic had been on his side, the delightfully bratty Charlie McCarthy would probably have dumped his stuffed-shirt partner Bergen and struck out on his own.

Born Edgar John Berggren in Chicago in 1903, Edgar Bergen grew up on a farm in Michigan with his Swedish immigrant parents. The shy, somewhat taciturn young man began studying ventriloquism at age 11, using the "belly talk" method developed by such past masters of the art as Fred Russell and the Great Lester to throw his voice and confuse his household. At age 16, Bergen paid Chicago bartender Theodore Mack $35 to carve him a wooden dummy, the face modeled on an Irish newsboy Edgar had known in childhood. The finished product was a red-headed urchin with long, gangly legs (the body built by Bergen himself) whom Edgar christened Charlie McCarthy. Except for shortening the legs, Edgar would make no significant physical changes to Charlie for the next 58 years.

Finding that he was able to overcome his nervousness in crowds by speaking through Charlie, Bergen worked his way through pre-med at Northwestern University by performing at small gatherings, eventually dropping out of college to give vaudeville a try. The story of Bergen's professional breakthrough has been told many times, most colorfully in the November 20, 1944, issue of *Time* magazine. Down and out in Chicago, Bergen and Charlie were given a week's tryout in a tiny nightclub. Launching their act at three in the morning, the ventriloquist and his dummy were greeted with bored indifference by the sparse audience until Charlie suddenly turned on Bergen and screamed, "Who in hell ever told you you were a good ventriloquist?"—then proceeded to insult each and every customer. Instead of rising as one to lynch Bergen, the audience roared with laughter. Backstage, Bergen expressed embarrassment over losing control, but admitted, "I just had to get that off my chest." In that single moment (I prefer to think the story isn't apocryphal), Edgar knew that he and Charlie were not only a winning combination but also the yin and yang of his own psyche. Bergen remained polite, reserved and self-effacing throughout his career, allowing Charlie McCarthy to purge him of all egomania, irreverence and hostility. One man's schizophrenia is another man's gold mine.

Soon Bergen was playing the big houses for the big money, touring the best theaters throughout the world and scoring a personal triumph at New York's Palace in 1930. Along the way he improved his act by removing Charlie's clichéd raggedy-newsboy costume and snazzing up the dummy with white tie and tails, a top hat and a monocle, a sophisticated facade that made Charlie's earthy comic vitriol and snarky schoolboy wisecracks all the funnier in contrast. Bergen occasionally experimented with other dummies, but Charlie remained his and the audience's favorite.

Also established during his first flush of success was Edgar's method of compensating for his lack of technical polish. Prior to Bergen, the star in a ventriloquism act was the ventriloquist and not his dummy. The *schtick* that was supposed to bring the house down was the ventriloquist's skill at tossing his voice without moving his lips, or while smoking a cigarette or drinking a glass of water. Try as he might, though, Edgar was unable to prevent his lips from moving, and when he did succeed in this endeavor his timing was thrown off. So Bergen reversed the standard operating procedure by forcing the audience's attention on Charlie McCarthy, making the dummy the star. To do this he invested Charlie with a brash and well-defined personality, totally the opposite of his own, and generously gave the dummy all the laugh lines. He also kept Charlie on the move as much as possible, with every nod, jerk and head-turn calculated to deflect attention from Bergen. When all else failed, Edgar garnered laughs by deliberately *drawing* attention to his own deficiencies: One of the best Bergen-McCarthy exchanges, immortalized in the 1938 feature film *Letter of Introduction,* has Charlie staring Edgar square in the face and declaring "*You* aren't so clever. I can see your lips move"—then turning to the audience and chuckling, "It burns him up when I say that!"

In 1930 Bergen and McCarthy followed the lead of several other New York–based stage performers by appearing in a group of one-reel comedies produced in Flatbush by the Vitaphone Corporation. Technically this represented the beginning of the ventriloquist's screen career, though 1930 is not the date listed at the top of this entry because Edgar had yet to appear on radio. Not that he hadn't *tried,* but virtually every stopover at a broadcast studio resulted in one of two putdowns: "Ventriloquists are a dime a dozen!" and "How will the audience know that you're talking to a dummy, and who cares?" With radio closed to him, Bergen settled for the easy work and quick money of the Vitaphone shorts.

Released in February 1930, the first one-reeler *The Operation* was based on a sketch Bergen had performed on stage, with Edgar as a sonorous doctor, Charlie as his nervous patient, and a pretty nurse with nice legs whom the wise-beyond-his-years Mr. McCarthy could ogle. Though in most of the 14 Vitaphone comedies Charlie is shorn of his tux, top hat and monocle, his basic personality is already firmly in place, as are many of his pet gag lines ("It's a long story—and a dirty one!"). Also honed to perfection is the impeccably timed give-and-take between Bergen and McCarthy, with Edgar's rapid questions and Charlie's barbed answers punctuated by throwaway lines like "I see," "You did?" "Uh huh," "Never mind," "That's all right" and "Yes, yes." Here as elsewhere, one can try as hard as possible to focus on Bergen's lips, but within a few seconds one is thoroughly convinced that the words are coming from Charlie's mouth, and that there are actually two human beings up there on screen instead of one guy with a block of pine on his knee.

What is missing in these shorts is the consistent sharpness of material that would be the hallmark of Bergen's later radio work, and also a clearly defined personality for Bergen himself. Made up to look like an elderly professor in *Two Boobs in a Balloon,* slicked down as a girl-happy football coach in *All-American Drawback,* posing as a gentleman hobo in *Free and Easy,* impersonating a judge in *Nut Guilty* and exchanging Burns & Allen material with a Dumb Dora straight woman in *At the Races,* Edgar has yet to find a proper niche in his own act beyond representing a stern father figure for the precocious Charlie. Overall, however, the Bergen-McCarthy Vitaphone shorts possess their own special charm, and some are better than average, notably those directed by Hal Roach alumnus Lloyd French and featuring such future Hollywood character comics as Shemp Howard and Donald MacBride.

Bergen was still occasionally filming at Vitaphone when a summons came from the J. Walter Thompson agency for an appearance on Rudy Vallee's radio show. The facts surrounding this momentous event are a bit muddled. We know that after Edgar and Charlie did their act at an Elsa Maxwell party in New York, they were hired for the Rainbow Room, located above NBC headquarters in Rockefeller Center, at the recommendation of Noël Coward. Some sources claim that Rudy Vallee was also in attendance at Elsa's party and invited Bergen to come on his radio program; others insist that two of Vallee's representatives caught the act at the Rainbow Room, then contacted Vallee. It doesn't really matter how Bergen got the *Royal Gelatin Hour* spot on that December evening in 1936; the important thing is that he *was* there, and he was a hit. So enthusiastic was listener response that Vallee signed Edgar and Charlie for an additional 13 weeks, which led to Bergen's own NBC program for Chase and Sanborn beginning May 9, 1937. *The Chase and Sanborn Hour* was a variety show in every sense of the word: Though Bergen and McCarthy were prominently billed, they were not at first the sole attraction, appearing primarily at the beginning and end of each broadcast while the rest of the program showcased the other regulars: singer-announcer Don Ameche, vocalists Nelson Eddy and Dorothy Lamour, the Stroud Twins and the Canova Family (featuring Judy Canova, who eventually went solo). In addition to the comedy routines and musical numbers, each episode featured a comic or dramatic playlet teaming Ameche with the evening's guest star. One of these was the infamous "Adam and Eve" sketch which succeeded in getting Mae West banned from radio for over two decades.

Soon comedian W.C. Fields, emerging from a lengthy illness-dictated sabbatical, became a *Chase and Sanborn Hour* quasi-regular. The 1937–38 season would be dominated by the verbal fisticuffs between the braying, braggadocio Fields and the irreverent, irrepressible Charlie McCarthy. As Edgar adopted a neutral stance, W.C. would sneeringly greet Charlie as "the woodpecker's pin-up boy," invite the little nipper to ride piggy-back on a buzzsaw, and threaten to slash him into Venetian blinds. Charlie gave back as good as he got, making pointed references to Fields' drinking ("You weren't born—you were squeezed out of a bar rag!") and prominent proboscis ("Is that your nose or are you eating a tomato?"). Friends of Fields insisted that the comedian genuinely detested the dummy, but curiously held little animosity for Bergen, whose ad libbing talent he admired. While such stories invariably improve with the telling, actress Constance Moore has given eyewitness testimony that during filming of the Bergen-Fields comedy *You Can't Cheat an Honest Man* (1939), Fields became so enraged by Charlie's insolence that at one point he banned the dummy from the set. Not Bergen. The dummy.

By late 1937 a major feature film appearance for Edgar Bergen was a foregone conclusion. Fields wanted Bergen to co-star with him in Paramount's *The Big Broadcast of 1938* (discussed elsewhere), but Edgar had already made a contractual commitment to independent producer Sam Goldwyn. Having tuned in on that fateful Rudy Vallee broadcast, Goldwyn immediately hired Bergen for a featured role in his long-in-preparation Technicolor musical *The Goldwyn Follies*. When this project was first publicly announced in 1932, it was to be an extravagant all-star revue in emulation of Goldwyn's idol, Broadway impresario Flo Ziegfeld—and like *The Ziegfeld Follies*, *Goldwyn Follies* was to be an annual event. For five years Goldwyn issued press releases announcing negotiations with such A-list talent as director René Clair and an honor roll of stars from every major studio. George Gershwin was engaged to compose what turned out to be his last original score, with Goldwyn hoping to fulfill his dream that the film would feature a ballet inspired by Gershwin's "An American in Paris." While this dream would not be realized until 1951, and then not by Sam Goldwyn but by Gene Kelly, most of Goldwyn's other goals for his *Follies* were met—save for the participation of René Clair, who was replaced by George Marshall, and the Ballet Russe, replaced by the American Ballet of the Metropolitan Opera.

During the development process, the concept of a plotless revue was scrapped when Goldwyn settled upon a "book" show with a proposed plotline involving a nasty Broadway critic, to be scripted by Dorothy Parker, Lillian Hellman or someone like that. It was Ben

Hecht who finally came up with a story about an ambitious Hollywood producer, who believing that he has lost the pulse of the public hires a young woman whom he feels represents a cross-section of America. Redubbed "Miss Humanity," the heroine advises the producer on the sort of entertainment ingredients the public craves, all of which are blended into the producer's next picture. Though Sam Goldwyn's business associates tried to argue that the title *Goldwyn Follies* did not apply to a "plotted" show—and might indeed be a detriment if a few clever critics decided to pounce upon the "Follies" part—Goldwyn stubbornly stuck with the film's original name if not its original intent.

Selecting his stars from every branch of popular entertainment, Goldwyn cast film actors Adolphe Menjou as producer Oliver Merlin and Andrea Leeds as Hazel "Miss Humanity" Dawes; lyric soprano Helen Jepson of the Metropolitan Opera; Norwegian ballet star Vera Zorina, with her then husband George Balanchine choreographing the film; Broadway luminaries Bobby Clark and Ella Logan; nightclub favorites The Ritz Brothers, borrowed from 20th Century–Fox in exchange for Goldwyn contractee Joel McCrea; and, from network radio, tenor Kenny Baker (who sings Gershwin's "Love Walked In" so often you want to throw something at him), comedian Phil Baker, and of course Edgar Bergen and Charlie McCarthy.

Goldwyn had signed Bergen at a time when the ventriloquist was willing to accept a modest $400 per week with an eight-week guarantee. But by the time *Goldwyn Follies* was ready to go before the cameras, Bergen calmly informed the producer that the original deal was made "a whole career ago." In the midst of weighing huge offers from every studio in Hollywood, Bergen politely insisted that if Goldwyn wanted to retain his services, he would have to pay Edgar at least half of the highest offer he had gotten elsewhere. Sam swallowed hard and accepted these terms, though with the warning that Bergen might never again be in such a bargaining position if the movie audience didn't like him. As the meeting ended, the producer turned to Bergen and coined one of his most famous "Goldwynisms": "It's a goddam sight easier to climb up a greased pole than to *stay* there!"

Bergen never fell off that pole in *this* picture. Seen today, *Goldwyn Follies* would be an utter waste of time were it not for the wonderful cross-talk vignettes between Bergen and Charlie McCarthy, and to a lesser extent the synchronized silliness of the Ritz Brothers. Edgar and Charlie are so at ease before the cameras, and so successful in persuading the viewer that two separate people are carrying on their conversations, that this writer is willing to believe the legend that Goldwyn's boom operator kept losing Bergen's voice on the soundtrack because he instinctively shifted the microphone from Edgar to Charlie and back again during their dialogue scenes! At one point, we are given a foretaste of the Bergen-McCarthy films to come when Charlie shares a tête-à-tête with co-star Vera Zorina—with Edgar nowhere in sight. In interviews of the period, Bergen indicated that this sort of suspension of disbelief would not occur again onscreen. That's what *he* thought.

Though *Goldwyn Follies* lost money by the bushel basket, those who saw the picture agreed with critics that Bergen and McCarthy were the real stars of the show. Katherine Best of *Stage* magazine qualified her tepid review of the film with, "Nothing seems to fit anywhere except Charlie McCarthy, who plays around in my mind with the seven dwarfs, and he's all right, even if his competition were worth mentioning. It isn't though." Likewise bypassing Bergen, the critic for *Literary Digest* had this to say about Mr. McCarthy: "No matter how faithful is your radio friendship for [Charlie], you will enjoy the back-talking sourpuss in person."

Bergen and McCarthy were seen to even better advantage in *Letter of Introduction* (1938), the first of their three Universal features. The "team" was reunited with their *Goldwyn Follies* co-stars Adolphe Menjou and Andrea Leeds in a sentimental comedy-drama about a fading Broadway matinee idol (Menjou at his Barrymoresque hammiest) who gives a break to his long-estranged daughter (Leeds) by choosing her as his new leading lady, precipitating unfounded gossip and unforeseen consequences when he refuses to reveal their actual relationship.

Billed third in the opening credits (with Charlie in fourth place), Bergen is the first of the film's stars to appear onscreen, battling his way through a New Year's Eve crowd to exchange pleasantries with aspiring actress Kay Martin (Leeds), a fellow tenant in a cheap theatrical boarding house. Suddenly a fire breaks out in their lodgings and both Kay and Edgar charge into the burning building, Kay to retrieve her letter of introduction to stage star John Mannering (Menjou) and Edgar to rescue his dummy Charlie. It is quickly established that not only is Kay an unemployed performer, but so is Edgar, who has been told by one booking office too many that ventriloquists are out of fashion in A.D. 1938. From this point on, Bergen's subplot in *Letter of Introduction* is a virtual replay of his actual rise to stardom. Thanks to the intervention of John Mannering, Edgar is invited to entertain at a Lamb's Club Gambol, which leads to a radio contract with Rudy Vallee (referenced but never seen in the picture). A later scene at a penthouse party offers a fascinating glimpse of Bergen and McCarthy's nightly act at the Rainbow Room; and the film's climax features Edgar and Charlie standing before a packed house in an NBC radio studio, their superstardom a *fait accompli*.

During the penthouse scene, Edgar brings forth a second dummy, a bucktoothed, droopy-eyed, arrested-development hayseed who introduces himself as "Elmer Morti-more Snerd." Charlie clearly regards this country bumpkin as a rival, and for the rest of the act he turns disdainfully away from Edgar and says not a word. Contrary to certain radio history books, Mortimer Snerd was not previously introduced on *The Chase and Sanborn Hour*; and contrary to press releases issued for *Letter of Introduction*, this film wasn't Mortimer's debut either. According to *Radio Mirror*, the simple-minded, unworldly Mortimer Snerd had been created to complement the quick-witted, urbane Charlie, and the original intention was to confine Mortimer to Bergen's appearances in nightclubs and films. The world at large first saw the new dummy (again calling himself "Elmer," with "Morti-more" as an afterthought) in Bergen's final Vitaphone one-reeler *A Neckin' Party* (1937). In a 1938 edition of Paramount's Technicolor short subject series *Unusual Occupations,* it was revealed that sculptress Virginia Austin had molded Mortimer's head from sketches provided by Bergen, incorporating all the "weak" physical features that the more assertive Charlie lacked. While Mortimer Snerd would never match Charlie's popularity, the enthusiastic audience response to his appearance in *Letter of Introduction* assured the public that they'd see—and hear—a lot more from him.

Director John M. Stahl was determined to make *Letter of Introduction* a hit after the debacle of his previous film, the infamous Clark Gable stinkaroo *Parnell*. Stahl liked Bergen and felt that by building up the ventriloquist as an active participant in the story and not confining him to a couple of specialties, the film would benefit immeasurably. The director was not only receptive to Edgar's on-set suggestions but even incorporated a few of them into the script, including a trick scene in which Charlie is shown sliding down a bannister. For his part, Bergen was eternally grateful to Stahl for allowing him to do some straight acting, which he pulls off magnificently. Rather than avoid exposing his genuine feelings of inadequacy away from Charlie, Edgar willingly lays himself bare in this film, which depicts him as too shy and tongue-tied to reveal his true emotions unless he's speaking through his dummy. Having lost the affections of heroine Kay to handsome hoofer Barry Paige (George Murphy), Edgar arises from his bed on a sleepless night, picks up his dummy from a chair, and says dolefully, "Talk to me, Charlie"—which Charlie does, harshly reprimanding Edgar for his self-defeating reticence! (Shed no tears for Bergen, folks: At the end of the film he finds romance in the person of Kay's wisecracking roommate, played by Eve Arden—in itself something of a reflection of real life, since Arden was at the time engaged to a man named *Edward* Bergen.)

Except for a closing gag involving Mortimer Snerd, *Letter of Introduction* does not repeat the illusion briefly sustained in *Goldwyn Follies* (and more extensively in the earlier Vitaphone shorts) that Bergen's dummies are capable of acting independently of the ventriloquist. If anything, the film goes to the opposite extreme, placing emphasis on the fact that Charlie really is a dummy and not a living person. On two occasions, the camera picks up a medium shot of Charlie sitting alone and motionless, staring blankly into the camera. The effect is not only startling but terrifying, reminding one of those Victorian photographs of dead infants propped up in their coffins. Throughout his career Bergen was extremely careful not to shatter the onstage perception of Charlie McCarthy as a genuine human being; Edgar never walked into the spotlight with Charlie hanging limply from his arm, and *absolutely* never allowed anyone to see him stuff his dummy into a suitcase. Undoubtedly as disturbed as the audience by the sight of a corpselike Charlie in *Letter of Introduction,* Edgar would not allow this to happen again in any future screen appearance.

With *Letter of Introduction* scoring at the box office, Bergen's price per picture climbed to $100,000—the same amount demanded by W.C. Fields when he signed a Universal contract in 1938, hot on the heels of his career reboot on *The Chase and Sanborn Hour.* For his first Universal feature *You Can't Cheat an Honest Man* Fields earned an additional $25,000 to write the screenplay, using his favorite *nom de plume* Charles Bogle. Promised full creative control over his Universal films (a promise not always kept), Fields immediately requested Bergen as co-star. The Fields-McCarthy radio feud had really blazed up by this time, fueled by the *Chase and Sanborn* broadcast of June 5, 1938, in which Fields allegedly walked off after being mercilessly needled by Charlie about the cancellation of his Paramount contract. Many media historians prefer to believe that this blowup was authentic, but a quick listen of the broadcast indicates that the barrage of insults and Fields' outraged exit were all planned in advance. At any rate, Fields appreciated the value of perpetuating the feud onscreen, so he wrote

This lobby card approximates the caricatures of (left to right) Charlie McCarthy, W.C. Fields and Edgar Bergen seen in the opening credits of Universal's *You Can't Cheat an Honest Man* (1939).

his screenplay with Edgar and Charlie in mind, incorporating several of his previous radio exchanges with Charlie into the dialogue. Fields of course was never averse to using tried-and-true material: In *You Can't Cheat an Honest Man,* his scenes with Eddie "Rochester" Anderson were adapted from an ages-old *Ziegfeld Follies* sketch originally performed by W.C. and black comedian Bert Williams.

Nor was *You Can't Cheat an Honest Man* itself all that new, being the latest version of a screen story Fields had been toying with since 1929. The comedian intended to cast himself as a shady but lovable circus manager, married to a trapeze artist named Gorgeous who is fatally injured in a fall. Fields promises the dying Gorgeous that he will do everything in his power to make sure that their children will enjoy a happy and prosperous adulthood. In this way, all of Fields' later acts of dishonesty and flim-flammery would be justified by a noble purpose, with audience sympathy firmly in his corner. Bergen's character in the revised script is an impoverished circus magician with whom Fields' daughter falls in love. Discovering that her daddy owes an enormous debt that he must pay immediately or lose his circus, the daughter prepares to enter into a marriage of convenience with a wealthy wastrel. As much as Fields dislikes Bergen—and Charlie McCarthy even more—he ultimately concedes that Edgar would be a better choice for his daughter than the rich man.

Just before shooting started in November 1938, Fields and Bergen conferred on their choice of director. Not unexpectedly Bergen wanted to go with *Letter of Introduction*'s John Stahl, but Fields felt that Stahl's comedy experience was insufficient and steered Edgar in the direction of *Goldwyn Follies*' George Marshall. As much as he hated to admit it, Fields knew that Bergen would be the bigger box-office attraction and was willing to evenly divide the comedy highlights between himself and his co-star. While Edgar's radio gag writers were responsible for the scenes in which he and Charlie perform a magic act with the fetchingly underclad Princess Baba (who really was a Eurasian princess, Baba of Sarawak), Fields scripted most of his exchanges with Charlie McCarthy, and was none too happy during story conferences in which Edgar, still a bit timid in the presence of the Great Man, objected to certain lines or bits of business by speaking through Charlie. This fed into the general perception that Fields genuinely hated the dummy, despite Edgar's later protests that W.C.'s animosity was "synthetic."

Fields had a tougher time with director George Marshall, who pressured the comedian to remove what turned out to be his funniest sequence, in which he single-handedly lays waste to a fancy society party. Things reached an impasse when Marshall flatly refused to work with Fields any more, whereupon two separate production units were established, Marshall remaining with Bergen (with whom the director got along famously, frequently spoiling takes by laughing out loud at Edgar's ad libs) and Fields working exclusively first with Edward Sedgwick and then with Eddie Cline. Only recently have Fields scholars gone into the main reason for his obstreperous behavior. The comedian's protests notwithstanding, Universal had cut out his character's backstory involving the death of his wife and his promise to move heaven and earth for the sake of their children. Minus this crucial sequence, Fields came off as thoroughly unsympathetic and (to non-fans of the comedian) utterly repulsive. The self-protective myth that Universal perpetuated in years to come had a drunken W.C. Fields staggering around the set, making ridiculous demands that the studio film a death scene for a character who wasn't even in the script.

While it's tough to give Universal an even break under these circumstances, we should note that the film as it stands could not have included the "Gorgeous" scenes without doing serious damage to the comedy flow. The melancholy opening scene might also have ruined the "plausible impossibility" of the routines with Bergen and McCarthy, which would have us believe that Charlie is able to move about on his own and go through such comic bits as sabotaging Fields' sharpshooting act without Edgar's assistance. In another scene, Fields vengefully tosses Charlie into the circus alligator pit, forcing Edgar to figure out which of the big lizards has swallowed his little pal *by following the direction of Charlie's voice*. And in the closing gag, Mortimer Snerd sits in the gondola of a balloon high above the ground, commenting on a chase scene occurring thousands of feet below him—in which Edgar Bergen is participating! The absurdity of Charlie and Mortimer functioning separately from Edgar could only be pulled off if the rest of the film was played as pure farce, which would have been problematic had the story opened with a realistic deathbed scene.

You Can't Cheat an Honest Man earned more money than any previous W.C. Fields picture, a fact that everyone at the time attributed to the presence of Edgar Bergen and his dummies. Youthful moviegoers of 1939 with only dim memories of Fields' past films tended to express impatience during his setpieces while howling with approval at Edgar and Charlie. This division of interest would be radically reversed in the late 1960s when the college counterculture crowd embraced Fields as an anti-establishment hero; during revival showings of *You Can't Cheat an Honest Man* the "kids" were known to hiss and boo during the Bergen-McCarthy scenes while laughing hysterically at everything Fields said and did. Safely removed from both these eras, we can state that the film benefits equally from Fields and Bergen's comic input. Back in 1939, however, Universal was of the opinion that Fields still needed a dynamic co-star to bring in crowds, so his next film *My Little Chickadee* teamed the comedian with Mae West. It was a different story with Bergen and McCarthy, who were allowed to carry their next picture by themselves. Directed by Frank Tuttle and released by Universal during Christmas Week of 1939, *Charlie McCarthy, Detective* is the only feature film that can be described as a Bergen-McCarthy vehicle pure and simple.

The pretense of Edgar being a struggling, impoverished ventriloquist is forever dashed in the very first scene of *Charlie McCarthy, Detective*, in which we see the highly successful Bergen performing his act in a lavish nightclub before a well-heeled audience of the Manhattan glitterati. Charlie likewise is a fully acknowledged celebrity, to the extent that he is allowed to perform the novelty song "I'm Charlie McCarthy, Detective," his inverness-and-deerstalker costume verifying his boast. After this promising start, the film becomes entrenched in a deadly serious murder mystery, demonstrating that Universal wasn't all that misguided when they excised the dramatic subtext of *You Can't Cheat an Honest Man*. Edgar's reporter pal Scotty Hamilton (Robert Cummings) is determined to get the goods on crooked editor Arthur Aldrich (Louis Calhern) after Scotty's pal Felton (Milburn Stone) is killed on the verge of exposing the unholy alliance between the editor and racketeer Tony Garcia (Harold Huber). During a weekend party at Aldrich's estate where Edgar and Charlie have been hired to entertain, Aldrich is shot to death and suspicion immediately falls on Scotty's fellow newshound Bill Banning (John Sutton). Since Edgar is a friend of Bill's songstress sweetheart Sheila Stuart (Constance Moore), he and Charlie decide to investigate Aldrich's murder themselves, much to the aggravation of police inspector Dailey (Edgar Kennedy).

So here we have two "real" murders and several lives in the balance. But never mind all that: Both Charlie McCarthy and Mortimer Snerd pop up at random moments while Edgar is supposedly somewhere else; Charlie and Mortimer carry on conversations with other characters of which Edgar is ignorant; and in the final skirmish between cops and gangsters, the two dummies take it upon themselves to hide in strange, confined places which could never accommodate a full-sized human ventriloquist. The audience is asked to accept the reality of both the straight murder story *and* the "look-no-hands" perambulations of Charlie and Mortimer—and we can't do it, I tell ya, *we just can't do it*! The limit comes when, during a gun battle between the good guys and the bad guys, Charlie McCarthy is shot, wounded, and rushed to a hospital emergency room.

Though there are plenty of amusing scenes in *Charlie McCarthy, Detective*, and at the very least Edgar Bergen and not Charlie is allowed to solve the mystery, the end result is more "funny-strange" than "funny-haha." Some observers in 1939 were willing to swallow the film's ludicrousness, *Film Daily* assuring exhibitors, "It's a Bergen-McCarthy-Snerd field day; should click easily." Others were not quite as enchanted, notably *Photoplay*: "Unfortunately, the idea of a ventriloquist's dummy (or dummies, considering Mortimer Snerd's in it, too) carrying a weak murder mystery to success is too much to hope for." The film wasn't a flop, but it was several furlongs removed from a hit.

While Bergen and McCarthy's screen career was in temporarily abeyance in 1940, the act was hotter than ever on radio, with the *Chase and Sanborn* program officially retitled *The Edgar Bergen/Charlie McCarthy Show*—and ultimately just *The Charlie McCarthy Show*. Now deemed worthy of a $150,000-per-film paycheck, Bergen entered into a motion picture package deal brokered by MCA's Lew Wasserman and including another NBC radio attraction, Fibber McGee and Molly (q.v.). MCA was given the selection of story, director, and supporting cast, while RKO Radio Pictures would be responsible for production costs, studio facilities and distribution. In the two films resulting from this arrangement, Bergen & McCarthy and Fibber McGee & Molly were given equal screen time, their respective radio writers (Zeno Klinker and Dorothy Kingsley for Edgar & Charlie, Don Quinn and Leonard Levinson for Fibber & Molly) prominently listed in the opening credits. However, in deference to their greater radio popularity, Bergen & McCarthy received top billing, and in both films Charlie McCarthy had the final close-up and last laugh.

Produced and directed by Allan Dwan, the initial RKO film *Look Who's Laughing* (1941) devotes its first reel to Edgar and Charlie, who are introduced at an NBC radio broadcast performing their old "Operation" routine with Lucille Ball, cast as Bergen's "Girl Friday" Julie Patterson and here dressed as a nurse (the scene sustains the popular illusion held by people who'd never attended a live radio broadcast that the performers appeared in full costume using props and elaborate sets, with no pesky microphones cluttering the stage). We learn that this is the final broadcast of the season and Bergen is about to go on vacation, while Julie intends to hand in her notice and marry Edgar's business manager Jerry Wood (Lee Bonnell). The stunned reaction to this news by Jerry's erstwhile sweetheart Marge (Dorothy Lovett), and the fact that Edgar and Julie are obviously devoted to each other, tips us off that Edgar will be paired with Julie and Jerry with Marge before the end title. This was the second cinematic attempt to pass off Bergen as a romantic lead, and is about as successful as the first, which is just barely. Having invested his dummies with all the "personality" in the act, Edgar is something of a hollow presence on screen, which does no harm to the comedy sequences but no good for any sort of love story. In *You Can't Cheat an Honest Man* Bergen was something of a weak sister, willing to allow his sweetheart to marry another man until Charlie shames him into speaking up for himself. In *Look Who's Laughing*, Edgar's preoccupation with his radio program and absent-mindedness in all other matters is the wedge that separates him from Julie until the final scene. Thanks to the vivacious Lucille Ball, the audience accepts that she and Edgar will live happily ever after, but it's an extremely close call.

While Edgar pilots his own plane towards his chosen vacation site, he and Charlie experience engine trouble and are forced to land in Wistful Vista, home town of Fibber McGee & Molly (Jim and Marian Jordan). Here the main plot gets underway, with Fibber endeavoring to persuade billionaire industrialist Hillary Horton (a blatant Howard Hughes clone, played by Neil Hamilton) to purchase an airstrip outside of town, while Fibber's perennial nemesis Throckmorton P. Gildersleeve (Harold Peary) tries to undermine these plans for his own gain. It turns out that Edgar is a friend of Horton and offers to stay in town as the McGees' house guest to help Fibber close the deal. All sorts of wackiness ensues until the fadeout, when Jerry Wood reveals that Edgar might have saved everyone a whole lot of trouble if he'd remembered that he holds a controlling interest in the Horton company and could have bought the airstrip himself in Reel Three—but then there wouldn't have been any movie, would there?

For the first 40 minutes or so, *Look Who's Laughing* maintains a surface credibility, never presenting Charlie McCarthy as anything other than a dummy operated by Bergen, not even in a party scene where Charlie flirts with a bevy of beautiful girls. (Charlie's makeup is smoother here than at Universal, where the ridges around his chin were more pronounced.) Yes, Edgar carries on conversations and arguments with Charlie as if his little friend is real, but we've come to accept this idiosyncrasy. Elsewhere, there is considerable emphasis on Bergen's skill as a ventriloquist *without* Charlie, as he stages an impromptu performance for Fibber's friends with a character named Ophelia, whom he had previously used in his nightclub act and as a warm-up for his radio audience. Reminiscent of Señor Wences' "Johnny," Ophelia is a literal hand puppet, her eyes painted on Bergen's closed fist, her mouth consisting of Edgar's thumb and forefinger, and a bandana draped over her "head." Ophelia would later graduate to dummy-hood as spinsterish Effie Klinker (in tribute to Bergen's head writer Zeno Klinker), who though she appeared on radio and later on TV (rechristened "Podine Puffington") would never show up in a motion picture.

Once the plot has gotten rolling, the impossibility factor again takes over and Charlie McCarthy begins exhibiting genuine human motor and cognitive skills. Bored with Wistful Vista and anxious to return to New York, Charlie is most receptive when Gildersleeve suggests that the dummy send a forged telegram to Bergen claiming that Julie is ill and needs Edgar to come home right away. Of course, Bergen knows *nothing* of this deception, and only after Charlie confesses to Julie does Edgar find out. When it becomes necessary to briefly get Charlie out of the way, Molly McGee calls him up using her little-girl "Teeny" voice, arranging a date at the local malt shop. Throughout the phone conversation we hear Charlie's filtered voice on the other end (remember that boom operator at Goldwyn?), with a few cutaway shots revealing that he is changing positions while sitting in his chair. And when he thinks he's been stood up, Charlie gets "drunk" on ice cream sodas—while Edgar is halfway across town rescuing Fibber and Molly from a runaway airplane! Only the dexterous direction of Allan Dwan saves these scenes from being hopelessly outlandish: After all, if Dwan could turn the Ritz Brothers into human beings in *The Three Musketeers* (1939), why shouldn't he be able to do the same for Charlie McCarthy?

Completed in late June 1941, *Look Who's Laughing* was released just before Pearl Harbor, precisely when audiences were desperate for a "laff riot" to take their minds off the sorry state of the world. While the *Montreal Gazette* reviewer felt that Marian Jordan came off best of the film's radio stars ("She has a nice friendly way about her that should delight all McGee fans and scores in her little-girl imitation"), many critics insisted that Charlie McCarthy stole the show. Only a few, like the *Pittsburgh Post-Gazette*'s Harold V. Cohen, disagreed, but that may have been because they, like Cohen, couldn't resist such quips as "Charlie McCarthy is a somewhat wooden actor." *Look Who's Laughing* was RKO's second biggest moneymaker of 1941 (Hitchcock's *Suspicion* was #1); its surprise success prompted MCA to hastily assemble another package deal with the studio for a reunion of Bergen & McCarthy and Fibber & Molly, released in 1942 with the appropriate title *Here We Go Again*. Dwan returned as producer-director, with Jim and Marian Jordan bringing along their radio cohorts Harold Peary as Gildersleeve and Isabel Randolph as Mrs. Uppington, and Bergen accompanied by his NBC orchestra leader Ray Noble—not to mention Mortimer Snerd, absent from the big screen since *Charlie McCarthy, Detective*. Singer Ginny Simms, who'd come to RKO as part of another MCA package involving bandleader Kay Kyser (q.v.), plays Bergen's love interest this time out (and like Lucille Ball must tolerate Edgar's absent-mindedness for most of the proceedings).

In "now it's your turn" fashion, the focus is on Fibber McGee and Molly rather than Bergen during the first reel of *Here We Go Again,* as the McGees plan to celebrate their 20th wedding anniversary by returning to the Ramble Inn where they'd spent their honeymoon. When they find that the inn has degenerated into a fleabag, Fibber and Molly book themselves into the exclusive Silver Tip Lodge on the shores of

Lake Arcadia (actually California's Big Bear Lake and Cedar Lake, where most of the exteriors were filmed), there to link up with their Wistful Vista neighbors Gildersleeve and Mrs. Uppington. Coincidentally, Edgar Bergen and Charlie McCarthy are camping out near the lodge; evidently having given up radio, Edgar is now an entomologist, in search of a rare silk-spinning moth that will greatly benefit the war effort. The two separate stories collide when Edgar discovers that a supposedly worthless synthetic gasoline in which Fibber has invested his last dime is the catalyst that will release the valuable silk threads from the moth cocoons. As if we've come to see *Here We Go Again* for the plot.

After treading a thin line between reality and fantasy in *Look Who's Laughing,* director Dwan throws in the towel in *Here We Go Again,* playing the whole picture like a live-action cartoon. Except for the genuine warmth and affection generated by Jim and Marian Jordan, there's barely a believable moment in the entire film. Typical gags include Charlie cooking breakfast over a geyser which erupts and sends him shooting into the air, and Edgar escaping from a hostile Indian tribe (in 1942?) by disguising himself as a Swedish-accented squaw and throwing his voice to make it appear that a totem pole has come to life. Even the scenes with Fibber have a loopy, cartoonish quality; his pool-game routine with Gildersleeve and a wild episode with an out-of-control model airplane are so laden with special effects that they look like something out of a George Pal Puppetoon.

But the film doesn't really go over Niagara Falls in a barrel until we see Charlie McCarthy and Mortimer Snerd actually walking around unassisted, with dwarf actor Jerry Maren (best known for his work in such films as *The Wizard of Oz* and the Marx Bros.' *At the Circus*) doubling for both dummies in the long shots. Depending on one's point of view, the high or low point of *Here We Go Again* is the musical production number "Delicious Delirium," in which the diminutive Charlie is shown dancing with a group of full-sized human chorus girls. RKO publicists had a jolly old time issuing press releases explaining how Jerry Maren rehearsed for hours on end to make Charlie's stiff movements look natural during his terpsichorean turns, just so audiences wouldn't assume that Maren himself was a puppet on strings. It says something about the state of American pop-culture journalism in 1942 that grown men could seriously discuss the credibility factor of watching a wooden dummy dance on-screen.

Critics tried to be friendly towards the film, but it was an uphill battle. The reviewer for the *Milwaukee Journal* sighed, "The radio abilities of all these people are such that even this movie cannot harm them. But we hope they stay away from cameras for awhile." That wartime audiences were hungry for escapist movie fare of this nature was proven anew when *Here We Go Again* posted a profit of $228,000. All that kept RKO from making a third Bergen-McGee vehicle was Jim and Marian Jordan's insistence upon starring by themselves in their next picture, and Bergen's crowded radio and USO tour schedule. One would like to believe that Bergen was absenting himself from films because he felt that RKO's insistence upon depicting Charlie McCarthy as a living, breathing small boy had been stretched as far as it could go, and he wanted to pull back to some semblance of reality. During this period, the trade papers began circulating the story that Edgar was planning to star in a remake of the 1929 musical melodrama *The Great Gabbo,* which starred Erich von Stroheim as a deranged ventriloquist whose obsession with his rather malevolent dummy alienates him from his sweetheart! While we'll give Bergen an "A" for Ambition, it's just as well that this project was dropped.

Edgar's next two films were guest star appearances. Like every other big name appearing in producer Sol Lesser's wartime musical *Stage Door Canteen* (1943), the ventriloquist donated his salary to the real Stage Door Canteen on 44th Street in New York, a recreational center where servicemen could mingle with showbiz celebrities before being shipped overseas. Showing up 21 minutes into the picture, Edgar and Charlie perform a mind-reading routine that had been in their repertoire for years (and continued into the 1970s). Like his penthouse party performance in *Letter of Introduction,*

Bergen's act is filmed in one long take (albeit unnecessarily interrupted with cutaways to the laughing audience), allowing us to fully appreciate the virtuosity of his performance. Mortimer Snerd shows up at the end of the turn as a messenger boy delivering a large crate containing British entertainer Gracie Fields, who in a triumph of dubious taste immediately launches into a cheerful ditty about killing "Japs."

Independently produced by Charles R. Rogers, *Song of the Open Road* started production in early 1944 as a vehicle for 14-year-old soprano Suzanne Burce, who had gotten an MGM contract largely on the strength of her radio appearances as Charlie McCarthy's "protégée." By the time she had been borrowed from MGM to appear in *Song of the Open Road,* Suzanne had decided to follow the lead of actors Anne Shirley and Gig Young by professionally adopting the name of her screen character, Jane Powell. This relentlessly propagandistic film concerns a pampered child actress (Jane) who runs away from her studio and joins a chapter of the Youth Hostel Association, a sort of junior-league Civilian Conservation Corps who are harvesting oranges in California. When it looks like there won't be enough orange pickers to save the crop before bad weather sets in, Jane rallies the local townsfolk to pitch in and help by staging a variety show with her Hollywood friends.

Evidently little Janie doesn't hang with entertainers her own age, since the musicale consists of Bergen & McCarthy, W.C. Fields and Sammy Kaye's orchestra. Charlie's eagerly anticipated rematch with Fields is a bit anticlimactic, cut short by W.C.'s horrified reaction to a miniature dummy named Charlie McCarthy Jr. For the remainder of their very limited footage, Edgar and his sidekicks Charlie and Mortimer come off better than Fields, who in addition to looking ill and unsteady is forced to deliver a distressingly straight patriotic speech to the gathered throng.

Bergen and his dummies make a more formal appearance in Disney's Technicolor animation–live action hybrid *Fun and Fancy Free* (1947), which consists of two cartoon featurettes linked together by the presence of Jiminy Cricket. After forcing the audience to suffer through an interminable animated adaptation of the Sinclair Lewis story "Bongo" narrated by Dinah Shore, the film picks up tremendously when Jiminy hops over to the home of Edgar Bergen, who is holding a birthday party for child actress Luana Patten. With Charlie and Mortimer also in attendance, Edgar reads a new version of "Jack and the Beanstalk," visualized in cartoon form with Mickey Mouse, Donald Duck and Goofy as the story's protagonists and Billy Gilbert providing the voice (and sneezes) of the Giant. The influence of Bergen's still-popular radio program is felt in the comic interpolations by his dummies (when Edgar reads that Happy Valley has been shrouded in misery, Charlie shoots back, "Just like the eighth grade"), and in the unseen presence of *Charlie McCarthy Show* vocalist Anita Gordon as the voice of the Singing Harp. The Disneyesque trappings are an ideal setting for Bergen, McCarthy and Snerd, and one regrets (and resents) the decision made for the 1960s TV anthology *Walt Disney's Wonderful World of Color* to remove the Bergen scenes and replace them with the ever-tiresome cartoon mallard Ludwig Von Drake.

Except for a pair of 1950 short subjects, *Fun and Fancy Free* represented Bergen & McCarthy's last screen appearance until 1979. On his own, Edgar played character parts in a few films, most memorably as Ellen Corby's starched-collar Swedish suitor in *I Remember Mama* (1948). Just after his radio show's cancellation on July 1, 1956, Bergen gave series television a try with a brief stint as host (along with his dummies) of the CBS quiz show *Do You Trust Your Wife?* (later taken over by Johnny Carson and retitled *Who Do You Trust?*). As in their film appearances, Bergen and Charlie somehow came off more persuasively on radio than in a visual presentation. With the venues for his act narrowing to TV guest spots, occasional nightclub gigs and state fairs, Edgar was unfairly dismissed by some observers as an elderly has-been who moved his lips too much. This opinion was not shared by such professional ventriloquists and puppeteers as Paul Winchell, Shari Lewis, and Jeff Dunham, who regarded him as the *maître* of the art, the man who rescued ventriloquism from a mere extra added attraction to top-of-the-bill status by pioneering the concept of "personality" dummies.

There were few bigger admirers of Edgar Bergen than Jim Henson, creator of the Muppets, who provided Edgar and Charlie with a choice cameo appearance in 1979's *The Muppet Movie* as the judges of a beauty contest entered by that vainglorious sock puppet Miss Piggy. Just before the contest results are announced, the camera closes in on Bergen & McCarthy, as sartorially splendid as ever:

> CHARLIE (to the camera): You're not gonna believe who the winner is, folks.
> EDGAR: Oh, come now, Charlie, it's their movie.
> CHARLIE: Oh, so it is, yes.

One could not ask for a more amusing and graceful exit from the big screen. As it happened, *The Muppet Movie* was released posthumously. On September 30, 1978, shortly after wrapping up a spectacularly successful farewell appearance at Caesar's Palace in Las Vegas, Edgar Bergen died peacefully in his sleep. The forever young Charlie McCarthy now resides in an honored place at the Smithsonian Institution.

The Bob Hope Connection: "Honey Chile" Wilder, "Brenda & Cobina," "Vera Vague" and Jerry Colonna (1938–1962)

It is hardly necessary to chronicle the amazing career of comedian Bob Hope (1903–2003) within these pages. From the moment the London-born, Ohio-raised Hope discovered his true calling as a monologist in 1928, his ascendancy to the highest strata of show business success was assured. Vaudeville, Broadway, films, radio, television—you name it, Bob conquered it, along the way becoming an entertainment icon for his tireless trouping overseas on behalf of America's fighting men. If ever there was a true "solo" performer, it was Bob Hope: always standing alone and naked unto his enemies (and friends) before a curtain or other backdrop, rattling off jokes at a rate of six per minute, and having the intestinal fortitude to remain stock still with a fixed glare on his face until the audience caught up with him. "My idea," he explained, "was to let them know who was running things." As the man in charge, Hope usually saw to it that no one got bigger laughs than him—and if his legions of gag writers couldn't do the trick, Bob himself would trump his competition with a quick, cutting ad lib.

Yet throughout his career Bob Hope would benefit from the comic input of co-stars and stooges. In his earliest two-reel comedy films for Vitaphone, he was usually seen fielding setups and punchlines for a variety of supporting players, including hawk-beaked Johnny Berkes and radio funster Tommy Mack ("Who's excited? *Who's excited?*") And of course many of his best feature films teamed him with his lifelong pal Bing Crosby, their ongoing war of ad libs and putdowns at times taking on Gettysburg dimensions.

During a mid–1930s vaudeville engagement at the Palace Theater, Bob had a blonde female foil in the statuesque form of Georgia-born showgirl Patricia "Honey Chile" Wilder (1913–1995). Hope later claimed that he hired Wilder as his partner the moment she opened her mouth and in a "thick spoonbread accent" greeted him with "Haaow you, Mistah Hope?" Chances are that if Bob hadn't discovered her, someone else would have. A superb deadpan comedienne, "Honey Chile" not only brightened Hope's Palace act but also his first important radio show *The Intimate Revue*, which bowed January 4, 1935, on NBC. Even before Hope made the transition to feature films, Wilder began appearing in such pictures as MGM's *Speed* (James Stewart's first starring vehicle) and RKO's *Off Again—On Again* (with Wheeler and Woolsey) and *New Faces of 1937* (featuring fellow radio performers Joe Penner, Bert Gordon and Parkyakarkus). A sample of the nonsensical material Hope did with "Honey Chile" on stage and radio can be heard in Bob's first Paramount feature *The Big Broadcast of 1938* (discussed elsewhere); she later showed up in the 1938 Hope vehicle *Thanks for the Memory*, the last of her seven films. Wilder might have become a permanent fixture in Hope's movie entourage were it not for two reasons: (A) For the most part Bob kept his radio and film work separate by playing different characters in the two mediums; and (B) "Honey Chile" was otherwise preoccupied with a very colorful social life. Squired by practically every eligible millionaire in New York's café society, she eventually settled down as the wife of a wealthy Austrian prince. It is said that Patricia Wilder was a primary inspiration for Holly Golightly in Truman Capote's *Breakfast at Tiffany's*.

Some of the other female members of Hope's radio stock company were as far removed from the sexy "Honey Chile" as Mars is from Pluto. During the first two seasons (1938–1940) of his weekly program for Pepsodent toothpaste, Hope traded quips with a couple of raucous husband-hunting debutantes named "Brenda and Cobina," a takeoff of real-life socialites Brenda Frazier and Cobina Wright, Jr. Played by Blanche Stewart (1903–1952) and Elvia Allman (1904–1992), Brenda and Cobina were uproariously wicked sendups of the entire "glamour girl" culture, the two ladies posing for publicity photos in hideous evening gowns, Medusa-like hairdos and grotesque facial makeup. Neither actress was the Miss America type, but they were nowhere near as homely as the characters they played. Reportedly, these two monstrosities were the basis for all those beastly animated-cartoon spinsters who ran around screaming "A *maaa-aan*!" whenever some unfortunate male crossed their path. Stewart and Allman were given their first screen exposure as Brenda and Cobina ("The Gusher Sisters") in the Paramount B-musical *A Night at Earl Carroll's* (1940), and it's really their picture despite the top billing bestowed upon Ken Murray. Of Brenda & Cobina's three subsequent films, the best—and the one most often revived today—is *Time Out for Rhythm* (Columbia, 1941), in which they share several scenes with the Three Stooges. When the Stooges confront the two deadly debutantes for the first time, Curly shudders and squeals, "Imagine five things like *us* in the same room? I can't stand it!!!"

Eventually the real Brenda Frazier and Cobina Wright, Jr. became fed up with the spoof and threatened legal action if Hope didn't drop the characters. This hardly fazed Bob, who simply filed all the "ugly" jokes he'd used on the two ladies for future reference (several of these questionable witticisms would be trotted out when the comedian worked with Phyllis Diller in the 1960s). Nor did Stewart and Allman suffer too much after their characters were taken from them, finding plenty of solo work on other radio comedy series like *The Jack Benny Program* and *The Abbott and Costello Show*. Outliving Blanche Stewart by forty years, Elvia Allman is perhaps best remembered today as social-climbing Selma Plout on the TV sitcom *Petticoat Junction*.

The unofficial replacement for Brenda and Cobina was Barbara Jo Allen (1904–1974), a Broadway-bred dramatic actress who'd made her earliest known radio appearance on the NBC West Coast network series *Signal Carnival*. Though she played all sorts of roles on radio (notably Beth Holly in the evergreen serial *One Man's Family*), she had an affinity for comedy parts. One of her favorite characters on *Signal Carnival* was a shrill, man-chasing spinster called Vera Vague, who greeted every male she met with a gushing "You *deeeear* boy!" The character received nationwide acclaim as a semi-regular on Bergen & McCarthy's *Chase and Sanborn Hour* during the 1939–40 season, then really caught fire when Allen joined the cast of Bob Hope's Pepsodent show in 1942. (The following year she married the comedian's producer Norman Morrell.) For her Hope appearances, the actress dressed in dowdy "old maid" outfits and gaudy flowered hats, a pince-nez or lorgnette topping off the characterization. In real life Barbara was an extremely attractive woman with a warm, sweet voice, but you'd never know it when she was jabbering away in full "Vera Vague" regalia.

The actress' film career began in 1938 with *Major Difficulties,* one of several RKO short comedies in which she co-starred with Leon Errol, often as Leon's shrewish wife. She made her feature film debut as a nondescript receptionist in MGM's all-female extravaganza *The Women* (1939), then landed a credited role in the Republic musical *Village Barn Dance* (1940), playing Vera Vague onscreen for the first time. The actress continued to be billed under her real name in subsequent films, though she was invariably cast as Vera Vague (as in *Ice Capades*) or a reasonable facsimile. From 1942's *Priorities on Parade* onward, the actress and her radio persona were forever fused, and she was billed in the opening credits solely as Vera Vague, even when her screen character had a different moniker (or even a different personality, as in 1945's *Snafu*).

In 1943 Miss Allen—hereafter "Vera" to avoid confusion—signed with Columbia Pictures to headline a series of two-reel comedies produced by the same unit responsible for the Three Stooges shorts. Some modifications were made in her established character: Gone are the frumpy spinster makeup and spectacles, allowing the actress to appear as her own lovely self and even wear fashionable outfits. Also, Vera no longer has problems snaring a man; if she isn't given a husband in her Columbia films, she is being ardently pursued by good-looking bachelors. She is even allowed to use her own voice in her first two-reeler *You Dear Boy* (1943), and in *Cupid Goes Nuts* (1947) she gets to play a dual role as a repressed college professor and her uninhibited twin sister.

Of the 16 "Vera Vague" shorts produced between 1943 and 1952, a handful are quite good, two of them—*The Jury Goes Round and Round* (1945) and *Hiss and Yell* (1946)—earning Academy Award nominations. (In both these films Vera co-starred with her ex-husband Barton Yarborough, then concurrently appearing in Columbia's *I Love a Mystery* series [q.v.].) Others were mere potboilers, recycling scripts originally written for Charley Chase and other past Columbia comedians. The weakest of the shorts were directed by Jules White, though in fairness he did a few of the better ones too. After clashing with director Harry Edwards on the set of *Strife of the Party* (1943), Vera insisted upon working exclusively with White, whom she personally liked. Since the actress had already indulged in onscreen slapstick in her feature work, she took to the roughhouse antics of the White comedies like a duck to water. The trouble came whenever Vera was expected to do a gag that robbed her of her femininity (breaking a light bulb in the mouth of her romantic rival in 1946's *Headin' for a Weddin'*), or appeared to be in genuine pain as the result of a physical gag. Particularly hard to take is the scene in *Miss in a Mess* (1949) in which Vera attempts to escape from a mad killer, only to be yanked to the ground by the rope tied around her neck.

Leaving Bob Hope's radio program, Vera joined Jimmy Durante's show that same year (1949), remaining with the Schnozzola until 1950. In the early days of network television she emceed a couple of game shows, *The Greatest Man on Earth* and *Follow the Leader,* still billed as Vera Vague. The actress reverted to her real name onscreen for a juicy supporting part in MGM's *The Opposite Sex* (1956), a musical remake of her first feature film *The Women*. Her billing alternated between Barbara Jo Allen and Vera Vague for the rest of her career, which included voiceover work in such Disney cartoon features as *Sleeping Beauty* (1959), wherein she was heard as the good fairy Fauna. After retiring from acting in the 1960s, she wrote the pro-ecology children's book *The Animal Convention* and became quite active in the burgeoning environmental movement.

No other radio comedy foil benefited as mightily from the Bob Hope Connection as Gerard Luigi "Jerry" Colonna (1904–1986). After attending high school in his native Boston, Colonna worked as a longshoreman by day and studied trombone and drums by night. By the time he joined the CBS radio orchestra in 1931, Jerry had adopted the bushy handlebar mustache that became his lifelong trademark. In later interviews he indicated that this hirsute ornament served as a cushion when he played his trombone, but fellow musician Merwin Bogue has said that Colonna grew the handlebars so that he wouldn't be just another face in the crowd, just as Bogue later adopted his attention-getting Beatle haircut when he became "Ish Kabibble" of the Kay Kyser Orchestra. During his early years with CBS, Jerry gained a reputation as a prankster, breaking up rehearsals and sometimes performances by making silly faces and rolling his saucerlike eyes. He would also sing along during rehearsals in an air-raid-siren tenor, regaling his coworkers with

Two of Bob Hope's funniest and most dependable radio foils, Jerry Colonna and Vera Vague (Barbara Jo Allen), combine forces in Paramount's *Priorities on Parade* (1942).

his ability to hold a high note in perfect pitch for as long as 72 seconds. A talent like this was too conspicuous to confine to mere orchestra work, and before long Jerry was supplementing his income as a musician with brief comedy bits on the radio shows of Walter O'Keefe and Fred Allen.

Hired as a trombonist for orchestra leader John Scott Trotter, Colonna joined the cast of Bing Crosby's *Kraft Music Hall* in 1935. During one of the show's weekly concert spots, generally the most serious portion of the program, Bing introduced Jerry as the only singer on Earth who started on a high note and worked his way up. As of yet Colonna wasn't doing jokes, but he'd learned how to make people laugh simply by showing up. A few New York nightclub engagements led to his film debut as a specialty singer in producer Walter Wanger's *52nd Street* (1937) and to small parts in other films.

While performing an uncredited cameo as a zany music professor in *College Swing* (1938), Colonna was invited by the film's leading man Bob Hope to join Bob's new radio program for Pepsodent. As noted by radio historian John Dunning, Jerry rapidly built a following as "perhaps the wildest comic presence" on network radio. On Bob's show he functioned in the same manner as Bert "The Mad Russian" Gordon on *The Eddie Cantor Show* (see **The Eddie Cantor Connection**), popping up without warning as a loony character known as "The Professor." Colonna may well have been the only comedian to upstage Hope on a weekly basis and live to tell the tale, fracturing audiences with his standard salutation "Greetings, Gate!" and supplying such other *Bob Hope Pepsodent Show* catchphrases as "Who's Yehoodi?" and "Gimme a drag on that before you throw it away" (a line that was dropped when listeners finally figured out what it meant!). Outside of these and other *bon* *mots*—seldom funny in themselves but made hilarious through his manic delivery—Colonna was most famous for his unique renditions of such standard songs as "The Road to Mandalay" and "Sonny Boy," holding high notes louder and longer than any other human being.

With the exception of Patricia "Honey Chile" Wilder, Colonna was the only one of Hope's radio supporting comics to appear onscreen with his boss, playing a sizable supporting role in *Road to Singapore* (1940) and cameos in *Star Spangled Rhythm* (1942), *Road to Rio* (1947) and *The Road to Hong Kong* (1962). His most characteristic moment came in *Road to Rio*, where after leading a troop of mounted soldiers to the rescue of Hope and Bing Crosby, he suddenly pulled up, stared at the audience and declared with a grin, "Well, waddya know? We never quite made it! *Exciting*, though, wasn't it?"

By the early 1940s, Colonna hardly needed Bob's patronage to land movie roles. He was seen to excellent advantage in such musicals as 1942's *Priorities on Parade* (cast opposite fellow Hope regular Vera Vague), 1944's *Atlantic City* and 1951's *Kentucky Jubilee,* in which he was not only billed above the title but appeared in caricature form as a harvest moon in the opening credits. Among his many other films were *True to the Army* (1942) with Judy Canova, *It's in the Bag* (1945) with Fred Allen (q.v.) and the all-star MGM musical *Meet Me in Las Vegas* (1956). Colonna also provided voices for Walt Disney's cartoon features, lending his distinctive touch to the narration of the "Casey at the Bat" sequence in *Make Mine Music* (1946) and excelling in the role of the March Hare (drawn to resemble Jerry) in *Alice in Wonderland* (1951). And let's not forget the scores of proxy Jerry Colonnas in such 1940s cartoon shorts as Warner Bros.' *The Wacky Worm, Greetings Bait* and *Daffy Doodles.*

In the midst of all this activity, Colonna found time to compose several popular songs ("At Dusk," "I Came to Say Goodbye"), and also toured extensively with Bob Hope's USO troupe throughout World War II (as recalled in his book *Who Threw That Cocoanut?*) and beyond. In 1946 Jerry *almost* preceded Hope as a television personality: Hired to appear in a comedy sketch on New York station WABD, Colonna stormed out of the studio when he realized that the sketch was merely a glorified Westinghouse commercial and his part had been trimmed to nearly nothing. Ultimately Jerry would embrace TV as an outlet for his talents, appearing in his own 1951 ABC program and as guest star on such series as *Super Circus, Climax!, The Gale Storm Show, The Shirley Temple Hour, McHale's Navy* and *The Monkees.*

While Bob Hope could frequently be cold-blooded in his professional relationships, he had a great deal of affection for Jerry Colonna. When he decided to fire Colonna from his radio show and replace him with singer Doris Day in 1948, Hope nonetheless continued to use Jerry in his TV specials and his USO unit. After Jerry suffered a debilitating stroke in 1966, Bob went out of his way to find nonstressful work for his longtime sidekick. Making his final appearance in Hope's 1976 special *Joys,* a frail-looking Jerry rose to the occasion with all his former gusto. And during his last days at the Motion Picture & Television Country House and Hospital, few people outside of his own immediate family paid as many visits to Jerry Colonna as his old pal Bob Hope.

Ahhhhh, yes. *Heartwarming,* isn't it?

From WXYZ Detroit: "The Lone Ranger" (1938–1939, 1956–1958, 1981, 2013); "The Green Hornet" (1940, 2011)

Purchased in 1929 by movie theater mogul John H. King and his business partner George W. Trendle, radio station WXYZ was initially the Detroit, Michigan, affiliate of the CBS network. In full charge of the station by 1932, Trendle made the first of several bold moves when he severed ties with CBS to develop his own network-quality programming with a top-notch acting repertory organized by director James Jewell. In choosing the flagship program for the "new" WXYZ, Trendle could not afford the sort of musical-variety offerings popular on network radio, so he chose to launch a dramatic series, traditionally the cheapest sort of programming to produce. A spirited debate rages to this day over who actually created the program that put Trendle's operation on the map, so we'll cut to the chase with an indisputable fact: *The Lone Ranger* made its first formal appearance on January 31, 1933. A western series with a Zorro-like masked hero, *The Lone Ranger* was in its early years written exclusively by Fran Striker, who recycled many of the story and character elements he'd developed on previous radio programs—most conspicuously the hero's reliance upon silver bullets. So successful was *The Lone Ranger* on a syndicated-transcription basis that Trendle was able to gather together several powerful radio stations outside of Michigan for the purpose of forming a new national network, the Mutual Broadcasting System.

The premise, format and trademarks of *The Lone Ranger* have been thoroughly documented and analyzed in dozens of authoritative works, and need not be recounted in these pages. It's worth noting that in its formative period the series emulated its role model Zorro by depicting the title character as a laughing-cavalier type. Before long, however, both character and program were religiously adhering to a strict set of guidelines established by Trendle and Striker, among them: "The Lone Ranger is never seen without his mask or a disguise"; "The Lone Ranger always uses perfect grammar and precise speech completely devoid of slang or colloquial phrases"; and, foremost, "When he has to use guns, the Lone Ranger never shoots to kill, but rather only to disarm his opponent as painlessly as possible."

The Lone Ranger traveled with his "faithful Indian companion" Tonto, whose monosyllabic grasp of the English language belied his great wisdom and vast resourcefulness. In keeping with the silver motif established by his specially molded bullets, the Ranger rode throughout the West astride a proud stallion named Silver—and if there were any doubts as to the horse's identity, they were removed by the hero's celebrated rallying cry "Hi-yo, Silver!" heard at the beginning and end of each half-hour episode. As famous as the star and his steed was the series' theme song, Rossini's "William Tell Overture," which like most of the incidental music heard on the program was lifted from royalty-free classic compositions. Other favored pieces included Liszt's "Les Preludes," Mendelssohn's "Fingal's Cave Overture," Tchaikovsky's "1812 Overture," and several Wagner compositions.

Nobody knew the Lone Ranger's true identity, nor where he came from—at least not until Republic Pictures optioned the film rights to the property for a 15-episode serial in 1938. The industry leader in thrill-a-minute chapterplays, Republic assembled a grade-A staff of scriptwriters (Barry Shipman, George Worthing Yates, Franklyn Adreon, Ronald Davidson, Lois Eby) and engaged a pair of ace action directors (William Witney, John English) to put *The Lone Ranger* together. Retained from the radio original were the two main characters, the mask, the Rossini theme music, and "Hi-yo, Silver!" Otherwise, and despite the "based on" credit given Fran Striker in the opening titles, Republic's *The Lone Ranger* was woven from whole cloth—including the backstory for the title character in Chapter One.

Set in the last months of the Civil War, the story is motivated by a rogue military officer named Smith (Stanley Andrews), who takes time off from plundering Texas to murder Marcus Jeffries, the territory's newly appointed minister of finance. Assuming Jeffries' identity, the villain uses his position of power to levy huge taxes and rule the populace with a dictatorial hand. Informed by his chief spy Joe Snead (Maston Williams) that a band of six Texas Rangers is on its way to check up on the activities of "Jeffries" and his henchmen, the criminal leader arranges an ambush, killing all but one of the Rangers. Rescued by the wandering Indian Tonto (played by Chief Thundercloud, the stage name of Native American actor Victor Daniels), the surviving Ranger—his face carefully averted from the camera—is nursed back to health. The dialogue between the two men ("Other rangers—all dead") would later be repeated *ad infinitum* on the radio series, as would the survivor's vow to track down the killers of his comrades and carry on an endless battle for justice as a "masked rider of the plains" known only as the Lone Ranger.

Republic goes all out in its promotion of the 1938 movie serial version of radio's *The Lone Ranger* in this trade ad from *Independent Exhibitors' Film Bulletin*.

This was the basic legend that, with a few variations over the years, would be accepted and adopted by the WXYZ version of *The Lone Ranger*. But Republic went one better, utilizing a plot device that would do yeoman service in several future serials (notably *The Masked Marvel*). Determining that the mysterious Lone Ranger is one of five young lawmen, "Jeffries" arranges for all five to be arrested and sentenced to death. In a darkened prison cell, the actual Lone Ranger identifies himself to the other four men, who take an oath that once they escape their present predicament they will carry on the Ranger's crusade to establish law and order in Texas—and if need be, each man will occasionally don the Ranger's mask to throw the villains off the scent. This Magnificent Five includes Allen King (Lee Powell), Bert Rogers (Herman Brix, aka Bruce Bennett), Bob Stuart (Hal Taliaferro, aka Wally Wales), Dick Forrest (Lane Chandler) and Jim Clark (George Letz, aka George Montgomery). But don't look for clues as to who's really who in the opening chapter: The voice of the Lone Ranger is provided by none of these five actors. Until the long-lost *Lone Ranger* serial was restored in the 1980s, it was assumed that the voice behind the mask was that of Earl Graser, then playing the character on radio—or possibly Graser's successor Brace Beemer, who played the role longer than any other actor, right up to the final first-run radio episode in 1955. But no: The words spoken behind that face-obscuring mask were supplied by veteran comedian and cartoon voiceover specialist Billy Bletcher, who in contrast with the six-foot-tall Lone Ranger stood five feet two inches in his stocking feet.

Through the process of elimination, the Lone Ranger is revealed to be Allen King in the serial's final chapter, enabling actor Lee Powell to subsequently embark on a circus tour billing himself as "The Original Lone Ranger of Talking Pictures." George Trendle, already displeased with Republic's adaptation of his pet property (about which more later), placed a restraining order on Powell, but a Federal judge ruled that the actor could exploit his Lone Ranger association whenever he felt like it (more on *that* later as well). Meanwhile, the success of the movie serial following its February 1938 release prompted Republic to consider fashioning the property into a feature film titled *The Lone Ranger Returns*. *Variety* reported in June 1938 that John Wayne had been selected to play the Masked Man, and that production would commence in the fall of that year. But for reasons unknown, Wayne was diverted to the studio's "Three Mesquiteers" B-western series—and the second *Lone Ranger* filmization, like the first, ultimately emerged as a 15-part serial.

Again directed by William Witney and John English, *The Lone Ranger Rides Again* (1939) is better constructed than its predecessor, perhaps because it has a less cumbersome plotline. Eschewing the mystery angle of the earlier serial, the screenplay goes the Zorro route by establishing the Lone Ranger's true identity from the outset. Star Robert Livingston had refused to spend the entire serial behind a mask, thus he is frequently seen bare-faced as young homesteader Bill Andrews. Working in tandem with Tonto (Chief Thundercloud again), our hero has sworn to topple the empire of evil cattleman Bart Dolan (Ralph Dunn), who as head of the Black Raiders is waging a campaign of terror to drive all settlers out of the San Ramon Valley. On this occasion the masked man also has a *second* faithful companion, Latino sidekick Juan Vasquez (Duncan Renaldo).

As mentioned, Trendle was unhappy with what Republic did to his "baby" in the studio's two *Lone Ranger* serials. It wasn't enough that the scriptwriters flew in the face of the Ranger's credo by having him shoot to kill on several occasions, and even lose his temper to the extent of lacerating a villain with a bullwhip. Trendle's chief gripe was that both serials had revealed the Ranger's identity, something the radio show scrupulously avoided in order to sustain the character's mystique. So riled was Trendle at Republic that he eventually bought up prints and negatives of the serials and had them destroyed. For decades *The Lone Ranger* and *The Lone Ranger Rides Again* were the Holy Grail for serial buffs, who refused to settle for the still-extant *Hi-yo Silver*, the 1940 feature-length adaptation of the first serial, and demanded to see "the real thing" from first to last. In the late 1970s and early 1980s several attempts were made to piece together the serials from dupe prints, foreign-language copies and snippets of *Hi-yo Silver,* but the ragged and blurred results were endurable only to diehard completists. It wasn't until 2009 that a fairly complete, decent-quality edition of the 1938 *Lone Ranger* was made available on DVD.

Though Trendle seldom had a pleasant word for Republic, this didn't stop him from appropriating a few of the serial's more attractive elements for his radio program. Republic's original musical cues, largely written by Alberto Colombo, Cy Feuer, and William Lava, subsequently became the standard background themes for radio's *Lone Ranger* and its TV spinoff. And as noted, Trendle had the first *Lone Ranger* serial to thank for establishing the character's "origin" story. It was tinkered with and elaborated upon over the airwaves for nearly a decade—including a curious 1941 variation, heard during the series' "Legion of the Black Arrow" story arc, which stated that the ambushed Ranger had been rescued from the brink of death by a beautiful young woman. The Ranger's backstory took its final form on the episode of June 30, 1948.

Unfortunately this broadcast is unavailable to collectors except in an abbreviated recreation released as a 45-rpm record premium by the series' sponsor General Mills. Even in this potted version, one can only marvel at how expertly the writing staff headed by Striker adapted the Gospel According to Republic Pictures for the purposes of the radio show. The bare bones of the legend are still present: The six rangers killed in an ambush, the survivor rescued by Tonto, the self-promise to carry on as "champion of justice" in the guise of the Lone Ranger. To further personalize the hero's crusade, it was now carved in stone that the ill-fated Rangers had been led to their rendezvous with destiny at Bryant's Gap (originally Grant's Pass) by Captain Dan Reid, elder brother of the young man who would soon be reborn as the Lone Ranger. Contrary to popular belief, Dan's kid brother was not specifically named John Reid on this program, nor at any other time during the radio series' 22-year run. No one would ever know the Lone Ranger's full identity so long as George W. Trendle had anything to say about it.

Other ingredients of the backstory (the silver mine that provided the Lone Ranger and Tonto with a perpetual source of income, the capture and taming of the magnificent stallion Silver) had been established in previous episodes, but it was not until this 1948 installment that all the pieces fell into place. The following year, the "origin" yarn served as the three-part opener for ABC's filmed TV series version of *The Lone Ranger* starring Clayton Moore and Jay Silverheels, who in the eyes of many aficionados (this writer included) are the definitive Lone Ranger and Tonto. Like its radio predecessor, this version of the legend solidified the identity of the outlaw leader who had orchestrated the fatal ambush as Butch Cavendish, played on TV by Glenn Strange (previously seen as a different bad guy in *The Lone Ranger Rides Again*). Trendle had no objection to committing his property to film under these circumstances, especially since his own company, the Lone Ranger Inc., was in charge of production; but a planned *Lone Ranger* feature film was thwarted by Trendle's exorbitant monetary demands and insistence upon total creative control.

By 1956, however, Trendle had little say in the matter. The Lone Ranger Inc. was now controlled by Texas oil millionaire Jack Wrather and his actress wife Bonita Granville, who would place their own stamp on the property with a group of 39 half-hour television episodes filmed in color for the series' final season. Though quite popular with the show's juvenile fans, the earlier black-and-white *Lone Ranger* TV seasons were often hobbled by cheap production values, poor sound recording, slovenly scripting and erratic direction. There was also that awkward period in 1952 when Clayton Moore and the series' then-producer Jack Chertok parted company over a salary dispute. Hired to play the Lone Ranger for 52 interim episodes, actor John Hart fit the mask and costume and very little else, his voice lacking the authoritative timbre that Moore brought to the role. Once the Wrather Corporation took the reins, the series began to display the same glossy production polish and consistent professionalism that were hallmarks of the Wrathers' other television property *Lassie*.

Before beginning production on the revitalized TV series, the Wrathers adapted *The Lone Ranger* as a theatrical motion picture. The producers were able to secure distribution and financial backing from Warner Bros., who in the process purchased the rights to 130 of the TV episodes and 1500 of the radio scripts, as well as all merchandising rights to the property. Released February 10, 1956, Warners' 83-minute, full-color film version of *The Lone Ranger* ranks among the finest studio westerns of the 1950s, and as a bonus adheres more faithfully to the radio original than any prior movie adaptation—though on at least one occasion the Lone Ranger breaks faith with his youthful fans by killing the man he is shooting at.

From the first scene onward, director Stuart Heisler (*The Biscuit Eater, The Glass Key*) establishes a breathless pace that never lets up, while cinematographer Edwin B. DuPar (later a mainstay of Warners' TV division) makes the most of some spectacular locations in and around Sonora, California. The screenplay is by Herb Meadow, best known to western buffs as the co-creator (with Sam Rolfe) of the classic television series *Have Gun—Will Travel*. The writer deftly interweaves three separate story threads, each of which could have easily stood on its own as a half-hour episode of the *Lone Ranger* TV show: the underhanded efforts by a greedy land baron to stir up a war between the white settlers and a nearby Indian tribe in order to gain control of a mountain rich with silver; the same land baron's pigheaded efforts to raise his young daughter as if she were a boy, the better to humiliate his aristocratic wife; and a power struggle between a pacifistic Indian chief and a hotheaded young brave. It is to Meadow's credit that these diverse plot devices are sewn into a unified whole with nary a stitch showing.

The performances in *The Lone Ranger* are first-rate. Clayton Moore and Jay Silverheels had never been better, with Moore having the time of his life temporarily dropping his Lone Ranger persona to disguise himself as a grizzled old prospector, and Silverheels carrying several key scenes—including an outsized brawl with a lynch-happy mob—all by himself. The villainy is in the capable hands of Lyle Bettger as the covetous landowner and Robert J. Wilke as his snarling henchman; Bonita Granville, the film's co-producer, gives an understated and nuanced performance as Bettger's long-suffering wife; and two of television's favorite Native American impersonators, Michael Ansara (Cochise on *Broken Arrow*) and Frank deKova (Wild Eagle on *F Troop*), lend credibility and poignancy to the Indian camp scenes. But the film's acting honors go to child performer Beverly Washburn, who as the villain's imperiled daughter runs through a wider gamut of emotions than any of her adult co-stars.

As part of the property's 25th anniversary celebration in 1958, the Wrathers assembled a follow-up *Lone Ranger* color feature for United Artists release: *The Lone Ranger and the Lost City of Gold,* again starring Moore and Silverheels and largely filmed in Tucson, Arizona. As before, the film is well produced, though without the financial backing of Warner Bros. the producers were forced to a cut a few corners. Scripted by Eric Friewald and Robert Schafer ("based on the Lone Ranger legend," or so the opening credits would have us believe), the plot once again revolves around an avaricious landowner who hopes to swipe a valuable chunk of property from a peaceful Indian tribe. This time the coveted turf is rumored to be located near one of the fabled Seven Cities of Gold that Spanish Conquistadors had sought but never found. Potentially more compelling than this storyline is a subplot dwelling upon the issue of racial prejudice, involving a young Native American doctor (Norman Frederic) who passes for white in a town populated almost exclusively by anti–Indian bigots. Though we don't know it until well into the film, this subplot is intimately related to the main narrative. Unfortunately, the individual storylines aren't quite as well unified as in the first *Lone Ranger* feature, nor does director Lesley Selander maintain the steady pace needed to bring these links together in a tidy fashion. Selander does a better job with the film's sporadic bursts of violence, especially a climactic shootout in a deserted adobe settlement.

Points in the film's favor include the performances by the stars, especially Silverheels, who as Tonto has a lot more to do—and does it with more panache—than in any previous appearance. Especially fascinating are those brief moments wherein Silverheels drops his standard "Tonto-ese" and converses in full, eloquent and often poetic sentences. Moore is likewise in fine fettle, though the Lone Ranger's masquerade as a Southern-accented bounty hunter isn't as much fun as his "Gabby" Hayes routine in the previous picture. Of the supporting players, Noreen Nash brings a unique slant to her role as the deceptively genteel landowner who is actually the brains behind all the villainy, playing her "mean" scenes with the same honey-dripping sweetness as her "nice" moments.

Though it doesn't quite live up the standards of the Wrathers' first Lone Ranger feature, *The Lone Ranger and the Lost City of Gold* has an advantage over its predecessor in providing a clearer explanation for the benefit of those who came in late as to who the title character is and how he came to be. In the first film, the Lone Ranger offers a 30-second verbal rundown of the massacre at Bryant's Gap and his emergence as the Masked Rider of the Plains. *Lost City of Gold* improves upon this with a pre-credits montage, complete with the newly composed ballad "Hi-Yo Silver," offering a Cliff's Notes version of the Ranger's backstory. This sequence is brief enough not to overwhelm the rest of the picture—which, alas, is just what happened in the next cinema adaption of this evergreen property, 1981's *The Legend of the Lone Ranger.*

The surprise success of the 1978 theatrical feature *The Magic of Lassie* encouraged the Wrathers to revive *The Lone Ranger* for the big screen. Ideally, the producers would have offered a cameo role to the actor most closely associated with the title character, but Clayton Moore and the Wrathers weren't speaking to each other except through attorneys. For nearly two decades after *The Lone Ranger and the Lost City of Gold,* Moore continued making personal appearances in his Lone Ranger mask and costume—and not always with permission from the owners of the franchise. It will be remembered that back in 1938 Lee Powell, star of the first *Lone Ranger* serial, was able to get legal dispensation to continue using the Lone Ranger name for live appearances; but it was a different story in 1975, when the Wrathers obtained a court order banning Moore from any further personal appearances in the familiar garb. The actor took to wearing a pair of shaded glasses in public, all the while waging a court battle to win back what he now considered his birthright. This legal contretemps was still going on as *The Legend of the Lone Ranger* went into production in 1979, thus the only former "Ranger" to whom the Wrathers extended an invitation to make a brief appearance in the picture was Moore's 1952 replacement John Hart, who gives a nice account of himself in the role of a newspaper editor named Striker (!).

Of course Hart was too far along in years to play the title character, while Jay "Tonto" Silverheels was mortally ill at the time and would pass away before the film's release. But the Wrathers had intended all along to hire a pair of unknowns to play the Lone Ranger and Tonto for their new production, lavishing a great deal of publicity on their intensive eight-month search to find these lucky fellows. One is tempted to respond to the previous sentence with "Eight months, and the best they could come up with was Klinton Spilsbury and Michael Horse?"—but that would be unfair to one of them. Klinton Spilsbury had been an art student and professional model before being tapped to don the familiar domino mask of the Lone Ranger. It is difficult to make a fair assessment of Spilsbury's acting ability, inasmuch as his voice has been dubbed by actor James Keach. A 2013 *Entertainment Weekly* article by Jeff Labrecque indicates that all of Spilsbury's dialogue was re-recorded because his thinnish voice didn't match his character, but speculation in 1981 was that the new Lone Ranger was hopelessly inept at line delivery. More embarrassing for the film's publicity team was Spilsbury's behavior during the location shoot in Arizona, ranging from fistfights with the production crew to rowdy displays of public drunkenness; as one observer noted at the time, Spilsbury seemed hell-bent on destroying his reputation before he had one. Meanwhile Michael Horse, the young Native American cast as Tonto, comported himself in a far more professional manner, and also made a much better impression onscreen. It isn't surprising that while *The Legend of the Lone Ranger* was Spilsbury's first and last film, Horse went on to a thriving career as a character actor in such efforts as David Lynch's cult TV classic *Twin Peaks*.

Not as bad a film as one might expect, *The Legend of the Lone Ranger* is gorgeously photographed (by Laszlo Kovacs) and fitfully enjoyable, but overall a lopsided and uneven enterprise. Several sequences seem to end before they're supposed to, characters are effusively introduced only to abruptly vanish, and an obviously expensive western town exterior set is barely shown at all. This sort of shortchanging is a sure sign that the film was originally longer than its present 98 minutes, and that wholesale cutting took place after a couple of previews. Another indication that several lengthy scenes went by the wayside is the fact that, after rolling along for nearly an hour before the Lone Ranger actually becomes the Lone Ranger, the film hastily sets up what was supposed to be its main plotline—a scheme to kidnap President Ulysses S. Grant—and then rushes headlong to an unsatisfying conclusion.

It has been claimed by some reviewers that *The Legend of the Lone Ranger* can't make up its mind whether to be serious or self-satirical. In truth, most of the film is played straight, with even so florid a performer as Christopher Lloyd enacting his scenes as the fanatical Butch Cavendish without a trace of tongue in cheek. Only occasionally are there intentionally funny bits, such as Jason Robards, Jr.'s boozy portrayal of President Grant; and seldom are there any *unintentional* laughs, unless one counts the shapeless and seemingly endless ballad "The Man in the Mask," performed off-screen by a dazed-sounding Merle Haggard.

The film's one admirable quality is its respectful treatment of the official Lone Ranger backstory. Director William Fraker and screenwriters Ivan Goff and Ben Roberts do a laudable job visualizing the legend's various points of interest, including the heretofore unfilmed (but described on radio) childhood friendship between the Lone Ranger and Tonto, affirmed by their mutual term of endearment "Kemo Sabe" (which really *does* mean "trusted friend" in the Potawatomi language). And in direct opposition to the clunky "five rangers" gimmick in the 1938 serial, all deviations from the Sacred Text in *The Legend of the Lone Ranger* are made *within* the legend itself. The hero is still the brother of ranger Dan Reid, albeit firmly identified as John Reid for the first time on screen *or* radio. In previous versions, the younger Reid was a novice ranger on the day of the Bryant's Gap massacre; here he isn't an official ranger at all, having been pressed into emergency service to help track down the killers of newspaper editor Striker. Butch Cavendish, the rather flea-bitten outlaw boss in the radio saga, is now a crazed paramilitary leader with his own private army, bent upon transforming Texas into a separate country with himself as Dictator for Life. And whereas all the familiar trademarks of the Lone Ranger (the mask, the silver bullets, etc.) were of his own invention on radio, in the film it is Tonto who introduces or inspires each and every trademark—and in flawlessly articulate English to boot.

Its few merits notwithstanding, *The Legend of the Lone Ranger* did so poorly at the box office that its distributor ITC was forced to retreat into the corporate maw of Tri-Star Pictures. Thus it is hardly surprising there were no other attempts to make a *Lone Ranger* film until the 2003 television movie starring Chad Michael Murray as the title character and Nathaniel Arcand as Tonto. Intended as a TV series pilot, this version went nowhere and stayed there—but amazingly, that was *not* the end of the story. As these words are being written, Disney has released a big-budget, high-concept *Lone Ranger* theatrical feature produced by Jerry Bruckheimer, directed by Gore Verbinski and starring Armie Hammer. In a surprising break with tradition and the dictates of political correctness, a non–Native American, Johnny

Depp, has been cast as Tonto—meaning that in *another* precedent-smashing move, for the first time in motion picture history Tonto receives top billing over the Lone Ranger. (P.S.: The movie stinks. Enough said.)

While *The Lone Ranger* has transcended its WXYZ radio roots and entered the realm of folklore, its companion series *The Green Hornet* does not seem to command the same awe and reverence, perhaps because of its "second-tier imitation" status. Casting about for a modern-dress variation of *The Lone Ranger* back in 1935, George Trendle conferred with Fran Striker and James Jewell to come up with the Green Hornet, a masked crimefighter with a Tonto-like companion and a Silver-like mode of transportation. Even the property's theme music invoked the Lone Ranger in its deployment of a classical composition, in this case Rimsky-Korsakov's "The Flight of the Bumblebee."

Beginning with its 20th century setting, *The Green Hornet* differed significantly from its Old West role model. For one thing, the audience was clued in from the beginning that the Hornet's true identity was Britt Reid, the young publisher of *The Daily Sentinel,* a crusading big-city newspaper. Having inherited the *Sentinel* from his wealthy father, Reid was regarded as a playboy and dilettante by everyone else in town, but this was only a charade. Whenever the need arose, Reid donned the mask of the Green Hornet to mete out justice to criminals and racketeers who carefully operated within the law and had eluded capture by the official authorities. Figuring that it takes a thief to catch a thief, the Hornet posed as a wanted criminal, the better to insinuate himself into various illegal operations for the purpose of playing one crook against another and forcing them into the open—and, inevitably, into jail. In a further break from the *Lone Ranger* formula, the Green Hornet was believed to be a fugitive outlaw by both the underworld and the police, meaning that Britt Reid had to be careful during his nocturnal forays into crimefighting. Clearly he succeeded, since every episode ended with a *Sentinel* paperboy shouting out the headline: "GREEN HORNET STILL AT LARGE!"

Britt Reid's "Tonto" was his faithful Oriental houseboy Kato, a master of martial arts (and yes, Kato *was* described as Japanese before he was firmly identified as a Filipino, but this metamorphosis occurred several years before Pearl Harbor). The Green Hornet's "Silver" was the Black Beauty, a "sleek, superpowered" roadster which he kept hidden in an abandoned warehouse, conveniently if somewhat illogically located next door to Reid's lavish penthouse apartment. And in place of the Lone Ranger's silver bullets, the guns wielded by Britt Reid and Kato emitted a harmless gas to render their victims unconscious. Finally, whereas the Lone Ranger and Tonto were the only "regulars" on their own program save for a few recurring characters like the Ranger's nephew Dan Reid (remember that name!), *The Green Hornet* boasted a large extended "family" including Britt Reid's secretary Lenore "Casey" Case, his Irish-accented bodyguard Mike Axford, fast-talking reporter Ed Lowry and intrepid female photographer Clicker Binney. None of these characters was privy to the Green Hornet's true identity, though Lenore Case, like Superman's Lois Lane, always harbored a few suspicions.

Debuting January 31, 1936, as a local Detroit program, *The Green Hornet* was picked up by Mutual in 1938, then by NBC-Blue the following year. In 1940 the property was optioned by Universal Pictures for a 13-episode movie serial, titled (they must have stayed up nights to come up with this) *The Green Hornet*. Five members of the Universal writing staff are given credit for the screenplay, with Fran Striker receiving a separate title card for originating the property. Unlike the situation with Republic's *The Lone Ranger,* Striker's template exerts a lot more influence here. In fact, the serial version of *The Green Hornet* is a virtual clone of the radio series—right down to the theme music and the ominous "buzz" of the speeding Black Beauty—with Britt Reid and Kato battling a different racket or racketeer in each episode. Bundling all this into a chronological scenario is the fact that each separate criminal operation is controlled by a mysterious mastermind whom the Green Hornet is finally able to expose in the last chapter. Upholding the integrity of the radio original, the Hornet himself is never unmasked in public, his true identity remaining a secret to everyone but himself and Kato right up to the final fadeout and beyond.

At first, Gordon Jones seems all wrong as Britt Reid, especially since most viewers can't help but associate the actor with his buffoonish sidekick roles in Roy Rogers westerns and his comic stint as Mike the Cop on TV's *The Abbott and Costello Show*. But Jones grows in stature as the serial progresses, albeit with the uncredited assistance of Al Hodge, who was then playing the Green Hornet on radio and here provides the Hornet's voice whenever Reid dons his mask. Other members of the cast include Keye Luke as Kato, Anne Nagel as Lenore Case and Wade Boteler as Mike Axford, all of whom deliver performances well in keeping with their radio prototypes. While directors Ford Beebe and Ray Taylor move the action along with swift assuredness, their principal function is to match up the actors with the miles of stock footage used to beef up the action highlights—especially in the final two chapters, which contrive to have the Green Hornet nearly consumed in a roaring circus fire lifted bodily from Universal's 1933 Clyde Beatty vehicle *The Big Cage*.

Released eleven months after the first serial, Universal's 15-episode *The Green Hornet Strikes Again* follows the pattern of each chapter essentially a self-contained story involving a separate illegal activity (mostly insurance and extortion scams), leading up to the exposure of a well-concealed master criminal. The cast is basically the same as in the first *Green Hornet*, with the exception of Warren Hull, who as Britt Reid is better suited to the part than Gordon Jones—and better-looking in the bargain. And on this occasion Ed Lowry is also part of the action, played by William Newell. Of interest in the supporting cast is Dorothy Lovett, better known as Nurse Judy Price in RKO's radio-inspired *Dr. Christian* movie series (q.v.), here playing a permanently-in-distress heiress; and Pierre Watkin, future Uncle Jim Fairfield in Columbia's *Jack Armstrong* serial (q.v.), cast against type as the erudite "Mr. Big" behind all the city's illicit operations.

Green Hornet devotees may wonder why neither of the Universal serials mentions a vital fact about the character—to wit, that the Hornet and the Lone Ranger had a lot more in common than their WXYZ parentage. Whenever Britt Reid donned his mask and ventured into the night, he was carrying on a tradition inherited from his own father Dan Reid (we *told* you to remember that name!), whose uncle was none other than the Lone Ranger himself. Universal made no mention of Britt Reid's noble lineage because no one was aware of it in 1940: The revelation that Britt was the grand-nephew of the Lone Ranger did not occur until the *Green Hornet* radio episode of November 11, 1947.

Once the Hornet's heritage was established, it was seldom mentioned again, and had been all but forgotten by the time the series ended its radio run on December 5, 1952. *The Green Hornet* itself was largely forgotten until entrepreneur Charles H. Michelson assembled 52 recordings of the original series (mostly culled from the 1945–46 season) for station-by-station syndication in 1963. Michelson also resyndicated *The Lone Ranger* at the same time, but while the adventures of the Masked Man had a timeless quality that allowed them to be accepted as viable entertainment by the mid–1960s crowd, *The Green Hornet* was so firmly locked into its 1940s timeframe that it had to coast on its nostalgia value. The fact that a *Green Hornet* television series debuted on ABC in the fall of 1966 had less to do with renewed interest in the property than with the recent spectacular success of *Batman*, another nostalgia-driven "masked crusader" series on the same network. Both *Batman* and *The Green Hornet* were produced by William Dozier's Greenway Productions for 20th Century–Fox, but there the resemblance ended. While *Batman* was promoted as "camp" and played for laughs, Dozier deliberately took a different approach with *The Green Hornet*, fashioning it into a straightforward, basically humorless half-hour adventure series.

The familial link between the Lone Ranger and the Green Hornet was never alluded to on the TV series, probably because Dozier didn't feel like paying license fees for two properties.

Though updated to the 1960s, *The Green Hornet* was the mixture as before, with youthful publisher Britt Reid (played by Van Williams) foiling the activities of "untouchable" crooks in the guise of the Green Hornet—"on police records a wanted criminal," as the narrator (producer Dozier) explained at the beginning of each episode. Gone was the abandoned warehouse that had formerly shielded the Black Beauty from public view: Britt Reid now had an elaborate system of sliding doors and sinking floors in his posh apartment, leading to the fully computerized garage which housed his customized Chrysler Imperial. Also, the Hornet's true identity was now known not only to Kato but to Reid's secretary Lenore Case (Wende Wagner) and District Attorney Scanlon (Walter Brooke)—though poor Mike Axford (Lloyd Gough) was still in the dark. While this might seem to be a violation of the Green Hornet Canon, it should be noted that by the time the radio original had run its course in 1952, "Casey" and several other people of importance were aware of Britt Reid's double life.

Telecast on Friday evenings at 7:30 p.m. *The Green Hornet* was unable to weather the competition of NBC's *Tarzan* and CBS's *The Wild Wild West* and was cancelled after 26 episodes. However, the series enjoyed a robust second life in off-network syndication, especially after the ascendancy to superstardom of Bruce Lee, the Chinese-American martial arts practitioner who had been cast as Kato allegedly because he was able to properly pronounce the name "Britt Reid." (I don't believe that one either.) Even during the series' original network run, the charismatic Lee so outshone his pleasant but unremarkable co-star Van Williams that it wasn't even a contest. After Lee's death in 1973, several episodes of the TV series were spliced together into an ersatz theatrical feature film—and guess who got top billing *this* time.

Television's *Green Hornet* was afforded a "marathon" showing by the Me-TV cable channel in 2011 to cash in on the release of a $120,000,000 theatrical feature based on the property. That film might have been produced as early as 1992 had the property's owner Leisure Concepts and potential distributor Universal Pictures been satisfied with the preliminary screen treatment, and had George Clooney agreed to star in the title role. But Clooney always seemed to be busy elsewhere, obliging the producers to consider several other actors for the dual role of Britt Reid and the Green Hornet. One of the candidates was Greg Kinnear, an actor more closely associated with comedy parts than action roles, indicative of the direction the film would ultimately take. In 2001 Miramax secured the rights to the Green Hornet character, whereupon Kevin Smith, *auteur* of the low-budget slacker comedy *Clerks*, was proposed to write the screenplay and Jake Gyllenhaal was announced as star, with Jet Li as Kato. None of these personalities were available by the time producer Neal H. Moritz and Columbia Pictures took over the property from Miramax-Universal. Accelerating the project was an overwhelming desire to capitalize on the moneyspinning *Batman* movie franchise—and in a reversal of the situation when *The Green Hornet* came to TV in 1966, it was decided to counter the now heavily-somberly-serious *Batman* films with a satirical and slapsticky approach to *The Green Hornet*. In this spirit, comic actor Seth Rogan was engaged to star as Britt Reid and co-write the screenplay with his frequent collaborator Evan Goldberg (*Superbad, Pineapple Express*). After negotiations with Hong Kong filmmaker Stephen Chow to direct the film and appear as Kato fell through, Kevin Gondry, who'd been associated with the project off and on since 1997, was chosen as director, while Taiwanese musical star Jay Chou signed on as Kato. (We do this research so you don't have to.)

The characters in the 2011 filmization of *The Green Hornet* bear the same names as those on radio, and there's even a fleeting reference to the Lone Ranger, but otherwise we're in virgin territory here (if "virgin" is the appropriate word for a Rogan-Goldberg effort). For the first time ever we are provided with a backstory for the title character, beginning with a pre-credits scene in which coldhearted billionaire James (not Dan) Reid humiliates his pudgy little son Britt by decapitating the boy's superhero doll. Twenty years later, James Reid dies and his dissolute playboy son Britt inherits the old man's publishing empire, as well as James' Oriental chauffeur Kato. Taking belated revenge for past cruelties, Britt drunkenly talks Kato into helping him knock the head off a statue of James Reid. In the process, Britt accidentally breaks up a crime in progress, and thus the epiphany comes to pass. Urged on by the resourceful Kato, young Reid dedicates his life to bringing criminals to justice in the guise of the Green Hornet, utilizing the ultra-cool Black Beauty and a limitless arsenal of custom-made weaponry—not to mention Kato's special "Katovision," enabling him to instantly locate and analyze the weapons carried by the bad guys. Foremost among these rapscallions is hyperparanoid Russian *mafioso* Chudnofsky, a role inherited by *Inglourious Basterds* star Christoph Waltz after the defection of Nicolas Cage (who'd perversely intended to play Chudnofsky with a Jamaican accent). Posing as a criminal, Britt Reid cannot count on the support of DA Scanlon (David Harbour), who is himself in cahoots with Chudofsky. Meanwhile, the exploits of the Green Hornet are given screaming-headline treatment by the *Daily Sentinel,* which now boasts a considerably elevated Mike Axford (Edward James Olmos) as managing editor.

Longtime fans of *The Green Hornet* have always suspected that Kato and not Britt Reid is the brains of the organization. The 2011 film version not only confirms this, but also depicts Reid as an imbecilic schlepper who probably can't tie his own shoes without Kato's assistance. This of course feeds into the derisively comic tone of the entire enterprise, which substitutes chaos and car crashes for wit and intelligence. While enough filmgoers were satisfied with this approach for *The Green Hornet* to earn a fair worldwide gross, many jaundiced observers will find the whole imbroglio a waste of time—save for the appealing performance by Cameron Diaz as Lenore "Casey" Case, here not only Reid's secretary but also a capable journalist in her own right. The film's most satisfying moment occurs when, after discovering that she has been an unwitting dupe for Britt and Kato, the outraged Casey beats the snot out of *both* of them.

There was a third major adventure series on WXYZ radio, *Sergeant Preston of the Yukon,* assembled by the same personnel as *The Lone Ranger* and *The Green Hornet* but produced across the border from Detroit in Windsor, Ontario. Though *Sergeant Preston* never graduated to theatrical feature status, a reasonably successful TV version of the property ran on CBS from 1955 to 1958 starring Richard Simmons (*not* the exercise guru by a long shot!).

"The Aldrich Family" [Henry Aldrich] (1939–1944)

Technically, the *Henry Aldrich* B-movie series had its roots in a Broadway play rather than a radio series, but it is included here because the films probably wouldn't have been made were it not for the popularity of the radio version— and in fact, the Broadway play owed a lot of its success to radio as well.

The son of a high school principal, Clifford Goldsmith (1899–1971) aspired to be a writer but met with little success until 1938, when he decided to write a play based on the people he'd met while earning a living as a touring high school lecturer (He also drew some inspiration from the antics of his own teenage sons, who once their dad became famous joshingly handed him bills "for services rendered.") Goldsmith's *What a Life!,* set in its entirety in the principal's office of Central High School, was originally a serious ensemble piece unified by the character of Principal Bradley. Producer-director George Abbott felt that *What a Life!* would work better as a pure comedy, especially if Goldsmith built up the secondary character of trouble-prone student Henry Aldrich, an ideal role for Abbott protégé Ezra Stone. The playwright complied, focusing his rewrite on hapless Henry's efforts to attend the spring dance despite having been suspended for flunking his history exam, complicated by the messes our hero gets into thanks to the practical jokes perpetrated by swellheaded jock George Bigelow. Along the way, bashful Henry works up the nerve to ask class president Barbara Pierson to the dance.

Opening on April 13, 1938, at New York's

Biltmore Theater, *What a Life!* was greeted with critical indifference and got off to a slow start until star Ezra Stone made a tour of New York high schools to drum up an audience. At the same time, Rudy Vallee saw the play, liked it, and invited Goldsmith to write a seven-minute "Henry Aldrich" sketch for Vallee's radio show; this in turn led to a regular featured spot for Stone and the rest of "The Aldrich Family" on *The Kate Smith Hour*. All this network-radio exposure had the desired effect of stirring up additional interest for *What a Life!*, which ended up a solid 538-performance hit. In the bargain, the Kate Smith program's "Aldrich Family" sketches ran for 39 weeks under the direction of Bob Welsh, the man responsible for coming up with the property's famous opener:

MRS. ALDRICH: Hen-*reeee*! Henry Aldrich!
HENRY: C-coming, Mother!

While Henry's mother had appeared in the original play (though not identified as Alice as she would be on radio), his attorney father was only spoken of. For the purposes of *The Kate Smith Hour* Mr. Sam Aldrich made regular appearances in the person of actor House Jameson, along with Mrs. Aldrich (Katherine Raht) and Henry's sister Mary the campus belle, a role created for radio and initially played by Betty Field, who'd been seen as Barbara Pierson in *What a Life!* After its trial run on Kate Smith's show, *The Aldrich Family* was rewarded with its own separate half-hour timeslot on July 2, 1939, as a summer replacement for NBC's *The Jack Benny Program*, underwritten by Benny's sponsor Jell-O. On October 10, 1939, *The Aldrich Family*—still "brought to you" by Jell-O—became a weekly NBC fixture, remaining on the air through several cast and sponsor changes until April 19, 1953.

Even without its radio tie-in, *What a Life!* was deemed worthy enough for Paramount Pictures to option the play for a film version, adapted for the screen by no less than Billy Wilder and Charles Brackett and released on October 6, 1939. While Jackie Cooper took over from Ezra Stone in the role of Henry, several of the original Broadway actors recreated their roles in the movie version, notably Betty Field as Barbara, Vaughn Glaser as Principal Bradley and James Corner as George Bigelow. Though *What a Life!* was intended as a one-shot, the continuing popularity of the radio series was impossible for Paramount to ignore, thus Jackie Cooper reprised his starring role in the 1941 sequel *Life with Henry*, which the studio touted as being inspired by the radio version. Accordingly, Henry's father Mr. Aldrich made his first screen appearance, played by former film director Fred Niblo, as did Henry's flirtatious sister Mary, enacted by Kay Stewart. (As in *What a Life!*, Mrs. Aldrich was played by Hedda Hopper, then just starting her second career as a gossip columnist.) Another character who hadn't appeared on Broadway but had been developed for radio was Henry's goofy best pal Homer, played on the NBC version by Jackie Kelk. In *Life with Henry*, the Homer character is rechristened Dizzy Stevens and portrayed by Eddie Bracken, previously seen in a small role in the Broadway version of *What a Life!* and as Henry himself in the touring company. The critical consensus was that Bracken stole the show, especially in the scenes where he attempts to woo the fickle Mary Aldrich.

By the time Paramount formally launched a series of *Henry Aldrich* second features, both Jackie Cooper and Eddie Bracken had outgrown their roles. Though the studio tested the original "Henry" Ezra Stone for their new series, the part went instead to James Lydon, then building a reputation as a dramatic juvenile actor in such films as *Tom Brown's School Days*. Somewhat reluctantly, Lydon agreed to imitate the adenoidal, high-pitched Henry Aldrich voice established by Ezra Stone on radio, and in so doing became the actor most closely associated with the role in the eyes of the public. The part of Dizzy went to Charles Smith, who likewise found himself typecast. Though the character of Mary Aldrich was eliminated, Henry's parents were still very much a part of the action, with John Litel (late of Warner Bros.' *Nancy Drew* series) as Sam Aldrich and Olive Blakeney (who in real life became James Lydon's mother-in-law) as Alice Aldrich. Of the original Broadway cast, only Vaughn Glaser survived the cut, continuing to play Principal Bradley for eight of the nine subsequent *Henry Aldrich* entries.

Many film buffs have a soft spot in their hearts for the *Henry Aldrich* series, if only because the films provide a farcical antidote to the sickly wholesomeness of MGM's concurrently produced *Andy Hardy* films. No idealized "typical American teenager" like Andy Hardy, Henry has been succinctly pigeonholed by B-movie historian Don Miller as the "typical American lunkhead." Henry's metamorphosis from the recognizable human being of *What a Life!* to the cartoonish ignoramus of the Paramount series began with the radio program, in which Henry had an uncanny knack for transforming minor problems into major cataclysms. "Henry found more ways to turn the ordinary into complete chaos and disaster than Mack Sennett ever devised for his old two-reel chase films," notes radio expert John Dunning. But compared to the film series, the radio version only scratched the surface when it came to the disastrous consequences wrought by Henry's presence on Planet Earth.

The first series entry *Henry Aldrich for President* (1941) wastes no time establishing the tone for all the rest, with Henry accidentally knocking down several people in the school hallway before fomenting slapstick chaos in the classroom of science teacher Mr. Crosley (Lucien Littlefield). Henry's convoluted but undeniably impressive explanation of "centrifugal force" attracts the attention of arrogant student Irwin Barrett (Kenneth Howell), who is running for class president against the more deserving Phyllis Michael (Mary Anderson). Scheming to siphon votes from Phyllis, Irwin arranges for Henry to run as a "third party" candidate, with Mr. Crosley secretly aiding Irwin in this devious scheme. Already we perceive that the *Henry Aldrich* formula is beginning to lose touch with reality, but you ain't seen nothin' yet. Thanks to Irwin's machinations, Henry is accused of stuffing the ballot box with counterfeit votes and is expelled on the spot by Principal Bradley. The only way Henry can redeem himself is to locate the printer responsible for the phony ballots—and the only way to get the printer to show up at Central High before the election is via airplane. So it is that Henry Aldrich, with only an instruction book titled *How to Land* as his guide, ends up flying the plane himself and crash-landing on Central's football field. Happens every day.

If anything, Henry's subsequent misadventures are even more ridiculous. *Henry and Dizzy* (1942) finds Henry facing a jail term unless he can pay for damages inflicted upon an expensive speedboat, a crisis that can apparently only be resolved by a neck-risking boat race at Lake Wopacotapotalong. In *Henry Aldrich, Editor* (1942), Henry writes a series of newspaper stories predicting where a mad arsonist will strike next—little imagining that the source of his information, mild-mannered Nero Smith (Francis Pierlot), is the guy who is starting the fires. *Henry Aldrich Gets Glamour* (1942) whisks our hero off to Hollywood and into the arms of movie queen Hilary Dane (Frances Gifford). *Henry Aldrich Swings It* (1943) gets the poor boy mixed up with criminals, one of whom is played by Bernard Nedell, in real life the husband of "Mrs. Aldrich" Olive Blakeney. On the strength of the title alone, one can get a pretty good idea what to expect from *Henry Aldrich Haunts a House* (1943), and one will not be disappointed. *Henry Aldrich, Boy Scout* (1944) ends with the obligatory climax of *all* Boy Scout films, with Henry and Dizzy rescuing a youngster (Darryl Hickman) who is clinging precariously to a slim ledge on a high cliff. And in *Henry Aldrich Plays Cupid* (1944), Henry endeavors to avoid expulsion (again) by finding a bride for Mr. Bradley, coming up with brassy showgirl Wild Rose (Barbara Pepper) before producing a more suitable candidate in the form of the widowed Mrs. Terwilliger (played by radio comedienne Vera Vague). The final series entry *Henry Aldrich's Little Secret* (1944) is the most conventional and "realistic" of the batch—and the least entertaining.

All nine *Henry Aldrich* pictures were directed by former film editor Hugh Bennett; all ran between 64 and 75 minutes; and all were excellent showcases for such promising Paramount starlets as Diana Lynn, Gail Russell, Martha O'Driscoll, Noel Neill and Mimi Chandler, the latter less renowned for her cinematic achievements than her status as the daughter of future baseball commissioner Happy Chandler. Fans of the original *What a Life!* and the *Henry Aldrich* radio program were apparently unperturbed by the comic overkill of the film series, and there might have been even more than nine entries if Paramount hadn't decided to fold its B-picture division in 1944 and turn all second-feature production over to the independent Pine-Thomas unit.

For those with an insatiable desire to see as well as hear *The Aldrich Family,* an NBC television adaptation premiered on January 2, 1949, with Robert Casey as the first TV Henry. Casey would in later seasons be succeeded by Richard Tyler, Henry Girard, Kenneth Nelson and Bobby Ellis, the last-named actor the only carryover from the radio version. This adaptation of *The Aldrich Family* ran until May 29, 1953, outlasting the radio series by approximately six weeks. Since that time, TV's *Aldrich Family* has been cited negatively in many books and articles about the Blacklist era, thanks to the 1950 decision by sponsor General Foods to fire the actress playing Mrs. Aldrich, Jean Muir, who had been named as a Communist sympathizer in *Red Channels*. Muir's replacement was former movie-musical favorite Nancy Carroll.

As a postscript, it's worth mentioning that *What a Life!* author Clifford Goldsmith never abandoned the family-sitcom genre, continuing to pen scripts for such TV series as *Leave It to Beaver* and *The Donna Reed Show*. Also of interest (at least to me) is the fact that four of the actors who played Henry Aldrich on radio and in films—Ezra Stone, Jackie Cooper, James Lydon and Norman Tokar—would mature into talented TV writer-directors, with Cooper advancing to production head of Columbia's TV subsidiary Screen Gems and Lydon assuming several executive producer positions at Warner Bros. Television.

"Dr. Christian" (1939–1941)

The story of *Dr. Christian* begins with the story of Dr. Allan Roy Dafoe, a Canadian obstetrician who on May 26, 1934, had greatness thrust upon him when he assisted in delivering the Dionne quintuplets. Journalists from around the world descended upon the Dionne family farm in Ontario, transforming both Dafoe and the five infant girls into overnight celebrities. Too poor to afford proper treatment for the quints, "Papa" Dionne signed a contract to exhibit his daughters at the Chicago World's Fair, a move that brought down the wrath of the Canadian prime minister, who made the children wards of the state—whereupon Canada itself profited enormously from displaying the girls before thousands of tourists at a large building complex called Quintland (are you listenin', Mr. Disney?). Then followed a maelstrom of merchandising, including dolls, toys, coloring books and commercial endorsements—with Dr. Dafoe, who was not quite the humble old country physician he claimed to be, accumulating vast riches from lectures, book contracts, advertising tie-ins and his salary as the quints' appointed guardian. Only in hindsight can one realize the negative effect this ceaseless and shameless exploitation would have on the Dionne girls in later life as they struggled to establish their individual identities, their own claim to the millions earned by everyone but themselves, and their long-overdue right to privacy.

When the Fox Film Corporation purchased the movie rights to the Dafoe-Dionne story in 1935, the studio's publicity department suggested that the good doctor initially resisted such a transaction because he'd only seen one movie in his life and didn't like it (though one suspects that he was simply holding out for the best offer). Will Rogers was slated to play Dafoe on film, but after Rogers was killed in a 1935 plane crash the part went to Jean Hersholt on the strength of his similar characterization in the 1934 medical drama *Men in White*.

Born into a Copenhagen theatrical family in 1886, Jean Hersholt made his movie debut in 1905 in the first film ever produced in Denmark, a job that he claimed netted him the equivalent of 75 cents. It was some time in 1913 or 1914 that Hersholt arrived in Hollywood wearing a specially tailored dress suit, the sight of which so impressed producer Thomas Ince that he hired the young actor on the spot for a munificent 15 dollars per week. Working his way up from the extra ranks, Hersholt established himself in the 1920s as one of moviedom's most reliable "heavies," playing unpleasant and unsavory roles in such films as *Tess of the Storm Country, Greed* and *Stella Dallas.* The actor's lilting, gently accented voice enabled him to alter his image when talkies came in, making him an ideal choice for the (publicly) kind-hearted and selfless Allan Roy Dafoe in the 1936 20th Century–Fox production *The Country Doctor,* which ended with a wonderfully spontaneous sequence wherein, with palpable mutual affection, the actor and the Dionne quints played a game together. (This scene was filmed in Canada; the girls never set foot on a Hollywood soundstage.) Hersholt and his five "leading ladies" would repeat their characterizations in two equally well-received sequels, *Reunion* (1936) and *Five of a Kind* (1938).

An early–1940s trade advertisement for Jean Hersholt's radio and movie series *Dr. Christian.*

A word of clarification here. Though most publications of the 1930s and many film history books have stated that Hersholt played Dr. Dafoe, in point of fact his character was named Dr. John Luke, just as the Dionne girls themselves were rechristened the Wyatts. Be that as it may, when representatives of the Vaseline company decided in 1937 to parlay the Dionne movies into a weekly radio series, Hersholt was the first and only choice to play Dr. Dafoe on the air. Only this time around the real Dafoe refused to have anything to do with the project no matter how they renamed the character. So the "quintuplet" element was dropped, the locale of the proposed series moved from Canada to Minnesota, and Hersholt was penciled in to play a small-town general practitioner rather than a specialist in obstetrics. In choosing a name for the character, Hersholt suggested Dr. Paul Christian, a decision many observers have attributed to the actor's high regard for the work of Danish fantasist Hans Christian Andersen (Hersholt owned the largest personal collection of Andersen books in the world). But in a UPI article of September 13, 1939, Frederick C. Othman reported that the character's name was recommended to Hersholt by the Danish Consul of New York as a "typical" moniker of the actor's homeland.

Joining the CBS Wednesday night lineup as *The Vaseline Program: Dr. Christian of River's End* on November 4, 1937, the new half-hour dramatic series was set in the fictional Minnesota community of River's End, where kindly Dr. Christian dispensed medical treatment and homespun philosophy with the help of his attractive young nurse Judy Price, originally played by Rosemary DeCamp. Many of his ministrations were philanthropic in nature for the benefit of the poorer residents, though he was known to accept farm-grown foodstuffs as payment from his grateful patients. Occasionally Dr. Christian played Cupid for those star-crossed lovers who seemed to breed like mink on radio programs, and every so often his skills were challenged to the utmost by a life-or-death catastrophe, frequently with himself in more danger than anyone.

Hersholt made such a powerful impression

as Dr. Christian that in the first year of the series alone he received 75,000 letters from listeners, many of whom believed he was a genuine doctor and solicited his advice on medical matters. The generosity and compassion of Dr. Paul Christian was no mere actor's trick, but the real deal. Throughout his career Hersholt devoted countless hours to a multitude of charitable concerns, among them the establishment of the Motion Picture Relief Fund to help industry members who could no longer help themselves. During World War II he disseminated pro-democracy propaganda to Nazi-occupied Denmark via short wave radio, putting his film career on hold for the duration to concentrate on this sort of work—a selfless decision that in 1946 earned him a knighthood from his homeland's King Christian X. His legacy lives on today in the form of the Academy of Motion Picture Arts and Sciences' Jean Hersholt Humanitarian Award, established shortly after the actor's death in 1956.

Despite being dismissed as corny and provincial by "in the know" showbiz pundits, *Dr. Christian* was an immediate success—and with similar immediacy, several Hollywood studios began courting Hersholt to star in a film series based on his radio character. In 1939 Hersholt's agent William Stephens solicited financial aid from one Howard Lang to form Stephens-Lang Productions, an independent unit designed to produce low-budget *Dr. Christian* films for RKO Radio release. Stephens-Lang's first contract called for at least three films starring Hersholt, who would receive a percentage of profits in lieu of salary.

While filming the first entry *Meet Dr. Christian* (1939), Hersholt noted that the only difference between this picture and his previous efforts was his own financial interest: "It used to be that I didn't care how much time the producers wasted, or how many mistakes they made. But now I even keep an eye on my watch to stop the day's shooting exactly on the dot so we don't have to pay the carpenters overtime." Hersholt admitted that the experience "has given me a completely new outlook on the movie business. I've about decided that if all actors, directors, and writers could be paid on a percentage basis, motion pictures probably would be a lot better than they are."

Directed by Bernard Vorhaus, the 68-minute *Meet Dr. Christian* fades in on what became the series' standard opening, with cast and production credits printed on the pages of a medical appointment pad. Introduced to the movies are two recurring characters from the radio series, Nurse Judy Price and Christian's no-nonsense housekeeper Mrs. Hastings. The latter role was played on both film and radio by Maude Eburne, while Judy was enacted by RKO starlet Dorothy Lovett, borrowed from the studio to appear in five of the six *Dr. Christian* efforts (Lovett was introduced to the series' fans in the opening episode of the radio show's third season, "Once Around the Block," not as Judy but as "Kit McKenzie, a worried young mother"). The screenplay was by Ring Lardner, Jr. and Ian McLellan Hunter, two socially conscious young men who got a rush from injecting as much political commentary into their work as they could get away with—a practice that would cause both of them grief during the Blacklist of the 1950s.

In *Meet Dr. Christian,* it is established that the title character has done so much gratis work for his less fortunate patients that he is heavily reliant on his salary as health commissioner of River's End. After endorsing the mayoral bid of lumberyard owner John Hewitt (Paul Harvey), Christian is dismayed by Hewitt's subsequent fondness for making expensive cosmetic changes in the city's landscape, all the while insisting that there is no money in the budget for a new hospital. (You can't trust those dirty capitalists.) When Christian challenges Hewitt at a town picnic, the new mayor spitefully removes the doctor from his commissioner's post, all but breaking the heart of Mrs. Hewitt (Enid Bennett), who had once been Christian's sweetheart. It takes a serious auto accident caused by Hewitt's ne'er-do-well son Don (Jackie Moran), which in turn necessitates a delicate brain operation for Don's sister Patsy (Patsy Lee Parsons), for Hewitt to appreciate the full value of that "mid–Victorian fussbudget" Dr. Christian, and to drop an unnecessary road-improvement project in order to fund the hospital.

Some humor involving the precocious Patsy's interference in the romance between Don and fickle bobbysoxer Marilee (Marcia Mae Jones), and Don's courting of "older woman" Nurse Judy to the chagrin of her druggist beau Roy Davis (Robert Baldwin), leavens the otherwise soggy proceedings. Also good for laughs is the ice cream–juggling prowess of supporting player Frank Coghlan, Jr., whose skill at tossing scoops of vanilla in the air and catching them in a dish without spilling a drop earned the spontaneous applause of the film crew—and nearly spoiled a perfect take. Budgeted at $116,000, the maiden entry in the Dr. Christian series earned $400,000, getting the property off to a flying start despite reviews like the one in *Commonweal*: "*Meet Dr. Christian* introduces the radio character in his first film, but surrounds him with so many clichés that we feel we've seen him many times before."

Assembled by the same director-writer team, the second entry *Courageous Dr. Christian* (1940) is widely regarded as the best of the series. Drama, comedy, romance, medical crisis, suspense, pathos and pungent social commentary are combined satisfactorily if not perfectly into a neat 66-minute package. If screenwriters Lardner and Hunter were wearing their liberal hearts on their sleeves in the first film, they're practically carrying placards down Main Street in this one. Much of the action takes place in Squatter's Town, the disease-ridden slum section of River's End. The doctor is appalled by the living conditions of the community's down-and-outers and lobbies the city council to build decent low-cost housing closer to town, so that the indigents can live in dignity and seek out employment. The class-conscious battle lines are sharply drawn from Scene One onward. Cocky young hobo Dave Williams (Tom Neal doing a John Garfield imitation) spouts reams of radical venom about how the Privileged are always playing angles to keep Dave and his kind festering in squalor. At the same time, the prosperous council members led by usurious banker Harry Johnson (George Meader in a mustachio-twirling performance) lounge around the local golf club and haughtily dismiss Dr. Christian as a fuzzy-headed idealist.

Comedy is injected into this Clifford Odets atmosphere as Christian pays a visit to wealthy widow Mrs. Hastings (Vera Lewis) in hopes of purchasing a valuable plot of land on which the new housing project can be erected. A string of misunderstandings leads Mrs. Hastings to believe that Christian will marry her if she agrees to sell, and for a while it looks as if the doc will have to make the supreme sacrifice for the greater good. Meanwhile, Dave Williams attempts to cram social awareness down the throats of River's End by moving all of Squatter's Town onto Mrs. Hastings' property, right down to the last tar-paper shack. All that prevents a full-scale riot between the squatters and the cops is Dr. Christian's grim announcement that spinal meningitis has broken out in the poor community. With dialogue like "Meningitis hits all ages—and classes" bandied about, the "respectable" people in town reveal their essential decency, enthusiastically pitching in to help Christian wipe out the deadly disease and minister to those already stricken. Of course, everything ends happily—except for viewers who have grown heartily sick of "adorable" child actors Bobby Larson and Babette Bentley as a pair of obnoxious and extremely destructive slum kids. After suffering through five minutes of these two little cretins, a good case of measles is the kindest fate one can wish for them.

One lasting legacy of *Courageous Dr. Christian* is the musical theme "Presenting the Doctor," written by William Lava and first heard over the film's opening credits. Like many another Lava composition, this theme would soon be folded into a library of stock music available for rental to other producers. One can hear the strains of "Presenting the Doctor" flowing gently through everything from the TV series *Lassie* to the Ed Wood, Jr., exploitation epic *Glen or Glenda!*

The "crusading" aspect of Dr. Christian's moral makeup is carried over into the third series entry, *Dr. Christian Meets the Women* (1940), directed by William McGann and written by Marion Orth. This time Christian crosses swords with phony dietician Prof. Kenneth Parker (Rod La Rocque), who sets up shop in River's End with hometown boy Bill Ferris (Frank Albertson) as his advance man. After a few lighthearted scenes at the expense of the town's more corpulent Women's Club members, things take a serious turn as Dr. Christian vainly argues against the faddish "one size fits all" diet programs which fail to take individual health needs into account. Though the ladies turn against Christian in favor of the charismatic Parker, the truth of the doctor's warning strikes home when young Kitty Browning (Marilyn Merrick), starving herself to follow Parker's regimen, collapses of malnutrition. At this point Christian discovers that Parker, who holds no physician's license, has been administering the potentially lethal prescription drug benzedrine sulfate to his customers. The premise of a charming quack promoting crash diets, injurious exercises and dangerous "miracle" drugs is surprisingly timely, though its treatment in the film is strictly routine. The most noteworthy element of *Dr. Christian Meets the Women* is the casting of comic actor Edgar Kennedy as grocer George Browning, father of the ill-fated Kitty. Except for a single slow burn—and that after several reels of provocation—Kennedy delivers a straight dramatic performance, and most effectively.

Once the initial three-picture contract was fulfilled, Stephens-Lang Productions entered into an arrangement with RKO for an additional three *Dr. Christian* efforts. RKO decided not to include the doctor's name in the titles of these three films, concerned that the public might confuse the new releases with the old ones. For reasons that were evidently never articulated in print (but probably had something to do with diminishing box-office receipts), a further decision was made to downplay the "medical" aspect of the property in favor of stories designed to appeal to a wider demographic than the faithful followers of the radio show. As a result, Dr. Christian hardly does any doctoring at all, placing a considerable distance between the three final film entries and the original radio version. As a matter of fact, these low-budget potboilers are so far removed from radio's Dr. Christian that Hersholt might just as well be Dr. Pepper.

Directed by Erle C. Kenton from a script by Lee Loeb, *Remedy for Riches* is played strictly for laughs, with Edgar Kennedy reverting to type in the now-comical role of George Browning—performing both a slow burn and a double take *in his very first scene,* with plenty more where that came from. Hersholt himself indulges in a Three Stooges–style cooking routine with town constable Walter Catlett, a scene so jam-packed with hokum that we're surprised the scriptwriter forgot to include "separate two eggs." The only pill-pushing done by Dr. Christian is to supply a few Vitamin B capsules to a pair of elderly spinsters who behave exactly like the "Pixilated Sisters" in Capra's *Mr. Deeds Goes to Town* (and small wonder, since one of the old biddies is played by the earlier picture's Margaret McWade). Oh, we forgot to mention that the Vitamin B is swallowed by a chicken, who instantly morphs into a slapstick prop.

We also forgot to mention the film's plot, or maybe we just wanted to forget it. Warren Hull plays silver-tongued Tom Stewart, a college buddy of Nurse Judy's boyfriend Roy (whom we haven't seen since *Courageous Dr. Christian*). Tom shows up in town as the front man for grandiloquent con artist D.B. Vandeveer (Jed Prouty) who convinces the townsfolk that there's an oil well on a piece of land that has been cleared for a new hotel. But Dr. Christian smells a rat (or rats, as the case may be), and he manages to expose the fraud and the fraudsters before everyone in town has hocked the family jewels to invest in the nonexistent gusher. Real-life home economist Prudence Penny plays herself in the final scene of *Remedy for Riches,* apparently because she had nothing else to do that day.

Nineteen forty-one's *Melody for Three* (working title: *Prodigy*), again directed by Kenton and co-written by Loeb (with Walter Ferris), trades belly laughs for bathos as Dr. Christian blithely disregards 57 varieties of professional ethics to reunite a long-divorced couple, local music teacher Mary Stanley (Fay Wray) and world-famous orchestra leader Antoine Pirelle (Walter Woolf King), for the sake of their musical-prodigy son Billy (very well played by 13-year-old violin virtuoso Schuyler Standish). A few particles of gold can be found among the dross of this dreary drama, notably an extended scene in a radio studio where Christian and Billy are taken on a guided tour by page Richard Webb (who seems to be auditioning for his later TV role as Captain Midnight). There's a measure of authenticity in this scene, which closely resembles the actual tours conducted by the big networks in the early 1940s, complete with a practical demonstration of that "latest scientific marvel" television, and an amusing sound-effects display featuring several of the genuine props used to create aural imagery over the air. (Incidentally, one of the tourists taking in this little show is a young and immediately recognizable Imogene Coca.)

Still another child prodigy is the central figure in 1941's *They Meet Again* (working title: *Interlude*), the final film in the series. This time it's a Deanna Durbin wannabe named Anne Bennett, who is cast as Janie Webster, the daughter of a bank teller (Barton Yarborough) falsely accused of embezzling $3,000. Again directed by Kenton, who does what he can with the paste-and-paper screenplay by Peter Milne, this is the sort of picture in which the arrest, trial and conviction of the teller all take place in approximately three days, and in which the allegedly intelligent daughter knows nothing about her dad's plight even though it's splattered all over the front page. And despite dialogue that carefully establishes him as a statewide celebrity, Dr. Christian is not only prevented from seeing the governor (Neil Hamilton) to beg clemency for the hapless teller, but is thrown in the pokey for his troubles. As for the musical portion of the program, Anne Bennett doesn't appear to be doing her own singing in the "La Traviata" finale—and besides, she's totally overshadowed by fellow child actor Leon Tyler, who does a wowser of a jumpin' jive number in the opening scene.

There might have been further timewasters like *They Meet Again* if Hersholt hadn't decided to pull out of the Dr. Christian series—and, as previously mentioned, out of moviemaking completely for the duration of World War II. Three years after the series' cessation, Stephens-Lang Productions sued RKO Radio Pictures, citing improper distribution charges and the studio's refusal to enforce contracts for theaters that wouldn't run the Christian pictures. The moment the case was settled, a handful of *Dr. Christian* films went into reissue, so someone must have made some money somewhere.

Just as the *Dr. Christian* film series was withering on the vine, the radio series was about to enter its best and most creative period. In 1942, the show's sponsor Vaseline launched a contest allowing listeners to submit scripts for the show, with awards for those selected ranging from $150 to $2,000. Some of these amateur scenarios turned out to be quite entertaining and innovative, launching a number of fledgling authors into professional writing careers: among the lucky winners was a young sprout named Rod Serling.

Remaining one of CBS's most dependable Wednesday night entries, *Dr. Christian* left the air on January 6, 1954. Once again it was Hersholt's decision to close up shop, after setting a record for never missing a single broadcast in 18 seasons. Having just accepted his only film acting role since 1941 in the James Cagney western *Run for Cover,* the actor explained to columnist Bob Thomas, "I want to see if I can get away with doing something else. After all, Dr. Christian is such a sweet, sentimental fellow. I'd hate to be stuck with playing only him the rest of my life."

The last anyone heard of *Dr. Christian* was a filmed half-hour television series, syndicated by Ziv Productions in the fall of 1956, a few months after Hersholt's death. As originally conceived, the 39-week series was to have featured Hersholt in 13 episodes, with Paul Christian gradually turning over his entire practice to his nephew Mark (Macdonald Carey). But by the time the series went into production, Hersholt weighed only 95 pounds and was suffering from terminal cancer. Even so, the tireless old trouper insisted upon rising from his sickbed and appearing in the pilot episode. He was a thorough professional and gallant gentleman to the last.

Kay Kyser (1939–1944)

As Rudy Vallee learned the hard way with his 1929 screen debut *The Vagabond Lover* (q.v.), while it was enough on radio for a bandleader to merely wield a baton and make sure his musicians started and finished on time, you can't build a feature-length film on that basis. This didn't stop Hollywood from insisting upon giving bandleaders roles to play and lines to speak. While a handful of popular radio kapellmeisters—Phil Harris, Bob Crosby, Spike Jones—turned out to be satisfactory actors, most of them (think Glenn Miller or Henry King) were roughly on the same thespic level as boxers and baseball players. As such they were seldom given any real characters to play, and often as not were shunted away to specialty numbers or single scenes in films while the brunt of the comedy or dramatics were carried by the romantic leads and comic relief. Like a record player, a bandleader was expected to make music when turned on and keep quiet when turned off.

Kay Kyser—born King Kern Kaiser in Rocky Mount, North Carolina, in 1906—was an exception. During his nine-film movie career, he was top-billed in seven of those films, not as a specialty or sidelines attraction but as an actual screen character whose contributions were vital to the plot. Nor was he merely playing an extension of his radio role as a quiz show host; his scriptwriters went into overtime creating a distinct (if not always credible) movie persona of a likable, naïve young fellow who couldn't seem to steer clear of the troubles and perils contrived by the story men.

Kyser didn't come to movie acting "cold." In addition to studying music at the University of North Carolina–Chapel Hill, Kay was active with the university's prestigious dramatic department the Carolina Playmakers, the spawning ground for such notable show biz personalities as Andy Griffith, George Grizzard and Louise Fletcher. Kyser was thoroughly trained in all aspects of acting, from outdoor drama to theater in the round. That he was grateful for this training was reflected in his many references to North Carolina in his films, notably the stage backdrop used in the opening "broadcast" scene of his 1940 vehicle *You'll Find Out,* which was decorated with paintings of various UNC–Chapel Hill landmarks. Off-screen, he contributed substantially to his alma mater, in 1941 establishing the Kay Kyser Foundation to provide annual fellowships to promising drama students, notably in the field of playwriting (Kyser's own written legacy to Chapel Hill was the deathless UNC cheerleading song "Split It for the Team").

While he enjoyed performing before live audiences, the bookish, bespectacled, reedy-voice Kyser realized he wasn't leading man material; and besides, music was his first love. He put acting on the back burner when he organized his own band in 1926. Small engagements led to bigger things, and in 1933 Kyser's band got its best booking to date at Chicago's Blackhawk Hotel, where he broke attendance records; that same year he made his radio debut in a remote broadcast from the Bal Tabarin in San Francisco. In the years that followed, Kyser began incorporating novelty songs and comedy into his act, notably with the aid of a gangling mop-haired cornettist named Merwin A. Bogue, better known as Ish Kabibble. Other personalities gaining prominence with Kyser in the 1930s were vocalist-musicians Harry Babbitt and Sully Mason, songstress Ginny Simms, and Kay's indispensable music arranger George Duning, whose imaginative stagings and orchestrations would become a Kyser hallmark. Kay sustained his personality-oriented band by encouraging loyalty and teamwork. Rare among Big Band leaders, he was universally regarded as a kind, considerate and generous employer.

Through the efforts of the MCA talent agency's Lew Wasserman, Kyser hit radio's Big Time on March 30, 1938, with NBC's *Kollege of Musical Knowledge,* which utilized Kay's college background by establishing his on-the-air character "The Old Perfessor." Outfitted in collegiate robes and mortar board, Perfessor Kyser presided over a weekly 60-minute musical program, gaining an enormous audience with radio's first major-league quiz show. In a manner that would become *de rigueur* for this genre, Kyser would gently rib his "civilian" contestants, coyly drop hints that would lead them to the correct response, and provide wish fulfillment to millions at home by establishing a top prize of $400. An offbeat added attraction was the weekly true-or-false session where contestants were rewarded for providing the "false" answers. Kyser's catchphrase "That's Right, You're Wrong"—or conversely, "That's Wrong, You're Right"—and his appeals to the "Students" (the studio audience) to help out the confused contestants, always paid off in big laughs.

By 1939, a movie contract for Kyser was inevitable. Through a package deal arranged by his old benefactor Wasserman, Kyser and his band were contracted to star in a feature film for RKO Radio, a profit-sharing deal for which Kay and company received a $75,000 advance. Unlike some bandleaders, Kyser did not have to be dragged kicking and screaming before the cameras. Though in later years he tended to be dismissive and apologetic about his film career, in 1939 he felt that a starring motion picture was an excellent career move, not only actively campaigning for the assignment but also investing some of his own money in his first RKO production.

That's Right—You're Wrong was filmed during Kyser's summer hiatus from his radio series under the guidance of producer-director David Butler, an old hand at musical comedy. Perhaps defensively, the screenplay by William Conselman and James V. Kern got around the "How do we make a movie about a bandleader?" dilemma by concocting a tale which precisely addresses this very problem. Much of the humor herein can be interpreted as a dig at Hollywood's Procrustean habit of reshaping unique talents to fit established patterns and clichés. In the film's plotline, "Four-Star Studios" has hastily signed Kyser to a movie contract on the strength of his radio fame, only to have second thoughts about the salability of their unprepossessing new star. A conniving producer (Adolphe Menjou), unwilling to simply buy out Kyser's contract, tries to get the bandleader to break the agreement on his own by subjecting Kay to a series of humiliations—including a ridiculous screen test involving an ill-fitting Romeo costume, a Venetian gondola and a haughty movie queen (Lucille Ball). Ultimately the plan to dishearten Kyser by turning him into something he's not is foiled when the Four-Star executives realize, via a nicely staged recreation of a *Kollege of Musical Knowledge* broadcast, that Kyser is most effective simply being his own "Evenin' folks, how y'all?" self.

This key scene contains the film's most sustained example of Kyser's audience rapport; the rest of *That's Right—You're Wrong* tends to take the same attitude adopted by Menjou, that Kay is unable to carry a picture by himself. Though the movie is "about" Kyser, far more screen time is devoted to Kay's fast-talking manager (Dennis O'Keefe) and a pair of what-the-hell screenwriters (based on RKO's own Gene Towne and Graham Barker, and played by Edward Everett Horton and Hobart Cavanaugh) who'd rather indulge in their various hobbies than hunker down to crafting a suitable Kyser vehicle. While these characters tend to reduce the star to a feckless punching bag, the end result turns out beneficially for the overall film. By having the rest of the actors dominate and condescend to Kyser, *That's Right—You're Wrong* creates automatic audience empathy for the bandleader, which might not have been possible if Kyser had been portrayed as the quick-witted, confident, organized and financially secure celebrity he really was.

Earning a profit of $219,000, *That's Right—You're Wrong* was RKO's fifth biggest moneymaker of 1939. It was only natural that the studio would combine forces with MCA for a quartet of additional films, and that the formula established in the first picture would be followed in Kyser's subsequent vehicles. For the rest of his RKO career, Kay would appear under his own name in the role of a radio star, with his band members in tow. He would be surrounded by top supporting players and excellent production values. His character would be a well-meaning schnook who'd end up as a victim of circumstances created by others, but it would always be Kay's proactive response to the plot convolutions that would lead to the happy ending. And of course, there would be plenty of music, including at least one "story" number per picture—a production piece that would

The December 1940 edition of *Photoplay* yielded this marvelously composed advertisement for Kay Kyser's best-known (but far from best) RKO feature film.

follow a scenario and be acted out by the likes of Sully Mason, Harry Babbitt and Ish Kabibble. The Story Number in *That's Right—You're Wrong* is "Little Red Fox," complete with a variety of vocal inflections and costume changes.

Kyser's next picture, 1940's *You'll Find Out* (working title: *The Old Perfessor*), was almost as huge a box office attraction as his first ($167,000 profit on a $500,000 investment),

though for contemporary viewers it is handicapped by the fact that it promises far more than it delivers. *You'll Find Out* is a "scare comedy," in its time a surefire moneymaking genre as witness Bob Hope's *The Ghost Breakers* and Abbott & Costello's *Hold That Ghost*. RKO boosted the film's salability with the casting of Boris Karloff, Peter Lorre and Bela Lugosi, the only occasion that these three "Titans of Terror" appeared in the same picture. Returning director David Butler sustains a suitably spooky mood, enhanced by a new sound-effect gimmick: the Sonovox, a device that enabled a person to "speak" through musical instruments via electronic vibration (*a la* the famous "singing guitar" of jazz musician Alvino Rey). This device serves the double function of providing eerie vocal accompaniment to a séance sequence and being the central "character" in the closing production number.

Alas, the film's potential is muted by its overlength (96 minutes) and its squandering of the Karloff-Lorre-Lugosi team. Only Bela, as a phony swami, has a role really worth playing; both Boris and Peter merely coast along on their reputations. Worse, we are robbed of one of the great pleasures of "old dark house" films, that of guessing who's responsible for the skullduggery (in this case the attempted murder of heroine Helen Parrish, whose romance with Kyser's business manager Dennis O'Keefe [again] is the catalyst that brings Kay and his band into the intrigue) and of weeding out the red herrings from the genuine culprits. Though Karloff, Lorre and Lugosi were advertised as "Masters of Mystery," the mystery is over halfway into the film when it is revealed that all three horror veterans really *are* the Bad Guys. Kyser himself is let down by the surprisingly mediocre screenplay by David Butler and James V. Kern, and the limp "special material" by Monte Brice, Andrew Bennison and R.T.M. Scott, which hauls out every bedraggled old haunted house gag known to mankind.

Kyser's best moments occur at the beginning and end of the picture, when he is allowed to appear as the glib, audience-conscious radio personality that his fans had come to admire. A minute or so before the final fadeout, Kay breaks the "fourth wall" by addressing the movie audience directly, informing them that Karloff, Lorre and Lugosi are really nice guys, and promising to return for his regular Wednesday night broadcast. (The planned finale, with his three sinister co-stars likewise breaking character to exchange one-liners with Kyser, was abandoned when it was determined that the picture was already too long.) The moment he stops talking, Kay is "evaporated" before our eyes by a bolt of electricity, a far funnier and more inventive gag than anything else in the film.

The one saving grace of *You'll Find Out* is its musical program, with the "story" number "Bad Humor Man," orchestrated for toy instruments, a singular highlight. This segment might have been even more enjoyable had RKO carried out its original intention of having one of the song's verses performed by Karloff, Lorre and Lugosi! If nothing else, it would have conveyed the genuinely festive mood that permeated the set during shooting. Director Butler has gone on record insisting, "The picture was one of the happiest I ever did. Everybody had fun making it."

Kyser's third RKO vehicle *Playmates* (1941) has an even poorer reputation among film buffs than *You'll Find Out,* by virtue (if that is the word) of its being the screen swan song of John Barrymore, here cast as "himself"—or rather the bloated, besotted self-caricature he had become in the years just prior to his death. Through no fault of his own, Kyser wound up as a spectator at the career low points of several performers: first the ill-served horror icons in *You'll Find Out,* and now John Barrymore.

So seedy is the premise of *Playmates*—Kyser and Barrymore's respective press agents come up with a joint publicity stunt whereby Barrymore will give Kay acting lessons in preparation for a musical version of *Romeo and Juliet*—and so pathetic is the participation of the one-time "Great Profile," that many people remember the picture as being even worse than it is. In truth, Barrymore was handled more respectfully in *Playmates* by star Kyser, director David Butler and screenwriters James V. Kern, M.M. Musselman and Arthur Phillips than he was in his embarrassing guest appearances on Rudy Vallee's radio programs of the early 1940s. In one particularly effective scene, the other cast members coax Barrymore into reciting Hamlet's "To be or not to be." As recalled by *Playmates* co-star Patsy Kelly in a 1968 interview with Leonard Maltin: "Then [Barrymore] stood up, and he did the soliloquy. And the stagehands, everyone on the set, spoiled the take, because they stood to their feet and gave him a standing ovation, which was the most thrilling thing you've ever seen." Barrymore is seated in the take used in the film, but his abbreviated rendition of the soliloquy is every bit as enthralling as Kelly remembered it; it is said that the actor broke down in tears at the end of the scene.

Elsewhere, the script takes pains to have Kyser constantly refer to his co-star as a "great artist." Even in the climax, in which Kyser thwarts Barrymore's plan to sabotage the bandleader's Shakespearean debut by tricking the actor into spraying his throat with alum (that's the caliber of jokes in this picture), Kay reiterates his on-screen respect for the faded matinee idol by telling a theater audience that his "Swinging Shakespeare" program would never have seen the light of day without the help and support of the great John Barrymore. Kyser's warmth and sincerity stand out like an oasis in a desert of tawdriness, and we come out of *Playmates* liking Kyser rather than condemning him as an accessory to RKO's exploitation of Barrymore's downfall.

Oddly, the film wasn't criticized as harshly when it first came out as it has been in recent years. *Variety* commented that the combination of Kyser and Barrymore would result in "big box office" and lavished praise on the musical numbers, which the reviewer felt were thoroughly accurate portrayals of actual nightclub and musical-comedy productions. (Contrary to expectations, the mini-opera "story" number "Romeo Smith and Juliet Jones" is rather pleasant, with a more restrained performance than usual from Ish Kabibble—adding credence to the legend that Butler wanted to spin this freakish clown off into a film series of his own.) Even the supporting appearances of Patsy Kelly and Lupe Velez, which today seem far more excruciating than Barrymore's turns, were regarded as major contributors to the film's success!

Playmates was the first of Kyser's RKO films that doesn't contain a romantic subplot with secondary characters. The studio was experimenting with allowing Kay to have an on-screen romance of his own by building up an implicit mutual attraction between him and vocalist Ginny Simms. In real life, Kay and Ginny had been an "item" for several years; actress Louise Currie, who appeared in *You'll Find Out,* has insisted that the bandleader was "madly in love" with the singer throughout filming. But by the time of *Playmates,* Ginny's ardor had cooled, even though Kay had proposed marriage. Significantly, this was Simms' last film appearance with Kyser; they parted amicably, and Ginny's contractual commitment to MCA and RKO was satisfied by casting her as Edgar Bergen's love interest in another radio-inspired "package," the Bergen & McCarthy-Fibber McGee & Molly vehicle *Here We Go Again* (1942), discussed elsewhere in this book.

The important consideration here is that no one in the movie audience felt uncomfortable with the suggested Kyser-Simms liaison in *Playmates,* encouraging RKO to give Kay a screen wife, played by Ellen Drew, in his fourth endeavor *My Favorite Spy* (1942). Rushed into production to capitalize on America's entry into World War II, this comedy-adventure is probably the most coherent of Kay's RKO vehicles. No longer does the plot grind to a halt for the musical numbers; the two songs are carefully integrated into the story, with "Got the Moon in My Pocket" serving a vital plot function as a Morse code message beaming information to enemy agents. Nor is Kyser obliged to share screen time with a "big name" like Barrymore or Karloff. Though *My Favorite Spy* has a particularly stellar supporting cast (Drew, Jane Wyman, Robert Armstrong, Una O'Connor and William Demarest), Kyser carries the whole picture on his bony little shoulders.

Perhaps Kay's dominance of *Spy* is due to some sidelines coaching by comedian Harold Lloyd, who produced the picture for RKO. Though not as intimately involved with all production aspects as he had been in his own starring pictures, Lloyd was known to drop in on the sets of his two RKO productions (the other was *A Girl, a Guy and a Gob*) and make a suggestion here and there, or help the actors pull off a tricky gag or bit of physical business. Throughout *My Favorite Spy,* Kyser, who physically resembles Lloyd right down to the horn-rimmed glasses, utilizes many of Lloyd's familiar gestures, facial expressions and body movements.

Interestingly, the one routine that screams "Harold Lloyd," in which Kyser subdues a nest of Nazi spies by covering the villains in a heavy theatrical curtain and knocking them out one by one, actually has its roots in a similar gag from the 1926 silent screwball comedy *The Cruise of the Jasper B*, co-scripted by *My Favorite Spy*'s director Tay Garnett. The rest of the film is the same slightly unsettling mixture of high comedy and tense melodrama that Garnett imbued in most of his productions, including the director's morbid trademark of unexpectedly killing off a likable supporting character (the luckless victim is Kyser's amiably goofy musical arranger, played by Edmund Glover). Unfortunately, Garnett is a bit off his mark here, making Kyser's character too realistic and vulnerable to be totally amusing. The scenes in which Kay is ordered by the Intelligence chief to be publicly humiliated in order to convince the enemy spies that he's willing to work with the Nazis, and the running gag of Kay's unconsummated wedding night with his new bride, should have been hilarious; but since our hero looks like he's really hurting, the effect is more melancholy than funny. Nor does it help any that the other characters in the film, from American spy Jane Wyman to Nazi ringleader Robert Armstrong, seem to take sadistic delight in Kay's suffering. At one point, Intelligence officer Vaughn Glaser responds to Kay's pitiful story of how his wife has left him by bursting out laughing!

Nor does the star receive much support from the uneven script by M. Coates Webster, Sid Herzig, William Bowers and Frank Ryan, who themselves were working under the handicap of being answerable to the War Department's Motion Picture Board Review, which ordered three revisions—each one less funny than its predecessor—before they'd allow Kyser to portray an Army Intelligence agent. As originally conceived, Kay was to have been recruited for spy duty as an Army officer the moment he was drafted; this was objected to on the grounds that his character had received no proper Intelligence training. Once this matter was straightened out, the War Department groused that Kyser's character was an "object of ridicule" and thus unfit for an officer's commission. Finally it was established that Kay had been discharged from the Army as a 4-F (for flat feet), so that he could function as a civilian secret agent, casting no aspersions on anyone. You'd *really* think that the Motion Picture Board Review would have more important things to worry about than Kay Kyser tarnishing the Army's image.

As in the case of *You'll Find Out*, most of the people who worked on *My Favorite Spy*, including Kyser, Wyman and Garnett, would later recall having a great deal of fun during production—though Garnett qualified this by wishing that some of the fun had carried over into the picture. Audiences in 1942 agreed; *My Favorite Spy* was Kyser's least financially successful film thus far. But Kay's radio popularity continued unabated, and there was still one picture left on his contract. Perhaps reasoning that the failure of *Spy* was due to its paucity of music and preponderance of plot, RKO responded by assembling a film that was virtually all music and no plot.

Kyser worked tirelessly on behalf of the USO and the war effort: He was the first big musical star of World War II to play at military bases, paying his own expenses and ultimately making more personal appearances for servicemen than any other bandleader. This was the inspiration for *Around the World* (1943), directed with economy and efficiency by Allan Dwan from a script by Ralph Spence and Carl Herzinger. The film is a romanticized account of Kay's recent tour of American bases in Australia, India, Chungking, Cairo and North Africa; thus we see plenty of the Kyser band (and much too much of Ish Kabibble) performing seven numbers, from the enjoyable "Candlelight and Wine" to the idiotic "The Moke from Shamokan." To blur the line between fact and fiction, most of the performers appear as themselves: Kay Kyser as Kay, Mischa Auer as Mischa, Joan Davis as Joan, Marcy McGuire as Marcy, and even uncredited bit players Barbara Hale, Joan Barclay and Rosemary LaPlanche as Barbara, Joan and Rosemary.

Had RKO stuck to this docudrama approach, everything would have come up roses. Instead, the screenwriters insisted upon shoehorning in a secondary story involving Axis spies, as well as a lachrymose subplot in which singer Marcy McGuire discovers that her military officer father has been killed in action. While the speech delivered by Army captain Robert Armstrong, exhorting Marcy to smile through her tears and give the boys the best show possible, was meant as a morale booster for 1943 audiences, it comes off as so artificial that the film is virtually unwatchable today.

This ended Kyser's obligation to RKO, though he kept busy throughout the rest of 1943 with guest appearances in the all-star movie musicals *Stage Door Canteen* and *Thousands Cheer* (his only Technicolor appearance). With his NBC radio program still selling plenty of Lucky Strike cigarettes, Kyser was hired by MGM for a one-shot project, the Tim Whelan–directed *Swing Fever* (1944), representing the only time the bandleader ever played a character other than himself. As aspiring songwriter Lowell Blackford, the star gets involved with gangsters who try to use his special "whammy"—a stare that renders people immobile—to fix a series of fights involving brainless pug Maxie Rosenbloom. While such Kyser regulars as Ish Kabibble, Sully Mason, Harry Babbitt, Julie Conway and Trudy Erwin are on hand, the main musical attraction in *Swing Fever* is Lena Horne's rendition of "You're So Indifferent."

From MGM it was onward and downward to Columbia for Kyser's last starring film *Carolina Blues* (1944), directed by Leigh Jason. This one begins as a quasi-sequel to *Around the World* with Kay (again as "himself") and his band coming back to the States after his USO tour; but soon the film becomes mired in a story involving the underhanded efforts by the impoverished Victor Moore to wangle a singing job with the Kyser band for his pretty daughter Ann Miller. The cheapest and sloppiest of all the Kyser vehicles, *Carolina Blues* nonetheless has some nifty musical numbers, including the all-black ensemble piece "Mr. Beebe," featuring Harold Nicholas, the Four Step Brothers, Julie Bryant and June Richmond. And while the law of diminishing returns has lessened the comic appeal of Kay Kyser and Ish Kabibble, some sparkling moments are provided by comic actor Moore, who with the help of trick photography plays not only the black sheep of a long line of industrialists, but the rest of his family as well (including one female member). The most fascinating aspect of *Carolina Blues* is its strange twist on Kyser's private life. In the film, Kay loses his vocalist Georgia Carroll (who'd made her screen debut in *Around the World*) when she retires from the band in favor of marriage, leaving the field open for Ann Miller to become the star's love interest. In real life, Georgia Carroll really did retire from show business in 1944 to get married—to Kay Kyser!

Though *Carolina Blues* spelled *finis* to Kyser's film career, his influence would continue to be felt in another aspect of cinematic art with his 1948 recording of "The Woody Woodpecker Song," subsequently the official theme tune for that particular cartoon favorite. Kyser enjoyed continued success on radio until 1949 (albeit in a different 30-minute format), and that same year brought his old *Kollege of Musical Knowledge* to television. The newest member of his professional entourage was singer and future talk show host Mike Douglas, who never grew tired of recalling Kyser's insistence that he would retire from performing and devote his life to the Christian Science Movement as soon as he'd earned a million dollars. In 1954 Kay did just that, moving back to North Carolina with his wife and three daughters. He became an accredited Christian Science practitioner, relocating to the denomination's Boston headquarters in 1974. Though he would produce several documentary films on behalf of his church, he never again appeared before a camera himself, politely refusing all entreaties to discuss his career in show business, and only reluctantly allowing fans to screen his old films in his presence. Kay Kyser died in 1985, a few months short of his 79th birthday.

Grand Ole Opry (1940) and *The National Barn Dance* (1944)

A separate book could be written on the multitude of country-western performers in the 1930s and 1940s who expanded upon their radio success by branching out into motion pictures. The popularity of this particular brand of musical entertainment reached a high point during the World War II years, when so many soldiers and sailors were recruited from the Southern and Western states, all demanding their favorite songs from radio stations located near military camps and from such specialized operations as the Armed Forces Network. At this time, the proliferation of disc jockey shows and live variety programs trafficking in C&W was borne of necessity: With ASCAP demanding ever-increasing royalties from performances and broadcasts of popular songs, and with American Federation of Musicians president James C. Petrillo at one point imposing a ban on records featuring union musicians until his demands were met, radio producers had to turn to the less restrictive Broadcast Music International (BMI) and its huge inventory of cowboy and hillbilly songs—most of them performed and recorded by non-union artists.

The two best-known and most widely heard weekly country-music programs of the 1940s were *The National Barn Dance,* created by Chicago radio station WLS in 1924, and *The Grand Ole Opry,* first broadcast on Nashville's WSM in 1925 and still on the air as of this writing. Though essentially a local program, *Grand Ole Opry* was picked up by NBC beginning October 14, 1939, with a 30-minute segment of the weekly four-hour Nashville broadcast heard regionally and later nationally until 1957. The series had landed its network slot and the sponsorship of the R.J. Reynolds Tobacco company thanks largely to the star power of singer Roy Acuff and his Smoky Mountain Boys, who'd spent three years trying to get on the *Opry* before finally making their bow in 1938. While the series' other regulars—notably emcee George Dewey Hay, aka "The Solemn Old Judge," and banjoist Uncle Dave Macon and his son Dorris—were household names in those states within range of WSM's 50,000-watt signal, Roy Acuff and his band were the show's main attraction with such hit songs as "Wabash Cannonball" and "Night Train to Memphis."

Even before *Grand Ole Opry* launched its network run, Hollywood's Republic Pictures was scouting the series for a possible film adaptation. Catering primarily to rural and small-town audiences, Republic knew that a film version of the series would have guaranteed appeal for its base. Initially, however, the studio planned to use only the name of the show as the title of a vehicle for their in-house singing cowboy Gene Autry. But after the radio show's successful network breakthrough, Republic invited Acuff, the Smoky Mountain Boys, the "Solemn Old Judge" and the Macons to their San Fernando Valley studios. Still, Republic hedged its bets by including another of its own popular C&W attractions, the Weaver Brothers and Elviry, as the film's top-billed stars.

Directed by Frank McDonald and scripted by Dorrell and Stuart McGowan (later the producers of TV's *Death Valley Days*), the 1940 filmization of *Grand Ole Opry* wove its musical specialties into one of Republic's most frequently used storylines: the efforts by a group of hometown folk to pass legislation that will benefit the farmers, and the simultaneous machinations of greedy city slickers to push through their own self-serving legislation at the farmers' expense. We all know who's going to win this tug of war, so there's no point in scrutinizing the story any further. It should be noted that while the film is bursting at the seams with cornball rustic comedy from the Weaver Brothers and Elviry, the *Grand Ole Opry* guest stars are treated with dignity—though this apparently was not the original intention. Upon arriving at Republic, Acuff and his band were escorted to the wardrobe department and outfitted with ludicrous cowboy costumes. But Acuff wasn't about to let a bunch of Tinseltown sharpsters monkey around with the Smoky Mountain Boys' established practice of appearing onstage in the casual, unpretentious outfits that one might see at a Sunday picnic in the Ozarks—and besides, nothing riled Roy more than being called a cowboy. Though Acuff and his band would go on to star in a group of Republic B westerns and make a guest appearance in the Columbia programmer *Cowboy Canteen* (1944), it would always be on Roy's own terms—and in duds of his own choosing.

Appropriately holding its world premiere at

The clown princes of NBC's *National Barn Dance,* the Hoosier Hot Shots (from the 1940 edition of the annual *WLS Family Album*): Left to right, Kenny Trietsch, Frank Kettering and Gabe Hawkins. Overwhelmed by instruments on the floor: Paul "Hezzie" Trietsch.

Nashville's Paramount Theater on June 28, 1940, *Grand Ole Opry* is not meant to be an authentic reproduction of the radio version, nor does it have to be, since we now have plenty of those thanks to kinescopes and videotapes of the program's many television broadcasts from 1955 onward. The film's enduring value is as a permanent record of the legendary Uncle Dave Macon, who died three years before the *Opry* made its TV debut, in his only screen appearance. Whenever a film clip of Uncle Dave is shown on a Nashville music retrospective, it has always been lifted from 1940's *Grand Ole Opry*—and thanks to the excellent preservation of most Republic films of its era, those clips are invariably in pristine condition.

The National Barn Dance made its network radio premiere on September 30, 1933, and yet the property wasn't transferred to film until 1944, four years after the upstart *Grand Ole Opry*. Surprisingly, it was not Republic who beckoned the *Barn Dance*'s stars to Hollywood but instead Paramount Pictures, who hadn't had a major "rural" attraction since the departure of Arkansas-bred comedian Bob Burns in 1940. Hardly an A picture but too elaborately mounted for a B, Paramount's *The National Barn Dance* represented the final directorial effort of Hugh Bennett, a former film editor who had piloted all of the studio's "Henry Aldrich" pictures (q.v.) from 1941 through 1944.

Whereas the plot of *Grand Ole Opry* is focused on the problems of the down-home folks, for most of its running time *The National Barn Dance* seems to think that we care more about the trials and tribulations of Johnny Burke (played by Clark Gable lookalike Charles Quigley), a young Chicago feller who hopes to land a job at a major radio advertising agency. Johnny is convinced that his scheme to book small-town hillbilly groups for a network program sponsored by Garvey's Soups will be his ticket to the Big Time. Posing as a representative of the ad firm that has yet to hire him, Johnny heads to a farming village in southern Illinois and signs up such musical acts as Lulu Belle and Scotty, the Hoosier Hot Shots, Arkie the Arkansas Woodchopper and the Dinning Sisters. He also promises radio work to a couple of farm boys with unusual voices, Joe Kelly and Pat Buttram. In case you haven't already figured it out, all of the above-named personalities were in 1944 regulars on radio's *National Barn Dance* (Kelly was the announcer, Buttram the lead comic), and all appear in this film under their own or their professional names—though not playing professional entertainers, at least not during the first few reels.

Scriptwriters Lee Loeb and Hal Fimberg devise all manner of setbacks and disappointments for Johnny's clients until ulcerated advertising executive Mr. Mitcham (how did Robert Benchley get involved in this?) is persuaded by baskets and baskets full of fan mail that country-western music is the Coming Thing. In the end, Mitcham arranges for a battery of WLS microphones to broadcast the would-be performers during their regular weekend barn dance (thought we'd *never* get there, didn't you?). There's also a romantic subplot involving Johnny and Lulu Belle's younger sister, a character played by Jean Heather. This young Paramount contractee had come to prominence with her supporting role in *Going My Way* opposite fellow newcomer James Brown, and was supposed to have been reteamed with Brown in *The National Barn Dance* before Charles Quigley was cast instead.

Though the film's storyline is for the birds, the musical performances are uniformly enjoyable, especially the novelty numbers by the Hoosier Hot Shots. It's also fun to see Pat Buttram going through exactly the same paces that would make him a sitcom favorite on TV's *Green Acres* in the 1960s. However, most of Paramount's publicity for the film was lavished upon the close-harmony Dinning Sisters (Lou, Ginger and Jean), who are *very* easy on the eyes and at the time were enormously popular on the USO circuit. But as far as this writer is concerned, the hit of the show is veteran humorist Robert Benchley, who wraps things up by performing the only square dance in his illustrious career.

The original *National Barn Dance* kept promenadin' along the network airstreams until 1950, then reverted to a local attraction via Cincinnati's WLW until 1960, finally landing on Chicago's WGN for another ten years. A handful of television versions were seen throughout the 1950s and 1960s, the last of these a widely syndicated half-hour program from WGN television hosted by that station's longtime agricultural reporter Orion Samuelson.

"The Great Gildersleeve" (1940–1944)

The Great Gildersleeve has been described as radio's first "spinoff" program, in which a supporting character in a highly rated series is deemed popular enough to star in a series of his or her own—a practice elevated to an art form in the 1970s by such TV producers as Norman Lear and Gary Marshall. Like many other showbiz "firsts," *Gildersleeve*'s claim to that title is questionable, given the murky history of radio's early years: Journalists in the 1940s played safe by describing the program as "one of the first" or "possibly the first." Whatever the case, it is safe to say that *The Great Gildersleeve* was the first truly successful network spinoff, outlasting its "parent" radio program *Fibber McGee and Molly* (q.v.) by a full year.

The son of Portuguese immigrants, Harold José Pereira De Faria was born in San Leandro, California, in 1908. Adopting the professional name Harold Peary, he made his first radio appearance in 1923 as a boy soprano on Oakland station KZM, continuing to work steadily as a singer and actor in California radio throughout the 1930s. Settling in Chicago in 1937, he could be heard on such series as *Road to Romance* and *Little Orphan Annie,* using his flexible voice and talent for dialects to play as many as six roles in a single broadcast. As a utility actor on the comedy series *Fibber McGee and Molly* he returned to California in 1938, shortly thereafter making his first appearance as one of several pompous, self-infatuated characters named Gildersleeve, all of whom resided in the McGees' home town of Wistful Vista. Finally on September 26, 1939, Peary was established as Fibber McGee's bloviating next-door neighbor and eternal nemesis Throckmorton P. Gildersleeve. Though essentially a two-dimensional antagonist at this point, Gildersleeve won the hearts of listeners with his inimitable "dirty laugh" (a slightly sinister giggle that started high and ended guttural), his sarcastic references to his "little chum" Fibber, and his funereal catchphrase "You're a haaard man, McGee!"

Peary was only nine or ten months into this characterization when he was signed along with several other second-echelon radio personalities to appear in the 63-minute Paramount musical comedy *Comin' Round the Mountain* (1940). Though studio publicity boasted that the producers had spent a lot of time and money harvesting scores of authentic "hillbilly" songs for the film, *Comin' Round the Mountain* was strictly B-grade, budgeted at $150,000—not including the $85,000 salary of its star, Arkansas comedian-philosopher Bob "Bazooka" Burns (see **The *Big Broadcast* Films**). Paramount's efforts to promote Burns as the new Will Rogers, successful at first, had just crashed and burned with the box office failure of his 1940 vehicle *Alias the Deacon,* but the comedian's play-or-pay contract required the studio to churn out one more film before giving him the air. As much in a hurry to part company with Paramount as they were with him, Burns broke a long-standing promise to himself never to appear in a film that depicted his fellow "mountain folk" in a derisive manner, and as a result angered a considerable portion of his fan base with *Comin' Round the Mountain,* which focused on a clichéd feud between a pair of backwoods families named the Blowers and the Beagles. Cast as traveling salesman Jed Blower, Burns brings peace to his home turf by convincing his family to drop their shootin' irons, gather together their homemade musical instruments and become radio stars, a move that enriches the impoverished village of Monotony and ends up getting Jed elected mayor.

Several of the radio performers in *Comin' Round the Mountain* had built their reputations upon rustic characterizations. Cliff Arquette, who later achieved talk show and game show fame as Charley Weaver, is seen in his role as "The Slaphappy Grandpappy" from the NBC variety series *Avalon Time.* Marjorie O'Neill Bauersfeld, who when not performing was a recognized horticultural expert, is billed on-screen only as "Mirandy," the character she'd made famous on NBC's *National Farm and Home Hour.* Pat Barrett, who like "Mirandy" had spent many years performing with a country-

Harold Peary as the Great Gildersleeve.

western singing group called the Beverly Hill Billies(!), was seen as Uncle Ezra Watters, the "old man with young ideas" that he played on *The National Barn Dance* (q.v.). And 27-year-old Bill Thompson, one of *Fibber McGee and Molly*'s most versatile supporting players, appears under mounds of age makeup in his familiar role as the Old Timer ("That ain't the way *I* heerd it!"), here teamed with Richard Carle as a pair of superannuated storekeepers—roles originally intended for the radio comedy duo Lum & Abner (q.v.).

To broaden the appeal of *Comin' Round the Mountain* beyond the corn-belt trade, three slightly more sophisticated radio second bananas were added to the cast. Jerry Colonna, Bob Hope's perennial wild-eyed foil, plays a zany balloon ascensionist who breaks the heart of nominal heroine Una Merkel. *Jack Benny Program* announcer Don Wilson shows up as "himself," sneaking in a plug for Benny's sponsor Jell-O. And last but not least, Peary makes his first screen appearance as Throckmorton P. Gildersleeve, who on this occasion is a decidedly unpleasant character, a small-town mayor who hides behind a mask of benevolence to bilk his constituents and mistreat the residents of the local poorhouse. Though his screen time is limited, Gildersleeve has the advantage of being the first radio "crossover" to appear in the film, looking a bit downtrodden as he implores W.P.A. clerk Walter Catlett to find him a job—thereby anticipating the delicious comeuppance that befalls "Gildy" at the end of the story. So that he'd more closely resemble his radio image, the youthful, slender Peary applied a few gray streaks to his temples, donned a bushy moustache and gained 20 extra pounds.

His next movie appearance as Gildersleeve was again designed to inject an urban note into an essentially rural setting. The 74-minute Republic musical *Country Fair* was supposed to have been the first starring assignment for Gene Autry's trusty sidekick Smiley Burnette, cast as a bumptious backwoods blacksmith who, much to his and everyone else's amazement, becomes governor of his state. But when the screenplay began showing signs of favoring Eddie Foy, Jr. in the role of a city-slicker campaign manager, Burnette dropped out and Guinn "Big Boy" Williams took his place.

The storyline plays the romance between Johnny Campbell (Foy) and heroine Pepper Wilson (June Clyde) against the backdrop of a gubernatorial race pitting crooked Stogie McPhee (William Demarest) against slightly less crooked incumbent Throckmorton P. Gildersleeve. Realizing his chances are akin to a snowball in hell, McPhee places a huge bet against himself, only to run afoul of shady gambler Cash Nichols (Harold Huber) when he unexpectedly wins. McPhee dashes off to parts unknown, leaving his doltish running mate Gunther Potts (Williams) to accept the nomination. Harold Peary's participation in the picture is minimal, strictly to cash in on his *Fibber McGee and Molly* name value. Of more importance to the proceedings are the film's other radio carryovers Lulubelle and Scotty and Whitey "Duke of Paducah" Ford, musical headliners on *The National Barn Dance*; and the Vass Family, a South Carolina singing group (husband, wife, seven kids) who had starred in their own NBC series from 1932 through 1937.

Country Fair was released on May 5, 1941. On August 31, Peary parted company with *Fibber McGee and Molly* to star in his own weekly 30-minute NBC comedy series *The Great Gildersleeve,* which like *Fibber* was created by Don Quinn. In the evolution process from supporting to main character, the disreputable side of Gildersleeve's personality was muted in favor of a more lovable—but no less bombastic—characterization. Though Gildy's actual age and profession was seldom alluded to on *Fibber McGee,* the first episode of his own series established him as a 42-year-old bachelor (ignoring earlier references to a Mrs. Gildersleeve), owner of the Gildersleeve Girdle Factory in Wistful Vista. Journeying to the town of Summerfield to take over the affairs of his late brother-in-law Ed Forrester, Gildy would soon settle down in his new home permanently as guardian of his orphaned niece Marjorie and nephew Leroy.

None of this was mentioned in the 1941 RKO feature *Look Who's Laughing,* a package deal brokered by the MCA talent agency. It combined the talents of Fibber McGee and

Molly (Jim and Marian Jordan) and Edgar Bergen and Charlie McCarthy (q.v.) within a single picture. As part of the package, three members of the *Fibber McGee* supporting cast also appear in *Look Who's Laughing*: announcer Harlow Wilcox, Isabel Randolph as Mrs. Uppington, and Harold Peary as you-know-who. Modern viewers might wonder why "Gildy" is not seen in his familiar role as water commissioner of the town of Summerfield. The answer is twofold: This film was in preparation before Peary was spun off into his new series; and his appointment to water commissioner didn't occur on *Great Gildersleeve* until the episode of October 18, 1942.

In *Look Who's Laughing*, Gildersleeve adopts a difference appearance than in his first two films. His hair is no longer smooth and gray, but has reverted to its naturally curly black; his moustache is of the more realistic and manageable "caterpillar" variety; and he has gained at least 20 more pounds, reportedly on orders from RKO. These cosmetic changes aside, Gildy continues in the comic-heavy mode established in his earlier screen appearances, as he works in league with a shady realtor to undermine Fibber McGee's plan to build an airplane factory near Wistful Vista. The part gives Peary full scope to play the vainglorious Gildersleeve to the hilt, catchphrases and all: By this time, his "You're a haaard man, McGee" is so well known that another actor beats him to it! Gildy is also the link between the two separate plotlines involving Fibber & Molly and Edgar Bergen, as he conspires with Bergen's "protégé" Charlie McCarthy to get Edgar out of town before the ventriloquist can queer a crooked land deal. (It is a testament to the consummate acting skill of Peary that he can carry on a long conversation with a wooden dummy without coming off as a delusional crackpot.) And since Gildy was never really *all* bad on the radio show, he is allowed to redeem himself—but not before getting a thorough trouncing by his ex-partner in crime.

By the time Peary made his second and final screen appearance with Fibber and Molly in *Here We Go Again* (RKO, 1942), *The Great Gildersleeve* was well on its way to becoming one of radio's most popular situation comedies, as well as a bountiful source of revenue for its sponsor, the Kraft Food Company. In keeping with the more sympathetic version of the character on his own series, in *Here We Go Again* Gildersleeve has been exorcised of all villainous vestiges, though his relationship with Fibber is just as adversarial as ever. Reacting to one of his "little chum"'s lousy jokes, Gildy grumbles "Listen, McGee, vaudeville is dead. And if you don't want to join it, you'll keep quiet." The character's connection with the plotline is more tenuous than in *Look Who's Laughing,* beyond establishing his attractive sister Jean Gildersleeve (played by vocalist Ginny Simms) as romantic interest for co-star Edgar Bergen. Peary's best scene in the picture is a tricked-up game of pool with Jim "Fibber McGee" Jordan, though both actors are upstaged by the special effects.

Approximately six weeks after the release of *Here We Go Again,* Gildersleeve was seen as a secondary rather than primary character for the last time in the all-star RKO musical *Seven Days' Leave* (1942). The plot, involving the efforts by wolfish GI Victor Mature to wed blue-blooded socialite Lucille Ball in order to secure a $100,000 inheritance, is merely an excuse to toss in as many guest performers from as many branches of entertainment as possible into an 87-minute mulligan stew with songs by Jimmy McHugh and Frank Loesser. In addition to established film personalities Victor Mature, Lucille Ball, Wallace Ford and Walter Reed, the film showcases nightclub entertainers Peter Lynd Hayes, Mapy Cortes and Lynn, Royce & Vanya; two big-name bands headed by Freddie Martin and Les Brown; and radio favorites Peary, Ginny Simms and Arnold Stang, the latter then playing prominent comedy roles in seven different programs. Also recruited from the ranks of radio row are abridged versions of two popular network weeklies: the CBS human-interest series *Court of Missing Heirs,* a broadcast of which apprises the hero of his inheritance; and Ralph Edwards' zany NBC audience-participation show *Truth or Consequences,* wherein Lucille Ball gets to satisfy the urge of many a 1940s moviegoer by throwing a pie at Victor Mature. As Harold V. Cohen of the

Pittsburgh *Post-Gazette* pontificated, "There have been worse musicals than *Seven Days' Leave*."

Billed in the opening credits as "Harold Peary (The Great Gildersleeve)," the actor originally was to have been confined to a cameo role as the executor of Mature's estate. But fortunes had shifted since Peary had been willing to accept a subordinate assignment in *Comin' Round the Mountain,* and he threatened to walk off the set of *Seven Days' Leave* unless his part was beefed up. And that is why Peary is seen singing and dancing alongside Peter Lynd Hayes, Victor Mature and newcomer Marcy McGuire (advertised by RKO as "the female Mickey Rooney") in the rambunctious specialty number "A Touch of Texas."

During its first season on NBC, radio's *The Great Gildersleeve* not only established Peary as a star in his own right but also familiarized the public with a number of other memorable characters. As played respectively by Lurene Tuttle and Walter Tetley, Gildy's wards Marjorie and LeRoy were not the usual smart-aleck juvenile characters—though wisecracks were a vital part of their repertoire—but instead personalities of considerable depth. (Tuttle was succeeded first by Louise Erickson and then by Mary Lee Robb, who held down the role for the longest time.) Similarly, Gildersleeve's housemaid Birdie Lee Coggins transcended the standard black stereotype of the era as a character possessed of a ready wit, a bottomless supply of common sense and resourcefulness, and a heart as big as all outdoors. Birdie was played throughout all manifestations of *The Great Gildersleeve* in radio, movies and television by the wonderful Lillian Randolph.

Without Fibber McGee to kick around any more, Gildersleeve found a new and even worthier adversary in the irascible form of Judge Horace Hooker (played on radio by Earl Ross), who in the early episodes did his utmost to place the guardianship of Marjorie and Leroy in more "capable" hands, but eventually mellowed into grudgingly accepting Gildy as both a suitable substitute parent and a fellow member in good standing of a local male fraternity called the Jolly Boys Club. And whenever Gildersleeve strolled into the local pharmacy, he was greeted by mealy-mouthed druggist Mr. Peavy, who contributed the series' most beloved catchphrase by countering Gildy's strongly held opinions with a fence-straddling "Well, now, I ... wouldn't say that." Richard LeGrand, a show business veteran of 40 years' standing, was coaxed out of retirement to play Peavy, remaining in the role until illness forced him to bow out in favor of sound-alike actor Forrest Lewis in the 1950s.

What made *The Great Gildersleeve* so fresh and funny back in its days of glory—and can still elicit chuckles today—was the series' abstention from gratuitous jokes and one-liners in favor of humor arising from the characters and situations. Too, despite the series' many wartime-themed episode, the comedy does not date as much as other radio programs from the same period because of its universality. Take away the references to rationing and scrap-metal drives and replace them with comments about post-recession economizing and conservation, and the scripts would play just as well now as they did back in the day.

In mid–1942 RKO signed Peary to star in a group of inexpensive feature films based on *The Great Gildersleeve.* Since the radio version didn't take a summer break, Peary was obliged to arrange his filming schedule around his broadcast duties. Under these conditions, four films were ground out between 1942 and 1944, all running between 62 and 64 minutes, and all produced by Herman Schlom, who later supervised another quartet of RKO "Bs" based on Chester Gould's comic strip *Dick Tracy.* The four *Gildersleeve*s were directed by Gordon Douglas, who had been borrowed from Hal Roach Studios for the first effort and then signed to a long-term RKO contract on the strength of his ability to make 'em fast, funny and cheap. Douglas would later graduate to the major leagues with such prestige productions as the science fiction classic *Them!,* the 3D western *The Charge at Feather River,* the Elvis Presley musical *Follow That Dream,* and no fewer than five Frank Sinatra vehicles, beginning with *Young at Heart* and wrapping up with *Lady in Cement.*

The *Gildersleeve* series' uniformity extended to the supporting casts, with Lillian Randolph as Birdie and teenager Freddie Mercer as Leroy in every film. (Walter Tetley, the radio show's Leroy, was in his late 20s and as such an inappropriate choice to play the role on screen, though he was compensated with a bit part as a bellboy in the series' third entry *Gildersleeve on Broadway*.) Appearing in his familiar guise as Peavy in three of the pictures was Richard LeGrand, one of those lucky radio performers who looked exactly as he sounded without the aid of makeup (LeGrand was in his early 60s at the time). And Charles Arnt was seen twice as Judge Hooker, a role taken on as a one-scene cameo by Dink Trout in the final entry *Gildersleeve's Ghost*. The biggest actor turnover in the series was in the role of Marjorie, played by Nancy Gates in the first two films, Margaret Landry in the third, and Margie Stewart (then a minor celebrity as the only "official" Army poster girl of World War II) in the series finale.

Scripted by Jack Townley and Julian Josephson, the opening series salvo *The Great Gildersleeve* (1942) exhibits both the virtues and the shortcomings of all four films. It moves quickly, delivers laughs with expertise and assurance, and boasts an appealing cast, but the "heart" of the radio version is largely lacking, except for the affectionate and supportive relationship among the members of the Gildersleeve household. Also, too much of the comedy relies more upon slapstick and stock gag situations than the natural humor of the situation or Peary's characterization. Backtracking to the earliest days of the radio series, the film finds Gildersleeve in danger of losing legal guardianship of his niece and nephew. Giving Gildy ten days to find a wife or give up custody, conniving Judge Hooker drops a few hints here and there that he'll rule in Gildy's favor provided that the portly bachelor proposes marriage to Hooker's spinster sister Amelia (played by the ubiquitous Mary Field). To save "Uncle Mort" from this grisly fate, Marjorie and Leroy mount a citywide campaign to convince the judge that Gildy would be unanimously chosen as Summerfield's leading citizen if given the chance. This fails, as does Gildy's attempt to beat the judge in a bicycle race when he ends up pedaling backward down a hill. It isn't until the governor (Thurston Hall), traveling incognito through the state, makes the chance acquaintance of Leroy that the machinery is set in motion for Gildy's ultimate triumph and Hooker's humiliating defeat.

Billed second in the role of Gildy's Aunt Emma, Jane Darwell demonstrates that her recent Oscar win for her heartrending performance as Ma Joad in *The Grapes of Wrath* had not made her hesitant or self-conscious in the least about participating in *The Great Gildersleeve*'s farcical plot convolutions—including such sight-gag highlights as a perilous ride in a runaway sidecar. If the RKO press releases can be believed, Darwell thoroughly enjoyed the company of Harold Peary, exchanging jokes and friendly putdowns with her co-star between scenes. The actress would also appear in the next *Gildersleeve* film.

Peary himself gives his liveliest performance to date, notably during an elaborate practical-joke sequence in the final reel. A few dim viewers like the *Pittsburgh Post-Gazette*'s house curmudgeon Harold V. Cohen felt that Peary was "not very interesting" as an actor, but audiences in 1942 were decidedly less critical, and *The Great Gildersleeve* more than paid its way.

The second entry *Gildersleeve's Bad Day* (1943) is probably the best of the series, its incident-packed screenplay (again by Jack Townley) copacetically blending sharply etched characterizations, verbal wit, situational humor, running jokes, sight gags, farce, suspense, and even a bit of social satire regarding the pitfalls of taking one's civic duties a bit too seriously. Despite a few ludicrous and overexaggerated moments, it comes closer to the spirit of the radio original than any of the other *Gildersleeve* entries. It was also one of the few Hollywood "series" films to warrant a half-hour adaptation on the prestigious radio anthology *Screen Guild Theater*.

Summoned for jury duty in Judge Hooker's court, Gildersleeve spends the night before the trial poring through every law book he can get his hands on. By the time he shows up in court he considers himself such a legal expert that he issues objections from the jury box. When time comes to render a verdict, everyone votes guilty but our hero, who argues that the evidence against defendant Louie Barton (Douglas Fowley) is purely circumstantial. In most comedies of this nature, the sole jury holdout is eventually proven right. Here, however, the audience already knows that Barton is guilty as hell, and that his two henchmen (Alan Carney, Frank Jenks) have tried to bribe the jury. In fact, their note promising big bucks for a "not guilty" verdict goes straight to Gildersleeve, though he never even peeks into the envelope and is thus pure of heart as he sways the jury to set Barton free.

Shortly afterward, Gildy receives another envelope containing $10,000, which he assumes is an anonymous donation to Marjorie's school canteen fund. Only after the money leaves his hands does he learn that it was stolen from Judge Hooker's safe. Before he or we quite know what is happening, Gildy is running for his life clad only in his underwear, pursued by both cops and crooks. Counterpointing the main action is the ever-mounting frustration of a fellow juror (Grant Withers) whose honeymoon is delayed by Gildy's obstinance—a running gag with a payoff that dovetails magnificently into the "chase" finale. Only in its haste to wrap things up near the end (a potentially exciting car chase is abruptly terminated with a stock-footage crash that was still being hauled out for TV's *The Untouchables* 20 years later!) does *Gildersleeve's Bad Day* betray its humble B-picture status.

The third and fourth *Gildersleeve* pictures were written by Robert E. Kent, a hardened veteran of the low-budget-filler mills. From the looks of things, Kent prepared for these two assignments by screening dozens upon dozens of old comedy short subjects. *Gildersleeve on Broadway* (1943), for example, is less a feature film than a bloated Leon Errol two-reeler, right down to the obligatory "high and dizzy" gag in which the protagonist must escape from a particularly sticky situation by crawling onto a skyscraper ledge. It should go without saying, then, that the film's relationship to the *Great Gildersleeve* radio show extends no further than the use of several principal characters and its deployment of the show's familiar plot device of getting self-styled *bon vivant* Throckmorton P. Gildersleeve innocently involved with more than one woman at a time.

The story finds Gildersleeve heading to New York on a double mission: to locate niece Marjorie's long-absent sweetheart Jimmy Clark (Michael Road), and to help his druggist pal Peavy persuade a major pharmaceutical supplier to stay in business. In short order, Gildy becomes the reluctant heart balm of dizzy widow Laura Chandler (Billie Burke), who happens to be the supplier Peavy hopes to win over—and whose addlepated brother (Hobart Cavanaugh) likes to shoot arrows at people. As if that wasn't enough to keep him occupied, Gildy is also targeted for matrimony by brassy blonde Francine (Claire Carleton), who thinks that he's a millionaire—while *he* labors under the misapprehension that Francine has stolen Jimmy away from Marjorie. The complications pile up thick and juicy when Gildy's fiancée Matilda (Ann Doran) shows up in the Big Apple, leading to a mix-up involving a valuable fur coat and several suspicious cops. Pretty soon Gildy is in such deep excrement that he can only be rescued by having Peavy don female drag and pose as Mrs. Gildersleeve (the writer didn't miss a trick, did he?) While radio buffs might be pleased that Richard LeGrand as Mr. Peavy has a lot more to do in *Gildersleeve on Broadway* than in *Gildersleeve's Bad Day*, it is our sad duty to report that LeGrand grows less funny the longer he remains on screen.

From Leon Errol–land we move to Three Stooges–ville for the final series offering *Gildersleeve's Ghost* (1944) which nowadays seems to show up on TV with more frequency than the other three *Gildersleeve* films. Those special qualities that endeared Peary and his radio series to millions of listeners are either ignored or trashed in *Gildersleeve's Ghost,* a run-of-the-mill "scare" comedy that could have starred any moderately talented comedian. Peary's best scene is at the beginning of the film, in which the spirits of Gildersleeve's ancestors Jonathan and Randolph (both Peary) rise from their graves to discuss Throckmorton's current campaign for the office of Summerfield police commissioner. They figure that Gildy won't have a ghost of a chance (yes, that one is in there too) unless he can perform an act of incredible courage. The gruesome twosome maneuver our hero in the direction of a spooky old mansion where a mad scientist (Frank Reicher) and his hulking assistant (Joseph Vitale) are conducting invisibility experiments, with hard-boiled chorus girl Terry Vance (Marion Martin) and a playful gorilla (Charles Gemora) as their guinea pigs. Terry has a habit of appearing and disappearing at the most inopportune moments, and it isn't long before everyone thinks Gildy has gone goofy as he claims to see the little blonde who isn't there.

If there are *any* musty old "terror" jokes overlooked by Robert E. Kent's screenplay, we sure couldn't remember them: That antediluvian routine in which a genuine gorilla is mistaken for a guy in a gorilla suit is trotted out no fewer than three times. Still, one cannot deny that *Gildersleeve's Ghost* does provide a few healthy laughs, most of them courtesy of Marion Martin as the dematerializing damsel and Nick "Nicodemus" Stewart as the traditionally terrified black chauffeur, an inherently embarrassing role that the gifted Stewart manages to slyly satirize throughout.

We mustn't be too hard on RKO's *Great Gildersleeve* films, since they never aspired to be anything more than double-bill fodder. Besides, they provided an excellent opportunity for the people handling the radio series to audition the property for the much-anticipated advent of network television. The *New York Times* reviewer glommed onto this back in 1942 with his summary of the initial *Gildersleeve* effort: "And so the film goes, more or less as [Peary's] radio show would appear if it were televised." And in a 1945 interview, Peary expressed optimism that the four *Gildersleeve* pictures had proven beyond doubt that both he and his series were TV-ready.

Unfortunately, he didn't get the chance to find out. Following a bitter court battle in which Peary vainly tried to claim all legal rights to the Gildersleeve character, the actor left both the series and its network to launch a new CBS comedy, *Honest Harold,* in the fall of 1950. His replacement on *The Great Gildersleeve* was 36-year-old Willard Waterman, who sounded enough like Peary to please the crowd but still managed to put his own distinctive stamp on the character. As a result, it was Waterman and not Peary who starred in a 39-week *Great Gildersleeve* television series, filmed by NBC in 1955 and widely syndicated throughout North America—one of the few examples of a TV adaptation that was a marked improvement over the motion picture version.

Peary continued working in radio, films and television (notably as Mayor LaTrivia on the short-lived TV edition of *Fibber McGee and Molly*) until his death in 1985. Likewise remaining active professionally after the termination of radio's *The Great Gildersleeve* on March 21, 1957, Willard Waterman died in 1995, having spent a goodly portion of his last years on earth patiently explaining to autograph seekers that they were thrusting 8 × 10 glossies of Harold Peary at him by mistake.

"Lum & Abner" (1940–1946; 1956)

Lum & Abner could be described as Amos 'n' Andy in whiteface—literally. Chester Lauck (1902–1980) and Norris Goff (1906–1978) were both Arkansas boys, childhood chums who enjoyed entertaining their friends and family with impromptu comedy routines involving mimicry and broad regional dialects. After briefly attending college, Lauck (the tall one) and Goff (the short one) settled down in Lauck's hometown, married a couple of local girls and took on steady non-showbiz employment, continuing to entertain at parties, lodge halls and such with a blackface routine. Then came a 1931 flood-relief fundraiser held by radio station KTHS in Hot Springs Arkansas. Among the many amateur acts invited to perform on this program, Lauck and Goff arrived at the station only to find themselves surrounded by other blackface comedians. Then and there they decided to drop their "colored" makeup and switch to a hillbilly routine (though both men hated that designation and never used it during their professional careers).

The act went over well enough for KTHS to sign the duo for a regular comedy series beginning April 26, 1931. Under the title *Lum and Abner*, the daily 15-minute offering was broadcast over NBC starting May 22, 1933.

"Sophisticated" journalists dismissed *Lum and Abner* as a rube act for a rube audience. The reviewer for *Radio Fan-Fare* thought it was funny to repeat the phrase "hick dialect" over and over, wrapping up his September 1933 critique with "Entertaining sketches for those who enjoy a good hick dia—now, now. Put down that brick. I'll quit." But the Horlick's Malted Milk company thought enough of the property to sponsor *Lum and Abner* over two different networks from 1934 through 1938, followed by Postum (a coffee substitute), who kept the show going on a Monday-Wednesday-Friday basis from 1938 through 1940, and Miles Laboratories, who underwrote the two comedians on NBC Pacific and the Blue Network (later ABC) for *four* days a week from 1941 through 1947. Something about this laid-back, pleasantly amusing series proved irresistible to 25,000,000 listeners of the Depression and World War II eras—not to mention the scores of latter-day fans comprising the National Lum and Abner Society, created in 1984 and still active as of this writing.

Most of the action in *Lum and Abner* transpired within the cluttered confines of the Jot 'Em Down Store in Pine Ridge, Arkansas (a fictional village which became factual when in 1936 the Arkansas town of Waters officially changed its name to Pine Ridge). Connected to the rest of the community by a single telephone party line ("I believe that's our ring, Abner"), the little general store was owned by a pair of bucolic senior citizens, self-proclaimed manager Columbus "Lum" Edwards (pronounced Ed-erds) and inveterate horse-trader Abner Peabody. When they weren't on the job, which was most of the time, Lum & Abner whiled away the hours discussing their own problems and those of their friends and neighbors. In the series' early years Lauck and Goff played all the characters, including Abner's perennial checkers opponent Grandpappy Spears, slow-witted blacksmith Cedric Wee-hunt, cheerful postmaster Dick Huddleston, fatuous loan shark-con artist Squire Skimp, and the rest. As with *Amos 'n' Andy*, recurring female characters like Abner's wife Lizzabeth and Aunt Charity Spears were mentioned but never heard; only when the necessity arose for women to take an active part in the serialized storylines were actresses hired, notably Lurene Tuttle. The two stars wrote all the scripts themselves until 1941, and thereafter continued contributing isolated jokes and random catchphrases like "By-Grannies" and "By-Doggies."

Somewhere around 1937, Lauck and Goff began expressing interest in a motion picture version of *Lum and Abner*. At the same, a man named Jack William Votion became convinced of *Lum and Abner*'s movie potential. A war hero in his native Belgium, Votion came to Hollywood in 1922, taking a variety of menial studio jobs as he worked his way up to the position of talent scout at Paramount Pictures in the mid–1930s. Among his many discoveries was Dorothy Lamour. He moved on to the same job at RKO, then set up his own talent agency. Though he had Hollywood connections to spare, Votion was unable to convince any major studio to bankroll a *Lum and Abner* feature film—least of all RKO, who were still smarting from the lumps they'd taken from the 1930 Amos 'n' Andy vehicle *Check and Double Check* (q.v.). After three years of rejections, Votion sold his spacious Southern California ranch, and with matching funds from one Roger Mardiette he went into partnership with songwriter Sam Coslow ("Cocktails for Two," "Sing You Sinners") to set up Voco Productions, expressly for the purpose of producing as many as three *Lum and Abner* pictures. This time around, RKO was responsive, agreeing to distribute the films. The RKO deal made headlines in Hollywood, prompting Paramount to offer Lauck and Goff a guest spot in the Bob Burns musical *Comin' Round the Mountain* (1940)—but now *they* were in a position to refuse.

The manner in which Lauck and Goff prepared the radio audience for their film debut was nothing short of inspired. In a continuity beginning March 4, 1940, Pine Ridge is invaded by bank robbers who end up being captured single-handed by Abner's wife Lizzbeth. The ensuing publicity attracts a Hollywood scout named Mr. Votion (where did they come up with a moniker like *that?*), who hopes to sign Lizzbeth to a contract to appear in westerns. She turns out to be the wrong type, but Votion has taken such a shine to the wholesome, unspoiled atmosphere of Pine Ridge that he signs Lum & Abner to star in a movie instead. This occurs on March 11; on March 20, the film's script arrives at the Jot 'Em Down Store, with the actual authors mentioned by name (Abner complains that he's never heard of them, while Lum bristles at being described as a "backwoods storekeeper"). The story thread continues for a few more episodes as the boys "modernize" their store to make it look nice in pictures, only to be told that the studio wants the place to retain its old-fashioned charm. Finally on March 29, Lum & Abner receive a phone call from director Harold Young (again, the real name) instructing them to close the store and turn it over to the movie people. At this point Lum makes a call of his own to "everybody," saying that he hopes they'll like the picture and asking them to write a letter of thanks to their sponsor, the Postum company. Still in character, the boys bid their audience an emotional goodbye, bringing an end to the 1939–40 season of *Lum and Abner*—and the end of Postum's sponsorship.

Filmed on the RKO-Pathé lot, the first *Lum and Abner* entry went into production as *Money Isn't Everything*, a title changed to *Dreaming Out Loud* to accommodate a song of that name written by Sam Coslow. Creating a believable backlot facsimile of Pine Ridge—a masterpiece of forced perspective by Universal art director Bernard Herzbrun—proved less of a challenge than convincing the audience that 38-year-old Chester Lauck and 33-year-old Norris Goff were a pair of sixty-somethings named Lum Edwards and Abner Peabody. The actors had previously donned heavy two-dimensional age makeup for publicity photos, but in films the cosmetics had to be credible from all angles. Each morning Lauck and Goff submitted to a three-hour makeup session, then had to virtually live at the studio to stay within the tight shooting schedule, a regimen followed in all six *Lum and Abner* pictures. The results were never entirely satisfactory, the actors often resembling a pair of college kids wearing muslin Halloween masks. *Photoplay* snippishly reviewed one *Lum and Abner* effort by commenting on the "thirtyish-looking" Lauck and the "even more thirtyish-looking" Goff. Fortunately, the acting skills and body language of the two stars went a long way towards maintaining a facade of authenticity.

Dreaming Out Loud differs from the subsequent *Lum and Abner* entries in several respects: its 81-minute length, more appropriate to an "A" feature than a modest programmer; its specially composed theme music, eschewing the radio show's signature tune "Evalena" (heard over the opening credits in the other five entries); the presence of two additional radio stars in the supporting cast, Frances Langford (who gets to sing) and Phil Harris (who doesn't); and the absence of the familiar secondary characters from the radio original. Squire Skimp wouldn't make an appearance until he was played by Oscar O'Shea in the series' second film *The Bashful Bachelor* (1942), though the character would show up in the four remaining efforts, with Dick Elliott replacing O'Shea in the final two films. Likewise making the first of three series appearances in *Bashful Bachelor* is Cedric Weehunt, an uncharacteristic "dimwit" portrayal by comic actor Grady Sutton. And after a trial run in the bit role of Ulysses the postman in Entry No. 3, *Two Weeks to Live* (1943), Danny Duncan was seen as Grandpappy Spears in the remaining three installments. The radio show's seldom-heard female characters occasionally dropped in as well: Sarah Padden played Aunt Charity Spears in Entry No. 4, *So This Is Washington* (1943); and Abner's elusive spouse Lizzbeth was enacted by Pamela Blake in the last RKO-released *Lum and Abner* film, *Partners in Time* (1946).

What really sets *Dreaming Out Loud* apart from the rest of the series is its screenplay and story by Barry Trivers, Robert D. Andrews and Howard Green. It's an odd and unsettling mixture of whimsical humor and stark melodrama, the like of which was *never* heard on the radio show. Put simply, *Dreaming Out Loud* has more mood swings than a 14-year-old girl.

The comical establishing sequence in the Jot 'Em Down Store, which includes a Harold Hill–like sales pitch from traveling peddler Phil Harris, in no way prepares us for the sudden death of a little girl in a hit-and-run accident. From here we move to a silly, slapsticky segment with Lum & Abner trying to track down the homicidal motorist—their antics provoking chuckles from everyone including the victim's grieving father! It's crisis time again as young physician Kenneth Barnes (Robert Wilcox) is barred from marrying postmistress Alice (Frances Langford) because her wealthy, self-centered Aunt Jessica (Clara Blandick of *Wizard of Oz* fame, here acting less like Auntie Em than Elvira Gulch) harbors a lifelong grudge against Kenneth's father, kindly "Doc Walt" Barnes (Frank Craven). Once that's established, we're back to the broad comedy of Abner's one-man checkers game (a routine he'd made famous on radio) and a running gag involving the town loafer, who spends his days snoozing next to the Jot 'Em Down Store's pot-bellied stove. Now that we're in the mood for a few more chuckles, the rug is pulled from under us again when Alice's kid brother Jimmy (the ever-whiny Bobs Watson) catches a vicious case of pneumonia. Valiant old Doc Walt spends several sleepless nights saving the boy's life, only to drop dead himself, setting us up for a funeral scene straight out of John Ford. But all ends merrily when Aunt Jessica sees the error of her ways, allows Alice and Kenneth to wed, and contributes a small fortune to finance Pine Ridge's new mobile first-aid unit—where, ha ha ha, the town loafer has already curled up for another nap. By-Grannies!

Dreaming Out Loud is seen at a disadvantage today, since all public-domain copies derive from a choppy TV print with at least 15 minutes missing. Perhaps in the film's complete and unedited form, director Harold Young was able to segue from comedy to tragedy and back again with more agility and less abruptness than in the existing version. Still, one might expect devotees of the essentially lighthearted radio *Lum and Abner* to sit through the picture scratching their heads and wondering if they'd entered the wrong theater. But that doesn't seem to have been the case: Opening simultaneously in four different Arkansas cities on September 30, 1940, *Dreaming Out Loud* turned out to be a hit far beyond RKO's modest expectations. In some cities where program pictures usually ran no more than seven days, the film was held over four weeks, with people who otherwise never went to the movies turning out in droves to break house records everywhere. When the final returns came in, *Dreaming Out Loud* had earned nearly $745,000. Apparently the Hollywood poobahs had miscalculated back in 1937 when they declared that Lum & Abner were too limited in appeal for movie success. (Trivia note: On May 7, 1940, Chester Lauck and Norris Goff made history of sorts when they were shown filming a scene from *Dreaming Out Loud* in a live experimental broadcast over Los Angeles television station W6XAO.)

The plan was to begin production on the series' second film *The Bashful Bachelor* in early 1941. This was delayed by a contract dispute between Jack Votion and his financial backer Roger Mardiette, who claimed that under the terms of their agreement he was to receive 15 percent of the series' profits. It would be nearly a year before this matter was settled, and as a result *The Bashful Bachelor* was still in production when America entered World War II. Receiving a commission in the Army, Jack Votion was stationed in London for the duration, obliging him to turn over the line-producer duties on the remaining four *Lum and Abner*s to production manager Ben Hersh. But no matter how far from home Votion traveled during the War (and that was far indeed when he was promoted to a colonel in Military Intelligence), Lauck and Goff continued soliciting his creative advice and submitting jokes for his approval by way of V-Mail.

The budget for *Bashful Bachelor* was about the same as *Dreaming Out Loud*, a fact reflected in the supporting cast. Both Frances Langford and Phil Harris had agreed to lower their asking price from the earlier film as a favor to the producer and the stars, but Votion could not always count on major radio performers to extend this courtesy. Thus, the biggest "name" in the second *Lum and Abner* picture is the not-too-high-priced ZaSu Pitts, cast as Lum's middle-aged heartthrob Geraldine, a character never mentioned on radio (though Pitts would join the regular *Lum and Abner* cast when the series' format changed from a 15-minute serial to a 30-minute comedy-variety weekly in 1948). The film's ingénue Marjorie is played by another economical performer, talented B-western and serial stalwart Louise Currie. The tight budget notwithstanding, RKO gave Voco Productions the go-ahead to extend *Bashful Bachelor*'s running time to 75 minutes in order to obtain top-of-the-bill bookings, indication that the studio expected the picture to match the spectacular box office of *Dreaming Out Loud*.

As mentioned, *Bashful Bachelor* was the first entry to include characters from the radio show: In addition to Oscar O'Shea as Squire Skimp and Grady Sutton as Cecil, Constance Purdy is seen as "Widder" Abernathy, another of those phantom ladies frequently alluded to but seldom heard. This gesture of fidelity to the broadcast original was due to the fact that Lauck and Goff wrote the film's story themselves, with Chandler Sprague handling the screenwriting duties. The stars dispensed with the turgid dramatics of *Dreaming Out Loud*, and as a result comedy lives everywhere in *Bashful Bachelor*—which can be a questionable virtue at times. Though the film is consistently funny, it also tells us something about Lauck and Goff that we'd rather not know: The two actors were quite capable of sacrificing the charm and integrity of their radio characters for the sake of an easy laugh.

A comedy film needs a comedy director, so Jack Votion hired Malcolm St. Clair, a Sennett graduate who had specialized in frothy, sophisticated romantic comedies in the silent era, then trafficked in broad, noisy farces in the 1930s, notably 20th Century–Fox's *Jones Family* series. Forced out of pictures in 1940 by illness, St. Clair was brought back for *Bashful Bachelor* through the kindness of producer Votion, who hadn't forgotten the helping hand St. Clair had extended him during his early days in Hollywood. Though he could still stage an isolated gag or comedy setpiece with élan, St. Clair had somewhere along the way forgotten how to tell a coherent story. His two *Lum and Abner* films are episodic and disjointed, a shortcoming St. Clair would carry over to his subsequent Laurel & Hardy comedies for Fox. (Some of the bits of comic business in his *Lum and Abners*—not always the good ones—ended up recycled for Stan and Ollie.)

Despite the film's unevenness, the basic story material is in keeping with the spirit of the radio series, as timid Lum first tries to impress his object of affection Geraldine with various acts of bravery, then gets into trouble when a love poem intended for Geraldine is misdelivered to the highly resistible "Widder" Abernathy. Meanwhile, Abner's fondness for horse-tradin' results in his swapping the Jot 'Em Down Store's delivery truck for a broken-down nag named Sky Rocket, who with the input of Marjorie as trainer wins an important race and prevents the store's mortgage from falling into the hands of shifty Squire Skimp.

The biggest laughs arise from Abner's efforts to transform Lum into a "knight in shining armor" for the sake of Geraldine with a series of neck-risking stunts, allowing himself to be tied to the railroad tracks so Lum can race to the rescue (he almost doesn't make it) and faking a kidnapping by unwittingly hiring a couple of thugs who aren't faking. Unfortunately these comedy highlights are at the expense of Lum & Abner's established characterizations. Instead of playing a couple of amiable hayseeds, they come across as brainless nincompoops. This might work for a lesser comedy team, but it's something of an affront to Lauck and Goff—and the actors have only themselves to blame.

Wartime audiences in dire need of laughs weren't bothered by the deficiencies of *The Bashful Bachelor*, and as RKO predicted the film was a box office goldmine. The studio gave Voco Productions (renamed Jack William Votion Productions Inc. with the abdication of Sam Coslow) permission to allow the third *Lum and Abner* offering *Two Weeks to Live* to run long (73 minutes), again to secure preferred bookings. Beginning with this film, Lauck and

Goff were billed onscreen only as Lum and Abner, following the example of fellow radio stars Fibber McGee and Molly (q.v.) in *their* RKO releases.

Two Weeks to Live and its follow-ups *So This Is Washington* and *Goin' to Town* (1944) contrive to yank Lum & Abner out of Pine Ridge for various big-city escapades, suggesting that in Jack Votion's absence interim producer Ben Hersh took it upon himself to transform the two old duffers into Ma and Pa Kettle (who hadn't been invented yet, but you get the drift). The foolhardy facsimiles of Lum & Abner in *The Bashful Bachelor* are MENSA students compared with the imbeciles who plod their way through *Two Weeks to Live*. With only the crazy-quilt screenplay by Roswell Rogers and Michael L. Simmons to work with, director Mal St. Clair has abandoned all hope of making any sense of the situation.

The "story" begins as Lum and everybody else in town invest their life savings in a railroad that Abner has inherited. Arriving in Chicago to survey this legacy, the boys find only an abandoned engine car and a hovel of a terminal. While trying to raise $10,000 to reimburse the investors, Abner tumbles down a flight of stairs and is rushed to a doctor's office. A stupid nurse mixes up two different diagnoses, convincing healthy-as-a-horse Abner that he has but two weeks to live (from the motion picture of the same name). Only mildly perturbed over his partner's plight, Lum advertises Abner's services as a "daredevil" willing to take on high risks for high pay. After messing up such death-defying jobs as flagpole painter and tightrope walker, Abner agrees to deliver a violin case to a "haunted" house from which no man has ever emerged alive, little suspecting that he's been set up as a dead duck in an insurance scam and that the case contains a time bomb. Showing up at the wrong house, Abner escapes unscathed but manages to blow up a nest of Nazi spies. Finally Lum makes a deal with a nutty scientist to shoot Abner to Mars in an experimental rocket. By the time Abner finds out that he's not going to die and that his "worthless" railroad has been sold for $20,000, it is Lum who has been blasted into the stratosphere (a sublimely rotten special effect).

The so-called plot of *Two Weeks to Live* goes off on so many tangents that halfway through the proceedings the filmmakers have to invent a character (played by Charles Middleton) to remind Lum & Abner why they've come to Chicago in the first place. The

A contemporary DVD sleeve for the 1943 Lum & Abner vehicle *Two Weeks to Live,* based on an original lobby poster. Abner (Norris Goff, right) is apparently listening to Lum's (Chester Lauck) ear-beat.

chaotic scenario brings to mind a review for St. Clair's later Laurel &Hardy opus *The Dancing Masters*: "You ask me what this picture is about. What *isn't* it about?" Paradoxically, while *Two Weeks to Live* may be the worst of the *Lum and Abner* films, it is also the one that delivers the biggest laughs when seen today. As a bonus, Lauck and Goff forged a strong on-set friendship with co-star Kay Linaker (cast as one of the villains) upon realizing that they were well acquainted with the actress' kinfolk back in Pine Bluff, Arkansas.

So This Is Washington is an improvement over *Two Weeks to Live,* if only because it is nine minutes shorter: Also, director Raymond Mc-Carey (brother of Leo) has a much firmer grasp on storytelling logic than St. Clair. Now teamed with Edward James, the earlier film's screenwriter Roswell Rogers still has trouble focusing on a single plotline for more than a few minutes at a time, but at least each of the film's individual episodes dovetails into the next. Best of all, the essential warmth, humanity and "horse sense" of the two leading characters is back, especially during a lengthy non-comic passage in which Lum explains to Abner the patriotic significance of such D.C. landmarks as the Capitol dome, the Lincoln Memorial and the Washington Monument (though the effectiveness of this scene, like its counterpart in Universal's *Sherlock Holmes in Washington,* is diminished by the glaringly obvious back projection).

Filmed during the second year of America's involvement in World War II, *So This Is Washington* is the most "topical" of the team's features, and consequently the most dated (though not in a negative sense) for 21st century viewers. After several joshing references to rationing, air raid wardens, blackouts and the like, Lum & Abner hear a radio broadcast by Chester W. Marshall (Alan Mowbray), self-styled champion of the "common man," who invites anyone with an invention that might aid the war effort to visit his office in Washington. The boys decide to take him up on his offer after Abner, trying to stir up a batch of licorice, creates what seems to be synthetic rubber. Once in D.C., our heroes are subjected to a lot of cartoonish verbal and visual gags about the overcrowding in the Nation's capitol, and while searching for a place to rest their weary bones they slump down on a park bench next to a pair of politicians who are expressing concern over the constituents' wartime needs. Offering some friendly common-sense agricultural advice to the two pols, Lum & Abner soon find themselves hailed throughout Washington as geniuses, and before long they are consulting hundreds of V.I.P.s from all over the country, dispensing sage philosophy from their park bench like a couple of cracker-barrel Bernard Baruchs.

Inevitably crossing paths with Marshall, Lum & Abner are invited to give a practical demonstration of their synthetic rubber before the press, but Abner suffers an accidental blow on the head and loses his memory. He not only forgets his rubber formula, but also his own identity, assuming that his name is Buster V. Davenport because of the initials on his underwear. From this moment on, *So This Is Washington* totally falls apart and sputters to a nonsensical conclusion, but for the first 45 minutes it's a worthy effort. Unfortunately, the film was withheld from a significant portion of its potential audience when the War Department Office of Censorship, its undies in a bundle over the script's irreverent treatment of rationing laws and the character of an Army doctor, barred RKO from sending *So This Is Washington* overseas.

Written by Charles E. Roberts and Charles R. Marion and directed by Leslie Goodwins (an alumnus of RKO's two-reel comedy division), the 69-minute *Goin' to Town* begins as Lum & Abner fall victim to a practical joke perpetrated by playful oil tycoon M.A. Parker (Andrew Tombes), who convinces the boys that there's a potential gusher beneath the surface of Pine Ridge. This seemingly harmless prank snowballs into a potential disaster as everyone in town invests in L&A's newly formed "Pine Ridge Oil and Development Company." When their oil "derelict" proves to be a bust, the two storekeepers make their second movie-series trip to Chicago in hopes of getting Parker to reimburse them. Thanks to the conclusion-jumping of Jimmy Parker (Dick Baldwin), an employee of Parker's chief business rival Wentworth (Herbert Rawlinson), the movers and shakers of Chicago's oil industry enter into a bidding war over Lum & Abner's nonexistent gusher, resulting in an $80,000 profit for the folks back in Pine Ridge. *Goin' to Town* has no more connection with reality than the previous *Lum and Abner* entries, but it moves quickly and amusingly, highlighted by the boys' pose as a pair of "Pine Ridge Playboys" and Abner's misadventures in a wild conga line at a Windy City nightspot featuring the Nils T. Grantlund chorus girls. The film also affords an early screen opportunity to RKO starlet Barbara Hale, cast as Parker's secretary, and introduces the character of Lum's would-be sweetheart Abigail, played by Florence Lake in *Goin' to Town* and by Phyllis Kennedy in the team's final RKO film, *Partners in Time*.

Directed by William Nigh from a screenplay by Charles E. Roberts, *Partners in Time* marks a near-total departure from the established *Lum and Abner* movie formula. While the basic storyline is standard stuff involving a highly suspicious land grant held by the eternally untrustworthy Squire Skimp, the bulk of the story is told in flashback, as Lum & Abner try to convince a pair of disillusioned young lovers (John James, Teala Loring) not to forsake their hopes and dreams by recalling their own experiences way back in 1904. For the first time in films Lauck and Goff appear without their old-codger makeup, and the results are quite appealing, especially Goff's metamorphosis from a cranky geezer to a youthful gay blade with an eye for the ladies. While comedy abounds in the 1904 sequences—notably the offhand remarks about the ready availability of butter, sugar, gasoline and other items that were still being rationed in early 1946—there are also moments of truly moving pathos, mostly centered around the star-crossed romance between youthful Lum Edwards and Elizabeth "Lizzabeth" Meadows (Pamela Blake), the pretty schoolteacher who would later become the wife of Abner Peabody. Never even so much as hinted at in the radio series, this bittersweet backstory provides *Partners in Time* with a touchingly enigmatic finale, as clueless Abner is allowed to go on believing that Lum fabricated the story about his courtship of Lizzbeth just to make the flashback more interesting. Reviewers in 1946 regarded *Partners in Time* as the best of the *Lum and Abner* films, some critics expressing the wish that it had been the first entry in the series rather than the last.

Though all their vehicles had been huge moneymakers, Lum & Abner's movie career effectively came to an end when producer Jack Votion accepted a position as head of RKO's London department. The radio series continued as a CBS half-hour until April 26, 1950, then reverted to a 15-minute serialized daily on ABC, surviving in this format until May 15, 1953. During this period, Lauck and Goff tackled the challenge of television with a half-hour *Lum and Abner* TV pilot, broadcast November 2, 1949, on CBS. It has been claimed that this potential TV series failed because of a lack of sponsor interest, though in truth the main obstacle was Goff's fragile health.

After the cessation of their network radio series and a season's worth of syndicated broadcasts, both comedians felt fit enough to embark on a second TV project, resulting in three half-hour episodes filmed in Yugoslavia (!). Produced and directed by Hal Roach Studios functionary James V. Kern, this proposed series cast Lum & Abner as a pair of American goodwill ambassadors who travel throughout Europe solving problems and getting into mischief. A combination of health and financing difficulties, coupled with a total lack of sponsor and network interest, doomed this project to a quick demise, but in 1956 Howco Productions spliced the three pilot episodes into the jerry-built feature film *Lum and Abner Abroad*, which didn't get much theatrical play but was reasonably well syndicated to local TV outlets. Though the actors never left the Croatian city of Zagreb, an opening title assures us that the picture was "Actually Filmed in Europe (not Pine Ridge)," with two of the individual segments supposedly taking place in Paris and Monte Carlo. The predictably jumbled continuity finds an assortment of refugees, jewel thieves, crooked gamblers, impoverished aristocrats and gypsy vagabonds enlivening the boys' peregrinations. The best and pithiest comment regarding this patchwork affair was uttered by Goff during a 1970s guest appearance at a nostalgia convention. Asked if *Lum and Abner Abroad* was the team's last movie, Goff replied, "That one would have been *anybody*'s last movie."

"Scattergood Baines" (1941–1942)

Scattergood Baines was a much-beloved literary property for 20 years before either radio or the movies got their hands on it. It is included here because of the likelihood that the property's film adaptation was a direct result of the radio version's popularity.

Michigan-born Clarence Buddington Kelland (1881–1964) liked to describe himself as "the best second-rate writer in America." At one time he was also the most popular writer in America, responsible for over 400 short stories published by such prominent periodicals as *The Saturday Evening Post* and *The American Magazine*. Today he is forgotten, much to the dismay of such contemporary "writing machines" as Harlan Ellison, who in a 2008 interview with *The Onion AV Club*'s Tasha Robinson praised Kelland: "He was not William Faulkner, he was not Colette, but he certainly was a very good, decent writer." Though his fictional work covered everything from western yarns to children's tales, he had a strong preference for stories about country bumpkins who turned out to have a lot more common sense and innate decency than any city slicker, shyster lawyer or corrupt politician who might try to outwit them. One of Kelland's best stories, "Opera Hat," served as the inspiration for Frank Capra's *Mr. Deeds Goes to Town*.

Described on radio as "the best-loved, most cussed-at, and by all odds the fattest man" in the small Vermont town of Coldriver, Scattergood Baines was introduced in Kelland's story "Scattergood Baines—Invader," published in the June 30, 1917, edition of *The Saturday Evening Post*. The title character, explained the author, was not based on any one actual person, "but rather he expressed my notion of what a true Vermonter was like." The owner of a prosperous hardware store, Baines was wealthy but not ostentatious, preferring to wear his oldest clothes and relax on the "piazza" of his store in his stocking feet. Having intimate knowledge of everyone in Coldriver, he was not exactly a snoop or buttinsky, but (again quoting the radio version) he always "finds himself drawn into everything that happens to him." Be it a domestic squabble, an estranged parent and child, a financial crisis, a confidence scheme perpetrated by an "outsider," or even a murder mystery, Scattergood generally managed to resolve the problem at hand through shrewd observation of human nature, remarkable powers of persuasion and fundamental horse sense. His favorite phrase was "I calc'late," typical of a man who spoke in such New England colloquialisms as "sich" for "such," "figger" for "figure," "wuth" for "worth" and "'bleeged" for "obliged." Baines was married to the devoted Mirandy, and counted among his best friends the town's branch-line train conductor Pliny Pickett (Coldriver's stage driver in the days before the community had train service).

The first radio version of *Scattergood Baines* premiered over CBS's West Coast network on February 22, 1937, joining the full national chain on October 22, 1938. Originally a daily 15-minute serial, the program featured Jess Pugh as Scattergood, with Viola Berwick as Mirandy, Dink Trout as Pliny Pickett, Chuck Grant as the Baines' adopted son Jimmy, and John Hearne as Hippocrates "Hippy" Brown, the phlegmatic African American jack-of-all-trades who helped around the hardware store. Except for a four-month hiatus in 1941, this version ran until June 12, 1942.

A little over three years into the radio run, independent film producer Jerrold T. Brandt purchased 107 of Kelland's "Scattergood Baines" magazine stories in hopes of launching a B-movie series. With financial backing from New York's Irving Trust Company, Kelland was able to interest RKO Radio in distributing his series in the same manner that RKO had been handling two other radio-driven independent properties, *Dr. Christian* and *Lum & Abner* (both q.v.). Several candidates were announced for the role of Scattergood Baines, among them

Edgar Kennedy, Charles Coburn, Charles Winninger, Frank Craven, Charley Grapewin and George Barbier. Finally Brandt was successful in signing cherubic character actor Guy Kibbee as his star. A fixture of the Warner Bros. stock company in the early 1930s (he starred in the studio's 1934 adaptation of Sinclair Lewis' *Babbitt*), Kibbee had most recently been featured in such prestige efforts as *Mr. Smith Goes to Washington* and *Our Town,* but had no objections to fronting a B-picture property, especially since the price was right and he'd get his first top billing since 1937. To properly match Clarence Buddington Kelland's physical description of Scattergood Baines, the famously bald Kibbee was outfitted with a flowing silver toupee. Finally, producer Brandt took out a huge insurance policy on his 59-year-old star just in case his health failed him during production.

Brandt and RKO mapped out an infallible formula for financial success with the *Scattergood Baines* series. Each film was budgeted at $130,000 and not a penny more. Each was completed in two weeks under the direction of Christy Cabanne, who since the pre–World War I era had kept afloat in Hollywood on his reputation of seldom shooting any scene more than once. The major supporting players were paid a uniform $1,000 per week. There was no time wasted on developing new "discoveries": Even the ingénues, traditionally newcomers in such "B" efforts, were required to have prior film experience before being considered for a part. RKO charged a flat rental fee to local movie houses, allowing theater managers to show the pictures as often as they liked without any further expense. Banking upon the built-in popularity of "Scattergood Baines" as a literary and radio property, the films could not help but earn back twice their cost, providing RKO with a tidy profit and Jerrold Brandt with ten percent of the gross.

Released February 21, 1941, the inaugural entry *Scattergood Baines* devotes its early scenes to recounting the title character's first arrival in Coldriver, as set down in the initial Kelland short story "Scattergood Baines—Invader." The coal-black wig sported by Kibbee does not entirely persuade us that he's only 26 years old in these scenes, but no matter. Before long the Edward T. Lowe–Michael Simmons Jr. screenplay is brought up to 1941, with Baines firmly ensconced as Coldriver's ace hardware merchant, loving husband of Mirandy (Emma Dunn) and benevolent employer of the industriously lazy Hippocrates Brown (portrayed along stereotypical lines by Willie Best). Also on hand is Plinky Pickett, well played by Dink Trout, the sole carryover from the radio version; and two other prominent characters created by Kelland and heard on radio, garage mechanic Ed Potts (Lee "Lasses" White) and his nagging wife Clara (Fern Emmett). The plot is calculated to instantly endear the title character to those few stragglers unfamiliar with the property, as Scattergood foils a pair of shifty mill owners who have duped young lawyer Johnny Bones (John Archer), then smooths the course of true love for Johnny and pretty vaudevillian Helen Parker (Carol Hughes), who has been victimized by loose gossip. RKO's newspaper ads for *Scattergood Baines* mentioned the radio program only in passing, concentrating on such taglines as "Clarence Buddington Kelland's Lovable Character" and "Read by More Than 3,000,000 Readers."

The second film *Scattergood Baines Pulls the Strings* (1941) drew its title from a 1939 collection of Kelland stories published by Harper & Company, its screenplay weaving five separate yarns into a single narrative. On this occasion, Baines reunites itinerant laborer Ben Mott (Monte Blue) with his ten-year-old son (the insufferably weepy Bobs Watson). Emma Dunn, Dink Trout, Lee "Lasses" White and Fern Emmett reprise their roles from the first film, while Paul White of the Theater Guild brings a tad more dignity to the part of Hippocrates Brown than his predecessor Willie Best. Mildred Coles had been slated to play the ingénue, but she fell ill and was replaced by Susan Peters, a brilliant young actress whose career was tragically cut short in 1944 when she was crippled in a hunting accident. An RKO press release stated that Kibbee was particularly looking forward to making *Scattergood Baines Pulls the Strings* because of a scene in which he would be allowed to indulge in his favorite pastime of fishing. It's too bad that neither this film nor its follow-ups ever showcased Kibbee's prowess as a champion golfer.

Though critical response to the *Scattergood Baines* series was friendly at the outset, with the release of the third entry *Scattergood Meets Broadway* (1941) a few reviewers began to gripe that the property was drifting away from the no-frills formula established in the Kelland stories and the radio program. *Scattergood Meets Broadway* finds the protagonist heading off the Great White Way to act as "angel" for a play written by a Coldwater resident (William Henry), forcing him to match wits with a couple of shady producers (Frank Jenks, Bradley Page) and a predatory chorus girl (Joyce Compton). Evidently recovered from whatever malady kept her out of the previous film, Mildred Coles shows up as the heroine. The next offering *Scattergood Rides High* (1941) spends more time on the racetrack (location-filmed in Riverside, California) than the hardware store, with Scattergood helping a young man (Charles Knox) fulfill his dream of becoming a champion trotting racer, and settling a few domestic issues within the *nouveau riche* household of the aspiring jockey's sweetheart (Dorothy Moore).

Critical support for the series totally evaporated with Entry No. 5, 1942's *Scattergood Survives a Murder* (reissued as *The Cat's-Claw Murder Mystery*), involving the mysterious deaths of two wealthy recluses who have left their fortune to a pet cat. Though a mediocre entry, the film boasts a strong supporting cast including Margaret Hayes, whom producer Brandt managed to snag just as the actress was being released by Paramount, and Wallace Ford, who seemed to have been in every other picture made in the 1930s and '40s. The two murder victims are played by Margaret McWade and Margaret Seddon, the celebrated "pixilated sisters" from the Kelland-inspired *Mr. Deeds Goes to Town*. Willie Best is back as Hippocrates Brown, with all his eye-rolling, lip-quivering "skeered" reactions in full flower.

The sixth and last series entry *Cinderella Swings It* (1943) is a bush-league imitation of Universal's Deanna Durbin and Gloria Jean pictures, with Scattergood organizing a charity USO show to advance the career of teenage soprano Gloria Warren (some of whose songs were composed by comedian Georgie Jessel!) The fact that *Cinderella Swings It* does not include "Scattergood Baines" in its title would seem to indicate that the series had taken a financial dip and that RKO had lost faith in the character's pulling power. It has also been suggested that the series came to an end because its corresponding radio program had recently been cancelled. Actually, the termination of *Scattergood Baines* as a movie property had more to do with the fact that producer Jerrold T. Brandt had joined the Navy, where he spent the war years producing military training films. Though he returned to Hollywood after V-J Day, Brandt was never able to fulfill his great ambition of mounting a pageant-like film chronicling the history of radio, tentatively titled *Magic in the Air* or *Command Performance*.

Just as the RKO *Scattergood Baines* pictures were being released to television in 1949, the radio version was revived on the Mutual network, this time as a weekly series of half-hour playlets. Most of the *Scattergood Baines* episodes currently available are taken from this short (nine-month) run, which starred Wendell Holmes as Baines and featured Parker Fennelly—aka "Titus Moody" on *The Fred Allen Show*—as feed store bookkeeper Hannibal Gibbey.

"Mr. District Attorney" (1941–1942, 1947)

No one could have been further removed from the Phillips H. Lord who rose to radio fame as the folksy, avuncular Seth Parker (q.v.) in the early 1930s than the Phillips H. Lord who produced such blood-and-thunder radio crime series as *Gang Busters*, *Mr. District Attorney* and *David Harding, Counterspy*. All three of these properties would spawn motion picture versions (see separate entries), though none quite came up to the standards of the radio originals. This is especially true of *Mr. District At-*

torney, a weekly radio show that was hailed by a 1945 *Variety* article as "one of the great program success stories of recent years," setting itself apart from the general run of cops-and-robbers efforts by remaining "almost exclusively a reflection of current events, controversy and ideological matters."

Inspired by the racket-busting crusade of New York D.A. Thomas E. Dewey, *Mr. District Attorney* was created by former law student Edward A. Byron (still in radio in the mid–1960s as the guiding force behind the nightly dramatic anthology *Theater Five*). Producer Lord initially developed the property as a nightly 15-minute serial, a replacement for NBC's *Amos 'n' Andy* after that show moved to CBS. Debuting on April 3, 1939, the program originally starred Dwight Weist as the title character, who throughout his network run was never identified by any name other than "Mr. District Attorney"—not even by his closest associates, who addressed him as "chief" or "boss." During this formative period, actor Jay Jostyn was heard as one of the gangsters in charge of a vicious protection racket. The serial format was abandoned in favor of weekly, self-contained half-hour dramas on October 1, 1939—and after a few months with Raymond Edward Johnson (later the host of *Inner Sanctum*) as star, the role of Mr. District Attorney was taken over by a "reformed" Jay Jostyn, who remained with the series until its final ABC network broadcast on June 13, 1952. Other regulars included Vicki Vola as the hero's ultra-efficient secretary Miss Miller and Len Doyle as Mr. D.A.'s chief investigator Harrington, the closest the show came to a comic relief character.

With the careful guidance of Lord and his successor Jerry Devine, not to mention the brilliant script work of Robert Shaw, *Mr. District Attorney* expanded its crimefighting activities beyond mere racketeers to include scam artists, kidnappers, mad killers and, even before America entered World War II, enemy spies and saboteurs. Creator Ed Byron was a keen and knowledgeable student of crime and criminals (he owned one of the largest personal libraries on the subject), not only keeping abreast of late-breaking events but occasionally anticipating them, most famously with the episode of June 17, 1942, in which he dramatized the true story of Nazi submarines dropping secret agents along the Atlantic coast well before the FBI revealed the facts to the public. As noted by radio historian John Dunning, "Byron got a 'visit' from the FBI after his show." This ability to remain up-to-date and even court controversy by covering stories that were normally vetoed by network Standards and Practices as being too "hot" for public consumption kept *Mr. District Attorney* head and shoulders above its crime-show competitors.

One could not realistically expect a Hollywood treatment of the program to maintain this cutting-edge quality, but at the very least a movie adaptation of *Mr. District Attorney* should have *tried* to be as compelling as the radio model. For the most part, however, this was not to be. Though there were a few worthwhile moments here and there, none of the four films produced under the *Mr. District Attorney* imprimatur would measure up to the dramatic impact of the original.

First to acquire movie rights to the property was Republic Pictures, resulting in a well-assembled 1941 effort directed by William Morgan and titled simply *Mr. District Attorney*. In emulation of Columbia's (mis)treatment of the great fictional sleuth Ellery Queen, Republic decided to reconfigure the radio series as a comedy, adding murder and mystery almost incidentally. The initial 69-minute entry established a formula that would be followed in all subsequent *Mr. District Attorney* films: Splitting the protagonist in two. Inasmuch as Jay Jostyn's mature, authoritative radio voice didn't quite match his youthful appearance, Mr. District Attorney—here given the last name Winton—is played by 50-year-old character actor Stanley Ridges. However, the sleuthing and action scenes are handled by young *assistant* district attorney P. Cadwallader Jones, played by Dennis O'Keefe. The hero's character name is a dead giveaway that we aren't expected to take things seriously, a suspicion confirmed at film's end when Jones sheepishly explains that the "P" stands for "Prince ... but I didn't want to be whistled for." Scriptwriter Malcolm Stuart

Boylan dispenses with the radio show's Miss Miller by providing Jones with an attractive *vis-à-vis* in the form of intrepid gal reporter Terry Parker, played in the first film by Florence Rice.

Fresh out of Harvard Law School, P. Cadwallader Jones gets a job in Winton's office through the influence of a wealthy relative, but so badly bungles his first case that it looks like his legal career is over before it begins. Unable to fire Jones, Winton disposes of the boy by assigning him a "cold" case that no one else cares about, involving a counterfeiter named Hyde (played by a woefully underused Peter Lorre) who dropped out of sight years before. With Terry's help, Jones follows several seemingly unrelated leads that point in the direction of a vast conspiracy of corruption, apparently orchestrated by slick society lawyer Barrett (Minor Watson). Along the way a key character is murdered, but the killer is not whom Jones suspects—and in fact wouldn't have been revealed at all if Barrett hadn't brought the confessed culprit to the D.A.'s office. This would seem to confirm that Jones is in over his head, but he and Terry play a hunch and solve the bigger mystery of who is behind the conspiracy.

Originally planned as a programmer, *Mr. District Attorney* was given an expanded budget on orders from Republic chairman Herbert J. Yates, who liked what he saw in the rushes and elected to promote the picture as a "special." To that end, he hired playwright F. Hugh Herbert (*Kiss and Tell, The Moon Is Blue*) to contribute additional dialogue, which may explain why the witty badinage between O'Keefe and Rice is the best thing in the picture. Hardly "torn from today's headlines," the first *Mr. District Attorney* film bears no relation to the radio show, though as a brisk comedy-mystery it passes the time tolerably. And besides, how many other films can *you* think of which feature a brawl involving a bunch of jokers in Santa Claus suits?

Less costly but a notch better than its predecessor is the 67-minute *Mr. District Attorney in the Carter Case* (1941), directed by Bernard Vorhaus from a script co-written by Ben Roberts and a pre–*Windmills of the Gods* Sidney Sheldon. Again, the film delivers more laughs than thrills, and again its focus is not on a crime of national consequence but a simple murder mystery, this one involving the death of a fashion magazine publisher. James Ellison takes over as Jones, Virginia Gilmore steps into the role of Terry, and blustery Paul Harvey is cast as D.A. Winton. Though not widely seen in recent years, *Mr. District Attorney in the Carter Case* has assumed near-legendary status thanks to a bit of stunt casting described by movie historian William K. Everson: "It must be unique among all detective films; in picking the least suspicious character to be revealed as the killer, it went beyond all bounds of audience expectations and against all movie tradition and cliché." Even years after the fact, the revelation of the murderer can take one's breath away, though the surprise element was neutralized back in 1941 by Republic's decision to showcase this particular actor in a menacing pose—complete with low-key lighting—in the film's advertising posters. But to make sure we don't forget that *Carter Case* is essentially comic in tone, the film is climaxed by a wild and woolly slapstick chase, with actors Virginia Gilmore and Douglas Fowley careening down a treacherous hill on a runaway stretcher. Apparently Republic had absorbed some good vibes when the company moved into the old Mack Sennett studios back in 1935.

Technically, Republic produced three *Mr. District Attorney* films, and indeed the third entry was advertised as "based on" the radio program by Phillips H. Lord. But beyond the presence of leading characters Jones and Terry, *Secrets of the Underground* (1943) is an entity unto itself, with D.A. Winton (now played by Pierre Watkin) reduced to a bit role. William Morgan was back in the director's chair, while Geoffrey Homes (aka Daniel Mainwaring of *Build My Gallows High* fame) co-wrote the script with Ben Roberts. John Hubbard was the third actor in as many films to play assistant D.A. Jones, while Virginia Grey succeeded Florence Rice and Virginia Gilmore as Terry. This time around, the screwball-comedy content seriously erodes the film's effectiveness, particularly since the storyline deals with a weighty subject that would have done the original radio series proud: the counterfeiting of war savings

Leveling his gun at hoodlum Robert Barron (left), Adolphe Menjou (center) is clearly master of the situation as the title character in Columbia's *Mr. District Attorney* (1947). Assistant DA Dennis O'Keefe (standing just behind Menjou) holds an unknown player at bay.

stamps, which in 1942 were vital to the American defense budget. Boasting a strong supporting cast including Neil Hamilton, Lloyd Corrigan, Miles Mander and perennial comedy foil Olin Howlin in a standout role as a reluctant undercover agent, the 70-minute *Secrets of the Underground* is a decidedly mixed bag, with such action highlights as an attempted double murder in a grain silo undermined by such absurdities as the villains hiding a kidnapped woman in plain sight by wrapping her in bandages and placing her in the middle of a window display. (That sound you hear is Phillips H. Lord and Ed Byron banging their heads against the wall.)

The property would not see the light of a projection booth again until 1947, when Columbia Pictures came forth with a second film bearing the title *Mr. District Attorney*. On the credit side, this is the first picture in which the title character resumes pride of place and takes center stage, rather than being shunted to the background. In recognition of this, a "name" actor is cast in the role: Adolphe Menjou, seen to excellent advantage as hard-driving District Attorney Craig Warren. Also, for the first and only time the radio series' loyal supporting characters Harrington and Miss Miller appear on screen, respectively played by Michael O'Shea and Jeff Donnell. Finally, and despite the presence in the cast of the first film's P. Cadwallader Jones Dennis O'Keefe, there is next to no comedy in the Columbia incarnation of *Mr. District Attorney,* and this absence of frivolity goes a long way towards restoring the integrity of the NBC original.

As scripted by Ian McLellan Hunter, Ben Markson and Sidney Marshall, the 1947 version bears many of the hallmarks of *film noir,* right down to a spectacular opening-scene murder and the strategic casting of such *noir*-ish actors as George Coulouris and Steven Geray. Once again we are offered a dual-hero dichotomy, with O'Keefe carrying a significant portion of the story as embittered, disillusioned criminal lawyer Steve Bennett. Impressed by Bennett's willingness to resign his job rather than clear a shady client with false evidence, Craig Warren offers the young man a position in the D.A.'s office—and as his first assignment, Steve is to prosecute his former client. Things take a *Double Indemnity* turn when Bennett falls under the spell of femme fatale Marcia Manning (Marguerite Chapman at her slinkiest), who works for a crime kingpin with connections to Steve's quarry. Ending up as putty in the predatory female's hands, Steve is guilty of all sorts of ethical indiscretions, even covering up proof that Marcia is a murderess. But no matter how entangled he becomes in the villainess' web of deceit, D.A. Warren has faith that the wayward boy will eventually redeem himself.

Alas, the film never lives up to its promise, ponderously lurching from one loosely basted scene to another under the perfunctory direction of Robert B. Sinclair, and crawling along at a snail's pace throughout its 81 minutes despite a preponderance of plot. Given the straight-faced solemnity of the proceedings and the title character's active participation in the outcome, *Mr. District Attorney* should have been the best of the films based on the radio show, and the one with closest kinship to its source. Instead, it comes off as just another late–1940s Columbia potboiler, barely distinguishable from such other second-echelon melodramas as *Framed* and *The Devil's Henchman.*

If *Mr. District Attorney* really *had* to be converted from an aural to a visual attraction (a debatable point), the property was far better represented on television than in the movies. On October 1, 1951, it became the first radio mystery series to make the transition to live TV with the original cast intact. Under the supervision of Ed Byron, stars Jay Jostyn, Vicki Vola and Len Doyle played their familiar roles before the ABC network cameras on an alternate-week basis with *The Amazing Mr. Malone* until June 23, 1952, outlasting the radio version by ten days. Later that same year *Mr. District Attorney* was revived for radio syndication by producer Frederick Ziv with a transcribed version starring David Brian; in this one the title character was finally given a permanent name, Paul Garrett. Brian repeated the role in Ziv's subsequent filmed TV revival of *Mr. District Attorney,* likewise shown on a syndicated basis beginning in the spring of 1954. This slickly produced adaptation was still making new regional sales well into the 1960s, thanks to Ziv's foresighted decision to film most of the 50 half-hour episodes in color. For additional details, please reference the author's *Encyclopedia of Television Law Shows* (McFarland, 2009).

Pot o' Gold (1941)

In a saner world, a nine-day-wonder radio show like *Pot o' Gold* would hardly have qualified as a one-reel short, much less a big-budget musical feature. But given Hollywood's ongoing obsession with trying to make movie stars out of such ephemeral radio personalities as Jack "Baron Munchausen" Pearl and Bert "The Mad Russian" Gordon, it should surprise no one that *Pot o' Gold* would be given the same showcase treatment. Besides, when the son of the president of the United States says he wants to make a motion picture, who's going to argue him out of it?

American network radio's first major big-money giveaway show, *Pot o' Gold* was obliged to play dodgeball with the FCC before it was even allowed to premiere over NBC on September 26, 1939. There was a strict ban on holding radio lotteries, so the producers were forced to follow a rigid set of guidelines. Since the contestants were not required to put up any money to participate, that took care of the lottery angle; but neither could the contestants submit their names for consideration, since that would constitute a raffle, also *verboten* by the FCC.

When the decision was made to pick the winner's name at random from a phone book, the FCC insisted that any such selection on a network program could not be exclusively limited to the Metropolitan New York area, compelling the producers to collect phone directories from all over the country. And in order to choose those numbers, the producers had to jump through hoops on the air to prove that no favoritism was being practiced and that the winners really were randomly selected. This is why a huge "wheel of fortune" was featured on the program. The first spin of the wheel determined which state's phone book would be referenced; the second spin chose the page number from which the potential winner's name would be pinpointed; and the third spin chose the specific line number on the page. There was no way to determine if the call-ee would be home to answer his phone—but if a connection was indeed made and the listener correctly answered a query posed by announcer Ben Grauer, a prize of $1,000 would be sent via Western Union to the lucky contestant. If no one answered at the other end, $100 was sent to the chosen one just for being chosen, and $900 was added to the "pot o' gold" for the person selected the following week. A man in Jamestown, New York, would win $4,600 thanks to this laborious procedure.

Even allowing for the enticing prospect of becoming rich simply by sitting at home next to your phone on Tuesday (and later Thursday) night, *Pot o' Gold* would have been mighty dull had there been nothing but dead air between wheel spins, so a popular orchestra was needed to keep the program aurally stimulating during the selection process. Fortunately the series had been introduced as a local Cincinnati attraction by Horace Heidt (1901–1986), one of the finest novelty bandleaders in America. A versatile musician who indulged in such gimmickry as toy-piano compositions ("Tippy Tippy Tin"), nonsense tunes ("The Hut-Sut Song") and comedy monologues (Johnny Standley's "It's in the Book"), Heidt and his two biggest aggregations the Grenadiers and the Musical Knights had been radio stalwarts since 1932, while "Horace Heidt and His Californians" predated the star's radio career with a pair of one-reel films in 1929. Though Heidt went on to make more money than he ever had in show business as a real estate entrepreneur, his greatest personal triumph would remain his tenure as bandleader on NBC's *Pot o' Gold,* where each and every week listeners waited with bated breath for Ben Grauer to yell "*Stop, Horace!*"—signaling that the all-important phone call had gone through and the person on the other end was on the verge of winning a cool thousand (or more!).

As radio historian John Dunning has suggested, "The lure of *Pot o' Gold* was rooted in greed." Though the odds of being called by the program were approximately 20,000,000 to one, this didn't faze the series' loyal listeners, who broke dates, quit jobs and delayed weddings in order to be home just in case their numbers were chosen. At the height of the show's popularity, movie theater owners were known to offer their own $1,000 prizes to anyone who missed a call from *Pot o' Gold* while watching the picture.

Given that the excitement generated by the series was totally dependent on its immediacy and suspense, surely it would be impossible to duplicate this euphoria in any sort of film version of *Pot o' Gold*. Ah, but there was no such word as "impossible" in the lexicon of the Roosevelt family, especially after Franklin Delano Roosevelt had won an unprecedented third term as the nation's president. Like all of FDR's sons, James Roosevelt was fascinated with show business, and though he never went to the extreme of marrying movie star Faye Emerson like his brother Elliott, James was well-connected enough in Hollywood to wangle a job as a production assistant on Samuel Goldwyn's 1939 effort *Wuthering Heights*. Now that he knew all there was to know about filmmaking, the time was ripe for Jimmy Roosevelt to produce a whole entire feature-length movie all by himself. And the picture that young Mr. Roosevelt chose to produce through his own Globe Productions and release through United Artists was a cinema adaptation of the hottest show on radio: *Pot o' Gold,* featuring Horace Heidt and his Musical Knights, a project that UA had reportedly rejected when it was previously proposed by quickie producer Samuel Bronston.

Fine, except that a literal adaptation of the show would only run between 20 and 30 minutes—and while Globe Productions was then specializing in short subjects, James R. had loftier ambitions. So a story for *Pot o' Gold* had to be developed by Harry Tugend, Andrew Bennison and Monte Brice—or more specifically, a progression of events leading up to the story of the series. Perhaps audiences would be amused by a sequence in which the leading man (maybe Heidt would be the leading man, maybe not) was confronted by a representative of the FCC, who would tick off the many reasons that a giveaway show like *Pot o' Gold* could *not* be allowed on radio unless stringent guidelines were established. Okay. Now we've accounted for the final third of the film. The first two-thirds would be the buildup to the payoff. Could Horace Heidt and his band carry the entire weight of such a picture by themselves? Evidently the answer to that one was "Let's not take any chances."

Here's the plot that came out of the many pre-production brainstorming sessions. The hero is young harmonica-playing Jimmy Haskell, who'd rather run a musical instrument store than work for his uncle, millionaire health food manufacturer Charles Haskell. At the moment, Uncle Charley is taking legal action to close down the boarding house owned by Mom McCorkle, across the street from the elder Haskell's factory. The reason for this is twofold: Uncle Charley wants to tear down the boarding house so he can expand his business, and he can't stand the swing music played during the rooftop jam sessions held by star boarder Horace Heidt and his merry band. Meanwhile, Jimmy befriends Horace and the McCorkle family—which includes pretty aspiring singer Molly McCorkle—and secretly schemes to undermine his uncle without letting Molly know his true identity.

Tricking Charley into leaving town for awhile, Jimmy arranges for Heidt and Molly to appear on Haskell's weekly radio show. But upon discovering that Charley is Jimmy's uncle, Molly spitefully makes an announcement over the air that next week, and every week thereafter, Haskell will give away a thousand dollars to a lucky listener. The FCC swoops down and informs Jimmy that if he gives away the money, he'll be in violation of the agency's no-lottery rule, but if he *doesn't* give away the money, he'll be prosecuted for making false claims. "Either I give the money away and go to jail," moans Jimmy, "or I don't give the money away and go to jail." Literally overnight, Jimmy and his pals formulate the spinning-wheel, random-phone-number selection process to be followed on Haskell's radio program, now rechristened *Pot o' Gold*. Perpetuating the myth that the real *Pot o' Gold* was created on the spur of the moment via sheer improvisation, Jimmy and Molly personally lug hundreds of telephone books into the radio studio just minutes before the giveaway broadcast begins, then conspire to steal a "wheel of fortune" from a local carnival with only seconds to spare!

Despite the participation of James Roosevelt, there is no overt political message in *Pot o' Gold*, nor would such a message be appropriate in what was essentially a harmless entertainment. Even so, the viewer is given a tantalizing glimpse into the mindset of the FDR branch of the Roosevelt family. During the scene where Jimmy and the FCC official hash out a compromise that will allow *Pot o' Gold* to go on the air, all legal details must be followed to the letter, with every i dotted and t crossed. But when millionaire Charley Haskell justifiably hauls poor-but-proud landlady Ma McCorkle into court after someone in her boarding house throws a tomato at him, the kindly cop on the beat and the reactionary judge instantly take Ma's side, cheerfully denying any sort of due process to that filthy capitalist Haskell!

For the roles of Jimmy Haskell and Molly McCorkle, James Roosevelt wanted to borrow James Stewart and Judy Garland from MGM. Both actors were then working on *Ziegfeld Girl*, but Jimmy's shooting schedule allowed him sufficient time to appear in *Pot o' Gold*. Judy could not be released, so Roosevelt turned to Paramount and borrowed Paulette Goddard, with director George Marshall included in the deal.

In all future interviews, James Stewart would cite *Pot o' Gold* as his worst picture. Admittedly it is nothing to write home about, but Stewart's harsh assessment may stem from his inability to establish an on-set rapport with Goddard, who felt Jimmy wasn't romantic enough to be her leading man ("Anyone can gulp" was Paulette's snarky comment on the subject). Harmonica virtuoso Jerry Adler, who was hired to teach Stewart how to properly mime playing a mouth organ, has claimed in his autobiography that Jimmy was so unhappy with the picture that he frequently showed up "fairly inebriated" on the set. Since the actor was then suffering from a nasty head cold, he might merely have been overmedicated; but I like Adler's story better.

Paulette Goddard and James Stewart are the focal point in this lobby card for 1941's *Pot O' Gold*, at the expense of the star of the radio version, bandleader Horace Heidt.

Stewart had a happier working relationship with Charles Winninger, the ebullient old trouper cast as Uncle Charley Haskell. Jimmy also liked working with Horace Heidt and the Musical Knights, who from all reports were determined to have as much fun as possible during the shoot. Composer Frank DeVol, then a member of the Musical Knights, told interviewer Michael Seth Starr: "James Roosevelt produced *Pot o' Gold* about as well as I did; he just put his name on it. We had a very good cast, but it was a terrible picture.... We were in the band and sang 'A Knife, a Fork and a Spoon,' some piece of crap, but we had so much fun because we weren't in all the scenes. They had a big street scene for us, kind of an Argentinian thing they did. They had a stock of bananas and we started eating those bananas, and we were down to about four bananas by the time we were through."

While it is hard to spot DeVol among the sea of youthful faces in *Pot o' Gold*, another member of the Heidt unit, musician-comedian Art Carney, is instantly recognizable. Be advised that he speaks in a pear-shaped professional announcer's voice that sounds absolutely nothing like the "Hey, Ralphie Boy!" Carney that we've come to know and love.

All in all, Heidt and his boys come off better than practically anyone else in *Pot o' Gold*, making one regret that James Roosevelt didn't have enough confidence in the orchestra to give them the star treatment reserved for Stewart and Goddard. One of the film's most endearing aspects is that for the first five reels or so, there is no incidental music on the soundtrack. Instead, all of the music is performed on-screen, mostly by Heidt and company; and all of the tunes arise casually and naturally from the action, rather than being arbitrarily inserted just because Heidt happens to be in the picture. If Heidt is less effective in his big comic setpiece where he poses as a bearded psychiatrist, it is hardly his fault since he is forced to share camera space with the redoubtable Charles Winninger, who could have stolen a scene from King Kong.

The film's weakest sequence is the one that was potentially the most fascinating: the ceremonial spinning-wheel selection of the person whose thousand-dollar phone number is called over the air. Roosevelt and director Marshall must have known all along that the thrill inherent in this sort of "reality bite" could never be adequately replicated on screen, but the decision to hire character comedian Victor Potel (with a bad Scandinavian accent) to play the winner drives the final nail in the credibility coffin. How much more entertaining and believable it would have been had the filmmakers arranged to have a *genuine* winner from the *Pot o' Gold* program recreate his or her moment of triumph.

Critical reaction to the film was split down the middle. *Newsweek* commented, "James Stewart not only gives an interesting performance ... but sings on the screen for the first time—and not at all badly." Conversely, a Boston newspaper critic grumbled, "This picture, if nothing else, proves that Jimmy Roosevelt can't produce, Jimmy Stewart can't sing and Horace Heidt can't act." (Evidently *both* reviewers had either missed or forgotten Stewart's achingly sincere rendition of "Easy to Love" in the 1936 MGM musical *Born to Dance*.) Moviegoers greeted the film with a riot of silence, since not only had enthusiasm for radio's *Pot o' Gold* died down, but the show was on the verge of being cancelled, its integrity having been compromised by several lawsuits which raised some embarrassing questions about the infallibility of the winner-selection system. *Pot o' Gold* the movie opened on April 4, 1941; *Pot o' Gold* the radio show was terminated on June 5, 1941. Guess what impact *that* had at the box office.

Amazingly, radio's *Pot o' Gold* was exhumed by ABC—"by public demand," the network insisted—on October 2, 1946, this time with comedian Happy Felton as host and no "name" band on the premises. With big-prize giveaway shows the rule rather than exception in the postwar era, the revival made no dent whatsoever and came to an end on March 26, 1947. Around the same time, Astor Pictures reissued the film version of *Pot o' Gold* under the title *Jimmy Steps Out*, conclusive proof that there was no gold left in this particular pot.

Even if his movie had been a hit, James Roosevelt wouldn't have been able to capitalize on its success inasmuch as he had accepted a commission in the Marine Corps for the duration of World War II. Though in peacetime Roosevelt would serve six terms as Congressman from Los Angeles County, he never got show biz completely out of his blood. In 1981 he was screen-tested for the role of his own father Franklin D. Roosevelt in the TV miniseries *The Winds of War*—and while he didn't expect to be cast, he certainly didn't turn down the opportunity either. (Ralph Bellamy landed the role. Jimmy Roosevelt wasn't the type.)

Captain Midnight (1942)

Once they got their first radio series *The Air Adventures of Jimmie Allen* (q.v.) up and running, the writer-producer team of Bob Burtt and Bill Moore trafficked almost exclusively in juvenile aviation serials like *Hop Harrigan* and *Sky King*. In 1939 the team reunited with *Jimmie Allen*'s sponsor Skelly Oil for a new property in the same vein—and like *Jimmie Allen*, *Captain Midnight* began life as a regionally syndicated program.

Featuring future John Ford stock company member Willis Bouchey in the title role, the first 15-minute episode of *Captain Midnight* was broadcast by Chicago's WGN on October 17, 1939. Opening with the sound of a church bell tolling twelve times, the serial revolved around World War I flying ace Red Albright, who had earned his nocturnal soubriquet when he returned from a mission vital to the Allied victory precisely at the stroke of 12. The action of the serial transpired some 20 years after this epochal event, by which time Red Albright had for all intents and purposes *become* Captain Midnight, with not even his closest associates knowing his true identity. His top secret mission was to put a halt to the diabolical activities of "evil genius" Ivan Shark, an old enemy from the war years. Invariably dragging out his first name when identifying himself ("IIIIIIIvan Shark!"), the villain was aided in his perfidy by his equally evil daughter Fury (who looked like the Wicked Witch of the West in the show's publicity handouts) and their scurrilous toady Fang. But Captain Midnight's team was every bit as formidable as Ivan Shark's. This select group, known as the Flight Patrol, included the youthful Chuck Ramsay and Patsy Donovan, as well as grizzled mechanic Ichabod "Icky" Mudd.

The specter of the era's most popular kiddie serial *Jack Armstrong, the All-American Boy* (q.v.) loomed large over *Captain Midnight,* manifested not only in the hero's far-reaching airborne adventures but also in the presence of two comparative youngsters in Midnight's entourage. Chuck and Patsy were clearly inspired by Jack Armstrong's Billy and Betty Fairfield, right down to the "golly gee" dialogue: Patsy's oft-repeated "loopin' Loops" was a direct descendant of Billy Fairfield's favorite expletive "Gosh all fishhooks!" In other respects, *Captain Midnight* was cut from the same cloth as Burtt and Moore's *The Air Adventures of Jimmie Allen,* especially in the realm of sponsor-driven merchandising. Just as in the *Jimmie Allen* days, Skelly Oil used *Midnight* to promote scores of premiums, foremost among them the various products associated with membership in the Captain's "Flight Patrol," including identification cards, bronze medallions, and special decoder dials to decipher the secret messages transmitted on the program.

This sort of merchandising would reach a fever pitch after *Captain Midnight* was picked up by the Mutual network on September 30, 1940. The new sponsor was Ovaltine, who needed a series with established appeal to replace its recently cancelled *Little Orphan Annie.* Ovaltine instituted several changes in their new franchise, replacing star Willis Bouchey with Ed Prentiss and announcer Don Gordon with *Little Orphan Annie* alumnus Pierre André. The Flight Patrol was now known as the Secret Squadron, its members identified as SS-1, SS-2, SS-3 and so on—at least until the Nazis put an onus on those initials, whereupon the designations became SQ-1, SQ-2, SQ-3, etc. For reasons that must have had a legal foundation, the character of Patsy Donovan was changed to Joyce Ryan, though Chuck Ramsay, Ichabod Mudd, Ivan Shark and Fury were allowed to keep their original names.

The merchandising: To say that Ovaltine was aggressive in promoting its product by way of premiums and prizes would be the understatement of the 20th century. Hardly an episode went by without a closing exhortation by Pierre André to mail a label from an Ovaltine jar and ten cents in coin to receive the latest fabulous commercial tie-in—and as in the Skelly Oil era, secret decoders were the fastest-moving items. These devices, which over the years were molded in the shape of watches, keys and whistles, required the user to line up scrambled letters and numbers in order to decipher the messages that Captain Midnight imparted to all you "Fellows and Girls." The annually updated decoders were not only huckstered during the closing commercial but also within the episodes themselves. Radio historian Jim Harmon has noted a particularly brazen example during a story arc in which Ivan Shark had gotten his slimy hands on the latest decoder. There was no other alternative for Captain Midnight but to change the code overnight—and to prevent the listeners from missing out on any future dispatches from the Secret Squadron, it was imperative that they tear off that label, dig a dime out of the piggy bank, and send for the brand-spanking-new decoder without delay!

No Ovaltine was offered, displayed or consumed in Columbia Pictures' 1942 serial adaptation of *Captain Midnight,* though many of the radio version's other elements were in attendance—or at least they seemed to be. Actor-stuntman David O'Brien of *Pete Smith Specialties* fame sported a more lavish toupee than usual as the title character, who in transitioning from radio to film had borrowed some of the characteristics of another radio-movie crimefighter, *The Shadow* (q.v.). Most of the time, the hero goes by his given moniker Captain Albright, and in this capacity is a veritable flyin' fool. But when he needs to chip away at the conscience of one of the bad guys, Albright dons a mask and dark goggles to transform into Captain Midnight, swooping down as the clock strikes the Witching Hour to extract information from the miscreant at hand. This much was established in Chapter One of *Captain Midnight*; but as the story progressed, Albright assumed his Captain Midnight alter ego whenever he felt like it any time of the day—for what purpose we couldn't tell you, since even most of the villains had figured out that Albright and

Midnight were one and the same before the thirteenth and final chapter.

Featured in the cast as Chuck Ramsey is radio stalwart Sam Edwards, looking and sounding exactly as he would 25 years later on such TV programs as *Dragnet* and *Gunsmoke*. Arrow-narrow Guy Wilkerson, more at home as a western sidekick, was a laconic Icky Mudd. For the purposes of the screenplay, Joyce Ryan has become Joyce Edwards (played by David O'Brien's then-wife Dorothy Short), the eminently kidnappable daughter of distinguished scientist Dr. Edwards (Bryant Washburn). The doctor has invented a range finder that is much coveted by the unspeakable Ivan Shark (James Craven)—who spends half the serial terrorizing the populace with random bombing raids (Why bombing raids? Well, Columbia had a lot of aerial stock footage in its vaults. That's as good a reason as we're likely to get.)

Columbia's serials were traditionally the cheapest produced in Hollywood during the 1940s. This one looks as if it was filmed on a budget accumulated by auctioning off old *Captain Midnight* premiums. There doesn't even seem to be enough money in the till to purchase a properly villainous wardrobe for Ivan Shark and his daughter Fury (much prettier than her radio counterpart, and played by Luana Walters). Forget the lurid word pictures painted by the radio serial in which Ivan Shark sounded like Fu Manchu incarnate, replete with flowing robes and Mephistophelian beard. The movie serial's Ivan Shark wears an ordinary business suit and looks more like a salesman than a criminal mastermind. Similarly, Fury Shark, who at the very least should bear a passing resemblance to *Terry and the Pirates*' Dragon Lady, comes off about as menacing as a Simi Valley real estate agent.

Transcending the shoddy production values is the every-man-for-himself direction by James W. Horne, whose Columbia serials have been described by movie historian William K. Everson as "delightful forays into near-insanity." Obviously figuring that no one could take them seriously, Horne opted to play his serials for laughs, most conspicuously in his treatment of the subordinate villains. As one pores through the director's Columbia output, one finds a pair of henchmen playing patty-cake while awaiting further instructions from their boss, a band of outlaws greeting the delivery of an important package by shouting "Hooray!" in unison, and a group of thugs taking advantage of the head criminal's absence by donning ladies' hats and throwing a party. Devotees of this sort of subversive silliness will have a field day in *Captain Midnight*, with such choice tidbits as a minion of Ivan Shark reacting to the escape of the captured heroine and the arrest of Shark's daughter by sighing, "*This* is a fine kettle of fish!"

But the best lines are reserved for Ivan and Fury Shark themselves. Donning one of his many disguises in an early scene, Shark orders his daughter to pull the appropriate costume from the closet, whereupon the dialogue begins to sound like something out of *My Little Margie*:

> FURY: Really, Father, I don't know what you have in mind.
> SHARK: Of course you don't. If you did, *you'd* be running the place and *I'd* be getting the suit.
> FURY: Oh, you're impossible!

Radio's *Captain Midnight* managed to survive the movie serial's assault on the national intelligence, remaining on Mutual until December 30, 1949, by which time it had dropped the daily serialized format and switched to self-contained half-hour episodes (a comic book version, published first by Dell and then by Fawcett, ran from 1941 through 1948). The baby-boomer generation is perhaps most familiar with the 39-episode CBS television version of *Captain Midnight*, starring Richard Webb. Produced by Columbia's Screen Gems division, the series dropped all of the secondary characters except "Icky" Mudd, here played by Sid Melton. Olan Soulé, who had played Midnight's Secret Squadron second-in-command Kelly on radio, was seen in the TV adaptation as Professor Tutt. This Captain Midnight was a private citizen dedicated to battling "evil men everywhere"; he lived in a hi-tech mountain fortress equipped with its own airstrip, whence he blasted off each week in his jet *The Silver Dart*, "Courtesy of the Douglas Aircraft Company and the U.S. Navy." As in days of yore, Ovaltine sponsored the TV network run of

Captain Midnight, still peddling premiums and code devices with merry abandon. When the series went into off-network syndication without Ovaltine's patronage, its title was changed to *Jet Jackson: Flying Commando,* with all soundtrack references to Captain Midnight clumsily overdubbed. While *Captain Midnight* was part of the CBS weekend lineup from 1954 through 1957, *Jet Jackson* remained in distribution well into the early 1960s.

"Gang Busters" (1942; 1955–1957)

Screaming whistles! The pounding feet of prisoners marching in lockstep! Machine gun fire! The wail of police sirens! That was the unforgettable signature of the popular radio crime anthology that came on like ... like ... well, like *Gang Busters.*

Although *Mr. District Attorney* (q.v.) was the first of producer Phillips H. Lord's crime series to be adapted to film, Lord's *Gang Busters* had preceded *Mr. District Attorney* as an airwave attraction by four years. As part of an ongoing campaign to divest himself of his once popular but now discredited image as folksy New England philosopher Seth Parker (q.v.), Lord in 1935 came up with a radio concept to cash in on the publicity surrounding J. Edgar Hoover's Federal Bureau of Investigation after the death of Public Enemy #1 John Dillinger the previous year. The series signed on under the title *G-Men* over NBC-Blue on July 20, 1935, and as originally conceived would dramatize case histories drawn from the files of the FBI, with the more notorious felons—John Dillinger, Alvin Karpis, Baby Face Nelson—identified by their real names. But J. Edgar Hoover disapproved of the violence and gunplay on the series, and initially refused to cooperate with the producer. Mollified by the attorney general, who *did* like the series, Hoover agreed to open his files to Lord, but limited the choice of stories to cases that had already been closed.

After 26 weeks Hoover terminated his association with the series that had by now been retitled *Gang Busters.* Lord in turn eliminated all references to the FBI unless they were absolutely necessary, issuing city police badges to the authority figures on his program. *Gang Busters* now began each half-hour episode with the qualified assertion that the show was produced "in cooperation with police and federal law enforcement departments throughout the United States." Lord was still able to boast that *Gang Busters* was "the only national program that brings you authentic police case histories"—true enough in 1935 but less so in later years with the advent of such rival (and fully authorized) radio anthologies as *This Is Your FBI* and *The FBI in Peace and War.*

Gang Busters never had any regular characters beyond its two hosts, New York police commissioner Lewis J. Valentine and former New Jersey state police supervisor Col. H. Norman Schwarzkopf (father of the future Persian Gulf War hero). Though radio historian Jim Harmon has reported that both Valentine and Schwarzkopf appeared "by proxy"—*Gang Busters* code for "these are only actors pretending to be the real guys"—*On the Air* author John Dunning has stated that the actual men bearing those names were heard, and in fact were specifically selected by Lord because he knew that their presence would rankle the recalcitrant J. Edgar Hoover. (However, actor Don McLaughlin *is* known to have portrayed both Valentine and Schwarzkopf at certain junctures.) In each episode, the host would turn over the narration to the police official (again appearing "by proxy") whose case was being dramatized. The weight of the program was mostly carried by the villains, whose various schemes and skullduggeries were heard in progress. Among the actors playing these miscreants were Santos Ortega, Art Carney, Richard Widmark, Bryna Raeburn, Raymond Edward Johnson, and everyone's favorite gun moll Elspeth Eric. At the end of each episode the listener was given a detailed description of a criminal who was still at large, ending with, "If you have seen this man, notify the FBI, your local law enforcement agency, or *Gang Busters* ... at once!" (Hey, ma, they're talkin' about Uncle Louie. Gimme the phone, quick!)

Gang Busters still had no set protagonist when it was adapted as a comic book, first in

There were no "official" protagonists on the radio version of *Gang Busters* but Universal's 1942 serial adaptation had three: Kent Taylor, Irene Hervey and Robert Armstrong.

"Big Little Book" form in 1938 and then as a periodical the following year. Occasionally the stories would focus on an FBI agent named Winston, but that was about all. Only when *Gang Busters* was transformed into a 13-episode serial by Universal Pictures in 1942 could the property boast a consistent "hero"—and heroine. While the multi-story anthology format may have worked just fine on radio, for the purposes of the serial a single basic chronology with a limited cast of characters was established by screenwriters Morgan Cox, Al Morgan, Victor McLeod and George H. Plympton. The result was a storyline that might have been better suited to *Dick Tracy, The Green Hornet* or *The Shadow* than *Gang Busters,* though each episode was introduced with the same montage as the radio program, with an off-screen announcer declaiming a radiolike opening signature: "Calling the police! Calling the G-men! Calling all Americans to war on the underworld! *Gang Busters* with the cooperation of law enforcement officers of the United States presents a picture of the endless war of the police on the Underworld, illustrating the clever operations of law enforcement officers in the work of protecting our citizens. The All-American crusade against crime!"

A tired-looking Ralph Morgan is cast as Dr. Mortis, mastermind of a criminal organization known as the League of Murdered Men. The members of this select group are all criminals officially reported as deceased, but actually placed in suspended animation by Dr. Mortis with the help of a secret death-simulating drug. Their features altered by plastic surgery, the members of the League of Murdered Men carry out a variety of heinous crimes, every one of them publicly announced ahead of time by the brazen Dr. Mortis. This device enables each episode to begin with a newspaper headline heralding Mortis' latest threat, seguing into a brief summary of the previous chapter, usually parsed out in brief conversations between Police Chief O'Brien (Joseph Crehan) and Mayor Hansen (George Watts).

Forming a united front against the League are police detectives Bill Bannister and Tim Nolan, played respectively by Kent Taylor and Robert Armstrong. They are aided by intrepid female photojournalist Vicki Logan (Irene Hervey) and reporter Happy Haskins (Richard Davies), though the latter has a hidden agenda. Amidst the random perils and chapter-concluding death traps, a romance blossoms between Bill and Vicki, while in a separate development Bill is pulled off the investigation because of his dogged determination to avenge the death of his brother at Mortis' hands—precisely the sort of complication avoided on radio's *Gang Busters,* in which the authorities were emotionless automatons (Phillips H. Lord preferred to leave the hair-pulling histrionics to the bad guys). The conclusion of the serial (while escaping from his underground headquarters, Dr. Mortis is crushed to death by a subway train) might have been more shocking had not Universal released a production still of this gruesome moment.

Though there were no sequels to the Universal serial, the radio and comic book versions of *Gang Busters* were still thriving when, in 1952, the property was adapted as a half-hour filmed TV anthology, broadcast by NBC on an alternate-week basis with *Dragnet.* When the sponsor insisted that *Dragnet* be shown every week, *Gang Busters* was cancelled despite high ratings, though it continued to be seen in a syndicated-rerun package hosted by Chester Morris and retitled *Captured.* The property was given a second and final TV outing in first-run syndication in 1955, the same year that a feature-length *Gang Busters* movie was released theatrically. The film focuses on infamous real-life cop killer John Omar Pinson, who had been captured only a few years earlier following a macabre misadventure in which one of his minions buried him alive. Almost simultaneously with its national release, the *Gang Busters* film was re-edited and shown as a three-part story arc on the TV series titled "The Pinson Gang."

Research has not revealed whether the film had been made first for television and then distributed to theaters, or the other way around in the tradition of 1951's *Superman and the Mole-Men*—though the film version's threadbare production values and nonstellar cast (Myron Healey plays Pinson) would seem to suggest that it had been aimed at television all along.

There is no question that the 1957 theatrical film follow-up *Guns Don't Argue* was indeed cobbled together from three previously telecast *Gang Busters* episodes: "John Dillinger" with Myron Healey in the title role; "The Van Meter Case" starring Richard Crane as Dillinger crony Homer Van Meter; and "The Karpis Case" featuring Paul Dubov as Alvin Karpis and Jean Harvey as Ma Barker. *Guns Don't Argue* was still playing the drive-in circuit when radio's *Gang Busters,* now heard over the Mutual network, closed out its 22-year run on November 27, 1957.

Cosmo Jones in the Crime Smasher (1943)

Arguably the most obscure title in this book, *Cosmo Jones in the Crime Smasher* was based on a radio series originating from station KNX, the CBS-owned outlet in Los Angeles. The star was Detroit-born Frank Graham, who had launched his acting career in Seattle before relocating to California in 1937. Graham soon began popping up on practically every local program, dramatic and otherwise, emanating from KNX. Among his credits were the station's Monday-through-Friday *Night Cap Yarns* and the historical anthology *The Romance of the Ranchos,* narrating the latter series as "The Wandering Vaquero." Somewhere around 1939 Graham began a weekly 15-minute detective series known variously as *Cosmo Jones* and *The Crime Smasher.* Billed as the "one-man-theater," Graham wrote the scripts and played all the roles himself, including the eccentric, erudite correspondence school criminologist Professor Cosmo Jones. Though not heard in the East or Midwest, the series enjoyed wide West Coast distribution via the CBS Pacific hookup, which included such regional operations as the Arizona Radio Network.

Cosmo Jones was in its third year on the air when B-picture factory Monogram secured the film rights to the property. Throughout the 1940s, Monogram churned out a variety of inexpensive "series" films built around such fictional characters as the East Side Kids, Charlie Chan, the Cisco Kid, Joe Palooka and the Shadow (q.v.). What Monogram saw in *Cosmo Jones* is anyone's guess: Unlike its other series franchises, the radio show was by and large unknown to half the country. Perhaps both the show and its star came cheap—and if Monogram loved anything, it loved Cheap. At any rate, Frank Graham's screen debut *The Crime Smasher* was optimistically heralded as the "first" of the studio's *Cosmo Jones* efforts.

Billed fifth in his own picture, Graham doesn't make his initial appearance as Cosmo until nine minutes into the story, which concerns a bloody turf war between two rival criminal mobs in an unnamed big city. As if this crime wave wasn't irksome enough for irascible Police Chief Murphy, gang boss Biff Garr is set on kidnapping heiress Phyllis Blake and holding her for ransom. Cosmo is yanked into the story when, after stumbling upon the corpse of one of the bad guys, he offers his services as a special investigator to Murphy, who merely finds the little twerp annoying—as does the audience, especially since Professor Jones insists upon using shmancy words like "cerebrating" instead of "thinking" and "vocal prestidigitation" instead of "ventriloquism." During a shootout with the kidnappers, young Police Sgt. Callahan apparently wounds an innocent bystander and is demoted on the spot. Befriending both Callahan and the sergeant's girlfriend Susan Fleming, Cosmo hatchets a complex scheme to win back the boy's stripes, at the same time wiping out both gangs and rescuing the imperiled Phyllis.

Directed by James Tinling as if in a rush to go on his lunch break, *Cosmos Jones in The Crime Smasher* is chintzy even by Monogram standards, with wholesale corner-cutting throughout. The three main playing areas—a police station, a night club, a millionaire's mansion—all appear to be crowded into the same city block. Most of the interior sets threaten collapse, with the fashionable Diamond Club looking more like zircon. The "vast" criminal empires described in the film are whittled down to no more than four henchmen per gang, which is just as well since there are only about five guys on the police force. Screaming newspaper headlines cover up for scenes that were deemed too costly to shoot, with lame expositional dialogue and ridiculous coincidences substituting for logical story development. And in a sweeping economy move, screenwriters Walter Gehring and Michael L. Simmons eliminate the need for extra locations, camera angles and shooting days by jamming *all* the principal players into a single exterior set during the climactic plot resolution.

As with most Monograms of the period, the supporting cast of *Cosmo Jones* boasts some very talented people making lemonade from lemons. As the bombastic Chief Murphy, Edgar Kennedy surpasses himself with an average of five slow burns per reel, becoming so flustered at times that he audibly fluffs his dialogue. Matching Kennedy double-take for double-take is the immortal black comedian Mantan Moreland as Cosmo's reluctant aide Eustace Brown, who reaches a pinnacle of comic absurdity when he reacts in jibbering terror as the villains "torture" an apple before his eyes. In the potentially nondescript role of Susan Fleming, Gale Storm exhibits so much vivacity that one wonders why a lively lassie like Susan would waste time with a mope like Sgt. Callahan (played by the colorless Richard Cromwell).

Monogram showed great sagacity in assembling this strong cast of secondary players, since nominal star Frank Graham all but fades into the woodwork as the title character. It is true that he'd created the role on the airwaves, contemporary reviews indicating that he was most appealing before the microphone. And on film, Graham occasionally exhibits a flair for throwaway lines, as when he describes Chief Murphy as "a hail-fellow-well-forgotten." But for the most part, the wimpy, bespectacled, umbrella-toting Cosmo Jones is an empty suit—or to be precise, an empty raincoat. The filmmakers didn't help matters any by denying Graham sufficient screen time to show off the versatile voice work that had made him a radio favorite. Though the plot contrives to have Graham imitate Edgar Kennedy while making a phone call, the post-production people perversely sabotage the star by awkwardly dubbing in the real Kennedy's voice.

Cosmo Jones in The Crime Smasher turned out to be first and last entry in this putative series. Putting the experience behind him, Graham continued to prosper not only on radio but as a voice actor in animated cartoons, providing narration for such noteworthy efforts as Warner Bros.' *Horton Hatches the Egg,* Disney's *Chicken Little* and MGM's *The Blitz Wolf*; he was also heard as both title characters in Columbia's *The Fox and the Crow* cartoon series. Tragically, show business success did not translate into personal contentment, and in 1950 the 36-year-old Frank Graham committed suicide.

Reveille with Beverly (1943) and *Make Believe Ballroom* (1949)

As a slang designation for a radio performer who plays recorded music over the air, "disc jockey" did not exist until it was coined by Walter Winchell in 1935 to describe New York–based announcer Martin Block (about whom, more later). On the whole, disc jockeys were scarce during radio's Golden Age, particularly in the 1930s and early 1940s. Those few local air personalities who made their living spinning records and sustaining a steady stream of small talk between songs were operating under a handicap imposed by the Federal Communications Commission. Bowing to pressure from the American Society of Composers, Authors and Publishers (ASCAP), the FCC decreed that no disc jockey program could play a popular record until it was at least three years old, which not only forced these programs to rely on a repertoire of outdated tunes but also to fill the rest of their air time with foreign recordings of classical music and marching songs. Though the embargo on current songs was lifted in 1940, less than a year later a boycott organized by radio broadcasters against the high royalty fees imposed by ASCAP dealt another body blow to the "deejay" community, who for ten long and arid months were banned from playing any songs other than public-domain compositions by the likes of Stephen Foster.

The handful of deejays who flourished under these and other restrictive conditions were those with the talent and ability to entertain audiences—and, more importantly, sell their sponsors' products—through sheer force of personality. The most successful of these included Arthur Godfrey, Steve Allen and Jean Shepherd, all of whom would become major national names. Another important early deejay, for years known only as "Lonesome Gal," matriculated from a local Dayton program to a nationally syndicated "platters and chatters" party, due in great part to her come-hither voice and the aura of mystery surrounding her. (It wasn't until 1953 that she was publicly identified as Jean King, by which time she was pulling in $200,000 annually.) But the heyday of the disc jockey would not arrive until the collapse of network radio in the mid–1950s shifted the economics of broadcasting back to the local stations. From that point forward the airwaves proliferated with celebrity "jocks" like Alan Freed, Murray the K and Wolfman Jack, who wielded the power to bestow superstardom upon unknown recording artists; Gary Owens, Wally Phillips, Don Imus and Howard Stern (q.v.), whose iconoclastic humor meant more to their fans and sponsors than the records they played; and Larry King and Rush Limbaugh, who successfully deployed the "big sell" disc jockey format within the non-musical realm of talk radio.

Many deejays have appeared as "themselves" on film over the years. Alan Freed stars in 1957's *Mr. Rock and Roll,* sometimes described as a biopic but really a pastiche of lip-synching musical artists; and there's a whole battalion of regional radio personalities (among them Dick Clark, Howard Miller, Milt Grant and Dick Whitinghill) in another 1957 hodgepodge, *Jamboree*. Since we're presently talking about the 1940s, let's look at a couple of movies from that decade, both inspired by actual disc jockey programs. *Reveille with Beverly* (1943) and

Taking a few liberties with radio's *Reveille with Beverly*, the 1943 film version offers Ann Miller (center) as a decidedly demonstrative lady disc jockey.

Make Believe Ballroom (1949) will be jointly discussed in these pages for two reasons: Both were produced by Columbia, and both were basically the same picture.

Reveille with Beverly and *Beverly at Reveille* were used interchangeably to identify the early-morning record program hosted by 22-year-old Jean Ruth over Denver station KFEL. Ruth launched her show in 1941, coinciding with the influx of new draftees at the four Army posts in the Denver area. From 5:30 to 6:30 each weekday morning, "Beverly" Ruth played songs by request, delivered personal messages to the trainees and read Army camp bulletins, all with the blessing of the military brass. She also made personal appearances at dances and other social functions, dated boys at the camps, and in general boosted morale for thousands of homesick GIs. After being spotlighted in a 1942 *Life* magazine spread, she was hired by Los Angeles' powerful CBS affiliate KNX, where her platter-spinning program was recorded and shipped overseas for airplay on the Armed Forces Radio Network. The *Life* article also caught the corporate eye of Columbia Pictures, who contracted with producer Sam White to construct a low-budget musical around *Reveille with Beverly* as a vehicle for dancing star Ann Miller. In an early 1980s interview with film historian David Bruskin, White recalled,

> We tenuously hooked our storyline into all of the different recordings that [Beverly] played.... The basic "weenie" on which I was able to hang the musical reality occurred when she would get a request from a certain guy. There was a lot of byplay back and forth. She'd said, "David requested Bob Crosby and his band doing 'South Rampart Street Parade.' All right, David, are you listening? You better get your pants on because you're going to be late for roll call, but if you can spare a few minutes, here's your number. I hope it keeps you bouncing all day." As the turntable would start, the camera would move in on it and dissolve to the live band actually performing in a specialized set we designed.

Since there isn't a whole lot of intrigue in the premise of a pretty girl sitting at a turntable, screenwriters Howard J. Green, Jack Henley and Albert Duffy conjured up a slim but serviceable framing story in which Beverly Ross (Miller), switchboard operator at radio station KFEL, is given an opportunity to break into the performing end of the business as temporary replacement for the early-morning classical music show hosted by prissy Vernon Lewis (Franklin Pangborn). The show has been designed to entertain soldiers at a nearby army camp, but Beverly senses that the boys would prefer swing over symphony and revs up a stack of Count Basie, Duke Ellington, Bob Crosby, Freddie Slack and Mills Brothers records. Though she's fired by station manager Kennedy (Tim Ryan) for deviating from the approved playlist, Beverly scores a hit with the draftees and is brought back by popular demand. One of her biggest G.I. fans is incognito millionaire Barry Lang (William Wright), with whom Beverly falls in love, unaware that he's her show's biggest sponsor. This being a wartime musical, the plot is superseded by an overproduced last-reel stage show for the benefit of the boys in uniform, a tailor-made opportunity for Miller to finally get out from behind the microphone and let loose with a fabulous "V for Victory" tap dance specialty, complete with fireworks.

Made for a pittance, *Reveille with Beverly* turned out to be what White described as a "sleeper," the sort of small, unimportant film that gradually grows into a huge cash cow by word of mouth. But it wasn't the Ann Miller Fan Clubs who were responsible for the film's success. The big selling card for *Reveille with Beverly*—then as now—is the film's glittering array of musical guest stars. Though Charles Barton is the credited director, the specialty numbers were filmed under the supervision of White, who in the early 1930s had helmed a marvelous group of musical two-reelers for RKO featuring such artists as Ruth Etting and Ted Fio Rito. As he related to Bruskin, White recycled "every innovative idea I had developed at RKO with those band shorts," which explains why these segments outclass everything else in *Reveille with Beverly*.

Among the highlights is Duke Ellington's performance of the Billy Strayhorn jazz standard "Take the A Train," even though the song's title doesn't quite jibe with the segment's content. As everyone who'd ever been to Manhattan Island knew in 1943, the "A Train" was the crowded subway that took its passengers directly into Harlem. In *Reveille with Beverly*, however, the number is performed in a roomy and well-appointed private railroad car, hundreds if not thousands of miles removed from New York. White's rationale for altering the song's backdrop was that he needed a larger set to accommodate the lively dance number that accompanies the instrumentals. This sequence also represents the first time that the public ever heard the lyrics for "Take the A Train," courtesy of vocalist Betty Roche. At White's request, Ellington wrote the lyrics himself, in a single overnight session.

For all of its musical delights—Bob Crosby's "A Big Noise from Winnetka," Count Basie's "One O'Clock Jump," Freddie Slack and Ella Mae Morse's "Cow Cow Boogie," the Mills Brothers' "Cielito Lindo" et al.—the jewel in the film's crown, at least in terms of box-office pull, was the brief appearance by Frank Sinatra, crooning Cole Porter's "Night and Day" while duded out in a sharp tuxedo and surrounded by a dazzling female orchestra. *Reveille with Beverly* was Sinatra's third feature film appearance, and his first as a solo vocalist. Amazingly, White never took the usual movie-producer prerogative of claiming that he'd "discovered" Sinatra for the movies. On the contrary, White later confessed that he'd expressed skepticism when the singer's services were offered by MCA's Jimmy McHugh, fretting that Frankie was too "skinny" and "unphotogenic." As for Sinatra himself, even at this early date he knew precisely where he was going professionally and precisely how he'd behave when he got there. Upon completing the master shot of his big number, the singer rebelled at having to submit to a retake. When White ordered him to do so, Frankie grumbled, "Well, all right, but I'll never do that again." And with rare exceptions, he never did.

Since *Reveille with Beverly* went into release at the height of the "Swoonatra" craze, it was clear as glass that Sinatra was the film's main attraction. Even so, Frank was contractually bound to settle for only fifth billing—and at that, he was in a preferable position to nominal star Ann Miller, whose name didn't appear on-screen until after all the musical guest performers were billed, relegating her to *eighth* place. If Ann felt slighted by this, imagine the reaction of the film's formidable roster of comic supporting actors (Franklin Pangborn, Tim and Irene Ryan, Wally Vernon, Andrew Tombes, Doodles Weaver, Maude Eburne), none of whom received any billing at all!

Decades after her first flurry of national fame, the original "Beverly" Jean Ruth claimed that the Pentagon instructed her to mention requests over the air from military personnel for records that didn't exist. Only after the war ended was she informed that these requests were actually coded messages to the French underground. Stories like this are always hard to verify, but it is irrefutably true than among Ms. Ruth's fringe benefits from her association with the movie version of *Reveille with Beverly* was her 1945 marriage to one of the film's headliners, bandleader Freddie Slack. While the union didn't last long, Jean's show business career thrived well into the television era, when she became the national voice for Pillsbury's radio and TV commercials. Jean Ruth died in 2004 at the age of 84.

Though chronologically 1943's *Reveille with Beverly* must be dealt with first, the source material for the 1949 Columbia musical *Make Believe Ballroom* can be traced all the way back to 1932, and to the first-ever radio disc jockey. According to the *Gino's Place* web page, Canadian-born Al Jarvis was all of 23 years old when as a staff announcer at Los Angeles' KFWB he began hosting a daily, six-hour program called *The World's Largest Make Believe Ballroom*. Per its title, the show never left the confines of the radio studio as Jarvis played popular recordings and filled the gaps by providing his audience with information about each record. Though very popular within the range of KFWB's small signal, Jarvis' program was all but unknown to the rest of the country. It would take the efforts of 32-year-old Martin Block, an announcer for New York City's WNEW, to transform *Make Believe Ballroom* into a household word.

This came about indirectly starting February 3, 1935, while WNEW was providing coverage of the Lindbergh kidnapping trial. During a lengthy break in the courtroom proceedings, Block came up with the bright idea of spinning a few music records to hold the audience's attention. Like most radio stations of the period, WNEW had no music library, forcing Block to purchase a bunch of records with his own money. Playing five discs by bandleader Clyde McCoy back to back, Block introduced each song by conveying the illusion that he was transmitting a live dance hall remote. Once the trial ended, WNEW opted to retain Block's "Make Believe Ballroom" (the official title would come later) in answer to thousands of fan requests. Those thousands grew into millions in the months to come, and thanks to strong sponsor support, Block's spin party was expanded to two and a half hours per week. There were actually those who believed that the performances of "the country's foremost dance bands" were being broadcast live on four spacious bandstands from "the Crystal Studios of WNEW." Block was cagey about the whole charade, never blatantly insisting that he was anywhere else but a tiny studio with one microphone and two turntables, but whenever he'd make announcements like, "And now, Mr. Frank Sinatra ascends our revolving stage to sing 'Nancy with the Laughing Face,'" listeners were not discouraged from jumping to conclusions. Though *Make Believe Ballroom* was never given a national network slot, WNEW's powerful transmitter drew in listeners from Pennsylvania, New Jersey, Massachusetts and Connecticut. In addition, the program was widely syndicated to local stations beginning in 1948. California's Al Jarvis may have blazed the trial, and indeed had co-written a theme song for the program that resulted in a top-selling 1940 recording by Glenn Miller, but so far as the public at large was concerned, *Make Believe Ballroom* was the sole province of Martin Block.

That said, Columbia's 1949 filmization of *Make Believe Ballroom* was lensed in Hollywood and Al Jarvis was nearby and available, so Jarvis enjoyed ample screen time as "himself," though Block made a token uncredited appearance in the course of the film's 79 minutes, and both Block and Jarvis were listed in all advertisements. Directed by Joseph Santley, who like *Reveille with Beverly*'s Sam White had specialized in musical short subjects in the 1920s and 1930s, *Make Believe Ballroom* was co-scripted by *Reveille*'s Albert Duffy, relying heavily upon what had worked so well in the earlier film. As before, the plot is a paper-thin affair, this time concerning a contest devised by Jarvis' press agent Liza Lee (Ruth Warrick in an Eve Arden–ish performance that may astonish fans of her work as Phoebe Tyler on the TV soap opera *All My Children*). Her idea is that $5,000 will be given to the person who can identify the most performers and titles of the records played on Jarvis' daily radio show. Among the finalists are Gene Thomas (Jerome Courtland) and Josie Marlowe (Virginia Welles), carhops at the Hamburger Heaven drive-in. The two kids fall in love despite their ongoing competition, but trouble arises in the form of an amorous college professor (Ron Randell) and false accusations that Gene has bribed a radio station engineer (Louis Jean Heydt) to get the record titles in advance. As if we care, since the plot is merely a clothesline upon which to hang a series of specialty numbers, which in *Reveille with Beverly* fashion are introduced with an optical transition effect linking the spinning records with the live performances.

You wouldn't think an "all-star" musical would look any cheaper than *Reveille with Beverly*, but *Make Believe Ballroom* achieves this dubious distinction. In his screen debut Frankie Laine immortalizes "On the Sunny Side of the Street" while standing before a black curtain and a dollar-store table lamp; Kay Starr warbles "Lonesomest Gal in Town" while lounging in the tackiest apartment in town; the Nat King Cole trio barely have room to turn around in as they go through "The Trouble with Me Is You"; and Gene Krupa nearly reduces the canvas backdrop to rubble with "Disc Jockey Jump." Slightly better production values are afforded "Joshua Fit the Battle of Jericho," a battle-of-the-bands number featuring Krupa, Charlie Barnet, Ray McKinley, Pee Wee Hunt, Jan Garber and Jimmy Dorsey. But no lavish art direction trappings are really necessary for the film's star attraction, the peerless African American blues singer Toni Harper, then only ten years old and cute as all get out. Her delightful, full-throated renditions of "Miss In-Between Blues," "Candy Store Blues" and "Hamburger Heaven" (the last number performed with Jack Benny's Sportsmen quartet) are so vastly superior to the rest of the proceedings that one can only retroactively curse the de facto show biz segregation of 1949 which denied her the chance to become the Deanna Durbin of the postwar generation. (Coincidentally, like Deanna before her, Toni was under contract to comedian Eddie Cantor.)

Make Believe Ballroom came and went with none of the fanfare of *Reveille with Beverly,* and hasn't been widely seen since a few rounds of television exposure in the 1960s and 1970s. As for Martin Block and Al Jarvis, both men continued to prosper in the disc jockey field for the rest of their broadcast days, Block remaining in New York until his death in 1967 and Jarvis at his Hollywood post until his passing in 1970.

"The Crime Doctor" (1943–1949)

Polish-born Max Marcin (1879–1948) was one of those professional "writing machines" who proliferated in the early decades of the 20th century, efficiently churning out scores of plays, novels, short stories and films, few of which stand the test of time but all extremely popular and profitable in their day. He scored his first Broadway hit with *House of Glass* in 1916; Marcin's subsequent theatrical triumphs included the oft-filmed *The Eyes of Youth* and *Three Live Ghosts,* as well as such brisk entertainments as *See My Lawyer* and *Cheating Cheaters.* A former police reporter for the *New York World,* Marcin was frequently called upon by Hollywood to lend his expertise to such crime melodramas as *City Streets* (1931) and *Gambling Ship* (1933). (He also directed the latter, along with six other films.) Though he'd never written a radio script prior to 1940, Marcin thought that it would be an amusing challenge and dashed one off virtually overnight. The result was the first episode of his long-running CBS series *The Crime Doctor.*

The title character was Dr. Benjamin Ordway, who'd earned his soubriquet as one of America's leading criminal psychologists. Ordway came to his chosen profession in an unorthodox fashion: A onetime criminal himself, he'd suffered a blow to the head which rendered him an amnesiac. Mentored by a compassionate doctor, Ordway established an entirely new identity in the field of medicine—and upon learning of his unsavory past, he devoted his life to the study of the criminal mind. (Max Marcin claimed that his own knowledge of underworld matters was harvested from interviews with actual convicts and reformed crooks.) When the weekly 30-minute *Crime Doctor* series premiered on August 4, 1940, Ordway was appointed to the parole board of a large unnamed state. In each of the early episodes he listened to the case history of a specific prisoner seeking a parole in order to determine whether or not the poor soul had paid his debt to society. A studio audience, evenly comprised of men and women, rendered the final verdict—and as a pre-show publicity ploy for the inaugural episode, listeners at home were invited to phone in their verdicts, with prizes up to $200 awarded to those who'd voted in line with the studio "jury."

The format was altered during the war years, with Ordway's backstory largely forgotten upon his retirement from the parole board and his establishment of a consulting office in his own home. As the years went by, Ordway himself spent most of his time offstage, the first two-thirds of each episode devoted to setting up a murder mystery with an overabundance of suspects. Called into the case by the police at practically the last moment, Ordway would listen to all the evidence and alibis, then suddenly declare that the killer had made the One False Step which cooked his goose. At this point, the final Philip Morris cigarette commercial would cut in, prefaced by an assurance from announcer Ken Roberts: "Ladies and gentlemen, Dr. Ordway will be back in exactly 57 seconds with the solution to tonight's case." This is the one aspect of *The Crime Doctor* that would remain burned into the memories of its millions of fans—emphasis on "memories," since only a handful of recorded episodes are known to exist.

Ray Collins was the first actor to play Ordway on radio, followed by House Jameson (who appeared during the aforementioned transition period), John McIntire, Hugh Marlowe, Brian Donlevy and Everett Sloane. When Columbia Pictures purchased the film rights to the series, the studio conducted a search for a star who could convey the middle-aged dignity, bearing and experience of radio's Ordway, but at the same time project enough "romantic appeal" to bring in the ladies. Just such an actor all but fell into Columbia's lap when Warner Baxter emerged from a two-year "retirement" for a comeback role in Paramount's *Lady in the Dark* (1944).

Born in Columbus, Ohio, in either 1889 or 1892, Warner Baxter moved with his family to San Francisco, where they managed to survive the 1906 earthquake, a story that Baxter would dine out on for the rest of his life. Entering vaudeville in 1910, Baxter moved on to stock companies and Broadway before his screen debut in 1922. Among his starring assignments during the silent era was the title role in the original (and now sadly lost) adaptation of *The Great Gatsby* (1926). Making a spectacular switchover to sound, he earned the first Academy Award for Best Actor in a talking picture with his bravura portrayal of the Cisco Kid in Fox's *In Old Arizona* (1929). During the early 1930s he was the busiest male star on the Fox lot, headlining as many as five pictures per year. Playing in everything from historical melodrama (*The Prisoner of Shark Island*) to screwball comedy (*Wife, Husband and Friend*), the muscular, mustachioed Baxter's stock-in-trade was the strong, resilient, utterly dependable hero. At his peak popularity in 1936, Baxter earned $236,000, the highest-paid actor in Hollywood. Even then, however, the aging actor knew that his leading-man days were numbered; first announcing his planned retirement, he changed his tune and declared that he would limit himself to character roles. The studios, however, wouldn't hear of it, and continued casting him in star parts.

In 1940 Baxter suffered a severe nervous breakdown which forced the issue. Wealthy enough to give up show business if he chose, he repaired to his home in Malibu where his wife of 22 years, former actress Winifred Bryson, carefully monitored his diet, physical activities and involvement in local civic affairs (he served as the head of Malibu's civil-defense program during World War II, and was later elected mayor of the upscale beach community). The actor's return to films in 1943 prompted Columbia to offer him the leading role in their proposed *Crime Doctor* series, with the assurance that he would be limited to only two films per year and his shooting schedule would be as non-strenuous as possible. In a Columbia press release that we'd like to believe he wrote himself, Baxter stated, "Playing the same character over and over again in a series is likely to become monotonous. But with the Crime Doctor, the actor doesn't have to worry about that, thanks to the character himself—or should we say to Max Marcin, his creator, and the writers who have handled him since then? There is, of course, always the same stability—may I say 'guts?' But he is forever flexible, not just a stereotyped stick to do any of his own moulding. That's what makes him so arresting to both audiences and the player alike. To me he is one of the most interesting characters I have every played."

Following Columbia's established B-picture policy, each *Crime Doctor* entry was filmed on a set limited budget, the potential profits already calculated by the studio's accountants; each had a running time between 65 and 72 minutes; each was populated by up-and-coming Columbia contractees (Nina Foch, Lloyd Bridges) and established but not-too-expensive character players (Reginald Denny, Jerome Cowan, Steven Geray); and each was completed in a swift four weeks. Though Marcin received a contractual "created by" credit for every entry, neither he nor the radio show's staff writers had any actual input in the films.

Even so, the inaugural *Crime Doctor,* released under that title on June 22, 1943, harked back to the radio series' backstory, a decision that had less to do with fidelity to the original program than with studio economics. In pure dollars and cents, it lowered the overhead considerably to remake an earlier, similarly themed Columbia feature, *The Man Who Lived Twice.* This excellent 1936 programmer stars Ralph Bellamy as a ruthless, ugly gang boss who while fleeing the police ducks into a lecture given by an eminent surgeon (Thurston Hall), who theorizes that it is possible to completely alter one's personality on the operating table. Sensing a foolproof method of avoiding arrest, Bellamy volunteers to be the doctor's guinea pig. The operation is a complete success: Bellamy not only has absolutely no memory of his gangster past, but he has emerged from the bandages with a handsome countenance and a sunnier disposition. Several years pass, by which time Bellamy has become a noted physician and psychologist, working with the local parole board to rehabilitate criminals. Inevitably his past comes back to bite him, and at the urging of his sweetheart (Marian Marsh) Bellamy turns himself over to the authorities to answer for past sins. Though the Production Code insisted that "crime does not pay" whatever the circumstances, the audience would not have accepted an ending in which the now-sympathetic hero went behind bars for life, so director Harry Lachman and his four screenwriters devised a fiendishly clever newspaper-headline montage that allowed everyone to have his cake and eat it too.

Directed by Michael Gordon, the initial *Crime Doctor* lists none of the writers from *Man Who Lived Twice* in the opening credits, though enough remains of the earlier film to easily discern the source. To soften the pre– "good guy" character of Dr. Robert Ordway (his first name permanently changed for the film series), the film's Depression-era prologue never shows Ordway's hardboiled alter ego Philip Morgan committing any crimes, nor acting like a criminal except for a later sequence devised to fool Morgan's former cronies into believing that their "boss" has risen from the dead. Instead, we fade in as the wounded Morgan is thrown from a speeding car after being taken for a ride. Ray Collins, the first of radio's Crime Doctors, is here cast as the kindly surgeon who performs the character transformation on the unconscious gangster. Once again the passage of several years enables the "reborn"

Ordway to establish a spotless reputation as a brilliant and humane criminal psychologist, and in this capacity he is assigned to the state parole board where he unexpectedly comes in contact with past associates. *Crime Doctor*'s closing courtroom sequence streamlines the sleight-of-hand finale of *The Man Who Lived Twice* by having Ordway found guilty for crimes committed while traveling under the name Philip Morgan, only to be instantly given a suspended sentence and the full blessings of the court to continue his good works. This of course thrills Ordway's young sweetheart Grace Fielding (played by Margaret Lindsay, fresh from Columbia's recently terminated "Ellery Queen" series)—a character never to be seen again in future *Crime Doctor* entries, in which Ordway has no romantic entanglements of any kind, not even with his unfailingly gorgeous nursing staff. We would also never again hear of Ordway's criminal past, though he'd return to parole board duty for the series finale *Crime Doctor's Diary* (1949).

Although the murder-mystery angle is absent from *Crime Doctor,* the remaining nine films in the series made up for this oversight with at least two homicides per picture. Eschewing the radio-series format in which Dr. Ordway is barely present for most of the proceedings, Baxter's Ordway takes an active part in tracking down and subduing the villains from Reel One onward, occasionally indulging in fisticuffs (with the aid of a stunt double) and elaborate "disguise" sequences. In a refreshing departure from the usual detective-movie formula, Ordway is more often than not a reluctant sleuth who tries to beg off the case, arguing that the official police are better equipped to handle such matters,

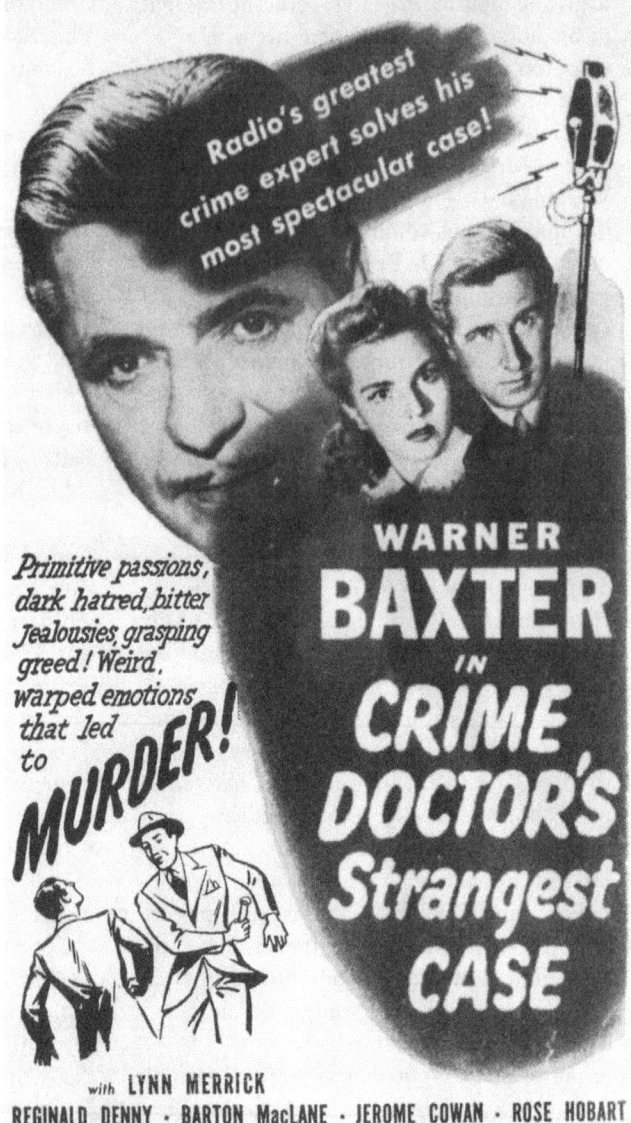

Star Warner Baxter looms large over this 1943 ad for the second entry in Columbia's *Crime Doctor* series, leaving little space for romantic leads Lynn Merrick and Lloyd Bridges.

but is inexorably drawn into the story by circumstances beyond his control. Only rarely does he inaugurate the investigation, as he does after being duped into administering a fatal vaccination in the opening scene of *Just Before Dawn* (1946).

Another noteworthy aspect of the *Crime*

Doctor series is the concerted effort to alter either the format or the locale in several of the entries. Both *The Crime Doctor's Strangest Case* (1943) and *Shadows in the Night* (1944) incorporate supernatural elements not found in the series' other films, while *The Crime Doctor's Courage* and *The Crime Doctor's Warning* (both 1945) are more in the *film noir* than the whodunit category. And on two occasions Dr. Ordway is forced to cut short a long-overdue vacation when murder rears its ugly head. In *The Crime Doctor's Gamble* (1947), an excursion to Paris is spoiled by some deadly intrigue surrounding a stolen painting; and in *The Millerson Case* (1947), the good doctor has the bad luck to go on a hunting-and-fishing trip in a backwoods "Peyton Place" replete with a quack medico who harbors deadly grudges, a murder victim who has apparently slept with every woman in town, a case of feigned insanity, and at least one Faulknerian idiot.

A few clumsy plot devices and too-obvious "surprise" killers notwithstanding, the ten *Crime Doctor* films maintain a fairly high batting average, with aficionados divided as to which entry is the series' best. Some have a preference for *Shadows in the Night*, wherein heroine Nina Foch suffers from a recurring nightmare in which a mysterious woman appears dripping wet in her room and lures her to a horrible death by drowning. Others are fondest of *Crime Doctor's Warning*, if for no other reason than the flamboyant performance of Eduardo Ciannelli (uncredited on screen but prominently billed on the advertising posters) as a Bohemian artist. And still others cast their vote for *Crime Doctor's Man Hunt* (1946), directed by William Castle from a script by Leigh Brackett (*The Big Sleep, The Empire Strikes Back*), which features Ellen Drew in a dual role and a terrific closing line by police detective William Frawley.

The radio version of *Crime Doctor* ended its CBS run on October 19, 1947, some five weeks before the release of the film series' ninth entry *Crime Doctor's Gamble*. For a while, it seemed as if Columbia was going to follow CBS's example by terminating the film version, but by 1948 Baxter was giving interviews indicating that the studio would continue the series, further insisting that playing the same character for six years hadn't worn him down in the least. Baxter echoed these sentiments for an interview with the AP's Bob Thomas in May 1949, a month and a half after *Crime Doctor's Diary* made its New York theatrical bow: "It's a very comfortable way to continue a long career. When you are doing a familiar character, he practically becomes a friend of yours, and more important, a friend of the audience." But while Warner Baxter would appear in three other films before his death in 1951, *Crime Doctor's Diary* turned out to be the series' swan song.

"Al Pearce and His Gang" and *Here Comes Elmer* (1943)

San Francisco–born comedian Al Pearce (1900–1961) wasn't just blowing air when he claimed to have headlined radio's first comedy-variety series. One of the true pioneers of the broadcast industry, Pearce started out singing, playing banjo and cracking jokes for the fun of it while accumulating millions of dollars selling real estate. But by age 28 he was flat broke and had to find another quick source of income. He might have gone back to his earlier vocation as an insurance salesman had he not joined his brother Cal to launch a San Jose–based radio program on San Francisco station KFRC in 1928. A year into the run of the Pearce brothers' *Happy-Go-Lucky Hour*, writer Jack Hasty penned a sketch in which Al played a bashful door-to-door peddler named Elmer Blurt (or Blurp, depending on the source). Drawing upon his experiences in this field of endeavor, Pearce made Elmer his own personal property with a timid, rhythmic knock on the door and the mumbled catchphrase "Hope there's nobody home, I-hope-I-hope-I-hope." Once a prospective client answered that knock, Elmer invariably went into his by-rote sales pitch in a breathless monotone, just as invariably taking his foot out of the door and inserting it in his own mouth.

Even at this early date there was a lot more to Pearce's show than a single routine; he'd also begun assembling a cast of regulars which he expansively referred to as his "gang." Among the first members of this entourage was Monroe Upton, playing a silly-ass Englishman named Lord Bilgewater who was incapable of understanding even the most infantile of Pearce's jokes. In 1933, Arlene Harris, a Canadian-born vaudeville monologist who'd retired from show business when she married a doctor, joined the cast with her ladies' club comedy routine as an overly garrulous housewife. Known as "The Human Chatterbox," Harris could rattle off 240 words a minute as she carried on nonstop telephone conversations with her friend Maizie. Other members of the "Gang" during this formative period included singer-guitarist Tony Romano, comedian Morey Amsterdam and his then wife Mabel Todd, and Bill Comstock in the drag role of Tizzie Lish, a broad parody of a typical cooking show hostess. It was a happy "all for one—one for all" bunch, with Pearce paying his regulars full salary even during layoffs, and gently advising them to salt away 40 percent of their earnings in a mutual trust fund in case the bubble ever burst.

In April 1934 an NBC talent agent, acting upon the advice of several California advertisers, offered Pearce and his Gang a weekly sustaining network program to try them out on a national scale. Pearce in turn offered to forego a salary for himself and his cast (that trust fund, remember?), in exchange for a three-day-per-week show that would let the public *really* get used to them. That's how it went over the coast-to-coast NBC-Blue chain from January 13, 1934, through March 29, 1935—and by May 13 of that year, *Al Pearce and His Gang* had landed the sponsorship of Pepsodent for a fat $10,000 per week. Before long the entire country was reveling in the antics of Pearce's prankish cohorts, who over time would include persimmon-faced character actor Will Wright playing Zeb to Pearce's Eb in a recurring hillbilly routine and Cheerily in the "Yahbut and Cheerily" sketches with Jennison Parker; Harry Stewart as Swedish novelty singer Yorgi ("I Yoost Go Nuts at Christmas") Yorgenson; and former portrait photographer Artie Auerbach as pixieish entrepreneur Mr. Kitzel, a character he'd later carry over to the Abbott & Costello and Jack Benny programs. Such catchphrases as Elmer Blurt's "Nobody home I-hope-I-hope-I-hope," Tizzie Lish's "Hello, folksies!" and Mr. Kitzel's "Mmmm... *could* be!" gained wide popularity in the 1930s and 1940s, no small thanks to repeated exposure in the Warner Bros. cartoons of the era (notably *Jungle Jitters* and *The Woods Are Full of Cuckoos*).

Pearce's subsequent Hollywood fortunes would be securely shackled to Republic Pictures, beginning with a good guest spot in the studio's all-star 1937 musical *The Hit Parade* (see separate entry), which features an Elmer Blurt sketch with Pearce, Monroe "Lord Bilgewater" Upton and Arlene "Chatterbox" Harris (though Harris was edited out of the film's 67-minute reissue version *I'll Reach for a Star*). Orchestra leader Carl Hoff, then pulling double radio duty on Pearce's show and *Your Hit Parade,* was also in the film. By the time Pearce and Republic again collaborated, six years had passed, during which Al and his Gang had continued to prosper over two different radio networks and with the patronage of such sponsors as Ford Motors, Grape Nuts, Dole Pineapple and Camel Cigarettes. Then on July 2, 1942, Pearce's series left the air for a nearly two-year hiatus. Never one to let grass grow under his

The eponymous star of radio's *Al Pierce and His Gang* strikes an affable pose as "himself," temporarily forsaking his bumbling alter ego Elmer Blurt.

feet, Al signed on for a second Republic picture and his first starring vehicle, bringing Arlene Harris, Bill Comstock, Will Wright and Artie Auerbach along.

This writer has been unable to locate a copy of *Here Comes Elmer* (1943), and don't think I haven't tried. Judging by contemporary reviews and production stills, the 74-minute musical comedy was a typically slick and efficient Republic A-minus or B-plus effort, though one does not expect miracles from any picture directed by the prolific but uninspired Joseph Santley (as witness *Make Believe Ballroom*, discussed elsewhere). While the film marked the first important musical assignment for Dale Evans and a screen comeback after four years' absence by Gloria Stuart, neither actress had much to say about the experience in their memoirs; Stuart could only recall that her co-star was Stuart Erwin, evidently confusing *Here Comes Elmer* with the 1939 feature *It Could Happen to You*. If for no other reason, the Republic film should have some merit in that its guest-star roster includes the (Nat) King Cole Trio, performing their hit tune "Straighten Up and Fly Right."

Its title notwithstanding, *Here Comes Elmer* stars Al Pearce as Al Pearce—at least at first. The producer of a small-town radio show, Al loses sponsor Horace Parrot (Will Wright) when he refuses to allow Horace's sister Arlene (Arlene Harris) to sing on the program. Though Al and his cosmetician fiancée (Gloria Stuart) are willing to cut their losses and remain where they are, his manager Joe (Frank Albertson) arranges to get Pearce and his cast a big-city radio tryout with the help of his girlfriend Jean (Dale Evans), the secretary of a network executive. It so happens that Jean is an aspiring singer who's been trying to land a spot with the Jan Garber Band (playing themselves), but that's neither here nor there: The plot really begins percolating when Al, having been unable to make the grade in network radio, takes a job as a vacuum cleaner salesman, teaming up with his exact lookalike Elmer Blurt (also played by Pearce). Again trying out for an important radio gig, Al regales the audience with an Elmer Blurt imitation, only to be accidentally rendered unconscious. Upon awakening, the amnesiac Al believes he actually *is* Elmer, leading to a mass of mistaken identity complications culminating in the real Elmer taking Al's place in a forced marriage to Arlene. Oh, and Jean gets that job with Jan Garber, in case you couldn't sleep nights without knowing.

Far be it from us to challenge Republic's assertion in *The Hollywood Reporter* that *Here Comes Elmer* generated so much "exhibitor demand from all over the country" that the studio signed Pearce for three more starring features, in which he was to repeat his Elmer Blurt characterization. But though *One Exciting Week* (1946), *Hitchhike to Happiness* (1947) and *The Main Street Kid* (1948) all reteamed Pearce with Arlene Harris, he didn't play Elmer in any of them. The one entry in the trio that would seem to have any tangible connection with *Here Comes Elmer* is *One Exciting Week,* wherein Pearce once again essayed a dual role, this time as a GI war hero and his gangster doppelganger.

Having returned to radio in 1944, Pearce was never quite able to recapture his prewar popularity and faded from the airwaves in 1947. A stab at a morning variety show on CBS television in 1952 was warmly received and well reviewed, but the network was unable to clear enough local affiliates to keep the project afloat. By then Pearce had recouped his fortune in real estate many times over, and was too rich to care that the parade had passed him by. But *Al Pearce and His Gang* would not recede into total obscurity so long as such former series regulars as Morey Amsterdam and Mel Blanc kept the legacy alive in print and media interviews. And who could forget Mr. Amsterdam's sentimental gesture to his late employer when he arranged for Arlene Harris to recreate her "Chatterbox" routine on a 1964 episode of *The Dick Van Dyke Show?*

"The Whistler" (1944–1948)

Just as *Suspense* is often confused with *Escape* and *X Minus One* is frequently mistaken for *Dimension X,* those with only a passing interest in old-time radio tend to regard the melodramatic anthologies *Inner Sanctum Mysteries* and *The Whistler* as interchangeable. True, both series were introduced by a sinister host and both dealt in stories heavily laden with suspense, irony and unsympathetic protagonists. Otherwise, the two programs were wholly different commodities.

For starters, throughout its 11-year history (January 7, 1941, through October 5, 1952), *Inner Sanctum Mysteries* was heard from coast to coast, first on NBC-Blue and then on CBS. *The Whistler* was for most of its 13-year lifespan (May 16, 1942, through September 8, 1955) a regionally broadcast program, heard almost exclusively on CBS's West Coast hookup and picked up for only two brief national runs. *Inner Sanctum* was introduced by a creaking door, radio's only copyrighted sound effect. *The Whistler*'s opening signature was an eerie 13-note theme song, composed by Wilbur Hatch and whistled by Dorothy Roberts. *Inner Sanctum*'s host was the malevolently mirthful Raymond (originally played by Raymond Edward Johnson), who showed up at the beginning, middle and end of each episode to crack grim jokes and ghoulish puns about the evening's story, which in contrast was played completely straight and usually narrated by the leading character. Once that character had met his or her grisly but well-deserved fate, Raymond returned for a few more fiendish funnies and his familiar sign-off, a chillingly cheerful "Good night ... pleasant *dreeeeams*." (Again the sound of that creaking door, full up to finish.) The titular emcee of *The Whistler* (played by Bill Forman) was a humorless, spectral presence, introduced with echoing footsteps and the solemn intonation "I am the Whistler, and I know many things for I walk by night. I know many strange tales, many secrets hidden in the hearts of men and women who have stepped into the shadows. Yes, I know the nameless terrors of which they dare not speak ..." In the play proper, the Whistler was a combination second-person-singular narrator and guilty conscience, and woe betide the foolhardy protagonist who paid him no heed. Even when it appeared that evil had triumphed and the villain would get off scot-free, the Whistler always returned after the final commercial with the "strange climax" to the story in which justice was finally meted out.

The biggest difference between the two programs is that *Inner Sanctum Mysteries* was based on a series of crime novels published by Simon & Schuster, while *The Whistler* was a radio original—which is why this entry is about *The Whistler* and not *Inner Sanctum Mysteries*. Yet still we must reference one property to place the other in its proper context when discussing the Columbia film series inspired by *The Whistler*.

"Inspired" may not be the appropriate word, for there was more imitation than inspiration in this case. Let's begin in June 1943, when Universal Pictures decided to promote their resident horror star Lon Chaney, Jr., as "The Screen's Master Character Actor" in a group of B-pictures that allowed Chaney to appear without makeup and in non-monstrous roles. Acquiring the rights to the *Inner Sanctum* name from Simon & Schuster, Universal hardly touched the literary works published under this banner, nor did they use any of the radio series' trademarks. Replacing "Raymond" at the beginning of all but the final *Inner Sanctum* entry was actor David Hoffman as a disembodied head floating in a crystal ball, making oblique *Whistler*-like introductory comments: "This is the Inner Sanctum, a strange, fantastic world, controlled by a mass of living, pulsating flesh—the mind. It destroys, distorts, creates monsters, commits murder. Yes, even *you* without knowing can commit murder."

Mostly directed by Reginald LeBorg, the six *Inner Sanctum* films (*Calling Dr. Death, Weird Woman, Dead Man's Eyes, The Frozen Ghost, Strange Confession, Pillow of Death*) are set apart from the standard Universal horror product in that their plotlines are basically non-supernatural in nature, focusing on such normal, workaday story elements as greed, jealousy and revenge, and downplaying the use of blatant "fright" effects. It wasn't that Universal was trying to change its modus operandi after years in the scare-picture business; the studio was simply emulating the successful low-budget RKO melodramas produced by Val Lewton (*Cat People, I Walked with a Zombie*, etc.), which focused on psychological terror and the power of suggestion rather than overt horror gimmicks. Edward Dein, who wrote the script for the first *Inner Sanctum* film *Calling Dr. Death*, had in fact been recruited from the Lewton unit. Universal reasoned that if the first film in the Lewton-RKO series, *Cat People*, could earn a $4,000,000 profit on a $134,000 investment, they could earn just as much and spend even less on *Calling Dr. Death*.

Cast as a sympathetic character in some of the films and a villain in others, Chaney worked hard to convince us that he was really a doctor, psychiatrist or what have you. The kindest statement one can make about the results is that Chaney was capable of great things in the right role, but in the *Inner Sanctum* efforts he didn't always get the right role. Ironically, Chaney delivers one his weakest performances in the series' strongest film, 1944's *Weird Woman* (based on Fritz Leiber, Jr.'s classic *Conjure Wife*), while he is at his very best in one of the worst entries, 1945's *Strange Confession* (a tepid remake of the 1934 Claude Rains vehicle *The Man Who Reclaimed His Head*). Whatever the shortcomings of the films or their star, the *Inner Sanctums* all made money for Universal. And since Columbia Pictures wasn't in business for its health, the torch-lady studio took notice of what its rivals had been up to.

The prospect of a Lewton-like "psychological-terror" series that avoided costly special effects in favor of mood and atmosphere was quite appealing to Columbia, whose B pictures were among the cheapest of any major studio. The notion of basing this series on a pre-sold radio property like *Inner Sanctum* was another selling point, since Columbia was then doing just fine with their radio-inspired *Crime Doctor* pictures (q.v.). And the device of featuring the same star in each film *a la* Lon Chaney, Jr. was just the sort of set-up Columbia had been searching for since signing actor Richard Dix to a long-term contract in late 1943.

Born Ernest Carlton Brimmer in 1893, Dix had been a major movie star of the granite-jawed variety since 1921, successfully transitioning to talkies first at Paramount and then at RKO. His final film for the latter studio had been the Val Lewton production *The Ghost Ship*, so there was no loss of prestige for Dix to step into a new Columbia B-picture series inspired by the Lewton output. When journalists asked if the aging actor regarded his Columbia assignment as a comeback, Dix airily replied that Hollywood had previously insisted that he'd "come back" with the 1931 Oscar-winner *Cimarron*, and that according to studio publicists he had made two additional comebacks since. But as Dix noted in a January 1945 interview for the United Press, he had never really been away, though he'd occasionally taken an extended break from filmmaking and given serious consideration to retirement. "I guess [stage star] Richard Mansfield was dead right, when he said that once a man gets the smell of greasepaint, he'll never be satisfied with anything else."

Columbia's choice of *The Whistler* as the radio property to be adapted for their new Dix series was motivated by Universal's choice of *Inner Sanctum* for Chaney; like the casual radio

A studio portrait of sturdy leading man Richard Dix, several years before he became the star of Columbia's *Whistler* series.

listeners mentioned at the beginning of this entry, Columbia probably regarded the two programs as basically the same. In contrast with the Universal films, there was a firm tie-in between the radio and movie adaptations of *The Whistler*. Each of the eight Columbia films opened with Wilbur Hatch's spine-chilling theme tune, accompanied by a stylized visual representation of the shadowy title character and his famous introductory words "*I* am the Whistler. And I know many things..." etc. (Just as the identity of the actor playing radio's Whistler was kept secret for many years, Columbia never billed the voice of the unseen movie Whistler, though research has revealed that the performer was Otto Forrest.) Also, while only Simon & Schuster was credited in the *Inner Sanctum* pictures, both the CBS network and series creator J. Donald Wilson were duly acknowledged in the credits of the *Whistler* efforts.

Each of the *Whistler* films was budgeted at around $75,000, considerably less than their RKO and Universal counterparts—and every dollar that wasn't spent showed up on screen, notably in the rather mildewed interior sets and cramped studio exteriors. However, series producers Rudolph Flothow and William Picker were crafty B-picture veterans who knew every trick of transcending tiny budgets to come up with a quality product. Also rising above Columbia's parsimoniousness was director William Castle, who'd already proven that he could get a lot from a little with the studio's "Boston Blackie" entry *Chance of a Lifetime*, his feature film directorial debut. The four *Whistler* pictures helmed by Castle exhibit the same genius for evoking terror and suspense with the barest of production facilities that Castle would display in the horror films later made under his full creative control (*House on Haunted Hill, The Tingler, Homicidal*)—and *without* the crass gimmickry and blatant scare effects that ultimately became the director's stock-in-trade.

If we are to believe Castle's autobiography (an always risky proposition), the director regarded Eric Taylor and J. Donald Wilson's script for the inaugural entry *The Whistler* (1944) as "one of the most terrifying screenplays I'd ever read." Castle claims that he phoned Columbia CEO Harry Cohn at the stroke of midnight to assure Cohn, "I'll scare the shit out of the audiences." This much we can swallow, but Castle embroiders the story by claiming that he increased the scripted agitation of leading man Richard Dix by ordering the actor to give up smoking and going on a crash diet, then making him do multiple takes of each scene. Cute story, but it taxes credibility a bit to accept that an actor of Dix's stature would submit to such a harsh regimen, and that Cohn would allow Castle to strain an already tight budget with extensive retakes. Castle also insists that he used a handheld camera in some scenes, a claim easily disproven by viewing the picture. But considering what the director actually accomplished in bringing *The Whistler* to life, we can allow him a few harmless elaborations.

Running a few seconds short of an hour, *The Whistler* is a model B picture, as good a budget production as any studio ever made. Like Chaney in the *Inner Sanctums*, Dix alternates between heroes and villains in these pictures, playing for sympathy in the opening effort. The basic premise can be traced as far back as the 1916 Douglas Fairbanks vehicle *Flirting with Fate*, and probably wasn't new even then, but is just the sort of surefire yarn that never seems to lose its luster. Dix plays Earl C. Conrad, a man profoundly depressed by the news of his wife's death. With nothing to live for, Conrad arranges to have himself murdered by a paid assassin (J. Carrol Naish) who takes great professional pride in his work, and who of course refuses to break the contract when Conrad receives word that his wife may still be alive. In keeping with the film's predilection for implied rather than overt horror, once the assassin fails in his attempt to murder Conrad by orthodox methods, he adopts a new approach by planning to scare his client to death—a task made easier by the fact that Conrad has never met the killer face to face and has no idea where the man will strike next. In her final film appearance before her screen comeback in the 1980s, Gloria Stuart plays Conrad's secretary Alice Walker, who finds herself in the rock-and-hard-place position of being in love with her boss while still hoping that the information about Mrs. Conrad's survival is true for his sake.

The Whistler is very much in the spirit of the radio program, with the protagonist trapped by circumstances of his own making and forced to spend the bulk of the story extricating himself. The radio version's denouements were never in the hands of the main character but always determined by the inexorability of Fate. In the film, the Whistler informs us at the outset that "destiny" has decreed that one of the characters will die before the final fadeout, carefully neglecting to reveal which character it will be. As is his custom, the Whistler appears at various junctures in the story to comment on the action. However, for the first and last time either in films or on radio, the Whistler takes an active part in the story's development, with two of the characters commenting that they hear someone whistling somewhere. Just a few moments before the "End" title, the Whistler's presence so distracts one of the principal players that he brings about that person's fatal downfall—meaning that Destiny has very little to do with the outcome. The Whistler's jarring intrusion seems contrived to bring the story to a satisfying end which would otherwise not have been possible, a weak narrative device that the radio show always managed to avoid. It was a mistake that would not be repeated in any of the subsequent *Whistler* films, in which the title character observes but never intervenes. Otherwise, the initial series entry is superb, bolstered by the haunting cinematography of James Brown, Jr. and a hand-picked supporting cast including such uncredited thespians as Joan Woodbury (who *does* receive billing in the lobby posters), Don Costello, Cy Kendall, Billy Benedict, Robert E. Homans, Byron Foulger and George Lloyd.

Even better is Entry No. 2, *Mark of the Whistler* (1944), directed by Castle from a script written by George Bricker and fairly faithfully based on "Dormant Account," a story by Cornell Woolrich (*Phantom Lady, Rear Window*). Though not quite as sympathetic as in *The Whistler,* Dix is still in non-villainous mode as transient Lee Nugent, who chances upon a newspaper article about dormant bank accounts. One such account is in the name of "Lee Nugent," so *our* Lee Nugent decides to take advantage of the similarity in names—and the fact that the "real" Nugent has apparently vanished from the face of the earth—to claim the money. Ah, but it seems that the man Nugent is impersonating had a few skeletons in his closet, one of whom wears a coat of flesh and has murder on his mind. On this occasion, "destiny" returns to its proper place to dictate the strange (but logical) outcome of the story. Columbia contract starlet Janis Carter is the love interest, while character players Porter Hall and Paul Guilfoyle and dapper magician-turned-actor John Calvert (who later starred in a brace of *Falcon* movies) also figure into the scheme of things.

The two subsequent entries directed by Castle maintain the standards of his first two *Whistlers*. Co-written by Castle, Entry #4 *Voice of the Whistler* (1945) finds Dix in a characterization that starts out pleasantly enough but takes a dark turn by the final reel, while Fate plays its usual dirty trick on the one character who most deserves it, a mercenary nurse (Lynn Merrick). And in *Mysterious Intruder* (1946), the sixth film in the series and one of two without "Whistler" in the title, Dix manages to be both likable and detestable as a seedy private eye who wants to get his mitts on a set of priceless Jenny Lind recordings. Unsavory through Dix may be, he is well matched by duplicitous vixen Nina Vale and psychotic thug Mike Mazurki (who would still be up to no good in Castle's 1962 fantasy-comedy *Zotz*).

Without Castle's input, the *Whistler* series faltered a bit. Directed by Lew Landers, Entry #3 *Power of the Whistler* (1945) is arguably the weakest of the bunch, though redeemed by Dix's multilayered performance as an amnesiac who may or may not be a murderer and the presence of Janis Carter and Jeff Donnell as two refreshingly independent-minded leading ladies. Entry #5 *The Secret of the Whistler* (1946) is better, though George Sherman's direction is no match for Castle's. Dix again plays a man of dubious sanity, a famous artist whose wealthy but burdensome wife (Mary Currier) has died mysteriously and whose current *amour,* high-maintenance model Leslie Brooks, forges a potentially lethal bond with Dix's resentful housekeeper (Mona Barrie).

Directed by William Clemens, *The 13th Hour* (working title: *The Hunter Is a Fugitive*) was the seventh in the *Whistler* series and the last film ever made by Dix. The story is serviceable enough, with trucking company owner Dix, his son Mark Dennis and cop Regis Toomey all in love with diner operator Karen Morley, while rival trucker Jim Bannon plots to ruin Dix's business. A murder occurs and Dix finds himself on the run, forcing Morley to become the proactive member of the cast. The only problem here is that *The Whistler*'s distinctive "inevitability of fate" formula is abandoned in favor of a standard-issue crime melodrama that would have been more at home on radio's *Suspense*.

There is a common assumption that the *Whistler* series was terminated because of Dix's death on September 20, 1949. Actually *The 13th Hour* was released in 1947, and would most likely have been followed in short order by an eighth series entry had not Dix suffered the first of several heart attacks. After surviving his third attack, the actor issued press statements assuring the public that he'd return as soon as he was fully recovered. But when it became obvious that Dix was no longer able to work, Columbia dropped the *Whistler* franchise ... for a while. In 1948, the studio announced that it would revive the property on a one-time-only basis, and that the new film would deviate from the radio *Whistler*'s format by sidestepping the "Destiny" premise and focusing on characters who were victims of circumstance rather than their own actions.

Another Cornell Woolrich story, "All at Once, No Alice," was the basis for *The Return of the Whistler* (1948), and Columbia's all-purpose "B" director D. Ross Lederman was assigned to guide new leading man Michael Duane through the labyrinthine storyline. Unable to find a justice of the peace on a dark and stormy night, Ted Nichols (Duane) and his fiancée, self-described widow Alice Dupres Barkeley (Lenore Aubert), are forced to hole up in a small town hotel. Briefly leaving Alice behind to get his car repaired, Ted returns to find that the girl has vanished. Refusing to believe the hotel clerk's story that Alice has gone to New York without him, Ted engages the services of private detective Gaylord Traynor (Richard Lane, borrowed from Columbia's "Boston Blackie" series) to find her, unaware that Traynor is also in the employ of Mrs. Barkeley (Ann Shoemaker), the mother of Alice's first husband—who appears to be very much alive! The original Woolrich story was a scathing indictment of wealthy families who use money and influence to commit "undesirable" family members to disreputable mental institutions, but this story element doesn't surface until the final two reels of *The Return of the Whistler*, which is so full of plot twists that the viewer feels like a mouse in a maze. Like *The 13th Hour*, *The Return of the Whistler* bears scant resemblance to its radio role model, but is still a film well worth having if for no other reason than watching female lead Lenore Aubert, so often cast as a sinister *femme fatale* (as in *Abbott and Costello Meet Frankenstein*), playing victim rather than victimizer for a change.

The last of the Columbia series, *The Return of the Whistler* was released the same year that an independent programmer titled *Inner Sanctum,* starring Charles Russell and Mary Beth Hughes, was distributed by Film Classics. Unrelated to the Universal series but ostensibly based on the radio program, the circuitously plotted *Inner Sanctum* (a flashback detailing a murder concludes with the same murder occurring all over again) has more in common with another radio anthology, *The Mysterious Traveller.*

Then in 1954, *The Whistler* was adapted as a 39-week syndicated television series, regionally sponsored as on radio by the Signal Oil Company. Also in 1954, a 39-episode syndicated TV version of *Inner Sanctum,* underwritten by *its* radio sponsor Lipton Tea, was put on the market—and once again, those who hadn't paid much attention in the old days confused one program with the other. Adding to the confusion on the *Whistler* TV episode "Backfire" was the presence in the cast of *Inner Sanctum* alumnus Lon Chaney, Jr.!

Take It or Leave It (1944)

Devotees of Groucho Marx are well versed in the story of how Groucho did not achieve lasting radio success until he abandoned the scripted comedy-variety format for the largely ad libbed role of game show host on *You Bet Your Life*. These folks might not be aware that another popular comedian had gone the same route several years before Marx's show premiered in 1947. The biggest difference between *You Bet Your Life* and *Take It or Leave It* was that the latter series' host Phil Baker had, unlike Groucho, been quite successful on radio prior to assuming his quizmaster role. Yet the two shows can be mentioned in the same breath because, as in the case of Groucho's *You Bet Your Life*, Baker never did anything else on radio that brought him *more* fame and fortune than *Take It or Leave It*.

Born in Philadelphia in 1893, Phil Baker was 14 years old when he made his first stage appearance, and 19 when he formed a vaudeville partnership with another fledgling entertainer named Ben Bernie (see **The Winchell-Bernie "Feud"**). Phil played the accordion while Ben played his violin, both men throwing in jokes between renditions. On his own, Baker developed an act in which he'd walk on stage with his accordion, assure the audience that he'll give a musical performance, then adamantly refuse to play more than a couple of notes until he'd delivered a monologue. The comedian's relaxed, conversational style enabled him to get laughs without ever seeming to break a sweat; Jack Benny would later cite Phil Baker along with the similarly "intimate" monologist Frank Fay as the two biggest influences on his own comic style.

After great success on Broadway, Baker entered radio in 1931 with a brief CBS weekly. Two years later he struck pay dirt with his NBC-Blue series *The Armour Jester*, so named for its meat-packing sponsor. Though not the first comedian to use a heckling stooge in his act, Baker was the first to employ this device on radio, reportedly because having stooges to lean on enabled him to get over the "mike fright" which plagued him throughout his career. The hecklers in this case were a veddy-proper British butler named Bottle, played by Harry Naughton, and a disembodied voice named Beetle, who popped up without warning throughout *The Armour Jester* (and its successor shows *The Gulf Headliner* and the Dole Pineapple–sponsored *Honolulu Bound*) to give the star comedian a hard time. To enhance the "surprise" element of Beetle, the actor playing him never appeared onstage, speaking his lines through echo-chambered loudspeakers. Baker didn't bring Beetle or Bottle along with him in his two radio-related film appearances of the 1930s, *Gift of Gab* and *The Goldwyn Follies* (both mentioned elsewhere), though he'd drop occasional references to his twin nemeses when the spirit moved him.

Despite the sizable following Baker had built up during his first decade on radio, he felt that the public was growing weary of his act, and in 1939 voluntarily left the airwaves to concentrate on personal appearances. During his absence, CBS launched the Sunday night quiz show *Take It or Leave It* on April 21, 1940. Initially hosted by Bob Hawk, the series chose its contestants at random from the studio audience, using two glass bowls stuffed with ticket stubs and marked "Men" and "Women." The game itself was a question-and-answer, general-knowledge affair, with such categories as "Popular Songs," "Sports Figures," "Historical Highlights" "Famous Novels" and "Card Games" selected from a blackboard. The first prize was one dollar, the second doubled to $2, the third to $4, and so on up to the coveted "64 Dollar Question." Though many contestants considered themselves lucky if they guessed the $32 question, a few brave souls toughed it out to the top prize. But if they missed the big question, they lost all the money they'd previously earned. In other words, they could "take" what they had or "leave" empty-handed.

Emerging from his self-imposed exile, Baker accepted producer Bruce Dodge's invitation to take over the emcee duties on *Take It or Leave It* when Bob Hawk left for another CBS quizfest, *How'm I Doin'?* By the time Baker joined the show on December 27, 1941, America was at war, and a third bowlful of ticket stubs marked "Servicemen" had been added to the weekly lottery. It was during the Baker regime that *Take It or Leave It* really hit its stride, with the host genially ribbing the contestants and throwing in deliberately bad jokes just to keep the audience on its toes, providing accordion accompaniment whenever the quiz category had something to do with music, and resurrecting good ol' invisible Beetle to admonish players who dared to venture past the $32 prize and go all the way to $64 with a mocking "You'll be sorrrrree" (though usually the audience beat Beetle to it). By 1944 *Take It or Leave It* was the most popular quiz program on radio, its biggest and most enthusiastic fan base among servicemen, who packed the studio audience during the war years. As a both a tribute to this loyalty and a nod to patriotism, Baker enabled contestants in uniform to win up to $32 by making it *extremely* easy to provide the correct answers, his "subtle" clues stopping just short of giving the whole game away.

20th Century–Fox producer Bryan Foy exerted almost as little effort as those lucky servicemen when he set about to make a movie inspired by *Take It or Leave It*. In fact, Foy was able to find virtually every element in the picture right under his own nose. Baker had just completed work on the Fox musical *The Gang's All Here* and owed the studio one more picture—*any* picture. The rest of the cast was drawn from the Fox contract player roster, their combined salaries coming nowhere close to what Baker was getting. Leading man Edward Ryan had recently earned some good press for his work in Fox's *The Sullivans*; leading lady Marjorie Massow, a former cashier in the Fox commissary, had not yet appeared on film, thus this picture could qualify as her screen test (she was later signed by RKO under the name Madge Meredith); and comic relief Stanley Prager was fresh off the set of the studio's *The Eve of St. Mark,* the first step in a multifaceted career that would include a meaty role in the smash Broadway musical *The Pajama Game* and numerous directorial assignments on such New York–filmed TV series as *Car 54 Where Are You* and *The Patty Duke Show*. Foy had wanted the slightly higher-priced William Eythe and Mary Anderson for his leads, but you work with what you get.

In standard Hollywood tradition (see entries for *Breakfast in Hollywood* and *Queen for a Day*) the film's recreation of a "typical" *Take It or Leave It* episode was fleshed out by a fictional storyline. To that end, Foy plundered a property that Fox had had in its vaults since 1931, the Sally Eilers-James Dunn film vehicle *Bad Girl,* which theoretically was old enough that audiences wouldn't recognize the source. Screenwriters Mac Benoff, Harold Buchman and Snag Werris borrowed only the last two reels of *Bad Girl,* in which the impoverished hero goes to desperate lengths to hire an expensive obstetrician for his pregnant and slightly neurotic young wife. The material was updated so that the male protagonist is a soldier about to be mobilized, bringing him logically into the *Take It or Leave It* radio studio so that he can answer enough questions over a period of several weeks to cover the medical costs, but otherwise the progression of events is pretty much the same as in *Bad Girl*—though apparently not enough for Fox to bestow a screen credit upon the authors of the original film.

In its formative stages the film was to have used *Take It or Leave It* as the nucleus for an all-star Technicolor musical called *Movietone Follies,* a title Fox had previously trotted out for a couple of early talkies. Even when it was decided to pare down the budget to B-picture dimensions, the studio hoped to talk Jack Benny into making a cameo appearance, but Benny's agent turned down the offer on the grounds that Fox was liable to misleadingly advertise Jack as the picture's star. Fox *did* manage to talk Phil Silvers into a brief guest spot, however— and sure as shootin', Silvers was billed as star of the show in many of the regional ads.

Since the film's plotline and the quiz show device were not sufficient to fill up the allotted 70 minutes, musical highlights were called for—and here is where Foy truly lived up to his nickname "Keeper of the Bs." Why, reasoned Mr. Foy, should we go to the trouble of shooting new musical numbers when all we have to do is comb through the Fox archives and come up with excerpts from previous big-budget songfests? So it is that when the time comes for the hero to try for the $64 Question on *Take It or Leave It,* he chooses "Scenes from Motion Pictures of the Past" as his category. And despite the fact that we're supposed to be in a radio studio, Baker obligingly sets up projector and screen to regale us with the best that 20th Century–Fox has had to offer during the previous decade.

The first question involves Shirley Temple, so we see a film clip of the dimpled darling accompanying James Dunn in "Baby Take a Bow" from *Stand Up and Cheer* (1934). Subsequent questions yield clips from *Tin Pan Alley* (1940) with Betty Grable, Alice Faye and Billy Gilbert cutting a rug to "The Sheik of Araby"; *Orchestra Wives* (1942), spotlighting Glenn Miller and most of the rest of that film's cast; *The Great American Broadcast* (1941), highlighting specialties by the Wiere Brothers, the Ink Spots and the Nicholas Brothers; *One in a Million* (1936), featuring Sonja Henie and Borrah Minevitch and his Harmonica Rascals; *Rose of Washington Square* (1939), with Al Jolson (who threatened legal action for unauthorized use of his face and voice); *Hollywood Cavalcade* (1939), showing Buster Keaton throwing a pie at Alice Faye; *On the Avenue* (1937), showcasing the Ritz Brothers' "Oh Chychonya" number; and *King of Burlesque* (1936), with Fats Waller and Dixie Dunbar. (At one point Fox planned to use scenes that had been eliminated from previous films, such as the W.C. Fields segment in *Tales of Manhattan* [1942], but that really wouldn't have fit into the "Scenes from Motion Pictures of the Past" category.) Given the pastiche nature of the finished product, *Take It or Leave It* might as well have been titled *Take It, and Take It, and Take It, and Take It....*

In response to a popularity poll conducted among G.I. fans of the radio series, *Take It or Leave It* was shown to troops overseas before it was released in the United States—where, since the picture cost nothing to make, it could not help but earn a profit. We'll "Leave It" here to fill in the rest of the story, beginning with Baker's departure from the radio series in 1947 (except for a brief comeback in 1951), to be replaced by Garry Moore and then Eddie Cantor.

Retitled *The $64 Question* on September 10, 1951—by which time Jack Paar had taken over from Cantor—the series would continue until June 1, 1952. Throughout most of the radio run the producers had put up resistance to demands that they increase the grand prize from $64 to $640, but they eventually conceded, thereby paving the way for the enormously popular TV version of the 1950s, *The $64,000 Question*—and, many years and a few cheating scandals later, *The $128,000 Question*. Well into retirement during the heyday of the retitled TV incarnation of *Take It or Leave It,* Phil Baker died in 1963.

"I Love a Mystery" (1945–1946; 1973)

Whether or not *I Love a Mystery* was "the greatest radio program of all time!" as proclaimed (with exclamation point) by historian Jim Harmon, it was certainly the one adventure program that seems to have had the biggest impact on male listeners who grew up in the early 1940s. The program was created by Carlton E. Morse (1901–1993), the man also responsible for the polar-opposite soap opera *One Man's Family*. Having produced mystery melodramas since his early days in San Francisco radio, Morse saw *I Love a Mystery* as the apotheosis of all globetrotting soldier-of-fortune adventures—and to insure at least a surface authenticity, he buried himself in geographical reference works and books about archaic paganism and ancient superstitions.

Debuting as a nightly 15-minute serial over NBC's West Coast network on January 16, 1939, *I Love a Mystery* was the saga (and seldom has that word been more appropriate) of the three adventurers who comprised the A-1 Detective Agency, who worked sometimes for money, sometimes for duty, but mostly for the sheer excitement of it all. Jack Packard was the taciturn, maddeningly logical leader of the trio, a former medical student whose professional detachment when confronted by everything from serial killers to werewolves gave a new meaning to the word "stoic." His legendary imperviousness to the charms of the opposite sex was reportedly due to the unfortunate indiscretion in his youth that got him kicked out of college (or could it be that he was a ... ? *Naaaaw!*) In contrast, Jack's slightly ingenuous Texas-born sidekick Doc Long had a tongue hanging out for everything in skirts. A born scrapper, Doc's favorite expletive "Honest to my grandma" was most often uttered when he was confronted by a gang of murderous thugs, whom he delighted in taking on all at once; no fight was ever so enjoyable to Doc as when the odds were at least six to one against him. The third member of the team was Reggie Yorke, whose upper-crust British accent and inbred chivalry belied the fact that he could out-punch Jack and Doc combined. During the original Hollywood–based run of *I Love a Mystery* (which joined the full NBC web on October 2, 1939), Michael Raffetto, Barton Yarborough and Walter Paterson were respectively heard as Jack, Doc and Reggie.

The nature of the threesome's serialized adventures is implicit in such titles as "The Temple of Vampires," "Bury Your Dead Arizona," "Stairway to the Sun," "The Pirate Loot of Island of Skulls," "The Twenty Traders of Timbuktu" and "The Thing That Cries in the Night." For five years *I Love a Mystery* provided vicarious thrills to youngsters who dreamed of traveling to the farthest corners of the globe, battling villains both corporeal and spectral, and rescuing beautiful and grateful damsels. "Political correctness" was a concept unknown to *I Love a Mystery,* where violence, bloodshed and dismemberment were par for the course, the ladies wore next to nothing and sometimes not even that, and the best bad guys were those with the thickest accents and most fanatical religious convictions. It was ideal fare for the Theater of the Imagination, and any visual representation of the series could not help but fall short of expectations.

Not that Carlton E. Morse evinced any interest in transferring *I Love a Mystery* to the screen for the length its original radio run, during which the series changed networks to CBS and its format to 30 minutes per week. It was only after *I Love a Mystery* was cancelled on December 29, 1944, that Morse accepted an offer by Columbia Pictures to adapt the program as a B-picture series, in hopes of matching the popularity of the studio's other radio-generated movie franchises *Crime Doctor* and *The Whistler* (both q.v.). In an unusual move, Columbia engaged Barton Yarborough to recreate his radio role as Doc Long, which hardly involved much negotiation since Yarborough was already contracted to the studio. According to Jim Harmon, Michael Raffetto was not "deemed suitable" to play Jack Packard onscreen, so Columbia again dipped into its contract pool and came up with Jim Bannon, then quite busy both in films and on radio (he had at one point announced the commercials on *I Love a Mystery*). Those fans of the series who wonder why Reggie Yorke does not appear in the Columbia films are referred to John Dunning's *On the Air,* where it is chronicled that Reggie had been written out of the radio version in 1942 after the suicide of actor Walter Paterson. In the films, Yorke's erudition became a part of Jack

Jim Bannon, who played Jack Packard in Columbia's movie version of radio's *I Love a Mystery*, appears to be on his guard in this 1945 studio portrait for the first film in the series.

Packard's repertoire, essentially making Jack two characters in one.

Henry Levin directed all three *I Love a Mystery* films. The first series entry *I Love a Mystery* (1945) is introduced in radio fashion with an unseen narrator heralding "the adventures of Jack Packard and Doc Long"—though the original series' haunting theme song, Sibelius' "Valse Triste," is not used here nor in the two subsequent films. The screenplay was adapted by Charles O'Neal from Morse's 20-chapter *I Love a Mystery* radio continuity "The Decapitation of Jefferson Monk," a title referenced by the narrator during the opening credits. In later years Morse would admit that he wrote his radio scripts on the fly, never quite figuring out the resolution of the mystery or the identity of the killer until he came to the final chapter. But since its radio source story had already come and gone by 1945, the movie *I Love a Mystery* knows exactly where it is going from first frame to last, even audaciously opening with Jefferson Monk losing his head in an accident.

The rest of the film unfolds in flashback, and occasionally flashbacks within flashbacks; the question is not so much what is going to happen but how, why and who is responsible. Dominating the proceedings is the splendidly satanic George Macready as Monk, who has been given the prophecy that he will die of decapitation within three days. The coolheaded Jack and the hotheaded Reggie are drawn into the case by accident and indirection, but once committed the two adventurers are determined to either rescue Monk or find out who hates him enough to kill him—or, optimistically, both. Vital elements include a sinister Oriental cult, a million-dollar legacy, a wheelchair-bound wife (Nina Foch), a glib femme fatale (Carole Mathews), a shady psychiatrist (Lester Matthews), and a peg-legged stalker, who is revealed *not* to be the principal villain in a sudden, violent fashion. And despite a "logical" denouement, Jack Packard shares our doubts as to whether logic plays any role in what has gone before. Remarkably evocative of the radio program, *I Love a Mystery* packs a wealth of incident into a scant 69 minutes, but never feels rushed or forced. Though not as expansive in scope as the original radio serial, the film is one of the finest programmers Columbia ever turned out.

For the inaugural series entry, Bannon receives top billing, and Barton Yarborough is consigned to fourth place even though Jack and Doc function as a team throughout. This situation is reminiscent of an earlier dust-up that occurred in radio's *I Love a Mystery,* when after Michael Raffetto and Yarborough were promised star billing by Morse, the producer reneged on the deal, pleading "it was out of my hands." In letters written to his family, Bannon indicated that Morse's actual involvement in the Columbia series didn't extend much beyond granting the studio the film rights, so again he was powerless in matters of billing. In the second film in the series, *The Devil's Mask* (1946), Bannon is billed second to Anita Louise (which he apparently didn't mind since he enjoyed working with the actress), while Yarborough is consigned to fifth place. And in the third and final entry *The Unknown* (1946), Bannon is billed under Karen Morley and Yarborough has plummeted to sixth place. This cavalier treatment was reportedly the reason that Yarborough balked at recreating Doc Long in Morse's short-lived 1948 ABC radio spinoff *I Love Adventure* (for the first eight episodes, anyway), though the actor was content to play Clifford Barbour on Morse's NBC soaper *One Man's Family* until his death in 1951.

The Devil's Mask boasts a well-sustained atmosphere of nightmarish foreboding, and a few narrative grace-notes that would have done Morse proud, such as a string of cryptic clues lifted from "The Rime of the Ancient Mariner." Otherwise, the film doesn't quite live up to the standard set by *I Love a Mystery.* For all the exotica involving shrunken heads, poison darts and marauding panthers, *The Devil's Mask* is at heart a traditional grade-B mystery melodrama with such stock characters as the prime suspect who must have majored in Red Herring 101, and the "hidden" murderer whose identity is obvious ten minutes before any murder has been committed.

The last entry *The Unknown* is a heavily camouflaged rewrite of the *I Love a Mystery* radio serial "The Thing That Cries in the Night," involving madness and murder among the members of a dysfunctional family in a decaying Kentucky mansion—which, in a typical Columbia economy move, is the same backlot edifice that stood in for the lavish New York estate of Jefferson Monk in *I Love a Mystery*. The film's lengthy opening sequence is an unacknowledged swipe from Hitchcock's *Rebecca* (complete with elegiac off-screen narration by Karen Morley), with a bit of Edgar Allan Poe tossed in. Jack and Doc don't even show up until 15 minutes into the story, which thereafter moves along rather stodgily to a fairly exciting climax focusing on Columbia contractee Miss Jeff Donnell (as she was often billed) in a rare non-comic role.

The *I Love a Mystery* film series proved unsatisfying to devotees of the radio program ("Where are the vampire bats? The 9000-foot waterfalls? The slashed throats?") and not sufficiently profitable at the box office to warrant a continuation after the third installment. As for the radio version, after the previously mentioned attempt to redress the property as *I Love Adventure* the series assumed its original title for a nightly Mutual network run beginning October 3, 1949. Morse recycled many of the scripts from the earlier *I Love a Mystery,* but the cast was all new, with Russell Thorson as Jack, Robert Dryden as Doc, and 29-year-old Tony Randall as Reggie. Morse purists regarded the New York–based Mutual version (from which most currently available recordings are derived) to be but a pale shadow of the wild 'n' woolly Hollywood original, but the series' new fans kept the property alive and kicking until December 26, 1952.

Fifteen years later, the "camp" craze stimulated by the TV series *Batman* inspired Universal Television to get behind a 97-minute *I Love a Mystery* pilot film, written and directed by Leslie Stevens (*The Outer Limits*). Like *The Unknown,* the teleplay was based on Morse's "The Thing That Cries in the Night," with insurance investigators Jack, Doc and Reggie showing up at a mysterious mansion in search of a vanished billionaire, and running afoul of a demented matriarch and her three nubile daughters. Jack was played by former talk-show host Les Crane, Doc by *future* talk-show host David Hartman, and Reggie by former and future bit player Hagan Beggs. The uniquely eccentric daughters Faith, Hope and Charity from the radio original are portrayed by a trio of Universal starlets who spend a lot of time in bikinis, which takes our minds off their acting.

Either out of disregard or contempt for the source material, *I Love a Mystery* is played in the same self-consciously cartoonish manner as *Batman,* with the three heroes speaking in short stilted sentences and finishing each other's thoughts, coming off more like Huey, Dewey and Louie than Jack, Doc and Reggie. For no reason other than someone thought it would be funny, Terry-Thomas shows up for a deadly cameo, while the "surprise" of Don Knotts being revealed as the kidnapped billionaire is totally botched by giving the actor star billing in the credits. Only Ida Lupino as the villainess manages to survive this mishmash with her reputation and integrity intact. Deemed too horrible for television exposure even by 1967 standards, *I Love a Mystery* would rust on the shelf until a single NBC telecast on February 27, 1973. If it ever plays in your town, don't fail to miss it.

Duffy's Tavern (1945)

Born Eddie Poggenburg in 1905, Ed Gardner was a busy network radio director working through the J. Walter Thompson advertising agency when in 1939 he was assigned an episode of the CBS series *This Is New York*. Though he personally knew practically every radio actor from major star to bit player, Gardner simply could not find a performer to properly fill an important role on the program. The problem was the character's thick New York accent, which most of the auditionees were unable to master. In desperation, Gardner demonstrated exactly how the character should sound—and ended up playing the part himself. Fleshed out as a sardonic Manhattan tavern manager named Archie, this character would be provided with an expanded showcase in a tryout program heard July 29, 1940, on the CBS anthology

Forecast. This effort "flew," and on March 1, 1941, Ed Gardner's Archie swung open the doors of the weekly, half-hour situation comedy *Duffy's Tavern*.

Located on Third Avenue and 23rd Street, the titular tavern was advertised as "Where the Elite Meet to Eat," but there was nothing elite about the place beyond the slogan. Duffy's Tavern was internationally famous for its rotten food, rotten liquor, rotten service, rotten atmosphere and rotten manager Archie, who opened each episode by answering the phone and carrying on a conversation with the joint's never-seen owner Duffy. Other regulars included the owner's nasal-voiced daughter Miss Duffy, played by Gardner's wife Shirley (*Hazel*) Booth until their 1942 divorce, and thereafter by a number of actresses, most memorably Florence Halop and Sandra Gould; moronic steady customer Clifton Finnegan, whose every sentence began with a drawn-out "Duuuuuh" and who was played throughout the series' run by Charlie Cantor; and down-to-earth waiter Eddie, played by black actor Eddie Green, whose cynical give-and-take with Archie was the era's most racially liberated radio repartee this side of Jack Benny and Rochester.

For reasons nobody ever got around to explaining, dingy Duffy's Tavern was a favorite hangout for top-rank show biz celebrities, including movie stars James Cagney, Basil Rathbone and Madeleine Carroll, such Broadway luminaries as Gertrude Lawrence and Tallulah Bankhead, singers ranging from Dinah Shore to Lauritz Melchior, sports figures along the lines of Bill Tilden and Leo Durocher, acknowledged intellectuals like Deems Taylor, and on at least one occasion a fairly well-known "tavernkeeper" in his own right, Prince Michael Romanoff. One of the most consistently hilarious series of its time, *Duffy's Tavern* trafficked in a steady stream of wisecracks and insults, with all the aforementioned giants of the entertainment world (and many many others) enthusiastically getting down and dirty with Archie and his pals. And no discussion of the series would be complete without mentioning Archie's merciless mangling of the English language ("Leave us not jump to seclusions," "Don't infirm that I'm stupid," "Wait'll she gets a load of my personal maggotism"), assaulting the eardrums with more malaprops and mispronunciations than Amos 'n' Andy, Jimmy Durante, Leo Gorcey and Archie Bunker bundled together.

CBS (and later NBC) issued publicity shots of *Duffy's* showing Ed Gardner wearing a porkpie hat, clutching a telephone as if it were an assault weapon, and grimacing like a man who has just

Ed Gardner, creator-star of *Duffy's Tavern*, poses in his "lucky" apron, autographed by every one of the series' guest stars.

broken a tooth on a kumquat. Since everyone already knew what Archie looked like, there was little "surprise" value in launching a film version of *Duffy's Tavern* in late 1944, so Paramount Pictures had to dream up a different angle to draw in customers. That angle was one the studio had been playing since 1932's *The Big Broadcast* (q.v.)., and during the war years with extravaganzas like *Star Spangled Rhythm* and *Here Come the Waves*. The strategy was to populate the movie adaptation of *Duffy's Tavern* with practically every major name on the Paramount payroll. And why not? The radio series was already top-heavy with guest stars, and the movie would merely be a ten-reel extension of an established precedent. Or maybe "expansion" would be a more appropriate word. Well, all right then: an elephantization.

Worked over by nine credited writers (including the radio series' Abe Burrows and Bob Schiller, as well as Gardner himself) from a story by Norman Panama and Melvin Frank, the movie version of *Duffy's Tavern* took the liberty of blending the craven selfishness of the radio Archie with the milk of human kindness, albeit slightly curdled. A great pal of bibulous phonograph record manufacturer Michael O'Malley (Victor Moore)—and the would-be hubby of O'Malley's attractive daughter Peggy (Marjorie Reynolds)—Archie has been giving free food and drinks to fourteen workers from O'Malley's factory who were laid off by the wartime shortage of shellac. Of course he has done this without the pinchpenny Duffy's knowledge, so it's panic time when Miss Duffy (Ann Thomas, one of the few established radio actresses who *didn't* play this role on the air) shows up to examine the books. The fact that he loses Peggy's heart to handsome returning GI Danny Murphy (Barry Sullivan) doesn't vex Archie nearly as much as the realization that the bank has turned down O'Malley for a loan—and that the tavern's till is short by $1,200. To save both the tavern and the record plant from falling into the hands of creditors, Archie throws a huge fund-raising block party chock full of free entertainment. And *what* entertainment! By a miraculous stroke of fortune, Peggy works as switchboard operator at a posh hotel where several top Paramount film stars are stopping over—and, gloriosky, *every single one* of these superstars is willing to help put on Archie's show free for nothin'.

Chosen to direct this hodgepodge was Hal Walker, a former assistant director who'd gained a reputation in Hollywood for his skill at smoothing the ruffled egos of big stars while simultaneously persuading them to toe the line on the set. Bing Crosby, Bob Hope and Dorothy Lamour held Walker in such high esteem that they insisted he be promoted to full director for their joint starring effort *Road to Utopia*. *Duffy's Tavern* was his second such assignment, though thanks to Paramount's habit of overproducing and stockpiling their films *Duffy's* was released ahead of *Utopia*. It was lucky indeed for Walker that he'd already completed two more films before the world premiere of *Duffy's Tavern* on September 28, 1945: A picture like this could have been a career-killer for any fledgling director.

Our first inkling that *Duffy's Tavern* is going to be a bumpy ride is the opening scene in the tavern itself. To the studio's credit, Paramount engaged three of the stars of the radio version to recreate their roles on film: Gardner as Archie, Charlie Cantor as Finnegan, and Eddie Green as Eddie. But there's something a bit off-kilter here. The radio word pictures of Duffy's Tavern have conditioned us to anticipate a grease-splattered, vermin-infested pigsty, littered with dirty dishes, scummy shot glasses and rotting foodstuffs. But the tavern we see on screen is cozy, well-ordered and spotlessly clean, looking no different nor any worse than your favorite neighborhood pub. As for Archie, the craggy, wizened, unkempt Manhattanite of the publicity shots has been replaced by a freshly scrubbed, affable-looking chap with every button buttoned and every hair in place. He could almost pass as a real human being—and that's the last thing any true *Duffy's Tavern* fan wants from Archie. Similarly, Charlie Cantor bears no resemblance to the Finnegan of our imagination, nor even the squirrelly, chrome-domed Charlie Cantor we remember from his cameo appearances on TV's *Jack Benny Program*. He even sports a lavish toupee which makes him appear to be a slightly younger Ringo Starr. Only Eddie Green looks precisely the way he's supposed to look—and accordingly, he comes across as the most impressive of the three radio carryovers.

After spending what seems like a fortnight establishing the story, the film lulls us into the misapprehension that it's not going to be such a trial to sit through after all with a few truly funny vignettes. Preparing to visit his girlfriend, Archie can't find his aftershave and asks Eddie to go fetch the Bay Rum. Glaring back, Eddie replies contemptuously, "You done used up the Bay Rum on the Cuba Librés." And after going out on a bender, Archie and O'Malley groggily try to stuff themselves in the refrigerator to determine once and for all if the little light goes out when you shut the door.

Then the rot sets in. Hoping to contact the Paramount stars and ask them to entertain at the block party, Archie and O'Malley disguise themselves as painters and worm their way into a succession of celebrity suites. They come across Paulette Goddard in a bubble bath, a one-joke situation that goes nowhere. Betty Hutton mistakes the two bumblers for masseurs, leading to some limb-contortion gags that wouldn't have raised a chuckle in the Keystone days. And after overhearing a sinister scheme to blow up a war factory, Archie and O'Malley break down the door and tackle Alan Ladd to the ground—whereupon Veronica Lake testily explains that they're not planning any sort of sabotage but are instead (brace yourself for the shock) rehearsing a movie scene. The only spot gag that even remotely works was lifted from the Marx Brothers' *Monkey Business* (1931), in which a guy on a mission enters a door marked MEN, only to be violently tossed out on his ear when it is revealed that the first two letters of the word WOMEN have been covered up. Unfortunately, this gag was utterly neutered by the Hollywood censors, who demanded that *before* the unfortunate fellow (played by William Demarest) strolled through that door, it had to be laboriously established that he wasn't *really* entering the women's lavatory but instead merely a powder room "where women may be adjusting their makeup or perhaps sitting on a sofa—but nothing more."

Then there's the block-party variety extravaganza, which consumes nearly a third of the film's running time. On the plus side, every effort is made in this sequence to echo the roughneck charm of *Duffy's Tavern*. On the minus side, almost every effort fails miserably. No one expects subtlety or decorum from the raucous musical turns by Betty Hutton and Cass Daley, so we'll withhold comment except to say that both ladies are up to their usual standard. What really lays the climax low are the allegedly comic sketches by the "straight" actors, who generally come off even worse than those flavor-of-the-week guest stars on *Saturday Night Live*. While it is amusing to see Eddie Bracken playing the much-abused stunt double of a pampered cowboy star, we cannot say the same for a blackout sketch consisting of Veronica Lake getting slapped around by Howard da Silva while poker-faced Alan Ladd does nothing. The nadir arrives with two attenuated routines involving Bing Crosby, who almost without trying manages to seriously damage his reputation as America's Favorite Entertainer. In one yawn-provoking sequence, Robert Benchley gathers together Crosby's four real-life sons to tell them their father's life story. (Concerned about the boys' schooling, Bing's wife Dixie Lee would not allow the kids to appear in the film unless it was during Christmas break—the only time on record that the Crosby family ever botched up a Yuletide event.) And in the grand finale, Bing performs a self-referential takeoff of his recent *Going My Way* song hit "Swinging on a Star," with Dorothy Lamour, Betty Hutton, Cass Daley, Sonny Tufts, Billy De Wolfe, Howard da Silva and Diana Lynn contributing satirical lyrics of their own. You know you're in trouble when Sonny Tufts is the funniest guy in the room.

The only block party performers who are seen to their best advantage are the two least known members of the troupe, dancers Johnny Coy and Miriam Franklin. Their charming dance pantomime of a returning GI's courtship and marriage almost, but not quite, compensates for all the mediocrity surrounding them.

It's a shame that this number has nothing to do with either *Duffy's Tavern* or Ed Gardner.

Accruing better reviews and business than it deserved, *Duffy's Tavern* did no damage to the radio series, though it's worth noting that the program's guest-star roster slowly diminished after the film's release. *Duffy's* remained on NBC until 1952, by which time Gardner had moved the show, its cast and its crew to Puerto Rico as a tax shelter. (During this period he also produced a film in San Juan, *The Man with My Face,* in which he did not appear.) A syndicated half-hour TV sitcom version of *Duffy's Tavern* produced in 1954 brought Gardner back before the cameras, here looking far more like the "real" Archie than he had nine years earlier; but this version made very little impact and folded after 39 episodes. Gardner died in 1963, four years after his Archie voice had been cleverly approximated by Daws Butler for the character of feline gumshoe Super Snooper on the Hanna-Barbera TV cartoon series *Quick Draw McGraw.*

And speaking of cartoons, mention must be made of Warner Bros.' *Hush My Mouse* (1946), set in "Tuffy's Tavern" with Mel Blanc doing spot-on imitations of Gardner's Archie and Charlie Cantor's Finnegan, here reimagined as a pair of alley cats. Running a brisk seven minutes, *Hush My Mouse* manages to convey more of the fun and flavor of the original *Duffy's Tavern* than all 97 minutes of the benighted Paramount version.

People Are Funny (1946)

Only on radio could the idea of a spontaneous human interest "stunt" show have achieved lasting success in the 1940s. Certain vaudeville performers would occasionally invite people from the audience to participate in the frivolity on stage, but these participants were usually "plants" in the performer's employ. Olsen & Johnson's Broadway hit *Hellzapoppin'* incorporated audience members in a handful of sketches, but never throughout the entire show; also, these "civilians" were carefully coached onstage by Olsen & Johnson to deliver pre-written lines as buildup to a punchline delivered by one of the professional performers, so any actual spontaneity was minimal. But the freewheeling, largely ad libbed ambience of the average radio game show or contest program demanded the involvement of non-professionals from the audience, not only to play the game and win the prizes but also to provide the master of ceremonies with natural-born stooges and patsies. The one-on-one intimacy of live radio already made listeners feel as if they were part of the action; the audience participation program extended this feeling to its logical conclusion.

On most such programs—Kay Kyser's *Kollege of Musical Knowledge,* Phil Baker's *Take It or Leave It,* etc.—the emcee was the star. Producer John Guedel (1913–2001) reversed this setup by making the contestants the focal point of the show. After spending several years writing gags for comedy producer Hal Roach and various newspaper cartoonists, Guedel sweet-talked his way into a job with a radio ad agency, pitching an hour-long stunt show inspired by familiar parlor games, for which he made an audition record in 1938. This led to his first audience participation program *Pull Over Neighbor,* heard locally in Los Angeles; the program's inaugural stunt was persuading an audience member to sing "Smiles" while ice cubes were stuffed in his mouth. On this show and its successor *All Aboard,* Guedel came to realize that some of the biggest laughs on radio could be garnered from the humor inherent in average, everyday people, especially when encouraged to cut loose and act silly. It was only natural that *All Aboard* would ultimately matriculate into a show titled *People Are Funny.*

While producing Red Skelton's variety series in 1942, Guedel happened to read a trade paper article about a cancelled NBC radio program. He contacted the defunct program's ad agency and suggested that his new "human interest" show (the phrase used instead of "audience participation") would make an excellent replacement. Guedel's first choice as host for *People Are Funny* was freelance announcer Art Linkletter (1912–2010), who'd gained a measure of fame as radio director and resident interviewer for the 1939 San Francisco World's Fair. Throughout his six-decade broadcasting career, Linkletter would insist that he possessed no marketable skill other than the gift of gab. For Guedel, that was enough: The genial Linkletter's talent for ad libbing, moving a program along with speed and efficiency, and putting "average" people at ease before the microphone was just what Guedel needed to keep *People Are Funny* bouncing for 30 minutes weekly. However, NBC's choice for emcee was Art Baker, the host of such popular Los Angeles programs as *Tapestries of Hollywood* and *Art Baker's Notebook*. *People Are Funny* debuted April 10, 1942, with Baker as host and Linkletter as cohost—and from that moment on there was no love lost between the two lively Arts.

The key to *People Are Funny*'s success was the comedy of embarrassment: The more ridiculous the stunt (ranging from giving money away on the streets of Hollywood to registering a trained seal as a hotel guest), and the more humiliation piled upon the contestant, the more the audience howled—and human nature being what it is, no one laughed louder than the "victim." To heighten the hilarity, the contestants were set upon by antagonists who were actually working for *People Are Funny,* and whose job it was to make the player's task more difficult than under normal circumstances. In certain cases, a stunt would be drawn out over several weeks, with the amount of the prize increasing the more the contestant endeavored to fulfill his end of the bargain—the entertainment value likewise increasing as the hapless participant found himself sinking deeper and deeper into a comedy morass as the weeks rolled on. The listeners at home were also invited to participate in *People Are Funny* with a variety of write-in guessing games and nationwide treasure hunts, with the winners getting to appear on the program and collect their prizes.

Eighteen months into the show, the backstage animosity between Baker and Linkletter reached the crisis level; Baker was then fired and Linkletter promoted to full host. Thereafter, so far as the public was concerned Art Linkletter was *People Are Funny* and *People Are Funny* was Art Linkletter, and would remain so until the series ended both its radio and television runs in 1960. Thus, while Linkletter would be the last person on earth to call himself an actor (try sitting through his performance in the 1950 film *Champagne for Caesar*), there was no question of his appearing in the motion picture adaptation of *People Are Funny* being developed in late 1944 by Paramount's Pine-Thomas unit, which had paid $25,000 for the film rights.

After several years' experience as Paramount staff producers, William H. Pine and William C. Thomas set up their own independent unit at the studio in 1941, assembling low-budget action films with such second-echelon stars as Richard Arlen and Chester Morris. Pine and Thomas soon gained wide renown as the "Two Dollar Bills" because of their infallible knack for accruing huge profits on each picture while spending as little as possible on production. By 1944 the producers were showing signs of higher ambitions, interrupting their flow of aviation yarns, murder mysteries and outdoor actioners with the elaborate (but still modestly budgeted) musical *Take It Big*. Heading the cast was Broadway comedian Jack Haley, who despite his iconic performance as the Tin Man in *The Wizard of Oz* had never truly scored in films. Having recently endured the humiliation of playing second fiddle to Frank Sinatra in RKO's movie adaptation of his own Broadway hit *Higher and Higher,* Haley was most receptive when Pine-Thomas offered him the opportunity to appear in a string of films in which he was unquestionably the leading player. Also in *Take It Big* were bandleader Ozzie Nelson and his vocalist wife Harriet Hilliard (see separate entry).

Around this same time, producer Sam White (see entry for *Reveille with Beverly*) was invited to take over an entire B-unit at Paramount to produce musicals similar to *Take It Big*. White turned down the offer because he felt that being in charge of mass production tended to stifle creativity. Instead he accepted an offer from Pine-Thomas to produce their upcoming film version of *People Are Funny,* for which he was promised full creative control. Coincidentally, the film would be shot not on Paramount's main lot but in rented studio space on Santa Monica Boulevard, where Sam White's brother

A full-page magazine spread for the 1946 cinema adaptation of radio's *People Are Funny,* featuring virtually the entire cast.

Jack had once produced successful two-reel comedies for Educational Pictures.

Discussing *People Are Funny* for biographer David Bruskin, White recalled, "It was a very, very tough nut to crack in terms of a script into which you could inject musical numbers where they belong in the story.... The basic format [of the radio show] was funny, but to put it in a picture and get a story around it wasn't easy. I finally developed a storyline with Maxwell Shane, the key writer at Pine-Thomas." Either by accident or design, White and Shane hit upon the same formula used in a previous radio-to-movie adaptation, 1941's *Pot o' Gold* (q.v.) In that picture, the creation of the titular radio game show served as the climax to a story fictionalizing the events leading up to that creation. But unlike the 1941 film, which didn't even mention its radio show inspiration until after an hour or so of unrelated comic and romantic complications, *People Are Funny* featured an embryonic version of Guedel's radio series in its first two reels, then spent the remainder of the picture detailing the efforts made by Guedel to sell the program to a national network and sponsor.

As the story of *People Are Funny* would have it, John Guedel is an unsuccessful producer in desperate need of a program concept that will appeal to priggish sponsor Ormsby Jamison. Guedel solicits the aid of his erstwhile sweetheart, writer Corey Sullivan, who is presently in Las Vegas. Hitching a ride back to L.A. with saxophone player Leroy Brinker, Corey finds herself in the audience of a Clearwater, Nevada, radio station, watching a broadcast of a zany audience-participation show produced and directed by town druggist Pinky Wilson. Sensing that he could package this program himself and thus cheat Guedel out of the opportunity, Brinker (accurately described as a "first-class heel") conspires with Corey to steal a transcription of Pinky's broadcast, at the same time persuading the naïve Mr. Wilson to sign over all rights to his program. As it turns out, Corey is really working in Guedel's interests, intending to double-cross the eminently double-crossable Brinker. Coerced into heading to Hollywood to participate in the first national broadcast of his show, now titled *People Are Funny* and emceed by Art Linkletter, Pinky makes the colossal blunder of mistaking Ormsby Jamison for a contestant, running the outraged sponsor ragged with a particularly sadistic stunt and drenching him with seltzer. Feeling that he has been set up to look like a fool, the dejected Pinky prepares to return to Clearwater in disgrace, but changes his mind when *People Are Funny* turns out to be a smash success thanks to the persistence of Corey and Guedel, and the inherent humor of the contestants.

Jack Haley was already set to play Pinky Wilson (with Clara Blandick, *Wizard of Oz*'s Auntie Em, as Pinky's grandmother!), while up-and-coming Paramount contract actress Helen Walker was tapped for the part of Guedel's girlfriend Corey Sullivan. (It would have been nice if Corey had been played by the real Guedel's future wife, actress Helen Parrish, but you can't have everything.) Pine-Thomas managed to snag Rudy Vallee, then well into the second phase of his movie career as a character comedian, for the part of Jamison. Fresh from his wartime stint with the Coast Guard, Vallee was so enthusiastic about the project that he was willing to poke fun at his crooner image with a scene in which he fondly retrieves a megaphone from a place of honor in his trophy room. Producer Sam White had pleasant memories of Vallee (not everyone did!), claiming that the singer "especially wanted to meet me and inject his ideas into the script. With his typical 'down East' manner, he has a good sense of humor."

As the sneaky, duplicitous Leroy Brinker, Ozzie Nelson is a decidedly offbeat casting choice, since the character completely flies in the face of Nelson's amiable-bumbler TV image. Chances are that Oz was delighted to play the villain (albeit a charming and amusing one), especially since it was on behalf of his old friend and associate Guedel, who back in 1944 had encouraged Ozzie and Harriet Nelson to try their luck with a radio situation comedy. As for Guedel, he took a pass on playing "himself" in *People Are Funny*; the role went instead to Pine-Thomas contractee Philip Reed, a former RKO leading man who had just returned from military service. Both the script and Reed's performance capture many of the genuine eccentricities of Guedel, a man who in real life magnanimously bestowed the title of vice-president on every person in his production company—including himself.

Evidently screenwriter Maxwell Shane had solved the problem of logically integrating the songs into the story, since not one of the tunes nor any of the guest artists come off as arbitrary or gratuitous—even when they have nothing to do with the plot proper. The film opens during a broadcast of Guedel's soon-to-be-cancelled variety show, with Frances Langford singing "I'm in the Mood for Love," a number curiously missing from most available public-domain prints of *People Are Funny*. During Pinky Wilson's program on Clearwater station CRBC (strange call letters for a non–Canadian outlet), Bob Graham, then the vocalist on radio's *Duffy's Tavern,* portrays a contestant named Luke who takes part in a goofy stunt (a bear licks honey off his feet) before singing Duke Ellington's "Every Hour on the Hour." When Pinky's next-door neighbors hold a mini-fiesta, Pinky joins singer-guitarist Tito Guizar and dancers Lilian Molineri and Rosarita Valera for the exuberant production number "Hey Jose." In the midst of a business conference at NBC, Ormsby Jamison impulsively launches into a rondelay version of "Alouette," coercing several studio employees (including such familiar bit players as Eddie Kane, Billy Bletcher and Billy Benedict) to join in on each chorus. And weaving in and out of the picture as would-be radio artistes are the Vagabonds, a novelty quartet that producer White had developed while at Columbia Pictures. Other specialty performers include tangle-tongued monologist Roy Atwell (formerly of Fred Allen's radio program, and best known as the voice of Doc in Disney's *Snow White and the Seven Dwarfs*) as the mayor of Clearwater, and boogie-woogie pianist Ann Jenkins in one of the NBC studio segments.

The scenes which attempt to convey the ad libbed insanity of *People Are Funny* were inspired by authentic highlights from the radio program. During several broadcasts, Pine-Thomas rigged up a "Laff-o-Meter" to select the show's five funniest stunts. We've mention Bob Graham's close encounter with the sweet-toothed bear; other stunts recreated for the film include a man trying to roller-skate with a cake in his arms, another man sent out to Hollywood Boulevard to measure the runs in ladies' hoses, a vertigo-inducing spin in a prop airplane, and a William Tell act with the arrows shot by a supposedly nearsighted Indian.

These facsimile stunts get their fair share of laughs, and emcee Linkletter certainly works overtime to make it all look spontaneous. But in the final analysis *People Are Funny* suffers from the same handicap as every other film which has tried to visualize a genuine audience-participation program (*That's Right—You're Wrong, Radio Stars on Parade, Queen for a Day* et al.). Hiring Hollywood actors to portray the "real folks" contestants severely diminishes the verisimilitude needed to sustain the laughter. Had the film used a nonplussed nonprofessional as the poor schmo who is assigned to measure hosiery runs, the stunt would have been unbearably funny. Instead, the film uses comedian Joe DeRita, future "Curly Joe" of the Three Stooges—and because we are aware that he is a merely an actor being paid to make a fool of himself, our enjoyment of his embarrassment is considerably lessened.

Viewing a rough cut of *People Are Funny* shortly before its January 1946 release, Paramount production head Y. Frank Freeman enthused, "This is a real audience picture, and Paramount's going to make a lot of money out of it." Years later, White agreed, with qualifications: "It turned out to be a very good musical, but it didn't live up to my expectations. I didn't feel it had in it what I liked in a picture, basically because we didn't have the money to spend and because to adapt a radio show like that into a motion picture story was very superficial. It was difficult to get something in which you could actually believe the story." Having attended a screening of *People Are Funny* before an audience of Old Time Radio enthusiasts, this writer can affirm that the film still has the capability to entertain and amuse. And also that no one in that audience believed it for a minute, just as no one back in 1946 believed it for a minute—and didn't care that they didn't believe it. Heck, the war's over. Let's have some fun. People *are* funny, after all!

Breakfast in Hollywood (1946)

We now unfold a tale that may seem madness to a generation raised on such television personalities as Jerry Springer, Dr. Phil, Judge Judy and Kelly Ripa, and weaned on the plethora of squawk-shock-jocks that infest the radio airwaves before the noon whistle. And yet, it is all too true that there was once a time when the AM hours on both local and network radio were filled with middle-aged men sniggering like schoolboys, singing off-key, donning funny headgear and making cutesy-poo references to marriage, childbirth and body functions. All this for the benefit of studio audiences packed with blue-haired ladies wearing bad hats and worse jewelry, who giggled right along with those impish emcees, ritualistically played silly games, and accepted tacky little gifts as a reward for showing up in the same place at the same time. They were called "breakfast shows" in some markets, "morning shows" in others. Whatever the designation, this curious genre began in Chicago on June 23, 1933, with Don McNeill's daily NBC-Blue variety series *The Breakfast Club,* which somehow managed to survive on the Blue's successor ABC until December 27, 1968, along the way spawning scores of profitable imitations. Cincinnati broadcasting legend Paul Dixon was conducting a similar TV morning program as late as 1974, and he was far from the only laborer in this rich radio cornfield.

Second only to *The Breakfast Club* in coast-to-coast popularity was a daily meringue of entertainment, audience participation and human interest which premiered over Los Angeles station KFWB as *Breakfast on the Boulevard* on January 13, 1941, then was picked up for national play by NBC-Blue as *Breakfast at Sardi's* on August 3, 1942. Like McNeill's program, *Breakfast at Sardi's* relied heavily upon a live studio audience, with ladies sending in ticket applications months in advance for the opportunity to bask in the thrill of network radio. And like McNeill, *Sardi's* emcee Tom Breneman was a genial gent on the cloudy side of 40, who came to his current assignment with vast experience in several media venues (McNeill was a former newspaper journalist and radio comedian, Breneman an ex-vaudevillian and radio station manager). But while *Breakfast Club* was top-heavy with regular cast members, comedy routines, quizzes and cash prizes, *Breakfast at Sardi's* focused on playing the crowd, with Breneman strolling through the audience holding a portable baton-like microphone, asking non-rehearsed and often non sequitur questions of the gathered ladies just to see what sort of spontaneous answers he'd receive. If the answer provoked laughter, all the better: but if the answer was serious or elicited sympathy, that worked just as well. During the war years, Breneman's studio audience included male members of the armed forces, providing even more variety and stimulation to the give-and-take sessions.

Regular segments on *Breakfast at Sardi's* included "Wishing Ring," in which attractive rings supplied by Joseff's of Hollywood were given out to ladies who were then asked to reveal their fondest dreams; "Beauty Kit," wherein a case of cosmetics was raffled off to one of the lucky matrons; and a touching vignette which found Breneman presenting an orchid, delivered by "Joe the Express Boy," to the oldest woman in the audience. The daily ritual which invariably brought down the house was the moment when Breneman zeroed in on the female audience member wearing the silliest hat of the day— which he promptly placed upon his own head. There were actually publicity photos showing him doing this. Lots of them.

Two broadcasts of *Breakfast at Sardi's* were fed to the network each day to accommodate different time zones, with breakfast served in between; both broadcasts were completely unrehearsed, with Breneman often expressing on-air astonishment at how differently people behaved at 11 a.m. than at 8:30. Though the program originally emanated live from Sardi's restaurant on Hollywood Boulevard (except for the occasional location jaunt), in 1943 the title was changed to *Breakfast in Hollywood* to avoid confusion with the same-named dining establishment in New York. As the size of the studio audience continued to expand, Sardi's was no longer able to accommodate the crowd, so Breneman opened his own restaurant on Vine Street, where the series set up its microphones on March 10, 1945. It was "Breneman's in Hollywood" that served as the backdrop for the 1946 film adaptation of *Breakfast in Hollywood.*

Legend has it that producer Robert S. Golden had never heard of the radio series until he happened to stroll by Breneman's restaurant early one morn and got an eyeful of the block-long line of women waiting to get in even before the sun was up. This was incentive enough for

Golden to set up his own production firm and ink a deal with United Artists to release *Breakfast in Hollywood,* which began filming in the fall of 1945. The finished picture devotes over a third of its 90-minute running time (87 minutes in currently available prints) to a fairly accurate depiction of a "typical" *Breakfast in Hollywood* broadcast, with the plump and personable Breneman, portable mike in hand, wending his way through a maze of tables to make small talk with the audience and preside over the regular daily segments. Breneman delivers such an engagingly spontaneous performance throughout the film—even during the "plot" scenes—that his immense popularity should require no explanation for modern-day viewers.

The presence of celebrity guests on this particular broadcast may smack of contrivance, but in fact it was not unusual for film luminaries to drop in on *Breakfast in Hollywood,* either to perform or simply shoot the breeze with the host. Thus, there is nothing out of the ordinary for singer Andy Russell to perform three songs ("If I Had a Wishing Ring," "Magic Is the Moonlight," "Amor") nor for Spike Jones and his City Slickers to give out with a couple of cacophonous novelty numbers (including his hit single "Glow Worm"). Another of the film's musical acts, the (Nat) King Cole Trio, does not appear during the radio-show sequence, most likely because the producer was worried that their presence might cause the film distribution problems in the Jim Crow South. Still, the Trio is well represented with a brace of jumpin' jive tunes ("Solid Potato Salad," "It's Better to Be By Yourself"), strategically placed in scenes that could easily be removed from the film if necessary. Finally, gossip columnist Hedda Hopper shows up as part of the audience, bringing along a few "celebrity guests" of her own: the real-life mothers of Joan Crawford, Gary Cooper ... and Tom Breneman. The only aspect of the broadcast sequence that significantly strays from authenticity is the unlikely overabundance of familiar character actors like Sarah Padden and Robert Dudley in the "civilian" audience. Especially difficult to swallow—though highly hilarious—is the moment when Breneman interviews an engaged couple played by Amazonian Minerva Urecal and shrimpish Byron Foulger.

The radio-show sequence in itself would make an entertaining short subject, but with 60 minutes still to account for, *Breakfast in Hollywood* has to have some sort of plot. Screenwriter Earl Baldwin opts for the *Grand Hotel* device of spotlighting four seemingly unrelated characters whose personal stories are bound together by their attendance at a *Breakfast in Hollywood* broadcast. Going a step further, each of the main characters figures into one of the show's recurring segments. In order of billing, Bonita Granville plays small-town girl Dorothy Larsen, who shortly after arriving in L.A. to be reunited with her sailor fiancé participates in the show's "Wishing Ring" segment. Fifty-six-year-old Beulah Bondi is cast as 82-year-old widow Annie Reed, who as the oldest person on the show receives the coveted Orchid. Billie Burke portrays drab, neglected housewife Frances Cartwright, the winner of the "Beauty Kit" segment. And ZaSu Pitts does her usual as eccentric spinster Elvira Spriggins, whose sole purpose in life is to appear on *Breakfast in Hollywood* wearing a hat so ridiculous that Breneman will have no choice but to put it on himself.

Not content with this setup, Earl Baldwin conjures up ways to intertwine at least three of the subplots outside the walls of Breneman's. In fact, *Breakfast in Hollywood* comes off as a 1946 version of the 2004 Oscar-winner *Crash,* in which a number of disparate lives are woven together by a single traffic incident. On her way to the broadcast, Annie Reed is struck by a car driven by the philandering husband (Raymond Walburn) of Frances Cartwright. Annie is determined to get to *Breakfast in Hollywood* despite her injuries and does so, collapsing just before the program signs off. Elsewhere, Mrs. Cartwright takes advantage of her "Beauty Kit" prize by having a complete makeover—and as she leaves the salon she overhears her husband, who has just been released from jail, arranging a rendezvous with his current mistress. As for Dorothy Larsen, she attends the broadcast in the company of her fiancé's best friend Ken (Edward Ryan), who hasn't the heart to tell the girl that her dream lover is already married. By the time she learns the truth, Dorothy has fallen in love with Ken, though she refuses to admit it. All the loose plot ribbons are bowed up prettily when the hospitalized Annie gets a new lease on life by conspiring with Tom Breneman to bring Dorothy and Ken back together, using the girl's wishing ring as catalyst; and the newly glamorized Frances Cartwright finds herself in a position to give her husband the cold shoulder instead of the other way around—though she forgives him anyway. And just so no one is left out, Elvira Spriggins finally gets hold of a hat that is outlandish enough to warrant Breneman's attention, courtesy of Hedda Hopper. (Small wonder that this film's overseas title was *The Mad Hatter*.) Director Harold D. Schuster of *My Friend Flicka* fame handles the contrivances of *Breakfast with Hollywood* so adroitly that it seldom enters one's consciousness that Real Life *never* works out this conveniently.

The film's radio series source retained its popularly under the aegis of Tom Breneman until his sudden death at age 46 in May 1948. *Breakfast in Hollywood* limped along for a while with Garry Moore as host, but it just wasn't the same without Breneman; the program expired on January 13, 1950, gone and forgotten save for a couple of lukewarm revivals a few years later. And in case you're curious as to the fate of Breneman's of Hollywood, the restaurant eventually folded and the wired-for-sound building was converted into the West Coast branch of ABC Radio Center. .

Night Editor (1946)

Night Editor was one of several Golden Age radio series built around the versatility of a single actor. Elsewhere in this book we've cited Frank Graham's "one-man show" *Cosmo Jones, Crime Smasher*. Other protean actors like Paul Frees, Don Douglas and Marvin Miller were similarly heard in anthology series wherein all the voices were provided by one person—thus taxing the ingenuity of the writers, who had to stay up nights figuring out stories that didn't require any female characters. First heard on NBC's West Coast network in 1934, *Night Editor* was created by its star Hal Burdick (1893–1978), appearing under his own name as the title character. In each weekly 15-minute episode, "editor" Burdick related a human interest or crime yarn in flashback by changing his vocal inflection each time a new character was introduced. According to Burdick, the evening's story was always "suggested" by a reader of his newspaper, an agreeable artifice that proved remarkably durable. Sporadically picked up by the entire Blue Network and its successor ABC, *Night Editor* kept rolling along until 1945, then reverted to its regional status for an additional three years. (A TV series adaptation, also starring Burdick and following the same format, aired on the DuMont network in 1954.)

The series was sufficiently familiar to national audiences for Columbia to acquire the film rights in 1945 for a one-shot *Night Editor* B picture. At the time it was announced that William Gargan, previously seen in Columbia's "Ellery Queen" series, would play the title role. As the film's release date drew closer, more press releases surfaced indicating that young studio contractee Coulter Irwin, a former Associated Press reporter, would be seen as the Night Editor. But the Columbia flacks were wrong on both counts. When the 65-minute *Night Editor* was finally projected before a New York audience on March 29, 1946, it was Charles D. Brown who essayed the title character, renamed Crane Stewart. Irwin was seen as a novice reporter with a fondness for booze and babes, while Gargan was the poor moax whose melancholy history was related by Crane Stewart in flashback.

Directed by Henry Levin, the film was adapted by Hal Smith from "Inside Story," a *Night Editor* radio play written by Scott Littleton (and not, unfortunately, included in the group of series transcriptions currently available to collectors). As a warning to reckless young newshound Johnny (Irwin), the New York *Star*'s night editor Stewart recalls the story of homicide detective Tony Cochrane (Gargan), another man who was dissatisfied with his mundane life. Though he dotes on his young son (Michael Chapin), Tony has little time for his mousy wife Martha (Jeff Donnell), preferring the company of sexy sophisticate Jill Merrill (Janis Carter), the trophy wife of an elderly millionaire (Roy Gordon). Sneaking out for some clandestine canoodling along a deserted road, Tony and Jill witness a murder in progress. Knowing that they cannot reveal what they've seen without exposing their infidelity, the lovers swear one another to secrecy. It so happens, however, that Jill not only knows the murder victim personally, but also the murderer, whom she is currently blackmailing. Once his conscience catches up with him, Tony is willing to come clean and begs Jill to do the same: She doesn't, and tragedy ensues. An epilogue in "the present" finds Johnny expressing skepticism over Stewart's cautionary fable, until he learns the ultimate fate of Tony Cochrane's son—and there's still *another* surprise in store for him. (Twist endings were a specialty of the radio version, and this filmization disappointed no one.)

While it doesn't entirely transcend its B-picture trappings, *Night Editor* is a solid piece of filmmaking dominated by the alluring Janis Carter in one of the best of her many deadly-dame assignments. After languishing in obscurity for decades, a magnificently restored print of the film resurfaced in the early 21st century as part of Sony's *Bad Girls of Film Noir* DVD package.

Janis Carter gets all the attention in this ad for the 1946 filmization of the radio series *Night Editor,* though William Gargan (top right) and Frank Wilcox and Harry Shannon (lower left) struggle to draw focus to themselves—while the "Night Editor" himself, played by Charles D. Brown, is relegated to a tiny medium shot at the bottom of the page.

"Senator Claghorn" and *It's a Joke, Son* (1947)

With the exception of Minerva Pious' "Mrs. Nussbaum" in *It's in the Bag* (1945), comedian Fred Allen (q.v.) never brought along any members of his radio "family" when appearing in motion pictures. Nor would he have been able to feature the most prominent character in his "Allen's Alley" stock company, since this particular character didn't even exist until after *It's in the Bag* effectively ended Allen's sporadic stabs at movie stardom. One suspects, however, that if the aforementioned character *had* existed prior to 1945, Fred would have displayed enough showmanship to exploit it on screen. You've probably already guessed that we're discussing that big wind from the South known as Senator Beauregard Claghorn, whose popularity was phenomenal considering the fact that his weekly appearances on *The Fred Allen Show* never lasted any longer than two minutes.

"When I'm not appearing as Senator Claghorn, this is Kenny Delmar." In words to that effect, this was the standard self-introduction that the announcer for *The Fred Allen Show* gave himself at the beginning of each broadcast. Born in Allen's home town of Boston in 1910, Delmar spent his childhood touring in his mother and aunt's vaudeville act "The Delmar Sisters," taking time out in 1921 to make his film debut in D.W. Griffith's French Revolution epic *Orphans of the Storm*, playing Joseph Schildkraut's character as a boy. The Griffith picture was lensed in New York, where during the 1930s Delmar established himself as an actor and announcer in network radio. During Orson Welles' tenure as star of the weekly crime meller *The Shadow* (q.v.), Delmar was heard as Commissioner Weston, and later played a variety of *Shadow* supporting characters, usually villainous or maniacal in nature ("The branding iron is glowing now ... prepare yourself, Miss Lane!") Delmar also showed up on Welles' *Mercury Theater of the Air*, most notoriously during the Halloween 1938 broadcast of "War of the Worlds." Though CBS had imposed a ban upon depicting President Roosevelt in a dramatic context, Delmar's "Secretary of the Interior" sounded enough like FDR to convince many listeners that the president himself was authenticating the Martian invasion. (Welles would later chuckle that the panic really started the moment Delmar stepped before the microphone and implored the public to remain calm.)

Delmar's subsequent credits included commercial spokesman for Lucky Strikes on *Your Hit Parade* and master of ceremonies for *The RCA Victor Show*, along with the usual quota of acting roles. One of the many minor characters Delmar played during this period was a bellicose Southerner named Counsellor Cartenbranch, heard during the 1944–45 season of *The Alan Young Show*. The prototype for this character had been filed in Delmar's memory banks back in 1929, when while hitchhiking to California he accepted a ride from a Texas cattleman whom the actor later identified as Cactus Jack. Forced to shout over the sound of his sputtering car motor, the Texan had fallen into the pattern of half-repeating everything he said: "Ah started out plantin' wheat—wheat, that is. And now—ah say, and *now* ah've got 500 acres. Acres, that is!" This amused Delmar as much as Cactus Jack's habit of underlining his occasional efforts at humor with "That's a *joke*, son!" and his insistence upon receiving a response from his young passenger while simultaneously never letting the boy get a word in edgewise: "Speak up, boy! What do ya say? Come on, boy, speak up!"

Fondly recalling this experience in later years, Delmar enjoyed imitating Cactus Jack at social occasions. During one such get-together in 1945, actress Minerva Pious was so impressed by the routine that she invited him to audition for her boss Fred Allen, who was resuming his radio show after a year's hiatus. Allen hired Delmar as his announcer for a salary of $350 per week (raising the performer's total compensation for all his radio work to $1,550 weekly), and also encouraged Kenny to write a couple of "Southern windbag" routines to perform on the air.

On October 7, 1945, *The Fred Allen Show* launched its first broadcast of the season with the new announcer rattling off a list of the series' regulars, concluding with, "If anybody cares who I am, it's Kenny Delmar." Allen and Delmar then exchanged a few witticisms, interrupted by Portland Hoffa's familiar "Mr. A-aallen." Preparing to take their regular opinion poll in Allen's Alley, Fred and Portland established the question of the evening: "How is the housing shortage affecting you?" Of the Allen's Alley regulars, only Minerva Pious' Mrs. Nussbaum had been carried over from Fred's previous seasons. Newcomers included Parker Fennelly as dry-witted Yankee farmer Titus Moody and Delmar as Senator Claghorn, a Southern-fried spin on the "Senator Bloat" character played by J. Scott Smart (see *The Fat Man*) during Allen's *Texaco Star Theatre* days.

Five minutes and 25 seconds into the broadcast, Fred knocks on the first door of Allen's Alley. The door opens, and the occupant declares (in a surprisingly slow and measured cadence), "Somebody—ah say, somebody knocked. Who was it?" He then introduces himself: "Senator Claghorn's the name. Claghorn, that is." It turns out that the Senator is from Deep Down South, "so far down South that mah family's treadin' water in the Gulf Stream." First laugh from the audience. "Where ah live we call the people from Alabama 'Yankees.'" A bigger laugh, then Claghorn starts gathering steam: "Don't butt in when a body's talkin', son. Try listenin', ah say, try listenin', you're bound to learn somethin'. Anything gets me down it's two people tryin' to talk at the same time. Ah got the floor, son, don't filibuster!" Unaccustomed to hearing the mighty Fred Allen shouted down by a bit player, the audience is really pumped up now. Allen poses the evening's question, and Claghorn replies that he can't get a hotel room in D.C. "For 20 dollars a day they give me a chair in the lobby and a sleepin' pill." Moderate laugh. "*Pill,* that is." Guffaws. Finally, Claghorn suggests eliminating the Office of Price Administration, which throughout the war had been imposing price ceilings on everything: "You put four walls under them ceilings, you got housing. So long, son. So long, that is." Long applause, then Allen sticks in his own two cents: "You know, I think the Senator's got something there. Got something there." In just one minute and 35 seconds, a star was born.

The following week's broadcast (not presently available to collectors, worse luck) cemented Claghorn's most durable catchphrase. Asked a question about the postwar employment situation, the Senator assures Allen, "We're investigatin' it, son.... Senator Pepper is red hot on the subject." No reaction. Claghorn breaks the dead air with, "Red hot, ah say!" Allen tries to cut in, but the Senator is on a roll. "That's a *joke,* son! It's witty! Pay attention!" Immense laughter—and there's no turning back now. Beginning with the broadcast of October 22, Allen himself is writing the Claghorn segments, investing them with the satiric hyperbole he did so well. The Senator is so xenophobic a Son of the South that he only drinks out of Dixie cups, refuses to wear a Union Suit, limits his diet to Georgia Crackers, never drives through the Lincoln Tunnel, avoids any movie starring Cary Grant, and only goes to Yankee Stadium when Dixie Walker is playing. Claghorn can't even bring himself to say "No" because N-O is the abbreviation for North. *North,* that is.

In the weeks to come, the magnificently awful puns cascaded from the Senator's lips, all relating to current politicians. "Congressman Coffey is boilin'. Coffee's boilin', that's a joke son!" "Senator Glass is all broken up. Glass! Broken! That's a joke, son." "Senator Byrd is ravin'. Bird! Raven! That's a joke, son. Ah keep pitchin' 'em, you keep missin' em. Pay attention, son!" So it went, with people running down Senator Hill, everyone glad to see Senator Akin back, and the legislation which Senator Rankin filed. (Rank 'n' file. That's a *joke,* son!) By March of 1946—at which time Senator Claghorn had been on the air for a sum total of, oh, 44 minutes—Gene Cook of *Life* magazine was writing that the character "is unquestionably the most quoted man in the nation." Especially by rival comedians, newspaper humor columnists, advertising copywriters and the kids on the playground who were flogging the Senator's "That a *joke,* son!" to death—so much so that Delmar eventually dropped the phrase, explaining to Louella Parsons that it had lost its charm through overuse. Not that Delmar was complaining: Senator Claghorn had within six months of his first appearance become a merchandising bonanza, yielding toys, dolls, watches, coloring books, phonograph records, commercial endorsements, and even a novelty compass that only pointed South.

Though no one analyzed the phenomenon at the time, it's safe to assume that the public's response to Claghorn had something to do with instant recognition of the character's many real-life counterparts, especially during the postwar years when the issue of civil rights became a rallying point for genuine Southern politicians of the "Dixiecrat" variety. Willing to say or do anything that would assure them their constituents' votes, these unreconstructed Confederates wrapped themselves in the Bars and Stripes, shamelessly exploiting eighty years of Southern resentment against Damn Yankee "carpetbaggers" and progressive politicians who had the temerity to suggest that the Jim Crow laws were medieval and odious. (As cartoonist Bill Mauldin once described the Old South, it was dead but it wouldn't lie down.) Though Allen was careful never to bring the race issue into the Claghorn segments (his network and sponsors wouldn't have let him anyway), listeners on the same political wavelength as the liberal-minded comedian had no trouble reading between the lines.

The funny thing was than Southern listeners enjoyed the lampoonish elements of Senator Claghorn as much as Northerners—with such vociferous exceptions as the real-life Senator whom, it was whispered, served as one of the character's prime inspirations. Arguably the most virulently anti-North, anti-black, pro-lynching politician in America, Mississippi Senator Theodore G. Bilbo was enraged by Claghorn, referring to the character as "silly and puerile" and a "peckerwood"—not to mention a personal slam on him. Though neither Allen nor Delmar directly responded to these complaints, a United Press article of July 29, 1946, reported that Hollywood producers Bryan Foy and Aubrey Schenck, then preparing a film built around the Senator Claghorn character, had offered Bilbo $500 to play the Senator whom Claghorn would defeat in the screenplay written by Robert E. Kent and Paul Girard Smith. Despite assurances that Bilbo would be permitted to enact the role "in any manner he pleases," the Senator declined. In this puckish spirit, the scriptwriters went ahead with their intention to spoof the Senator's nickname "Theodore 'The Man' Bilbo" by christening their character Sen. Alexander P. "The Man" Leeds—though this pointed barb was missing from the completed film, no doubt at the behest of a nervous studio lawyer.

That studio was Producers Releasing Corporation (PRC), which in December 1945 had posted a decent profit on *How Dooooo You Do!*, a film starring another popular radio "second banana," *The Eddie Cantor Show*'s Bert Gordon (see **The Eddie Cantor Connection**)—and figured that if they liked it once they'll love it twice. Though Delmar had been forced to turn down an offer from former colleague Orson Welles to appear in a Broadway musical version of *Around the World in 80 Days,* the PRC picture would be made during Allen's summer layoff, giving Delmar plenty of time for a paid vacation to Tinseltown, as well as numerous live promotional appearances to and from the movie capital. And despite the actor's decision to eliminate his most celebrated catchphrase from his portfolio, Delmar's first starring film would bear the title *It's a Joke, Son.*

The presence of proven movie commodity Bert Gordon in *How Doooo You Do!* had enabled PRC to justify a higher budget than the studio usually bestowed upon their productions (some of which came in for as little as $20,000!), including the hiring of other radio celebrities, the inclusion of musical numbers, and a running time of 80 minutes. But since Senator Claghorn was a new kid on the block with no film track record, PRC played it safe by focusing primarily upon the star and the storyline with no costly added attractions, limiting the running time to 63 minutes to keep the lab costs low. The usual result from this sort of economizing was a B picture that would be sold at B picture rates. But changes were underway at PRC in the summer of 1946; the tiny film factory at 7324 Santa Monica Boulevard was in the process of being acquired by Eagle-Lion Pictures, a British firm owned by J. Arthur Rank. The main purpose for this transaction was to provide Rank with a reliable American distributor for his own films. PRC's new head of production Arthur Krim felt that it was necessary to increase the quality of the studio's Hollywood-made films to keep apace of the British product. Gradually Krim weeded out PRC's quota of bottom-budget crime dramas, slapstick comedies, horror films and series westerns, with plans to concentrate on fairly ambitious pictures with bankable stars and comparatively lavish budgets up to $500,000. The icing on the cake was the rechristening of PRC as Eagle-Lion, solidifying the link between the British and American divisions.

A caricatured Kenny Delmar (left), in costume as Senator Claghorn, helps congratulate Eagle-Lion Films on the success of their maiden effort *It's a Joke, Son!* (1947).

Still in the planning stages during the last months of the old PRC regime, *It's a Joke, Son!* would not reap the benefits of the more generous budgets and upped production values of subsequent Eagle-Lion productions, but it was clear from the finished product that the creative people involved regarded it as a "special." Though still essentially a B, the film had a more polished look than the general run of PRC efforts, with energetic direction by Benjamin Stoloff, a hand-picked supporting cast of surefire laugh-getters (including canine celebrity Daisy from Columbia's *Blondie* series), superbly textured photography by Clyde DeVinna, a wall-to-wall musical score by Alvin Levin, and solid, substantial-looking interior and exterior sets, some utilizing rented facilities on the RKO Pathé backlot. All in all, it was a worthy selection for the first official Eagle-Lion release on January 15, 1947.

In tackling the challenge of fleshing out a leading character who had previously been confined to a weekly two-minute comic harangue, the screenwriters decided to dish up an "origins" story, explaining how Senator Beauregard Claghorn came to be Senator Beauregard Claghorn. The writers also threw in a dash of W.C. Fields in order to turn what could have been an annoying and wearisome blowhard into a more human and sympathetic figure. At first, it doesn't look like they're going to pull it off: Early scenes find him holding court in the main street of his home town, bombarding a reporter with fatuous opinions and overbearing Southern chauvinism. Hmmm.... if this is how the rest the picture is going to go, Claghorn has already shot his wad and we may as well head for the exit. But, no! The moment Claghorn sets foot in his crumbling ancestral mansion, the lion turns into a lamb and he unprotestingly allows himself to be humbled and browbeaten by his shrewish wife Magnolia (Una Merkel), who is every bit as formidable as any of W.C. Fields' film spouses. The Fields connection is further underlined by the presence of Claghorn's daughter Mary Lou (June Lockhart), who loves her daddy without question and refuses to pass judgment on his character blemishes. Claghorn reciprocates by helping Mary Lou keep her dates with boyfriend Jeff Davis (Kenneth Farrell) despite Magnolia's objections, a bit of emotional generosity that will pay dividends at the end of the film.

Now on to the plot. The local chapter of the Daughters of Dixie selects Magnolia as the first woman candidate for State Senate. This does not sit well with the town's slimy political boss Dan Healey (Douglass Dumbrille) nor his squirrelly "bought and paid for" candidate Leeds (Jimmy Conlin), so Healey persuades the ingenuous Claghorn to run for the Senatorial office as a third-party candidate, thereby splitting the ticket and defeating Mrs. Claghorn. Upon realizing that he's merely a cat's paw—and worse, that Healey is just another a no-good Yankee—Claghorn tones down his bombast and delivers a serious, common-sense speech to the voters, who respond enthusiastically to his honest and no-frills solutions to the issues that personally affect them. Terrified that Claghorn might actually win after all, Healey orders his henchmen to kidnap the candidate so that he will miss an all-important Town Hall meeting and thus disqualify himself. Tied to a chair and resigned to his fate, Claghorn is suddenly galvanized into action when he hears a faraway hillbilly band playing "Dixie"—or, as he refers to it, the National Anthem. Beating the thugs black and blue, Claghorn escapes, wins the nomination and ever-so-gently puts his termagant wife Magnolia in her proper place (she's not such a bad kid after all, but you already knew that).

Throughout the film, Delmar is seen in the white suit coat, string tie and wide-brimmed that he wore for his radio publicity photos. Though only 36, the actor does not rely upon makeup to convey his character's age, but instead upon his booming voice and body language, pulling off the illusion so well that you'd never guess he was younger than his screen wife Una Merkel. Though Claghorn runs the risk of coming off as a one-trick pony when stretched over six reels, Delmar manages to invest quite a lot of variety in his character, convincingly seguing between his comic and his "straight" scenes. And while neither Delmar's dialogue nor the script as a whole ever rise to the level of the sharp, biting wit of Claghorn's *Fred Allen Show* vignettes, it is amazing how well the film's clichéd, formulaic comedy material works in context. A high point in low-comedy hilarity is achieved when Claghorn accidentally spikes the punch served to the Daughters of Dixie, a scene capped by dear old Ida Moore delivering a fiery temperance speech while stewed to the gills.

Given preferred bookings in hundreds of regional and big-city theaters (including a world premiere in Austin, Texas), *It's a Joke, Son!* racked up excellent box-office returns wherever it played. Its success proved to be a cornerstone in Eagle-Lion's expansion plans, and it wasn't long before the studio was inking fat percentage-of-profit deals with such top Hollywood names as Abbott & Costello, Zachary Scott, Sydney Greenstreet, Joan Leslie, Franchot Tone, Paul Henreid, Jimmy Durante, Dennis O'Keefe and producer Walter Wanger. In fact, Eagle-Lion strove so hard to become a "class" operation that there would be virtually no more room for an unpretentious little number like *It's a Joke, Son!* Though the events in the film would seem to anticipate a sequel, if not an entire series of Senator Claghorn films, this was not the creative direction that Eagle-Lion was taking, and Kenny Delmar would never again star onscreen.

Delmar continued pulling double duty as announcer and actor on *The Fred Allen Show* until its final broadcast on June 26, 1949. He then moved on to Broadway, playing a Claghorn-like leading role in the successful (293 performances) musical comedy *Texas Little Darlin'.* This assignment prevented him from participating in a recreation of "Allen's Alley" on a 1950 television special, obliging Allen to prerecord the regulars' voices and substitute a quartet of marionettes. Delmar continued playing character parts on such New York–based TV programs as *School House, All Star Revue, Armstrong Circle Theater, Mack and Myer for Hire* and *Car 54 Where Are You* into the early 1960s; he also did extensive cartoon voiceover work for Total Television, providing the voice of the Hunter on *King Leonardo,* Commander McBragg on *Tennessee Tuxedo and His Tales* and Colonel Kit Coyote on *Go Go Gophers,* among others. Not long before his death in 1984, Delmar was making plans for a one-man stage show based on Senator Claghorn, testing material on various late-night talk shows hosted by people like Tom Snyder and Larry King. Had this plan come to fruition, Delmar would have been in the curious position of having to ask permission to play the role he created—not, as one might assume, from the estate of Fred Allen, but from Warner Bros.

Many animation histories have suggested that the garrulous rooster character Foghorn Leghorn introduced in the 1946 Warner Bros. cartoon *Walky Talky Hawky* was an affectionate swipe of Delmar's Senator Claghorn. In later years, cartoon director Robert McKimson and voice artist Mel Blanc were both a bit vague concerning this matter, suggesting that while elements of Claghorn were incorporated in the rooster's voice and manner, the basic character had been developed separately ... and earlier.

Here are the facts, as chronicled in a February 2013 blog by cartoon historian Keith Scott: On January 13, 1945, nearly ten months before Delmar introduced Senator Claghorn on *The Fred Allen Show*, McKimson and Blanc recorded the soundtrack for *Walky Talky Hawky*—and it certainly sounds as if the essence of Claghorn is already part and parcel of the cartoon rooster, right down to his repetition of "I say" and his exhortation "Pay, attention, boy!" McKimson has acknowledged that a lot of this characterization was drawn from "The Sheriff," a hard-of-hearing rustic played by Jack Clifford on an early–1930s Los Angeles radio variety series. Too, Blanc's voice in *Walky Talky Hawky* sounds less like Claghorn than Yosemite Sam, with hardly a trace of a Southern accent. The blatant Claghorn imitation didn't begin until the rooster's second appearance in *Crowing Pains,* recorded in late 1945 A.D. (After Delmar) for a 1946 release. And the character wasn't given the derivative name Foghorn Leghorn until his third appearance in a 1946 cartoon bearing that title—which was also the first time that he pilfered Delmar's signature phrase "That's a joke, son."

Is everything clear now? Good. Then explain it to me. Explain it, that is.

Jack Armstrong, the All-American Boy (1947)

Jack Armstrong, the All-American Boy was the radio serial that every real All-American Boy (and a sizable contingent of All-American Girls) grew up with in the 1930s and 1940s. The daily 15-minute program was created in 1933 at the behest of radio producer and advertising executive Frank Hummert, who at the time was handling the General Mills account. The cereal company had been sponsoring a radio adaptation of Percy Crosby's juvenile comic strip *Skippy*, and was casting about for a program that would appeal to older kids and teenagers. Hummert's head writer Robert Hardy Andrews came up with a derivation of Burt L. Standish's popular "Frank Merriwell" stories, which focused on a college football hero. Andrews' slightly younger protagonist Jack Armstrong was B.M.O.C. at fictional Hudson High School.

When not scoring touchdown after touchdown, Jack chummed around with fellow students Billy and Betty Fairfield, nephew and niece of eminent scientist, inventor and globetrotting adventurer "Uncle Jim" Fairfield. An athletic-minded program needed an appropriate sponsor, so General Mills' breakfast cereal Wheaties was chosen to represent *Jack Armstrong, the All-American Boy,* an association that would last throughout the series' two-decade radio career. Like most Hummert projects, *Jack Armstrong* originated from Chicago, specifically the studios of CBS affiliate WBBM. Jim Ameche was the first of nine different actors who were heard in the title role.

The show's gridiron-star angle didn't last too long; in fact, when first heard on July 31, 1933, Jack, Billy and Betty were miles from home, visiting the Chicago World's Fair. It would be quite some time before they'd return to the playing fields of Hudson High, as they were quickly whisked off to an adventure in the frozen tundra of Canada. The show became a junior version of such rip-roaring action properties as *Doc Savage,* with the younger cast members accompanying the peripatetic Uncle Jim as he climbed aboard his streamlined hydroplane *Silver Albatross* and headed off to a variety of thrill-packed rendezvous throughout the world. Though it was harmless escapism, *Jack Armstrong* was frequently attacked by special interest groups who used isolated incidents to "prove" that the show was detrimental to youngsters—accusations that the producers quickly countered by hiring prominent child psychologist Dr. Martin L. Reymert to carefully monitor each episode. Evidently Reymert didn't object to the fact that the serial was primarily designed as a merchandising tool, not only pushing Wheaties by the barrel but also offering an endless supply of premiums, all obtainable in exchange for a couple of boxtops and a nominal cash fee. Over the years the *Jack Armstrong* premiums included toy planes, code books, whistles, maps, popguns, bombsights, rings, broaches, and especially pedometers (or "Hike-o-Meters," as General Mills liked to call them).

Given its enormous popularity, *Jack Armstrong* took its time making the transition from radio to film. It was not until 1947, fourteen years after the show's premiere, that the property was made into a movie serial. It has been speculated that the licensing fee demanded by the radio show's packagers was too high for any Hollywood producer to evince interest in a film version. However, by 1947 the show had suffered a severe eclipse in popularity, to the extent that a youngster would be "hooted off the sandlot" (in the words of essayist Brock Brower) if he admitted to being a *Jack Armstrong* fan; correspondingly, the license cost was made more affordable. This explanation makes sense in light of the fact that it was the notoriously frugal Sam Katzman who supervised production of the 15-chapter Columbia serial *Jack Armstrong, the All-American Boy.* John Hart, the actor who played Jack Armstrong, told interviewer Boyd Magers that Katzman was so cheap that he refused to refilm the serial's opening credit titles when Charles Middleton was hired to play the principal villain—and thus Middleton, whose character motivates the entire plotline, receives no billing whatsoever.

The radio version of *Jack Armstrong* was then on the cusp of a radical makeover dictated by its new network ABC, which would not only dispense with the daily serialized format in

The props outnumber the actors in this scene from Columbia's 1947 serial version of radio's *Jack Armstrong, the All American Boy*. From left: Wheeler Oakman, John Hart (as Jack Armstrong), Hugh Prosser, Zon Murray and Pierre Watkin.

favor of self-contained half-hour adventures, but also gradually phase out the surrogate-father character of Uncle Jim Fairfield, replacing him with the younger and more virile Victor Hardy. The Columbia serial was produced during this transitional period, meaning that both Uncle Jim (played by Pierre Watkin) and Vic Hardy (Hugh Prosser) were key players in the proceedings.

The serial opens with the same strident sennet heard on radio, as narrator Knox Manning shouts "Jack Armstrong!" three times, then adds "The All American Boy" almost as a postscript. Once established as the head of an aviation company specializing in atomic energy, Jim Fairfield receives word from his chief scientist Vic Hardy that someone outside the United States is conducting dangerous experiments with cosmic radioactivity. Hardy's subsequent disappearance prompts Fairfield to embark upon a search for the scientist, accompanied as always by Jack, Billy (Joe Brown Jr.) and Betty (Rosemary LaPlanche). The foursome end up on an uncharted island ruled by the well-named Allura (Claire James), who is under the influence of the malevolent god Xulta. Actually the voice of Xulta is being provided by the Ruler, a deranged scientist who plans to rule the world by firing off his deadly "cosmic annihilator ray" from the safety of the Aeroglobe, an orbiting space platform. Suspecting that the island's scuzzy trading post operator Jason Grood (Middleton) is in fact the mysterious Ruler, the good guys are unable to prove anything until another bad guy named Pierce (John Merton) forces Grood's hand. The presence of these and other slavering heavies, and the fact that Jack, Billy and Betty are constantly threatened with immolation in the "Pit of Everlasting Fire," would suggest that the radio series' watchdog Dr. Martin L. Reymert was not consulted on script content.

Jack Armstrong, the All-American Boy is superficially more elaborate than most of Katzman's Columbia serials, though it appears that the majority of the budget was blown on such geegaws as the Aeroglobe and Jack's futuristic automobile. Otherwise, the serial looks like it was lensed in its entirety on Columbia's B-western exterior sets, hastily refoliated to resemble a tropical isle. Directed by the no-nonsense Wallace Fox, the serial lacks the crazed campiness of director James W. Horne's freewheeling Columbia efforts (see *Captain Midnight*), though the script provides an abundance of unintentional laughs with its utter ignorance of the laws of science and physics. Outside of such veterans as Pierre Watkin and Middleton, the performances range from mediocre to appalling. Having once told an interviewer that there wasn't much an actor could bring to the role of Jack Armstrong, John Hart proceeds to prove his point throughout all 15 episodes.

After the Columbia serial ran its course, radio's *Jack Armstrong* continued in its new half-hour format until September 5, 1950, when in an overnight growth spurt unrivalled until the sudden maturation of Joey Stivic from infant to five-year-old on *All in the Family*, Jack Armstrong suddenly became a full-fledged adult, moving into a prime-time radio spy series titled *Armstrong of the SBI*. Betty and Billy were shunted into the background as Vic Hardy became Jack's permanent traveling companion in a passel of espionage adventures that were indistinguishable from *Dangerous Assignment*, *The Man Called X*, *Counterspy* and other like-minded radio shows. In this format, the aging property lasted only one season, joining both the movie serial and the short-lived (1947–1949) *Jack Armstrong* comic book in the Halls of Obscurity.

Sporadic efforts to transform *Jack Armstrong* into a TV series came to naught, though the property was ushered in through the back door when negotiations fell through for a Hanna-Barbera TV cartoon adaptation, whereupon the animation studio whipped up an imitation *Jack Armstrong* which premiered in the fall of 1964 as *Jonny Quest*. Finally, in 1997 Timothy Bottoms starred as an in-name-only Jack Armstrong in *American Hero*, originally designed as an interactive videogame movie for Jaguar (CD) but never given a wide release in any format due to irreparable damage incurred by the negative in the editing process.

"Big Town" (1947–1948)

On October 19, 1937, Warner Bros. film star Edward G. Robinson increased his already heavy workload with the weekly half-hour CBS radio newspaper drama *Big Town*. The series was produced and written by Jerry McGill, a former print journalist who seldom let facts get in the way of entertainment. Set in a mythical major metropolis—"Neither New York City, Chicago, St. Louis nor San Francisco" declared narrator Dwight Weist, but an amalgam of all the "Big Towns" of America—the show cast Robinson as Steve Wilson, crusading city editor of the *Illustrated Press*. His obligatory Girl Friday was plucky society editor Lorelei Kilbourne, played first by Claire Trevor and then by Ona Munson. Wilson's motto, as declared by a disembodied, echo-chambered voice at the beginning of each program, was "Freedom of the press is a flaming sword. Use it justly ... hold it high ... guard it well."

During the debut episode, the First Amendment handily outweighs Wilson's conscience, to which he refers as "the little something that creeps up in your soul." In a virtual replay of Robinson's 1931 film *Five Star Final*, Wilson all but destroys a society wedding by dredging up the unsavory past of the bride's mother Mrs. Lela Radcliffe, once the notorious "Pittsburgh Lil." Though he has berated his editor for "petty-larceny ethics," and despite Lorelei's pleas to let sleeping dogs lie, Wilson goes ahead with his exposé. Even when Mrs. Radcliffe threatens to kill him, Wilson is a newspaperman to the core, hoping that she'll go through with her threat so he'll get another headline out of the story!

In later episodes Wilson is more high-minded but no less high-handed, using his daily tabloid as a weapon to smite criminals, racketeers, dishonest businessmen and corrupt politicians, with a few arsonists, madmen, drunk drivers and abusive spouses thrown into the pot. Robinson delivered a virtuoso performance befitting the larger-than-life ambience of *Big Town*, which lived up to its title as a Big Hollywood Production with a full studio audience, Leith Stevens' booming orchestra and supporting players drawn from Radio Row's uppermost ranks. (These actors were required to show up when star Robinson and director William M. Robson conducted their intensive week-long rehearsals. The fact that the actors were not paid for these sessions, which often prevented them from accepting other more lucrative assignments, was one of the many reasons that the American Federation of Radio Artists came into being, but now is not the time to go into that.)

Though Robinson was heartened by the positive response from the series' fans, the actor departed *Big Town* at the end of the 1941–42 season, explaining in his autobiography that the series had become irrelevant in the light of the real-life drama then unfolding in Europe and the Pacific. CBS thought so too, and elected to cancel *Big Town*. Within a year, however, producer McGill revived the property with a scaled-down version produced in CBS's New York studios with Broadway actor Edward Pawley as Steve Wilson and soap-opera stalwart Fran Carlon as Lorelei, both considerably less expensive than the Hollywood stars. The economizing extended to the rest of the series, with the orchestra replaced by solitary organist John Galt and the studio audience eliminated entirely. This version of *Big Town* remained on the air until June 25, 1952, by which time Pawley had been replaced by Walter Greaza.

Inasmuch as *Big Town* had devolved from an "A" to a "B" production during its New York run, it makes sense that the long-overdue movie adaptation of the property would be entrusted to the Paramount B-picture division headed by William Pine and William C. Thomas, aka the "Two Dollar Bills" (see *People Are Funny*). Though by 1947 the Pine-Thomas unit had become more ambitious and expansive with A-grade pictures like *Albuquerque,* they would continue supplying Paramount with cheap but popular six-reelers until switching over entirely to more elaborate endeavors in 1949. Among the last of Pine-Thomas' B productions was the unit's only continuing series: a quartet of modestly mounted features inspired by the still-popular radio weekly *Big Town*.

All four entries were directed by co-producer Thomas, and all four starred Pine-Thomas contractee Philip Reed as Steve Wilson and freelance actress Hillary Brooke as Lorelei Kilbourne. Best known today for her frequent appearances with Abbott & Costello, Brooke brought the same brittle breeziness to Lorelei that she'd previously exuded in such films as *Jane Eyre, The Woman in Green* and *Monsieur Beaucaire*. Her co-star Reed had been a Hollywood leading man since the 1930s, but despite several adventure-film assignments (notably the role of Uncas in 1936's *Last of the Mohicans*) he didn't quite match the bare-knuckle dynamism that Edward G. Robinson and Edward Pawley had invested in the role of Steve Wilson. Perhaps aware of this shortcoming, the actor overplayed Steve to such an extent that, in the words of *Film Noir of the Week* blogger "Raven," Reed "packs about the same amount of emotion into his portrayal of Wilson as Moe Howard would playing Hamlet."

Sustaining the spirit of the Robinson radio version, the inaugural filmic entry *Big Town* (1947) quickly establishes Wilson as a mover and shaker *par excellence*. En route to his new position as managing editor of the *Illustrated Press,* he takes pictures of a train wreck, but the *Press'* conservative-minded head man Amos Peabody (Charles Arnt) buries the story and the paper is scooped by its rival, the *Chronicle*. This energizes Steve into a total makeover of the *Press* from a "respectable" rag to a scandal sheet, and never mind whose heart he stomps on in the process. Though Lorelei deplores Steve's ruthless methods, he is temporarily vindicated when the *Press* manages to track down and capture an elusive female bandit (Veda Ann Borg). Lorelei later quits the *Press* in a huff after Steve apparently buckles under pressure from his own advertising department to kill a story about a faultily constructed roller coaster that has already claimed one life (an extremely well-staged highlight). After Steve uses the *Press* to persecute a former mental patient known as "The Vampire Killer" whom Lorelei is trying to clear of a murder charge, the victimized man commits suicide in his jail cell. All is forgiven when the chastened Steve composes a *mea culpa* headline, whereupon Lorelei returns to the *Press* and Wilson's boss gives him the go-ahead for a major exposé of slum conditions.

Big Town was co-scripted by Pine-Thomas stalwart Maxwell Shane and Geoffrey Homes, who (writing under the name Daniel Mainwaring) was responsible for the *noir* classic *Build My Gallows High,* filmed in 1947 as *Out of the Past.* (Homes also co-wrote the final series entry *Big Town Scandal.*) The film's excess of plot and incident nicely compensate for its pinchpenny production values, resulting in excellent box office returns and positive critical response. As noted in *Independent Exhibitors' Film Bulletin,* "Pine-Thomas continue to turn out neat little action programmers, and this is one. Based on the radio program of the same name, *Big Town* follows the format of the air program and subordinates the love interest, an asset to a feature aimed at juvenile audiences and action houses."

The reviewer also advised exhibitors to capitalize on the film's built-in ties with authentic journalism: "Press cooperation might be obtained by circularizing newspaper editors, most of whom will be interested in the film's protest against yellow journalism. Civic betterment groups, municipal officials, physicians and clergymen should find the slum-clearance program outlined in the film of sufficient interest to merit their support." Paramount picked up on this, emphasizing the real-life accomplishments of crusading newspaper editors in its promotional copy. The studio's obvious goal was to not only grab the "juvenile audiences" but also adults who had over time become disenchanted with radio's *Big Town* and its increasingly simplistic plotlines and insubstantial scriptwork.

(By 1947 it seemed that every episode found Steve and/or Lorelei abducted by the villains 20 minutes into the story, squandering the last ten minutes on a lot of silly pseudo-tough dialogue and childish melodramatics—no better, and sometimes a bit worse, than the concurrently published *Big Town* comic books.)

The first two *Big Town* films were filmed and distributed so quickly in the early months of 1947 that in some cities the second entry *I Cover Big Town* was screened first. Adapted from a *Big Town* radio play by Whitman Chambers, this one finds Steve mounting a campaign to oust new police chief Tom Blake (Robert Shayne) because escaped killer John Moulton (Louis Jean Heydt) slipped through the authorities' fingers. At the same time, Lorelei persuades Steve to assign her to the police beat. The sound of a barking dog precipitates Lorelei stumbling upon a murder, which is blamed on architect Harry Hilton (Frank Wilcox), whose wife (Mona Barrie) was being blackmailed by the victim. The separate plot fragments crystalize when Hilton and the recaptured Moulton become cellmates, leading Steve and Lorelei on a covert mission which reveals the actual murderer and eliminates the ongoing threat of Moulton all at once. Yet another plot strand involves the underhanded methods used by *Chronicle* reporter Pete Ryan (Robert Lowery) to repeatedly scoop Lorelei.

With this film Vince Barnett becomes a series regular as a weasely little bail bondsman named Louie. And if your eyes are good, you might be able to spot child actor Freddie Bartholomew's aunt Cissie making her screen debut (at least that's what the publicity handouts claimed). *Film Bulletin* praised *I Cover Big Town* as "a credible melodrama.... The picture has plenty of plot development, a minimum of dialogue and good production values." The *St. Petersburg Times* reviewer also liked the picture, curbing his enthusiasm with an admonition: "But don't get the idea that's the life all newspapermen and women lead because it's not. It's all decked out in glamour and dressed up to suit the audience. And they eat it up."

Big Town radio writer Whitman Chambers was responsible for the original screenplay of

From *Big Town After Dark* (1947), third in Pine-Thomas' film series based on the radio program *Big Town*: Deceptively demure Susan Peabody (Ann Gillis) indulges in some slightly illegal gambling with crusading newspaper editor Steve Wilson (Philip Reed).

the next movie installment, *Big Town After Dark* (1947). With Lorelei quitting the *Illustrated Press* in disgust over Steve's unrepentant yellow journalism (guess how long *this* lasts), Steve replaces her with boss Peabody's niece Susan (Ann Gillis), of whom it can be said that butter wouldn't melt in her mouth. Susan's schoolgirl manners prove to be as phony as her journalistic credentials when she is allegedly kidnapped by gambling boss Chuck LaRue (Richard Travis), head of an operation which Steve has been trying to expose and smash. In truth, Susan is LaRue's wife, and almost as deeply involved in the town's illegal gambling emporiums as her husband. An offbeat performance by former child star Gillis and a tense finale involving a *really* high-stakes poker game notwithstanding, *Big Town After Dark* falls short of the quality established by its predecessors. "A weak, empty little action melodrama" was the verdict of *Film Bulletin*.

Another troublesome relative figures into the fourth and final entry *Big Town Scandal* (1948). This time it's Frankie Sneed (Carl "Alfalfa" Switzer), the teenage nephew of bail bondsman Louie Sneed (Barnett). When Lorelei argues in court on behalf of Frankie and his gang, she runs afoul of Steve, who believes that all juvenile delinquents should be locked up and the key thrown away. Imagine Steve's discomfort when Frankie and all his pals are paroled in his custody—but he soon gets over his mad-on when he realizes that his efforts to reform the youngsters will make a swell newspaper story. As often happens in postwar J.D. films, the fault lies not with the kids but with the adult villains, mobster Joe Moreley (John Phillips) and his torpedo Cato (Reginald Baldo), who attempt to strong-arm Frankie's pal Tommy (Stanley Clements) into throwing a basketball tournament. The film is fairly thrilling and occasionally shocking (one of the more sympathetic teens ends up dead), but falls apart in the basketball game finale, wherein the bad guys' behavior is so overt that it's surprising they weren't arrested on general principles when they bought their tickets. Of special interest in *Big Town Scandal* is the motley crew of juvenile actors hired to play the teenage gang members, including former *Our Gang*-ers Switzer and Tommy Bond (the latter cast as a deaf-mute), soon-to-be *Bowery Boys* stalwart Clements, versatile child actor and future TV producer Darryl Hickman, and dancer-choreographer Roland Dupree.

When the four *Big Town* films were reissued theatrically in the 1950s and later released to television, legal complications required title changes: *Big Town* was renamed *Guilty Assignment*, *I Cover Big Town* was rechristened *I Cover the Underworld*, *Big Town After Dark* became *Underworld After Dark* and *Big Town Scandal* emerged as *Underworld Scandal* (a subtle pattern is emerging). The property went on to enjoy enormous success as a TV series, which ran on both CBS and NBC from 1950 through 1956. Patrick McVey and later Mark Stevens starred as Wilson, with Mary K. Wells, Julie Stevens, Jane Nigh and Trudy Wroe as Lorelei. The TV incarnation of *Big Town* also underwent several title changes when the episodes entered off-network syndication: *Headline*, *Heart of the City*, *City Assignment* and *Byline: Steve Wilson*.

A Date with Judy (1948)

A Date with Judy was the brainchild of Aleen Leslie (*née* Wetstein), who had only recently graduated from Ohio State University when in 1933 she began her journalistic career with a weekly humor column for the *Pittsburgh Press*. Armed with her press pass and a healthy supply of *chutzpah*, Leslie stormed the gates of Columbia Pictures, where she launched her film career scripting two-reelers for such comedy stars as the Three Stooges and Charley Chase. This job didn't last long, but she found plenty of work writing radio material for youthful stars Deanna Durbin and Mickey Rooney, picking up a generous reserve of authentic teenage jargon along the way. Her subsequent film credits included the amiable Loretta Young-Ray Milland romantic comedy *The Doctor Takes a Wife* (1940) and several entries in Paramount's teen-centric *Henry Aldrich* series (q.v.). At the time of her death at age 101 in 2010, Aleen Leslie was the oldest member of the Writers Guild of America.

Conceiving a radio series built around a rambunctious teenage girl named Judy Foster, Leslie wrote the first scripts with her actress friend Helen Mack in mind for Judy. But Mack demurred for a variety of reasons, including the impending birth of a child and the inescapable fact that she was too old for the part. (Even when she *was* the proper age, Helen Mack had *never* been a typical ingénue, as witness such films as *Melody Cruise* and *The Son of Kong*.) Slated for a brief NBC run in 1941 as the summer replacement for Bob Hope, the project now known as *A Date with Judy* finally landed a leading lady when Hope suggested a fellow Paramount contract player: 14-year-old Ann Gillis, whose main claim to fame was the part of Becky Thatcher in Selznick's *The Adventures of Tom Sawyer* (1938). After a second summer stint for Hope in 1942, *A Date with Judy* returned for an equally brief run in 1943, this time as a hot-weather replacement for Eddie Cantor, with Dellie Ellis in the lead and 15-year-old Louise Erickson as Judy's friend Mitzi. Finally on January 30, 1944, the series won a full-time NBC slot, with Mack returning to the fold as the series' producer-director, the only woman to hold such a position in network radio at that time. Promoted to the title role, Louise Erickson would soon take her place in the minds and hearts of the series' millions of fans as the definitive Judy Foster.

Not too far removed from the wacky world of Aleen Leslie's Columbia two-reelers, *A Date with Judy* was a textbook example of "verbal slapstick," with each half-hour episode finding the hyperactive Judy building mammoth mountains out of minuscule molehills. The 16-year-old heroine lived at 123 State Street with her father Melvyn (owner of a local cannery), her mother Dora and her flippant kid brother Randolph. Faithful in her fashion to her lifelong sweetheart Ogden "Oogie" Pringle, Judy spent much of her time yakking on the telephone or waiting for the phone to ring as she lined up dates for the days to come. Convinced that her parents didn't understand her, Judy frequently scooted out of the house to join her pals Mitzi, Eleanor, Gloria and Jo-Jo at such favorite hangouts as Pop Scully's Soda Fountain. Barely pausing for breath as she chattered away about the latest crisis in her life—as far as she was concerned, nothing ever happened in her life that *wasn't* a crisis—Judy innocently left her long-suffering parents, her geeky boyfriend and her wide-eyed brother all reeling in her wake.

A typical episode found Judy and Oogie planning a date at the movies, a simple premise that snowballed into catastrophe with Judy watching the picture all by herself, Oogie forced to wash dishes at the soda shop to square his fountain bill, Mrs. Foster frantically phoning the Missing Persons Bureau to report a "kidnapped" daughter, and Mr. Foster landing in jail. *A Date with Judy* may not have been the wittiest situation comedy on radio, but it certainly was one of the fastest, and in terms of sheer laugh content miles ahead of such rival "teen-coms" as *Henry Aldrich, Archie Andrews* and *Meet Corliss Archer* (the latter based on a hit Broadway play but adapted for radio as CBS's "answer" to *Judy*).

It is not entirely accurate to say that Louise Erickson played the role of Judy Foster: To many of her friends and colleagues she *was* Judy, and indeed had to put a lid on her natural exuberance when playing such "ordinary" radio roles as Marjorie on *The Great Gildersleeve* (q.v.). Modern viewers can get an eyeful of Louise at full throttle as star of the 1944 Columbia B-musical *Meet Miss Bobby Socks*, a fair indication that it would have been no effort at all for her to repeat her radio characterization had *A Date with Judy* been purchased by Columbia. Instead, the movie rights were acquired by MGM, and Louise somehow sensed early on that the role of Judy would go to someone else in the film. As indicated in a May 1945 interview with the UP's Virginia McPherson, the 17-year-old actress was philosophical about the situation: "They haven't called me up or invited me [to MGM] to talk about it. So I guess they're going to put a big name actress in it. Maybe they'll get one who can sing and turn it into a musical."

Erickson turned out to be a prophet. By November 1945, the property was in the hands of MGM musical producer Joe Pasternak, the man who'd made a star of Deanna Durbin at Universal nine years earlier. Pasternak had every intention of fashioning *A Date with Judy* into a vehicle for his latest teenage-soprano protégée. In a studio press release, the producer made it official: The film version would star 16-year-old Jane Powell as Judy Foster.

This of course was assuming that *A Date with Judy* would ever go before the cameras—and for a long time, it appeared that the project would permanently languish in Development Hell. By the time Pasternak had sufficiently cleared his schedule in early 1947, MGM had lined up two more of their adolescent contractees for the supporting cast: 15-year-old Elizabeth Taylor and ten-year-old Margaret O'Brien. Exactly what part Margaret would have played is uncertain since she was dropped from the film almost as soon as she was added to the cast. Also, by 1947 Taylor had blossomed into a gorgeous young lady, appearing significantly older and more sophisticated than the now 18-year-old Jane Powell—who could still pass as a teenager well into her late 30s. One can safely assume that the relationship of the characters played by the two budding actresses (who were, and remained, good pals off-screen) had undergone several adjustments by the time the film finally went into production.

In keeping with the female-dominated creative staff of radio's *A Date with Judy,* Dorothy Cooper and Dorothy Kingsley were assigned the screenplay duties for the 1948 film version. The names of the main characters were retained, as were several other elements from the original source, including Pop Scully's Drug Store, the ever-busy telephone in the Foster house, the "backstory" of how Judy and Oogie first met (they'd run into each other's tricycles) and Judy's endearingly convoluted teenage logic, such as her explanation for breaking up with Oogie: "I just gave him up forever for a little while."

Elsewhere, significant changes were made. Judy's home town, unidentified on radio, was now Santa Barbara, California. The Foster household not only accommodated two parents and two kids, but also twinkly-eyed "Gramps" Foster and a psalm-singing black maid named Nightingale. Oogie now had a serious rival for Judy's affections, handsome twentysomething Stephen Andrews, who jerked sodas at Pop Scully's. Adding to the intrigue was another girl who'd set her cap for Stephen, Oogie's hitherto never-mentioned older sister Carol, the role created for Elizabeth Taylor. Though the script required Carol to be bitchy and imperious at times, MGM didn't want to stray too far from Liz's established screen image, so it is explained that Carol is a really a nice kid who acts the way she does because she is neglected by her wealthy father. And since Carol had to have a wealthy father, this meant that Oogie, who on radio was frequently so strapped for cash that he had to borrow date money from Judy with the promise that he'd "renoomerate" her later, now dwelled in a palatial mansion with a full retinue of servants.

While the principal plotline involved the Judy-Steve-Carol triangle, the screenwriters also had to bear in mind that MGM's longtime box-office magnet Wallace Beery had been cast as Judy's father Melvyn, receiving top billing over Jane Powell. So the Melvyn Foster character was fleshed out to a far greater extent than on radio with a subplot wherein Judy suspects that her dad is having an affair with a Latin lovely named Rosita, when in truth Mr. Foster is merely taking rhumba lessons in order to surprise his wife on their 20th anniversary. The sudden overemphasis on the Mr. Foster–Rosita business halfway into the picture suggests that this had been the intended main storyline for *A Date with Judy* until it was decided to build up Liz Taylor's part.

A Date with Judy co-stars Selena Royle (replacing the studio's first choice Mary Astor) as Mrs. Foster, Jerry Hunter as Randolph Foster, and onetime child star Scotty Beckett as Oogie. Marshall Thompson had originally been announced to play Stephen Andrews, but producer Pasternak decided to go with Robert Stack, a move that may have been engineered by the MGM publicity department. Having made headlines throughout the world for giving Deanna Durbin her first screen kiss in Pasternak's *First Love* (1939), Stack performs the same service for Jane Powell in *A Date with Judy*—though technically, it is Jane who kisses *him*.

The presence of orchestra leader Xavier Cugat as "himself" may smack of another MGM contrivance, though in fact his appearance is in keeping with the very brief "guest star" policy on radio's *A Date with Judy*, beginning with Joseph Cotten on the episode of February 6, 1945. This policy had been suggested by Louise Erickson in hopes that she'd eventually get to act with Frank Sinatra, which indeed happened the following week. While the celebrity guest device proved cumbersome and was eventually dropped from the radio show, it does no harm to MGM's *A Date with Judy*, especially since in the film it is established that Cugat is engaged to Rosita, who of course is crucial to the plot. Seen as Rosita is the film's other "special guest" Carmen Miranda, who except for a sizzling climactic performance of her big hit "Cuanto la Gusta" gives a remarkably subdued performance (by Carmen Miranda standards, anyway). A third specialty performer appears in the film with considerably less fanfare than Cugat or Miranda: fourteen-year-old drumming sensation Buddy Howard, cast as Oogie's buddy Jo-Jo on the strength of his show-stopping appearance in the LA–based stage revue *Ken Murray's Blackouts*. Though Pasternak lavished a great deal of pre-production publicity on his new "discovery," for reasons unknown Buddy Howard receives no billing in the cast credits.

Contemporary viewers unfamiliar with radio's *A Date with Judy* (and undisturbed by the liberties taken with the source material) will probably accept the film version at face value as a typical late–1940s MGM Technicolor musical, its lumbering pace and uninspired direction (by Richard Thorpe) made palatable by an attractive cast and a buoyant musical score. Especially appealing is the memorable tune "It's a Most Unusual Day," composed by Harold Adamson and Jimmy McHugh and sung in the finale by everyone in the cast—including Wallace Beery.

Moving from NBC to ABC in the fall of 1949, the radio version of *A Date with Judy* lasted until May 25, 1950. One year later it was revived for television as a live weekly half-hour sitcom, again by ABC. Patricia Crowley played Judy Foster for the first batch of TV episodes, with Mary Lynn Beller assuming the role for the final two seasons in 1952 and 1953.

The Life of Riley (1949)

The Life of Riley has frequently been described as radio's first "blue collar" situation comedy, vanguard of a TV subgenre that would eventually include *The Honeymooners, All in the Family, Married ... with Children, Roseanne* and *King of Queens*. While this point is debatable, it can be stated with some assurance that *Riley* was the first sitcom of the "Father Is an Idiot" classification. As noted by TV comedy historian Rick Mitz, the eponymous Chester A. Riley "was a bumbling bimbo—prototypically typical of a feast of fathers who would follow in his pratfalls. True, Riley was lovable ... but *so* stupid."

One of the standard trivia-contest questions of years gone by was, "Who was the original star of *The Life of Riley?*" If you answered "William Bendix," the questioner would giggle with patronizing glee and point to the many "official" Old Time Radio history books that listed gravel-voiced Lionel Stander as the very first Riley. That's true as far as it goes, but it doesn't go far enough. From April 12 through September 6, 1941, CBS ran a comedy weekly titled *The Life of Riley*, which indeed starred Stander as one J. Riley Farnsworth. But beyond the fact that the leading character, like the more familiar Riley, had a sweetheart named Peg, this program bore no resemblance to the *Life of Riley* we all know and love—and *that* program bore no resemblance to its original pilot episode, conceived and written by Irving Brecher as a vehicle for his friend and frequent collaborator Groucho Marx. *The Flotsam Family* starred Groucho as the long-suffering (but *not* stupid) patriarch of a "typical" small-town brood, and from all reports it was loaded with laughs if not logic.

Recorded some time between the Marx Bros. films *Go West* (1940) and *The Big Store* (1941), the pilot for *The Flotsam Family* was turned down by its potential sponsor, who could not envision the iconoclastic Groucho in such a conformist role. A year or so after this debacle, Brecher went to the movies and happened to see a Hal Roach "streamliner" (a feature film running approximately 45 minutes to accommodate short double bills) titled *The McGuerins of Brooklyn*. Starring in the role of a thickheaded *nouveau riche* cab driver was William Bendix, who'd been signed to a Roach contract on the strength of his first film assignment as a punch drunk bartender in MGM's *Woman of the Year* (1942). Born in Manhattan in 1906, Bendix did not entertain any thoughts of an acting career until the grocery store he operated was shuttered by the Depression. Joining the New Jersey Federal Theater Project, the 30-year-old Bendix soon found a thriving market for his beefy physique, his unique manner of slurring words and his projection of a tough but likable lug, as in his breakthrough Broadway role as Officer Krupp in William Saroyan's Pulitzer-winning *The Time of Your Life* (1939). From his first film appearance until his death in 1964, Bendix carved out a special niche in Hollywood as a seemingly typecast actor who nonetheless was capable of running the gamut from comic imbecility (the Hal Roach films) and sentimental pathos (*China, Guadalcanal Diary*) to thuggish menace (*The Glass Key, The Dark Corner*). So far as Brecher was concerned, Bendix was just what the doctor ordered for his heavily revised *Flotsam Family* pilot, now known as *The Life of Riley*.

Armed with inside information that Bendix's agent was shopping around for a radio program, Brecher recorded a second pilot with the actor playing Chester A. Riley, a solid family man with a heart of gold and a brain of lead, who faithfully brought home $110 per week from his job as a riveter at the Stevenson Aircraft factory. Riley lived in a modest Los Angeles bungalow at 1313 Blue View Terrace with his everlovin', ever-patient wife Peg, his teenage daughter Babs and his adolescent son Junior. Also on hand was Riley's neighbor, co-worker, fellow Brooklynite and best friend Jim Gillis, whose own wife was Honeybee and whose son went by the name of Egbert. Through a deal arranged by Groucho Marx's agent brother Gummo, the Blue Network picked up the property, and on January 16, 1944, *The Life of Riley* began a seven-season radio run, most of which was sponsored by the Pabst brewing company.

Each episode followed the unwritten Law of the Sitcom, that Chester A. Riley was never any better off at the end of the program than at the beginning, despite his pie-in-the-sky schemes to advance himself financially or make life easier for his family. Stubborn to a fault (usually his fault), Riley would stand upon his convictions by declaring, "My head is made up"—and the results were invariably disastrous. Forever jumping to the wrong conclusion, Riley's well-meaning efforts to straighten out the problems of his wife and children succeeded only in making matters worse, whereupon the exasperated Riley would moan his classic lament "What a revoltin' development *this* is!" (So closely associated was Bendix with this catchphrase that he even used it as a different character in the 1947 Bob Hope comedy *Where There's Life*.)

Though essentially grounded in reality, radio's *Life of Riley* boasted a touch of macabre surrealism in the person of Riley's friend Digby "Digger" O'Dell, "The Friendly Undertaker." The role was played to perfection by British-born actor John Brown, who also appeared on the series in the polar-opposite characterization of Gillis. Good for one brief appearance per week, usually at the point when Riley's bad fortunes couldn't get any worse, "Digger" would introduce himself in a funereal baritone by remarking, "You're looking fine, Riley—*very* natural" and proceed to color his advice to Riley with an endless supply of "death" and "burial" jokes ("I've covered a lot of ground today," "The grass is always greener on the other fellow" and so forth), then bid farewell with a clammy "Cheerio. I'd better be ... shovelling off."

During the series' first few years on the air, Brecher forsook an on-air writing credit at the request of his home movie studio MGM, who had given him dispensation for this "outside" project but didn't want to encourage their other house writers to do the same. But when his agent made what he later described as a "phenomenal deal" to write, produce *and* direct a Universal-International film version of *The Life of Riley*, Brecher could hardly turn down the opportunity to get his name all over the screen. Not that Brecher was ever modest about accepting credit: For the rest of his life he would tell anyone who'd listen that he was the first and only writer ever to receive a solo credit on a Marx Bros. picture, which, considering that the picture was *At the Circus*, was scarcely something to crow about.

Shooting began in late 1948 with Bendix, on loan from Hal Roach, assuming his proper place as Riley. Most of the radio actors, notably Paula Winslowe as Peg Riley, were bypassed in favor of Universal's own casting choices. The movie version of Peg was played by Rosemary DeCamp, who though only in her late 30s had since 1940 been firmly established onscreen in middle-aged maternal roles, most memorably as the mother of James Cagney (11 years her senior) in *Yankee Doodle Dandy*. Recognition of DeCamp's screen specialty occurred on the set of *The Life of Riley* when Dr. Paul Popenoe, founder of the American Institute of Family Relations, presented a statuette to the actress as "America's Mother of Distinction of 1948," for doing more than any other woman in the past decade "to glorify American motherhood through her inspiring film portrayals and exemplary life off the screen."

No awards were forthcoming to James Gleason, third-billed in *The Life of Riley* in the role of Gillis, though there certainly should have been some sort of Lifetime Achievement honor for this matchless character comedian. The casting of Gleason did not, however, mean that his radio counterpart John Brown was left in the cold: Brown was permitted to recreate his now-celebrated role of "Digger" O'Dell in all its crepe-hanging glory, and it is he who receives some of the best lines and biggest laughs. Other members of the cast included Meg Randall (later a semi-regular in the *Ma and Pa Kettle*

A family portrait from Universal-International's 1949 spin on the radio comedy series *The Life of Riley*. From left: Richard Long as Jeff Taylor, Rosemary DeCamp as Peg Riley, William Bendix as Chester A. Riley, Meg Randall as Babs Riley and Lanny Rees as Junior Riley. Guess which two of these people would like the other three to leave the room.

pictures) as Babs, Lanny Rees as Junior, Beulah Bondi as the Rileys' landlady Martha Bogle (the focus of a running gag in which Riley, several weeks behind in his rent, goes to Herculean lengths to avoid her baleful glance), a pre–*Big Valley* Richard Long as Martha's nephew and Babs' boyfriend Jeff Taylor, Mark Daniels as Jeff's wealthy rival Burt Stevenson, and popular radio announcer Bill Goodwin as Peg's self-aggrandizing former beau Sidney Monahan.

Released in April 1949, the 87-minute cinema adaptation of *The Life of Riley* has been described by Leonard Maltin as more "bittersweet" than the radio and TV show, but this is only in terms of the plotting. Having already overspent the household budget, Riley goes into further debt when he tries to impress his old nemesis Sidney by taking him to dinner at a swank French restaurant (imagine any establishment charging such exorbitant rates as $13.39 for a party of six!). Things begin to brighten when Riley unexpectedly receives a promotion at his job, little realizing that this was engineered by his boss' son Burt Stevenson, who is heavily in debt to a gambler (Ted De Corsia) and can only tap into his trust fund if he gets married—which is why he is so ardently squiring Riley's daughter Babs, much to the dismay of her regular beau Jeff. When Riley faces another huge financial crisis, Babs decides to sacrifice her happiness for the sake of her family by wedding Burt. But thanks to Junior Riley's prowess as an amateur detective (inspired by his favorite radio program *Sam Spade,* allowing

Howard Duff to make an unbilled voice cameo in the picture), Riley is able to expose Burt as a four-flusher before the wedding vows are exchanged. In the process, he also redeems himself in the eyes of his pal Gillis, who had broken off with Riley in the mistaken belief that Babs was being "sold" into marriage for her dad's benefit.

In the fine tradition of the radio series, Brecher masterfully undermines the potential syrup of the Babs-Jeff romantic subplot and the incipient melodrama surrounding Riley's monetary travails and his daughter's marriage of convenience by investing each scene with surefire laughs and boffo punchlines. When Riley contemplates suicide so that Peg can collect his insurance, and when he tearfully reveals something that no one has ever known before—"I'm a failure"—the effect is hilarious rather than heartrending. The same is true of Riley's roundabout blessing on the potential union of Babs and Jeff: "When two people are in love, there's only one way to stop it. Get married!" Even the traditional hugs-and-smiles ending cleverly sidesteps over-sentimentality: Forgiven for his past stupidities, Riley proudly proclaims that what makes him happiest of all is to be totally reconciled with the ones he loves best—whereupon he walks right past Peg and throws his arms around Gillis.

Even if *Life of Riley* had succumbed to seriousness at any point in the story, one could always rely upon Friendly Undertaker "Digger" O'Dell to restore the comic balance with such black-humor grace notes as relaxing at the beach by digging a six-foot-deep hole in the sand. And if there had been any doubts that *Riley* would lend itself to a film translation, these were efficiently disposed of by director Brecher. His firm grasp of screen comedy's visual dynamics is evident from start to finish, with such highlights as "Digger" O'Dell's first entrance in a darkened room illuminated by a single candle, and Riley's hesitant efforts to secure a raise from his boss during a seaside picnic—a scene filmed from knee level, allowing Bendix's bare legs to do all the "acting."

The reviews were on the whole friendly, exemplified by Lillian Blackstone's four-bell assessment in the *St. Petersburg* (FL) *Times*: "One laugh after another." Only a few, like Herb Miller of the *Bridgeport* (CT) *Sunday Herald,* found fault with the picture, citing the standard complaint that what plays on radio does not always go over on screen. Miller also had harsh words for what many modern-day observers regard as the best thing in the whole film: "John Brown, as the deep-down 'Digger' O'Dell the undertaker, [is] a diverting character until you have seen him a few scenes too often." Audiences chose to ignore criticism of this nature, enabling *The Life of Riley* to realize a profit of $2,000,000. "That gave me a lot of security," recalled Brecher in later years; he was now emboldened to carry out the big saturation campaign for the property that he had first set forward in a newspaper interview with Hollywood columnist Virginia Vale in March 1946. Not only was *Riley* destined to become a movie, but also a television series, a Broadway play and a daily comic strip.

The latter prediction only partially came to pass with a *Life of Riley* comic book, while no stage adaptation appeared beyond the usual amateur-show script prepared by Samuel French Inc. But by 1949 the TV series was a definite "go," especially since the property's radio sponsor Pabst Blue Ribbon had been so impressed by the film version. Pabst wanted to do *Riley* as a live TV show broadcast from New York, but Brecher wanted a filmed series so he wouldn't have to shuttle between the east and west coasts every week. Renting an empty store on Melrose Avenue in LA, Brecher set up a makeshift studio and filmed *Riley* on a weekly budget of $10,200, of which he had to supply $2,000 from his own pocket while Pabst bankrolled the rest.

A *Life of Riley* without William Bendix would seem to be the equivalent of H_2 without the O, but such was the dilemma facing Brecher when Bendix proved unavailable for the series due to previous movie commitments. The producer then hired a brash Broadway and nightclub comic named Jackie Gleason, who had yet to enjoy any sort of success in a filmed medium. Because Gleason was deemed too stout for the role of Riley, the comedian slimmed down almost to the point of emaciation, with the unanticipated result of lessening his comic appeal. Rosemary DeCamp, John Brown and Lanny Rees were all carried over from the film version to repeat their roles on TV; Gloria Winters, best known to baby boomers as Penny on *Sky King*, was cast as Babs, and Sid Tomack was seen as Gillis.

All 26 episodes of Jackie Gleason's *Life of Riley* are still extant, and some are well worth having, but none have the extra spark that Bendix would have brought to the enterprise. Despite winning an Emmy award, the 1949 TV edition of *Riley* was cancelled after a single season. Stories persist that the NBC network had decreed that Gleason had "no future in show business," but the decision to pull the plug was the sponsor's, who all along had intended the series as a merely a means of holding onto a weekly prime-time slot throughout the spring and summer of 1949 until the inauguration of Pabst's Madison Square Garden boxing matches in the fall of that year.

In 1952 NBC television licensed *Life of Riley* from Brecher for another filmed go-round, this one produced by Tom McKnight at Hal Roach Studios and thus fully benefiting from the presence of Roach contractee Bendix in the title role. Onetime movie ingénue Marjorie Reynolds (*Holiday Inn, Ministry of Fear*) was cast as Peg at the urging of her ex-husband, Roach studio executive Jack Reynolds. Rounding out the regulars were Lugene Sanders as Babs, Wesley Morgan as Junior, Tom D'Andrea as Gillis and Gloria Blondell (Joan's sister) as Gillis' wife Honeybee. A success from the get-go, this *Riley* lasted from January 2, 1953, to August 22, 1958, then lingered on for decades in rerun syndication.

Conspicuous by his absence in the second TV incarnation of *The Life of Riley* was John Brown as "Digger" O'Dell. Quoted in Earl Wilson's newspaper column of January 25, 1954, Bendix's explanation for the elimination of "Digger" not only ignored the character's omnipresence on the Jackie Gleason version of the series but also contradicted the known facts about audience response to "Digger"'s appearance in the 1949 movie adaptation. According to Bendix, the character "went well on radio, but not in the movie we made, and when television came along, Digger O'Dell was ... you'll pardon the expression ... dead." Conveniently unmentioned by either Bendix or Wilson is the fact that actor Brown was by 1954 *persona non grata* in both radio and television, having been blacklisted at the behest of *Red Channels* and other egregious Commie-hunting publications. As of May 16, 1957, Brown would be ... you'll pardon the expression ... dead at the age of 53.

"My Friend Irma" (1949–1950)

When the weekly, half-hour radio comedy *My Friend Irma* joined the CBS Friday night lineup on April 11, 1947, few could have predicted that it was the harbinger of a new CBS policy to build sitcoms around dynamic female personalities. Prior to *Irma,* programs in this genre—*The Life of Riley, The Great Gildersleeve*—tended to favor male protagonists. But within two years of its first broadcast, *My Friend Irma* was joined on the CBS manifest by *My Favorite Husband,* starring Lucille Ball, and *Our Miss Brooks,* starring Eve Arden. It could be said with only slight exaggeration that were it not for the success of *Irma* and her spiritual sisters, CBS's television division might never have given *I Love Lucy* a second glance.

The guiding force behind *My Friend Irma* was Cy Howard, who came to CBS in 1946 after extensive experience in local radio. He had been developing *Irma* in his mind for several years, but had yet to find an actress who was not only perfect for the part but would also endear herself to millions of listeners. While attending a performance of Ken Murray's long-running (3,587 performances) L.A. stage review *Blackouts,* Howard first became aware of the wide-eyed, well-proportioned blonde who served as a foil for some of Murray's raciest material: When this fair damsel explained that she was born "in Anaheim in a grapefruit grove," Murray leered at her heaving bosom and replied, "Well, that explains a couple of things." The joke, like most of the jokes in *Blackouts,* wasn't terribly funny in itself. What impressed Howard was the actress' ability to be sexy and funny all at once, and her skill at delivering lines with a wholly believable air of innocent bewilderment.

Though she always appeared younger than she was, Marie Wilson was no spring chicken when she joined *Blackouts* in 1941. She really *was* born in Anaheim, California, in 1916 as Katherine Elizabeth Wilson, and had been in Hollywood since 1932, making her uncredited movie debut as Mary Quite Contrary in Laurel & Hardy's *Babes in Toyland* (1934). A screen test at MGM did not result in any work at that studio, but Jack Warner was impressed by the test and signed the actress to a contract, intending at first to cast her in straight roles. Instead, Marie's inborn comic sense led to a great many dumb-blonde assignments, notably the pregnant waitress in Warner Bros.' *Boy Meets Girl* (1938). But stardom would elude Marie until after her contract expired and she signed with Murray, starting at $250 per week but rapidly working her way up to $1,000. Her character in *Blackouts* wasn't anything like Howard's concept of the title character in *My Friend Irma*, but he was enchanted by the actress' ability to project sexy naiveté without lapsing into archness. Wilson was just the sort of person who could object to compulsory military service because "a girl shouldn't have to go out with a sailor unless she wants to"—and make it sound as if she really meant it.

At first, Marie resisted Howard's offer of a radio series. She was growing weary of playing dumbbells, and was self-conscious about playing a leading role. Also, the prospect of reading a script into a microphone after only a few hours' rehearsal instead of studying and memorizing her part frightened her. But Howard persisted, and Wilson acquiesced—and after a brief battle of wills between Howard and CBS, who'd wanted a bigger name for the series, *My Friend Irma* finally made it to the air.

Opening each week to the strains of Cole Porter's "Friendship," the series delineated the adventures of two working girls (not *those* kind of working girls) who shared a small New York apartment. Irma Peterson (Wilson) worked as stenographer for bombastic Mr. Clyde (Alan Reed), who spent a lot of time suppressing the urge to strangle the girl after she'd pulled some well-intentioned blunder like filing a double tax return so that the IRS would think that Clyde's business was more successful. Irma's roomie and best friend Jane Stacy (Cathy Lewis) was as level-headed and logical as Irma was not, making no secret of her desire to land her wealthy boss Richard Rhinelander III (Leif Erickson) as her husband. Irma's brash boyfriend Al (John Brown), a Runyon character come to life, invariably greeted the girl with a jaunty "Hi'ya, chicken," just before getting her enmeshed in his latest get-rich-quick scheme. Other regulars included the girls' crotchety landlady Mrs. O'Reilly (Gloria Gordon) and elderly Professor Kropotkin (Hans Conried), violinist at a local burlesque house, who never let an opportunity pass to exchange insults with Mrs. O'Reilly or make an affectionate reference to Irma's vacuity.

There was a marked resemblance between *My Friend Irma* and the Joseph Fields-Jerome Chodorov stage play (and later motion picture) *My Sister Eileen,* which told of two small-town sisters—one a wisecracker, the other a gorgeous featherbrain—who came to New York to seek their fortune . The similarity did not go unnoticed by writer Arthur Kurlan, who in 1946 had been contracted by CBS to produce and script a radio version of *My Sister Eileen* starring Lucille Ball. (An announcement to this effect was made during a half-hour adaptation of *Eileen* on the May 18, 1946, broadcast of *Academy Award Theater.*) This project was cancelled at the last minute, but within the next year *My Friend Irma* signed onto the same network. Feeling that he'd been shabbily treated by CBS, Kurlan went to court, winning a sizable settlement and a financial piece of the *Irma* radio series and all future movie and print adaptations.

For her part, Wilson never issued a formal statement on this legal imbroglio; in fact, she was most often quoted in the press as "Irma" rather than herself, leading fans to conclude that the actress was just as stupid off-microphone as on. Hans Conried, who played Kropotkin on the radio show, spoke for the rest of the cast when describing the real Marie Wilson: "Marie is as good as Irma, with native kindness and an instinctive sense of justice. But Irma is dumb. Marie is not dumb." Like Gracie Allen before her, Wilson played her role so well that the public at large was convinced she was as big a dimwit as her character. Howard did nothing to discourage this presumption, stating in various interviews that most of the show material that he and co-writers Parke Levy, Stanley Adams and Roland MacLane came up with was inspired by Marie's zany offstage behavior and non sequitur pronouncements: "I have to rewrite the things she says to make them believable." Journalists picked up on this fantasy with such statements as "Marie is not only Irma on the air but in real life. She is the flutter-headed Samaritan who has the brains of a chipmunk."

A very savvy chipmunk, however, as Marie proved when Paramount producer Hal B. Wallis purchased *My Friend Irma* with the intention of making a film adaptation starring Betty Hutton as Irma Peterson. Contemporary news reports insisted that Wallis changed his mind only after receiving thousands of protest letters from the various Marie Wilson fan clubs throughout the land. Generally unmentioned was the fact that Marie herself had hired a press agent who'd lined up all those fans for a massive letter-writing campaign. Even in the face of this contrary evidence, Howard persisted in suggesting that Wilson was not quite "all there." In a 1949 *Radio Mirror* interview, he expressed outrage that the actress had called him up in the middle of the night to politely but firmly reject his screenplay for the film version, saying in a gentle voice, "I just feel you haven't captured my character, Cy"—which he apparently regarded as ingratitude born of stupidity. Only grudgingly did Howard admit that Marie was absolutely right, and that the script needed a total rehaul.

While Wallis bowed to pressure and cast Wilson in her familiar role for the film version, several other members of the radio cast were replaced. Paramount contractees Diana Lynn and John Lund took over in the roles of Jane and Al—with Lund getting his part only after Paramount was unable to borrow Jack Carson from Warner Bros.—while Don Defore was cast as Richard Rhinelander III. Conversely, Wallis retained the services of Gloria Gordon as Mrs. O'Reilly (a much smaller role on screen than on radio) and Hans Conried as Mr. Kropotkin. Actually, there are conflicting reports regarding Conried. In a 1970 interview with Leonard Maltin, the actor claimed that he'd turned down the film because he felt that he was too young-looking for the part; other sources indicate that Paramount never even considered the 32-year-old Conried, hiring Felix Bressart, then 57, to play Kropotkin. All this became a moot point when after a few days' shooting, Bressart died on March 17, 1949. As Conried recalled to Maltin: "Then the producer, who was an old friend of mine, said, 'Hans, you've got to fish us out.' So then I played the part; the close-ups are indeed little old me, and very badly performed, I was so obviously made up. The best parts of that performance are the long shots, in which Felix Bressart still crosses the camera field of vision." But as reported by Conried's biographer Suzanne Gargiulo, the actor was exercising his usual prerogative of not letting the facts spoil a good anecdote. An examination of the film reveals that Conried played Kropotkin all the way through, with no cutaways to Bressart in long shot. Some fast glimpses of Bressart remain in the film's nightclub scenes, but he and Conried are wearing different costumes, suggesting that the producer hoped audiences would assume that Bressart was merely an extra who happened to resemble Conried.

It's doubtful that anyone seeing *My Friend Irma* upon its August 16, 1949, release gave a tinker's dam who played Kropotkin—and there were probably those who weren't overly concerned with who played Irma either. Its main selling angle was the screen debut of Dean Martin and Jerry Lewis, then the hottest nightclub act in the country. Having signed them to a seven-picture, five-year contract beginning at $50,000 per film, Wallis thought it wise to test their movie potential in a proven property with built-in audience appeal. Billed fifth in the cast, Dean Martin is cast as Steve Laird, a character never heard on radio, who works at the orange juice stand frequented by Irma's beau Al. Discovering that Steve has a gorgeous singing voice, Al goes into the talent agent business with

Irma's dough, leading logically to the inevitable tunes by Jay Livingston and Ray Evans. Steve also serves a larger narrative purpose as the man with whom Jane falls in love despite her determination to wed Richard Rhinelander III. Jerry Lewis was billed sixth as doltish orange squeezer Seymour, a role invented at the last minute when preliminary screen tests indicated that Lewis was not yet a good enough actor to play any character other than himself. (The 23-year-old comedian had lobbied for the totally unsuitable part of Al until Wallis threatened to fire Jerry if he didn't shut up.) Despite the rawness of his performance and his minimal relevance to the storyline, Lewis manages to dominate every scene he's in.

The studio-dictated inclusion of Martin & Lewis aside, the filmization of *My Friend Irma* generally follows the pattern established on radio, with generous, good-hearted Irma doing her best to help Jane in her romantic pursuits but succeeding only in fouling things up almost beyond repair. Some of the script's best lines are holdovers from the radio version: When Jane sighs, "Wouldn't it be great if I wound up being Mrs. Richard Rhinelander the Third?," Irma asks "What good will that do if he's got two other wives?" Slightly jarring for fans of the series was the climactic sequence in which, after apparently ruining Jane's chances at romance and Steve's bid for show business success, Irma sadly ventures into the rainy night to commit suicide. Though of course nothing comes of this, the segment has the potential of leaving a sour taste in the mouth. Disaster is averted by Wilson's wonderful performance and the surehanded direction of George Marshall. Even when poised for her death leap into the East River, Irma is still Irma, carefully holding an umbrella over her head so she won't get her hair wet.

My Friend Irma was a gigantic box office success, though industryites recognized that it was Martin & Lewis and not Marie Wilson who packed 'em in. Verification of this can be found in the now-famous *New York Times* review by Bosley Crowther, who after dismissing the picture as worthless added, "Let us amend that ever so slightly. We could go along with the laughs that were fetched by a new mad comedian, Jerry Lewis by name.... As a hanger-on in the wake of Irma, he's the funniest thing in this film." To the surprise of no one, Wallis and Paramount decided to continue building up Martin & Lewis in the 1950 sequel *My Friend Irma Goes West*. In between the two Marie Wilson pictures, Dean and Jerry had starred in their own independently produced service comedy *At War with the Army,* in which both comedians

Marie Wilson gets to reprise her radio role as the title character in Paramount's *My Friend Irma* (1949), but Irma's shifty boyfriend Al is played by John Lund rather than John Brown on screen.

honed their screen acting skills to the point that they had outgrown the "extra added attraction" category. Nonetheless, their contract called for another "Irma" picture, so they were once again consigned to supporting roles. But with *At War with the Army* director Hal Walker at the helm, and the addition of an extended excerpt from the team's nightclub act with their regular bandleader Dick Stabile, there was little doubt as to whom the real stars of *My Friend Irma Goes West* (released several months before *Army*) were intended to be.

Ostensibly a sequel to *My Friend Irma,* the second film begins with a reprise of the first film's opening gag as clueless Irma falls down an open manhole. We then pick up where we left off with Al's never-ending efforts to make singer Steve Laird (Martin) a household name. With Richard Rhinelander III out of the picture (the double-wedding finale of *My Friend Irma* having been vague enough to allow for his absence), Jane willingly goes along with her new beau Steve, Irma, Al and Seymour to Hollywood under the misapprehension that Steve has been signed to a movie contract. But as luck and the scriptwriters would have it, the little party never gets any farther than Las Vegas, where Irma has opportunity aplenty to stroll around in a two-piece bathing suit and Jane must fight for Steve's affections with alluring movie starlet Yvonne Yvonne (played by Wallis "protégée" Corinne Calvet). Once again cast as Seymour, Jerry Lewis is given an even wider platform for his special brand of lunacy than in the team's starring picture *At War with the Army* as he romps through a Bette Davis imitation, lampoons a ten-gallon-hat gunslinger, and shares several routines with a remarkably well-trained chimpanzee. Though Lewis is overbearing at times (and would admit so himself when he saw the film's rushes), he remains the funniest and most compelling aspect of the sequel, which overall is pretty weak.

If Wilson was dissatisfied with the script of the first *Irma* film, one wonders what was running through her mind in this one, where she not only had to play third fiddle to Martin & Lewis but was also obliged to share screen space with Corinne Calvet, whom the producer obviously favored over Marie both photographically and otherwise. The film's nadir arrives when Irma is kidnapped by gangsters who are trying to muscle in on the "clean" Vegas casinos (Dean Martin must have gotten a guffaw out of *that!*) Driven crazy by Irma's incessant idiotic prattle, one of the thugs prepares to bump her off, whereupon she reacts not with comic fright but with genuine terror. In the best of circumstances, Irma's dumbness provided her with a shield of invulnerability: Like Gracie Allen, Wilson's character should never be in real jeopardy, or at the very least should remain oblivious to the danger. Showing a tremulous Irma desperately pleading for her life is a complete violation of form, and even the risible rescue efforts by Jerry Lewis do not absolve this scene of its sins.

Reviewing *My Friend Irma Goes West,* Herb Miller of the *Bridgeport* (CT) *Sunday Herald* declared, "Calling this *Martin and Lewis Go West* would describe the film much better because along the way 'Irma' seems to have been cut down to size to make room for the current entertainment favorites ... [T]he major share of the comedy belongs to Lewis, who appears to be able to go it alone any time he wants to." The cruelest blow to Wilson's ego came when some of the newspaper ads billed Martin & Lewis over the title, ignoring the actress completely. If not for the fact that Marie's then husband Allan Nixon was cast in the film at her request, *My Friend Irma Goes West* would have been of absolutely no value to the star either personally or professionally.

Fortunately the radio version of *My Friend Irma* was still in robust health in 1950, augmented by a series of comic books for Atlas (later Marvel) Publications and a daily Mirror Syndicate comic strip, both written by Stan Lee (the same) and drawn by Dan DeCarlo. There was also a three-act play adaptation of the property, written by James Reach and published for amateur theater consumption by Samuel French Inc. And in 1952 *My Friend Irma* was brought to live television (a few kinescopes still exist), again starring Wilson, Cathy Lewis and Gloria Gordon, with Sid Tomack as Al, Brooks West (the husband of Eve Arden) as Richard Rhinelander III, and Sig Arno as Kropotkin. Lewis quit both the radio and TV versions in 1953, whereupon Irma was given a new roommate named Kay Foster, played by Mary Shipp.

Faced with such heady competition as Lucille Ball, Joan Davis and Gale Storm, Wilson's dumb act inevitably began to wear thin on audiences, and in 1954 both network incarnations of *My Friend Irma* were cancelled. Marie went on to play character parts in such films as *Mr. Hobbs Takes a Vacation*, appear in nightclubs, and star in regional stage productions of *Born Yesterday* and *Gentlemen Prefer Blondes*. Shortly before her death in 1973, she provided the Irma-esque voice of Penny on the primetime Hanna-Barbera animated series *Where's Huddles?*

While dumb-blonde humor tends to go in and out of fashion with each new generation, the fundamental appeal of *My Friend Irma* is the same as that of such specialized comedians as Laurel & Hardy, the Three Stooges and Jackie Gleason, who also garnered huge laughs by making the audience feel superior to their characters. No one understood this better than Marie Wilson herself: "People like me because I'm dumb.... It gives them a good feeling to be smarter than I am."

"David Harding, Counterspy" (1950)

David Harding, Counterspy was the third title in producer Phillips H. Lord's "Triumvirate of Tension" (a phrase coined by radio historian Jim Harmon), following closely on the heels of his *Gang Busters* and *Mr. District Attorney* (both q.v.) Officially titled simply *Counterspy*, the weekly 30-minute series began its Blue Network run on May 18, 1942, five months after Pearl Harbor. Accordingly, the show was top-heavy with German and Japanese spies, none of whom proved to be a match for David Harding, special agent of the United States Counterspies.

If you've never heard of that particular government organization, that's because it didn't exist. Having had a certain amount of difficulty with J. Edgar Hoover over story content in *Gang Busters*, Lord wasn't about to identify any actual covert counterintelligence agency by name. Hence the fictional United States Counterspies, which not only operated with a completely free hand but was also apparently a law unto itself, replete with special holding cells to keep enemy agents out of circulation until Harding ordered their execution! Despite the "no names please" policy of the radio series, Lord continued courting the same controversy he'd stirred up on *Mr. District Attorney* by dramatizing actual cases of American counterespionage before they'd even been revealed to the public. (No, he didn't have moles within the FBI; he simply applied deduction and logic in coming up with his scenarios.)

Actor Don McLaughlin, then appearing concurrently on Lord's *Gang Busters*, brought plenty of gravitas to the role of David Harding, who in the earliest episodes did most of the legwork and spy-busting himself, but eventually turned over the rough stuff to his young and virile sidekick Peters, played by Mandel Kramer. (The two lead actors would occasionally be reunited on the long-running TV serial *As the World Turns*, on which McLaughlin played Chris Hughes for nearly 30 years.) Though *Counterspy* was aimed at a family audience, and in later years was sponsored by such kid-oriented products as Bit-o-Honey candy and Pepsi-Cola, the program was one of the most uncompromisingly grim and violent of its genre, with cold-blooded villains merrily slaughtering American agents, innocent bystanders and even their own henchmen in pursuit of their insidious goals. This carnage was well in keeping with the propagandistic nature of the program during the World War II years—Lord had in fact planned for the series to end once the war was over—but seemed a bit excessive after 1945 when Harding's foes became Communist agents and nonpolitical master criminals (mostly played by sandpaper-voiced Ralph Bell).

In the wake of their recent mass termination of the *Boston Blackie, Crime Doctor* and *Lone Wolf* series, Columbia Pictures decided in late 1949 to launch a new group of crime-and-punishment B pictures, again based on a proven property. *Counterspy* was chosen for this honor but McLaughlin was not brought along, even though he fit the physical requirements for the role. Instead, the studio went with one of their own contractees: Howard St. John, a 45-year-old stage actor of wide experience who'd made his screen debut in 1949's *Shockproof* (which didn't stop Columbia from giving the actor an "introducing" credit in the first *Counterspy* picture). The authoritative St. John is probably best known today for his Broadway and motion picture performance as double-dealing zillionaire General Bullmoose in the musical-comedy adaptation of Al Capp's *Li'l Abner*. (The actor can be heard talking—not singing, just talking—his big character song "Progress Is the Root of All Evil" on the original cast album.) In the tradition of the radio series, moviedom's David Harding was teamed with his younger and more athletic assistant Peters, played by future director Fred Sears.

Written by Tom Reed and directed by Ray Nazarro, the 71-minute *David Harding, Counterspy* (1950) opens with a prologue that is fascinating on a sociopolitical level. After delivering an impassioned opinion piece attacking the U.S. government for recently allowing enemy agents to get their hands on top-secret information, radio correspondent Ray Kingston (Alex Gerry) is kidnapped by two sinister-looking men. In a normal workaday crime melodrama, Kingston would then be taken for a one-way ride, or at the very least given a painful going-over on orders from a mysterious "Mister Big." Not this time, however: The correspondent's abductors turn out to be the *good guys,* operatives for U.S. Counterespionage chieftain David Harding. Calmly chastising Kingston for his reckless editorializing, Harding explains that the information about the stolen secrets was completely false, a subterfuge designed to mislead a gang of foreign agents. One might expect that Kingston will tear into Harding for violating his First Amendment rights, and for sending the whole country off on a wild goose chase. Instead, the reporter meekly apologizes and shuts up long enough for Harding to tell him a story of a similar false-intelligence strategy that occurred during World War II. If all this seems incredible to modern viewers inured by the whistle-blowing, tell-all journalism seen on the various cable news channels, remember that *David Harding, Counterspy* was made in the middle of the Cold War, when you just plain didn't question *any* action perpetrated by the U.S. Government (at least not out loud).

After this powerhouse opening, *David Harding, Counterspy* settles into a lethargically paced flashback to 1943. Naval officer Jerry Baldwin (Willard Parker) is dispatched by Harding to take over from an undercover agent working at a torpedo-manufacturing plant. The agent died in what appeared to be a workplace accident but Baldwin suspects it was murder. Making this assignment tougher is the fact that he'd once been in love with the dead man's widow Betty (Audrey Long), who also works at the plant. It gradually develops that Betty is in cahoots with the plant's house physician Dr. Vickers (Raymond Greenleaf), secretly the leader of a Nazi spy ring. A few gimmicky grace notes involving an infrared light and a mini-camera hidden in a false hearing aid do little to enliven the sluggish proceedings, though the film has a moderately exciting wrap-up staged in a darkened airport terminal where the Nazis await the arrival of secret information which, unbeknownst to them, has been fabricated by Harding to throw them off the track. (The plan must have worked: Look who won the war.)

Released four months after the first series entry, *Counterspy Meets Scotland Yard* (working title: *David Harding's Secret Mission*) is an improvement over its predecessor, perhaps because it is four minutes shorter, or perhaps because Seymour Friedman was a better director than Ray Nazarro. Scripted by Harold Greene, the second film adheres religiously to the formula established in the first: a counterintelligence operative sent to work at a top-secret defense plant to replace an agent who has died under mysterious circumstances; a romance involving the agent and a female employee at the same plant; sensitive information smuggled to the Enemy via a miniaturized device; and a staff physician who turns out to be a foreign spy. This entry is not set in the past but in "the present" (1950), and the female lead is not herself a subversive but instead an innocent pawn of the genuine villains.

Sensing that the suicide of a fellow agent was really murder, Harding assigns Scotland Yard operative Simon Langton (Ron Randell) to take over the dead man's job at a California factory specializing in the manufacture of guided missiles (which look like something out of *Flash Gordon*). The undercover Langton makes the acquaintance of secretary Karen Michele (Amanda Blake in one of her best pre–*Gunsmoke* performances), who is undergoing psychiatric treatment to overcome her wartime experiences in a Nazi concentration camp. We soon learn that "kindly" Dr. Vincent Gilbert (Lewis Martin)—real name Hugo Boren—is on the payroll of an unnamed foreign government, and that he has been plying the clueless Karen with truth serum so that she will reveal secrets regarding those missiles. This information is transcribed on a tiny tape recorder, whereupon the tape is secreted in the corks used in the water bottles regularly brought into and out of the office by the minions of water company executive Mr. Miller (Charles Meredith), ringleader of the enemy agents. So cunningly complex is Mr. Miller's scheme that one is almost pulling for him to get away with it!

The original *Counterspy* remained a weekly radio staple on ABC, NBC and Mutual until November 29, 1957, outlasting such similar programs as *Cloak and Dagger*, *This Is Your FBI* and *The FBI in Peace and War*. In 1958, producer Bernard L. Schubert revived the property as a TV series pilot, filmed in England and starring Don Megowan as David Harding. Though divested of the radio show's familiar opening signature—"Washington calling David Harding, counterspy! Washington calling David Harding, counterspy!" [beep-beep-beep of a telegraph key] "David Harding, counterspy, calling Washington!"—the TV version follows the usual pattern of Harding supervising covert activities from behind his desk while a lesser operative (in this case, a civilian scuba diver) does most of the physical work. And as on radio, the bad guys are so blatant that they might as well be wearing neon signs, especially the lead heavy who preaches a doctrine of world peace in a thick Boris Badenov dialect. *David Harding, Counterspy* never went to series; the pilot is available on several DVD "Golden Age of Television" collections.

From the second of Columbia's two radio-inspired *Counterspy* films: This 1950 ad is dominated by third-billed Ron Randell (top right), while nominal star Howard St. John (lower left) issues instructions via microphone.

The Goldbergs (1950)

The motion picture version of Gertrude Berg's venerable radio serial *The Goldbergs* was a long time coming—so long in fact that it just barely qualifies as a radio-to-film adaption, and might be more appropriately described as the first TV comedy series to be transformed into a movie.

Born in Harlem in 1899, Gertrude Edelstein grew up in a show business atmosphere as the daughter of a Catskill Mountains resort owner. She had been Mrs. Gertrude Berg for nearly a decade when, at age 29, she decided to try her luck writing for radio. Her first sketch was about a Bronx housewife saddled with a lazy, no-good husband (one hopes this was not autobiographical). But during the revision process the characters were changed to a gently counseling *Yiddishe mama,* her loving and industrious husband, and their two children, whom the mother believed should be allowed to determine their own destinies—a belief opposed by her dictatorial "old world" spouse, who nonetheless always seemed to come around to his wife's way of thinking. First heard as a one-shot on New York's WMCA, Mrs. Berg's fragmentary sketch (originally titled "Effie and Laura") blossomed into the daily, 15-minute serial *The Rise of the Goldbergs* on NBC-Blue beginning November 30, 1929. Like the popular *Amos 'n' Andy* (q.v.), the program followed a dramatic and sometimes poignant narrative in a basically comical fashion, and like *Amos 'n' Andy* the humor was ethnic in nature, the difference being that Berg was authentically Jewish and not an Anglo-Saxon made up to look Jewish. The original cast consisted of Berg as Molly Goldberg, James Waters as her tailor husband Jake, Alfred Ryder as their son Sammy and Roslyn Silber as their daughter Rosalie. The great Yiddish comedian Menasha Skulnik rounded out the regulars as the philosophical Uncle David, Jake's pet pinochle companion and verbal sparring partner.

From the beginning, the series was praised for its warmth, depth and authenticity, qualities maintained by Berg's periodic forays into real-life Bronx and Lower East Side neighborhoods to absorb local color. In the earliest episodes, Berg wrote her scripts in a thick Milt Gross–like Yiddish dialect, but as time went on, the actors would instinctively fall into the proper cadence without having their accents typed out. Though her program—its title eventually streamlined to *The Goldbergs*—seemed casual and spontaneous, Berg rehearsed her cast like a drill sergeant, sweating over the simplest line or sound effect for hours until it was performed to her satisfaction. The Goldbergs became a genuine family not only to the listeners but to themselves; there were no significant cast changes until the program had been on the air for nearly nine years, at which time Everett Sloane took over as Sammy. So secure was Berg with her program and co-stars that it was said that she could complete a *Goldbergs* script in less than half an hour—and if any last-minute emergencies arose, she could revise that script from top to bottom in as little as eight minutes.

The actress became so closely identified with Molly Goldberg that when she attempted a new characterization as a nagging *yente* on the 1935 radio serial *House of Glass,* her fans roundly rejected this stab at versatility. Except for a year-long hiatus during the experimental *House of Glass, The Goldbergs* remained on the air in its original daily quarter-hour format—and with the same theme music, "Toselli's Serenade"—over two different networks until March 30, 1945. Three years later Berg revived the property as a Broadway play, *Molly and Me,* which ran 156 performances; at the same time she began putting together a cast for a proposed weekly 30-minute TV version of *The Goldbergs.* The all-important role of Jake was filled by Philip Loeb, whose extensive stage work had been long familiar to Berg. Well liked among the Jewish theatrical community, Loeb was nonetheless regarded as a risky loose cannon because of his intense political beliefs and fervent left-wing activism; but Berg admired these qualities and felt they added a fiery subtext to the part of Jake (though no political philosophy of any kind was ever preached on the series). Other new members of the cast were Larry Robinson as Sammy, Arlene McQuade as Rosalie and Eli Mintz as Uncle David.

When NBC rejected *The Goldbergs* as being too verbose for television, Berg arranged an audition with CBS president William Paley, resulting in an immediate sale and the sponsorship of General Foods. The video version of *The Goldbergs,* telecast live from CBS's New York facilities, began running on January 10, 1949, and was an immediate hit in those areas where television had already gained a foothold. Berg's writing and the individual characterizations were as sharp as ever, with an added dimension of intimacy as Molly opened each show by sticking her head out of her Bronx apartment window to carry on a brief expository conversation with the folks at home. During these interludes Molly also unobtrusively pushed her sponsor's product, which even without the verbal backup was a constant presence by virtue of the Sanka coffee can that served as a flowerpot on Mrs. Goldberg's windowsill.

As this Emmy-winning incarnation of *The Goldbergs* launched its second season, the radio version was briefly revived on CBS, likewise in a weekly half-hour format and with the same cast that appeared on TV. Though they'd been together less than a year, the performers interacted as if they'd been an honest-to-goodness family for decades, and this ambience would be carried over into the long-overdue Hollywood movie version of *The Goldbergs*, filmed at Paramount in May 1950. Co-scripted by Berg and N. Richard Nash (*The Rainmaker*) and again featuring the television cast, *The Goldbergs* was directed by the TV version's resident megger Walter Hart (a graduate of the MGM short subject department) with the same swift and sure efficiency he'd established for the CBS program, including intensive rehearsals and the use of multiple cameras running simultaneously. Six of the script's pages had actually been lensed as makeup tests prior to the official starting date, but were deemed good enough to include in the finished film. Everyone on the Paramount lot marveled at how Berg and her closely knit unit were able to accomplish in a fast four weeks what normally took two to three months to complete: UP correspondent Patricia Clearly reported from the set, "The only time they stop is when the camera breaks down from overheating. Then Mrs. Berg, who wrote the movie script and rewrites it as she goes, works on next year's television story." *The Goldbergs* ultimately came in under schedule and, to the gratification of the studio accountants, under budget.

Gertrude Berg in her natural habitat as Molly Goldberg, adding motion pictures to her radio and TV triumphs.

Despite a popular assumption that *The Goldbergs* was based on the stage play *Molly and Me*, the story and its complications are unique to the film. The plot finds Jake putting on airs and stretching the household budget for a dinner party to impress a wealthy and important visitor, Molly's former beau Alexander "Abie" Abel (Eduard Franz in a beautifully delineated performance). Everyone is surprised when Abie, well into "the middle ages," shows up accompanied by his 23-year-old fiancée Debby Sherman (Barbara Rush in her screen debut). Not at all a gold-digger as the neighbors suspect, Debby is genuinely in love with Abie, or so she tells herself. In one of the film's many well-staged kitchen scenes, Molly determines without a single overt statement that Debby, the product of a broken home, has latched onto Abie as a surrogate father. The girl's resolve to go through with the marriage is weakened when, while attending Molly's weekly music appreciation class, she meets handsome young teacher Ted Gordon (Peter Hanson). Though sensing that Debbie and Ted would be a better match than Debbie and Abie, Molly works overtime to keep the two young people apart, but succeeds only in forcing them together, precipitating a chain reaction of wounded pride, shouting matches and the squelching of Jake's dream of opening a chain of clothing stores with Abie's financial support. But what seems an insurmountable catastrophe yields beneficial results, with Jake developing enough initiative to take business chances on his own, Debby and Ted falling in love without consequences, and Abie finding a more appropriate soul mate in the form of the widowed Mrs. Morris (Betty Walker), whose small son Uncle David occasionally babysits. The giddily artificial Hollywood ending, with Molly's fellow PTA members staging a "show and tell" of wedding gifts to reunite the temporarily estranged young lovers, is brought back to reality by Jake's realization that he will probably never become a prosperous manufacturer like Abie, and should count the blessings he already has.

Though for the most part acted and photographed like a stage play (or a live TV show), *The Goldbergs* boasts enough interplay, byplay, character business and throwaway comic lines—especially from David Opatoshu as Jake's harried accountant—to bring the film to life for any audience, Jewish or Gentile. Early concerns that the film might be too ethnocentric for general consumption were addressed by the trade and newspaper reviews, which lauded Berg for the authenticity of the dialects, gestures and family rituals, and also for resisting the temptation to poke fun at the characters' eccentricities. The *Los Angeles Times* predicted that "non–Jews should find it as recognizably human as the Gaelic characterizations of, say, *Going My Way*." But this didn't seem to be happening during the initial limited run of *The Goldbergs* in November 1950, when box office returns failed to meet expectations. Reasoning that the title might be a turn-off for those unattuned to Jewish humor, Paramount changed it to *Molly* for the film's general release in early 1951. Apparently this did the trick, for *Molly* not only earned back its cost but also rang up a respectable profit. The film proved especially attractive to moviegoers in those parts of the country without television coverage, who were still curious as to what Gertrude Berg and her radio family looked like. (Previously published reports that the actress appeared in the 1937 Bobby Breen musical *Make a Wish* are inaccurate, though she did co-write the screenplay.)

Molly was just making inroads theatrically when its TV source became embroiled in controversy. Co-star Philip Loeb had been labeled a Communist sympathizer in the odious publication *Red Channels,* and Berg was under great pressure to drop the actor from the cast. Though she put up a loyal and valiant resistance to this effrontery, Berg was ultimately forced to fire Loeb in 1951, replacing him first with Harold J. Stone and later Robert H. Harris. Berg did what she could to help Loeb through this harrowing period, paying him full salary for two years after his dismissal, but his inability to secure any other work, combined with profound personal difficulties, climaxed with his suicide in 1955 (a tragedy fictionalized in the 1976 blacklist drama *The Front,* with Zero Mostel as the Philip Loeb surrogate). By that time *The*

Goldbergs had left network television to become a sort of Kosher *Father Knows Best* in off-network syndication, with Molly and her family moving out of their Bronx tenement and into the white-bread suburb of Haverville for 39 filmed episodes.

Berg went on to win a Tony award for her performance in the successful 1959 Broadway comedy *A Majority of One* opposite Sir Cedric Hardwicke, with whom she also co-starred in the short-lived 1961 CBS sitcom *Mrs. G Goes to College* (the "G" this time standing for Green). The actress would star in one more Broadway production, the 1963 musical *Dear Me, the Sky Is Falling,* before her death in 1966.

The Fat Man (1951)

There is a common misapprehension that crime novelist Dashiell Hammett's radio detective "The Fat Man" was inspired by Kasper Gutman, the obese master criminal in Hammett's 1930 novel *The Maltese Falcon*. But as noted by radio historian Jim Harmon, the Fat Man was more likely based on a frequently referenced but unnamed detective in the "Continental Op" stories written by Hammett for *Black Mask* magazine in the 1920s and 1930s. It can be safely assumed, however, that the title *The Fat Man* was intended to evoke memories of Hammett's *The Thin Man,* which after enjoying success in book form was spun off into a popular MGM film series and a long-running radio mystery program. (The preponderance of Hammett characters with adjectives for names inspired radio comedy writer Aaron Ruben to develop a detective spoof titled *The Small Man,* starring comedian Bert Wheeler. *Billboard* magazine reported that the pilot episode was hysterically funny, but no series resulted.)

Premiering January 21, 1946, on ABC, the weekly half-hour *The Fat Man* chronicled the exploits of private sleuth Brad Runyon, who on each episode was introduced by a sultry feminine voice: "There he goes, into that drugstore.... He's stepping on the scale.... Weight? Two hundred thirty-seven pounds.... Fortune—danger! Whoooo is it?" Well, we *knew* who it was, but Brad Runyon told us anyway: "*The Fat Maaaaan.*"

Runyon worked alone with very little time for a social life, though for a guy of his bulk he seemed to do quite well with the ladies. The show's mystery element was usually established when Runyon's latest client came knocking at his office door to provide the corpulent crimefighter with just enough information for Brad to know he was in for another eventful day. Though he preferred relying upon dissemination of clues and fundamental logic (the latter a variable commodity given the whims of radio writers), Runyon could also be a man of action if the need arose, and by episode's end he always fingered the culprit—who on more than one occasion was the person who hired him in the first place. Unlike some other radio gumshoes, Runyon was on generally good terms with the official police authorities (notably Sgt. O'Hara, played by Ed Begley), who willingly opened their files to him so he could piece the weekly puzzle together.

Throughout the ABC run Brad Runyon was portrayed by J. Scott Smart (1902–1960), who as Jack Smart had already racked up a lengthy radio, stage and film career, often in comedy roles opposite Bob Hope, Jack Benny and Fred Allen (he was heard as blustery "Allen's Alley" resident Senator Bloat, precursor to the more celebrated Senator Claghorn). Befitting his most famous role, Smart not only had the advantage of being fat in real life but also sounding fat on the air: Even his *theme music* sounded fat. Particularly memorable was Smart's distinctive way of slurring words for emphasis—especially when referring to the gentle art of "*murrr-*der."

The film adaptation of *The Fat Man* was originally announced in 1949 by producer Hunt Stromberg as a potential Columbia release starring Sidney Greenstreet, who had played Kasper Gutman in the 1941 filmization of *The Maltese Falcon* and was then portraying Rex Stout's equally heavy hawkshaw Nero Wolfe on radio. Greenstreet's failing health put the kibosh on this project, whereupon the property was purchased by Aubrey Schenck for Universal-International. The decision to hire Smart to

Julie London clearly relishes the opportunity to jitterbug with J. Scott Smart, cast as the pudgy title character in Universal-International's *The Fat Man* (1951).

recreate his radio role was aesthetically satisfying but chancy in terms of box office, since Smart was a largely (in every sense of the word) unknown quantity to the average filmgoer. Thus, what had been intended as a Columbia "A" picture was scaled down to a budget-conscious Universal programmer, a not altogether bad thing at a time when the studio was excelling within these limitations with the "Francis" and "Ma and Pa Kettle" series, not to mention their endless parade of inexpensive Technicolor westerns. Assigned to direct *The Fat Man* was William Castle, already well-versed in economical but entertaining radio-to-movie adaptations (see separate entries on *The Crime Doctor* and *The Whistler*).

Scripted by Harry J. Essex and Leonard Lee, *The Fat Man* is not so much a whodunit as a why'd-he-do-it. The audience is treated to a full facial view of the man who murders dentist Henry Bromley (played *sans* screen credit by radio announcer Ken Niles) in the opening scene, but it takes the deductive prowess of Brad Runyon to figure out the motivation for the murder (the killer was after a set of incriminating dental X-rays). Runyon must also determine if an elusive young ex-convict was the killer—and once it is rather forcefully proven that he wasn't (the kid becomes a murder victim himself), how the former prisoner fits into the greater mystery involving a $500,000 armored car robbery. Essex and Lee don't have to work too hard to make Brad Runyon a likable screen presence, since it was already well known to his fans that beneath Brad's gruff exterior beat a 14-karat heart: When he finally says "*murrr*-der" in this picture, it's as a comic punchline.

The writers expand upon Runyon's established character traits by adding a fondness for gourmet food (in his very first scene he is found in the kitchen of a fancy restaurant, assisting the chef in preparing his favorite repast *just* so) and a hitherto untapped talent as a jitterbug dancer, showing the elephantine Mr. Smart cutting a rug with astonishing grace and agility. This, too, came as no surprise to Smart's loyal fans, who knew by heart the story of the actor winning a Charleston contest. Additionally, a *soupçon* of Nero Wolfe is thrown in by providing Runyon with a wisecracking "Archie Goodwin"–type legman named Bill Norton, played by Clinton Sundberg. A few of the radio series' devotees have objected to this emendation (Jim Harmon griped about the "whole crew of flunkies" forced upon Runyon in the movie), but the breezy rapport between Smart and Sundberg is quite appealing—and now that he has someone to talk to, Runyon doesn't have to rely upon first-person narration, a device that generally works better on radio than in the movies.

The film version of *The Fat Man* manages to convey many of the best qualities of the radio version in purely cinematic terms. As in the original program, overt violence is kept to a minimum: Once the rather vicious introductory murder is over and done with, plot and dialogue effectively carry the ball. When violence occurs again, director Castle handles it in an unfailingly surprising and offbeat manner. One sudden burst of gunfire occurs in the middle of a casual conversation, providing a real jolt; the capture of a suspect is climaxed by a slow-motion shot of his body falling towards the camera; and the unexpected murder of a principal character (and a sympathetic one to boot) is superbly staged with a medium shot of the victim blithely entering an office where the killer lurks in the shadows, followed by an extremely brief track-in to a closed door.

Also innovative was the decision to downpedal the film's romantic subplot, despite the luscious presence of singer Julie London as an outwardly hardboiled beauty who is revealed to be broken-hearted over her apparent betrayal by the aforementioned ex-convict. In a much larger role, Jayne Meadows plays a woman with seemingly no men in her life at all, save for her murdered boss and the guy who plans to bump *her* off. And as the ostensible romantic lead, 25-year-old Universal contractee Rock Hudson is seen only in flashback—one of these a flashback within a flashback—but the role is substantial enough to stand as one of the fledgling actor's best early showings.

In the months before the film was theatrically released in May 1951, the Universal publicity department did its usual efficient job of making the public *Fat Man*–conscious. A United Press tidbit of August 2, 1950, insisted that Smart almost lost out on the title role because he was *too* fat. Smart's studio contract stipulated that he tip the scales at no less than 230 nor more than 250 pounds. Dutifully shedding some of his 270 pounds, the actor was still ten pounds over the limit when he arrived on the set, and was forced into a dietary and exercise regimen that he openly despised. "It's ridiculous," Smart is quoted as saying. "Why should a fat man reduce in order to play a fat man? I owe it to my audiences to be as fat as I can get."

There was some highly suspect flackery in an Associated Press article from September 30, 1950, which if nothing else demonstrates that Castle was already practicing the sort of gimmickry that would draw customers to his later horror films *Macabre, House on Haunted Hill, The Tingler* and *13 Ghosts*. According to an AP correspondent, "Not even the cast knows who committed the four murders in *The Fat Man*. As an experiment in mystery story filming, director William Castle decided not to divulge the secret until the final scene. He says he wants to catch 'genuine bewilderment and surprise' on the actors' faces." Hold on, it gets better: "Castle concedes that the players are capable of simulating the expressions but 'I simply want to see surprise that is not simulated, and compare it with the synthetic variety. We'll shoot the ending twice and use the one with the best reactions.'"

Yeh, sure. Never mind that the face of the murderer is shown in the very first scene. Never mind that one of the principal characters spends an inordinate amount of screen time in heavy facial makeup, obscuring his features. Never mind that as written, the ending could *only* have been performed by the actor playing the killer. And never mind that even before the film's premiere, the identity of the killer was exposed in one press release after another. After all, reasoned Universal, we've gone to a lot of trouble and expense to hire Emmett Kelly, "The World's Greatest Clown," for his dramatic film debut (Kelly had come to Hollywood for a Barnum and Bailey picture planned but abandoned by David O. Selznick). Why not clue the public in to the fact that the beloved circus star is going to be cast totally against type as a pathetic murderer? "The kindly Kelly turns evil in the picture, and will wear no makeup" was the "exclusive" printed in Hedda Hopper's column of August 1, 1951, while the film was still in distribution and had barely reached the hinterlands.

Before you take this writer to task for giving away the ending, it must be noted that Kelly did a pretty thorough job of that himself. Interviewed by Fred Wright of the *St. Petersburg* (FL) *Independent* in December 1972, Kelly not only reiterated that he "done it" in *The Fat Man,* but also explained why he appeared in traditional clown-white makeup rather than as his copyrighted alter ego, hapless hobo Weary Willie: "I rebelled against playing Willie in that. I didn't want Willie to be associated with all of that. So I played a different clown in that movie, not Willie." (Some sources have gone so far as to state that this was Emmett Kelly's only unsympathetic screen turn, forgetting that he also shows up as drink-sodden swamp pirate "Bigamy Bob" in Nicholas Ray's 1958 melodrama *Wind Across the Everglades.*)

The above-cited spoilers should not diminish one's enjoyment of *The Fat Man,* any more than when the film was originally released. It might have resulted in a whole series of pictures starring Smart had not the radio version of *The Fat Man* been cancelled along with all the other Dashiell Hammett–derived programs (including *The Thin Man* and *Sam Spade*) in the wake of Hammett being branded a Communist sympathizer by the House Un-American Activities Committee. A somewhat emaciated radio revival of *The Fat Man* starring Lloyd Berrell ran in 1954 and 1955 on the Australian Broadcasting Corporation; and in 1958, Joseph H. Lewis directed the one-hour pilot episode for an unsold TV version of *The Fat Man* starring Robert Middleton as Detective Lucius Crane.

Queen for a Day (1951)

Queen for a Day was once described by the esteemed TV writer, comic book author and media historian Mark Evanier as "one of the most ghastly shows ever produced." Evanier then relaxed, thought it over for a while, and added that the show was "tasteless, demeaning to women, demeaning to anyone who watched it, cheap, insulting and utterly degrading to the human spirit."

Created by Raymond R. Morgan (see *Chandu the Magician*) and Robert Raisback, *Queen for a Day* signed on as a weekday Mutual radio series on April 30, 1945. It was designed to showcase the interviewing skills of its original host Dud Williamson, who on each 30-minute episode invited five ladies from the studio audience to express their fondest wishes to the nation. The audience would by their applause select the woman whom they felt deserved most to have her wish come true, whereupon she was crowned with a tacky tiara as "Queen for a Day," wrapped in a moth-eaten robe and bombarded with fabulous "in exchange for advertising" gifts. During its initial New York run the show was lighthearted in nature, and remained so when production moved to Hollywood and ex–

sideshow barker Jack Bailey (1907–1980) was hired as emcee. A mustachioed, oily-looking jasper who came off like the guy in the parking lot who sells you a microwave from his trunk, the leather-lunged Bailey was mischief incarnate as he played the crowd, cajoled the contestants into making embarrassing statements just prior to revealing their wishes, and performed silly *Truth or Consequences*–like stunts for the benefit of the hysterical crowd. Before long, the ladies at home just couldn't get through the afternoon unless they heard Bailey's booming intro "Would *you* like to be Queen for a Day?" and outro "This is Jack Bailey, wishing we could make *every* woman Queen for every day!"

This essentially humorous effort would by the end of the 1940s morph into a clone of the maudlin human-interest series *Strike It Rich,* wherein people down on their luck would relate their tales of woe in hopes of receiving huge cash donations from a call-in "heartline." The number of *Queen for a Day* contestants was reduced from five to three, the better to allow each luckless lady to swill in misery as she unraveled her sorry saga of the unrepaired leaky roof in her bedridden mother's shanty house, the expensive operation needed for her mentally unbalanced double-amputee soldier husband, or the summer-camp vacation that was the heart's desire of her blind, deaf and terminally ill son. (These are composite examples: The individual ones are even more wretched, but let's move on.) Put bluntly, the show's applause meter rewarded the winning contestant for being the biggest loser of the day.

This dismal state of affairs held true as *Queen for a Day* made the transition to television beginning in 1955 on NBC, moving to ABC before breathing its last in 1964. In today's post-feminist, post–Oprah era, one might assume that any halfway intelligent woman would run screaming from the set the moment Bailey's gnarly little head appeared onscreen. And yet at its height, *Queen for a Day* was viewed by 13,000,000 fans, and there is photographic evidence aplenty of thousands of *Monty Python*–esque hausfraus standing in line for hours to attend the various *Queen for a Day* remote telecasts throughout the continental U.S. (A 1969 syndicated TV revival was cancelled after disgruntled viewers discovered that the winners had been chosen in advance.)

With so much going against it, United Artists' 1951 film adaptation of *Queen for a Day* has no business being as good as it is. At first glance, producers Seton I. Miller (who also wrote the screenplay) and Robert Stillman appear to have drawn inspiration from the 1946 filmization of the daily audience participation show *Breakfast in Hollywood* (q.v.), in which the titular radio series served as a way station for four separate subplots involving a group of otherwise unrelated characters. Actually, the 107-minute *Queen for a Day* is more in the tradition of such "omnibus" films as *If I Had a Million* and *Tales of Manhattan,* in which a single item (a million-dollar legacy, a fancy dinner coat) is the catalyst for a collection of short playlets, each with a different cast. The structure of the 1951 film is also heavily influenced by the popular British multipart films *Quartet, Trio* and *Encore,* each of which features a star-studded cast in dramatizations of stories by W. Somerset Maugham. In this respect, *Queen for a Day* anticipates two better-known 20th Century–Fox omnibus efforts, *O. Henry's Full House* and *We're Not Married!* (see entry on **Fred Allen**).

The film's framing story is spread out over several *Queen for a Day* broadcasts on both radio and television, even though the source program hadn't yet made its TV bow. Coming off as the deadly alien spawn of Art Linkletter and Bob Barker, Jack Bailey cavorts about the stage like a giggling baboon, hectoring the contestants for the benefit of the studio audience but turning serious when seriousness is called for. As in the original radio version, three main stories are dwelled upon. Each is based on a short story by a different author, each is directed in a markedly different style by the versatile Arthur Lubin, and each boasts a distinctive musical score by Emil Newman.

In Story Number One, Faith Baldwin's "Gossamer World," young mother Marjorie Watkins (Phyllis Avery), who does not win on *Queen for a Day*, nonetheless writes a thank-you letter to the show. We then flash back to Marjorie and her husband Dan (Darren McGavin) allowing their six-year-old son Pete (Rudy Lee) to dwell in a fantasy world where the kid drills a well, tends a farm, repairs the plumbing, and best of all drives a train. It turns out that Pete is a victim of infantile paralysis, and that the toy train sent to him as a *Queen for a Day* consolation prize had enabled him to briefly live out his dreams to the fullest. This touching segment is delicately accompanied by background music played on toy instruments.

Less whimsical but equally dramatic is Story Number Two, adapted from John Ashworth's award-winning magazine piece "High Diver." The son of Polish immigrants, Chunk Nalawak (Adam Williams) plans to work his way through college, starting with a job as substitute for a carnival high-diver (yes, circus music is heard throughout this one). Just before making a perilous 110-foot dive, Chunk forms an affectionate bond with fellow carny performer Peggy (Tracey Roberts). Seconds after the big plunge, Chunk learns that he never had to go through with the stunt, since his mother (Kazia Orzazewski) has been chosen Queen for a Day and has won him a full scholarship. It's a happy ending for everyone but Peggy, who realizes that Chunk is now lost to her forever. The thematic resemblance between "High Diver" and the Charles Boyer–Barbara Stanwyck segment (involving a tightrope walker) in the 1943 omnibus picture *Flesh and Fantasy* was not lost on the United Artists publicity department, who featured an artist's rendition of Adam Williams leaping from a diving board in the print ads for *Queen for a Day*. (Another story involving a high-dive artist, "Gigolo and Gigolette," was dramatized in the Somerset Maugham portmanteau film *Encore,* released in the U.S. in 1952.) An uncredited Leonard Nimoy makes his first screen appearance in this episode.

After so much heavy going in the previous scenes, the audience is in the mood for a few laughs. The final segment, underscored with mocking oboe music, is adapted from "Horsie," a story by humorist Dorothy Parker. Played by Edith Meiser, the title character (real name Ella) is an incredibly homely spinster who works as a children's nurse. Her present assignment finds her caring for the wife and newborn child of obnoxious business executive Owen Cruger (Dan Tobin), who pokes cruel fun at Ella's equine facial features, incessant baby talk and gauche behavior. Imagine everyone's surprise when, while appearing on a TV broadcast of *Queen for a Day,* Ella asks for the prize of an electric shaver, which she intends to give to the "nicest, kindest" boss she's ever had—Mr. Owen Cruger.

For a while, the release title for *Queen for a Day* was *Horsie* (an unsubtle cash-in on director Arthur Lubin's popular talking-mule comedy *Francis*), thus the third segment received more press attention than the others. According to the United Artists flack squad, distinguished stage actress Edith Meiser implored the producers to cast her as "Horsie," only to be told that she was too attractive for the part. Undiscouraged, she auditioned with a ridiculous hairdo, a hideous hat and a set of false buck teeth—and nailed the role on the spot. For the film itself, makeup artist Lou Phillippi elongated her lovely features with soft sponge rubber, all the while referencing photographs of genuine "horsies."

Queen for a Day is one of those pleasant little independent films that popped up all over the place on television in the 1950s and 1960s, then abruptly vanished from sight. If you can find a copy, it's definitely a more pleasant way to spend your time than the ten known existing kinescopes of TV's *Queen for a Day*—which, all things considered, is approximately ten too many.

Ozzie and Harriet and *Here Come the Nelsons* (1952)

Please spare me your warnings. I am already aware that some readers will turn away from this entry in contempt and disgust. To many disillusioned baby boomers, *The Adventures of Ozzie and Harriet* represents the most egregious exemplification of the false values and empty ambitions pursued by the WASP nuclear families that proliferated in TV sitcoms of the 1950s and 1960s. The very title of the series has become an object of cruel derision: If ever there was a show that was less than "adventurous," it was *The Adventures of Ozzie and Harriet.*

Long before *Seinfeld, Ozzie and Harriet* was the original Show About Nothing; but unlike *Seinfeld* the Nothing here was *really* Nothing, ranging from Ozzie Nelson's anxious nocturnal search for a carton of tutti-frutti ice cream to Harriet Nelson's avowed desire to spend an entire day in bed (the same one that Ozzie and Harriet shared onscreen, a rather progressive move in TV's twin bed era—though few viewers could imagine the Nelsons actually *doing* anything under the covers). At a time when the youth of America was declaring its independence in a voluble and violent fashion, the Nelsons' *über*-conformist older son David continued coming home to Mom's cooking every night while attending college; and even after getting married and moving into a place of his own, he apparently found it impossible to tear himself away from his parents' living room. Worse, the insipid lifestyle celebrated by Ozzie and Harriet has often been held directly responsible for the perceived moral decay of their rebellious younger son Ricky in his final unhappy years. The ultimate slap in the face to the ludicrously idealized world of *Ozzie and Harriet* was administered by playwright David Rabe in his harrowing anti–Vietnam piece *Sticks and Bones,* in which Ozzie and Harriet are the names given to a conservative middle-class couple who are so discomfited by the inconvenient presence of their blind and embittered war veteran son that they politely invite the boy to slash his wrists—and even provide the knife.

And yet, a whole new generation has come to enjoy the reruns of the radio and TV versions of *Ozzie and Harriet,* recognizing that the couple's "adventures" are essentially fantasies and accepting them on those terms. Audio and video copies of the property have remained big sellers for the past twenty years, and cable television services can always rely upon a sizable audience when choosing the TV adaptation for their late-night schedules. The youthful enthusiasts of this time-honored property have no trouble accepting the radio version's opening declaration that Ozzie Nelson and Harriet Hilliard Nelson were indeed, once upon a time, "America's favorite young couple."

Born Oswald George Nelson in Jersey City in 1906, Ozzie worked his way through Rutgers University by organizing a dance orchestra, with himself on saxophone in emulation of his role model Rudy Vallee. Though he ultimately received a law degree, Nelson devoted himself to show business after a prestigious gig at the Glen Island Casino led to several radio and recording contracts. In 1932 he spotted a pretty young vaudeville singer in *The Campus Mystery,* a Paramount musical short. Coming into the world as Peggy Lou Snyder in 1909, the Iowa-born thrush had since adopted the stage name Harriet Hilliard. Hiring Harriet as a vocalist, Ozzie worked up an act in which she would sing a love ballad "straight," whereupon he would repeat the tune while Harriet made gently disparaging comments about his lyrical ardor. (A superb example of this routine can be seen in their "Why Don't You Fall in Love With Me?" duet in the 1943 Universal B-musical *Honeymoon Lodge.*) From the beginning, their rapport was infectious, and what started out as a felicitous business arrangement blossomed into romance, culminating in marriage on October 8, 1935—though for professional purposes Harriet retained the last name Hilliard for many years to come.

The couple's first important radio assignment commenced in 1933 on *The Baker's Broadcast* starring comedian Joe Penner (q.v.), who remained close to the Nelsons until his death in 1941. For all their witty bits of banter, this was a standard assignment for a bandleader and singer of the period, with Penner handling the bulk of the funny stuff. Nonetheless, Ozzie began thinking of himself as a comedian, while Harriet, under contract to RKO Radio, likewise aspired to the sort of humorous roles played by her friend and mentor Ginger Rogers. But for her early starring film appearances in RKO's *New Faces of 1937* and *The Life of the Party* (both discussed elsewhere), Harriet remained basically poker-faced while professional clowns Penner, Milton Berle, Parkyakarkus and Bert Gordon did the gagging. Both Ozzie and Harriet finally got their chance to spread their comedic wings when they were signed to NBC's *Red Skelton Show* in 1941, the same year that the Nelsons appeared together onscreen for the first time in Columbia's Ruby Keeler vehicle *Sweetheart of the Campus*. Skelton saw to it that Harriet played a variety of comic roles on his show, notably the long-suffering mother of Red's "Mean Widdle Kid" character. Meanwhile, Ozzie was permitted to crack wise with the star between numbers, writing his own material for the occasion.

When Skelton was drafted in March of 1944, the comedian's producer John Guedel suggested to Ozzie and Harriet that they branch out into their own radio comedy series. Too busy with such game show projects as *People Are Funny* (q.v.) to focus on a weekly situation comedy, Guedel helped to formulate the series, then granted Ozzie full creative rights to the property. From the outset, Ozzie was opposed to coming off as "the dumb cluck husband with the Phi Beta Kappa wife," a possible reference to the "foolish mister-sensible missus" setup on the popular *Fibber McGee and Molly* (q.v.), likewise starring a married couple. Though they would retain the characterizations established in their singing act (Ozzie the head-in-the-clouds idealist, Harriet the down-to-earth pragmatist), the Nelsons were determined to build their new series on a realistic foundation. To that end, they played "themselves," while the show's plotlines were based on events that either had, or conceivably *could* have, taken place in their own home. And since the Nelsons were the parents of two sons—David, born in 1936, and Eric, aka "Ricky," born in 1940—the real-life escapades of the children would also be grist for the comic mill. ("Reality" of course is in the eye of the beholder. Ozzie Nelson was far more of a workaholic and taskmaster than the character he portrayed, while Harriet Nelson, who seldom set foot in her own kitchen, was hardly an average everyday housewife.)

Making its CBS bow as *The Ozzie Nelson–Harriet Hilliard Show* on October 8, 1944, the series settled upon its more familiar title a few months later. In honor of their sponsor Rogers Brothers Silver, radio's Nelson family lived at 1847 Rogers Road (1847 being the year the company was founded) in the town of Hillsdale. The jokes about "What does Ozzie Nelson do for a living?" weren't yet in common coinage because most of the radio stories took place on weekends, with scattered references to Ozzie's weekday job as a bandleader (the show regularly featured musical numbers with Ozzie, Harriet and the King Sisters until it was decided that these interludes upset the flow of the storyline). While David and Ricky were also heard on the program, during the first few seasons they weren't *really* David and Ricky but a pair of professional child actors. In a 1951 interview with the AP's Bob Thomas, Harriet explained that she and Ozzie had not even considered subjecting their own kids to the pressures of show business until April 1949, when Bing Crosby's son Lindsay played a guest role on the series. "If Lindsay can play himself on radio, why can't we?" asked little Ricky. Good question. The show had already gone through two sets of juvenile actors and was just about to switch over to a new twosome, so why not let 13-year-old David and nine-year-old Ricky play themselves? Any doubts the Nelsons may have harbored about exposing their young'uns to the spotlight proved unfounded: Not only were both boys eager to perform on the show, but they also turned out to be natural-born actors—especially the youngest member of the clan, whose enthusiastic precocity earned him on-air billing as "the irrepressible Ricky."

Carefully controlling and monitoring every aspect of the show, Ozzie wrote most of the early episodes, which proved to be a mixed blessing. Though unerringly accurate and hilarious when recreating the natural speech and word patterns of the real Nelson household, he was less skillful handling the fictional supporting characters, who leaned toward such radio comedy stereotypes as the Nelsons' haughty next-door neighbor Mrs. Waddington and their whiny, doomsaying maid Gloria (both roles played by Bea Benaderet). Too, Ozzie had not yet fully emerged from the shadow of Red Skelton, inserting mother-in-law jokes and other tired wheezes into his scripts.

The series began to improve and stabilize when Ozzie turned over most of the writing duties to a regular staff including his brother Don Nelson, Bob Schiller and Sol Saks. This team enabled Ozzie (a far better story editor than storyteller) to keep the show and its characters human and credible even when the situations and predicaments were exaggerated for comic effect. "We stay within what I call 'farce believability,'" explained Nelson three years into the show's run. True, Ozzie always managed to cause trouble with his various mental tangents, making an ass of himself while trying to prove that "men are superior to women" or "a father should be a pal to his sons." In contrast with the rival radio sitcom *The Life of Riley* (q.v.), Ozzie's problems were not the result of stupidity but of stubborn pride—and he was never *too* proud to admit by episode's end that he should have looked before he leaped. As for Harriet, though she always came across as the more level-headed of the two (John Guedel admired the actress' "Myrna Loy quality"), she was also capable of getting into jams by misinterpreting facts and jumping to conclusions, harmless character flaws with which most of her fans could readily identify.

New supporting characters were introduced after the elimination of such cardboard cutouts as Mrs. Waddington and Gloria; they too seldom strayed too far from believability. Ozzie's next-door neighbor "Thorny" Thornberry (played by the ineluctable John Brown) may have been a cornucopia of bad jokes and worse advice, but everyone knew a "Thorny" in their own neighborhood; moreover, this character was rooted in fact, his name lifted from Nelsons' real-life neighbor Syd Thornbury. Similarly, hyperactive teenager Emmy Lou (Janet Waldo) was but a slight exaggeration of the genuine bobby-soxers found in virtually every American high school of the late 1940s.

In his pursuit of verisimilitude, Ozzie liked to sustain the illusion that the Nelsons were making up their own dialogue. Thus for several years he would not bestow on-air credit on any of his writers, not even brother Don. While this might smack of egotism, it was a decision in keeping with the series' premise that the Ozzie, Harriet, David and Ricky we heard on radio were the real McCoy—er, Nelson. And in at least one case, life imitated art: When Don Nelson came up with a characteristically flip remark for his nephew Ricky, "I don't mess around, boy!," the youngster fell in love with the line and adopted it as his very own, both on- and off-microphone. By the time the Nelson family appeared in the 1952 Universal-International feature film *Here Come the Nelsons,* Ricky's catchphrase was so well known that it was even uttered by supporting actor Gale Gordon!

Having previously run on both the CBS and NBC radio networks, *The Adventures of Ozzie and Harriet* was picked up by ABC beginning October 14, 1949, (it would continue to play on radio until 1954). The youngest and hungriest of the four major webs, ABC willingly acceded to Ozzie's demand that he retain full creative control over his series, with no network or sponsor interference. At the same time, ABC was granted the option to adapt the property as a television series. "We knew that we would eventually make the transition to television," recalled Ozzie in his autobiography, "but we also wanted to make sure that we didn't make the move prematurely." Had *Ozzie and Harriet* crossed over to TV in late 1949 or early 1950, the series would most likely have been telecast live. This would have been no difficulty for the adult members of the cast, but might have proved problematic for David and Ricky, who though skilled at reading lines off a piece of paper had never been required to memorize a script, nor deliver a sustained 30-minute performance (the radio version was taped to allow for any gaffes on the part of the kids). If Ozzie didn't want his sons to again be replaced by strangers—the Nelsons' deal with the radio network stipulated that the boys' contracts could be cancelled at any time—his series would have to be filmed, a rarity on network TV at the time. And even if ABC green-lighted a filmed program, there was still no guarantee that David and Ricky would not freeze up in front of a camera.

Here the legends begin to conflict: Either ABC wasn't altogether sure that *The Adventures of Ozzie and Harriet* would work on television, or Ozzie himself wasn't entirely certain; *or,* Ozzie wanted to find out if his sons could withstand the rigors of filmmaking (and still give convincing performances) before embarking on such a project. Whatever the case, everyone dragged their feet until the fall of 1950, when Universal-International producer Aaron Rosenberg approached Ozzie for the purpose of making a theatrical feature based on the radio series. (Nelson's autobiography states only that Rosenberg had wanted to do a film for some time; there's no indication who first came up with the idea, the producer or Ozzie.) In addition to bringing added revenue to the Nelson bank account, a movie adaptation could also serve as the pilot for a prospective TV series—and, making the project more attractive to Universal, it could be filmed entirely on the studio back lot for peanuts.

In the spring of 1951, Ozzie wrote the script for *Here Come the Nelsons* in collaboration with his brother Don and Bill Davenport. In July of that year, the cameras started rolling under the direction of Fred de Cordova, who'd already demonstrated a facility for getting value for money with his economical Technicolor costumers *Buccaneer's Girl* and *The Desert Hawk*. De Cordova had also been the man behind the megaphone for the deathless *Bedtime for Bonzo* (1951), an honor that his future boss Johnny Carson would never let him forget. If de Cordova had the patience and dedication to coax a persuasive performance from a chimpanzee, he certainly would encounter no difficulty whatsoever wrangling David and Ricky Nelson. Fulfilling all expectations, de Cordova kept the plot-heavy picture moving at a fast clip, every so often pausing for such charming comic vignettes as the scene in which a roomful of noisy children abruptly lapses into silence while the kids stare at Ozzie and Harriet exchanging a kiss.

Having its world premiere in Pittsburgh on January 16, 1952, the 76-minute *Here Come the Nelsons* starts off confidently with the same main- and secondary-theme music (by Billy May) heard on the radio show, and a gag opening title introducing David and Ricky Nelson as "two characters created by Ozzie and Harriet," just the sort of droll remark that was a Harriet Nelson specialty. An establishing scene outside the Nelson home allows Ozzie and Harriet to indulge in their patented kidding-on-the-square banter, with Ozzie pretending not to recognize his wife and Harriet making veiled threats to walk out on her husband if he doesn't come down to breakfast soon. When Ozzie bumps his head on the window sill, we sense that the comic tone of the radio show, which was always slightly broader than the subsequent TV series, will be maintained to the best of everyone's ability.

The radio version's predilection for the comedy of misunderstanding and conclusion-jumping is played to the hilt in the film adaptation. A professional astrologer warns Harriet that men born under Ozzie's zodiac sign tend to get frisky and flirtatious in the spring, and that under such circumstances Harriet should cut her husband some slack and not display any jealousy. Meanwhile, Ozzie has an unexpected reunion with Barbara, the attractive younger sister of his old friend Gordon Schutzendorf. A professional rodeo rider, she is in Hillsdale to appear in the town's Centennial celebration, and sees nothing wrong with Ozzie's invitation (extended before he fully realized that "little Barbara" is now all grown up) to stay at the Nelson house during her stopover, though Ozzie worries that Harriet will be jealous. Of course Harriet *is* jealous, but she chooses to follow the astrologer's advice by feigning indifference to Barbara's presence. This puzzles Ozzie, who can't understand why his wife is so understanding. Thanks to the needling of next-door neighbor Joe Randolph, Oz gets it into his head that Harriet has lost interest in him and has possibly fallen for another man—and when Barbara's handsome former beau Charlie Jones insinuates himself into the Nelson household, Ozzie is convinced that Harriet's heart has strayed.

Now we've arrived at the old *Ozzie and Harriet* radio standby of Ozzie stubbornly determined to prove a point even if it kills him. To demonstrate to Harriet that he is just as youthful and virile as Charlie, he vows to win a prize at the Centennial rodeo by riding a fierce bucking bronco named (inevitably) Dynamite. While all this is transpiring, David and Ricky jump to a conclusion of their own when they

Ricky Nelson (left) and his brother David think they've stumbled upon the truth about their parents' houseguest Rock Hudson in the 1952 "Ozzie and Harriet" feature film *Here Come the Nelsons* (courtesy Jim Feeley).

notice that Charlie Jones' suitcase is embossed with the letters F.B.I., then overhear Charlie tell Barbara that he's working for Uncle Sam! Though the kids are just as much on the wrong track as their parents, at least *their* misapprehension makes some sense.

So far, *Here Come the Nelsons* hasn't drifted significantly from the established radio formula, though the "farce believability" has been stretched a few degrees beyond its usual limits. But in the course of events there are certain deviations from the norm that might prove unsettling to longtime fans of the Nelsons. First and foremost, *Ozzie Nelson actually has a job*: He works for an advertising agency headed by H.J. Bellows, a bombastic back-slapper who speaks in fluent sports metaphors. Ozzie has been assigned to come up with a winning ad campaign for Bellows' latest client, a manufacturer of ladies' undergarments—and if this seems to be a gratuitous gag, wait until the final scene where the client's new line of girdles resolves everyone's problems in one fell snap (two words: "Elastic Roadblock"). Even with Ozzie's uncharacteristic visible means of support in the film, the scriptwriters manage to sneak in a reference to his real vocation, when his exasperated boss issues an ultimatum that either Ozzie come up with an ad campaign before nightfall or he can go back to "playing a trombone." "Saxophone," Ozzie mutters sheepishly.

For Ozzie, the most salutary result from the box office success of *Here Come the Nelsons* "was that it demonstrated to us that our type of comedy projected just as well on screen as it did on the radio, and that the transition from radio to television would not be too difficult." Seeing the film today, one has the feeling that Ozzie was also using it as an experimental lab to test out what *wouldn't* work on television. We've mentioned the decision to show Ozzie working at an identifiable job, a one-time-only device that would be rejected out of hand for the TV version: As Nelson once explained, "by not designating the kind of work I did, people were able to identify with me more readily." The heaviest concentration of misfire ideas occurs during the film's final 20 minutes. It's no fun at all to see Ozzie and Harriet engaging in a bitter and mutually recriminating quarrel, nor can we reconcile ourselves to the spectacle of Harriet bursting into tears. The script also clumsily tosses in a couple of gun-wielding crooks who steal the rodeo receipts, then kidnap Ricky while making their getaway. Really? Little Ricky in danger? The most danger anyone *ever* encountered on TV's *Ozzie and Harriet* was trying to carry on an intelligent conversation with David's troglodyte college pal Wally. Admittedly, on its own merits the chase finale is both funny and exciting, with such incidental gags as the local constabulary arguing over whose jurisdiction has the authority to capture the criminals, and the ease with which Ricky—having the time of his life as a hostage—repeatedly outsmarts his dull-witted captors. But this sort of zaniness is more suited to one of Universal's Ma and Pa Kettle comedies than the cozy domesticity of *Ozzie and Harriet*. Ozzie Nelson must have sensed this, for no such thrill climax would ever again be attempted on his watch.

On the plus side, the film's supporting cast is generously stocked with radio comedy favorites, including Gale Gordon as Ozzie's windbag boss, Sheldon Leonard as the (marginally) smarter of the two holdup men, and a surprisingly unbilled Frank Nelson (the "Yesssssss" man from *The Jack Benny Program*) as the unctuous astrologer who sets the plot in motion. Playing the secondary heroine, junoesque Barbara Lawrence (who towers over both Ozzie and Harriet) is totally convincing as a zesty female bronc buster. In his second radio-to-movie adaptation (*The Fat Man* [q.v.] was the first), Rock Hudson is given an early opportunity to flex his comedy muscles in the role of Charley Jones, notably during the climactic chase in which he is seen awkwardly astride a circus dancing horse that haughtily refuses to break into a gallop. And in a piquant bit of casting, the Nelsons' neighbors Joe and Clara Randolph are played by Jim Backus and Ann Doran, three years before their reteaming as James Dean's parents in *Rebel Without a Cause.*

Best of all, 15-year-old David and 11-year-old Ricky are natural, unaffected and totally at ease in their screen debut. If indeed Ozzie intended the film to prove that his boys were ready for prime time, he succeeded beyond his wildest dreams. Both Ozzie and David have since credited the sensitive direction of Fred de Cordova for the youngsters' excellent performances, but in all fairness de Cordova had the advantage of working with a pair of juvenile actors bubbling over with charisma and charm. Even at this early stage of the game, the "irrepressible" Ricky handily upstages his sober-sided older brother David, though in the film's final close-up both boys are evenly matched as they launch into their own devastatingly accurate impersonations of dear old dad Ozzie.

Here Come the Nelsons can be summed up as "Ozzie and Harriet for people who don't like Ozzie and Harriet." Once the family's TV series commenced on October 3, 1952, the freshness and novelty of the film version faded into the woodwork as cuteness and predictability took over. Now directing as well as producing, co-writing and co-starring, Ozzie fell into an assembly-line pattern that his older fans found comfortable and reassuring while driving younger viewers up a wall—at least until Ricky Nelson emerged as a teenage singing idol in 1957, at which point the kids at home were willing to tolerate the show's banalities in order to savor those precious few minutes of Ricky warbling "Hello, Mary Lou" and "I'm Walkin'." (At the apex of his popularity in 1959, Universal reissued *Here Come the Nelsons,* which must have been a bewildering experience for those fans who knew Ricky only from his more recent appearances.) Somehow or other *The Adventures of Ozzie and Harriet* managed to remain on ABC's evening lineup until March 26, 1966, the longest-running American TV sitcom until its record was broken by *The Simpsons* in 2005.

Seven years after his show's cancellation, Ozzie made a game effort to relate to a new generation with *Ozzie's Girls,* a syndicated comedy series wherein Ozzie and Harriet rented their sons' old rooms to a pair of nubile coeds (Brenda Sykes, Susan Sennett). Despite a strong lineup of local stations including ABC's owned-and-operated outlets, *Ozzie's Girls* was gone after a single season; by 1975 Ozzie was gone as well, succumbing to liver cancer at age 69. Rick Nelson (no longer Ricky) continued his singing career with variable success until he was killed in a plane crash in 1985; Harriet Nelson made a few noteworthy television guest appearances before she died in 1994; and David Nelson was an established TV commercial producer at the time of his death in 2011. *The Adventures of Ozzie and Harriet* continues to play on cable TV, almost as if the Nelsons were still, per their onscreen billing, "America's favorite family."

Pete Kelly's Blues (1955)

Several of the films referenced in this book were unsuccessful adaptations of successful radio properties. *Pete Kelly's Blues,* the last of the Golden Age radio adaptations, reversed this procedure: It was a successful film inspired by a series that had made no impact at all on radio.

Mention the name Jack Webb today and you're likely to get a sonorous "dum-da-dum-dum" in reply, or perhaps a mocking "Just the facts, ma'am" or joking reference to "Blue Boy." There's no getting around it: The ferret-faced, icy-voiced Webb (1920–1982) will forever be associated with his greatest radio and TV achievement, the pioneering procedural cop drama *Dragnet.* There was, however, a time when the actor-director-producer had a lot more creative irons in the fire, and when his famously monotonal voice actually showed vestiges of versatility. Before the radio debut of *Dragnet* on June 3, 1949, Webb had starred in his own sketch comedy series (which contrary to expectations was frequently hilarious), played all the roles in an exhausting array of dialects on the anti-prejudice dramatic weekly *One Out of Seven,* and was a member in good standing of the "Wisecracking Private Eye vs. Stupid Cops" league with his work in *Pat Novak for Hire* and *Johnny Madero: Pier 23.* Even while *Dragnet* was establishing itself as the best crime drama in any medium, Webb could be seen playing comic, sarcastic and menacing roles in such films as *Sunset Blvd., Appointment with Danger, The Men, The Halls of Montezuma* and *You're in the Navy Now.* Thus it was hardly out of character for Webb to take on an entirely different role than Sgt. Joe Friday in a dramatic series that replaced Walter Schumann's portentous four-note theme song with blue-ribbon Dixieland music.

Conceived by Webb and his favorite writer Richard L. Breen, the weekly 30-minute *Pete Kelly's Blues* took place in Kansas City "on the Missouri side" around 1927. The principal setting was George Lupo's speakeasy at 417 Cherry Street, where the title character (Webb), a Bix Beiderbecke–style cornet player, fronted a jazz combo called Pete Kelly's Big Seven. Pete and his boys weren't at all concerned about Lupo's shady business dealings, his rough-looking clientele or his cheap liquor, so long as they were allowed to play the music they loved: "We start every night about ten and play 'til the customers get that first frightening look at each other in the early light." Though not a detective of any sort, Kelly always managed to get involved in someone else's problems, usually of the kind that earned him a pummeling from a couple of thugs after gentler efforts to persuade him to "lay off" had failed.

For years, only one episode of this program was available to collectors. The unearthing of additional episodes has revealed that *Pete Kelly's Blues,* like its spiritual ancestor *Pat Novak for Hire,* tended to tell the same story every week in the same metaphorical purple prose (penned by Breen, Jim Moser and Jo Eisenger). Still, the show scored on its atmosphere, colorful characters, staccato pacing, and especially the music, with at least two hot Dixieland numbers played without interruption in each episode; some of these tunes were originals, written by Arthur Hamilton. The Pete Kelly Seven included cornet player Dick Cathcart (who ghosted for Webb), late of the Bob Crosby band; clarinetist Matty Matlock, who also did the arrangements;

and trombonist Elmer "Moe" Schneider, pianist Ray Sherman, guitarist Bill Newman, bassist Marty Carb and drummer Nick Fatool. All these men received billing at the end of each episode, along with announcer George Fennemann and such *Dragnet* perennials as Herb Butterfield, Peggy Webber and Vic Perrin. (William Conrad, an old pal of Webb's who was barred from the reality-grounded *Dragnet* because of his too-theatrical voice, was allowed to appear on the more melodramatic *Pete Kelly's Blues,* invariably as a villain.) Outside of Webb, the series' only regular actor was blues artist Meredith Howard, cast as speakeasy singer Maggie Jackson. The character was supposed to be a black woman, but this wasn't over-stressed.

Debuting over NBC as a summer replacement series on July 4, 1951, *Pete Kelly's Blues* ran concurrently with Jack Webb's *Dragnet* until September 19 of that year. Critics were kind, but the show was never able to attract a sponsor and was not picked up for renewal after its initial 11-week run. Webb tucked it away for further use, possibly as a TV series to be aired after the video version of *Dragnet* (which also premiered in 1951) had run its course. He had in fact begun working on such a project in 1952, and when *Dragnet* showed no signs of abatement he seriously considered dropping out of his signature program to play Pete Kelly on television. But when Webb approached NBC with this suggestion, the network heads turned him down. *Dragnet* was their number one TV hit, and they weren't about to mess with success; nor did NBC allow Webb to cancel the radio version, which continued playing until 1957.

Meanwhile, the financial success of Warner Bros.' 1954 movie version of *Dragnet* had made Webb as hot a commodity on the big screen as on the 21-inch tube. Since Webb had already persuaded Warners to let him direct and star in a feature-length *Pete Kelly's Blues* as his next picture, it looked like the studio had another hit on its hands. Against his better judgment, Webb agreed to shoot the picture in Technicolor and CinemaScope—he would have preferred the black-and-white and standard-aspect of his TV show—but in exchange he would receive 50 percent of the film's profits (compared to 25 percent on *Dragne*t) and be allowed to retain Richard L. Breen as screenwriter. In addition to keeping up the momentum of Webb's film career, *Pete Kelly's Blues* would also prove to NBC that a visual translation of his old radio property could fly as a weekly series. Before long, he was referring to his latest project as "the most expensive pilot in history."

Since the Pete Kelly Seven had stayed together after the termination of the radio series, Webb was able to record most of the film's musical numbers during the pre-production stage. *Pete Kelly's Blues* itself was completed in a little over five weeks, an eternity by Jack Webb standards but remarkably fast for a big-budget picture in 1955. Most of the credit for the film's eye-popping visual design and color scheme goes to Harper Goff, a Walt Disney Studios technician whom Webb had met while filming

Janet Leigh and Jack Webb pose for a 1955 TV-magazine cover heralding the release of the motion picture version of the radio series *Pete Kelly's Blues.* Don't make me repeat that.

the TV *Dragnet* on the Disney lot (Goff also plays a small role in the film).

Another of Jack's Disney acquaintances was singer Peggy Lee, who'd just finished her voice-over-songwriter duties on the animated feature *Lady and the Tramp*. Though Peggy hadn't done much straight acting to this point, she delivers a heartbreaking performance as gangster's moll Rose Hopkins, who is forced on Pete Kelly as a vocalist and who comes to a sorry end when her sadistic boyfriend knocks her down a flight of stairs (actually the fall is taken by stunt woman Carol Thurston). Earning the singer an Oscar nomination, her performance as Rose Hopkins made so deep an impression on Peggy Lee that for the rest of her life she would refer to Rose in the third person, as if she actually existed. Another popular singer of the era, Ella Fitzgerald, was cast in what she considered *her* finest screen role as jazz singer Maggie Jackson, whose ripsnorting rendition of "Hard Hearted Hannah" is to die for.

The rest of the cast is equally impressive. Though Edmond O'Brien and Janet Leigh are typecast as slimy protection racketeer Fran McCarg and thrill-seeking heiress Ivy Conrad (described by *Harrison's Reports* as "reminiscent of an F. Scott Fitzgerald characterization"), others are so far removed from type that they are recognizable only by face and voice. Any other director would have cast craggy Lee Marvin as hotheaded drummer Joey Firestone and cherubic Martin Milner as oversensitive clarinetist Al Gannaway; only Webb, who'd worked with both actors on *Dragnet* and knew their true potential, would have had the guts to reverse their roles. And imagine anyone other than Webb tapping into the dark side of lovable, ratchet-voiced comic actor Andy Devine by casting him as brutish Kansas City cop George Tennell.

Film theorist Michael Jarrett has described *Pete Kelly's Blues* as "a disguised western set in the Jazz Age." Making his living as a saloon entertainer in a wide-open Missouri town, Pete (the peaceable drifter) doesn't want any trouble, so he puts up very little resistance when Fran McCarg (crooked rancher–gambling boss) muscles in, charging the musicians (farmers) exorbitant protection rates and telling them where they can play (graze) and where they can't. Gathering at a roadhouse (nearby ranch), all the local bands are for putting up a stand against McCarg, but Kelly figures it's better for everyone's health if they capitulate. The murder of drummer (saddle pal) Joey begins to arouse Pete's sense of justice, as does the cruel treatment doled out to McCarg's mistress Rose (jaded dance hall gal), yet still our hero does nothing until he has positive proof who's behind all the skullduggery. The story ends with a violent showdown between hero and villain, who exchange gunfire not in Main Street at High Noon but in a darkened dance hall, where Kelly finally regains his self-respect as his girl Ivy (no schoolmarm, but she'll do) looks on adoringly.

Just before the film's release on July 31, 1955, Webb and his cast went on a 12,000-mile national tour to promote the picture, bringing along the Pete Kelly Seven for musical entertainment. It's hard to say if the tour, the TV popularity of Webb, or the ongoing 1950s nostalgia for the 1920s was responsible, but *Pete Kelly's Blues* was a box office bonanza, earning $5,000,000 on a $2,000,000 investment and ending up as the year's 14th top-grossing film. That it isn't a conspicuously good film hardly seems to matter in the face of these statistics, but we should at least touch upon this subject. Unlike the story-driven but stylish *Dragnet*, *Pete Kelly's Blues* is all style and practically no story. What stands out in the viewer's memory is not the routine plotting or the laughable *film noir* dialogue exchanges, but a handful of isolated episodes. The best of these is the lengthy pre-credits prologue (a Richard Breen specialty) that fades in on the "jazz funeral" of a black musician; a cornet placed upon the coffin falls off unnoticed, then passes through several hands over the years until it is finally won in a dice game by returning World War I vet Pete Kelly. Other bravura vignettes include a haunting visit to the mental hospital where Rose Hopkins, whose injuries have left her with the mind of a five-year-old, will remain for the rest of her life; and the climactic gun duel, illuminated by flashes of light reflected in a rotating chandelier.

Reviewer François Truffaut was perfectly satisfied with Webb's gossamer virtuosity: "[He] is a filmmaker who is more skillful than gifted, more sincere than brilliant, more likable than prestigious. Which is to say that the film is nice to see...." Truffaut added, "Jack Webb, who is a shrewd man, knows perfectly well that one-half of the young audience likes jazz and the other half like fights. So he made a film about jazz with fights...." A few other critics weren't at all impressed, the *New York Times* writing off the picture as "an incredible waste of tantalizing music and décor." Even those who enjoyed the show were not enraptured by Webb's performance, more than one observer echoing *Photoplay*'s dismissive capsule critique "*Dragnet* with a trumpet." By 1955, Webb had become so locked into the role of stiff-necked Joe Friday that it was impossible to imagine him playing an insouciant cornet player. It's *still* impossible.

But the fact remains that *Pete Kelly's Blues* was a successful movie commodity despite its disappointing shakedown period on radio, and this was motivation enough for Webb—who referred to it as "the best damned picture I ever made"—to refashion the property into a TV series. But not for another four years, and again only as a replacement for another show. Debuting April 5, 1959, this version of *Pete Kelly's Blues* starred William Reynolds as Pete, Than Wyenn repeating his film role as the speakeasy owner, and Connee Boswell, who'd been showing up in radio-to-film adaptations since 1932's *The Big Broadcast,* as cabaret singer Savannah Brown. As before, Dick Cathcart dubbed in Pete's cornet licks, this time receiving the screen credit that eluded him for the film version. Though attractively mounted and with a wealth of old-style optical transition effects, *Pete Kelly's Blues* lasted only 13 weeks, another in a long line of NBC casualties opposite CBS's Sunday night dreadnaught *The Ed Sullivan Show.*

Howard Stern and *Private Parts* (1997)

With big-time network radio long dead and buried, and local radio "narrowcasting" to specific rather than general tastes, there is as of this writing not much of a market for a wide-release motion picture capitalizing on the fame of individual radio personalities and programs, or for films designed to broaden the appeal of those personalities and programs beyond their fan base. Which is why the spectacular success of the 1997 Paramount release *Private Parts* is all the more incredible. The star of the picture is also an anomaly in an era of hunk heroes and buff heroines: gangly, gawky, curly-haired "shock jock" Howard Stern, self-proclaimed King of All Media. Whether he deserves that appellation is open to debate, but there's no denying that for all its 1990s *zeitgeist* and R-rated language, Stern's film is at base an "old school" success story about one radio star's rise from total obscurity to the pinnacle of popularity. In this respect it is in the same league with earlier films starring Rudy Vallee and Kate Smith, and previous pictures built around such programs as *Pot o' Gold* and *People Are Funny* (all q.v.). The fact that *Private Parts* could never have been filmed during the heyday of the Hollywood studio system—nor even gotten past the concept stage—does not alter its pedigree nor lessen its entertainment value.

Born in Jackson Heights, New York, in 1954, Howard Allen Stern was attracted to radio at an early age while visiting the recording studio owned by his father Ben, who was also an engineer for Manhattan radio station WHOM. At Boston University, Howard launched his own program on campus station WTBU. He entered professional broadcasting at WNTN in Newtown, Massachusetts. Howard moved on to a performer-programmer job at WRNW in Briarcliff Manor, New York, then in 1979 landed a spot as morning DJ at Hartford, Connecticut, station WCCC. Among his fellow record spinners was Fred Norris, destined to become the longest-lasting of Stern's staff members. After a rewarding gig at Detroit's WWWW in 1980, Howard moved to Washington DC station WWDC in 1981. Here he formed a professional alliance with newscaster Robin Quivers, who followed Howard to New York's WNBC as co-host and sidekick for an afternoon drive-time show beginning in 1982. Fired by WNBC three years later, Howard and

Robin switched to another New York outlet, WXRK (K-Rock), which beginning in 1986 simulcast Stern's program with stations in Philadelphia and Los Angeles. Publishing his memoirs in 1993, he did programs on both over-the-air radio and commercial TV until 2004, when he signed with Sirius XM Satellite Radio. Stern's other credits include the starring role in his own biopic *Private Parts* and a stint as judge on TV's *America's Got Talent*. And if this paragraph were any drier, we'd all die of thirst.

Let's flesh things out so we can understand why this guy was considered movie-worthy. Born into a Jewish household, Howard went through a big-time culture shock as virtually the only white student at South Side High School in Rockville Center, New York. While working at WTBU he launched *The King Schmaltz Bagel Hour*, a raucous parody of the syndicated rock-music program *King Biscuit Flour Hour*. After a few unhappy experiences at WRNW (including being forced to fire people he liked), he submitted an outrageous audition tape to WCCC, featuring an abundance of flatulence and body-function jokes; once he was hired, he stirred up trouble for his bosses with a two-day personal boycott of the Shell Oil Company. After a few weeks at WWWW going through the motions of a typical rock-jock (a *schtick* he was never comfortable with), Howard decided to be true to himself and indulge in the raunchy comedy he loved, breaking down as many broadcast barriers as he could get away with. In concert with Robin Quivers at WWDC he challenged the station's rigid format and ramped up the sex-and-fart jokes and the nothing-sacred irreverence. Gays, religious groups, celebrity deaths and the mentally challenged were all fair game for our boy. WWDC responded with a TV ad campaign labeling Howard a "pervert," and ratings for the station soared.

Hired sight unseen by WNBC, Stern appalled management with his no-holds-barred comedy style and was placed under the thumb of programmer Kevin Metheny, whom Howard referred to on the air as "Pig Virus." Stern continued doing it all his own way with such stunts as inviting sexy young ladies to enter his studio and disrobe entirely while he lovingly described their attributes for the benefit of his audience. An appearance on David Letterman's show brought Howard to the attention of a greater audience than ever before, delighting WNBC's promotional department as the station grabbed a 5.7 percent market share. In 1985 Stern and Quivers were fired for "conceptual differences" with management, though Howard insisted that millions loved him and the complaint had come from one lone executive. While with K-Rock from 1985 to 1992, he persisted in courting controversy and baiting censors. Extending his act to TV, during the 1992 *MTV Video Music Awards* he was lowered from the ceiling garbed in an electrified blouse and an open-rear pair of jeans as the parody superhero "Fartman" (we'll leave his special powers to your imagination). Along the way he built up an on-air entourage including his old sidekick Fred Norris, described as "strange" no matter what he said or did; call screener "Stuttering John" Melendez, whose offensive ambush interviews of celebrities were both praised and damned by showbiz insiders; and producer Gary Dell'Abarte, aka "Baba Booey!" Repeatedly running afoul of the FCC, Stern finally gave up commercial radio in favor of regulation-free Sirius XM, where he remains to this day.

Having previously appeared in the 1986 quickie *Ryder PI*, Howard had intended to make his film starring debut in 1992 with a feature-length version of "Fartman." But potential distributor New Line Cinema was aiming for a PG film, and whatever else Howard Stern may be, he certainly isn't PG or even PG-13. So he forgot about movies for a while and accepted a million dollar advance to write his memoirs in collaboration with Larry Sloman. The engagingly obscene tome called *Private Parts* tempered the truth with some gross (in every sense of the word) exaggerations. Published in October 1993, it turned out to be the fastest-selling book in Simon & Schuster's history, with 1,200,000 hardback copies sold during the first two weeks. Those who dismissed Stern as an overgrown adolescent with a puerile sense of humor were amazed that his fan base extended beyond the "11-year-old-with-dirty-magazines-under-his-bed" demographic. Also amazing to Howard's non-fans was that the book actually made the author come off as warm and cuddly: For all his foul-mouthed harangues and public hubris, the "real" Howard Stern was apparently a nice Jewish boy who just wanted everyone to love him. Especially charming was the impression that *Private Parts* was a valentine to Alison Berns Stern, Howard's wife and the mother of his three daughters. The reader came away with

From *Private Parts* (1997): Radio shock-jock Howard Stern is uncomfortably shoehorned into a country-western format.

the feeling that after fifteen years of connubial bliss, Howard could still not believe that a schlub like him could ever have wooed and won a marvelous girl like Alison.

As producer Ivan Reitman (a longtime fan of Stern) began assembling the pieces for Paramount's filmization of *Private Parts* in late 1995, Stern envisioned the project as a comic version of Sylvester Stallone's *Rocky* (1976), to the extent that his first choice for director was John G. Avildsen. Given full story approval, Stern rejected several scripts (some with jokes even more infantile than his own) before settling upon a screenplay written by Len Blum and Michael Kalesniko—all the while assuming that the filmmakers would allow him to "wing" his dialogue in the stream-of-consciousness fashion of his radio show.

In the absence of Avildsen, Betty Thomas was tapped as director. Seldom exhibiting a discernable style of her own, she was masterful in adapting to, and improving upon, the style established by her scripts, as indicated by her earlier *The Brady Bunch Movie* (1995). The decision had been made with *Private Parts* to avoid the standard straight-biopic trappings in favor of the hyperbolic hilarity of Stern's book, in the tradition of *Great Balls of Fire!* (1989), the over-the-top movie biography of Jerry Lee Lewis.

Thomas responded to this concept by creating a living cartoon populated with living cartoon characters (including "Fartman" in a riotous recreation of the *MTV Awards Show* incident), pausing every so often for an honest moment so audiences would accept the essential truth of the story.

Like the book, the reality of the film is filtered through Stern's skewered perspective. It may be hard to swallow that Stern's boss at WRNW was really as insanely irrational as he comes off in the film, but that's how Howard saw him and it's Howard's story. The image of a female listener getting so aroused by a sensual Stern monologue that she begins using her radio as a sex toy might well be entirely a product of Howard's imagination, but it's faithful to the tone of the picture. When we finally get to an incident that actually happened beyond question, such as the scene in which Howard invites a lady to the WNBC studio to simulate fellatio with an enormous kielbasa, so many other absurdities have already been presented as fact that we're willing to buy the reality of the situation.

When shooting began in May 1996, Betty Thomas faced the formidable challenge of persuading Howard Stern the radio star to believe in Howard Stern the movie star. All the brazen bravado Stern displayed on radio and in interviews vanished when he was confronted with the prospect of playing himself on-screen. He had never hidden the fact that his rebellious nature was a byproduct of deeply ingrained insecurities, but he'd been able in the past to put up a good bluff. Not this time. Memorizing scripted lines was difficult enough for a man who'd built his reputation on ad libs (his only extemporaneous speech occurs at the very end of the picture). Putting even more pressure on Stern was the fact that he was doing his K-Rock show all the time he was making the film, rushing from the set to the radio studio promptly at 4 p.m. each day. He became so convinced that he wouldn't be able to give his all to the movie that he begged to be replaced with actor Jeff Goldblum. Thomas finally deduced that Howard felt lost in his new surroundings because there was no one from the world of radio to talk to. Hence the casting of Thomas' old friend Michael Gwynne, a musician and former disc jockey who'd been popularly known as Lee Vaunce at KGFJ in Los Angeles.

Quoted by Stern's biographer Rich Mintzer, Gwynne explains that Howard "had never been an actor, and [Thomas] really did not want him crashing on the set or falling apart. She knew I had done radio and thought that perhaps having me around as a safety device to talk radio might be helpful to Stern to keep him in his comfort zone." In the film Gwynne plays the Duke of Rock, early-morning DJ at Detroit station WWWW. Watching with amusement as newcomer Stern hauls in a bulky box of props while wearing a silly hat, the Duke turns to his mike and introduces Howard to Detroit as "Big Bird," then bids him farewell with the ad libbed line, "Whatever you do, don't hurt yourself." Between takes, Gwynne calmly discussed the mechanics of moviemaking with Howard and encouraged the star to swap "war stories" about their respective radio careers. Before long Howard was totally at ease, and the shoot proceeded smoothly thereafter. Gwynne recalls that Stern never pulled rank, never ego-tripped, and never complained: "He put himself in a position to let things happen rather than making the mistake a lot of big stars make by trying to be in control all the time."

A minor crisis arose when, after Ivan Reitman was unable to get Julia Louis-Dreyfus to play Howard's wife Alison, Mary McCormick was hired for the role. McCormick was not a fan of Stern and thoroughly disapproved of his radio act, feelings she had trouble suppressing during her first few scenes. But by the time production reached the midway point, Mary had been won over by Howard's sincerity, generosity and strong work ethic, and by film's end she was one of his biggest boosters (though one suspects she never did become a regular listener). As for the genuine Alison Stern, you can spot her in the tiny role of a WNBC receptionist—one of the few real-life personalities not seen as herself in the film. Elsewhere, Robin Quivers is provided with a generous amount of screen time, looking a bit uncomfortable but still coming across most effectively, particularly in what must have been a very difficult scene wherein she blames Howard for getting her fired. Fred Norris offers an intriguing portrayal of himself as an all-but-mute introvert who springs to life only when he's on the air. Gary Dell'Abarte is seen along with *Howard Stern Show* writer Jackie Martling in a handful of "reality bites," ad libbing with abandon as he sets up tacky-looking location shots, annoys cops and pedestrians, and hits on various well-endowed females while filming the transitional inserts for *Private Parts*. And "Stuttering John" Melendez shows up just long enough to unleash a torrent of profanities because he wasn't invited to be in the movie. (There are also a number of celebrity cameos, including an amusingly ironic vignette with Ozzy Osbourne.)

Private Parts may not have ended up looking like *Rocky* as Stern had hoped, but there are plenty of quotes from other films throughout its 109 minutes. The framing device of Howard telling his life story (up to 1985) to an initially uninterested fellow plane passenger is a steal from 1994's *Forrest Gump* (the passenger is played by supermodel Carol Alt, an inside joke referring to Stern cohort Fred Norris' derisive on-air comments about Alt's acting skills). The scenes of Howard's angst-ridden childhood and his lack of success on the college dating scene—even a blind girl refuses to go out with him—are straight out of Woody Allen. The occasional cutaways to Howard's associates and loved ones discussing him for the benefit of an unseen interviewer smack of Bob Fosse's *Lenny* (1974). And Howard's windmill-tilting battles with the humorless radio Establishment (especially fictional WNBC program director Kenny "Pig Vomit" Rushton, overplayed by Paul Giamatti as a combination Captain Hook and Cosmo Spacely) are reminiscent of Armed Forces Radio deejay Robin Williams' confrontations with the military brass in *Good Morning Vietnam* (1987)—prompting one wag to label this film *Good Morning New York*.

Just as MGM "humanized" the anarchistic Marx Brothers in *A Night at the Opera, Private Parts* goes a long way towards making the iconoclastic Stern more palatable for mainstream consumption. No matter how far he pushes the envelope both personality and professionally, there's a sweetness of spirit to the man that is almost irresistible. It must be emphasized that this warm feeling toward the protagonist is only possible when the film is seen as a whole and not as a bunch of out-of-context episodes. When Howard mortifies Alison by delivering a comic radio monologue about her recent miscarriage, the danger exists that the scene will come off as cruel and callous—unless one is forearmed with a previous scene in the couple's bedroom, showing both of them making sick jokes about their personal tragedy as a defense mechanism. Thus, Howard's embarrassed explanation to Alison that he honestly thought she'd find his monologue funny comes off as wholly sincere and rather touching. In moments like these, you want to take Howard Stern home with you.

Not everything in the film works. Visualizing the *Howard Stern Show* call-in personality known as "The Leather Weather Lady" isn't quite as effective as imagining what this weirdo looks like; and the moment in which Fred Norris unexpectedly breaks his silence and tells one of Howard's detractors where to get off should have had the same impact as the scene where the "whispering" TV comedy writer suddenly develops a voice in *My Favorite Year* (1982), but doesn't because of an inadequate buildup. These are minor quibbles, however. In the wider scheme of things, *Private Parts* succeeds where other films built around radio personalities have failed, transforming a specialized performer with a basically limited appeal into a widely popular attraction.

It would be small of us to make a snide comment about the post–*Private Parts* breakup of the "perfect" marriage between Howard and Alison Stern, especially since the two ex-spouses have remained good friends ever since. It wouldn't be small at all to mention that *Private Parts* was as big and astonishing a success as its literary source, earning over $85,000,000. You still may not fully appreciate Stern's comic vision (I certainly don't), but you can't deny that this picture grabbed practically everyone's attention. And look, we're *talking* about Howard, aren't we? That's all the dear lad really wants out of life anyway.

A Prairie Home Companion (2006)

It is altogether appropriate for a book focusing on radio-to-movie adaptations of the 1930s, 1940s and 1950s that the final film listed herein was inspired by a modern-day program that is universally acknowledged as an affectionate throwback to the great variety shows of radio's Golden Age. The Peabody Award–winning *A Prairie Home Companion* has been favorably compared to such earlier airwave favorites as *Grand Ole Opry,* Gene Autry's *Melody Ranch, The Arthur Godfrey Show* and especially the Minnesota–based programs of newscaster-raconteur Cedric Adams—who though he may not be a familiar name to you and me, just so happens to be the personal idol of *Prairie Home Companion* creator Garrison Keillor.

Born in Anoka, Minnesota, in 1942, Gary Edward "Garrison" Keillor grew up within a strict religious sect that forbade him to watch television and only allowed him to listen to radio under supervision. Like millions of other Midwesterners, Keillor was enthralled by the broadcasts of the folksy, gregarious Cedric Adams over Minneapolis' WCCO. While attending the University of Minnesota, Keillor decided to follow in Adams' footsteps, performing on Minnesota Public Radio station KSJR beginning in 1969. Garrison's three-hour morning show was a potpourri of country music, friendly chatter and lengthy monologues about the fictional Minnesota community of Lake Woebegon and its colorful residents. After publishing his first *New Yorker* story in 1970, he delved further into his radio heritage by digging up tapes of old programs like *Fibber McGee and Molly* (q.v.) and the aforementioned *Melody Ranch*. In 1971 he rechristened his KSJR program *A Prairie Home Companion*, a title whimsically borrowed from a local cemetery. While researching a *New Yorker* article on the final Ryman Auditorium broadcast of *Grand Ole Opry*, Keillor's random dreams of launching an old-style radio variety show crystalized, and on July 6, 1974, *A Prairie Home Companion* became a weekly, 90-minute music-and-comedy offering. In 1978, the program moved from its tiny radio studio to St. Paul's venerable World Theater in order to accommodate a studio audience and an ever-growing cast of regular performers. *Prairie Home Companion* was then offered to National Public Radio for widespread syndication but was considered too regional in appeal, so Minnesota Public Radio set up its own network, American Public Radio (now known as American Public Media), for national distribution beginning in 1980. During the 1994 centennial for Minnesota-born novelist F. Scott Fitzgerald, the World Theater became the Fitzgerald Theater, the now-permanent home of Keillor's weekly two-hour broadcast—which by 2009 was boasting a 500-station lineup and some five million regular listeners.

Strange as it seems, it is quite possible to adore *A Prairie Home Companion* without being enamored of its host. The public's divided attitude towards Keillor is similar to that of another highly specialized radio star, Howard Stern (q.v.), with a slight difference. With Stern, you either love or hate him. With Keillor, you either take him or leave him. Millions of listeners cherish Keillor's lengthy, rambling "News from Lake Woebegon" monologues, his satirical sketches focusing on such eccentrics as seedy 1940s-style private eye Guy Noir and flea-bitten cowboys Dusty and Lefty, and his faux commercials for imaginary sponsors Ralph's Pretty Good Grocery, Guy's Steel-Toed Shoes, Bertha's Kitty Boutique, Fritz Electronics, the Ketchup Advisory Board, the American Duct Tape Council and Mournful Oatmeal. Less sympathetic listeners regard the host's monologues as boring and pointless, his sketches as a bit too derivative of Bob & Ray and other radio humorists, and his fake commercials as slightly condescending. But even those who tend to tune out whenever Keillor steps up to the microphone are united in their affection for the musical portions of the program, featuring such gifted and versatile performers as the Powdermilk Biscuit Band (Mary Du Shane, Bob Douglas, Dick Rees), the Guys All-Star Shoe Band (Pat Donohue, Andy Stein, Gary Rainor, Arnie Kinsella), keyboardist-vocalist-music director Richard Dworsky, bass saxophonist-tuba player Vince Giordano, string specialist Peter Ostroushko, clarinetist Butch Thompson, trumpeter-pianist Randy Sandtke, harmonica artist Greg Brown, brass master Scott Robinson, percussionists J.T. Bates and Peter Johnson, and singers Jearlyn & Jevetta Steele, Robin & Linda Williams and Prudence Johnson. In an era of canned, computerized and digitalized music, the sound of live musicians performing live selections before a live audience is positively enthralling.

Keillor has over the years extended his creative outlets to novels, voiceovers and political commentary, but until the first decade of the 21st century he did not evince any interest in motion pictures. Around that same time, legendary film director Robert Altman (*MASH, Nashville, The Player*) was pondering another of his "chamber" pieces (a film with minimal cast and settings deliberately aimed at a limited audience), this one built around a radio broadcast. An American expatriate of long standing, Altman had never heard of *Prairie Home Companion* until the program was brought to his attention by his wife. "I didn't see the film in it," Altman recalled to the *Washington Post*'s Peter Kaufman. "It was a real challenge: How can we make this work?" For Keillor's part, he would have been happy with a film that featured a typical *Prairie Home Companion* broadcast and nothing else, but admitted to Kaufman that the entertainment value of "a bunch of actors standing around holding scripts" might be minimal. "I mean, that would be funny for 45 seconds."

With Altman directing and Keillor scripting (with story construction assistance from Ken LaZebnik), the two men collaborated on a framing device which imagines that the broadcast of *A Prairie Home Companion* enacted in the 2006 film of that title is the absolute final show of the series: The film's working title was indeed *The Last Broadcast*. According to this scenario, fictional St. Paul radio station WLT, which carries the program, has been sold to a Texas conglomerate whose soulless executives plan to tear down the Fitzgerald Theater and toss all the *Prairie Home Companion* performers out on the street. As Keillor and his confreres gather for their farewell performance (bringing along a lot of emotional baggage), an ethereal young lady identified in the script as "Dangerous Woman" wafts through the proceedings, ultimately revealing herself as the Angel of Death—but what exactly is her mission on this fateful evening?

Auteurists have in recent years opined that the film is a remake of the ultra-cheap 1954 musical film *Corn's-a-Poppin*, for which Altman co-wrote the screenplay (and has long since disowned it). But beyond the earlier film's plot device of a country-music TV show sponsored by a regional popcorn firm threatened with extinction in a hostile takeover by big-city popcorn interests (*are* there big-city popcorn interests?), its connection to the film version of *Prairie Home Companion* is as thin as a cobweb. Other observers have theorized that Keillor was using his film's Texas–based corporate villain as a savage attack on his own personal *bête noire*, President George W. Bush. But Keillor has pooh-poohed this notion, telling About.com Guide's Rebecca Murray, "I wanted to finish a piece of work on time and have it not be embarrassing. That was my goal. I was really working on assignment from Mr. Altman.... I volunteered to do it in order to keep somebody else from doing it because I could think of people I would not want to write a screenplay about *A Prairie Home Companion*. It was a sort of a dog in the manger act on my part. It had very little to do with wanting to express something. Anything you want to say you can say on the radio or almost any place." At the same time, the notion of a final broadcast was definitely in keeping with Keillor's oft-repeated "*Every* show's the last show, that's my philosophy."

We'll never know what the earlier drafts of the screenplay looked like, since Keillor expunged them from his laptop each time he conferred with Altman, whose only comment was, "You're getting warm." During production both Altman and Keillor publicly praised one another. "It was a pleasure to have somebody else be the boss," Keillor insisted to Murray. "It wouldn't have been so much fun any other way. [Altman has] been around and he's made a lot of movies, and he's a great straightforward person to work for.... It was an amazing experience as a writer to be in the middle of the maelstrom—and have a good time." But many people close to the film have revealed that Keillor and Altman didn't always see eye to eye. Temperamentally, the only thing the two had in common was that they were born in Minnesota. Both men were long accustomed to being the kings of their respective castles; both were stubborn and set in their ways; and neither responded well to criticism. Altman was a bit more candid than Keillor when he told Peter Kaufman, "It's very difficult for [Keillor]. It's the first time he's had anybody that can override him.... I have the editing control. But he's smart enough—he knows that."

With the conspicuous exception of Lily Tomlin, here cast as one-half of the singing Johnson Sisters (an amiable spoof of the Carter Family Singers), most of the starring actors were making their first appearance in an Altman film—and every one of them jumped at the chance, all willing to work for scale and none asking for nor receiving preferential treatment. These high-profile performers were delighted with the creative freedom Altman had always afforded his actors, allowing them to ad lib and improvise on-camera and often adjusting the screenplay to accommodate these artistic indulgences. Cast member Virginia Madsen spoke for many when she thanked Altman for the opportunity to "dare to be bad."

The communal on-set atmosphere enabled the "name" actors to blend in seamlessly with the carryover regulars from radio's *Prairie Home Companion,* among them Tim Russell (cast as the show's stage manager), Sue Scott (as the makeup lady), sound effects man Tom Keith, singers Prudence Johnson, Robin & Linda Williams and the Guys All-Star Shoe Band, and of course Keillor himself. Actually he almost *wasn't* himself, feeling so edgy about delivering a self-portrayal that he wanted to be cast as "Carson Wyler," one of his frequent aliases from the radio show (in which Keillor was never identified on the air as himself except for the initials G.K.). As it turned out, Keillor's thoroughly natural and unaffected performance is one of the picture's highlights, with even his tendency to speak in fluent Anecdote both on- and off-stage coming across as 100 percent credible—though it's a bit surprising to watch Keillor, a notorious control freak, exercise so much *lack* of control over his cast and crew members in the film.

The decision to shoot on location at the Fitzgerald Theater posed a few difficulties. When the theater's interior proved too small to accommodate some of the backstage scenes, other nearby structures were substituted; however, all of the actual radio show scenes were filmed on the Fitzgerald stage. But this was hardly the most daunting problem during the four-week shoot. Hovering over the entire enterprise was the specter of death, with Altman in the final stages of the leukemia that would claim his life only a few months after wrapping up the picture. Because no insurance company was willing to underwrite the production, Paul Thomas Anderson, who'd previously helmed the Altman-like *Magnolia Departed,* was hired as backup director. Typically, Altman treated Anderson's presence in a jocular fashion, insisting that his potential replacement be given a canvas director's chair labeled "Pinch Hitter." Anderson was never called up from the bullpen: Altman finished the job through sheer force of will.

Taking into consideration Altman's failing health and his impressive body of work prior to 2006, the director can be forgiven for borrowing heavily from himself in the film version of *Prairie Home Companion.* The final efforts of John Ford and Howard Hawks were decidedly self-referential, so why not Altman's? Thus in *Prairie Home Companion* we have a trio of obtuse males embarrassing the radio show's very pregnant floor director Molly (wonderfully played by Maya Rudolph) by forming a circle and chiding her for not being married, a scene reminiscent of the more spectacular public humiliation of Sally Kellerman in *MASH* (1970). We have elderly country-western favorite Chuck Akers (a character based on Chet Atkins and played by L.Q. Jones) singing a valedictory song just before he drops dead, similar to Margaret Hamilton's decorous departure in *Brewster McCloud* (1971). We have the show's makeup lady unknowingly carrying on a conversation with Chuck Akers' corpse, just as half the cast of *A Wedding* (1978) unwittingly chattered away at the deceased Lillian Gish. And in emulation of *Nashville* (1975), singer Yolanda Johnson (Meryl Streep) has a mini-breakdown during an onstage performance (Ronee Blakely in *Nashville*) while her daughter Lola (Lindsay Lohan) closes the show with an uninhibited—and wholly unexpected—rendition of "Frankie and Johnny" (Barbara Harris in the earlier film). Finally, Altman's love affair with smooth-but-complex tracking shots, most memorably expressed in *The Player* (1996), permeates *Prairie Home Companion* from start to finish, a testament to the brilliance of cinematographer Edward Lachman.

Though these echoes of past Altman glories are effective, the director seems off his feed in other parts of the film. Inasmuch as some of the longer Altman pictures can be a challenge to the kidneys, we should be grateful that the 98-minute *Prairie Home Companion* moves at such a rapid pace; unfortunately, at times this swiftness suggests that the director merely wanted to get it all over with in a hurry. Altman's genius for tossing out a bunch of seemingly random bits and pieces and then fusing them into a unified whole is largely absent here, notably in the much-admired scene wherein Keillor and his crew are forced to ad lib a duct tape commercial when Molly drops the script: It's funny, yes, but

A radiant Meryl Streep and a dour Garrison Keillor share the microphone in this scene from Robert Altman's 2006 film version of Keillor's radio series *A Prairie Home Companion*.

it doesn't really jell and the chaos tends to wear down the viewer after a few minutes. Finally, the director's willingness to let his actors extemporize to their heart's content has in the past resulted in scenes that are pure gold; but when in *Prairie Home Companion* Meryl Streep and Lily Tomlin (as the Johnson Sisters) are allowed to improvise their dialogue at great and interminable length, the viewer might well stop listening and start asking such embarrassing questions as "Why don't Meryl and Lily look more like sisters?" or "Why is Lily's Wisconsin accent thicker than Meryl's?"

Most of *Prairie Home Companion*'s weaknesses can be laid at the feet of screenwriter Garrison Keillor. For starters, its premise is absurd. Maybe we can believe that the *Prairie Home Companion* performers would have trouble finding other show biz jobs if they were suddenly fired *en masse*; and given the present state of the economy, we can accept the possibility that Keillor himself would have to settle for a menial job as a parking ramp attendant. But a vastly popular radio program that we see playing to a capacity theater audience coming to a permanent end just because a radio station has been sold and a building has been razed? Spare us.

And since all the film's characters are of Keillor's invention, he must be held responsible for the misfire idea of having private eye Guy Noir—played by Keillor in his radio sketches and Kevin Kline on-screen—serve as the film's narrator and the audience's "eyes." Even on radio, Guy Noir is a Johnny One-Note, good for maybe five minutes' airtime at most. When stretched to feature-film length, the character's Chandleresque *patois* and outdated attitudes—apparently intended to represent the anachronistic nature of *Prairie Home Companion*—become awfully tiresome, helped not at all by the decision to saddle Guy with lame Clouseau-like slapstick. Also, the sinuously silent and langorously lethal Dangerous Woman (Virginia Madsen), the personification of *Prairie Home Companion*'s imminent extinction, grows less effective the longer she remains on-screen. And when she opens her mouth to speak, out comes dialogue that sounds like a high schooler's rewrite of Emily Webb in the third act of *Our Town*.

The only allegorical character in the film with any lasting value is the Axeman, the heartless representative of the corporation that intends to kill *A Prairie Home Companion* for all time. Tommy Lee Jones frowns his way through the role, his face demonically underlit and his every word and gesture invoking Charles Foster Kane at Xanadu. Yet for all its blatancy, the character performs the valuable service of clueing us in as to what Keillor and Altman truly regard as priorities. When the Axeman comments that *Prairie Home Companion* looks like it should have died 50 years ago, we aren't really expected to be offended, especially since one of Keillor's favorite quips is that his fans listen faithfully to *Prairie Home Companion* because most of them live in nursing homes and can't reach the radio dial. No, that's not enough to despise the Axeman. What is really supposed to roil us about the character—and to cheer on his ultimate doom at the hands of Dangerous Woman—is that not only does the Axeman plan to tear down the Fitzgerald Theater, *he has never even heard of F. Scott Fitzgerald*! Get a rope, boys.

Now the really good stuff. The sequences purporting to show an episode of *Prairie Home Companion* in progress, though taking a few liberties with the source material (Lake Woebegon is never mentioned), are almost uniformly excellent, making one wish that Keillor had at least tried to make a film consisting of nothing but the broadcast scenes. Everyone in the cast sings and plays instruments magnificently, especially Streep and Tomlin, thanks in great part to the patient tutelage of *Prairie Home Companion* bandleader Rich Dworsky. Lindsay Lohan, a variable actress in other films, gives a standout performance as Lola Johnson, the disenfranchised daughter and niece of the Johnson Sisters who spends her early scenes fuming over her relatives' spiteful reminiscences and writing suicidal poetry. Yet elsewhere backstage she enjoys being in the company of Keillor and the other *Prairie Home Companion* regulars, and is enlivened by their remembrances of things past.

When in the climax Lola discovers that she thrives in the spotlight as a performer herself (albeit very briefly), we know that for all the "death" imagery in the film there is at least one natural-born survivor who is capable of carrying the torch of *joie de vivre* passed along by Keillor's weekly program. As a result, Lola is one of the few of the film's characters whom we genuinely care about.

Best of all are Woody Harrelson and John C. Reilly as Dusty and Larry, the lonesome cowboys played on radio by Keillor and Tim Russell and here elevated to the level of performing artists. Though professional singers Tom Waits and Lyle Lovett were originally considered for these roles, it is hard to imagine anyone other than Harrelson and Reilly successfully socking across their big number "Bad Jokes (Lord I Love 'Em)," an outrageous musical medley of dirty jokes that are older than your grandpa. ("I think my wife died." "Waddya mean, you think?" "Well, the sex is the same but the dishes are stackin' up.") It's also hard to imagine two performers deriving as much sheer adolescent enjoyment out of singing such deliberately dreadful material. Thank your lucky stars that Altman persuaded Keillor to add this genially ribald number so that the director wouldn't suffer the onus of making a PG movie, insisting upon something—*anything*—that would bump him into the PG-13 category.

Produced independently, *A Prairie Home Companion* became the object of an intense bidding war involving several distributors, with Picturehouse Entertainment winning the prize. Released to select cities on a limited basis, it earned around $25,000,000, no blockbuster but fairly respectable for its low budget and modest expectations. Reviewers tended to echo one another by classifying it as a film about death, citing the end of the show, the end of the Fitzgerald, the onscreen demise of Charley Akers, Lola Johnson's Sylvia Plath–like poetry, the sledgehammer symbolism of Dangerous Woman, and of course the tragically inescapable fact that this was Altman's last film. Molly Haskell of *The Village Voice* went off on a different tangent, characterizing the film as a tribute to the immutability of the show's music, songs that will linger in our collective memory long after the musicians have shuffled off to the Undiscovered Country: "[Music is] like a river, running through the film, running through their life. They contribute to it, are united for a time, lose out, die out, but the music, as the last scene suggests, continues."

In a way, these words can also apply to the rarefied world of Old Time Radio. Most of the programs listed in these pages have long since been cancelled and the performers' voices eternally stilled. Yet many can still be heard in recordings and on film, and will continue to be heard as long as recordings and film exist. Though the Golden Age of Radio was officially declared dead with the final CBS broadcasts of *Yours Truly, Johnny Dollar* and *Suspense* on September 30, 1962, thanks to the magic of microphones and movies it is alive and well and living in our hearts.

Bibliography

Books

Adler, Jerry. *Living from Hand to Mouth: My Memoir*. Bloomington, IN: AuthorHouse, 2005.

Antler, Joyce. *You Never Call! You Never Write! A History of the Jewish Mother*. New York: Oxford University Press, 2007.

Backer, Ron. *Mystery Movie Series of 1940s Hollywood*. Jefferson, NC: McFarland, 2012.

Bakish, David. *Jimmy Durante: His Show Business Career, with an Annotated Filmography and Discography*. Jefferson, NC: McFarland, 1995.

Bannon, Jim. *The Son That Rose in the West*. Plano, TX: Devil's Hole Printery, 1975.

Barbas, Samantha. *The First Lady of Hollywood: A Biography of Louella Parsons*. Berkeley: University of California Press, 2005.

Barbour, Alan G. *Days of Thrills and Adventure*. New York: Collier, 1970.

_____. *A Thousand and One Delights*. New York: Collier, 1971.

Barnouw, Eric. *A History of Broadcasting in the United States, 1933–53*. 3 vols.: *A Tower in Babel*, *The Golden Web* and *The Image Empire*. New York: Oxford University Press, 1966–1970.

Barrios, Richard. *A Song in the Dark: The Birth of the Musical Film*. New York: Oxford University Press, 1995.

Beck, Jerry, and Will Friedwald. *Looney Tunes and Merrie Melodies: A Complete Guide to the Warner Bros. Cartoons*. New York: Henry Holt, 1989.

Behlmer, Rudy, ed. *Memos from David O. Selznick*. New York. Viking, 1972.

Blanc, Mel. *That's Not All, Folks: My Life in the Golden Age of Cartoons and Radio*. New York: Warner, 1988.

Boardman, Gerald. *American Theater: A Chronicle of Comedy and Drama, 1930–1969*. New York: Oxford University Press, 1995.

Bogdanovich, Peter. *Who the Devil Made It*. New York: Knopf, 1997.

Bogue, Merwin. *Ish Kabibble*. Baton Rouge: Louisiana State University Press, 1989.

Bruskin, David N. *The White Brothers: Jack Jules & Sam White*. Metuchen, NJ: Scarecrow, 1990.

Cahn, William. *A Pictorial History of the Great Comedians*. New York: Grosset & Dunlap, 1970.

Castle, William. *Step Right Up! ... I'm Gonna Scare the Pants Off America*. New York: Putnam, 1976.

Cocchi, John. *Second Feature: The Best of the B's*. Secaucus, NJ: Citadel, 1991.

Coghlan, Frank, Jr. *They Still Call Me Junior: Autobiography of a Child Star, with a Filmography*. Jefferson, NC: McFarland, 1993.

Cox, Jim. *Historical Dictionary of Radio Soap Operas*. Lanham, MD: Scarecrow, 2005.

Cozad, W. Lee. *More Magnificent Mountain Movies: The Silver Screen Years, 1940–2004*. Lake Arrowhead, CA: Sunstroke Media, 2006.

Cullen, Frank, Florence Hackman, and Donald McNeilly. *Vaudeville, Old and New: An Encyclopedia of Variety Performers in America*. New York: Routledge, 2007.

Curtis, James. *W.C. Fields: A Biography*. New York: Knopf, 2003.

DeLong, Thomas A. *Radio Stars: An Illustrated Biographical Dictionary of 953 Performers, 1920 through 1960*. Jefferson, NC: McFarland, 1996.

Dick, Bernard F. *Hal Wallis: Producer to the Stars*. Lexington: University Press of Kentucky, 2004.

Dixon, Wheeler Winston. *The Early Film Criticism of François Truffaut*. Translations by Ruth Cassel Hoffman, Sonja Kropp, and Brigitte Formentin-Humbert. Bloomington: Indiana University Press, 1993.

Dooley, Roger. *From Scarface to Scarlet: American Films in the 1930s*. New York: Harcourt Brace Jovanovich, 1981.

Dunning, John. *On the Air: The Encyclopedia of Old-Time Radio*. New York: Oxford University Press, 1998.

Elliot, Marc. *Jimmy Stewart: A Biography*. New York: Harmony, 2006.

Ely, Melvin Patrick. *The Adventures of Amos 'n' Andy: A Social History of an American Phenomenon*. New York: Free Press, 1991.

Etling, Laurence. *Radio in the Movies: A History and Filmography, 1926–2010*. Jefferson, NC: McFarland, 2011.

Eyman, Scott. *The Lion of Hollywood: The Life and Legend of Louis B. Mayer*. New York: Simon & Schuster, 2005.

Fein, Irving. *Jack Benny: An Intimate Biography*. New York: Putnam, 1976.

Fletcher, Anthony L. *Don't Dare Miss the Next Thrilling Chapter.* Minneapolis: Mill City Press, 2009.

Flom, Eric L. *Silent Film Stars on the Stages of Seattle.* Jefferson, NC: McFarland, 2009.

French, Warren. *The South and Film.* Jackson: University Press of Mississippi, 1981.

Friedman, Ryan. *Hollywood's African-American Films.* New Brunswick: Rutgers University Press, 2011.

Friedwald, Will. *A Biographical Guide to the Great Jazz and Pop Singers.* New York: Pantheon, 2010.

Furia, Philip, and Laurie Patterson. *The Songs of Hollywood.* New York: Oxford University Press, 2010.

Gargiulo, Suzanne. *Hans Conried: A Biography, with a Filmography and a Listing of Radio, Television Stage and Voice Work.* Foreword by Leonard Maltin. Jefferson, NC: McFarland, 2002.

Garnett, Tay. *Light Up Your Torches and Pull Up Your Tights.* New Rochelle, NY: Arlington House, 1973.

Gaver, Jack, and Dane Stanley. *There's Laughter in the Air! Radio's Top Comedians and Their Best Shows.* New York: Greenberg, 1945.

Gibson, Walter B., with Anthony Tollin. *The Shadow Scrapbook.* New York: Harcourt Brace Jovanovich, 1979.

Giddins, Gary. *Bing Crosby: A Pocketful of Dreams—The Early Years, 1903–1940.* Boston: Little, Brown, 2001.

Goldberg, Lee. *Unsold Television Pilots: 1955 through 1989.* Jefferson, NC: McFarland, 1990.

Goldman, Herbert J. *Banjo Eyes: Eddie Cantor and the Birth of Modern Stardom.* New York: Oxford University Press, 1997.

Goulart, Ron, ed. *The Encyclopedia of American Comics: From 1897 to the Present.* New York: Facts on File, 1990.

Harmon, Jim. *The Great Radio Heroes.* Garden City, NY: Doubleday, 1967.

_____. *Radio Mystery and Adventure and Its Appearances in Film, Television and Other Media.* Jefferson, NC: McFarland, 2003.

Hayde, Michael. *My Name's Friday: The Unauthorized But True Story of Jack Webb.* Foreword by Harry Morgan. Nashville: Cumberland House, 2001.

Hemming, Roy, and David Hajdu. *Discovering Great Singers of Classic Pop.* New York: Newmarket, 1991.

Higby, Mary Jane. *Tune in Tomorrow.* New York: Cowles, 1968.

Hollis, Tim. *Ain't That a Knee-Slapper: Rural Comedy in the Twentieth Century.* Jackson: University Press of Mississippi, 2008.

Horn, Maurice, ed. *100 Years of American Newspaper Comics: An Illustrated Encyclopedia.* New York: Gramercy Books, 1996.

Irvin, Sam. *Kay Thompson: From Funny Face to Eloise.* New York: Simon & Schuster, 2010.

Jewell, Richard B. *RKO Radio Pictures: A Titan Is Born.* Berkeley: University of California Press, 2012.

_____, with Vernon Harbin. *The RKO Story.* New York: Arlington House, 1982.

Josefsberg, Milt. *The Jack Benny Show.* New Rochelle, NY: Arlington House, 1977.

Kanin, Garson. *Hollywood.* New York: Viking, 1974.

Kenney, Dave. *Twin Cities Picture Show: A Century of Moviegoing.* St. Paul: Minnesota Historical Society Press, 2007.

King, John P. *Wicked Tales from the Highlands.* Charleston, SC: History Press, 2011.

Lamparski, Richard. *Whatever Became Of . . . ?* Various vols. New York: Crown, 1968–1978.

Lawrence, A.H. *Duke Ellington and His World.* London: Psychology Press, 2001.

Lee, Judith Yaross. *Twain's Brand: Humor in Contemporary American Culture.* Jackson: University Press of Mississippi, 2012.

Lennig, Arthur. *The Immortal Count: The Life and Times of Bela Lugosi.* Lexington: University Press of Kentucky, 2003.

Lord, Phillips H. *Seth Parker and His Jonesport Folks.* Philadelphia: John Winston, 1932.

Louvish, Simon. *Man on the Flying Trapeze: The Life and Times of W.C. Fields.* New York: Norton, 1997.

Maltin, Leonard. *The Disney Films.* New York: Crown, 1973.

_____. *The Great American Broadcast: A Celebration of Radio's Golden Age.* New York: Dutton, 1997.

_____. *The Great Movie Shorts.* Foreword by Pete Smith. New York: Crown, 1972.

_____. *Movie Comedy Teams*, rev. ed. Foreword by Billy Gilbert. New York: New American Library, 1985.

_____. *The Real Stars.* New York: Curtis, 1972.

Mank, Gregory W. *Karloff and Lugosi: The Story of a Haunting Collaboration.* Jefferson, NC: McFarland, 1990.

Marmorstein, Gary. *A Ship Without a Sail: The Life of Lorenz Hart.* New York: Simon & Schuster, 2012.

Martin, Len D. *The Republic Pictures Checklist: 1935–1959.* Jefferson, NC: McFarland, 1998.

Martin, Linda, and Kerry Seagrave. *Women in Comedy.* Secaucus, NJ: Citadel, 1986.

McGee, Kristin A. *Some Liked It Hot: Jazz Women in Film and Television, 1928–1959.* Middletown, CT: Wesleyan University Press, 2009.

McGilligan, Pat, ed. *Backstory 2: Interviews with Screenwriters of the 1940s and 1950s.* Berkeley: University of California Press, 1991.

Medved, Harry, and Michael Medved. *The Hollywood Hall of Shame: The Most Expensive Flops in Movie History.* New York: Perigree, 1984.

Miller, Don. *B Movies.* New York: Curtis, 1973.

Mintzer, Rich. *Howard Stern: A Biography.* Westport, CT: Greenwood, 2010.

Mitz, Rick. *The Great TV Sitcom Book.* New York: R. Marek, 1980.

Nachman, Gerald. *Raised on Radio.* Berkeley: University of California Press, 2000.

Nelson, Ozzie. *Ozzie.* Englewood Cliffs, NJ: Prentice Hall, 1973.

Okuda, Ted, with Ed Watz. *The Columbia Comedy Shorts: Two-reel Hollywood Film Comedies, 1933–1958.* Introduction by Edward Bernds. Jefferson, NC: McFarland, 1986.

Osgood, Dick. *Wyxie Wonderland: An Unauthorized Fifty-Year Diary of WXYZ, Detroit.* Bowling Green, OH: Bowling Green University Press, 1981.

Parish, James Robert. *The Great Movie Series.* New York: A.S. Barnes, 1971.

_____, William T. Leonard, Gregory W. Mank, and Charles Hoyt. *The Funsters.* New York: Arlington House, 1979.

Peters, Margot. *The House of Barrymore.* New York: Knopf, 1990.

Pitts, Michael R. *Famous Movie Detectives Two.* Metuchen, NJ: Scarecrow, 1991.

Quirk, Lawrence J., and William Schoell. *The Rat Pack: Neon Nights with the Kings of Cool.* New York: HarperCollins, 1998.

Reid, John. *Popular Pictures of the Hollywood 1940s.* Lulu.com, 2011.

Rhodes, Gary Don. *Lugosi: His Life in Films, on Stage, and in the Hearts of Horror Lovers.* Jefferson, NC: McFarland, 1997.

Ritchie, Michael. *Please Stand By: A Prehistory of Television.* New York: Overlook, 1994.

Rothel, David. *Who Was That Masked Man? The Story of the Lone Ranger.* Cranbury, NJ: A.S. Barnes, 1976.

Schlappi, Elizabeth. *Roy Acuff: The Smoky Mountain Boy.* Gretna, LA: Pelican, 1993.

Secrest, Meryle. *Somewhere for Me: A Biography of Richard Rodgers.* New York: Knopf, 2001.

Sennett, Ted, ed. *The Old-Time Radio Book.* New York: Pyramid, 1976.

Server, Lee. *Screenwriter: Words Become Pictures.* Pittstown, NJ: Main Street Press, 1987.

Settel, Irving. *A Pictorial History of Radio.* New York: Grosset & Dunlap, 1967.

Sheward, David. *It's a Hit! The Back Stage Book of Longest-Running Broadway Shows: 1884 to the Present.* New York: Back Stage Books, 1994.

Shimeld, Thomas. *Walter B. Gibson and the Shadow.* Jefferson, NC: McFarland, 2003.

Sikov, Ed. *Dark Victory: The Life of Bette Davis.* New York: Henry Holt, 2007.

Smith, Glenn D., Jr. *"Something on My Own": Gertrude Berg and American Broadcasting.* Syracuse: Syracuse University Press, 2007.

Smith, Kate. *Upon My Lips a Song.* New York: Funk & Wagnalls, 1960.

Starr, Michael Seth. *Art Carney: A Biography.* New York: Fromm, 1997.

Sterling, Christopher H., Cary O'Dell, and Michael C. Keith, eds. *The Biographical Encyclopedia of American Radio.* New York: Routledge, 2011.

Stern, Howard, with Larry Sloman. *Private Parts.* New York: Simon & Schuster, 1993.

Strom, Robert. *Miss Peggy Lee: A Career Chronicle.* Jefferson, NC: McFarland, 2005.

Tackley, Catherine. *Benny Goodman's Famous 1938 Carnegie Hall Concert.* New York: Oxford University Press, 2013.

Taylor, Robert. *Fred Allen: His Life and Wit.* Boston: Little, Brown, 1989.

Terrace, Vincent. *Radio Programs, 1924–1984: A Catalog of Over 1800 Shows.* Jefferson, NC: McFarland, 1999.

Weiss, Ken and Ed Goodgold. *To Be Continued.* New York: Bonanza, 1972.

Wurtzler, Steve J. *Electric Sounds: Technological Change and the Rise of Corporate Mass Media.* New York: Columbia University Press, 2007.

Zinman, David H. *Saturday Afternoon at the Bijou.* New Rochelle, NY: Arlington House, 1973.

Zuckoff, Mitchell. *Robert Altman: The Oral Biography.* New York: Borzoi Books, 2009.

Selected Articles, Short Works and Dissertations

Clayton, Edward T. "The Tragedy of Amos 'n' Andy." *Ebony,* Oct. 1961.

Evanier, Mark. "Bottom of the Barrel." *News from Me* blog, Feb. 10, 2010.

Kelland, Clarence Buddington. "Scattergood Baines-Invader." *Saturday Evening Post,* June 30, 1917.

Murray, Rebecca. "Garrison Keillor Discusses the *A Prairie Home Companion* Movie." *About.com Guide,* June 6, 2006.

Ness, Richard R., West Illinois University. "From a Voice in the Night to a Face in the Crowd: The Rise and Fall of the Radio Film." Paper delivered to the AEJMC Conference in San Francisco, Aug. 2006.

Review of *Dreaming Out Loud. The Magazine of Sigma Chi* 31 no. 2, 1941.

Saunders, Allen. "Did Movie Magnates Put Radio Stars in Bad Films to Wreck Them?" *Toledo News-Bee,* Sept. 18, 1934.

Scott, Keith. "The Origin of Foghorn Leghorn." *Apatoons* #150, 2008. [Reprinted on the *Cartoon Brew* website].

Twynham, Leonard. "Seth Parker, Vermonter." *The Vermonter,* June 1932. [Reprinted in *The Hartford Historical Society Newsletter,* Nov.–Dec. 2007]

Frequently Referenced Newspapers and Periodicals (Past and Present)

Billboard
Bridgeport [CT] *Herald*
Broadcasting (Broadcasting and Cable)
Chicago Tribune
Entertainment Weekly
Exhibitor's Herald-World
Film Bulletin
Film Daily
Films in Review
Hollywood Reporter

Independent Exhibitors' Film Bulletin
Jet Magazine
Life Magazine
Meriden [CT] Daily Journal
Metropolitan News-Enterprise
Milwaukee Journal-Sentinel (separate newspapers prior to 1995)
Montreal Gazette
Motion Picture Daily
Motion Picture News
New Movie Magazine
New York Times
The New Yorker
The Onion
Photoplay
Pittsburgh Post-Gazette
Pittsburgh Press
Portsmouth [NJ] Times
Radio Digest
Radio Fan-Fare
Radio Guide (Movie-Radio Guide)
Radio Mirror (Radio and TV Mirror)
Rochester [NY] Evening Journal
St. Petersburg [FL] Times
Screen Facts
Sponsor Magazine
Time Magazine
TV Guide
Variety
Village Voice
Washington Post

Video

Hollywood, The Golden Era: The RKO Story (3-part television documentary). Arts & Entertainment Network, July 24–Aug. 7, 1987.

Frequently Referenced Websites

All-Rovi Guide http://www.allrovi.com/movies
American Radio History http://americanradiohistory.com/index.htm
The Classic TV Archive Homepage http://ctva.biz
Film Noir of the Week http://www.noiroftheweek.com
Gino's Place http://www.geocities.ws/doo wop gino/index–2 html
Google News Archive Search http://google.com/archives.search
Greenbriar Picture Show http://greenbriarpictureshows.blogspot.com
Internet Archive Media History Digital Library http://archive.org/details/mediahistory
Internet Movie Database http://imdb.com
Lum and Abner Museum and Jot 'Em Down Store http://lum-n-abner.com
Media History Digital Library http://mediahistoryproject.org
Old Time Radio Researchers Library http://otrrlibrary.org
Rudy Vallee-Official Website http://rudyvallee.com
Third Banana http://thirdbanana.blogspot.com
Thrilling Days of Yesteryear www.thrillingdaysofyesteryear.blogspot.com
Travalanche travsd.wordpress.com
Turner Classic Movies www.tcm.com
Wanna Buy a Duck? (The Joe Penner Project) http://craighodgkins.com/joepenner/index.html
Western Clippings http://www.westernclippings.com
Wikipedia http://wikipedia.org
William K. Everson Collection http://www.nyu.edu/projects/wke/notes.htm

Index

Page numbers in ***bold italics*** indicate pages with illustrations.

A&P Gypsies 6
Abbott, George 77, 145
Abbott and Costello 5, 7, 80, 204, 234
The Abbott and Costello Show 131, 143
ABC *see* American Broadcasting Company
Aber, Nestor (Michael Stuart) 29
Academy Award Theater 249
Ace, Goodman, and Jane (The Easy Aces) 7
Acuff, Roy 161
Adams, Cedric 278
Adams, Franklyn P. 7
Adams, Stanley 250
Adamson, Harold 89, 243
Adler, Jerry 187
Adler, Larry 40
Adreon, Franklyn 135
The Adventures of Ozzie and Harriet: radio series 3, 265, 266–267, 268, 269; TV series 264–265, 270, 271; *see also* Nelson, Harriet; Nelson, Ozzie
Ainsley, Norman 106
Air Adventures Corporation 84
The Air Adventures of Jimmie Allen 83–84, 188, 189; *see also Sky Parade*
Al Pearce and His Gang 117, 204, 205
Alba, Maria 31
Alberni, Luis 113
Albert, Eddie 89
Albertson, Frank *23*, 24, 152, 205
The Aldrich Family: radio series 4, 146, 147, 148; TV series 148; *see also* Henry Aldrich, film series
Alexander, A. L. 7
Alias the Deacon 40, 164
Alice in Wonderland 134
All Aboard 220
All-American Drawback 119
"All at Once, No Alice" *see The Return of the Whistler*
All-Star Bond Rally 103
Allen, Barbara Jo (Vera Vague) 131–132, ***133***, 134, 147
Allen, Fred 7, 60–67, ***67***, 68–71, 90, 95, 133, 134, 224, 228–229, 234, 259
Allen, Gracie 250, 252; *see also* Burns and Allen
Allen, Woody 277

Allman, Elvia *see* Brenda and Cobina
Allwyn, Astrid 106
"Alouette" 224
Alt, Carol 277
Altman, Robert 279, 280, 281, 283
Amadeus 112
The Amazing Mr. Malone 184
Ameche, Don 70, 120
American Ballet of the Metropolitan Opera 120
American Broadcasting Company (ABC) 7, 9, 32, 138, 143, 171, 177, 181, 184, 188, 225, 227, 235, 244, 255, 259, 263, 267, 270, 271
American Federation of Musicians 161
American Federation of Radio Artists 238
American Hero 237
American magazine 178
American Public Radio (American Public Media) 279
American Society of Composers, Authors and Publishers (ASCAP) 161, 195
American Tobacco Company 84
America's Got Talent 275
"Amor" 226
Amos 'n' Andy (Freeman Gosden and Charles Correll) 2, 15–18, ***18***, 19–20, 32, 37–38, 55, 170, 171
Amos 'n' Andy: animated cartoon adaptations 7, 20; radio series 7, 15–20, 21, 57, 181, 256; TV series 19
Amsterdam, Morey 204, 205
Anders, Lynn 106
Andersen, Hans Christian 149
Anderson, Eddie "Rochester" 65, 66, 68, 93, 124, 217
Anderson, Ivy 87
Anderson, Marjorie 107
Anderson, Mary 147, 212
Anderson, Paul Thomas 281
André, Pierre 189
Andrews, Robert D. 172
Andrews, Robert Hardy 235
Andrews, Stanley 135
Andy Hardy: film series 147
The Animal Convention 132
Ansara, Michael 139

AP *see* Associated Press
Apfel, Oscar 23
Arcand, Nathaniel 141
Archer, John 179
Archie Andrews 242
Arden, Eve 88, 122, 248, 252
Arizona Radio Network 194
Arkie the Arkansas Woodchopper 163
Arlen, Richard 41, 221
Armbrister, Cyril 31, 32
Armed Forces Radio Service 7, 196
Armetta, Henry 113
The Armour Jester 211
Armstrong, Louis 44
Armstrong, Robert 158, 159, 160, ***192***, 193
Armstrong of the SBI see *Jack Armstrong, the All-American Boy*, radio series
Arnaz, Desi 83
Arnheim, Gus 45
Arno, Sig 252
Arnold, Dorothy 114
Arnt, Charles 168, 238
Around the World 159–160
Around the World in 80 Days 231
Arquette, Cliff 164
Arthur, Art 95
The Arthur Godfrey Show 278
Artists and Models Abroad 65
As the World Turns 253
ASCAP *see* American Society of Composers, Authors and Publishers
Ashworth, John 264
Associated Press (AP) 203, 227, 261, 266
Astaire, Fred 22, 43, 44
Astor Pictures 188
"At Dusk" 134
At the Circus 128, 245
At the Races 119
At War with the Army 251, 252
Ates, Roscoe 19
Atkins, Chet 281
Atlantic City 134
Atlas Publications 252
Atwell, Roy 6, 224
Aubert, Lenore 210
Auer, John H. 88, 89, 114

289

Auer, Mischa 159
Auerbach, Artie (Mr. Kitzel) 204, 205
Austin, Gene 45
Austin, Virginia 122
Australian Broadcasting Corporation 262
Autry, Gene 25, 114, 168, 165, 278
Avalon Time 164
Avery, Phyllis 263
Avery, Tex 74, 101
Avildsen, John G. 276
Ayres, Lew 92

Babbitt, Harry 154, 156, 160
Baby Rose Marie 6, 37
"Baby Take a Bow" 213
The Bachelor and the Bobby Soxer 68
Backus, Jim 270
Bad Girl 212
"Bad Humor Man" 157
"Bad Jokes (Lord I Love 'Em)" 283
Bailey, Jack 263
Baker, Art 221
Baker, Kenny 38, 43, 88, 121
Baker, Phil 45, 76, 91, 96, 121, 211–213, 220
The Baker's Broadcast 72, 73, 75, 76, 265
Bal Tabarin (San Francisco) 154
Balanchine, George 113, 121
Baldo, Reginald 240
Baldwin, Alec 111
Baldwin, Dick 176
Baldwin, Earl 226
Baldwin, Faith 263
Baldwin, Robert 151
Ball, Don 36
Ball, Lucille 76, 83, 126, 127, 155, 166, 248, 249
Ballet Russe 120
Ballew, Smith 6
Bankhead, Tallulah 217
Bannon, Jim 214, *214*, 215
Banyard, Beatrice 59
Barbas, Samantha 115
Barbier, George 35, 73, 179
Barclay, Joan 159
Bard, Ben 52
Baringer, Barry 31
Barker, Graham 155
Barker, Ma 193
Barnes, Binnie 45, 69, 70
Barnes, George 116
Barnet, Charlie 44, 199
Barnett, Vince 239, 240
Baron Munchausen *see* Pearl, Jack
Barrett, Pat 164–165
Barrie, Elaine 92
Barrie, Mona 210, 239
Barrie, Wendy 38
Barron, Robert *183*
Barry, Pete 109
Barrymore, John 62, 92, 157–158
Bartholomew, Freddie 239
Barton, Charles 80, 197
Baruch, Andre 85
The Bashful Bachelor 172, 173–174, 175
Basie, Count 88, 197
Batchelor, Walter 67

Bates, J.T. 279
Batman: film series 111, 144; TV series 143, 216
Battle, George Gordon 26
Bauersfeld, Marjorie O'Neill "Mirandy" 164
Baxter, Warner 200–201, 202, *202*, 203
Beal, John 33
Beale Street Boys 45
Beatty, Clyde 143
Beaudine, William 109
Beck, Arthur F. 84
Beck, Jackson 7
Beckett, Scotty 243
Bedtime for Bonzo 268
"The Bee" (Schubert) 64
Beebe, Ford 143
Beech-Nut Gum 28–29
Beemer, Brace 137
Beery, Wallace 243, 244
Beggs, Hagan 216
Begley, Ed 259
Behind the Mask 108, 109
Behlmer, Rudy 50
Bell, Ralph 253
Bellamy, Ralph 188, 201
Beller, Mary Lynn 244
Beloin, Ed 66, 67, 68
Ben Bernie and All the Lads 91
Ben Bernie, the Old Maestro 91
Benaderet, Bea 266
Benchley, Robert 69, 163, 219
Bendix, William 70, 244, 245, *246*, 247, 248
Benedict, Billy 209, 224
Benett, Anne 153
Bennett, Enid 150
Bennett, Hugh 147, 163
Bennett, Joan 27
Bennison, Andrew 157, 186
Benny, Jack 2, 5, 38, 39, *39*, 40, 41, 42, 58, 7, 60–67, *67*, 68–71, 75, 79, 90, 93, 95, 96, 98, 199, 204, 211, 212, 217, 259
Benoff, Mac 212
Bentley, Babette 151
Berg, Gertrude 256, 257, *257*
Bergen, Edgar 2, 5, 7, 40, 100, 101, 118–123, *123*, 126–130, 131, 158, 166
Bergen, Jerry 99
Berkeley, Busby 116
Berkes, Johnny 130
Berle, Milton 43, 75, *78*, 79, 83, 265
Berlin, Irving 50
Bernie, Ben 64, 90, 91, 92, 93, 94, 95, 96, 211
Berrell, Lloyd 262
Berwick, Viola 178
Best, Katherine 121
Best, Willie 179, 180
Bettger, Lyle 139
Beverly Hill Billies 165
Beverly Hills Friar's Club 83
The Big Broadcast 2, 33, *34*, 35–36, 45, 47, 84, 218, 274
The Big Broadcast of 1936 20, 37–38
The Big Broadcast of 1937 38–39, *39*, 40, 41, 63

The Big Broadcast of 1938 5, 40–41, 120, 130
The Big Cage 143
The Big Liar see Meet the Baron
"A Big Noise from Winnetka" 197
The Big Store 244
Big Town: film series 238–241; 1947 film 238–239, 241; radio series 237–238, 239; TV series 241
Big Town After Dark 240, *240*, 241
Big Town Scandal 239, 240–241
Bigard, Barney 19
Bilbo, Theodore G. 231
Billy Gray's Band Box 83
Biograph Studios 87, 114
Black Mask magazine 259
Blackhawk Hotel (Chicago) 154
Blackmer, Sidney 62
Blackstone, Lillian 247
Blake, Amanda 254
Blake, Ben K. 7, 87
Blake, Pamela 172, 177
Blakely, Ronee 281
Blakeney, Olive 146, 147
Blanc, Mel 66, 73, 205, 220, 234
Blandick, Clara 173, 223
Blane, Sally 13, 14, 47, 48, 49, 105
Blessed Event: play and film 92
Bletcher, Billy 137, 224
The Blitz Wolf 195
Block, Martin 195, 198, 199
Blondell, Gloria 248
Blondie: film series 233
Blue, Monte 179
Blue Coal 104, 105, 109
Blue Coal Radio Revue 104; *see also The Shadow*, radio series
Blue Network 8, 171, 227, 245, 253; *see also* American Broadcasting Company; National Broadcasting Company
Blum, Len 276
BMI *see* Broadcast Music International
Boasberg, Al 58–59
Bob and Ray 37, 279
Bogue, Merwin A. (Ish Kabibble) 132, 154, 158, 159, 160
Boland, Mary 38, 73, 88
Boleslawski, Richard 53
Bond, Ford 112
Bond, Lillian 27
Bond, Tommy 241
Bondi, Beulah 226, 246
Bonnell, Bonnie 59
Bonnell, Lee 126
Booth, Shirley 217
Borg, Veda Ann 107, 239
Born to Dance 188
Borrah Minnevitch and His Harmonica Rascals 88, 213
Boston Blackie: film series 208, 210, 253
Boswell, Connee 2, *34*, 44, 63, 274; *see also* Boswell Sisters
Boswell Sisters 2, 6, *34*, 35, 36, 63
Boteler, Wade 143
Bottoms, Timothy 237
Bouchey, Willis 188
Bourbon Street Shadows see *The Invisible Avenger*

Index

Bowers, William 159
Bowman, Lee 98
Box Office magazine 99
Boy Meets Girl 249
Boyd, William "Stage" 55
Boyer, Charles 264
Boylan, Malcolm Stuart 181–182
Boyle, Peter 111
The Boys from Syracuse: play and film 77
Bracken, Eddie 146, 219
Brackett, Charles 146
Brackett, Leigh 203
The Brady Bunch Movie 276
Brainard, Bertha 11
Brande, Dorothea 92
Brandt, Jerrold T. 178, 179, 180
Breakfast at Sardi's see *Breakfast in Hollywood*, radio series
Breakfast at Tiffany's 131
The Breakfast Club 225
Breakfast in Hollywood: 1946 film 212, 225–227, 263; radio series 225–227
Breakfast on the Boulevard see *Breakfast in Hollywood*, radio series
Brecher, Irving 43, 244, 245, 247, 248
Breen, Bobby 78, 258
Breen, Richard L. 271, 272, 273
Bregman, Martin 110
Brenda and Cobina (Blanche Stewart, Elvia Allman) 44, 131
Breneman, Tom 225–226, 227
Brenton, William 36
Bressart, Felix 250
Brewster McCloud 281
Brewster Twins 93, 95
Brian, David 184
Brian, Mary 72
Brice, Monte 157, 186
Bricker, George 209
Bridgeport (CT) *Sunday Herald* 252
Bridges, Lloyd 201, **202**
Briskin, Sam 43
Brix, Herman (Bruce Bennett) 137
Broadcast Music International (BMI) 161
The Broadway Melody of 1936 42, 63
A Broadway Romeo 61
Broadway Through a Keyhole 2, 92
Broderick, Helen 44, 75, 80
Brokenshire, Norman 36
Bronston, Samuel 186
Brooke, Hillary 238
Brooke, Walter 144
Brooks, Albert 79
Brooks, Leslie 210
Brooks, Mel 43, 69
Brophy, Ed 85
Brower, Brock 235
Brown, Charles D. 227, **228**
Brown, Greg 279
Brown, James 163
Brown, Joe, Jr. 236
Brown, Joe E. 55, 56
Brown, John 245, 247, 248, 249, 267
Brown, Les 166
Brown, Melville 16, 19
Brown, Wally 44
Bruckheimer, Jerry 141

Bruskin, David 196, 222
Bryan, Arthur Q. 101
Bryant, Julie 160
Bryson, Winifred 201
Buchman, Harold 212
Buck Benny Rides Again 5, 66, 68
Bulldog Drummond 35, 108
Bullock, Walter 88
Burce, Suzanne see Powell, Jane
Burdick, Hal 227
A Burglar to the Rescue 105
Burke, Billie 169, 226
Burke, James 81
Burnette, Smiley 114, 165
Burns, Bob "Bazooka" 2, 39–40, 43, 162, 164
Burns, George 71; see also Burns and Allen
Burns and Allen (George Burns and Gracie Allen) 2, 32, 33, **34**, 35, 36–37, 38–39, **39**, 40, 41, 42, **42**, 58, 60, 63, 72, 78, 98
Burrows, Abe 218
Burtt, Robert M. "Bob" 83, 84, 171, 188, 189
Burum, Steven H. 111
Bush, George W. 280
Butler, David 155, 157, 158
Butler, Daws 220
Butterfield, Herb 272
Buttram, Pat 163
Byron, Edward A. 181, 183, 184

Cabanne, Christy 179
Caesar, Arthur 55
Caesar's Palace (Las Vegas) 130
Cage, Nicholas 145
Cagney, James 51, 153, 217, 245
Cahn, Sammy 114
Calhern, Louis 125
Callahan, George 108
Calling Dr. Death 206, 207
Calloway, Cab 2, 6, **34**, 35, 36, 37, 113
Calvert, John 209
Calvet, Corinne 252
Campbell's Soups 115, 117
The Campus Mystery 265
The Canada Dry Program 61
Candid Microphone: radio and film series 7
"Candlelight and Wine" 159
"Candy Store Blues" 199
Canin, Stuart 64
Canova, Judy 25, 120, 134
Cantor, Charlie 217, 218–219, 220
Cantor, Eddie 4, **4**, 51, 55, 62, 72, 77–81, 93, 96, 199, 213, 241
Capote, Truman 131
Cappy Bara Boys 44
Capra, Frank 152
Captain Midnight: 1942 film serial 6, 189–190; radio series 84, 188–189, 191; TV series 190–191
Captured see *Gang Busters*, TV series
Carb, Marty 272; see also The Pete Kelly Seven
Carey, Macdonald 153
Carlay, Rachel 113

Carle, Richard 165
Carleton, Claire 169
Carlisle, Mary 41
Carlon, Fran 238
Carney, Alan 44, 169
Carney, Art 7, 187, 191
Carney, "Uncle" Don 6
Carol, Sue 17
Carole, Joseph 82
Carolina Blues 160
Carpenter's 116
Carradine, John 69
Carrillo, Leo 113
Carroll, Georgia 160
Carroll, John 88, 89
Carroll, Madeleine 217
Carroll, Nancy 22, 62, 63, 148
Carson, Jack 76
Carson, Johnny 129, 268
Carter, Janis 209, 228, **228**
Carter Family 289
"The Case of the Cotton Kimono" see *The Shadow*, 1954 TV pilot
Casey, Robert 148
Castle, Nick 89
Castle, William 203, 208, 209, 260, 261–262
Cat People 207
The Cat's-Claw Murder Mystery see *Scattergood Survives a Murder*
Cathcart, Dick 271, 274; see also The Pete Kelly Seven
Catlett, Walter **94**, 152, 165
Cavalcade of Stuff 37
Cavanaugh, Hobart 155, 169
CBS see Columbia Broadcasting System
Chambers, Whitman 239
Chance of a Lifetime 208
Chandler, George 109
Chandler, Happy 148
Chandler, Lane 137
Chandler, Mimi 147–148
Chandu on the Magic Island see *The Return of Chandu*
Chandu the Magician: 1932 film 3, 25, 28, 29–30, **30**, 31; radio series 28–29, 31–32
Chaney, Lon, Jr. 206, 207, 208, 210
"Change of Heart" (song) 89
Change of Heart see *The Hit Parade of 1943*
Chapin, Michael 227
Chaplin, Saul 114
Chapman, Marguerite 184
Charley's Aunt 69
Charlie Chan: film series 108
Charlie McCarthy, Detective 125–126, 127
The Charlie McCarthy Show 126, 129; see also Bergen, Edgar
Charlot, Harry Engman 104
The Charm School see *Collegiate*
Chase, Charley 10, 241
Chase and Sanborn 78, 79, 120
The Chase and Sanborn Hour 40, 41, 120, 122, 123, 126, 131; see also Bergen, Edgar
Check and Double Check 2, 16–18, **18**, 19–20, 21, 22, 24, 25, 32, 37,

48, 50, 55, 171; *see also* Amos 'n' Andy
Chicago Daily News 15
Chicago Defender 16
Chicago Tribune 15
Chicken Little 195
Chico and the Man 103
The Chief (*The Fire Chief*) 2, 25, 54–56, 59, 60; *see also* Wynn, Ed
Chief Thundercloud 135, 137
The Choclateers 43
Chodorov, Jerome 249
Chou, Jay 144
Chow, Stephen 144
Ciannelli, Eduardo 203
"Cielito Lindo" 197
Cimarron 207
Cinderella Meets Fella 74
Cinderella Swings It 180
The Circus Show-Up 105
Cities Service Concerts 38
Clair, René 36, 120
Clarence *see* Hedges, Ray
Clark, Bobby 121
Clark, Buddy 95
"Clean as a Whistle" 52
Clearly, Patricia 257
Clemens, William 210
Clements, Stanley 240, 241
Cleveland, George 101
Clifford, Jack 234
Cline, Eddie 124
Cliquot Club Eskimos 6
Cloak and Dagger 255
Clooney, George 144
Clyde, June 165
Coblentz, Edmund D. 25
Coburn, Charles 179
Coca, Imogene 153
Cocomalt 75
Coghlan, Frank, Jr. 151
Cohen, Harold V. (Harold W. Cohen) 20, 127, 166, 168
Cohn, Harry 208
Cole, Nat King 199, 226
Coleman, Georgia 74
Coles, Mildred 179, 180
College Holiday 41, 63, 64
College Humor 41
College Rhythm 41, 72–73, 74
College Swing 42, 133
Collegiate 41, 74, 98
Collins, Dorothy 89
Collins, Ray 200, 201
Collins, Ted 46, 47, 49
Collins, Tom 32
Colombo, Alberto 138
Col. Lemuel Q. Stoopnagle (F. Chase Taylor) 37
Colonna, Jerry 5, 7, 42, 69, 132–133, *133*, 134, 165
Colony Pictures 106
Columbia Broadcasting System (CBS) 2, 7, 9, 19, 33, 37, 39, 40, 43, 44, 45, 46, 57, 58, 61, 72, 75, 76, 79, 85, 87, 89, 90, 96, 104, 109, 115, 117, 129, 132, 134, 149, 153, 166, 170, 177, 178, 181, 190, 191, 193, 196, 199, 203, 205, 206, 208, 211, 214, 216, 235, 237, 238, 241, 242, 244, 248, 249, 257, 259, 266, 274, 284
Columbia Pictures Corporation 7, 44, 45, 80, 81, 82, 87, 101, 105, 107, 131, 132, 143, 144, 145, 160, 161, 181, 183, 184, 189, 190, 195, 196, 198, 200, 201, 202, 206, 207, 208, 210, 214, 215, 216, 224, 227, 233, 235, 236, 237, 241, 242, 253, 259, 260, 266
Columbia Records 46
Columbo, Russ 2
The Comedy of Errors (Shakespeare) *see The Boys from Syracuse*
Comer, Russell C. 83
Comer, Twila 84
Comin' Round the Mountain 101, 164–165, 167, 171
Commonweal 151
Community Sing 43, 79
Como, Perry 63, 97
Compton, Joyce 180
Comstock, Bill "Tizzy Lish" 204, 205
Condos Brothers 93
Conlin, Jimmy 59, 233
Conn, Harry 62, 75
Connecticut Yankees 11, 12; *see also* Vallee, Rudy
Conners, Barry 27, 29
Conrad, William 272
Conried, Hans 249–250
Conselman, William 155
Consolidated Laboratories 84
Conway, Julie 160
The CooCoo Nut Grove 92
Cook, Donald 27
Cook, Gene 230
Coons, Robin 68
Cooper, Betty Jane 74
Cooper, Dorothy 242
Cooper, Gary 226
Cooper, Jackie 146, 148
Cooper, Jerry 115, 117
Cooper, Melville 88
Cooper, Sanford L. 84
Corby, Ellen 129
Cormack, Bartlett 27
Corman, Roger 60
Corner, James 146
Corn's-a-Poppin 280
Correll, Charles *see* Amos 'n' Andy
Corrigan, Lloyd 183
Cortes, Mapy 166
Cortez, Ricardo 28
Coslow, Sam 49, 171, 172, 174
Cosmo Jones (aka *The Crime Smasher*): radio series 193–194, 227
Cosmo Jones in the Crime Smasher: 1943 film 194–195
Costello, Don 209
Cotten, Joseph 243
Cotton Club Orchestra 19; *see also* Ellington, Duke
The Coty Program 38
Coulouris, George 184
Counterspy see David Harding, Counterspy
Counterspy Meets Scotland Yard 254–255, **255**
The Country Doctor 149
Country Fair 165
Courageous Dr. Christian 151
Court of Human Relations: radio and film series 7
Court of Missing Heirs 166
Courtland, Jerome 199
"Cow Cow Boogie" 197
Cowan, Jerome 43, 201
Coward, Noël 120
Cowboy Canteen 161
Cox, Morgan 192
Coy, Johnny 219
Cramer, Richard 107
Crane, Les 216
Crane, Richard 193
Craven, Frank 173, 179
Craven, James 190
Crawford, Joan 62, 226
"Crazy People" 36
Creelman, James, Jr. 12
Crehan, Joseph 109, 192
Crime Doctor: film series 200, 201, 202–203, 207, 214, 253, 260; 1943 film 201–202
The Crime Doctor: radio series 3, 199–200, 201, 203
The Crime Doctor's Courage 203
The Crime Doctor's Diary 202, 203
The Crime Doctor's Gamble 203
Crime Doctor's Man Hunt 203
The Crime Doctor's Strangest Case **202**, 203
The Crime Doctor's Warning 203
Cromwell, Richard 194
Crosby, Bing 2, 5, 19, 32, 33, **34**, 35, 36, 37, 38, 39, 41, 47, 72, 73, 95, 130, 133, 134, 218, 219, 266
Crosby, Bob 154, 197, 271
Crosby, Lindsay 266
Crosby, Percy 235
Cross, Ben 110
Crowing Pains 234
Crowley, Patricia 244
Crowther, Bosley 251
The Cruise of the Jasper B. 159
"Cuanto la Gusta" 243
The Cuckoos 17
Cugat, Xavier 243
Cummings, Robert 125
Cupid Goes Nuts 132
Currie, Louise 158, 174
Currier, Mary 209
Curry, Tim 112

Dabney, Virginia 114
Dafoe, Dr. Allan Roy 148, 149
Daisy 233
Daley, Cass 219
Damerel, Donna *see* Myrt and Marge
The Dancing Masters 176
D'Andrea, Tom 248
Dandridge, Dorothy 38, 88
Dandridge Sisters 38
Daniels, Marc (Mark) 110, 246
Dare, Danny 88
"Dark Eyes" 116
Darkman 110
Darro, Frankie 22–23
Darwell, Jane 168
da Silva, Howard 219

A Date with Judy: 1948 film 242–244; radio series 3, 241–242, 243, 244; TV series 244
Davenport, Bill 268
David Harding, Counterspy: 1950 film 253–254; 1958 TV pilot 255; radio series 25, 180, 253
Davidson, Ronald 135
Davies, Marion 115
Davis, Bette 23, 24, 116, 117
Davis, Joan 65, 93, 95, 159
Davis, Johnny "Scat" 116, 117
Davis, Rufe 44, 99
Davis, Sammy, Jr. 78
Day, Dennis 66
Day, Doris 134
A Day at the Races 87
The Day the Bookies Wept 76, 77
Dean, James 270
Dear Me, the Sky Is Falling 259
"Dearest, Darest I" 68
Dearing, Edgar 84
DeCamp, Rosemary 149, 245, *246*, 248
"The Decapitation of Jefferson Monk" see *I Love a Mystery*, 1945 film
DeCarlo, Dan 252
de Cordova, Fred 268, 270
De Corsia, Ted 246
DeFore, Don 250
DeForest Phonofilm 91
De Francesco, Louis 29
Dein, Edward 207
deKova, Frank 139
de Leon, Walter 72, 74
"Delicious Delirium" 128
Dell comics 190
Dell'Abarte, Gary 275, 277
Delmar, Kenny (Senator Claghorn) 229–230, 231, *232*, 233–234
Demarest, William 85, 158, 165, 219
DeMille, Katherine 84
Denison, Leslie 81
Dennis, Mark 210
Denny, Reginald 22, 201
Depp, Johnny 141–142
DeRita, Joe 224
Derr, Richard 109
The Detective Story Hour 104; see also *The Shadow*, radio series
Detective Story Magazine 104, 105
The Devil's Mask 215
Devine, Andy 66, 273
Devine, Jerry 181
DeVol, Frank 187
Dewey, Thomas E. 181
De Wolfe, Billy 219
The Diary of Anne Frank 56
Diaz, Cameron 145
The Dick Van Dyke Show 37, 82, 205
Diller, Phyllis 131
Dillinger, John 191, 193
DiMaggio, Joe 114
Dinning Sisters (Lou, Ginger and Jean) 163
Dionne Quintuplets 148
"Disc Jockey Jump" 199
Disney Studios 56, 89, 102, 103, 129, 132, 134, 141, 195, 272–273
Dix, Richard 207, *207*, 208, 209, 210

Dixon, Paul 225
Do You Trust Your Wife? (*Who Do You Trust?*) 129
Dr. Christian: film series 143, 150–153, 178; radio series 2, 148, 149–150, 153; TV series 153
Dr. Christian Meets the Women 151–152
Dodge, Bruce 211
Dolores Divine, Guilty or Innocent: novel and radio serial 27; see also *The Trial of Vivienne Ware*
Don Lee Network 29, 32
Donald Duck 129
Donlevy, Brian 200
Donnell, Jeff 183, 209, 216, 228
"Don't Believe Everything You Dream" 44
Doran, Ann 169, 270
"Dormant Account" see *Mark of the Whistler*
Dorsey, Jimmy 199
Double or Nothing 38
Douglas, Don 102, 227
Douglas, Gordon 167
Douglas, Mike 160
Downey, Morton, Sr. 6, 11
Downey Sisters 45
Doyle, Len 181, 184
Dozier, William 143, 144
Dracula 29
Dragnet: 1954 film 3, 272; radio series 1, 271, 272; TV series 193, 272, 273, 274
Dragonette, Jessica 38
Dreaming Out Loud 172–173, 174
Dressler, Marie 14
Drew, Ellen 66, 158, 203
Droopy 101
Dryden, Robert 216
Duane, Michael 210
Dubov, Paul 193
Duchin, Eddie 54, 87
Duck Soup 55, 56
Dudley, Robert 226
Duff, Howard 247
Duffy, Albert 196, 199
Duffy's Tavern: 1945 film 218–220; radio series 82, 216–220, 224; TV series 220
Dugan, Tom 109
Dumbrille, Douglass 233
Dumont, Margaret 75
DuMont Network 227
Dunbar, Dixie 213
Duncan, Danny 172
Dunham, Dorothea 88
Dunham, Jeff 129
Duning, George 154
Dunn, Eddie 36
Dunn, Emma 179
Dunn, James 212, 213
Dunn, Ralph 137
Dunne, Irene 43
Dunning, John 133, 147, 181, 185, 191, 214
DuPar, Edwin B. 139
Dupree, Roland 241
Durante, Mrs. Jean 53, 234
Durante, Jimmy 51–52, 53, 132

Durbin, Deanna 22, 78, 180, 199, 241, 242, 243
Durkin, James 105
Durocher, Leo 217
Dvorak, Ann 113
Dwan, Allan 53, 101, 126, 127, 128, 159
Dworsky, Richard 279, 283

Eagle-Lion Pictures 231, 233, 234; see also Producers' Releasing Corporation
Earl Carroll Vanities: 1945 film 81
Earl Carroll's Vanities: stage show 29
Earnshaw, Harry A. 28, 29, 32
"Easy to Love" 188
Ebony magazine 20
Eburne, Maude 150, 198
Eby, Lois 135
The Ed Sullivan Show 274
The Eddie Cantor Show 77–78, 79, 80, 82, 133, 231; see also Cantor, Eddie
Eddy, Nelson 44, 120
The Edgar Bergen/Charlie McCarthy Show 126; see also Bergen, Edgar
Educational Pictures Corporation 32, 37, 43, 222
Edwards, Gus 50
Edwards, Harry 132
Edwards, Joan 89
Edwards, Ralph 44, 166
Edwards, Sam 190
Effie Klinker (Podine Puffington) see Bergen, Edgar
Eilers, Sally 212
Einstein, Bob 79
Einstein, Harry (Parkyakarkus) 4, 5, 43, 75, 76, 78, *78*, 79, 130, 265
Eisenger, Jo 271
Ellery Queen: film series 181, 202, 227
Ellington, Duke 19, 87, 197
Elliott, Dick 172
Ellis, Bobby 148
Ellis, Dellie 241
Ellis, Kenneth M. 25, 27
Ellis, Marvin 27
Ellis, Robert 31
Ellison, Harlan 178
Ellison, James 182
Ellsler, Effie 55
Elmer Fudd 101
Elting, Lawrence 6
Emerson, Faye 185
Emmett, Fern 179
Encore 263, 264
English, John 135, 137
Ennis, Skinnay 42, 44
Enright, Ray 101
Entertainment Weekly 140
Epstein, Philip 43
Eric, Elspeth 191
Erickson, Leif 41, 249
Erickson, Louise 167, 241, 242, 243
Errol, Leon 131, 169
Erwin, Stuart (Stu) *34*, 35, 36, 51, 205
Erwin, Trudy 160
Escape 205
Essex, Harry J. 260, 261
Estabrook, Howard 101

Etting, Ruth 45, 197
"Evalena" 172
Evanier, Mark 262
Evans, Dale 205
Evans, Ray 251
Everson, William K. 24, 182, 190
"Every Hour on the Hour" 224
Exhibitor's Herald-World 14
Eythe, William 212

Fadiman, Clifton 7
Falkenberg, Jinx 80
"Falling in Love with Love" 77
Famous Studios 7; *see also* Paramount Pictures
Farrell, Glenda 117
Farrell, Kenneth 233
The Fat Man: 1951 film 259–260, 270, **260**, 261–262; radio series 259, 261, 262; TV pilot 262
Fatool, Nick 272; *see also* The Pete Kelly Seven
Fawcett Publications 190
Fay, Frank 61, 211
Fay, Larry 92
Faye, Alice 65, 72, 93, 94, **94**, 95, 213
FBI *see* Federal Bureau of Investigation
The FBI in Peace and War 191, 255
FBO Pictures 11, 12
FCC *see* Federal Communications Commission
Federal Bureau of Investigation (FBI) 191
Federal Communications Commission (FCC) 184–185, 186, 275
Feld, Fritz 76
Felton, Verna 188
Fennelly, Parker 180, 229
Fennemann, George 272
Ferris, Walter 152
Feuer, Cy 138
Fibber McGee and Company 99
Fibber McGee and Molly (Jim and Marian Jordan) 2, 5, 96–97, **97**, 98–103, 126–128, 158, 165–166, 175
Fibber McGee and Molly: radio series 96–97, 99–100, 101, 103, 126, 127, 164, 165, 166, 266, 279; TV series 101, 170
Fidler, Jimmy 65
Field, Betty 146
Field, Mary 168
Fields, Benny 40
Fields, Dorothy 51
Fields, Gracie 129
Fields, Joseph 249
Fields, Shep 41
Fields, Stanley 23
Fields, W.C. 37, 40–41, 60, 73, 90, 120, 123, **123**, 124–125, 129, 213, 233
52nd Street 133
Figueroa Playhouse (Los Angeles) 115
Film Bulletin 89, 95, 239, 240
Film Classics 210
Film Daily 24, 49, 126
Film Noir of the Week 238
Fimberg, Hal 163

Finlayson, James 98
Fio Rito, Ted 197
The Firehouse Five Plus Two 89
First Love 243
Fisher, Eddie 78
Fiske, Robert 84
Fitzgerald, Ella 273
Fitzgerald, F. Scott 279, 283
Fitzgerald Theater (St. Paul, MN) 279, 280, 281, 283
Five of a Kind 149
Five Star Final 237
Flagstad, Kirsten 41
Flavin, James 109
Fleischer, Max 6, 73
Fleischmann Yeast 72
The Fleischmann Yeast Hour 11; *see also The Rudy Vallee Hour*
Flesh and Fantasy 264
Fletcher, Lucille 3
"The Flight of the Bumblebee" (Rimsky-Korsakov) 142
Florey, Robert 99
Flothow, Rudolph 208
The Flotsam Family see The Life of Riley, radio series
Flying High 46, 49
Foch, Nina 201, 203, 215
The Foghorn Leghorn 234
Follow the Leader: 1930 film 54; radio series 132
Follow Your Heart 85
Fontaine, Frank 89
Ford, John 188
Ford, Wallace 166, 180
Ford, Whitey (The Duke of Paducah) 165
Forest, Frank 38–39
Forman, Bill 206
Forrest, Otto 208
Forrest Gump 277
42nd Street: novel 85
Foulger, Byron 209, 226
Four Step Brothers 160
Fowley, Douglas 169, 182
Fox, Wallace 237
The Fox and the Crow: cartoon series 195
Fox Film Corporation 15, 24, 25, 28, 29, 31, 32, 148, 200, 212; *see also* 20th Century-
Fox West Coast Bulletin 43
"Foxhound" *see International Crime*
Foy, Bryan 59, 212, 231
Foy, Eddie, Jr. 59, 60, 165
Fraker, William 141
Francis 264
Frank, John 83
Frank, Melvin 218
"Frank Merriwell" stories 235
Frankel, Harry (Singing Sam the Barbasol Man) 6
"Frankie and Johnny" 281
Franklin, Miriam 219
Franz, Eduard 258
Frawley, William 92, 203
Frazier, Brenda 131
The Fred Allen Show 180, 229, 234; *see also* Allen, Fred
Frederic, Norman 139

Free and Easy 119
Freed, Alan 195
Freeman, Y. Frank 224
Frees, Paul 227
French, Lloyd 119
Friedman, David 43
Friedman, Seymour 254
Friend, Cliff 87
"Friendship" 249
Friewald, Eric 139
Friganza, Trixie 59
Froman, Jane 43
The Front 258
Fun and Fancy Free 129
Funt, Allen 7

G-Men *see Gang Busters*, radio series
Galt, John 238
Gang Busters: 1942 film serial 192, **192**, 193; 1955 film 193; radio series 25, 180, 191–192, 193, 252; TV series 193
The Gang's All Here 212
Garber, Jan 44, 88, 199, 205
Garbo, Greta 63
Gardel, Carlos 38
Gardner, Ed 216–217, **217**, 218, 220
Gargan, William 84, 227, **228**
Gargiulo, Suzanne 250
Garland, Judy 186
Garlock, Mickey 91
Garnett, Tay 159
Gates, Nancy 168
Gehring, Walter 194
Gemora, Charles 170
The General Died at Dawn 99
General Foods 148
General Mills 138, 235
General Motors Promenade Concerts 41
The Gentle Maniacs (Paul "Mousie" Garner, Sam Wolf, Dick Hakins) 87
The George Burns and Gracie Allen Show: TV series 82; *see also* Burns and Allen
George White's Scandals: film version 72; stage version 79
Geray, Steven 184, 201
Gerry, Alex 254
Gershwin, George 120, 121
Geva, Tamara 113
"The Ghost of the Manor" *see The Shadow Strikes*
The Ghost Ship 207
Giamatti, Paul 278
Gibson, Walter B. (Maxwell Grant) 104, 106, 107, 110
Gifford, Frances 147
Gift of Gab 45, 211
Gilbert, Billy 75, 76, 80, 129, 213
Gildersleeve on Broadway 168, 169
Gildersleeve's Bad Day 168–169
Gildersleeve's Ghost 168, 169–170
Giles, Erva 21
Gillis, Ann 240, **240**, 241
Gilmore, Virginia 182
Gino's Place 198
Giordano, Vince 279
Girard, Henry 148

Index

A Girl, a Guy and a Gob 158
Gish, Lillian 281
"Give a Man a Job" 51
Givot, George 79, 87
Glaser, Vaughn 146, 159
Glasgow Herald 29
Glass, Myrtle 59
Gleason, Jackie 247–248
Gleason, James 95, 113, 114, 245
Glen Island Casino 265
Globe Productions 185, 186
Glorifying the American Girl 14
Glover, Edmund 159
"Glow Worm" 226
Go Chase Yourself 76
Go-Go Gophers 234
Go West 244
"God Bless America" 50
Goddard, Paulette 186, 187, **187**, 219
Goff, Harper 272–273
Goff, Ivan 141
Goff, Norris 178; *see also* Lum and Abner
Goin' to Town 175, 176–177
Going My Way 163, 219
Goldberg, Evan 144
The Goldbergs: 1950 film 256, 257–258; radio series 3, 57, 256; TV series 256, 257, 258–259
Goldblum, Jeff 277
Golden, Robert S. 225–226
Golden Gate Quartet 88
Goldsmith, Clifford 145, 148
Goldsmith, Jerry 111
Goldwyn, Sam 4, 40, 77, 79, 120, 185
The Goldwyn Follies 44, 120–121, 122, 124, 211
Gondry, Kevin 144
Gone with the Wind: novel 116
"Goo-Goo I Go Ga-Ga Over You" 73
Good Morning Vietnam 278
Goodkin, Alice 60
Goodman, Benny 40, 116, 117, 213
Goodwin, Bill 89, 246
Goodwins, Leslie 76, 176
Goofy 129
Gordon, Anita 129
Gordon, Bert (The Mad Russian) 5, 43, 75, 79, **81**, 130, 133, 184, 231, 265
Gordon, C. Henry 38, 55
Gordon, Don 189
Gordon, Gale 101, 267, 270
Gordon, Gloria 249, 250, 252
Gordon, Mack 73, 74, 94, 95
Gordon, Michael 201
Gordon, Roy 228
Gosden, Freeman *see* Amos 'n' Andy
"Gossamer World" *see* Queen for a Day, 1951 film
"Got the Moon in My Pocket" 158
Gough, Lloyd 144
Goulart, Ron 105
Gould, Sandra 217
Goulding, Edmund 53
Grable, Betty 74, 76, 98, 213
Graham, Bob 224
Graham, Frank 193, 194–195, 227
Grand Hotel 62, 226
Grand National Pictures 106

Grand Ole Opry: 1940 film 161–162, 163; radio series 1, 161, 162, 278
Granet, Bert 76
Grant, Cary 68
Grant, Chuck 178
Grant, Maxwell *see* Gibson, Walter B.
Grantlund, Nils T. 177
Granville, Bonita 138, 139, 226
Grapewin, Charley 49, 179
Graser, Earl 137
Grauer, Ben 85, 86, 185
Gray, Glen 44
The Great American Broadcast 213
Great Balls of Fire! 276
The Great Gabbo 128
The Great Gatsby 200
The Great Gildersleeve *see* Peary, Harold
The Great Gildersleeve: 1942 film 168; radio series 2, 163–164, 165, 166, 167, 168, 169, 170, 242, 248; TV series 170
The Great Man 56
Greatest Man on Earth 132
Greaza, Walter 238
Green, Eddie 217, 218, 219
Green, Howard J. 172, 196
Green, Johnny 44
Green, Mitzi 63
Green Acres 163
The Green Hornet: 1940 film serial 142–143; radio series 142, 143, 144, 145; 2011 film 1, 144–145; TV series 143–144
The Green Hornet Strikes Again 143
Greene, Harold 254
Greene, Vernon 107
Greene, Walter R. 14
Greenleaf, Raymond 254
Greenstreet, Sidney 234, 259
Greenway Productions 143
Greer, Sonny 19
Grey, Harry 113
Grey, Virginia 182
Grier, Jimmy 97
Griffith, Charles B. 60
Griffith, D.W. 229
Guedel, John 220–221, 222, 223, 266, 267
Guilfoyle, Paul 209
Guilty Assignment see *Big Town*, 1947 film
Guizar, Tito 6, 41, 224
Guns Don't Argue 193; *see also Gang Busters*, TV series
Guys All-Star Band (Pat Donohue, Andy Stein, Gary Rainor, Arnie Kinsella) 279, 281
Gwynne, Michael (Lee Vaunce) 277
Gyllenhaal, Jake 144

Haas, Charles 109
Haas, Robert M. 117
Haggard, Merle 141
"Hail to the Baron Munchausen" 52
Hale, Barbara 102, 159, 177
Haley, Jack 93–94, **94**, 221, **222**, 223
Hall, Cliff 50, 51
Hall, Porter 98, 209
Hall, Thurston 105, 168, 201

Halop, Florence 217
"Hamburger Heaven" 199
Hamilton, Margaret 281
Hamilton, Neil 126, 153, 183
Hammer, Armie 141
Hammett, Dashiel 259
Hampton, Lionel 117
Handman, Lou 87
Hanna-Barbera Productions 101, 237, 253
Hanson, Peter 258
The Happiness Boys (Billy Jones and Ernie Hare) 6
"Happy Days Are Here Again" 86
Happy-Go-Lucky Hour 203
Harbour, David 145
"Hard Hearted Hannah" 273
Hardwicke, Sir Cedric 259
"Harlem Sandman" 89
Harling, Jack 45
Harmon, Jim 213, 259, 261
Harper, Toni 199
Harper & Company 179
Harrelson, Woody 283
Harris, Arlene "Chatterbox" 82, 87, 204, 205
Harris, Barbara 281
Harris, Phil 5, 64, 65, 66, 154, 172, 173
Harris, Robert H. 258
Harris, Theresa 66, 68–69
Harris, Tommy 97
Harris, Val 10
Harrison's Reports 273
Harry Horlick and His Gypsies 6
Harry Rever and His Eskimos 6
Hart, John 138, 140, 235, **236**, 237
Hart, Lorenz 51, 53, 73, 77
Hart, Walter 257
Hartman, David 216
Harvey, Jean 193
Harvey, Paul 150, 182
Haskell, Molly 283–284
Hasty, Jack 203
Hatch, Wilbur 206, 208
Hathaway, Joy 21
Have Gun—Will Travel 139
Hawk, Bob 211
Hay, Dewey (The Solemn Old Judge) 161
Haydn, Richard 82
Hayes, Grace 59
Hayes, Margaret 180
Hayes, Peter Lynd 166, 167
Hayward, Susan 88
Hazard, Lawrence 47
"He and She" 77
Headin' for a Weddin' 132
Healey, Myron 193
Healy, Ted 51, 52, 59, 60, 87, 117
Hearn, Lou 106
Hearn, Sam "Schlepperman" 40
Hearne, John 178
Hearst, William Randolph 115
Heather, Jean 163
Heavenly Days 101–103
Hecht, Ben 120–121
Hedges, Ray ("Clarence") 58, 59, 60
Heidt, Horace 185, 186, 187, 188
Heigh-Ho Club 11

Heisler, Stuart 139
Hellman, Lillian 120
Hello, Everybody! (*Queen of the Air*) 47–50; *see also* Smith, Kate
"Hello, Mary Lou" 270
Helmore, Tom 109
Henie, Sonja 92, 213
Henley, Jack 196
Henreid, Paul 234
Henry, Louise 85
Henry, William 180
Henry Aldrich: film series 4, 145, 146–147, 163, 241; *see also The Aldrich Family*
Henry Aldrich, radio series *see The Aldrich Family*
Henry Aldrich, Boy Scout 147
Henry Aldrich, Editor 147
Henry Aldrich for President 147
Henry Aldrich Gets Glamour 147
Henry Aldrich Haunts a House 147
Henry Aldrich Plays Cupid 147
Henry Aldrich Swings It 147
Henry Aldrich's Little Secret 147
Henry and Dizzy 147
Henson, Jim 130
Herbert, F. Hugh 182
Herbert, Hugh 117
Here Come the Nelsons 3, 267, 268–269, **269**, 270; *see also The Adventures of Ozzie and Harriet*
Here Come the Waves 218
Here Comes Elmer 89, 205
"Here Lies Love" 36
Here We Go Again 100, 101, 102, 127–128, 158, 166
Herman, Woody 89
Hersh, Ben 173, 175
Hersholt, Jean 148–149, **149**, 150, 152, 153
Hervey, Irene 77, **192**, 193
Herzbrun, Bernard 172
Herzig, Sid 159
Herzinger, Carl 159
"Hey Jose" 224
Heydt, Louis Jean 199, 239
Hi-yo Silver, film *see The Lone Ranger*, 1938 film serial
"Hi-yo Silver" (song) 140
Hickman, Darryl 147, 241
Hickson, John 31
Hidden Hollywood II 96
Higby, Mary Jane 115
High and Happy see *The Hit Parade of 1947*
"High Diver" *see Queen for a Day*, 1951 film
Higher and Higher 221
Hilliard, Harriet *see* Nelson, Harriet
Hirsch, Walter 87
Hiss and Yell 132
The Hit Parade: 1937 film 85–86, **86**, 87–88, 112, 113, 114, 204
The Hit Parade: film series 45, 84–89; *see also Your Hit Parade*
The Hit Parade of 1941 88
The Hit Parade of 1943 88–89
The Hit Parade of 1947 89
The Hit Parade of 1951 89
Hitchcock, Alfred 69, 127

Hitchhike to Happiness 205
Hodge, Al 143
Hoff, Carl 86, 204
Hoffa, Portland 61, 64, 65, 229
Hoffman, David 206
Hoffman, Howard 32
Hold on to Your Hats 80
Hollywood and Highland Center 115
Hollywood Bowl 116
Hollywood Canteen 44, 69
Hollywood Cavalcade 213
Hollywood Hotel: 1937 film 44, 115–117; radio series 85, 115–116, 117
Hollywood Hotel (building) 114–115
Hollywood on the Air 27
Hollywood Party 53
Hollywood Reporter 49, 205
Hollywood Revue of 1929 32
Hollywood Revue of 1933 see *Hollywood Party*
Holmes, Wendell 180
Holt, David 38
Homans, Robert E. 209
Homes, Geoffrey (Daniel Mainwaring) 182, 239
Honest Harold 170
Honeymoon Lodge 265
"Hooray for Hollywood" 116
The Hoosier Hot Shots (Gabe Hawkins, Frank Kettering, Kenny and Paul Trietsch) **162**, 163
Hoover, J. Edgar 191, 253
Hope, Bob 2, 4–5, **5**, 40–41, 42, 44, 103, 130–132, 133–134, 165, 218, 241, 245, 259
Hopkins, Robert E. 55
Hopper, Hedda 146, 226, 262
Horlick's Malted Milk 171
The Horn Blows at Midnight 69, 71
Horne, James W. 107, 190, 237
Horne, Lena 160
Horse, Michael 140, 141
Horsie see *Queen for a Day*, 1951 film
Horton, Edward Everett 42, 155
Horton Hatches the Egg 195
House of Glass 256
The House of Mystery 105
How Doooo You Do! 81–82, 231
Howard, Buddy 243
Howard, Cy 248, 249, 250
Howard, Meredith 272
Howard, Shemp 119
Howard, William K. 27
The Howard Stern Show 277, 278; *see also* Stern, Howard
Howco Productions 177
Howe, Ann ("The Radio Girl") 1, 9–10
Howe, James Wong 109
Howell, Kenneth 147
Howlin, Olin 183
Hoyt, Harry 84
Hubbard, John 182
Huber, Harold 125, 165
Hudson, Rock 261, 270
Hughes, Carol 179
Hughes, Mary Beth 210
Hulick, Budd 37; *see also* Col. Lemuel Q. Stoopnagle

Hull, Warren 143, 152
Hummert, Anne 112
Hummert, Frank 112, 113, 235
Hunt, Marsha 41
Hunt, Pee Wee 199
Hunter, Ian McLellan 150, 151, 184
Hunter, Jerry 243
Hunter, Raymond 21
Hurst, Fannie 47
Hush My Mouse 220
Hutton, Betty 219, 250
Hutton, Ina Ray and the Melodears 38
Hyams, Leila **34**, 35

"I Came to Say Goodbye" 134
I Cover Big Town 239, 241
I Cover the Underworld see *I Cover Big Town*
"I Feel Like a Feather in the Breeze" 74
I Know Everybody and Everybody's Racket 6
I Love a Mystery: film series 132, 214–216; 1945 film **214**, 215, 216; 1967 TV pilot 216; radio series 3, 213–214, 215, 216
I Love Adventure 215, 216
I Love Lucy 248
I Remember Mama 129
"I Want to Be in Winchell's Column" 95
"I Wished on the Moon" 37
If I Had a Million 263
"If I Had a Wishing Ring" 226
If I'm Lucky 63
Ilf, Ilya 69
I'll Reach for a Star see *The Hit Parade*, 1937 film
"I'm Always Chasing Rainbows" 103
"I'm Charlie McCarthy, Detective" 125
I'm from the City 77
"I'm in the Mood for Love" 223
"I'm Like a Fish Out of Water" 116
"I'm the Power Behind the Throne" 80
"I'm Walkin'" 270
In Old Arizona 200
Ince, Thomas 149
Independent Exhibitors' Film Bulletin 87, 99, 239
Industrial Light and Magic 111
Inescourt, Frieda 102
Information Please: radio and film series 7
The Ink Spots 213
Inner Sanctum: film series 206–207, 208; 1948 film 210; TV series 210
Inner Sanctum Mysteries: radio series 181, 206, 207, 210
"Inside Story" *see Night Editor*, 1946 film
International Crime 106
International House 15, 36–37, 40
International Shoe Company 84
The Intimate Revue 130
The Invisible Avenger 110; *see also The Shadow*, 1958 TV pilot
Irving, George 76

Irving Trust Company 178
Irwin, Coulter 227
Is My Face Red? 92
It Pays to Be Ignorant: radio series and film 7
"It Was Sweet of You" 63
ITC 141
It's a Joke, Son! 231, **232**, 233–234; see also Delmar, Kenny
"It's a Most Unusual Day" 243
"It's Better to Be BY Yourself" 226
It's Chesterfield Time 85
It's in the Bag 69–70, 134, 228
"It's the Animal in Me" 38
"I've Got a Heartful of Music" 117

J. Walter Thompson Agency 72, 73, 119, 216
Jack Armstrong, the All-American Boy: 1947 film serial 6, 143, 235, 236, **236**; radio series 189, 235, 236, 237
The Jack Benny Program 43, 64, 66, 93, 98, 99, 131, 146, 165, 218, 270; see also Benny, Jack
Jack Oakie's College 43; see also Oakie, Jack
The Jack Pearl Show 51; see also Pearl, Jack
Jack William Votion Productions 174; see also Voco Productions
Jackson, Thomas 58, 81, 106
Jaguar (CD) 237
Jam Session 44
Jamboree 195
James, Claire 236
James, Edward 176
James, Harry 117
James, John 177
Jameson, House 146, 200
Jarrett, Michael 273
Jarvis, Al 198, 199
Jasmyn, Joan 59
Jean Hersholt Humanitarian Award 150; see also Hersholt, Jean
Jell-O 146, 165
Jenkins, Ann 224
Jenks, Frank 169, 180
Jepson, Helen 121
Jergens Lotion 90
Jerome, M.K. 59
Jessel, George 6, 180
Jet Jackson: Flying Commando see *Captain Midnight*, TV series
Jewell, James 142
Jimmie Allen and the Air Mail Robbery 83
Jimmy Steps Out see *Pot o' Gold*, 1941 film
The Joe Penner Show 75, 76; see also Penner, Joe
Johnny Madero: Pier 23 271
Johnson, Erskine 69
Johnson, Jack 111
Johnson, Nunnally 63, 71
Johnson, Peter 279
Johnson, Prudence 279, 281
Johnson, Raymond Edward 181, 191, 206
Johnson's Wax 96
Johnston, Arthur 49

Johnstone, Bill 107
Jolson, Al 39, 80, 92, 213
Jones, Allan 77
Jones, Gordon 143
Jones, L.Q. 281
Jones, Marcia Mae 151
Jones, Spike 154, 226
Jones, Tommy Lee 283
Jonny Quest 237
Jordan, Jim, and Marian see Fibber McGee and Molly
Jordan, Louis 44
Jory, Victor 107
Josefsberg, Milt 65–66
Josephson, Julia 168
"Joshua Fit the Battle of Jericho" 199
Jostyn, Jay 181, 184
Joyce, Peggy Hopkins 37
Joys 134
Juelle, Don 91
Jungle Jitters 204
The Jury Goes Round and Round 132
Just Before Dawn 202
Just Off Broadway 27

Kabibble, Ish see Bogue, Merwin A.
Kalesniko, Michael 276
Kalmar, Bert 17, 18, 54–55, 75
Kane, Eddie 224
Karloff, Boris 7, 45, **156**, 157, 158
Karlson, Phil 108, 109
Karpis, Alvin 191, 193
Kate Smith and Her Swanee Music 46; see also Smith, Kate
The Kate Smith Hour 146; see also Smith, Kate
Katzman, Sam 235, 237
Kaufman, Joseph 108
Kaufman, Peter 279, 280
Kaye, Sammy 129
Keach, James 140
Keaton, Buster 52, 58, 213
Keeler, Ruby 92, 266
Keillor, Garrison 278–280, 281, 282, **282**, 283
Keith, Tom 281
Keith-Albee-Orpheum Circuit 11
Kelk, Jackie 146
Kelland, Clarence Buddington 178, 179, 180
Kellerman, Sally 281
Kelly, Emmett 262
Kelly, Gene 120
Kelly, Joe 7, 163
Kelly, Patsy 63, 88, 94, **94**, 157–158
Kelsey, Fred 81
Kelton, Pert 85
Kemp, Hal 43
Ken Murray's Blackouts 243, 248, 249; see also Murray, Ken
Kendall, Cy 209
Kennedy, Edgar 117, 125, 152, 179, 194, 195
Kennedy, Joseph P. 10, 11
Kennedy, Phyllis 177
Kennedy, Tom 76, 88
Kent, Dorothea 109
Kent, Robert E. 169, 170, 231
Kenton, Erle C. 152, 153
Kentucky Jubilee 134

Kenyon, Curtis 92, 95
Kern, James V. 155, 157, 177
KFEL (Denver) 196, 197
KFRC (San Francisco) 203
KFWB (Los Angeles) 198, 225
KGFJ (Los Angeles) 277
KHJ (Los Angeles) 28, 32, 115
Kibbee, Guy 179–180
"Kickin' the Gong Around" 36
Kid Boots 77
The Kid from Spain 77
Kieran, John 7
Kilpack, Bennett 21
King, Henry 81
King, Jean (Lonesome Gal) 195
King, John H. 134
King, Larry 234
King, Walter Woolf 80, 152
King Christian X 150
King Cole Trio see Cole, Nat King
King Kong 19, 31
King Leonardo 234
King of Burlesque 213
The King of Jazz 32
The King Schmaltz Bagel Hour 275
King Sisters 266
The King's Men 103
Kingsley, Dorothy 126, 242
Kingsley, Grace 21
Kinnear, Greg 144
Klein, Philip 27, 29
Kline, Kevin 282
Klinker, Zeno 126
Knight, June 45
Knotts, Don 216
Knox, Charles 180
KNX (Los Angeles) 10, 193, 196
Kober, Arthur 51
Koepp, David 110, 111
Kolker, Henry 51
Kollege of Musical Knowledge 154–155, 160, 220; see also Kyser, Kay
Kovacs, Laszlo 141
Kraft Food Company 166
Kraft Music Hall 39, 42, 133
Kramer, Mandel 253
Krasna, Norman 51
Krim, Arthur 231
KRLA (Little Rock, AK) 27
Krueger, Lorraine 76
Krupa, Gene 40, 117, 199
Krupp, Roger 112
KSJR (University of Minnesota) 279
KTHS (Hot Springs, AK) 171, 172
Kupperman, Joel 7
Kurlan, Arthur 249
Kyser, Kay 2, 5, 44, 127, 154–156, **156**, 157–160, 220
KZM (Oakland, CA) 164

Labrecque, Jeff 140
Lachman, Edward 281
Lachman, Harry 201
Ladd, Alan 219
Lady and the Tramp 273
Lahr, Bert 46, 95–96
Laine, Frankie 199
Lake, Florence 177
Lake, Veronica 219
Lamb, Gil 89

Lamour, Dorothy 41, 65, 120, 171, 218, 219
Land of the Lost: radio series and animated cartoon adaptation 7
Landers, Lew 209
Landry, Margaret 168
Lane, Lola 117
Lane, Richard 43, 76, 210
Lane, Rosemary 77, 117
Lanfield, Sidney 92
Lang, Eddie 36
Lang, Howard 150
Langford, Frances 6, 42, 44, 74, 85, 87, 88, 114, 115, 116, 172, 173, *222*, 223
Lanson, Snooky 89
LaPlanche, Rosemary 159, 236
Lardner, Ring, Jr. 150, 151
La Rocque, Rod 106, 151
Larson, Bobby 151
LaRue, Frank 107
Lassie 139
Lauck, Chester *see* Lum and Abner
Laugh Your Blues Away 80
Laurel and Hardy 22, 53, 98, 174, 176, 249
Lava, William 138, 151
Lawrence, Barbara 270
Lawrence, Gertrude 217
LaZebnik, Ken 280
"Learn to Croon" 41
Leave It to Me 68
Le Baron, William 11, 12, 15
LeBorg, Reginald 210
LeCurto, James 104, 105
Lederman, D. Ross 210
Lee, Bruce 144
Lee, Dixie 219
Lee, Leonard 260, 261
Lee, Peggy 273
Lee, Rudy 264
Lee, Stan 252
Leeds, Andrea 121, 122
Leeds, Thelma 79
The Legend of the Lone Ranger: 1981 film 1, 140–141; *see also The Lone Ranger*
LeGrand, Richard 167, 168, 169
Leiber, Fritz, Jr. 207
Leigh, Douglas 111
Leigh, Janet *272*, 273
Leisen, Mitchell 40, 41
Leisure Concepts 144
Lenny 278
Leo, Maurice 116
Leonard, Sheldon 44, 270
Leslie, Aleen 241
Leslie, Joan 234
Lesser, Sol 31, 128
"Let That Be a Lesson to You" 116
Let's Have Fun 80
Letter of Introduction 119, 121–123, 128
Letterman, David 275
Letz, George (George Montgomery) 137
Levant, Oscar 7, 71, 91
Levey, Jules 77
Levin, Henry 215, 227
Levine, Nat 85

Levinson, Leonard N. 100, 126
Levy, Parke 250
Lewis, Cathy 249, 252
Lewis, Forrest 167
Lewis, Jerry 250, 251–252
Lewis, Jerry Lee 276
Lewis, Shari 129
Lewis, Sinclair 129
Lewis, Ted 11, 113
Lewis, Vera 151
Lewton, Val 206, 207
Li, Jet 144
Life Begins at 8:40 43
Life magazine 196, 230
The Life of Riley: 1949 film 245–246, *246*, 247, 267; 1949 TV series 247–248; 1953 TV series 248; radio series 3, 244–245, 248
The Life of the Party 75, 76, 80, 265
Life with Henry 146
Li'l Abner 254
Linaker, Kay 176
Lindsay, Margaret 202
The Linit Bath Club Revue 61
Linkletter, Art 220–221, *222*, 223, 224
Lipton Tea 210
Litel, John 146
Literary Digest 121
Little Orphan Annie 112, 189
"Little Red Fox" 156
Little Shop of Horrors 60
The Little Show 71
Littlefield, Lucien 147
"The Living Shadow" 104
Livingston, Jay 251
Livingston, Robert 137
Livingstone, Mary 61, 62, 64, 66, 67, 98, 99
Lloyd, Christopher 141
Lloyd, George 209
Lloyd, Harold 158, 159
Lockhart, June 233
Loeb, Lee 152, 163
Loeb, Philip 256, 258
Loesser, Frank 66, 166
Logan, Ella 121
Lohan, Lindsay 281, 283
Lombardo, Guy 33, 85
London, Julie *260*, 261
Lone, John 111
The Lone Ranger: 1938 film serial 6, 135, *136*, 137–138, 140; 1956 film 139; radio series 135, 137, 138, 142, 143, 145; 2003 TV film 141; 2013 film 141–142; TV series 138–139; *see also The Legend of the Lone Ranger*
The Lone Ranger and the Lost City of Gold 139–140
Lone Ranger Inc. 138
The Lone Ranger Rides Again 137, 138
"The Lone Tiger" *see The Shadow*, 1940 film serial
The Lone Wolf: film series 253
"Lonesomest Gal in Town" 199
Long, Audrey 254
Long, Richard 246, *246*
Look Who's Laughing 100, 101, 126–127, 128, 165–166

Lopez, Vincent 2, 6, *34*, 35, 36
Lord, Phillips H. 20–22, *23*, 25, 48, 180, 181, 182, 183, 191, 193, 253
Lord, Sophia 20–21, 25
Lord of the Rings 112
Loring, Teala 177
Lorre, Peter *156*, 157, 182
Los Angeles Times 85, 258
Louis-Dreyfus, Julia 277
Louise, Anita 215
Louvish, Simon 40
Love and Hisses 95–96
"Love Is Good for Anything That Ails You" 87
Love Story Dramas 104; *see also The Shadow*, radio series
Love Thy Neighbor 5, 66–67, *67*, 68–69, 95
"Love Walked In" 121
Lovett, Dorothy 126, 143, 150
Lovett, Lyle 283
Lowe, Edmund 29, *30*, 45
Lowe, Edward T. 179
Lowery, Robert 239
Loy, Myrna 68
Lubin, Arthur 263, 264
Lubitsch, Ernst 69
"Lucky Day" 86
Lucky Strike cigarettes 50, 85, 89, 160
Lugosi, Bela 29, 30–31, 45, *156*, 157
Lukas, Paul 45
Luke, Keye 81, 143
Lulu Belle and Scotty 163, 165
Lum and Abner (Chester Lauck, Norris Goff) 165, 171–175, *175*, 176–177
Lum and Abner: film series 171–178; radio series 2, 171–172, 173, 174, 177; TV pilot film 177
Lum and Abner Abroad 177–178
Lund, John 250, *251*
Lupino, Ida 216
Lux Radio Theater 95
Lydon, James 146, 147, 148
Lynch, Dennis 110
Lynn, Diana 147, 219, 250
Lynn, Royce, and Vanya 166
Lynn, Sharon 35

Macauley, Richard 116
MacBride, Donald 119
MacFarlane, Bruce 33
Mack, Helen 60, 72, 73, 241
Mack, Theodore 118
Mack, Tommy 43, 75, 79, 130
Mack, Willard 58
Mackaill, Dorothy 55
MacKenzie, Gisele 89
MacLane, Roland 250
Macon, Dorris 161
Macon, Uncle Dave 161, 162
Macready, George 215
The Mad Russian *see* Gordon, Bert
Madison Square Garden 80
Madsen, Virginia 280, 282
Magers, Boyd 235
"Magic Is the Moonlight" 226
The Magic of Lassie 140
Magnolia Departed 281

Mail Call: radio and film series 7
The Main Street Kid 205
Mainwaring, Daniel *see* Homes, Geoffrey
Major Bowes' Amateur Theater of the Air 6
Major Bowes and the Original Amateur Hour 6
Major Difficulties 131
Major, Sharp & Minor 36
A Majority of One 259
Make a Wish 258
Make Believe Ballroom: 1979 film 196, 198–199; radio series 198
Make Mine Music 134
Malkames, Don 37
The Maltese Falcon 259
Maltin, Leonard 157, 246, 250
Man About Town 65, 66, 98
"The Man in the Mask" 141
The Man Who Lived Twice 201
The Man with My Face 220
Mander, Miles 183
Manhattan Mary 54
Manhattan Merry-Go-Round: 1937 film 87, 112–114; radio series 112–113, 114
Manhattan Music Box see *Manhattan Merry-Go-Round*, 1937 film
Mankiewicz, Herman J. 51
Manley, William Ford 33
Manning, Knox 236
Marcelli, Rico 97
Marcin, Max 199, 200
Marcus, Sidney 84
Mardiette, Robert 171, 173
Maren, Jerry 128
Marin, Chinita 89
Marion, Charles R. 176
Marion, George, Jr. 33, 72
Mark of the Whistler 209
Markson, Ben 184
Marlowe, Hugh 200
Marsh, Marian 201
Marshall, George 120, 124, 186, 187, 251
Marshall, Sidney 184
Martin, Al 106
Martin, Dean 250, 251–252
Martin, Francis 72, 74
Martin, Freddie 88, 166
Martin, Hugh 114
Martin, Lewis 255
Martin, Marion 170
Martin, Mary 67, *67*, 68
Martling, Jackie 277
Marvin, Lee 273
Marx, Groucho 211, 244, 245; *see also* Marx Brothers
Marx, Gummo 245; *see also* Marx Brothers
Marx Brothers 55, 56, 58, 75, 87, 128, 219, 244, 245, 278
Mary Poppins 56
Mascot Pictures 84, 85
MASH 281
Mason, Melissa 44
Mason, Sully 154, 156, 160
Massow, Marjorie 212
Mathews, Carole 215

Matlock, Matty *see* The Pete Kelly Seven
Matthau, Walter 71
Matthews, Grace 107
Matthews, Lester 215
Mature, Victor 166, 167
Maugham, W. Somerset 263, 264
Mauldin, Bill 231
Maxwell, Elsa 120
The Maxwell House Showboat 72
May, Billy 268
Mayer, Arthur 48
Mayer, L.B. 13
Mayfair Productions 77
Mayfair Theater (New York City) 19
Mazurki, Mike 209
MCA *see* Music Corporation of America
McCarey, Raymond 176
McCarthy, Charlie *see* Bergen, Edgar
McCormick, Mary 277
McCoy, Clyde 198
McCrea, Joel 121
McDermott, Joe 72
McDonald, Frank 89, 161
McDonald, Marie 89
McGann, William 151
McGavin, Darren 264
McGill, Jerry 237, 238
McGowan, Dorrell, and Stuart 161
The McGuerins of Brooklyn 244
McGuire, Marcy 159, 160, 167
McHugh, Jimmy 51, 66, 166, 197, 243
McIntire, John 200
McKellen, Ian 112
McKimson, Robert 234
McKinley, Ray 88, 199
McKnight, Tom 248
McLaughlin, Don 191, 253
McLean, Murray, Jr. (Jimmie Allen) 83
McLeod, Victor 192
McManus, Marion 113
McNamee, Graham 27, 54, 56
McNeill, Don 225
McPherson, Virginia 242
McQuade, Arlene 256
McVey, Patrick 241
McWade, Margaret 152, 180
ME-TV 144
Meader, George 151
Meadow, Herb 139
Meadows, Jayne 261
Meany, Don 10
Meet Corliss Archer 242
Meet Dr. Christian 150–151
Meet Me at Parky's 82
Meet Miss Bobby Socks 242
Meet the Baron 25, 50, 51–52, 53, 59, 60; *see also* Pearl, Jack
Megowan, Don 255
Meins, Gus 85
Meiser, Edith 264
Melchior, Lauritz 217
Melendez, "Stuttering John" 275, 277
Melnick, Marty 87
Melody for Three 152–153
Melody of Spring 73
Melody Ranch 278, 279

Melton, Sid 190
Men in White 148
Menjou, Adolphe 121, 122, 155, 183, *183*
Menzies, William Cameron 29
Mercer, Freddie 168
Mercer, Johnny 116
Mercury Theater of the Air 229
Meredith, Charles 255
Meredith, Madge *see* Massow, Marjorie
Meridian Productions 109
Merkel, Una 81, 165, 233
Merman, Ethel 38
Merrick, Lynn (Marilyn) 152, *202*, 209
The Merry Macs 66
Merton, John 236
Metheny, Kevin 275
Metro-Goldwyn-Mayer (MGM) 2, 7, 13, 32, 39, 50, 51, 52, 53, 54, 56, 59, 60, 62, 63, 129, 130, 131, 132, 147, 160, 186, 188, 195, 242, 243, 244, 245, 249, 257, 259, 278
Meyers, Victor Aloysius 63
MGM *see* Metro-Goldwyn-Mayer
Michelson, Charles B. 110, 143
Mickey Mouse 51, 52, 129
Middleton, Charles 82, 175, 235, 236, 237
Middleton, Robert 262
Mighty Like a Moose 10
Miljan, John 70
Milland, Ray 39, 241
Miller, Alice Duer 74
Miller, Ann 43, 44, 88, 160, 196, *196*, 197, 198
Miller, Don 147
Miller, Glenn 5, 198
Miller, Herb 252
Miller, Jack 46
Miller, John "Skins" 45
Miller, Marvin 227
Miller, Mildred 48
Miller, Penelope Ann 111
Miller, Seton I. 263
The Millerson Case 203
Millionaire Playboy 77
Mills, Billy 99
The Mills Brothers 2, 32, *34*, 35, 36, 197
Milne, Peter 153
Milner, Martin 273
Milwaukee Journal 128
Minnesota Public Radio 279
Minnevitch, Borrah, and His Harmonica Rascals 88, 213
Mintz, Eli 256
Mintzer, Rich 277
Miramax 144
Miranda, Carmen 243
"Miss Brown to You" 38
Miss in a Mess 132
"Miss In-Between Blues" 199
The Missing Lady 108, 109
Mississippi 73
"Mr. Beebe" 160
Mr. Deeds Goes to Town 152, 178, 180
Mr. District Attorney: 1941 film 181–182; 1947 film 183, *183*, 184; radio

series 25, 180–181, 182, 183, 184, 191; TV series 184
Mr. District Attorney in the Carter Case 182, 253
Mr. Doodle Kicks Off 77
Mr. Keen, Tracer of Lost Persons 112
Mr. Rock and Roll 195
Mitchell, Geneva 105
"Moke from Shamokan" 159
Molasses and January *see* Pick and Pat
Molineri, Lillian 224
Molly see The Goldbergs, 1950 film
Molly and Me 256, 258
Monitor 103
Monkey Business 219
Monogram Pictures Corporation 44, 81, 84, 107–108, 194
Montreal *Gazette* 127
"Moon Song" ("That Wasn't Meant for Me") 49
Moore, Clayton 138, 139, 140
Moore, Constance 89, 120, 125
Moore, Dorothy 180
Moore, Garry 213, 227
Moore, Ida 234
Moore, Roger 107
Moore, Victor 44, 45, 70, 75, 80, 160, 218
Moore, Wilfred G. "Bill" 83, 84, 188, 189
Moore, William *see* Potter, Peter
Moorehead, Agnes 105, 107
Moran, Jackie 150
Moran and Mack 17
Moreland, Mantan 194
Morgan, Al 192
Morgan, Ralph 192
Morgan, Raymond R. 28, 29, 32, 262
Morgan, Wesley 248
Morgan, William 181, 182
Moritz, Neal H. 144
Morley, Karen 28, 216
Morrell, Norman 131
Morris, Chester 45, 193, 221
Morrison, Brett 107
Morrison, Ernie 88
Morrison, Joe 38
Morrow, Bill 66, 67, 68
Morse, Carlton E. 213, 214, 215, 216
Morse, Ella Mae 82, 197
Mortimer Snerd *see* Bergen, Edgar
Morton, Charles 17
Mosher, John 75
Mostel, Zero 258
Moster, Jim 271
Motion Picture Daily 60
Motion Picture Herald 27
Motion Picture News 14, 20
Motion Picture Relief Fund 150
Movie-Radio Guide 67
Movietone Follies: film series 32, 212
Movietone News 87
Mowbray, Alan 117, 176
Mrs. G Goes to College 259
MTV Video Music Awards 275, 276
Muir, Jean 148
Mulcahy, Russell 111
Mundin, Herbert 29
Munson, Ona 237

The Muppet Movie 130
Murfin, Jane 21–22
Murphy, George 122
Murphy, Ralph 82
Murray, Chad Michael 141
Murray, Ken 131, 248, 249
Murray, Rebecca 280
Murray, Zon *236*
Music Corporation of America (MCA) 100, 126, 127, 154, 155, 158, 165, 197
The Music Maids 88
Musselman, M.M. 157
Mutual Broadcasting System 2, 7, 9, 29, 32, 38, 82, 105, 106, 135, 142, 180, 189, 193, 216, 255, 262
My Favorite Husband 248
My Favorite Spy 158–159
My Favorite Year 278
My Friend Irma: 1949 film 250, 251, *251*, 252; radio series 3, 248, 249–250, 251, 252; TV series 252
My Friend Irma Goes West 251, 252
"My Heart Belongs to Daddy" 68
My Little Chickadee 125
"My, My" 66
My Sister Eileen 249
Myrt and Marge (Myrtle Vail, Donna Damerel) 57, *57*, 58–60
Myrt and Marge: 1933 film 3, 58–60; radio series 57–60
Mysterious Intruder 209
The Mysterious Traveller 210

Nagel, Anne 143
Naish, J. Carrol 208
Nancy Drew: film series 146
Nash, Clarence 77
Nash, N. Richard 257
Nash, Noreen 140
Nashville 281
The National Barn Dance: 1944 film 162–163, 165; radio series 86, 161, 162, *162*, 163
National Broadcasting Company (NBC) 1, 2, 3, 5, 7, 9, 10, 11, 12, 15, 16, 18, 21, 27, 33, 37, 38, 39, 41, 50, 54, 57, 63, 71, 76, 82, 85, 86, 89, 91, 96, 98, 100, 103, 120, 126, 127, 130, 131, 146, 148, 154, 160, 161, 164, 165, 166, 167, 171, 181, 183, 184, 193, 204, 213, 214, 215, 216, 220, 221, 224, 227, 241, 244, 248, 255, 257, 263, 266, 267, 272, 274
National Council of Jewish Women 74
The National Farm and Home Hour 164
National Lum and Abner Society 171
National Public Radio 279
Naughton, Harry 211
Nazarro, Ray 254
NBC *see* National Broadcasting Company
NBC-Blue 9, 25, 27, 41, 61, 72, 75, 90, 112, 142, 191, 204, 206, 211, 225, 256; *see also* American Broadcasting Company; Blue Network; National Broadcasting Company
NBC-Red 9; *see also* National Broadcasting Company

Neal, Tom 151
A Neckin' Party 122
Nedell, Bernard 147
Neilan, Marshall 13, 16
Neill, Noel 147
Nelson, David 265, 266, 267–269, *269*, 270, 271
Nelson, Don 267, 268
Nelson, Frank 270
Nelson, Harriet: as Harriet Hilliard 43, 72, 75, *78*, 221, 265; as Harriet Nelson 223, 265–271
Nelson, Kenneth 148
Nelson, Ozzie 72, 73, 221, *222*, 223, 265–271; *see also* The Adventures of Ozzie and Harriet
Nelson, Ricky 265, 266, 267–269, *269*, 270, 271
Nemec, Joseph C., III 111
Nero Wolfe 259, 261
Nesbitt, John 7
The New Deal see Myrt and Marge
New Faces of 1937 43–44, 75, 76, *78*, 79–80, 130, 265
New Line Cinema 275
New Movie magazine 21
New York American 25, 26
New York Daily Mirror 90
New York Graphic 90
New York Times 56, 63, 65, 74, 75, 170, 251, 274
New York World 199
New York Yankees 114
New Yorker 29, 75, 279
Newell, William 143
Newman, Bill 272; *see also* The Pete Kelly Seven
Newman, Emil 263
Newsweek 188
Niblo, Fred 146
"Nice Girl" *see Hello, Everybody!*
Nicholas, Harold 160
Nicholas Brothers 38, 213
Nichols, Nellie V. 113
Nick Kenny's Radio Thrills 6
Niessen, Gertrude 44
Nigh, Jane 241
Nigh, William 177
"Night and Day" 197
A Night at Earl Carroll's 131
A Night at the Opera 58, 278
Night Editor: 1946 film 226–227, *227*; radio series 227
Night Spot 80, 81
"Night Train to Memphis" 161
Niles, Ken 115, 117, 260
Nimoy, Leonard 264
Nixon, Allan 252
Noble, Edward J. 9
Noble, Ray 38, 101, 127
Nolan, Bob 89
Norris, Fred 274, 275, 277, 278
Northwestern University 118
Novis, Donald 2, 6, 35, 81
Nugent, Eddie 13
Nugent, Frank 65, 74
Nut Guilty 119

The O. Henry Twins *see* Fibber McGee and Molly

O. Henry's Full House 71, 263
Oakie, Jack 38, 41, 43, 72, 74
Oakland, Vivien 10
Oakman, Wheeler **236**
O'Brien, David 189, 190
O'Brien, Edmond 273
O'Brien, Margaret 242
O'Connell, Hugh 45
O'Connor, Nick 113
O'Connor, Una 158
O'Driscoll, Martha 147
"Oh Chychonya" 213
Okay, America! 92
O'Keefe, Dennis 155, 157, 181, 183, *183*, 184, 234
O'Keefe, Walter 133
"The Old Ox Road" 41
Oldham, Vera 28, 29, 32
Olexiewicz, Dan 111
Oliver, Edna May 51, 52
Oliver, Gordon 102
Olmos, Edward James 145
Olsen and Johnson 220
On-Broadway 90
On the Air 191, 214
On the Avenue 213
"On the Sunny Side of the Street" 199
One Exciting Week 205
One in a Million 92, 213
One Man's Family 131, 213, 215
"One O'Clock Jump" 197
One Out of Seven 271
O'Neal, Charles 215
The Onion AV Club 178
"Opera Hat" *see Mr. Deeds Goes to Town*
The Operation 119
The Opposite Sex 132
Orchestra Wives 213
Ornitz, Samuel 85
Orphans of the Storm 229
Ortega, Santos 191
Orzazewski, Kazia 264
Osborne, Ted 115
Osborne, Will 44
Osbourne, Ozzy 277
O'Shea, Danny 13
O'Shea, Michael 183
O'Shea, Oscar 172, 174
Ostroushko, Peter 279
Other People's Business see Way Back Home
Othman, Frederick C. 149
Our Gang 85, 241
Our Miss Brooks 3, 248
Out of This World 81
Outside of Paradise 80
Ovaltine 189, 190–191
Owen, Seena 98
Owens, Gary 113
Owlsley, Monroe 85
Ozzie and Harriet see The Adventures of Ozzie and Harriet
Ozzie's Girls 271

Paar, Jack 91, 213
Pabst Blue Ribbon 91, 245, 247, 248
Padden, Sarah 172, 226
Page, Bradley 180
Paige, Raymond 115, 116

Pallette, Eugene 102
The Palm Beach Story 15
Palmer, Effie 21
Pan, Hermes 88
Panama, Norman 218
Pandit, Korla 32
Pangborn, Franklin 197, 198
The Paramount Newsreel 99
Paramount on Parade 32
Paramount Pictures 2, 3, 5, 6, 7, 11, 14, 15, 17, 20, 32–42, 43, 45, 47, 48, 50, 51, 54, 61, 63, 65–66, 72, 73, 74, 75, 80, 81, 84, 97, 98, 99, 101, 108, 122, 123, 131, 134, 146, 147, 148, 162, 163, 164, 171, 180, 186, 207, 218–219, 220, 221, 223, 224, 238, 239, 241, 250, 251, 257, 258, 265, 274, 276
Parke, Harry *see* Einstein, Harry
Parker, Dorothy 37, 120, 264
Parker, Frank 63
Parker, Jennsion 204
Parker, Willard 254
Parkyakarkus *see* Einstein, Harry
Parrish, Helen 157, 223
Parsons, Louella 64, 115, 117, 230
Parsons, Patsy Lee 150
Partners in Time 172
The Passing Parade: radio and film series 7
Pasternak, Joe 242, 243
Pat Novak for Hire 271
Paterson, Walter 214
Patrick, Gail 38
Patten, Luana 129
Paulson, Wayne 80
Pawley, Edward 238
Pearce, Al 87, 203–204, **204**, 205
Pearce, Cal 203
Pearl, Jack (Baron Munchausen) 5, 50–51, *51*, 52–53, 59, 71, 184
Peary, Harold (The Great Gildersleeve) 100, 126, 127, 164, **164**, 165, 166, 167, 168, 169, 170
Pecora, Ferdinand 26
Peil, Edward, Sr. 107
Pelletier, Wilfred 41
Pendleton, Nat 55
Penner, Joe 2, 5, 7, 41, 43, 71–72, **72**, 73–77, **78**, 79, 80, 98, 130, 265
Penny, Prudence 152
People Are Funny: 1946 film 221–222, **222**, 223–224, 266, 274; radio series 220–221, 222, 223, 224, 266
Peoples, Neva 88
Pepper, Barbara 147
Pepsodent 15, 42, 204
The Pepsodent Show Starring Bob Hope 44, 131, 133; *see also* Hope, Bob
The Perfect Fool 53, 54
Perkins, Osgood 33
Perrin, Nat 43
Perrin, Vic 272
The Pete Kelly Seven 271–272, 273, 274
Pete Kelly's Blues: 1955 film 1, 271, 272, **272**, 273–274; radio series 3, 271–272; TV series 274
Peters, Susan 179
Peterson, Dorothy 23

Petrillo, James C. 161
Petrov, Yevgeni 69
Petticoat Junction 131
Pettis, Don 91
The Phantom, radio serial *see The Phantom of Crestwood*
The Phantom of Crestwood **26**, 27–28
Phillip Morris cigarettes 200
Phillippi, Lou 264
Phillips, Arthur 157
Phillips, John 240
Photophone 10, 14
Photoplay 14, 19, 66, 126, 172, 274
Pick and Pat (Pick Malone, Pat Padgett) 87
"Pickaninnies' Heaven" 49–50
Pickens Sisters 6
Picker, William 208
Pickford, Mary 13, 115
Picture Snatcher 51
Picturehouse Entertainment 283
The Pied Pipers 44
Pierlot, Francis 147
Pigskin Parade 92
Pillsbury 198
Pine, William H. 221, 238
Pine-Thomas Productions 148, 221, 222, 223, 224, 238, 239
Pinson, John Omar 193
Pious, Minerva 70, 228, 229
Pitts, ZaSu 27, 51, 52, 63, 174, 226
Pittsburgh Courier 16
Pittsburgh Post-Gazette 20, 127, 167, 168
Pittsburgh Press 18, 84, 241
The Player 281
Playmates 157–158
"Please" 36
Plympton, George H. 192
"Poor Butterfly" 58
Popenoe, Dr. Paul 245
Poppin' the Cork 43
Porter, Cole 68, 197, 249
Portsmouth (OH) *Times* 80
Postum 171, 172
Pot o' Gold: 1941 film 184, 185–187, **187**, 188, 222, 274; radio series 184–186, 188
Potel, Victor 188
Potter, Peter (William Moore) 106
Powdermilk Biscuit Band (Mary Du Shane, Bob Douglas, Dick Rees) 279
Powell, Dick 44, 63, 92, 116, 117
Powell, Jane 129, 242, 243
Powell, Lee 137, 140
Powell, Russell 18
Powell, Teddy 44
"Powerhouse" 95
Prager, Stanley 212
A Prairie Home Companion: radio series 1, 278, 279–280, 281, 282, 283; 2006 film 279–282, **282**, 283
Pratt, Purnell 55
PRC *see* Producers Releasing Corporation
Prentiss, Ed 189
"Presenting the Doctor" 151
Presley, Elvis 167
Prima, Louis 44, 113, 114

Princess Baba of Sarawak 124
Principal Distributing Corporation 31
Priorities on Parade 132, **133**, 134
Prival, Lucien 31
Private Parts: book 275–276, 278; 1997 film 1, 274, 275, 276, **276**, 277–278
Proctor, Kay 67
The Producers 43
Producers Releasing Corporation (PRC) 80, 81, 231, 233
Professor Quiz 44
Prosser, Hugh 236, **236**
Prouty, Jed 152
Pryor, Roger 45, 113
Pugh, Jess 178
Pull Over Neighbor 220
Purdy, Constance 174

Quartet 263
Queen for a Day: 1951 film 212, 263–264; radio series 3, 262–263; TV series 263, 264
Queen of the Air see *Hello, Everybody!*
Quick Draw McGraw 220
Quigley, Charles 163
Quinn, Don 96, 99, 100, 101, 126, 165
Quivers, Robin 274, 275, 277
The Quiz Kids: radio and film series 7

Rabe, David 265
Radio City Music Hall 43, 44
Radio City Revels 43–44
Radio Corporation of America (RCA) 10–11, 14, 16, 21
Radio Digest 48
Radio Fun-Fare 171
Radio Guild 115
Radio Mirror 59, 122, 250
Radio Revels 32, 42; see also *Radio City Revels*
Radio Rhythm 11
Radio Rogues (Jimmy Hollingwood, Eddie Bartell, Henry Taylor) 45
Radio Stars on Parade 44
Radioland 58
Raeburn, Bryna 191
Raffeto, Michael 214, 215
Raht, Katherine 146
Raimi, Sam 110, 112
Rainbow Room (New York City) 120
Rainger, Ralph 36
Rains, Claude 207
Raisback, Robert 262
The Ramblers 17
Ramblin' Round Radio Row: film series 6
Ramos, Harry 89
Randall, Meg 245, **246**
Randall, Tony 216
Randell, Ron 199, 254, **255**
Randolph, Isabel 97, 100, 127, 166
Randolph, Lillian 167, 168
Rank, J. Arthur 231
Rapf, Harry 50, 51, 53, 54
Rathbone, Basil 217
"Raven" 238
Rawlinson, Herbert 177
Raye, Martha 2, 39, 40, 41, 42, 77

Raymond, Gene 62, 75, 80
Raymond, Paula 109
RCA see Radio Corporation of America
Reach, James 252
Readick, Frank 105
Rebel Without a Cause 270
Red Channels 148, 248, 258
The Red Scare 105
The Red Skelton Show 266; see also Skelton, Red
Reed, Alan 249
Reed, Barbara 108, 109
Reed, Philip **222**, 223, 238, **240**
Reed, Theodore Luther 41
Reed, Tom 254
Reed, Walter 166
"Reefer Man" 37
Rees, Lanny 246, **246**, 248
Regan, Phil 44, 80, 85, 113
Reicher, Frank 170
Reilly, Howard 67
Reilly, John C. 283
Reiner, Carl 82
Reisman, Don 6
Reisner, Charles F. 53, 54, 113
Reitman, Ivan 276, 277
Remedy for Riches 152
Renaldo, Duncan 137
Republic Laboratories 84
Republic Pictures 45, 80, 81, 85–89, 112, 113, 114, 131, 135, 137, 161, 181, 182, 204–205
The Rescuers 103
The Return of Chandu: 1934 serial and feature film 31–32; see also *Chandu the Magician*
The Return of the Whistler 210
Reunion 149
Reveille with Beverly: 1943 film 44, 45, 195–196, **196**, 197–198, 199; radio series 2, 196, 198
Revel, Harry 73, 74, 95
Reville, Alma 69
The Revuers (Judy Holliday, Adolph Green, Betty Comden, Alvin Hammer) 89
Rey, Alvino 44, 157
Reymert, Dr. Martin L. 235, 237
Reynolds, Jack 248
Reynolds, Marjorie 218, 248
Reynolds, William 274
The Rhythm Boys (Bing Crosby, Harry Barris, Al Rinker) 19, 33; see also Crosby, Bing
Rhythm on the Range 39
Rice, Florence 182
Rich, Freddie 6
Richmond, June 160
Richmond, Kane 107, 108
Ridges, Stanley 181
Rifkin, Allen 51
Riley, Mike 36
Rio Rita 14
Rippling Rhythm Revue 41
The Rise of the Goldbergs see *The Goldbergs*, radio series
Ritz Brothers 77, 121, 127, 213
R.J. Reynolds Tobacco Company 161
RKO-Pathé 31, 172, 233

RKO Radio Pictures 2, 7, 10–15, 16–17, 18–19, 20, 21, 22, 24, 25, 27–28, 32, 33, 42–44, 48, 50, 51, 74–77, 79–80, 81, 100–103, 126, 127, 128, 130, 131, 143, 150, 152, 153, 155, 156, 157, 158, 159, 160, 165, 166, 167, 168, 170, 171, 172, 173, 174, 175, 176, 177, 178, 179, 180, 197, 206, 207, 208, 212, 221, 223, 265
Roach, Hal 10, 85, 119, 167, 177, 220, 244, 245, 248
Road, Michael 169
Road to Hong Kong 134
"The Road to Mandalay" 134
Road to Rio 134
Road to Singapore 134
Road to Utopia 218
Robards, Jason, Jr. 141
Robb, Alex 18
Robb, Mary Lee 167
Roberti, Lyda 38, 72, 73
Roberts, Ben 141, 182
Roberts, Charles E. 176, 177
Roberts, Dorothy 206
Roberts, Ken 200
Roberts, Tracey 264
Robin, Leo 36
Robinson, Bill 38
Robinson, Edward G. 237–238
Robinson, Larry 256
Robinson, Scott 279
Robinson, Tasha 178
Roche, Betty 197
Rochester (NY) *Evening Journal* 52
Rochester see Anderson, Eddie "Rochester"
"Rock and Roll" 63
Rocky 276, 277
Rodgers, Richard 51, 53, 73, 77
Rodriguez, Estelita 89
Rogan, Seth 144
Rogell, Albert S. 88
Rogers, Charles "Buddy" 6, 98, 99
Rogers, Charles R. 129
Rogers, Ginger 22, 43, 44, 116, 265
Rogers, Roswell 175, 176
Rogers, Roy 89, 143
Rogers, Will 25, 40, 49, 61, 71, 148
Rogers Brothers Silver 266
Rolfe, Sam 139
Roman Scandals 77
Romance and Rhythm see *The Hit Parade of 1941*
The Romance of the Ranchos 193
Romano, Tony 44, 204
Romanoff, Constantine 116
Romanoff, Prince Michael 217
"Romeo Smith and Juliet Jones" 158
Rooney, Mickey 83, 241
Roosevelt, Elliott 185
Roosevelt, Franklin Delano 185, 188, 229
Roosevelt, James 185, 186, 187, 188
Ropes, Bradford 85, 88
Rose Marie see Baby Rose Marie
Rose of Washington Square 213
Rosen, Phil 108
Rosenberg, Aaron 268
Rosenbloom, Maxie 160
Ross, Earl 167

Index

Ross, Lanny 72–73
Ross, Shirley 39, 41, 98
Rowland, Richard 53
Rowland-Brice Productions 6
The Royal Gelatin Hour 118, 120; see also *The Rudy Vallee Hour*
Royle, Selena 243
Rubber Heels 54
Ruben, Aaron 259
Ruben, J. Walter 28
Ruby, Harry 17, 19, 54–55, 75
Rudolph, Maya 281
The Rudy Vallee Hour 72; see also Vallee, Rudy
Ruggles, Charlie 38, 73
Run for Cover 153
Rush, Barbara 258
Russell, Andy 226
Russell, Charles 210
Russell, Gail 147
Russell, Tim 281, 283
Ruth, Jean "Beverly" 196, 198
Ryan, Edward 212, 226
Ryan, Frank 159
Ryan, Irene 198
Ryan, Tim 197, 198
Ryder, Alfred 256
Ryder PI 275
Ryman Auditorium (Nashville) 279
Ryskind, Morrie 69, 70

St. Clair, Malcolm 174, 175, 176
St. John, Howard 253–254, **255**
St. Petersburg (FL) *Independent* 262
St. Petersburg (FL) *Times* 239, 247
Saks, Sol 267
Saks Fifth Avenue 90
Sally, Irene and Mary 65
Sam 'n' Henry 15; see also Amos 'n' Andy, radio series
Sam Spade 246, 262
Samuel French Inc. 247, 252
Samuelson, Orion 163
San Francisco Examiner 114
Sanders, Lugene 248
Sandrich, Mark 65, 66, 68
Sandtke, Randy 279
Santley, Joseph 199
Sarnoff, David 10–11
Saroyan, William 244
Saturday Evening Post 178
Sauber, Harry 82, 113
Saunders, Allen 56
"Say It (Over and Over Again)" 66
Saylor, Sid 84
Scattergood Baines: literary property 178, 179; 1941 film 179; radio and film series 4, 178–180
"Scattergood Baines—Invader" 178, 179
Scattergood Baines Pulls the Strings 179–180
Scattergood Meets Broadway 180
Scattergood Rides High 180
Scattergood Survives a Murder 180
Schafer, Robert 139
Scharf, Walter 89
Schenck, Aubrey 231, 259
Schildkraut, Joseph 229
Schiller, Bob 218, 267

Schlesinger, Leon 68
Schlickter, Jack 84
Schlom, Herman 167
Schneider, Elmer "Moe" see *The Pete Kelly Seven*
Schubert, Bernard L. 255
Schuster, Harold D. 227
Schwarkopf, Col. H. Norman 191
Scott, Keith 234
Scott, R.T.M. 157
Scott, Randolph 47, 49
Scott, Raymond 89, 95
Scott, Ruth 88
Scott, Sue 281
Scott, Zachary 234
Screen Gems see Columbia Pictures Corporation
Screen Guild Theatre 168
Screen Songs 6
Sealed Lips 105
Sears, Fred 254
The Secret of the Whistler 209–210
Secrets of the Underground 182–183
Seddon, Margaret 180
Sedgwick, Edward 124
Seinfeld 265
Seiter, William A. 22, 24, 48, 49, 75
Selander, Lesley 139
Sellon, Charles 13
Selznick, David O. 25, 50, 51, 52, 53, 262
Senator Claghorn see Delmar, Kenny
Sennett, Mack 32, 63, 85, 182
Sennett, Susan 271
Sergeant Preston of the Yukon 145
Serling, Rod 153
Server, Lee 43
Seth Parker see Lord, Phillips H.; *Sunday Evening at Seth Parker's*
Seven Days' Leave 166–167
The Shadow: comic book and strip 107, 109; literary property 104, 194; 1940 film serial 107; 1954 TV pilot 109; 1958 TV pilot 109–110; 1994 film 110–112; radio series 104, 105–106, 107, 109, 110, 112, 189, 229
Shadow Detective Series: film series 105
"The Shadow Laughs" 104
The Shadow Magazine 104, 106, 107, 109
The Shadow Returns 108, **108**, 109, 110
The Shadow Scrapbook 104, 105
The Shadow Strikes 106
Shadows in the Night 203
Shane, Maxwell 222, 223, 239
Shannon, Frank 105
Shannon, Harry **228**
Shayne, Robert 239
Sheldon, Sidney 182
Sherlock Holmes in Washington 176
Sherman, George 209
Sherman, Ray 272; see also *The Pete Kelly Seven*
Sherwood, Robert E. 16
She's Got Everything 80
"The Shiek of Araby" 213
Shimono, Sab 112

Shipman, Barry 135
Shipp, Mary 252
Shoemaker, Ann 75, 210
Shoot the Works 92
Shore, Dinah 78, 81, 129, 217
Shores, Lynn 106
Short, Dorothy 190
Show Business 81
The Show of Shows 32
Signal Carnival 131
Signal Oil Company 210
Silber, Roslyn 256
"Silhouetted in the Moonlight" 116
Silverheels, Jay 138, 139, 140
Silvers, Phil 63, 88, 212
Simmons, Michael L. 175, 179, 194
Simmons, Richard 145
Simms, Ginny 127, 154, 158, 166
Simon, Neil 71
Simon, Simone 95
Simon & Schuster 206, 208, 275
The Simpsons 270
Sinatra, Frank 6, 95, 167, 197, 198, 243
Sinclair, Robert B. 184
Sing Baby Sing 92
Sing for Your Supper: film 80
"Sing for Your Supper" (song) 77
"Sing Sing Sing" 117
Sirius XM Satellite Radio 275
Sisk, Robert 76
Six Hits and a Miss 88
The $64 Question and *The $64,000 Question* see *Take It or Leave It*, radio series
Skelly Oil Company 83, 84, 188, 189
Skelton, Red 5, 220, 266
Skippy 235
Skirball, Jack 69
Skulnik, Menasha 256
Sky Parade 83–84
Slack, Freddie 197, 198
Sleeping Beauty 132
Sloane, Everett 200, 256
Sloman, Larry 275
Smackout 96
Small, Edward 43, 62, 101
Smart, J. Scott (Jack) 229, 259–260, **260**, 261, 262
Smith, Charles 146
Smith, Hal 227
Smith, Kate 2, 6, **34**, 35, 36, 45–46, **46**, 47–50, 146, 274
Smith, Kevin 144
Smith, Paul Girard 77, 231
Smoky Mountain Boys see Acuff, Roy
Snyder, Tom 234
So This Is Washington 172, 175, 176
The Soldier Voting Act 103
"Solid Potato Salad" 226
Song of the Open Road 129
Song Parade see *The Hit Parade of 1951*
"Sonny Boy" 134
The Sons of the Pioneers 89
Sorry, Wrong Number 3
Sothern, Ann 73
Soulé, Olan 190
Sparks, Ned 74, **94**, 98
Spence, Ralph 159

The Spider 29
Spilsbury, Klinton 140–141
Spivak, Charlie 38
"Split It for the Team" 154
Sportsmen Quartet 199
Sprague, Chandler 174
Stabile, Dick 251
Stack, Robert 243
Stafford, Jo 44
Stage Door Canteen 56, 128–129, 160
Stage magazine 76, 121
Stahl, John M. 122, 124
Stand Up and Cheer 213
Stander, Lionel 244
Standing, Sir Guy 38
Standish, Burt L. 235
Standish, Schuyler 153
Stanwyck, Barbara 3, 264
A Star Is Born 116
Star Reporter 38
Star Spangled Rhythm 134, 218
Starbuck, Betty 33
Starr, Kay 199
Starr, Michael Seth 187
Start Cheering 44
Staub, Ralph 87
"Stay as Sweet as You Are" 73
Steele, Jearlyn, and Jeyetta 279
Stein, Jules 115
Steinhauser, Si 18
Stella Dallas 112
Stephens, William 150
Stephens-Lang Productions 150, 152, 153
Stern, Alison Berns 276, 277, 278
Stern, Howard 1, 77, 195, 274–276, *276*, 277–278
Stevens, George 53
Stevens, Julie 241
Stevens, Leith 238
Stevens, Leslie 216
Stevens, Mark 241
Steward, Nick "Nicodemus" 170
Stewart, Blanche *see* Brenda and Cobina
Stewart, Gretchen 103
Stewart, Harry "Yorgi Yorgenson" 204
Stewart, James 130, 186–187, *187*, 188
Stewart, Kay 146
Stewart, Marjorie 168
Sticks and Bones 265
Stillman, Robert 263
Stokowski, Leopold 39–40
Stone, Ezra 145, 146, 148
Stone, Harold J. 258
Stone, James 105
Stone, Milburn 125
Stoopnagle and Budd *see* Col. Lemuel Q. Stoopnagle
Storck, Shelby 84
Storm, Gale 194
Strange, Glenn 138
Strange Confession 206, 207
Strayhorn, Billy 197
Streep, Meryl 281, 282, *282*, 283
Street & Smith 104, 105
Strife of the Party 132
Strike Me Pink 4, 79, 81

Striker, Fran 135, 142
Stromberg, Hunt 259
Stroud Twins 120
Stuart, Gloria 45, 205, 208
Sturges, Preston 15
Styne, Jule 88, 89
Sullivan, Barry 218
Sullivan, Ed 61, 91
Sunday Evening at Seth Parker's 2, 21, 22, 24, 25; *see also* Lord, Phillips H.
Sundberg, Clinton 261
The Sunshine Boys 71
Superman and the Mole Men 193
Suspense 1, 205, 284
Suspicion 127
Sutherland, Eddie 77
Sutton, Grady 172, 174
Sutton, John 125
Sweet, Blanche 13
"Sweet Georgia Brown" 91
Sweetheart of the Campus 266
Sweethearts of the U.S.A. 81
Swickard, Josef 31
Swing Fever 160
Swing Parade of 1946 44
"Swinging on a Star" 219
Switzer, Carl "Alfalfa" 240, 241
Sykes, Brenda 271
Syncopation 11

Taft, Sen. Robert A. 103
"Take a Number from One to Ten" 73
Take It Big 221
Take It or Leave It: 1944 film 212–213; radio series 3, 211–212, 213, 220
"Take the A Train" 197
Tales of Manhattan 263
Taliaferro, Hal (Wally Wales) 137
Talley, Marion 85
Tamiroff, Akim 38, 99
Tarzan the Fearless 31
Taurog, Norman 37, 72
Taxi Driver 112
Taylor, Deems 7, 217
Taylor, Elizabeth 242, 243
Taylor, Eric 208
Taylor, F. Chase *see* Col. Lemuel Q. Stoopnagle
Taylor, Kent 84, *192*, 193
Taylor, Marion Sayles (The Voice of Experience) 7, 87
Taylor, Ray 31, 143
Tayo, Lyle 36
Tedrow, Irene 32
Temple, Shirley 83, 213
"The Temple Bells of Neban" 111; *see also The Shadow*, radio series
Tennessee Tuxedo and His Tales 234
Terhune, Max 86–87, 114
Terry-Thomas 216
Tetley, Walter 167, 168
The Texaco Fire Chief 54, 56
Texaco Gasoline 54
Texaco Star Theater 229; *see also The Fred Allen Show*
Texas Little Darlin' 234
Thank Your Lucky Stars 44, 81
Thanks a Million 63–64, 92
Thanks for the Memory: 1938 film 130
"Thanks for the Memory" (song) 41

That's Right—You're Wrong 155
Theater Five 181
"There's a Lull in My Life" 95
They Meet Again 153
The Thin Man 259, 262
"The Thing That Cries in the Night" 214, 215, 216; *see also I Love a Mystery*
The 13th Hour 210
This Is New York 216
This Is the Army 50
This Is Your FBI 191, 255
This Way Please 66, 97–99, 100
Thomas, Ann 218
Thomas, Betty 276, 277
Thomas, Bob 71, 153, 203, 266
Thomas, Frank M. 76
Thomas, Jameson 27
Thomas, Thomas L. 112
Thomas, William C. 221, 238
Thompson, Bill 97, 100–101, 165
Thompson, Butch 279
Thompson, Duane 115–116
Thompson, Kay 85, 113, 114
Thompson, Marshall 243
Thorgersen, Ed 87
Thorpe, Richard 243
Thorson, Russell 216
Thousands Cheer 160
The Three Cheers 88
"Three Little Words" 19
The Three Musketeers 127
The Three Stooges (Moe and Curly Howard, Larry Fine) 51, 52, 59–60, 131, 132, 241
Thurber, James 60
Thurston, Carol 273
Tic Toc Girls 86
Tilden, Bill 217
Time magazine 118
The Time of Your Life 244
Time Out for Rhythm 44, 131
Tin Pan Alley 213
Tinling, James 194
Tinsley, Ted 106
Tizol, Juan 19
To Be or Not to Be 5, 69
Tobin, Dan 264
Todd, Mabel 117, 204
Tokar, Norman 148
Toledo News-Blade 56
Toler, Sidney 70
Tollin, Anthony 105
Tom Brown's School Days 146
Tomack, Sid 248, 252
Tombes, Andrew 176, 198
Tomlin, Lily 280, 282, 283
Tomlin, Pinky 113
Tone, Franchot 234
"Toselli's Serenade" 256
Total Television 234
Touché Turtle 101
The Town Crier 45
The Town Criers 44
Town Hall Tonight 63, 64, 65, 68; *see also The Fred Allen Show*
Towne, Gene 155
Townley, Jack 168
Tracy, Arthur (The Street Singer) 2, 6, *34*, 35, 36

Tracy, Lee 92
Transatlantic Merry-Go-Round 62–63
Trapped 105
Travis, Richard 240
Trendle, George W. 134–135, 137, 138, 142
Trevor, Claire 237
Tri-Star Pictures 141
The Trial of Vivienne Ware: 1932 film 27, 28; novel 27; radio serial 25–27
Trio 263
Trivers, Barry 172
Trotter, John Scott 133
"The Trouble with Me Is You" 199
Trout, Dink 168, 178, 179
Trowbridge, Charles 102
Truffaut, François 273–274
Truth or Consequences 44, 166
Tufts, Sonny 219
Tugend, Harry 92, 186
Tuttle, Frank 36, 125
Tuttle, Lurene 167, 171
The Twelve Chairs 69
20th Century–Fox 27, 63–64, 65, 69, 87, 89, 92, 93, 95, 121, 143, 149, 174, 212–213
Twenty Million Sweethearts 44, 92
Two Boobs in a Balloon 119
Two Weeks to Live 172, 174–175, **175**, 176
Tyler, Leon 153
Tyler, Richard 148

Underworld After Dark see *Big Town After Dark*
Underworld Scandal see *Big Town Scandal*
United Artists 62, 69, 139, 185, 226, 263, 264
United Press International (UPI) 149, 231, 242, 257, 261
United States Department of the Treasury 103
Universal-International 245, 259, 260, 261, 262, 267, 268, 270
Universal Pictures 6, 24, 32, 45, 58, 77, 92, 104–105, 111, 121, 123, 124, 125, 127, 142, 143, 144, 172, 176, 180, 192, 193, 206, 207, 208, 210, 242, 265; see also Universal-International
Universal Television 216
University of North Carolina–Chapel Hill 154
The Unknown 215–216
Unusual Occupations 122
Upon My Lips a Song 47
Upton, Monroe "Lord Bilgewater" 87, 204
Urecal, Minerva 226

The Vagabond Lover 1, 2, 12–15, 16, 25, 32, 35, 47, 50, 154; see also Vallee, Rudy
The Vagabonds 224
Vail, Myrtle see Myrt and Marge
Vale, Nina 209
Vale, Virginia 247
Valentine, Lewis J. 191
Valera, Rosalita 224

Vallee, Rudy 1, 6, 10–12, **12**, 13–15, 20, 22, 25, 32, 35, 36, 37, 44, 47, 70, 72, 118, 119, 120, 122, 146, 154, 157, **222**, 223, 265, 274
"Valse Triste" (Sibelius) 215
Van Beuren Productions 7, 20
The Vanderbilt Revue 72, 76
Van Meter, Homer 193
Van Rooten, Luis 32
Variety 6, 24, 36, 49, 54, 57, 73, 76, 99, 106, 137, 158, 181
Varnel, Marcel 29
Varsity Show 116
Vaseline 149, 153
The Vaseline Program: Dr. Christian of River's End see *Dr. Christian*, radio series
Vass Family 145
Vass Sisters 43
Vaudeville News 90
Velez, Lupe 53, 158
Vera Vague see Allen, Barbara Jo
Verbinski, Gore 141
Vernon, Wally 198
Vienna Boys' Choir 38
Village Barn Dance 131
The Village Voice 283
Vincent, Romo 99
Vinson, Helen 45
Vitale, Joseph 170
Vitaphone Corporation 5, 6, 10, 11, 52, 72, 92, 119, 122, 123, 130; see also Warner Bros. Pictures
Vlasek, June (June Lang) 29
Voco Productions 171, 174
Vogt, Eleanor May 76
The Voice of Experience: radio and film series 7
Voice of the Whistler 209
Vola, Vicki 181, 184
Vonn, Veola 32
von Stroheim, Eric 128
Von Zell, Harry 81, 82
Vorhaus, Bernard 150, 182
Vorhees, Don 54
Votion, Jack William 171, 173, 174, 175, 177

"Wabash Cannonball" 161
WABD-TV (New York City) 134
Wadsworth, Henry 38
Wagner, Sen. Robert F. 26
Wagner, Wende 144
Waite, Malcolm 13
Waits, Tom 283
Wake Up and Dream 2
Wake Up and Live: book 92; 1937 film 92–94, **94**, 95
Walburn, Raymond 63, 102, 226
Wald, Jerry 6, 116
Waldo, Janet 267
Walker, Betty 258
Walker, Cheryl 82
Walker, Hal 218, 251
Walker, Helen **222**, 223
Walker, Nella 13
Walker, Sid 45
Walky Talky Hawky 234
Wallace, Richard 69, 101
Waller, Fats 213

Wallington, Jimmy 36, 44
Wallis, Hal B. 250, 251, 252
Walt Disney's Wonderful World of Color 129
Walter Winchell's Jergens Journal 90–91
Walters, Luana 190
Waltz, Christoph 145
Wanger, Walter 133, 234
War Department Office of Censorship 176
"War of the Worlds" 5, 229
Ware, Irene 29
Waring, Fred 11, 116
Warner, Jack 115, 249
Warner Bros. Pictures 6, 7, 15, 32, 43, 44, 50, 69, 74, 81, 92, 95, 101, 111, 115, 134, 139, 146, 148, 179, 195, 204, 234, 237, 249, 272; see also Vitaphone Corporation
Warren, Gloria 180
Warrick, Ruth 199
"Was It Rain?" 87
Washburn, Beverly 139
Washburn, Bryant 190
Wasserman, Lew 126, 154, 155
Waterman, Willard 170
Waters, Ethel 45
Waters, James 256
Watkin, Pierre 108, 143, 182, 236, **236**, 237
Watson, Bobs 173, 179
Watson, Minor 182
Watts, George 192
Way Back Home (*Other People's Business*) 2, 20, 21–23, **23**, 24–25, 32, 48, 50; see also *Sunday Evening at Seth Parker's*
Way Down East 24
Wayne, John 137
WBBM (Chicago) 235
WCCC (Hartford, CT) 274, 275
WCCO (Minneapolis) 278
WEAF (New York City) 11
Weaver, Doodles 198
Weaver, Marjorie 65
Weaver Brothers and Elviry 161
Webb, Clifton 71
Webb, Jack 271, **272**, **272**, 273, 274
Webb, Richard 153
Webber, Peggy 272
Webster, M. Coates 159
A Wedding 281
Weems, Ted 97
Weidler, Virginia 38
Weird Woman 206, 207
Weist, Dwight 181, 237
Welker, Frank 111
Welles, Orson 5, 105, 107, 229, 231
Welles, Virginia 199
Wells, Billy 50, 51
Wells, Mary K. 241
Welsh, Bob 146
Wences, Señor 127
We're Not Dressing 38
We're Not Married! 71, 263
Werris, Snag 212
West, Brooks 252
West, Buster 44
West, Mae 48, 60, 120, 125

Westcott, Helen 110
Westinghouse 134
Westmore, Ern 24
WGN (Chicago) 15, 31, 163, 188
WHAM (Rochester, NY) 35
What a Life!: 1939 film 146, 147; play 145–146, 148; *see also* Henry Aldrich, film series
Wheaties 235
Wheeler and Woolsey 17, 22, 43, 130
Whelan, Tim 160
"When the Moon Comes Over the Mountain" 47
Where There's Life 245
Where's Huddles? 253
The Whistler: film series 105, 206, 207–210, 214, 260; 1944 film 208–209; radio series 2–3, 206, 207–208; TV series 210
White, Alice 45
White, Jack 222
White, Joseph M. (The Silver Masked Tenor) 93
White, Jules 56, 132
White, Lee "Lasses" 179
White, Paul 179
White, Sam 196, 197, 198, 221–222, 223, 224
White Horse Inn 44
Whiteman, Paul 33
Whiting, Richard A. 116
Whitley, Hobart Johnson 114
Whitman, Gayne 28
"Who Am I?" (Gordon and Revel) 74
"Who Am I?" (Styne and Bullock) 88
Who Threw That Cocoanut? 134
WHOM (New York City) 274
Whoopee 4, 77
"Why Don't You Fall in Love with Me?" 265
"Why Stars Come Out at Night" 38
WIBO (Chicago) 96
Widmark, Richard 191
Wiere Brothers 213
Wilcox, Frank **228**, 239
Wilcox, Harlow 82, 97, 101, 166
Wilcox, Robert 173
Wild Waves 33, 35; *see also* The Big Broadcast
The Wild Westerner 10
Wilder, Billy 146
Wilder, Patricia "Honey Chile" 41, 43, 75, 130–131, 134
Wilke, Robert J. 139
Wilkerson, Guy 190

"William Tell Overture" (Rossini) 135
Williams, Adam 264
Williams, Bert 124
Williams, Guinn "Big Boy" 165
Williams, Maston 135
Williams, Robin, and Linda 279, 281
Williams, Van 144
Williamson, Dud 262
Willie, West and McGinty 38
Wilson 103
Wilson, Don 43, 44, 66, 165
Wilson, Earl 248
Wilson, J. Donald 208
Wilson, Marie 249–250, 251, **251**, 252–253
Wilson, Teddy 117
Winchell, Paul 129
Winchell, Walter 6, 28, 43, 64, 90–92, 93, 94, **94**, 95, 96, 103, 195
The Winds of War 188
Windsor, Claire 82
Winninger, Charles 179, 187
Winslowe, Paula 245
Winters, Gloria 248
Winters, Jonathan 112
Withers, Grant 84, 169
Witney, William 135, 137
The Wizard of Oz 128, 173, 221, 223
WJZ (New York City) 25, 27, 54, 91
WLS (Chicago) 161, 163
WLW (Cincinnati) 163
WMAQ (Chicago) 15, 96
WMCA (New York City) 256
WNAC (Boston) 79
WNBC (New York City) 274, 275, 276, 277, 278
WNEW (New York City) 198
WNTN (Newtown, MA) 274
Wolff, Steven 111
Wolfson, P.J. 51
Woman of the Year 244
The Women 131, 132
Wons, Tony 96
Wood, Sam 51, 53
Woodbury, Joan 209
The Woods Are Full of Cuckoos 43, 92, 204
"The Woody Woodpecker Song" 160
Woollcott, Alexander 45
Woolrich, Cornell 209, 210
World Theater *see* Fitzgerald Theater
Wrather, Jack 138
Wrather Corporation 138–139, 140
Wray, Fay 152
Wright, Cobina, Jr. 131
Wright, Fred 262

Wright, Will 204, 205
Wright, William 197
Wrigley's Gum 28, 57, 58
Writers Guild of America 241
WRNW (Briarcliffe Manor, NY) 274, 275, 276
Wroe, Trudy 241
WSM (Nashville) 161
WSXAO (Los Angeles) 173
WTBU (Boston University) 274, 275
Wuthering Heights 185
WWDC (Washington, DC) 274, 275
WWWW (Detroit) 274, 275, 277
WXRK (K-Rock, New York City) 275
WXYZ (Detroit) 134–135, 137, 142, 143, 145
Wyenn, Than 274
Wyman, Jane 158, 159
Wynn, Ed 2, 5, 50, 53–55, **55**, 56, 59, 61
Wynn, Nan 44

A Yank in Libya 80–81
Yankee Doodle Dandy 245
The Yanks are Coming 81
Yarborough, Barton 132, 153, 214, 215
Yates, George Worthing 135
Yates, Herbert J. 84–85, 182
Yellin, Jack 92
Yokel Boy 77
Yost, Dorothy 47
You Bet Your Life 211
You Can't Cheat an Honest Man 120, 123, **123**, 124–125, 126
You Dear Boy 132
"You Hit the Spot" 74
You'll Find Out 156, **156**, 157, 158, 159
Young, Alan 229
Young, Clara Kimball 31
Young, Harold 172
Young, Loretta 241
Young, Polly Ann 105
Your Hit Parade: radio series 85, 86, 88, 89, 112, 204, 229; TV series 89
"You're So Indifferent" 160
Yourman, Alice 60
Yours Truly, Johnny Dollar 1, 284
Youth Hostel Association 129

Zanuck, Darryl F. 2, 64, 92, 93
Ziegfeld, Flo 32, 120
Ziegfeld Follies 50, 53, 77, 120, 124
Ziegfeld Follies of the Air 40
Ziegfeld Girl 186
Ziv, Frederick 184
Ziv Productions 153
Zorina, Vera 121

www.ingramcontent.com/pod-product-compliance
Lightning Source LLC
Chambersburg PA
CBHW081540300426
44116CB00015B/2696